THE PHYSICAL CHEMISTRY PROBLEM SOLVER

Staff of Research and Education Association,
Dr. M. Fogiel, Director

Research and Education Association
505 Eighth Avenue
New York, N. Y. 10018

THE PHYSICAL CHEMISTRY PROBLEM SOLVER

Printed in the United States of America

Library of Congress Catalog Card Number 81-52778

International Standard Book Number 0-87891-532-X

Revised Printing, 1983

WHAT THIS BOOK IS FOR

For as long as physical chemistry has been taught in schools students have found this subject difficult to understand and learn because of the unusually large number of concepts involved. Despite the publication of hundreds of textbooks in this field, each one intended to provide an improvement over previous textbooks, physical chemistry remains particularly perplexing and the subject is often taken in class only to meet school/departmental requirements for a selected course of study.

In a study of the problem, REA found the following basic reasons underlying students' difficulties with physical chemistry taught in schools:

(a) No systematic rules of analysis have been developed which students may follow in a step-by-step manner to solve the usual problems encountered. This results from the fact that the numerous different conditions and principles which may be involved in a problem, lead to many possible different methods of solution. To prescribe a set of rules to be followed for each of the possible variations, would involve an enormous number of rules and steps to be searched through by students, and this task would perhaps be more burdensome than solving the problem directly with some accompanying trial and error to find the correct solution route.

(b) Textbooks currently available will usually explain a given principle in a few pages written by a professional chemist who has an insight in the subject matter that is not shared by students. The explanations are often written in an abstract manner with involved procedures which leave the students confused as to the application of the principle. The explanations given are not sufficiently detailed and extensive to make the student aware of the wide range of applications and different aspects of the principle being studied. The numerous possible variations of principles and their applications are usually not discussed, and it is left for the students to discover these for themselves while doing exercises. Accordingly, the average student is expected to rediscover that which has been long known and practiced, but not published or explained extensively.

(c) The illustrations usually following the explanation of a principle in physical chemistry are too few in number and too simple to enable the student to obtain a thorough grasp of the principle involved. The illustrations do not provide sufficient basis to enable a student to solve problems that may be subsequently assigned for homework or given on examinations.

The illustrations are presented in abbreviated form which leaves out much material between steps. As a result, students find the illustrations difficult to understand— contrary to the purpose of the illustrations.

Illustrations are, furthermore, often worded in a confusing manner. They do not state the problem and then present the solution. Instead, they pass through a general discussion, never revealing what is to be solved for.

Illustrations, also, do not always include diagrams, wherever appropriate, and students do not obtain the training to draw diagrams to simplify and organize their thinking.

(d) Students can learn the subject only by doing the exercises themselves and reviewing them in class, to obtain experience in applying the principles with their different ramifications.

In doing the exercises by themselves, students find that they are required to devote considerably more time to physical chemistry than to other subjects of comparable credits, because they are uncertain with regard to the selection and application of the principles involved. It is also often necessary for students to discover those "tricks" not revealed in their texts (or review books), that make it possible to solve problems easily. Students must usually resort to methods of trial-and-error to discover these "tricks," and as a result they find that they may sometimes spend several hours to solve a single problem.

(e) When reviewing the exercises in classrooms, instructors usually request students to take turns writing solutions on the board and explaining them to the class. Students often find it difficult to explain in a manner that holds the interest of the class, and enables the remaining students to follow the material written on the board. The remaining students seated in the class are, furthermore, too occupied with copying the material from the board, to listen to the oral explanations and concentrate on the methods of the solution.

This book is intended to aid students in physical chemistry to overcome the difficulties described, by supplying detailed illustrations of the solution methods which are usually not apparent to students. The solution methods are illustrated by problems selected from those that are most often assigned for classwork and given on examinations. The problems are arranged in order of complexity to enable students to learn and understand a particular topic by reviewing the problems in sequence. The problems are illustrated with detailed step-by-step explanations of the principles involved, to save the students the large amount of time that is often needed to fill in the gaps that are usually omitted between steps of illustrations in textbooks or review/outline books.

The staff of REA considers physical chemistry a subject that is best learned by allowing students to view the methods of analysis and solution techniques themselves. This approach to learning the subject matter is similar to that practiced in the medical fields, for example, and various scientific laboratories.

In using this book, students may review and study the illustrated problems at their own pace; they are not limited to the time allowed for explaining problems on the board in class.

When students want to look up a particular type of problem and solution, they can readily locate it in the book by referring to the index which has been extensively prepared. It is also possible to locate a particular type of problem by glancing at just the material within the boxed portions. To facilitate rapid scanning of the problems, each problem has a heavy border around it. Furthermore, each problem is identified with a number immediately above the problem at the right-hand margin.

To obtain maximum benefit from the book, students should familiarize themselves with the section, "How To Use This Book," located in the front pages.

To meet the objectives of this book, staff members of REA have selected problems usually encountered in assignments and examinations, and have solved each problem meticulously to illustrate the steps which are usually difficult for students to comprehend. For their outstanding effort and competence in this area, special gratitude is due to Carl Adler, John Aibangbee, and David Isemin. Thanks are, furthermore, due to several contributors who devoted brief periods of time to this work.

The manuscript that was evolved with its endless inserts, changes, modifications to the changes, and editorial remarks, must have been an arduous typing task for Louise Dennis, Yvette Fuchs, Sophie Gerber, and Sara Nicoll. These ladies typed the manuscript expertly with almost no complaints about the handwritten material and the numerous symbols that require much patience and special skill.

For their efforts in the graphic-arts required in the layout arrangement, and completion of the physical features of the book, gratitude is expressed to Bruce Arendash, Vivian Lopez, and Robert Puig.

The difficult task of coordinating the efforts of all persons was carried out by Carl Fuchs. His conscientious work deserves much appreciation. He also trained and supervised art and production personnel in the preparation of the book for printing.

Finally, special thanks are due to Helen Kaufmann for her unique talents to render those difficult border-line decisions and constructive suggestions related to the design and organization of the book.

Max Fogiel, Ph.D.
Program Director

HOW TO USE THIS BOOK

This book can be an invaluable aid to students in physical chemistry as a supplement to their textbooks. The book is subdivided into 15 chapters, each dealing with a separate topic. The subject matter is developed beginning with the kinetic theory of gases and extending through the laws of thermodynamics, equilibrium, solutions, electrochemistry, chemical kinetics, and colloids. Separate sections are included on quantum chemistry, solid state, nuclear chemistry, and macromolecules.

TO LEARN AND UNDERSTAND A TOPIC THOROUGHLY

1. Refer to your class text and read there the section pertaining to the topic. You should become acquainted with the principles discussed there. These principles, however, may not be clear to you at that time.

2. Then locate the topic you are looking for by referring to the "Table of Contents" in front of this book, "The Physical Chemistry Problem Solver."

3. Turn to the page where the topic begins and review the problems under each topic, in the order given. For each topic, the problems are arranged in order of complexity, from the simplest to the more difficult. Some problems may appear similar to others, but each problem has been selected to illustrate a different point or solution method.

To learn and understand a topic thoroughly and retain its contents, it will be generally necessary for students to review the problems several times. Repeated review is essential in order to gain experience in recognizing the principles that should be applied, and to select the best solution technique.

TO FIND A PARTICULAR PROBLEM

To locate one or more problems related to a particular subject matter, refer to the index. In using the index, be certain to note that the numbers given there refer to problem numbers, not to page numbers. This arrangement of the index is intended to facilitate finding a problem more rapidly, since two or more problems may appear on a page.

If a particular type of problem cannot be found readily, it is recommended that the student refer to the "Table of Contents" in the front pages, and then turn to the chapter which is applicable to the problem being sought. By scanning or glancing at the material that is boxed, it will generally be possible to find problems related to the one being sought, without consuming considerable time. After the problems have been located, the solutions can be reviewed and studied in detail. For this purpose of locating problems rapidly, students should acquaint themselves with the organization of the book as found in the "Table of Contents."

In preparing for an exam, it is useful to find the topics to be covered in the exam from the Table of Contents, and then review the problems under those topics several times. This should equip the student with what might be needed for the exam.

CONTENTS

CHAPTER 1

GASES AND KINETIC THEORY

TEMPERATURE AND PRESSURE DEPENDENCE

• PROBLEM 1-1

The temperature of a given gas is $-10^\circ C$. What are the equivalent Fahrenheit and absolute Kelvin scales?

Solution: a) $$\frac{F - 32}{9} = \frac{C}{5} \qquad (1)$$

where F = Fahrenheit scale
C = Celsius or Centigrade scale

The problem states that the Celsius scale is $-10^\circ C$. Therefore, using equation (1),

$$\frac{F - 32}{9} = \frac{-10}{5}$$

or

$$5(F - 32) = 9(-10)$$
$$5F - 160 = -90$$
$$5F = 70$$
$$F = 70/5 = 14^\circ$$

b) $0^\circ C$ is equivalent to $273^\circ K$ where K = absolute Kelvin scale. To convert C to K, use the relationship K = 273 + C. The problem above indicates that $C = -10^\circ$ therefore $K = 273 + (-10) = 273 - 10 = 263^\circ$.

• PROBLEM 1-2

If the temperature of the air in a chemistry laboratory is ambient ($77^\circ F$), what is the equivalent scale in Kelvin?

Solution: K = 273 + C. First, convert 77° Fahrenheit ($^\circ F$) to Celsius ($^\circ C$). Then convert Celsius ($^\circ C$) to the absolute temperature scale, Kelvin ($^\circ K$). Using $\frac{F - 32}{9} = \frac{C}{5}$, substitute the value of F to obtain

$$\frac{77 - 32}{9} = \frac{C}{5}$$

or

$$5(77 - 32) = 9C$$
$$5(45) = 9C$$
$$C = 25^\circ$$

$$K = 273 + C$$
$$K = 273 + 25 = 298^\circ .$$

• PROBLEM 1-3

The bar is a unit of pressure defined as 1.00×10^6 dynes/cm^2, or 1.00×10^5 N/m^2. What is the equivalent of the bar in units of mm Hg?

Solution: This is a matter of scale conversions. In a problem dealing with pressure, it is reasonable to use a scale of One Atmospheric Pressure = 1.013×10^5 N/m^2 = 760 mm Hg for conversions. Note the convenience in appropriate scale choice. If an inappropriate scale had been chosen, another conversion to some other scale would be needed before converting to the desired scale. Since 1.013×10^5 N/m^2 is equivalent to 760 mm Hg, therefore 1.00×10^5 N/m^2 will be equivalent to

$$\frac{1.00 \times 10^5 \text{ N/m}^2}{1.013 \times 10^5 \text{ N/m}^2} \times 760 \text{ mm Hg} = 750 \text{ mm Hg}.$$

• PROBLEM 1-4

The density of liquid gallium is 6.09 g/cm^3 at 35°C. If this element is employed in a barometer instead of mercury, what is the height of a column of gallium sustained in the barometer at 1 atm pressure?

Solution: The gallium column can be computed by the use of the definition:

$$(h_{Ga})(d_{Ga}) = (h_{Hg})(d_{Hg})$$

where

h = height of a column,
d = density,

therefore

$$h_{Ga} = \frac{(h_{Hg})(d_{Hg})}{(d_{Ga})}$$

1 atm pressure = h_{Hg} = 760 mm Hg = 76.0 cm Hg . The density of mercury = d_{Hg} = 13.6 gm/cm^3 . Therefore,

$$h_{Ga} = \frac{(76.0 \text{ cm Hg})(13.6 \text{ gm/cm}^3)}{(6.09 \text{ gm/cm}^3)}$$

$$= 169.7 \text{ cm Ga} = 1697 \text{ mm Ga}$$

• PROBLEM 1-5

If the height of a water column is 600 mm, what will be the height of the mercury column?

Solution: The height of the mercury column will correspond to the pressure of the atmosphere. Now, by definition

$$(h_{water})(d_{water}) = (h_{mercury})(d_{mercury})$$

where

d = density
h = height .

From the mathematical relationship given,

$$(600\text{ mm})(1 \times 10^3\text{ kg/m}^3) = (h_{mercury})(13.6 \times 10^3\text{ kg/m}^3)$$

$$h_{mercury} = 600\text{ mm}\left[\frac{1 \times 10^3\text{ kg/m}^3}{13.6 \times 10^3\text{ kg/m}^3}\right]$$

or

$$h_{mercury} = \left[\frac{600}{13.6}\right]\text{ mm Hg} = 44.1\text{ mm Hg} .$$

• PROBLEM 1-6

In a popular laboratory experiment in general chemistry, a gas is collected in an inverted tube. A typical situation at the end of the experiment is shown in Figure 1. If the difference in levels of the liquid surfaces is 172 mm, the specific gravity of the liquid is 1.23, and atmospheric pressure is 763 mm Hg, find the pressure of the gas in mm Hg.

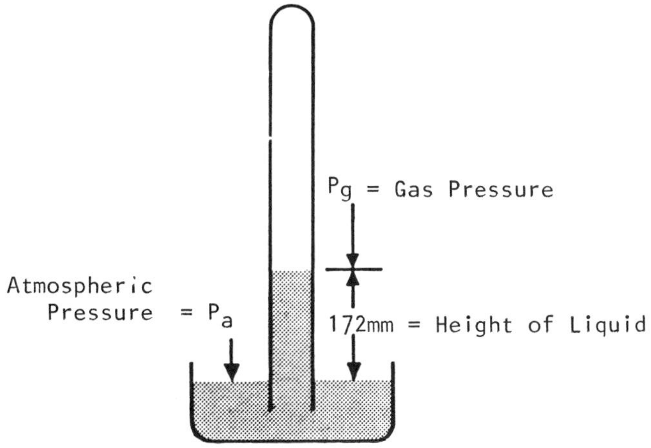

Fig. 1

Solution: To obtain the pressure of the gas in mm Hg, it is necessary to find the P_{Hg} that is equivalent to 172 mm of the liquid of specific gravity 1.23. By definition,

$$P_{Hg}\, d_{Hg} = P_{liq}\, d_{liq}$$

where P_{Hg} = pressure of mercury

P_{liq} = pressure of liquid

d_{Hg} = density of mercury

d_{liq} = density of liquid.

Therefore

$$P_{Hg} = \frac{(P_{liq})(d_{liq})}{(d_{Hg})}$$

$$d_{Hg} = 13.6 \text{ gm/cm}^3$$

$$d_{liq} = 1.23 \text{ gm/cm}^3$$

Here the density of the liquid is the same as the specific gravity because the specific gravity is given by

$$\frac{\text{density of substance}}{\text{density of water at } 4^\circ\text{C}}$$

Density of liquid = (specific gravity)(density of water at 4°C) .

But the density of water at 4°C = 1.00 grams/cm^3 .

Density of liquid = specific gravity.

Therefore the specific gravity is numerically equal to density in the metric system. Specific gravity is dimensionless (has no units) whereas density has units of gm/cm^3 in the metric system. From the mathematical relationship,

$$P_{Hg} = \frac{(172 \text{ mm})(1.23 \text{ gm/cm}^3)}{(13.6 \text{ gm/cm}^3)} = 15.55 \text{ mm Hg} .$$

Since atmospheric pressure supports the gas pressure and height of liquid, the following relationship is true.

$$P_a = P_g + P_{Hg} .$$

Remember that P_{Hg} is the pressure equivalent to the height of liquid.

$$P_a = 763 \text{ mm Hg}$$

$$P_{Hg} = 15.55 \text{ mm Hg}$$

$$P_g = 763 - 15.55 = 747.45 \text{ mm Hg}.$$

• PROBLEM 1-7

An open end mercurial manometer shown below in Fig. 1 is connected to a gas tank. The mercury meniscus in the left leg of the manometer is opposite 33.8 cm on the meter stick; in the right leg it is opposite 16.2 cm. Atmospheric pressure is 747 mm Hg. Find the pressure of the gas.

Solution: Always equate pressures at the lower liquid surface, that is, $P_g = P_a + P_{Hg}$. The gas pressure is greater than atmospheric pressure

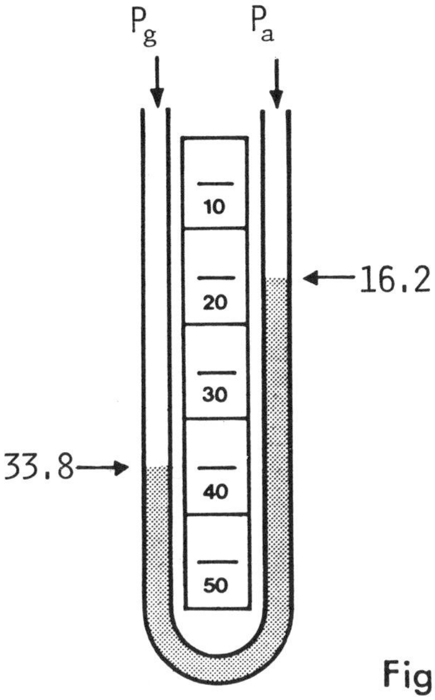

Fig. 1

as shown in Fig. 1. The diagram shows the gas supporting both the mercury and the atmosphere.

The difference between atmospheric and gas pressures is always equal to the difference in levels of the mercury in the two legs of the manometer. This difference is 33.8 - 16.2 = 17.6, or 176 mm. Since the gas pressure is greater than atmospheric pressure,

$$P_g - P_a = 176 \text{ mm Hg}$$

$$P_a = 747 \text{ mm Hg}$$

$$P_g = 747 + 176.0$$

$$= 923 \text{ mm Hg.}$$

• PROBLEM 1-8

> If P_a = 755 mm Hg, find the gas pressure in the demonstration setup in Figure 1.

Solution: From the figure, it can be seen that, the gas pressure P_g is less than atmospheric pressure P_a. Recall that the difference between atmospheric and gas pressures is always equal to the difference in levels of the mercury in the two legs of the manometer. This difference is 75.6 - 20.3 = 55.3 cm or 553 mm.

Then one can write,

$$P_a - P_g = 553 \text{ mm Hg}$$

since

$$P_a = 755 \text{ mm Hg}$$

$$P_g = 755 - 553 = 202 \text{ mm Hg.}$$

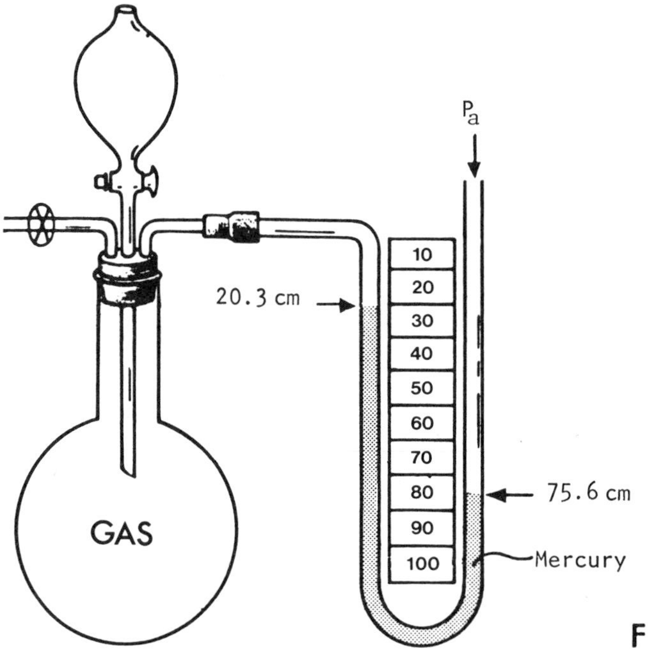

Fig. 1

TRANSPORT PROPERTIES OF GASES

• PROBLEM 1-9

A gaseous mixture of 90 mole percent hydrogen and 10 mole percent deuterium at 25°C and a total pressure of 1 atm effuses through a small pin hole of area $0.30mm^2$. Calculate the composition of the initial gas that passes through.

Solution: The rate of molecular flow or effusion in molecules per-second is given by, dn/dt . Thus rate of flow of

$$H_2 = \frac{dn_{H_2}}{dt} \tag{1}$$

where n_{H_2} is in $\frac{\text{molecules}}{cm^3} = n_{H_2} \bar{c}_{H_2} A$ and $\bar{c}$ is the average speed in cm/sec and A is the area in cm^2. The rate of effusion of

$$D_2 = \frac{dn_{D_2}}{dt} = n_{D_2} \bar{c}_{D_2} A \tag{2}$$

The ratio of equation (1) to equation (2) is

$$\frac{dn_{H_2}/dt}{dn_{D_2}/dt} = \frac{n_{H_2} \bar{c}_{H_2} A}{n_{D_2} \bar{c}_{D_2} A}$$

$$= \frac{n_{H_2}}{n_{D_2}} \cdot \frac{\bar{c}_{H_2}}{\bar{c}_{D_2}} .$$

$$\frac{n_{H_2}}{n_{D_2}} = \frac{\text{number of molecules of } H_2/cm^3}{\text{number of molecules of } D_2/cm^3} .$$ The volumes cancel in both the numerator and the denominator. To solve the problem molecules should be changed to moles.

$$\frac{\text{number of moles of } H_2}{\text{number of moles of } D_2} = \frac{\text{number of molecules of } H_2/\text{Avagadro \#}}{\text{number of molecules of } D_2/\text{Avagadro \#}} .$$

So the ratio of mole percent equals the ratio of molecular percent. Therefore,

$$\frac{dn_{H_2}/dt}{dn_{D_2}/dt} = \frac{90}{10} \frac{\bar{c}_{H_2}}{\bar{c}_{D_2}} \tag{3}$$

But the rate of effusion is inversely proportional to the $m^{\frac{1}{2}}$ in g/mole. The root-mean-square velocities are proportional to arithmetical mean velocities, and since the proportionality constant cancels out, equation (3) is written as

$$\frac{dn_{H_2}/dt}{dn_{D_2}/dt} = \frac{90}{10}\sqrt{\frac{M_{D_2}}{M_{H_2}}}$$

$$= \frac{90}{10}\sqrt{\frac{4.028}{2.016}}$$

$$= 9\sqrt{2.0}$$

$$= 12.7$$

Thus 12.7 molecules of H_2 per molecule of D_2 effuses, and the percent composition of the initial gas passing through will be

$$\text{mole \% } D_2 = \frac{1 \times 100}{12.7 + 1}$$

$$= 7.30\%$$

$$\text{mole \% } H_2 = 100 - 7.30$$
$$= 92.7\%$$

• PROBLEM 1-10

One side of a glass cylinder is initially filled with H_2 at a pressure P and the other side with N_2 at a pressure 2P.

This glass cylinder is closed at both ends and a glass filter in the middle of the cylinder divides it into two compartments of equal volume.

Describe what happens, starting at $t = 0$, at constant temperature and assuming that the pores of the filter have a diameter much smaller than the mean free paths of the gases.

Solution: The total number of molecules striking the unit area of the wall of the cylinder is given by,

$$Z_{wall} = \frac{1}{4} n\bar{C}$$

$$= \frac{1}{4}\left(\frac{PN}{RT}\right)\bar{C}$$

$$= \frac{1}{4}\left(\frac{PN}{RT}\right)\left(\frac{8RT}{\pi M}\right)^{\frac{1}{2}}$$

$$Z_{wall} = \frac{1}{4}\frac{N}{RT}\left(\frac{8RT}{\pi}\right)^{\frac{1}{2}}\frac{P}{M^{\frac{1}{2}}} .$$

N is the Avogadro's number and M = molecular weight. Thus it follows that at constant temperature the rate of effusion varies inversely as the square root of the molecular weight, M.

Therefore, the effusion of H_2 is proportional to $P_{H_2} M_{H_2}^{-\frac{1}{2}}$ and effusion of N_2 is proportional to $P_{N_2} M_{N_2}^{-\frac{1}{2}}$

$$\frac{Z_{H_2}}{Z_{N_2}} = \frac{P_{H_2}/M_{H_2}^{\frac{1}{2}}}{P_{N_2}/M_{H_2}^{\frac{1}{2}}}$$

$$\frac{Z_{H_2}}{Z_{N_2}} = \frac{P/(2)^{\frac{1}{2}}}{2P/(28)^{\frac{1}{2}}}$$

$$= \frac{1}{(2)^{\frac{1}{2}}}\left[\frac{(28)^{\frac{1}{2}}}{2}\right]$$

$$\frac{Z_{H_2}}{Z_{N_2}} = 1.87$$

or $$Z_{H_2} = 1.87\, Z_{N_2}$$

Thus the rate of effusion of H_2 into the N_2 compartment is 1.87 times faster than that of N_2 into the H_2 compartment of the cylinder.

• PROBLEM 1-11

a) Cl_2 (chlorine gas) is pumped into a 1-dm^3 vessel at a temperature of 300°K and a pressure of 1 mm Hg (torr). Determine how long it would take for the pressure to fall to 0.5 mm Hg (torr) if a small hole 0.2μm in diameter is punctured in the vessel, and the gas effuses into a vacuum.
b) Identify and justify the assumption that you made in the calculation.

Solution: a) Assuming that the 1-dm^3 vessel is occupied by N particles, the molecular concentration is thus,

$$n = \frac{N}{V}$$

where V is the volume of the vessel. The total number of molecules striking the unit area of the wall, Z_w, per second is given by:

$$Z_{wall} = \frac{1}{4} n \bar{C} \qquad (1)$$

where $\bar{C}$ is the mean speed of the molecules given by,

$$\bar{C} = \left(\frac{8RT}{\pi M}\right)^{\frac{1}{2}} \quad \text{and} \quad n = \frac{N}{V} .$$

From equation (1),

$$Z_{wall} = \frac{1}{4} \frac{N}{V} \bar{C} \qquad (2)$$

But, N/V = PL/RT where P is the pressure and L is the Avogadro number. Therefore, equation (2) becomes

$$Z_{wall} = \frac{1}{4} \frac{PL}{RT} \bar{C}$$

Define dn/dt = moles striking the small hole of area A per sec.

= rate of change in moles of gas per sec.

$$-\frac{dn}{dt} = Z_{wall} \frac{A}{L}$$

$$= \frac{1}{4} \frac{PL}{RT} \bar{C} \times \frac{A}{L}$$

$$-\frac{dn}{dt} = \frac{PA\bar{C}}{4RT} \qquad (3)$$

From ideal gas law,

$$PV = nRT$$

or

$$n = PV/RT \qquad (4)$$

Differentiating equation (4) with respect to P and V,R,T, held constant gives,

$$dn = \frac{V\,dP}{RT}$$

substitute dn = VdP/RT into equation (3). This gives

$$-\frac{V}{RT} \frac{dP}{dt} = \frac{PA\bar{C}}{4RT}$$

or

$$-\frac{V}{RT} \frac{dP}{P} = \frac{A\bar{C}}{4RT} dt$$

$$-\frac{V}{RT} \int_{P_1}^{P_2} \frac{dP}{P} = \frac{A\bar{C}}{4RT} \int_0^t dt$$

$$-\int_{P_1}^{P_2} \frac{dP}{P} = \frac{A\bar{C}}{4V} \int_0^t dt$$

$$-\ln P \Big|_{P_1}^{P_2} = \frac{A\bar{C}}{4V} t$$

$$-\ln \frac{P_2}{P_1} = \frac{A\bar{C}}{4V} t$$

$$-\ln \frac{0.5}{1.0} = \frac{\pi r^2 \bar{C}}{4V} t$$

$$0.693 = \frac{\pi\left[\left(\frac{0.2\times10^{-6}\text{m}}{2}\right)\left(\frac{100\text{ cm}}{1\text{m}}\right)\right]^2\left(2.993\times10^4\text{cm sec}^{-1}\right)t}{4(10^3\text{ cm}^3)}$$

$$0.693 = 2.351 \times 10^{-9}\text{ sec}^{-1}t$$

$$t = \frac{0.693}{2.351 \times 10^{-9}\text{ sec}^{-1}}$$

$$= 2.948\times10^8 \text{ sec}$$

$$t = (2.948\times10^8\text{ sec})\left(\frac{1\text{ hr}}{3600\text{ sec}}\right)$$

$$t = 8.18 \times 10^4 \text{ hr}.$$

b) The assumption made in the calculation was that the mean free path λ of the gas was very much larger than the diameter of the hole. To justify this, look at the average number of collisions experienced by one molecule per second, given by

$$Z = 2^{\frac{1}{2}}\pi N d^2 \bar{C}.$$

In this time, the molecule has traveled a distance $\bar{C}$. The mean free path λ is therefore $\bar{C}/Z$, or

$$\lambda = \frac{1}{2^{\frac{1}{2}}\pi N d^2} \qquad (5)$$

where N is the number of molecules = PL/RT and d is the diameter of hole. From (5) then

$$\lambda = \frac{1}{2^{\frac{1}{2}}\pi \frac{PL}{RT} d^2} \qquad (6)$$

$$\frac{PL}{RT} = \frac{(1/760\text{ atm})(6.02\times10^{23})}{(82.06)(300)}$$

$$= 3.2 \times 10^{16}$$

and

$$d = 3.70 \times 10^{-8}\text{ cm}.$$

Substituting d and PL/RT into (6) gives

$$\lambda = \frac{1}{\sqrt{2}\,\pi\left(3.2\times10^{16}\right)\left(3.70\times10^{-8}\right)^2}$$

$$\lambda = 5.11 \times 10^{-3}\text{ cm}$$

Thus λ is $\gg$ diameter of hole.

• PROBLEM 1-12

Kinetic theory of gases predicts that the viscosity of a gas is proportional to $T^{\frac{1}{2}}\sigma^{-2}$ where T is the temperature and σ is the molecular diameter. Give an explanation of why viscosity a) increases with temperature, b) depends on the diameter of the molecules, and c) is independent of pressure at constant high temperatures.

Solution: a) Gas viscosities are determined by the rate at which momentum is transported between adjacent layers of fluid that are moving at different speeds. Viscosity increases with increasing temperature because the mean speed, $\bar{C}$, of the molecules is proportional to $T^{\frac{1}{2}}$. This arises because at higher temperatures momentum is transported more rapidly through a given area, and so force has to be increased to maintain the motion of the layers of gas.

Another way of looking at it is to consider that molecules are not actually hard spheres, but somewhat soft and surrounded by force fields. Thus the higher the temperature, the faster the molecules move, and the deeper one molecule can penetrate into the force field of another, before repulsion.

b) An increase in molecular diameter of the gas molecules results in frequent collisions with other molecules, and hence a shorter mean free path for the molecules.

This reduction in the mean free path of the molecules results in a reduction in the average momentum difference between the layers of the gas between which the molecules travel in each free path. Thus, viscosity decreases with increasing molecular diameter.

c) The frequency of momentum - transporting molecules or molecules moving back and forth between layers increases in proportion to the pressure, but the mean free path, or effective distance between layers, decreases in proportion to the pressure. These two effects just cancel with respect to the momentum transport per unit distance.

The above explanation is true at high pressures. At very low pressures the mean free path does not increase further and so the viscosity approaches zero as the pressure approaches zero.

• PROBLEM 1-13

One of the two principal methods for the determination of viscosities of gases is the Poiseuille's flow experiment. In this experiment, a sample of air at 298°K was allowed to flow through a tube with radius 1mm and length 1m. Pressures at both ends of the tube were 765 mm Hg and 760 mm Hg respectively. A volume of 90.2 cm^3 measured at the lower pressure of 760 mm Hg passed through the tube after 100 sec. Calculate the viscosity of air at this temperature.

Solution: The Poiseuille's equation can be written as

$$\frac{dV}{dt} = \frac{(P_1^2 - P_2^2)\ \pi R^4}{16\ell\eta\ P_0} \qquad (1)$$

or

$$\eta = \frac{(P_1^2 - P_2^2)\ \pi R^4}{16\ell\left(\frac{dV}{dt}\right) P_0}$$

where V is the flowing volume, P_1 and P_2 are the pressures at each end of the tube of length ℓ, and P_0 is the pressure at which the volume is measured. η is the coefficient of viscosity (or viscosity) and is defined as a measure of the friction present when adjacent layers of the gas are moving at different speeds. Evaluating $(P_1^2 - P_2^2)$ in equation (1) gives

$$(P_1^2 - P_2^2) = \frac{(765^2 - 760^2)\text{mmHg} \times (1.0135 \times 10^5\ \text{Nm}^{-2})^2}{(760\ \text{mm Hg})^2}$$

$$= 1.356 \times 10^8\ \text{N}^2\text{m}^{-4}$$

From the data of the problem set,

$$\frac{dV}{dt} = \left(\frac{90.2\ \text{cm}^3}{100\ \text{sec}}\right)\left(\frac{1\text{m}}{100\ \text{cm}}\right)^3$$

$$= 9.02 \times 10^{-7}\ \text{m}^3\ \text{s}^{-1}$$

Thus from (1)

$$\eta = \frac{(1.356 \times 10^8\text{N}^2\text{m}^{-4})(\pi)(0.5 \times 10^{-3}\text{m})^4}{16(1\text{m})(1.0135\times10^5\text{Nm}^{-2})(9.02\times10^{-7}\text{m}^3\text{s}^{-1})}$$

$$= \frac{0.267\times10^8\times10^{-12}}{146.27\times10^{-7}\times10^5} = \frac{0.267\times10^{-4}}{146.27\times10^{-2}}$$

$$= 0.00182 \times 10^{-2}$$

$$\eta = 1.82 \times 10^{-5}\text{kg m}^{-1}\ \text{s}^{-1}$$

• PROBLEM 1-14

Knudsen effusion technique was used to determine the vapor pressure of scandium and the following data were obtained

temperature, 1555.4°K
time, 110.5 min
weight loss and diameter of orifice were 9.57 mg and 0.2965 cm, respectively.

Use the above data to estimate the vapor pressure of scandium at 1555.4°K and 1 atm.

Solution: In the Knudsen method, the weight of gas effusing through a small orifice in a given time interval is monitored and this is proportional to the vapor pressure, P.

$$P = Z\left(\frac{2\pi RT}{M}\right)^{\frac{1}{2}} \quad (1)$$

where Z is the collision frequency and is given by

$$Z = \frac{\Delta m}{A\Delta t} = \frac{\Delta m}{\pi r^2 \Delta t}$$

where

A = area of container
m = weight loss .

Therefore,

$$Z = \frac{(9.57\ \text{mg})\left(\frac{1\text{g}}{1000\ \text{mg}}\right)}{\pi(0.2965/2)^2(110.5\ \text{min})\left(\frac{60\ \text{sec}}{1\ \text{min}}\right)}$$

$$= 2.08 \times 10^{-5}\text{g cm}^{-2}\ \text{sec}^{-1} .$$

Using this value in equation (1) gives

$$P = 2.08 \times 10^{-5}\text{g cm}^{-2}\ \text{sec}^{-1}\left[\frac{2\pi(8.314 \times 10^7\ \text{ergs}\ {}^\circ\text{K}^{-1} - \text{mole}^{-1})\ (1555.4^\circ\text{K})}{44.96\ \text{g/mole}}\right]^{\frac{1}{2}}$$

$$= 2.80\ \text{dynes cm}^{-2}$$

$$P = (2.80\ \text{dynes cm}^{-2})\left(\frac{9.87 \times 10^{-7}\ \text{atm}}{1\ \text{dyne cm}^{-2}}\right)$$

$$P = 2.77 \times 10^{-6}\ \text{atm} .$$

• PROBLEM 1-15

A sample of beryllium powder was placed in a box having an effusion hole of 3.18 mm in diameter. After 15.2 min and a temperature of 1537°K , 8.88 mg of the powder had effused. Use the method of Knudsen to determine the vapor pressure of Be at 1537°K .

Solution: In the method of Knudsen, if a solid has a vapor pressure, P, and is enclosed in a box with a small hole, the rate of loss of mass from the box is proportional to P. Therefore P may be determined if the mass loss is known. Let the total mass diffused = M_T .

Inside the container, the number of collisions per unit time per unit area is

$$Z = \frac{1}{4}\left(\frac{\bar{C}NM}{L}\right) \quad (1)$$

where Z is the collision frequency and $\bar{C}$ is the mean speed of molecules given by

$$\bar{C} = \left(\frac{8RT}{\pi M}\right)^{\frac{1}{2}}$$

But

$$P = NRT/L \quad (2)$$

Rearranging equation (1) to solve for L gives

$$L = \frac{\bar{C}NM}{4Z} \text{ .}$$

Inserting this in equation (2) yields

$$P = \frac{NRT}{\left(\frac{\bar{C}NM}{4Z}\right)} = \frac{NRT}{1} \times \frac{4Z}{\bar{C}NM}$$

$$P = \frac{Z4RT}{M\bar{C}} \tag{3}$$

Moreover, the definition of Z indicates that

$$Z = \frac{M_T}{tA} = \frac{M_T}{t\pi r^2} \text{ .}$$

Hence, equation (3) becomes

$$P = \frac{M_T}{tr^2}\left(\frac{2RT}{\pi M}\right)^{\frac{1}{2}}$$

$$= \frac{0.00888}{15.2 \times 60 (0.159)^2}\left(\frac{2.8314 \times 10^7 \times 1537}{3.14 \times 9.012}\right)^{\frac{1}{2}}$$

$$= 36.60 \text{ dynes cm}^{-2}$$

$$= 3.61 \times 10^{-5} \text{ atm.}$$

• PROBLEM 1-16

Calculate the average velocity of Caesium atoms forming an atomic beam emerging from a small hole of a wall of an oven. The oven contains a sample of Caesium and is heated to 500°C.

Solution: Assume that the atoms impinging on the wall of the oven are doing so from the x-direction, so only their velocity components in that direction need be considered. The velocity of the atoms are thus between zero and infinity. The mean velocity $<V_x>$, of a particle is given by

$$<V_x> = \int_0^{\infty} V_x f\left(V_x\right) dV_x \tag{1}$$

where $f\left(V_x\right)$ is the velocity distribution given as

$$f\left(V_x\right) = \left(m/2\pi kT\right)^{\frac{1}{2}} \exp(-\tfrac{1}{2} m V_x^2/kT) \tag{2}$$

Also $$\int_{-\infty}^{\infty} f\left(V_x\right) dV_x = 1$$

The velocity component lies in the range $-\infty \leq V_x \leq +\infty$; hence, its probability must be unity.

In order to make the integral $\int_0^{\infty} f(V_x)dV_x = 1$, it is necessary to multiply the right-hand side of equation (2) by 2. Therefore from equation (1)

$$<V_x> = 2\left(m/2\pi kT\right)^{\frac{1}{2}} \int_0^\infty V_x \exp(-mV_x^2/2kT)dV_x$$

$$= 2\left(m/2\pi kT\right)^{\frac{1}{2}} (kT/m) = \sqrt{(2kT/\pi m)} \ .$$

For Caesium at 500°C,

$$<V_x> = \left[\frac{(2/\pi) \times \left(1.381 \times 10^{-23}\ JK^{-1}\right) \times (773\ K)}{(132.9) \times (1.6605 \times 10^{-27}\ kg)}\right]^{\frac{1}{2}}$$

$$<V_x> = 175.5\ m-s^{-1} \ .$$

• PROBLEM 1-17

The escape velocity, the speed at which molecules can escape the earth's gravitational field, is approximately 1.1×10^6 cm sec^{-1} (about 7 miles sec^{-1}). At what temperature, approximately, will the root mean square velocity value for H_2 be equal to the escape velocity?

($R = 8.3 \times 10^7$ erg $mole^{-1}$ deg^{-1} ;

at. wt: H = 1)

Solution: The root mean square velocity is defined by

$$U_{rms} = \sqrt{\bar{U}^2} \tag{1}$$

where $\bar{U}^2$ = average of the square of the velocity

U_{rms} = root mean square velocity.

From the $P - \bar{V} - KE$ relationship,

$$P\bar{V} = \frac{1}{3} M\bar{U}^2 = \frac{2}{3} \overline{KE} \tag{2}$$

where P = Pressure

$\bar{V}$ = molar volume

KE = Kinetic energy

M = molecular weight

But $P\bar{V} = RT$. Therefore equation (2) becomes

$$RT = \frac{1}{3} M\bar{U}^2 \tag{3}$$

where R = universal gas constant

T = temperature.

Rearranging equation (3) to solve for $\bar{U}^2$ gives

$$\bar{U}^2 = \frac{3RT}{M} \tag{4}$$

Substituting equation (4) into equation (1) gives

$$U_{rms} = \sqrt{\frac{3RT}{M}} = \left(\frac{3RT}{M}\right)^{\frac{1}{2}} \quad (5)$$

Squaring both sides of equation (5) gives

$$U_{rms}^2 = \frac{3RT}{M}$$

Solving for T, the equation becomes

$$T = \frac{MU^2_{rms}}{3R} \quad (6)$$

From the given data,

$$T = \frac{(2 \text{ g mol}^{-1})(1.1 \times 10^6)^2 \text{ cm}^2 \text{ sec}^{-2}}{(3)(8.3 \times 10^7 \text{ ergs mol}^{-1} \text{ deg}^{-1})}$$

$$T = \frac{2.42 \times 10^{12} \text{ g cm}^2 \text{ sec}^{-2}}{24.9 \times 10^7 \text{ ergs deg}^{-1}}$$

The units above might seem strange but erg is an energy unit in the cgs system. One form of energy that is well known is the kinetic energy and it's given by $\frac{1}{2}mv^2$. In cgs units, m = g, v = cm sec^{-1} and $v^2 = cm^2 \ sec^{-2}$. Consequently, kinetic energy = $\frac{1}{2}mv^2 = g \ cm^2 sec^{-2}$. But $g \ cm^2 \ sec^{-2}$ = erg. Therefore, the units cancel to give

$$T = \left[\frac{2.42 \times 10^{12}}{24.9 \times 10^7}\right] \text{deg.}$$

This is absolute (as usual).

$$T = \left[\frac{2.42}{24.9} \times 10^5\right] {}^{\circ}K = 0.0972 \times 10^5 \ {}^{\circ}K$$
$$= 9.72 \times 10^3 \ {}^{\circ}K$$

COLLISIONS

• PROBLEM 1-18

Air is estimated to be 20 mole percent O_2 and 80 mole percent N_2 and the total external surface area of an average human being is 2.0m^2. Estimate the number of collisions of air molecules per second with the surface of an average human being at 25°C and 1 atm.

Solution: Assume a one dimensional problem; consequently, only collisions in the positive x-direction will be considered. The mean velocity $\bar{c}_x$ is given by the integral of $c_x f(c_x)$ between the limits of $c_x = 0$ and $c_x = \infty$. That is,

$$\bar{c}_x = \int_0^{\infty} c_x \, f\left(c_x\right) dc_x \tag{1}$$

where $f(c_x)$ is some exponential function of c_x given by

$$f\left(c_x\right) = \left(\frac{m}{2\pi kT}\right)^{\frac{1}{2}} \exp\left(\frac{-\frac{1}{2}mc_x^{\;2}}{kT}\right) \tag{2}$$

Multiply the right-hand side of (2) by 2 so that $\int_0^{\infty} f\left(c_x\right) dc_x = 1$

Equations (1) and (2) become

$$\bar{c}_x = 2(m/2\pi kT)^{\frac{1}{2}} \int_0^{\infty} c_x \exp\left(\frac{-mc_x^2}{2kT}\right) dc_x$$

$$= 2\left(\frac{m}{2\pi kT}\right)^{\frac{1}{2}} (kT/m)$$

$$= \sqrt{\frac{2kT}{\pi m}}$$

$$\bar{c}_x = \sqrt{\frac{2RT}{\pi M}}$$

The collision frequency, Z is given by

$$Z = \frac{1}{2} N\bar{c}$$

where N is the number of molecules and $\frac{1}{2}$ is the fraction of molecules moving toward the surface.

$$Z = \frac{\frac{1}{2} \times 1 \text{ atm} \times 6.023 \times 10^{23} \text{ molecules mole}^{-1}}{82.06 \text{ cm}^3 \text{ atm deg}^{-1} \text{ mole}^{-1} \times 298 \text{ deg}} \times \sqrt{\frac{2 \times 8.314 \times 10^7 \times 298}{\pi}} \left(\frac{0.2}{\sqrt{32}} + \frac{0.8}{\sqrt{28}}\right)$$

$$= 2.885 \times 10^{23} \text{ collisions cm}^{-2} \text{ sec}^{-1}.$$

But the number of collisions = ZA, where A is the area.

$$ZA = \left(2.885 \times 10^{23} \text{collisions cm}^{-2} \text{sec}^{-1}\right)\left(\frac{100 \text{ cm}}{1\text{m}}\right)^2 (2.0 \text{ m}^2)$$

or

$$ZA = 5.77 \times 10^{27} \text{ collisions sec}^{-1}$$

• PROBLEM 1-19

A sample of caesium is heated in an oven to 500°C. Calculate

a) the number of collisions a single Cs atom makes inside the oven per second;

b) the number of collisions all the atoms make per second. Assume the volume of the oven to be 50 cm^3, the vapor pressure of Cs at 500°C is 80 mm Hg, and $\bar{C} = 351$ m sec^{-1}.

Solution: a) The number of collisions a single atom makes per unit time is called the collision frequency and is given by

$$Z = \sqrt{2}\,\sigma\,\bar{C}N/V \qquad (1)$$

where σ is the area of oven $= \pi d^2$ and d is the cross-section. $\bar{C}$ is the mean speed of the atoms, V is the volume of the oven and N is the number of molecules per unit volume.

From equation (1)

$$\frac{N}{V} = \frac{nL}{V} = \frac{P}{kT}$$

where P is the pressure

$$Z = 2^{\frac{1}{2}}\,\sigma\,\bar{C}\left(\frac{P}{kT}\right)$$

$$\sigma = \pi d^2$$

The cross-section of the oven is given as $5.40\ \text{Å} = 540 \times 10^{-12}\text{m}$

$$\sigma = \pi \times (540 \times 10^{-12}\text{m})^2$$

$$\sigma = 9.2 \times 10^{-19}\text{m}^2$$

Also

$$P = \left(\frac{80\ \text{mm Hg}}{760\ \text{mm Hg}}\right)(1.0133 \times 10^5\ \text{Nm}^{-2})$$

$$= 1.07 \times 10^4\ \text{Nm}^{-2}$$

Substituting for P, σ and $\bar{C}$ in equation (1) gives

$$Z = \frac{2^{\frac{1}{2}}(9.2 \times 10^{-19}\ \text{m}^2)(351\ \text{m-s}^{-1})(1.07 \times 10^4\ \text{Nm}^{-2})}{(1.381 \times 10^{-23}\ \text{JK}^{-1})(773°\text{K})}$$

or

$$Z = 4.6 \times 10^8\ \text{s}^{-1}\ .$$

b) The total number of atomic collisions is given by

$$Z_{CsCs} = \tfrac{1}{2}\,Z\,N/V = \tfrac{1}{2}\,Z(P/kT)$$

$$= \frac{\tfrac{1}{2}(4.6 \times 10^8\ \text{s}^{-1})(1.07 \times 10^4\ \text{Nm}^{-2})}{(1.38 \times 10^{-23}\ \text{JK}^{-1})(773°\text{K})}$$

$$= \left(2.31 \times 10^{32}\ \text{s}^{-1}\ \text{m}^{-3}\right)\left(\frac{1\text{m}}{100\ \text{cm}}\right)^3$$

$$Z_{CsCs} = 1.16 \times 10^{28}\ \text{sec}^{-1}$$

• PROBLEM 1-20

A gas in two dimensions is enclosed in a rectangular container. Calculate the number of molecular collisions on a unit length of the container.

Solution: A gas in two dimensions comprise a system of molecules having kinetic energy due to motion along two directions in space, say the x- and y-directions. In this problem collisions are directed at a 1 cm length, therefore only components of velocity in the positive x-direction are considered.

Assume there are N molecules per unit area in the container, then from the Boltzman equation, the number of molecules with velocities between u and u + du are

$$N\,P(u)du\ .$$

The total number of molecules striking the unit area of the container per second in this velocity range are

$$N\,uP(u)du\ . \tag{1}$$

Therefore the collision frequency, Z, per unit length is obtained by integrating (1) between the limits of u = 0 and u = +∞ . Thus,

$$Z = N\int_0^\infty uP(u)du$$

The integral can be evaluated easily using the explicit form of the velocity distributions.

$$Z = N\left(\frac{m}{2\pi kT}\right)^{\frac{1}{2}} \int_0^\infty \exp\left[\frac{-mu^2}{2kT}\right] u\,du$$

$$= N\left(\frac{m}{2\pi kT}\right)^{\frac{1}{2}} \left(\frac{2kT}{2m}\right)$$

$$Z = N\left(\frac{kT}{2\pi m}\right)^{\frac{1}{2}}$$

The two dimensional average speed follows in the same manner and is given by

$$\bar{c} = \int_0^\infty p(c)cdc$$

$$= \frac{m}{2k}\int_0^\infty c^2 \exp\left[\frac{-mc^2}{2kT}\right] dc$$

$$= \frac{m}{kT}\ \frac{\pi}{4}\left(\frac{2kT}{m}\right)^{3/2}$$

$$\bar{c} = \left(\frac{\pi kT}{2m}\right)^{\frac{1}{2}}\ .$$

Therefore

$$\frac{\bar{c}}{\pi} = \left(\frac{kT}{2m\pi}\right)^{\frac{1}{2}}$$

or

$$Z = \frac{N\bar{c}}{\pi}$$

• PROBLEM 1-21

The concentration of hydrogen atoms in intergalactic space at a temperature of 7.8×10^{50}K is about 1 atom per 100 liter. Assuming the collision diameter of the hydrogen atom is 2.0Å calculate a) the mean free path of an atom in light-years.
b) The approximate average time, in years, between collisions of a given atom.

Solution: a) The mean free path, λ, is a measure of the average distance that a molecule travels between successive collisions and is defined as

$$\lambda = \frac{\bar{c}}{Z} \quad (1)$$

where $\bar{c}$ is the mean speed of the atoms and Z is the collision frequency.

Equation (1) can also be written as

$$\lambda = \frac{\bar{c}}{2^{\frac{1}{2}}\pi\sigma^2\bar{c}c}$$

or

$$\lambda = \frac{1}{2^{\frac{1}{2}}\pi\sigma^2 c}$$

where c is the concentration

$$\lambda = \frac{1}{2^{\frac{1}{2}}\pi\left(10^{-5}\text{atom cm}^{-3}\right)\left(4\times10^{-16}\text{cm}^2\right)}\left(\frac{1\text{ light-yr}}{9.464\times10^{17}\text{cm}}\right)$$

$$\lambda = 59 \text{ light-yr}$$

b) The mean speed is given by

$$\bar{c} = \sqrt{\frac{8RT}{\pi M}}$$

where M is the molecular weight of hydrogen and R is the gas constant. Inserting the respective values into the equation yields

$$\bar{c} = \sqrt{\frac{8(8.314)(10^7)(7.8\times10^5\text{erg}(\text{g atom})^{-1}}{\pi(1.008\text{g}(\text{g atom})^{-1})}}$$

$$= \sqrt{1.64 \times 10^{14} \text{ erg g}^{-1}}$$

$$\bar{c} = 1.28 \times 10^7 \text{ cm sec}^{-1}$$

$$\text{Time}, t = \frac{\lambda}{\bar{c}}$$

$$= \frac{59\text{ light-yr}\left(9.464\times10^{17}\text{ cm(light-yr)}^{-1}\right)}{1.28 \times 10^7 \text{ cm sec}^{-1}}\left(\frac{1\text{ yr}}{3.156\times10^7\text{sec}}\right)$$

$$= 138.2 \times 10^3 \text{ yr}$$

or

$$t = 1.382 \times 10^5 \text{ yr}$$

IDEAL GASES

• PROBLEM 1-22

The following equation is given for 1 mole of a gas

$$V = f(P,T) \quad (1)$$

Derive the ideal gas equation.

Solution: The $V = f(P,T)$ expression means that molar volume is a function of pressure and temperature. If the molar volume is a property of the system, then equation (1) can be differentiated to give

$$dV = \left(\frac{\partial V}{\partial P}\right)_T dP + \left(\frac{\partial V}{\partial T}\right)_P dT \tag{2}$$

Since V is a function of pressure and temperature and an ideal gas is being considered, the appropriate formulas to use are Boyle's and Gay-Lussac's laws. These are $VP = k$ and $V = k'T$ respectively. They will be useful in evaluating $(\partial V/\partial P)_T$ and $(\partial V/\partial T)_P$. Note that k and k' are proportionality constants. From Boyle's law, $(\partial V/\partial P)_T = -k/P^2$. But $k = VP$. Therefore,

$$\left(\frac{\partial V}{\partial P}\right)_T = -\frac{VP}{P^2} = -\frac{V}{P}$$

and from Gay-Lussac's law,

$$\left(\frac{\partial V}{\partial T}\right) = k' = \frac{V}{T}.$$

Substituting these into equation (2) gives

$$dV = -\frac{V}{P}dP + \frac{V}{T}dT$$

and separating variables yields

$$\frac{dV}{V} = -\frac{dP}{P} + \frac{dT}{T}$$

or

$$\frac{dV}{V} + \frac{dP}{P} - \frac{dT}{T} = 0 \tag{3}$$

Integrating equation (3) gives

$$\ln V + \ln P - \ln T = \ln R \tag{4}$$

where R = integration constant.

Equation (4) can also be put in the form

$$\ln\left(\frac{VP}{T}\right) = \ln R .$$

Taking the exponents of both sides gives

$$e^{\ln(VP/T)} = e^{\ln R}$$

or

$$\frac{VP}{T} = R .$$

Note that R is the universal gas constant.

• PROBLEM 1-23

A sample of an ideal gas at 27°C and 380 torr occupied a volume of 492 cm^3. What was the number of moles of gas in this sample? ($R = 0.082$ liter atm $mole^{-1} deg^{-1}$).

Solution: Because the gas is ideal, the Ideal Gas law applies and the problem becomes merely an exercise in choosing the correct units. These units can be chosen correctly by converting the units of the values given to the units of the gas constant, R. Therefore, the volume must be in liters and the pressure, in atm. The temperature must be absolute (°K). The ideal gas law is represented by the formula PV = nRT where P is the pressure in atmospheres, V is the volume in liters, n is the number of moles, R is the Universal Gas constant in liters-atm/mole-°K, and T is in degrees kelvin. Thus,

$$\frac{380\ \text{torr}}{760\ \text{torr/atm}} = .500\ \text{atm}, \quad 27^\circ\text{C} + 273 = 300^\circ\text{K},$$

$$492\ \text{cm}^3 \times \frac{1\ \text{liter}}{1000\ \text{cm}^3} = .492\ \text{liters}.$$

$$PV = nRT \quad \text{or} \quad n = \frac{PV}{RT} = \frac{.500\ \text{atm} \times .492\ \text{liters}}{.0821\ \text{liters atm/mole}^\circ\text{K} \times 300^\circ\text{K}}$$

$$= .0100\ \text{moles}.$$

• PROBLEM 1-24

Calculate the number of moles of air in a column 1 cm^2 in area and rising from sea level to an altitude of 1.5×10^6 cm (about 10 miles), allowing for the barometric decrease in pressure. Assume air to be a uniform gas of molecular weight 29, and a uniform temperature of 0°C. Note that the atmospheric pressure is equal to the total weight of gas in a column of unit area and of infinite height. Conversion factors: R = 0.082 liter-atm/mole-deg = 8.31×10^7 ergs/mole-deg = 1.98 cal/mole-deg; 1 atm = 760 mm Hg = 1×10^6 dynes/cm^2.

Solution: The column of air at a uniform temperature is subject to a gravitational field of acceleration, g. Due to this field, the forces acting upon the lower and upper boundaries are not the same. The difference is equal to the weight of the fluid between the boundaries.

Thus,

$$-df = \pi r^2 \rho g\, dh \tag{1}$$

where f = force, ρ = density, dh = difference in height and g = gravity constant. But the difference in the force per unit area is equal to the pressure difference between the lower and upper boundaries. Therefore, equation (1) takes the form

$$\frac{-df}{\pi r^2} = -dP = \rho g dh \tag{2}$$

The minus sign indicates that the pressure decreases with increasing altitude. For ideal gases,

$$\rho = \frac{PM}{RT} \tag{3}$$

where M = molecular weight.

Using equation (3) appropriately, equation (2) becomes

$$-dP = \frac{PM}{RT} gdh$$

or

$$\frac{dP}{P} = - \frac{Mg}{RT} dh \qquad (4)$$

Integrating equation (4) gives

$$\int_{P_1}^{P_2} \frac{dP}{P} = - \frac{Mg}{RT} \int_0^h dh$$

But $P_1 = 1$ atmosphere. Therefore

$$\int_1^{P_2} \frac{dP}{P} = - \frac{Mg}{RT} h$$

or

$$\ln P \Big|_1^{P_2} = - \frac{Mg}{RT} h \quad ,$$

which becomes

$$\ln\left(\frac{P_2}{1}\right) = - \frac{Mg}{RT} h$$

$$= - \frac{(29)(980)(1.5 \times 10^6)}{(8.31 \times 10^7)(273)}$$

$$= - 1.879$$

$$P_2 = e^{-1.879} = 0.153 \text{ atm}$$

Since the weight of a column of air extending down to sea level is 1×10^6 dynes cm^{-2} , the weight of a column extending down only to a given altitude will be 0.153×10^6 dynes cm^{-2}. Therefore, the weight of the column between the sea level and this given altitude is $1 \times 10^6 - 0.153 \times 10^6 = 0.847 \times 10^6$ dynes cm^{-2}. The weight of this column between the sea level and the given altitude is given by

$$w = nMg \qquad (5)$$

where w = weight

n = number of moles.

Rearranging equation (5) to solve for n gives

$$n = \frac{w}{Mg} = \frac{(0.847 \times 10^6)}{(29)(980)}$$

$$n = 29.8 \text{ moles.}$$

• PROBLEM 1-25

A 2-liter Dumas bulb contains n moles of nitrogen at 0.5 atm pressure and at T°K. On addition of 0.01 moles of oxygen, it is necessary to cool the bulb to a temperature of 10°C in order to maintain the same pressure. Calculate n and T.

Solution: Using the ideal gas formula, we have

$$PV = nRT \tag{1}$$

and

$$n = \frac{PV}{RT} \tag{2}$$

After the addition of oxygen equation (2) becomes

$$(n + .01) = \frac{PV}{RT} = \frac{(.5)(2)}{(0.082)(283)} = 0.0432$$

$$n = 0.0432 - 0.01 = 0.0332 .$$

Now, use equation (1) PV = nRT, to solve for T

$$(.5)(2) = (0.0332)(0.082)\ T$$

$$T = \frac{(.5)(2)}{(0.0332)(0.082)} = 367°K$$

• PROBLEM 1-26

Under what conditions will a pure sample of an ideal gas not only exhibit a pressure of 1 atm but also a concentration of 1 mole $liter^{-1}$?

Solution: In taking a first look at the problem, it might seem out of place because of the word concentration. However, its units are moles/liter. In the ideal gas law n = number of moles and liters represent the volume. Therefore,

$$c = 1 \text{ mole liter}^{-1} = \frac{n}{V}$$

where c = concentration. The ideal gas law is defined as

$$PV = nRT \tag{1}$$

where P = Pressure, V = volume, R = gas constant and T = temperature. Rearranging equation (1) to solve for P gives

$$P = \frac{n}{V} RT . \tag{2}$$

Observe that the n/V term in equation (2) is the definition of concentration. Therefore,

$$P = cRT$$

or

$$1 \text{ atm} = 1 \frac{\text{mole}}{\text{liter}} RT . \tag{3}$$

The R in the right side of equation (2) has units of $0.082 \frac{\text{liter atm}}{\text{mole deg°K}}$

Hence, equation (3) becomes

$$1 \text{ atm} = \left(1 \frac{\text{mole}}{\text{liter}}\right)\left(0.082 \frac{\text{liter atm}}{\text{mole deg}}\right) T$$

Solving for T gives

$$T = \left[\frac{1}{0.082}\right] \text{deg} .$$

Note that deg is always absolute.

$$T = 12.19^\circ K$$

Consequently, an ideal gas will exhibit a pressure of 1 atm and a concentration of mole liter^{-1} only when the absolute temperature is $12.19^\circ K$.

• PROBLEM 1-27

a) Show that the pressure of the column of air at the height x in Figure 1 is given by

$$P = P_0 \exp\left(-\frac{Mgx}{kT}\right) .$$

P_0 is pressure at $x = 0$, g is the accelaration due to gravity and M is the average molecular mass of molecules in air. Assume a uniform air temperature T in the gravitational field of the earth.

b) What is P when $P_0 = 760$ mm Hg, $T = 273^\circ K$ and x is 8km ?

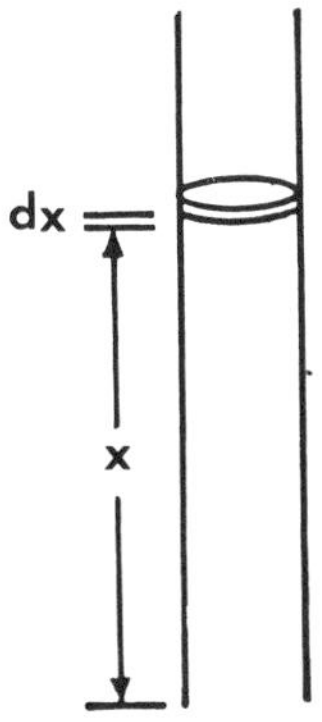

Fig. 1

Solution: a) Consider a column of air of unit cross-sectional area, and dx cm thick at an altitude, x, above the surface of the earth. Due to gravitational forces, the density and consequently the pressure of the earth's atmosphere is not uniform. The pressure decreases with increasing altitude. Therefore, the forces acting upon the top and bottom boundaries of the disc are not the same. The difference in these forces is equal to the weight of the disc. Thus,

$$-df = \rho g dx .$$

The difference in the force per unit area is equal to the pressure difference between the top and bottom boundaries of the disc:

$$-df = -dp = \rho g dx \qquad (1)$$

where g is the acceleration due to gravity and ρ is the density. Notice the minus sign which indicates that the pressure decreases with increasing altitude. Equation (1) may be rewritten as

$$df = dp = -\rho g dx . \qquad (2)$$

But

$$\rho = PM/RT$$

where M is the average molecular mass of air and R is the gas constant, therefore equation (2) changes to

$$dp = \frac{-PM}{RT}\, gdx \,. \tag{2}$$

Applying the boundary condition that at $x = 0$, $P = P_0$. Equation (2) can be integrated after separating the variables and using the appropriate limits. Thus,

$$\int_{P_0}^{P} \frac{dP}{P} = -\frac{Mg}{RT} \int_0^x dx$$

$$\ln P \Big|_{P_0}^{P} = -\frac{Mg}{RT}\, x$$

or

$$\ln \frac{P}{P_0} = -\frac{Mgx}{RT}$$

Taking the exponent of both sides gives

$$\frac{P}{P_0} = e^{-Mgx/RT}$$

or

$$P = P_0\, e^{-Mgx/RT} \tag{3}$$

b) Using $x = 8$ km, $P_0 = 760$ mm Hg and $T = 273\,^\circ K$ in equation (3) gives

$$P = 760 \text{ mm Hg } e^{-\frac{\left(29 \text{ gmole}^{-1}\right)\left(\frac{1 \text{ kg}}{1000 \text{ g}}\right)\left(9.8 \text{ m sec}^{-2}\right)\left(8000 \text{ m}\right)}{\left(8.314 J\,^\circ K^{-1} \text{ mole}^{-1}\right)\left(273\,^\circ K\right)}}$$

$$= 760 \text{ mm Hg} \exp \frac{-\left(29 \text{ gmole}^{-1}\right)\left(\frac{1 \text{ kg}}{1000 \text{ g}}\right)\left(9.8 \text{ m sec}^{-2}\right)\left(8000 \text{ m}\right)}{\left(8.314 \frac{m^2 kg}{sec^2}\,^\circ K^{-1} \text{ mole}^{-1}\right)\left(273\,^\circ K\right)}$$

The exponential term is dimensionless as expected. Thus,

$$P = 760 \text{ mm Hg} \exp(-1.0017)$$

$$= 760 \text{ mm Hg}(0.3672)$$

or

$$P = 279 \text{ mm Hg}.$$

• PROBLEM 1-28

The stopcock between a 3-liter bulb containing oxygen at 195 torr and a 2-liter bulb containing nitrogen at 530 torr is opened. After equilibration, what is the final pressure? Assume that T is constant.

Solution: The ideal gas law is given by $PV = nRT$. In this problem,

P = final pressure
V = final volume
n = total moles of oxygen and nitrogen
R = universal gas constant
T = temperature .

By Dalton's law of partial pressures, the total final pressure is equal

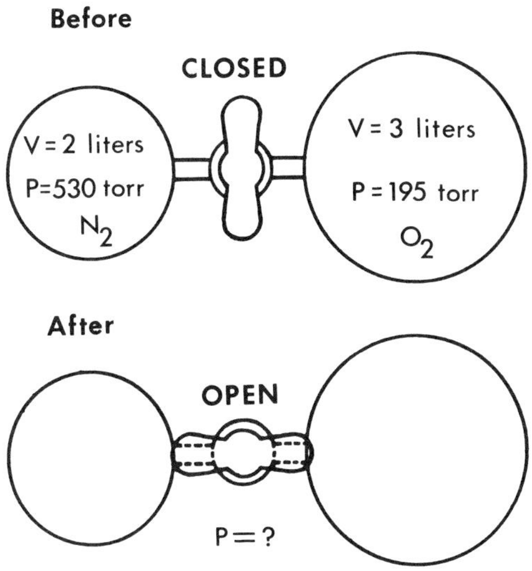

to final pressure of oxygen plus the final pressure of nitrogen. Therefore,

$$P_{final} = P_{O_2} + P_{N_2} = n_{O_2}\frac{RT}{V} + n_{N_2}\frac{RT}{V} \quad . \qquad (1)$$

Note that $V = 3 + 2 = 5$ liters because the P_{final} of the system is being considered after equilibriation.
Note that T is not known. It is assumed to be constant and may cancel.
Using original conditions, n_{O_2} and n_{N_2} can be calculated as follows:

$$n_{O_2} = \frac{P_{O_2}V_{O_2}}{RT} = \frac{(195 \text{ torr})(3 \text{ liters})}{RT}$$

and

$$n_{N_2} = \frac{P_{N_2}V_{N_2}}{RT} = \frac{(530 \text{ torr})(2 \text{ liters})}{RT}$$

From these, $n_{O_2}RT = P_{O_2}V_{O_2}$ and $n_{N_2}RT = P_{N_2}V_{N_2}$. Adding up both equations give

$$n_{O_2}RT + n_{N_2}RT = P_{O_2}V_{O_2} + P_{N_2}V_{N_2}$$

or

$$RT(n_{O_2} + n_{N_2}) = (195)(3) + (530)(2) .$$

Observe that if this equation is divided by V, it becomes equation (1), which is the equation for solving for P_{final} . That is,

$$\frac{RT}{V}(n_{O_2} + n_{N_2}) = \frac{(195)(3) + (530)(2)}{V}$$

Recall that V = 5. Therefore,

$$P_{final} = \frac{585 + 1060}{5} = 329 \text{ torr.}$$

• PROBLEM 1-29

Two flasks of equal volume are filled with nitrogen gas and, when both are immersed in boiling water, the gas pressure inside the system is 0.5 atm. One of the flasks is then immersed in an ice-water mixture, keeping the other in the boiling water. Calculate the new pressure for the system.

Solution: In this problem, the number of moles of gas remains the same. Therefore, using $n = PV/RT$, when the two flasks are immersed in boiling water,

$$n = n_1 + n_2 = \frac{P}{R}\frac{V_1}{T_1} + \frac{P}{R}\frac{V_2}{T_2} = \frac{P}{R}\left(\frac{V_1}{T_1} + \frac{V_2}{T_2}\right)$$

But $V_1 = V_2 = V$ at the initial stage

$$n = \frac{.5}{R}\left(\frac{V}{373} + \frac{V}{373}\right) = \frac{.5}{R}\left(\frac{2V}{373}\right) = \frac{.5V}{R}\left(\frac{2}{373}\right)$$

when one of the flasks is immersed in an ice-water mixture

$$n = n'_1 + n'_2 = \frac{P'}{R}\left(\frac{V}{273} + \frac{V}{373}\right) = \frac{P'V}{R}\left(\frac{1}{273} + \frac{1}{373}\right)$$

Now n'_1 = number of moles of gas in flask 1 immersed in ice-water mixture

n'_2 = number of moles of gas in flask 2

Equating both mathematical expressions for n,

$$\frac{.5V}{R}\left(\frac{2}{373}\right) = \frac{P'V}{R}\left(\frac{1}{273} + \frac{1}{373}\right)$$

$$P' = \left[\frac{.5V}{R}\left(\frac{2}{373}\right)\right] \Big/ \left[\frac{V}{R}\left(\frac{1}{273} + \frac{1}{373}\right)\right]$$

$$= [(0.5)(546)] \big/ (646) = 0.423 \text{ atm.}$$

• PROBLEM 1-30

The helium content of the atmosphere at sea level is about 5×10^{-4} mol %. A round 100-cm^3 Pyrex flask with wall thickness of 0.7 mm is evacuated to 10^{-12}atm and sealed; calculate the pressure in the flask at the end of one month due to inward diffusion of helium. At 20°C the permeability of Pyrex glass to helium is given as $4.9 \times 10^{-13} cm^3 s^{-1}$ per millimeter thickness and per millibar (m bar) partial pressure difference.

Solution: The volume of helium flowing through the wall of the flask varies linearly with the partial pressure difference and inversely with the thickness of the wall. Define dV_s/dt = rate of flow in cc(STP) per sec.

$$\frac{dV_s}{dt} = \frac{k(P_0 - P)\,A}{d} \qquad (1)$$

where k = permeability (cc gas(STP) per sec per cm^2 of surface per millimeter thickness per millibar partial pressure difference)

P_0 = pressure of helium outside of flask (m bar)

P_1 = pressure of helium inside of flask (m bar)

A = surface area of flask (cm^2)

d = thickness of wall (mm)

$$V_s = \frac{VT_sP}{P_sT}$$

$$V_s = \frac{(100\ cc)(273.15^\circ K)(P\ m\ bar)}{(1013.3\ m\ bar\ atm^{-1})(1\ atm)(293.15^\circ K)}$$

$$V_s = 0.09195\ P$$

Taking derivatives of both sides with respect to time yields,

$$\frac{dV_s}{dt} = 0.09195\ dP/dt \qquad (2)$$

Combining equations (1) and (2) gives,

$$\frac{dP}{dt} = \frac{k(P_0 - P)A}{0.0915\ d} \qquad (3)$$

By definition,

$$A = 4\pi r^2 \quad \text{and} \quad V = 4/3\ \pi r^3\ .$$

Solving for r from the V expression gives

$$r^3 = \frac{3V}{4\pi}$$

or

$$r = \left(\frac{3V}{4\pi}\right)^{\frac{1}{3}}$$

Squaring r yields

$$r^2 = \left(\frac{3V}{4\pi}\right)^{\frac{2}{3}}$$

Substituting this into the A expression yields

$$A = 4\pi\left(\frac{3V}{4\pi}\right)^{\frac{2}{3}} = 4\pi\left(\frac{3 \times 100}{4\pi}\right)^{2/3}$$

$$A = 104.2\ cm^2$$

From equation (3),

$$\frac{dP}{(P_0-P)} = \frac{kA}{0.0915\ d}\ dt$$

$$\frac{dP}{(P_0-P)} = \frac{(4.9 \times 10^{-13})(104.2\ cm^2)}{(0.0915)(0.7)}\ dt\ . \qquad (4)$$

Integrating equation (4) gives,

$$\int_0^{P_0} \frac{dP}{P_0-P} = 7.932 \times 10^{-10} \int_0^t dt$$

$$\ln \frac{P_0}{P_0 - P} = 7.932 \times 10^{-10}\ t$$

$$t = 30 \times 24 \times 3600$$
$$= 2.592 \times 10^6 \text{ sec}$$

$$P_0 = X_{He}\ P_{total}$$
$$= (5 \times 10^{-6})(1013.3)$$
$$= 5.066 \times 10^{-3} \text{ m bar}$$

$$\frac{P_0}{P_0 - P} = e^{(7.932 \times 10^{-10})(2.592 \times 10^6)}$$
$$= 1.002058$$

$$P_0 = 1.002058(P_0 - P)$$

$$P_0 = 1.002058\ P_0 - 1.002058\ P$$

$$1.002058\ P = P_0(1.002058 - 1)$$

$$1.002058\ P = 5.066 \times 10^{-3} \text{ m bar } (0.002058)$$

$$1.002058\ P = 1.0426 \times 10^{-5}$$
$$P = 1.04 \times 10^{-5} \text{ m bar}$$

• PROBLEM 1-31

The gauge pressure in an automobile tire when measured during the winter at 32°F was 30 pounds per square inch (psi). The same tire was used during the summer, and its temperature rose to 122°F. If we assume that the volume of the tire did not change, and no air leaked out between winter and summer, what is the new pressure as measured on the gauge?

Solution: From one season to another, the only properties of the gas that will change are pressure and temperature. The mass (hence the number of moles) and the volume will remain the same. If it is assumed that this gas is ideal, then

$$PV = nRT \tag{1}$$

where

P = Pressure of the gas
V = Volume of the gas
n = number of moles
R = gas constant
T = Temperature of the gas.

Rearranging equation (1) to solve for P gives,

$$P = (n/V)RT\ . \tag{2}$$

Since n and V are constant, equation (2) shows that pressure is directly proportional to temperature. That is, $P/T = nR/V$ = constant. Therefore,

$$\frac{P_1}{T_1} = \frac{P_2}{T_2} = \frac{n_1 R}{V_1} = \frac{n_2 R}{V_2} \tag{3}$$

where P_1 = initial pressure
T_1 = initial temperature
P_2 = final pressure
T_2 = final temperature

n_1 and n_2 = initial and final moles respectively. V_1 and V_2 = initial and final volume respectively.

The moles and volume are not changing; therefore, $n_1 = n_2$ and $V_1 = V_2$. Consequently, equation (3) can be written as

$$\frac{P_1}{T_1} = \frac{P_2}{T_2} . \tag{4}$$

Before equation (4) can be used, the pressure and temperature must be in absolute scales.

$$\frac{°C}{5} = \frac{°F-32}{9} \tag{5}$$

and

$$P = 14.7 \text{ psia} + \text{psig} \tag{6}$$

where °C = degrees centigrade
°F = degrees farenheit
Psia = absolute psi
Psig = gauge psi

Using equations (5) and (6),

$$122°F = 50°C = (50 + 273)°K = 323°K$$

and

$$P = 14.7 + 30 = 44.7 \text{ psia} .$$

These can now be inserted into equation (4) to give,

$$\frac{44.7}{273} = \frac{P_2}{323} .$$

Therefore,

$$P_2 = \left[\frac{(44.7)(323)}{273}\right] \text{psia}$$

$$= 52.9 \text{ psia}$$

or from equation (6),

$$52.9 \text{ psia} = 14.7 \text{ psia} + x \text{ psig}$$

$$P_2 = (52.9 - 14.7) \text{psig}$$

$$= 38.2 \text{ psig}$$

• PROBLEM 1-32

A Dumas bulb is filled with chlorine gas at the ambient pressure and is found to contain 7.1 g of chlorine when the temperature is T°K. The bulb is then placed in a second thermostat bath whose temperature is 30°C hotter than the first one. The stopcock on the bulb is opened so that the chlorine-gas pressure returns to the original value. The bulb is now found to contain 6.4 g of chlorine. Calculate the value of the original temperature. If the volume of the bulb was 2.24 liters, what was the ambient pressure? The atomic weight of chlorine is 35.5.

Solution: The procedure used is to compare the two cases that involve the same volume and pressure. Therefore,

$$n_1T_1 = n_2T_2 \tag{1}$$

where

n_1 = moles of first gas

n_2 = moles of second gas

The molecular weight of chlorine is 71. Therefore 7.1 gm corresponds to

$$(7.1\ g)\left(\frac{\text{mole}}{71\ g}\right) = 0.1\ \text{mole}.$$

Since the final 6.4 gm corresponds to 10% less,

$$n_2 = .1 - 10\%\ \text{of}\ .1$$
$$= .1 - (10/100)(.1) = .1 - .01$$
$$= .09\ \text{moles}.$$

Using equation (1), $.1T_1 = .09T_2$. But $T_2 = T_1 + 30$

$$.1T_1 = .09(T_1 + 30)$$
$$.1T_1 = .09T_1 + 2.7$$
$$.1T_1 - .09T_1 = 2.7$$
$$0.01T_1 = 2.7$$
$$T_1 = 2.7/.01 = 270^\circ K$$

Now V = 2.24 liters. Using PV = nRT, it follows that

$$P = \frac{nRT}{V}$$

$$= \frac{(0.1\ \text{mole})\left(\frac{0.082\ \ell\text{-atm}}{^\circ K\ \text{mole}}\right)(270^\circ K)}{22.4\ \ell}$$

$$P = 0.99\ \text{atm}$$

• PROBLEM 1-33

Two separate bulbs contain ideal gases A and B, respectively. The density of gas A is twice that of gas B, and the molecular weight of gas A is half that of gas B; the two gases are at the same temperature. Calculate the ratio of the pressure of gas A to that of gas B.

Solution: Using PV = nRT, $P_AV_A = n_ART_A$ for gas A and

$$P_BV_B = n_BRT_B \quad \text{for gas B}.$$

The problem states that $T_A = T_B = T$. So $P_AV_A = n_ART$ and $P_BV_B = n_BRT$ after substitution. Values for n and V are not given. However, it is known that

density = mass/volume

volume = mass/density

Now

$$P_A\left(\frac{M_A}{P_A}\right) = \left(\frac{M_A}{MW_A}\right) RT$$

and

$$P_B\left(\frac{M_B}{P_B}\right) = \left(\frac{M_B}{MW_B}\right) RT$$

where

M = Mass
MW = Molecular Weight
ρ = Density

The problem also states that $\rho_A = 2\rho_B$ thus, $\rho_B = \rho_A/2$, $MW_A = \frac{1}{2} MW_B$ and $MW_B = 2MW_A$

Using the ideal equation with appropriate substitution,

$$P_A\left(\frac{M_A}{\rho_A}\right) = \left(\frac{M_A}{MW_A}\right) RT \qquad (1)$$

and

$$P_B\left(\frac{M_B}{\rho_A/2}\right) = \left(\frac{M_B}{2MW_A}\right) RT \qquad (2)$$

Dividing (1) by (2),

$$\frac{P_A\left(\frac{M_A}{\rho_A}\right)}{P_B\left(\frac{2M_B}{\rho_A}\right)} = \frac{\left(\frac{M_A}{MW_A}\right) RT}{\left(\frac{M_B}{2MW_A}\right) RT}$$

$$\frac{P_A}{P_B} = \left[\left(\frac{2M_B}{\rho_A}\right)\left(\frac{M_A}{MW_A}\right)\right] \bigg/ \left[\left(\frac{M_A}{\rho_A}\right)\left(\frac{M_B}{2MW_A}\right)\right] = \left[\frac{2M_B M_A}{\rho_A MW_A}\right] \bigg/ \left[\frac{M_A M_B}{\rho_A 2MW_A}\right]$$

$$= \frac{2M_B M_A}{\rho_A MW_A} \times \frac{\rho_A 2MW_A}{M_A M_B} = 4$$

$$P_A/P_B = 4$$

• PROBLEM 1-34

An iron pipe 2m long and closed at one end is lowered vertically into water until the closed end is flush with the water surface (see Fig. 1 below). Calculate the height h of the water level in the pipe. Miscellaneous data: 25°C, diam. of pipe is 3 in., density of water is 1.00 g/cc, barometric pressure is 1.00 atm. Also, 1 atm = 10^6 dynes/cm^2 = 10 m hydrostatic head of water (neglect the effect of water vapor pressure).

Solution: The equation $P_1V_1/T_1 = P_2V_2/T_2$ is applicable here. But $T_1 = T_2$, $P_1V_1 = P_2V_2$ where

P_1 = initial pressure

P_2 = final pressure

V_1 = initial volume

V_2 = final volume

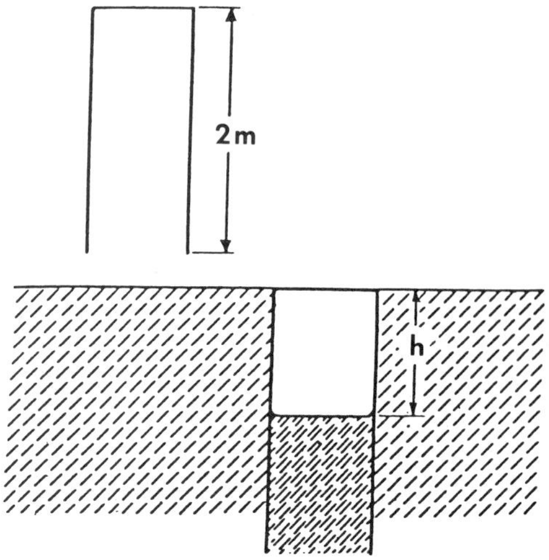

Fig. 1

$$P_2 = P_1\left(\frac{V_1}{V_2}\right) = P_1\left(\frac{2 \times \text{area of pipe}}{h \times \text{area of pipe}}\right) \qquad (1)$$

$$P_2 = 2P_1/h .$$

In this problem P_1 = 1 atm = 10m hydrostatic head and P_2 = (10+h)meters. From equation (1) we have

$$10+h = \frac{2(10)}{h} = \frac{20}{h}$$

$$h(10+h) = 20$$

$$h^2 + 10h = 20$$

$$h^2 + 10h - 20 = 0$$

This is a quadratic equation and there are two possible values for h. First both h values are found and then it is determined which one is suitable to the problem.

Using the "almighty" formula for solving quadratic equations,

$$h = \frac{-b \pm \sqrt{b^2 - 4ac}}{2a}$$

where b = coefficient of h = 10 in this case

a = coefficient of h^2 = 1 in this case

c = the constant = -20 in this case .

$$h = \frac{-10 \pm \sqrt{10^2 - (4)(1)(-20)}}{2(1)}$$

$$= \frac{-10 \pm \sqrt{100 + 80}}{2} = \frac{-10 \pm \sqrt{180}}{2}$$

The answers are either

$$\frac{-10 + \sqrt{180}}{2} = \frac{3.42}{2} = 1.71\text{m} ,$$

or

$$\frac{-10 - \sqrt{180}}{2} = \frac{-10 - 13.42}{2} = \frac{-23.42}{2} = -11.71\text{m} .$$

Both answers are mathematically valid for our equation. But physically, h is never negative. Therefore -11.71m is discarded. The final answer is h = 1.71m .

• PROBLEM 1-35

> What volume (in liters) will a 0.17 g sample of H_2S gas occupy at 27°C and 380 torr?

Solution: Assume that the H_2S gas is ideal. Then the relation, PV = nRT can be used.

P is the pressure of the gas, V = volume, n = number of moles, R = gas constant and T = temperature.

Before the above equation can be used to evaluate the volume, the number of moles need to be known. This is defined as the ratio of the mass of the gas to its molecular weight.

That is, n = g/mol.wt. where g stands for the mass of the sample. g is given to be 0.17 g and the molecular weight of H_2S = 2 + 32.06 = 34.06 g mol^{-1}. Therefore,

$$n = \frac{0.17g}{34.06\ g\ mol^{-1}}$$

$$= 0.005\ mol$$

Solving the ideal gas law for V gives

$$V = \frac{nRT}{P} = \frac{(0.005)RT}{P} \tag{1}$$

R = 0.082 liter atm mol^{-1} K^{-1} . Since R is in liter atm mol^{-1} K^{-1}, T has to be converted to K and P to atm. Thus,

$$T = 27°C = (27 + 273)°K = 300°K$$

and

$$P = 380\ torr = \frac{380\ torr}{760\ torr\ atm^{-1}} = 0.50\ atm.$$

Substituting these into equation (1) gives

$$V = \frac{(0.005\ mol)(0.082\ liter\ atm\ mol^{-1}\ K^{-1})(300K)}{(0.50\ atm)}$$

Observe that all the units cancel out except the liter, which is what the problem requires.

$$V = 0.246\ liter.$$

• PROBLEM 1-36

> Consider the apparatus in the diagram. If the temperature of the oil is raised from 68°C to 136°C, how large is the final volume compared to the initial? (Ignore the small effect of pressure change; i.e., assume that the pressure remains constant.)

Solution: Here, the properties of the oil that are changing are volume and temperature.

If this is ideal, then

$$PV = nRT \tag{1}$$

where P = pressure, V = volume, n = number of moles, R = constant and T = temperature. Since n and P are constant,

$$V \propto T$$

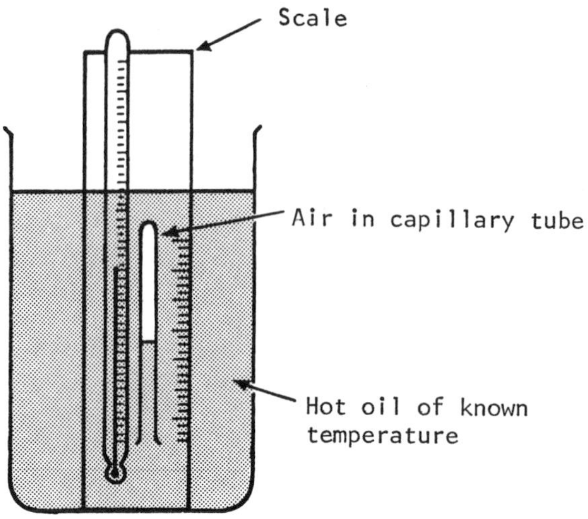

or

$$\frac{V}{T} = \frac{nR}{P} \tag{2}$$

Equation (2) can be written in the form

$$\frac{V_1}{T_1} = \frac{V_2}{T_2} = \frac{n_1R}{P_1} = \frac{n_2R}{P_2} \tag{3}$$

But $n_1 = n_2$ and $P_1 = P_2$. Therefore equation (3) becomes

$$\frac{V_1}{T_1} = \frac{V_2}{T_2} \tag{4}$$

where V_1 and V_2 = initial and final volumes respectively and T_1 and T_2 = initial and final temperature respectively. Since T is supposed to be in absolute scale, $T_1 = 68 + 273 = 341°K$

$$T_2 = 136 + 273 = 409°K$$

Using these in equation (4) yields

$$\frac{V_1}{V_2} = \frac{T_1}{T_2} = \frac{341}{409} = 0.833$$

$$V_2 = \frac{V_1}{0.833} = 1.2\ V_1$$

Thus the final volume is about 20% larger than the initial volume.

• PROBLEM 1-37

A pioneer aeronaut is planning the design of a hot-air balloon. What volume of air at 100°C should be used if the balloon is to have a gross lifting power of 200 kg (defined as the mass of displaced air minus the mass of hot air)? The ambient temperature and pressure are 25°C and 1 atm, and the average molecular weight of air is 29 g/mole, whereas that of the hot air is 32 g/mol (due to the presence of some CO_2).

Solution: Since $n = \frac{\text{weight or mass}}{\text{molecular weight}} = W/M$ = number of moles, the ideal gas equation can be written as

$$PV = \frac{W}{M} RT \tag{1}$$

where P = pressure
V = volume
R = gas constant
T = temperature in °K

The problem states that $W_{air} - W_{hot\ air} = 200$ kg or 2×10^5 gm. From equation (1)

$$W_{air} = \frac{VPM_{air}}{RT_{air}}$$

$$W_{hot\ air} = \frac{VPM_{hot\ air}}{RT_{hot\ air}}$$

$$W_{air} - W_{hot\ air} = \frac{VP}{R}\left(\frac{M_{air}}{T_{air}} - \frac{M_{hot\ air}}{T_{hot\ air}}\right) = 2 \times 10^5 \text{ gm}$$

$$2 \times 10^5 \text{ gm} = \frac{VP}{R}\left(\frac{M_{air}}{T_{air}} - \frac{M_{hot\ air}}{T_{hot\ air}}\right)$$

and

$$V = \frac{2 \times 10^5 \text{ gm} \times R}{P\left(\frac{M_{air}}{T_{air}} - \frac{M_{hot\ air}}{T_{hot\ air}}\right)}$$

$$= \frac{(2 \times 10^5 \text{ gm})(0.082 \text{ liters atm } {}^\circ K^{-1} \text{ mole}^{-1})}{1 \text{ atm}\left(\frac{29 \text{ g mole}^{-1}}{298^\circ K} - \frac{32 \text{ g mole}^{-1}}{373^\circ K}\right)}$$

$$= \frac{(2 \times 10^5 \text{ gm})(0.082 \text{ liters atm } {}^\circ K^{-1} \text{ mole}^{-1})}{1 \text{ atm}(0.0115) \text{ g mole}^{-1}/{}^\circ K}$$

$$V = 1.42 \times 10^6 \text{ liters.}$$

• PROBLEM 1-38

Air is approximately 80% nitrogen and 20% oxygen (on a mole basis). If 4.0 g of hydrogen is added to a 22.4-liter flask maintained at 0°C and initially filled with air at 1 atm pressure, what will be the molecular weight (i.e., the average molecular weight) of the hydrogen-air mixture?

Solution: There are 22.4 liters of air at STP (0°C and 1 atm). Therefore, there is 1 mole of air. Also, there are 4 gm of hydrogen, which is equivalent to

$$\frac{4 \text{ gm}}{2 \text{ gm/mole}} = 2 \text{ moles.}$$

By definition,

$$M_{average} = \left[\sum_{i=1}^{3} n_i M_i\right] \Bigg/ \left[\sum_{i=1}^{3} n_i\right]$$

where n_1 = moles of oxygen in air

n_2 = moles of nitrogen in air

n_3 = moles of hydrogen

M_1 = molecular weight of oxygen

M_2 = molecular weight of nitrogen

M_3 = molecular weight of hydrogen.

$$M_{average} = \frac{n_1M_1 + n_2M_2 + n_3M_3}{n_1 + n_2 + n_3}$$

$$= \frac{(.2)(32) + (.8)(28) + 2(2)}{.2 + .8 + 2} = \frac{32.8}{3} \text{ gm/mole}$$

$$= 10.9 \text{ gm/mole} .$$

• PROBLEM 1-39

An 11-liter flask contains 20 g of neon and an unknown weight of hydrogen. The gas density is found to be 0.002 g/cc at 0°C. Calculate the average molecular weight and the number of grams of hydrogen present, and also the pressure. The atomic weight of neon is 20 g/mole.

Solution: The gas density = $0.002 \text{ gm/cm}^3 = 0.002 \text{ gm/cm}^3 \times \frac{1000 \text{ cm}^3}{1 \text{ liter}}$

$= 2$ gm/liter.

Note that this is nothing more than conversion of scales. Also 11 liters could have been converted to cm^3.

Since the gas density is 2 gm/liter (that is, 2 gm in every liter), the 11 liters will contain 22 gm; but the flask contains 20 gm of neon. Therefore, there are 22-20 = 2 gm of hydrogen. Therefore, there exists 1 mole of each gas or 2 moles total.

Thus, the average molecular weight = $\frac{20 + 2}{2} = 22/2 = 11$ gm/mole.

Using PV = nRT which upon rearranging and substitution yields

$$P = \frac{(2)(0.082)(273)}{11} = 4.07 \text{ atm.}$$

Remember that temperature is in absolute kelvin.

• PROBLEM 1-40

Calculate the composition in weight percent of a mixture of 5.00 g of helium and argon occupying a volume of 10.0 liters at 25°C and 1.00 atm.

Solution: Define W_{Ar} and W_{He} as the weight of argon and helium in grams respectively. Define also P_{Ar} and P_{He} as the partial pressures of argon and helium respectively.

Therefore

$$W_{Ar} + W_{He} = 5.00 \text{ g} \quad (1)$$

and

$$P_{Ar} + P_{He} = P_{total} = 1.00 \text{ atm} \quad (2)$$

The molecular weight of a gas is given by

$$M = \frac{W}{n} \tag{3}$$

where W and n are the total weight and number of moles respectively. From equation (2),

$$P = P_{Ar} + P_{He}$$

But $P = nRT/V$. Therefore,

$$P = n_{Ar}\frac{RT}{V} + n_{He}\frac{RT}{V} \tag{4}$$

From equation (3), $n = W/M$. Therefore, equation (4) becomes

$$P = \frac{W_{Ar}RT}{M_{Ar}V} + \frac{W_{He}RT}{M_{He}V}$$

From (1) $W_{Ar} = 5.00\,g - W_{He}$

$$P = \frac{\left(5.00\ g - W_{He}\right)RT}{\left(39.9\ g\ mole^{-1}\right)V} + \frac{W_{He}RT}{\left(4.00\ g\ mole^{-1}\right)V}$$

$$P = \left(\frac{5.00\ g - W_{He}}{39.9\ g\ mole^{-1}} + \frac{W_{He}}{4.00\ g\ mole^{-1}}\right) \times \frac{\left(0.0821\ell\ atm\ K^{-1}mol^{-1}\right)(298°K)}{10.0\ell}$$

$$P = 4.00\left[\frac{(5.00 - W_{He}) + 39.9\ W_{He}}{159.6}\right](2.44)$$

$$P = 1\ atm$$

$$159.6 = (20 + 35.9\ W_{He})\ 2.44$$

$$159.6 = 48.8 + 87.5\ W_{He}$$

$$W_{He} = 1.26\ g$$

$$\text{Weight percent He} = \frac{1.26\ g}{5.00\ g} \times 100 = 25.2\ \%$$

$$\text{Weight percent Ar} = 100 - 25.2$$

$$= 74.8\%$$

• PROBLEM 1-41

Hydrogen gas will dissociate into atoms at a high enough temperature, i.e., $H_2 = 2H$. Assuming ideal gas behavior for H_2 and H, what should be the density of hydrogen at 2000°C if it is 33% dissociated into atoms? The pressure is 1 atm.

Solution: Use as a basis 1 mol hydrogen before dissociation (which has a weight of 2 gms). After 0.33 moles have dissociated, then we have

0.67 mole H_2 left.

Therefore, there are 0.66 moles of H. The total number of moles are 0.67 + 0.66 = 1.33 moles.

For a mixture of gases, the density

$$\rho = \frac{PM_{average}}{RT} \quad \text{where } M_{average} = \frac{\text{total weight}}{\text{total moles}} = \frac{2\ gm}{1.33\ mol}$$

Note that the units of $M_{average}$ are consistent with the units of molecular weight. This is very important.

Therefore,

$$\rho = \frac{(1)(2/1.33)}{(0.0082)(2273)} = 8.07 \times 10^{-3} \text{ gm/liter}$$

• PROBLEM 1-42

Calculate the minimum work that must be expended in the compression of 1 kg of ethylene from $10^{-1}m^3$ to $10^{-2}m^3$ at a constant temperature of 300°K, assuming the gas to be
a) ideal b) Van der Waals.

Solution: a) The work done in an isothermal compression of an ideal gas is given by

$$W = -\int PdV \tag{1}$$

But $P = \frac{nRT}{V}$. Substituting $P = nRT/V$ into equation (1) gives

$$W = -\int nRT \frac{dV}{V}$$

Since nRT is constant,

$$W = -nRT \int_{V_1}^{V_2} \frac{dV}{V}$$

or

$$W = -nRT \ln \frac{V_2}{V_1} \tag{2}$$

The number of moles of C_2H_4 are

$$n = \left(1 \text{ kg } C_2H_4\right)\left(\frac{1000 \text{ g}}{1 \text{ kg}}\right)\left(\frac{1 \text{ mole } C_2H_4}{28.05 \text{ g}}\right)$$

$$n = 35.65 \text{ moles.}$$

Hence equation (2) becomes

$$W = -(35.65 \text{ moles})\left(8.314 \text{ J°K}^{-1}\text{mol}^{-1}\right)(300°\text{K}) \ln\frac{10^{-2}m^3}{10^{-1}m^3}$$

$$= 2.047 \times 10^5 \text{ J}$$

or

$$W = 204.7 \text{ kJ}.$$

b) Again the work done is given by

$$W = -\int PdV.$$

For a gas that obeys the Van der Waals equation, P is given by

$$P = \frac{nRT}{V-nb} - \frac{n^2a}{V^2}$$

where a and b are Van der Waals constants given as $4.47\ \ell^2 \text{ atm mol}^{-2}$ and $0.0571\ \ell \text{ mol}^{-1}$ respectively.

Substituting for P gives

$$W = -\int PdV = -\int \left[\frac{nRT}{V-nb} - \frac{n^2a}{V^2}\right] dV$$

or

$$W = -\int_{V_1}^{V_2} \frac{nRT}{V-nb} dV + \int_{V_1}^{V_2} \frac{n^2a}{V^2} dV$$

Taking out the constants from the integral gives

$$W = -nRT \int_{V_1}^{V_2} \frac{dV}{V-nb} + n^2 a \int_{V_1}^{V_2} \frac{dV}{V^2} \qquad (3)$$

To evaluate the integral

$$\int_{V_1}^{V_2} \frac{dV}{V-nb},$$

let $y = V-nb$ where n and b are constants

$$dy = dV$$

$$\int_{y_1}^{y_2} \frac{dy}{y} = \ln y \Big|_{y_1}^{y_2} = \ln \frac{y_2}{y_1}$$

Equation (3) becomes

$$W = -nRT \ln \frac{V_2 - nb}{V_1 - nb} + n^2 a \left(\frac{V_2 - V_1}{V_2 V_1}\right)$$

$$= -(35.65 \text{ moles})\left(8.314 JK^{-1} mol^{-1}\right)(300°K) \ln\left(\frac{10^{-2} - (35.65)(0.0571 \ell mol^{-1})}{10^{-1} - (35.65)(0.0571 \ell mol^{-1})}\right)$$

$$+ (35.65 \text{ moles})^2 \left(4.47 \ell^2 atm\ mol^{-2}\right)\left(\frac{10^{-2} - 10^{-1}}{\left(10^{-2}\right)\left(10^{-1}\right)}\right)$$

$$W = -515{,}320\ \ell\text{-atm}$$

REAL GASES

• PROBLEM 1-43

A certain substance obeys the van der Waals equation, and its constants a and b are known. Name six types of properties or coefficients that may be calculated for this substance, using the above information.

Solution: If van der Waals forces are included the equation used is

$$\left(P + \frac{n^2 a}{V^2}\right)(V-nb) = nRT$$

where P = pressure
n = moles
V = volume
a and b = constants
R = gas constant
T = temperature .

Looking at the above equation it is possible to compute (a) P, V, or T if the other two are known. (b) Its critical point. At the critical point the P, T and V in the equation are replaced by P_c, T_c and V_c, respectively. P_c is the critical pressure, V_c, the critical volume, and T_c, the critical temperature. Since the van der Waals constants, a and b are known it is possible to express the critical pressure, temperature and volume in terms of these constants. Thus

$$V_c = 3b; \; P_c = \frac{a}{27b^2}; \; T_c = \frac{8a}{27bR}$$

(c) The vapor pressure of the liquid; (d) Compressibility factor, Z. Z is written as $\frac{P_c V_c}{RT_c}$; (e) The heat of vaporization; (f) coefficient of thermal expansion.

• PROBLEM 1-44

Determine the equation of state for a certain hypothetical gas whose thermal coefficient of expansion,

$$\alpha = \frac{1}{V}\left(\frac{\partial V}{\partial T}\right)_P = k_1\left(\frac{C_P}{C_V}\right)T^{(C_P/C_V)-1}$$

and the coefficient of isothermal compressibility,

$$\beta = -\frac{1}{V}\left(\frac{\partial V}{\partial P}\right)_T = \frac{k_2}{P}.$$

In this problem, assume that C_P, C_V, k_1 and k_2 are constants.

Solution: If temperature, T and pressure, P are chosen to be independent variables, then, volume, V is some function of T and P. Thus,

$$V = f(T,P).$$

Writing the change in volume in differential form gives

$$dV = \left(\frac{\partial V}{\partial T}\right)_P dT + \left(\frac{\partial V}{\partial P}\right)_T dP \qquad (1)$$

The quantities $\left(\frac{\partial V}{\partial T}\right)_P$ and $\left(\frac{\partial V}{\partial P}\right)_T$ can be determined using α and β

$$\alpha = \frac{1}{V}\left(\frac{\partial V}{\partial T}\right)_P = k_1\left(\frac{C_P}{C_V}\right)T^{(C_P/C_V)-1}$$

or

$$\left(\frac{\partial V}{\partial T}\right)_P = \frac{k_1 C_P T^{(C_P/C_V)-1} V}{C_V} \qquad (2)$$

$$\beta = -\frac{1}{V}\left(\frac{\partial V}{\partial P}\right)_T = \frac{k_2}{P}$$

or

$$\left(\frac{\partial V}{\partial P}\right)_T = \frac{-k_2 V}{P} \qquad (3)$$

Substituting equations (2) and (3) into equation (1) yields

$$dV = \frac{k_1 C_P T^{(C_P/C_V)-1} V}{C_V} dT - \frac{k_2 V}{P} dP$$

or

$$\frac{dV}{V} = k_1 \frac{C_P}{C_V} T^{(C_P/C_V)-1} dT - k_2 \frac{dP}{P} \quad (4)$$

Integrating equation (4) gives

$$\ln V = k_1 \frac{C_P}{C_V} \cdot \frac{C_V}{C_P} T^{C_P/C_V} - k_2 \ln P + \text{constant}$$

$$\ln V = k_1 T^{C_P/C_V} - k_2 \ln P + \text{constant}$$

$$V = e^{k_1 T^{C_P/C_V}} - k_2 P + \text{constant}$$

or

$$P^{k_2} V = k \exp\left(k_1 T^{(C_P/C_V)}\right)$$

Hence the desired equation of state is

$$P^{k_2} V = k \exp\left(k_1 T^{C_P/C_V}\right) .$$

• PROBLEM 1-45

At high pressures and temperatures a quite good equation of state is $P(V - nb) = nRT$, where b is a constant. Find $(\partial V/\partial T)_P$ and $(\partial V/\partial P)_T$ from this equation and hence dV in terms of $P, T, V\text{-}nb$, dT and dP.

Solution: Expanding the given equation of state, $P(V - nb) = nRT$, gives $PV - Pnb = nRT$ and rearranging to solve for V gives

$$V = \frac{nRT}{P} + nb \quad (1)$$

where V = volume, n = number of moles, P = pressure, R = gas constant and T = temperature. Differentiating equation (1) with respect to T and keeping P constant yields

$$\left(\frac{\partial V}{\partial T}\right)_P = \frac{nR}{P} \quad (2)$$

But $P = \frac{nRT}{V\text{-}nb}$. Therefore,

$$\left(\frac{\partial V}{\partial T}\right)_P = \frac{nR}{\left[\frac{nRT}{V\text{-}nb}\right]} = \frac{nR}{nRT} \times V - nb$$

$$= \frac{V\text{-}nb}{T} \quad (2a)$$

Note that the subscript P signifies that the pressure is being held constant while equation (1) is being differentiated. Now, differentiating with respect to P and holding T constant gives

$$\left(\frac{\partial V}{\partial P}\right)_T = -\frac{nRT}{P^2} = -\left(\frac{nRT}{P}\right)\frac{1}{P} \quad (3)$$

Observe that equation (1) can be rearranged to give $V\text{-}nb = \frac{nRT}{P}$.

Therefore,

$$\left(\frac{\partial V}{\partial P}\right)_T = -\left(\frac{nRT}{P}\right)\frac{1}{P} = -(V - nb)\frac{1}{P} \quad (3a)$$

Volume as a function of pressure and temperature can be represented as

$$V = f(P,T) \; . \qquad (4)$$

If the volume is a property of the system for which $P(V - nb) = nRT$, then it has an exact differential,

$$dV = \left(\frac{\partial V}{\partial P}\right)_T dP + \left(\frac{\partial V}{\partial T}\right)_P dT \qquad (5)$$

using equations (2a) and (3a), equation (5) becomes

$$dV = -\left(\frac{V-nb}{P}\right) dP + \left(\frac{V-nb}{T}\right) dT$$

$$= (V-nb)\left[-\frac{dP}{P} + \frac{dT}{T}\right] .$$

• PROBLEM 1-46

a) Estimate the Boyle temperature for a certain non-ideal gas whose equation of state is

$$P\bar{V} = RT + APT - BP,$$

where $\bar{V}$ is the molar volume and A and B are constants.

b) Determine whether this gas has a critical point.

Solution: Rearranging the equation $P\bar{V} = RT + APT - BP$ gives

$$P\bar{V} - APT + BP = RT$$

or

$$P(\bar{V} - AT + B) = RT .$$

Solving for P yields

$$P = \frac{RT}{\bar{V}-AT+B} \qquad (1)$$

$$= \frac{RT}{\bar{V}\left(1-(AT/\bar{V})+(B/\bar{V})\right)}$$

$$P = \frac{RT}{\bar{V}\left(1+(B-AT)/\bar{V}\right)}$$

$$P\bar{V} = \frac{RT}{\left[1 + (B-AT)/\bar{V}\right]} \qquad (2)$$

Consider the term $|(B-AT)/\bar{V}|$ to be very much less than 1, then equation (2) can be rewritten as,

$$P\bar{V} = RT[1 - (B-AT)/\bar{V}] \qquad (3)$$

The Boyle temperature of a gas according to one definition is the temperature, T_B, at which

$$\lim_{\bar{V}\to\infty} \left[\frac{\partial(P\bar{V})}{\partial(1/\bar{V})}\right]_T = 0$$

at which point $P = 0$ and $T = T_B$. Thus, from equation (3),

$$B - AT_B = 0$$

or

$$T_B = B/A .$$

b) To be able to ascertain whether a gas has a critical point, the first and second derivative of the equation of state for such a gas with respect to V at constant T must vanish.
Therefore from (1)

$$\left(\frac{\partial P}{\partial \bar{V}}\right)_T = \frac{-RT}{(\bar{V}-AT+B)^2} \quad (4)$$

$$\left(\frac{\partial^2 P}{\partial \bar{V}^2}\right)_T = \frac{2RT}{(\bar{V}-AT+B)^3} \quad (5)$$

At the critical point $(\partial P/\partial \bar{V})_T = 0$ and $(\partial^2 P/\partial \bar{V}^2)_T = 0$. The right hand sides of (4) and (5) can only be 0 if $T = 0$ or $\bar{V} - AT + B$ is infinite. Therefore this gas does not have a true critical point.

• PROBLEM 1-47

Express the Boyle temperature of a van der Waals gas in terms of the constants a,b, and R. The final expression for T_B must contain only a,b, and R.

Solution: It is not easy to rearrange the van der Waals equation into the virial form, which would allow T_B to be evaluated by inspection. Therefore, the van der Waals equation to be used is

$$P = \frac{nRT}{V-nb} - \frac{n^2 a}{V^2} \quad (1)$$

where P = pressure, V = volume, n = number of moles, T = temperature and R = gas constant. Multiplying both sides of equation (1) by V gives

$$PV = nRT\left(\frac{V}{V-nb}\right) - \frac{n^2 a}{V} \quad (2)$$

Differentiating equation (2) partially with respect to P, keeping T constant, gives

$$\left(\frac{\partial (PV)}{\partial P}\right)_T = \left[\frac{nRT}{V-nb} - \frac{nRTV}{(V-nb)^2} + \frac{n^2 a}{V^2}\right]\left(\frac{\partial V}{\partial P}\right)_T \quad (3)$$

At $P = 0$, $\left[\frac{\partial (PV)}{\partial P}\right]_T = 0$. Therefore,

$$\left[\frac{nRT}{V-nb} - \frac{nRTV}{(V-nb)^2} + \frac{n^2 a}{V^2}\right]\left(\frac{\partial V}{\partial P}\right)_T = 0 \quad (4)$$

Under all conditions $(\partial V/\partial P)_T < 0$; therefore, the expression in square brackets in equation (4) must equal to zero. That is

$$\frac{nRT}{V-nb} - \frac{nRTV}{(V-nb)^2} + \frac{n^2 a}{V^2} = 0 \quad (5)$$

Multiplying equation (5) through by $V^2(V-nb)^2$ gives

$$nRTV^2(V-nb) - nRTV^3 + n^2a(V-nb)^2 = 0$$

or

$$nRTV^2(V-nb) - nRTV^3 = -n^2a(V-nb)^2 .$$

Therefore,

$$RT = \frac{a}{b}\left[\frac{V-nb}{V}\right]^2 = \frac{a}{b}\left[\frac{V}{V} - \frac{nb}{V}\right]^2$$

$$= \frac{a}{b}\left[1 - \frac{nb}{V}\right]^2 \tag{6}$$

At the Boyle point $T = T_B$, $P = 0$ and $V = \infty$, so $RT_B = a/b$ or

$$T_B = \frac{a}{Rb} .$$

Another method of doing this is to set $n/V = c$. So, the van der Waals equation of state becomes

$$P = \frac{cRT}{1-bc} - ac^2 \tag{7}$$

From equation (7),

$$PV = n\left[\frac{RT}{1-bc} - ac\right] \tag{8}$$

Using the chain rule to differentiate equation (8) partially with respect to P gives

$$\left(\frac{\partial(PV)}{\partial P}\right)_T = \left(\frac{\partial(PV)}{\partial c}\right)_T \left(\frac{\partial c}{\partial P}\right)_T = n\left[\frac{bRT}{(1-bc)^2} - a\right]\left(\frac{\partial c}{\partial P}\right)_T . \tag{9}$$

Observe that $\left(\frac{\partial c}{\partial P}\right)_T = \frac{1}{(\partial P/\partial c)_T} = \left(\frac{\partial P}{\partial c}\right)_T^{-1}$. From equation (7),

$$\left(\frac{\partial P}{\partial c}\right)_T = \left[\frac{bcRT}{(1-bc)^2} + \frac{RT}{1-bc} - 2ac\right]^{-1} \tag{10}$$

Observe that equation (10) reduces to

RT as $P \to 0$ and $c \to 0$ or $\left(\frac{\partial c}{\partial P}\right)_T = 1/RT$.

Since $1/RT \neq 0$ and $n \neq 0$, the term in the square brackets in equation (9) must vanish at $c = 0$ and $T = T_B$. That is,

$$bRT_B - a = 0 \tag{11}$$

Solving for T_B changes equation (11) to

$$T_B = \frac{a}{bR} .$$

• PROBLEM 1-48

Gases A,B,C, and D obey the van der Waals equation, with a and b values as given (liter-atm system of units):

	A	B	C	D
a	6	6	20	0.05
b	0.025	0.15	0.10	0.02

Which gas has the highest critical temperature, the largest molecules, the most nearly ideal behavior at STP?

Solution: Looking at $\frac{P_c V_c}{RT_c} = \frac{(a/27b^2)(3b)}{(R)(8a/27Rb)}$ it is seen that T_c is proportional to a/b. If this ratio is computed for the various gases, then gas A, a/b = 6/0.025 = 240; For gas B, a/b = 6/0.15 = 40; For gas C, a/b = 20/0.10 = 200 and for gas D, a/b = 0.05/0.02 = 2.5. These values show that gas A (with the highest a/b ratio) has the highest T_c.

The constant b gives a measure of molecular volume (that is, $V_c = 3b$). Therefore, gas B has the largest molecules. At STP, the gas that has the lowest critical temperature and pressure will be most ideal. Gas D has the lowest a/b ratio, hence lowest T_c. The same gas also gives the lowest a/b^2 ratio, hence the lowest critical pressure P_c.

• PROBLEM 1-49

The van der Waals constants for gases A, B, and C are:

Gas	a, liters^2-atm/mole	b, liters/mole
A	4.0	0.027
B	12.0	0.030
C	6.0	0.032

Which gas has (a) the highest critical temperature, (b) the largest molecular volume, and (c) most ideal general behavior around STP?

Solution: The van der Waals equation is

$$\left(P + \frac{n^2 a}{V^2}\right)\left(V - nb\right) = nRT$$

where P = pressure
T = temperature
V = volume
n = number of moles.

a and b are van der Waals constants.

(a) It is known that T_c, the critical temperature is proportional to the ratio a/b. Computing the a/b ratios for the three gases yields:

for gas A $\frac{4.0}{0.027} = 148.15$

for gas B $\frac{12.0}{0.030} = 400$

for gas C $\frac{6.0}{0.032} = 187.5$

Since the ratio for gas B is the largest, gas B has the largest T_c. This question could have been answered by mere inspection. It can be seen that the constant b has almost the same value for the three gases. So, the larger a value means greater intermolecular forces. A larger T_c would be needed to overcome them. Since gas B has the largest a value, its T_c will be the largest.

(b) The constant b is proportional to V_c. Therefore gas C has the largest V_c.

(c) The b values are almost the same. Therefore ideality will be determined by the a values. Looking at the original equation, it can be seen that it is near ideality for values of the constants close to zero. Since gas A has the smallest a value, it should be the most ideal in behavior. Remember that for ideality, the expression is PV = nRT.

• PROBLEM 1-50

Given the following data for a certain nonideal gas at 25°C:

ρ/P, g/liter-atm:	10	11	10	(ρ = density)
P, atm:	1	10	20	

The critical pressure of this gas must then be (greater than 10 atm, greater than 20 atm, between 1 and 20 atm, between 1 and 10 atm, less than 20 atm, can't tell).

Solution: $\text{Density} = \frac{\text{weight}}{\text{volume}} = \frac{W}{V}$

$$\frac{\text{density}}{\text{pressure}} = \frac{W/V}{P} = \frac{\rho}{P} \qquad (1)$$

where $\rho = W/V$.

$$\text{Compressibility factor} = \frac{PV}{RT} \qquad (2)$$

Therefore, comparing (1) and (2), it is observed that ρ/P is inversely proportional to the compressibility factor at a given temperature, so the maximum in ρ/P means a minimum in PV/RT. In plots of PV/RT vs. P/P_c, such a minimum occurs only for $T < T_c$ and $P > P_c$ where T_c and P_c are critical temperature and pressure, respectively. The data tells us that this minimum is between 1 atm and 20 atm. Therefore P_c could be greater or less than 1 atm and greater or less that 10 atm, but it must be less than 20 atm.

• PROBLEM 1-51

Consider an equation of state in the form

$$P = \frac{RT}{V - b} \cdot e^{-A/RT^{3/2}\bar{V}}$$

for an arbitrary gas. Show that the critical constants are given by

$$T_c = \left(\frac{A}{4bR}\right)^{2/3},$$

$$\bar{V}_c = 2b \quad \text{and} \quad P_c = \frac{R}{b}\left(\frac{A}{4bR}\right)^{2/3} e^{-2}$$

Solution:

$$P = \frac{RT}{(\bar{V} - b)} \circ e^{-A/RT^{3/2}\bar{V}} \qquad (1)$$

Differentiate equation (1) twice with respect to $\bar{V}$ at constant temperature, T to generate two new equations. That is,

$$\left(\frac{\partial P}{\partial \bar{V}}\right)_T = \frac{RT}{(\bar{V} - b)} e^{-A/RT^{3/2}\bar{V}}\left(\frac{A}{RT^{3/2}\bar{V}^2} - \frac{1}{(\bar{V} - b)}\right) \qquad (2)$$

and

$$\left(\frac{\partial^2 P}{\partial \bar{V}^2}\right)_T = \left\{\left[\frac{A}{RT^{3/2}\bar{V}^2} - \frac{1}{(\bar{V} - b)}\right]\left[\frac{-1}{(\bar{V} - b)^2} + \frac{A}{RT^{3/2}\bar{V}^2}\right] + \left(\frac{1}{(\bar{V} - b)}\right)\left[\frac{-2A}{RT^{3/2}\bar{V}^3} + \frac{1}{(\bar{V} - b)^2}\right]\right\} RTe^{-A/RT^{3/2}\bar{V}} \qquad (3)$$

The first and second derivatives dissappear at the critical point, therefore

$$\left(\frac{\partial P}{\partial \bar{V}}\right)_T = 0 \quad \text{and} \quad \left(\frac{\partial^2 P}{\partial \bar{V}^2}\right)_T = 0$$

From equation (2), since $\frac{RT}{(\bar{V} - b)} e^{-A/RT^{3/2}\bar{V}}$ can not be zero, then

$$\frac{A}{RT_c^{3/2}\bar{V}_c^2} - \frac{1}{\bar{V}_c - b} = 0 . \qquad (4)$$

In equation (3), the first term is also zero; consequently, the second term will disappear only when

$$\frac{-2A}{RT_c^{3/2}V_b^3} + \frac{1}{(\bar{V}_c - b)^2} = 0 \qquad (5)$$

Dividing equation (4) by equation (5) yields

$$\frac{2}{V_c} = \frac{1}{(\bar{V}_c - b)}$$

$$2(\bar{V}_c - b) = V_c$$

$$2\bar{V}_c - 2b = V_c$$

and

$$\bar{V}_c = 2b \qquad (6)$$

Substituting equation (6) into equation (4) gives

$$\frac{A}{RT_c^{3/2}(2b)^2} - \frac{1}{2b - b} = 0$$

$$\frac{A}{RT_c^{3/2}\,4b^2} - \frac{1}{b} = 0$$

$$RT_c^{3/2}\, 4b^2 - Ab = 0$$

$$RT_c^{3/2}\, 4b - A = 0$$

$$T_c^{3/2} = \frac{A}{4bR}$$

or

$$T_c = \left(\frac{A}{4bR}\right)^{2/3} \tag{7}$$

Combining equations (6), (7), and (1) gives

$$P_c = \frac{R\left(\frac{A}{4bR}\right)^{2/3}}{(2b - b)} \quad e^{-A/R(A/4bR)2b}$$

or

$$P_c = \frac{R}{b}\left(\frac{A}{4bR}\right)^{2/3} \quad e^{-2} .$$

• PROBLEM 1-52

A gas obeys the van der Waals equation, with $P_c = 30$ atm and $T_c = 200°C$. The compressibility factor PV/RT will be more than one (at $P = 50$ atm, $T = 250°C$; at $P = 1$ atm, $T = 100°C$; $P = 500$ atm, $T = 500°C$; none of these). Calculate the van der Waals constant b for this gas.

Solution: For a compressibility factor greater than unity, P = 500 atm and T = 500°C (that is the highest P and T) are chosen. The constant $b = V_c/3$. It is known that

$$\frac{P_cV_c}{RT_c} = \frac{\left(\frac{a}{27b^2}\right)(3b)}{R\left(\frac{8a}{27Rb}\right)} = \frac{3}{8}$$

for a van der Waals gas. Therefore, $V_c = \dfrac{3RT_c}{8P_c} = \dfrac{(3)(.082)(473°K)}{(8)(30\ atm)}$

$V_c = 0.4848$ and $b = \dfrac{0.4848}{3} = 0.162$ liter/mole.

• PROBLEM 1-53

Derive the relations between the constants a, b, and R of the Berthelot equation,

$$P = \frac{RT}{(\bar{V} - b)} - \frac{a}{T\bar{V}^2} ,$$

and the critical parameters. Express the equation of state in terms of reduced variables.

Solution:

$$P = \frac{RT}{(\bar{V} - b)} - \frac{a}{T\bar{V}^2} \tag{1}$$

Taking the first derivative with respect to V at constant temperature

gives

$$\left(\frac{\partial P}{\partial \bar{V}}\right)_T = \frac{-RT}{(\bar{V} - b)^2} + \frac{2a}{T\bar{V}^3} \qquad (2)$$

The second derivative is

$$\left(\frac{\partial^2 P}{\partial \bar{V}^2}\right)_T = \frac{2RT}{(\bar{V} - b)^3} - \frac{6a}{T\bar{V}^4} \qquad (3)$$

Applying the critical isotherm conditions, that the partial derivatives with respect to volume at constant temperature is zero, equations (2) and (3) become

$$\left(\frac{\partial P}{\partial \bar{V}}\right)_T = \frac{-RT}{(\bar{V} - b)^2} + \frac{2a}{T\bar{V}^3} = 0 \qquad (4)$$

and

$$\left(\frac{\partial^2 P}{\partial \bar{V}^2}\right)_T = \frac{2RT}{(\bar{V} - b)^3} - \frac{6a}{T\bar{V}^4} = 0 \ . \qquad (5)$$

Solving equations (4) and (5) simultaneously yields

$$\frac{2}{\bar{V}_c - b} = \frac{3}{\bar{V}_c}$$

$$3(\bar{V}_c - b) = 2\bar{V}_c$$

$$3\bar{V}_c - 3b = 2\bar{V}_c$$

$$3b = \bar{V}_c$$

$$b = \bar{V}_c/3 \ .$$

Substitute $b = \bar{V}_c/3$ into equation (4) and solve for a. That is,

$$\frac{-RT_c}{\left(\bar{V}_c - \bar{V}_c/3\right)^2} + \frac{2a}{T_c\bar{V}_c^3} = 0$$

or

$$2a\bar{V}_c^{\ 2}(1 - \tfrac{1}{3})^2 - RT_c^2\,\bar{V}_c^3 = 0$$

$$2a = \frac{RT_c^2\,\bar{V}_c^3}{\frac{4}{9}\,\bar{V}_c^2}$$

$$2a = \frac{9RT_c^2\,\bar{V}_c}{4}$$

$$a = \frac{9RT_c^2\,\bar{V}_c}{8} \qquad (5)$$

Substituting $a = 9RT_c^2\,\bar{V}_c/8$ and $b = \bar{V}_c/3$ into equation (1) gives

$$P_c = \frac{RT_c}{\left(\bar{V}_c - \bar{V}_c/3\right)} - \frac{\frac{9RT_c^2\,\bar{V}_c}{8}}{(T_c)\,(\bar{V}_c^2)}$$

$$= \frac{RT_c}{\bar{V}_c(1 - \frac{1}{3})} - \frac{9RT_c^2\,\bar{V}_c}{8T_c\,\bar{V}_c^2}$$

$$= \frac{RT_c}{\frac{2}{3}\bar{V}_c} - \frac{9RT_c}{8\bar{V}_c}$$

$$P_c = \frac{3RT_c}{2V_c} - \frac{9RT_c}{8\bar{V}_c}$$

$$= \frac{12RT_c - 9RT_c}{8\bar{V}_c}$$

$$P_c = \frac{3RT_c}{8\bar{V}_c}$$

and

$$R = \frac{8P_c\bar{V}_c}{3T_c}$$

Substituting $R = 8P_c\bar{V}_c/3T_c$ into (5) gives

$$a = \frac{9(8P_cV_c)T_c^2\bar{V}_c}{24T_c}$$

or

$$a = 3P_c\bar{V}_c^2T_c$$

Now, define the reduced variables as π, φ and θ, corresponding to reduced pressure, volume and temperature respectively.

$$\pi = \frac{P}{P_c} \qquad (6)$$

$$\varphi = \frac{\bar{V}}{\bar{V}_c} \qquad (7)$$

and

$$\theta = \frac{T}{T_c} \qquad (8)$$

From equation (6) $P = \pi P_c$ and from equations (7) and (8)

$$\bar{V} = \varphi\bar{V}_c \quad \text{and} \quad T = \theta T_c \quad \text{respectively.}$$

Substituting $P = \pi P_c$, $\bar{V} = \varphi\bar{V}_c$, $T = \theta T_c$, R, b and a into equation (1) gives

$$\pi P_c = \frac{\frac{8P_c\bar{V}_c}{3T_c}(\theta T_c)}{\varphi\bar{V}_c - \bar{V}_c/3} - \frac{3P_c\bar{V}_c^2T_c}{\theta T_c\varphi^2\bar{V}^2}$$

$$= \frac{8P_c\bar{V}_c\theta T_c}{3T_c\bar{V}_c(\varphi-\frac{1}{3})} - \frac{3P_c}{\theta\varphi^2}$$

$$\pi P_c = \frac{8P_c\theta}{3(\varphi-\frac{1}{3})} - \frac{3P_c}{\theta\varphi^2}$$

or

$$\pi = \frac{8\theta}{3\varphi-1} - \frac{3}{\theta\varphi^2} \qquad (9)$$

Equation (9) is the equation of state in terms of reduced variables.

Some P-V plots are shown below for a gas that obeys the van der Waals equation. Calculate the constants a and b for this gas. Since your calculation is necessarily approximate, it is necessary to show very clearly just how you have obtained numbers from the graph below and how you have used them. Give the units of a and b also. (HINT: The 300°C isotherm is closest to critical point.)

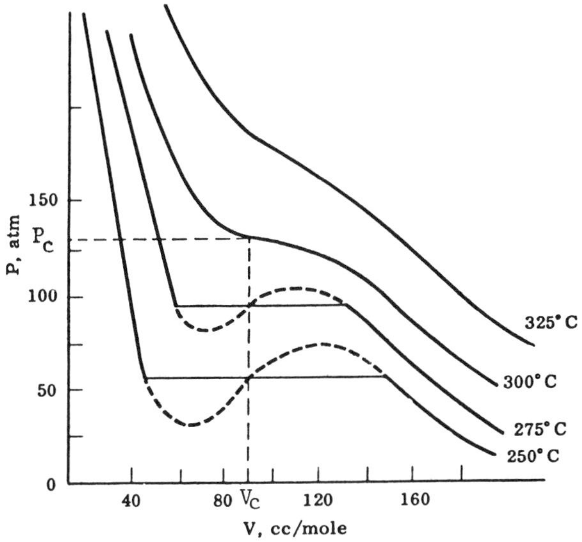

Solution: Since this problem requires approximate values, it is not necessary to interpolate or extrapolate. For the purposes of the problem, the 300°C isotherm (which is the closest to the critical point) is good enough.

Isotherm means, for any pressure and volume on that line, the temperature remains the same (300°C in this case). The terms P_c and V_c can be estimated from the point of inflection. Therefore $P_c \approx 130$ atm, $V_c \approx 90\ cm^3/mole$ and $T_c = 300°C = 573°K$.

For a van der Waals gas, $V_c = 3b$ and $P_c = \frac{a}{27b^2}$.

A system of two equations and two unknowns can now be presented. Thus,

$$90 = 3b \qquad (1)$$

and

$$130 = \frac{a}{27b^2} \qquad (2)$$

From (1) $b = 90/3 = 30\ cm^3/mole$. Substituting this value into (2),

$$130 = \frac{a}{27 \times 30^2}.$$

$$a = (130 \times 27 \times 30^2) cc^2\ atm/mole^2$$

$$= 3159000\ cc^2\ atm/moles^2$$

$$= 3.16 \times 10^6\ cc^2\ atm/moles^2.$$

An equation of state due to Dieterici is

$$P(V - nb')\exp \frac{na'}{RTV} = nRT \quad (1)$$

Evaluate the constants a' and b' in terms of the critical constants P_c, V_c, and T_c of a gas.

Solution: Rearranging equation (1) to solve for P gives

$$P = \frac{nRT}{V - nb'} e^{na'/RTV}$$

For 1 mole,

$$P = \frac{RT}{V - b'} e^{a'/RTV} \quad (2)$$

where P = pressure, R = gas constant, V = volume and T = temperature. Differentiating equation (2) with respect to V gives

$$\frac{dP}{dV} = -\frac{P}{V - b'} + \frac{a'P}{RTV^2} \quad (3)$$

and

$$\frac{d^2P}{dV^2} = \frac{a'^2 P}{(RTV^2)^2} - \frac{2a'P}{RTV^3} \quad (4)$$

At some point on a P-V diagram, the curve is horizontal and this part can be mathematically expressed as $dP/dV = 0$. Also, the highest temperature (maximum) at which such a horizontal line can still exist is called the critical temperature and at this point

$$\frac{d^2P}{dV^2} = 0 .$$

So, using these two conditions for equations (3) and (4), they can be rewritten as

$$0 = -\frac{P}{V - b'} + \frac{a'P}{RTV^2} \quad (3a)$$

$$0 = \frac{a'^2 P}{(RTV^2)^2} - \frac{2a'P}{RTV^3} \quad (4a)$$

Since there are two equations and two unknowns, the equations can be solved simultaneously. Simplfying equation (4a), it becomes

$$a'\left(\frac{a'P}{R^2T^2V^4} - \frac{2P}{RTV^3}\right) = 0$$

From this, observe that there are two possible values for a'. That is, $a' = 0$ and $a' = 2RT_cV_c$. The trivial solution is discarded, so that $a' = 2RT_cV_c$. Putting this into equation (3a) gives

$$0 = -\frac{P}{V_c - b'} + \frac{2RT_cV_cP}{RT_cV_c^2}$$

or

$$0 = -\frac{P}{V_c - b'} + \frac{2P}{V_c} = P\left(-\frac{1}{V_c-b'} + \frac{2}{V_c}\right)$$

From this, $-\frac{1}{V_c - b'} + \frac{2}{V_c} = 0$ or

$$\frac{1}{V_c - b'} = \frac{2}{V_c} \qquad (5)$$

The reciprocal of equation (5) is

$$V_c - b' = \frac{V_c}{2} ,$$

or

$$-b' = \frac{V_c}{2} - V_c = -\frac{V_c}{2} .$$

$$b' = \frac{V_c}{2} .$$

• PROBLEM 1-56

The critical temperature and pressure for NO gas are 177°K and 64 atm, respectively, and for CCl_4 they are 550°K and 45 atm, respectively. Which gas (a) has the smaller value of the van der Waals constant b, (b) the smaller value of the van der Waals constant a, (c) is most nearly ideal in behavior at 300°K and 10 atm?

Solution: For any gas that obeys van der Waals equation, $V_c = 3b$, $P_c = a/27b^2$ and $T_c = 8a/27bR$.

(a) If we take the ratio T_c/P_c, we have

$$\left[\frac{8a}{27bR}\right] \times \left[\frac{27b^2}{a}\right] = \frac{8b}{R}$$

Therefore b is directly proportional to T_c/P_c. Also it is observed that $V_c = 3b$ is proportional to T_c/P_c.

T_c/P_c for NO gas = 177/64 = 2.766.

T_c/P_c for CCl_4 = 550/45 = 12.22.

Therefore NO should have the smaller b value.

(b) The constant a is proportional to $P_c V_c^2$ or to T_c^2/P_c. Therefore it will be smaller for NO.

(c) NO should be more ideal since 300°K is above its critical temperature, but below that of CCl_4.

• PROBLEM 1-57

A nonideal gas of molecular weight 150 obeys the van der Waals equation; its critical pressure and temperature are 100 atm and 100°C, respectively.

(a) The compressibility factor PV/RT will be greater than unity at (500 atm and 80°C, 500 atm and 120°C, 50 atm and 60°C, 50 atm and 120°C, none of these).

(b) Calculate the value of the compressibility factor at the critical point.

Solution: The van der Waals equation is

$$\left(P + \frac{n^2 a}{V^2}\right)(V - nb) = nRT \tag{1}$$

(a) For the compressibility factor to be greater than unity, what is needed is a high pressure and temperature. By this it is meant that the required temperature and pressure must both be greater than the values at the critical point. Hence 120°C and 500 atm is the correct answer.

(b) Compressibility factor at the critical point $= \frac{P_c V_c}{RT_c}$, where the subscript c means the properties at the critical point. For a gas that obeys the van der Waals equation,

$$T_c = \frac{8a}{27Rb},$$

$V_c = 3b$ and $P_c = \frac{a}{27b^2}$ where a and b are constants (as in equation (1)).

Now after substituting these values into $\frac{P_c V_c}{RT_c}$, it yields

$$\frac{\left(\frac{a}{27b^2}\right)(3b)}{(R)\left(\frac{8a}{27Rb}\right)}$$

$$\text{Compressibility factor} = \frac{3ab}{27b^2} \times \frac{27Rb}{8aR} = \frac{3}{8}.$$

• PROBLEM 1-58

Carbon dioxide is assumed to follow the equation of state

$$\left(P + \frac{n}{V^2 T^{\frac{1}{2}}}\right)(v-m) = RT$$

where n and m are constants for any gas. Given that the critical pressure and temperature of carbon dioxide are 72.9 atm and 304.2°K respectively, determine the compressibility factor of the gas at 100°C and at a volume of 6.948 cubic decimeters per kilogram.

Solution:

$$\left(P + \frac{n}{V^2 T^{\frac{1}{2}}}\right)(V - m) = RT$$

solving for P gives

$$P = \frac{RT}{V-m} - \frac{n}{V^2 T^{\frac{1}{2}}} \tag{2}$$

Differentiate equation (2) twice with respect to V at constant T and set them equal to zero because at the critical point

$$\left(\frac{\partial P}{\partial V}\right)_T = \left(\frac{\partial^2 P}{\partial V^2}\right)_T = 0$$

Therefore at the critical point

$$\left(\frac{\partial P}{\partial V}\right)_T = -\frac{RT_c}{(V_c - m)^2} + 2\frac{n}{V_c^3 T_c^{\frac{1}{2}}} = 0 \tag{3}$$

$$\left(\frac{\partial^2 P}{\partial V^2}\right)_T = \frac{2RT_c}{(V_c - m)^3} - 6\frac{n}{V_c^4 T_c^{\frac{1}{2}}} = 0 \tag{4}$$

Equation (3) can also be written as

$$\frac{RT_c}{(V_c - m)^2} = \frac{n}{T_c^{\frac{1}{2}}} \frac{2}{V_c^3} \tag{5}$$

and equation (4) as

$$\frac{RT_c}{(V_c - m)^3} = \frac{n}{T_c^{\frac{1}{2}}} \frac{3}{V_c^4} \tag{6}$$

Divide equation (5) by equation (6) to get

$$V_c - m = \tfrac{2}{3} V_c$$

from which

$$m = \tfrac{1}{3} V_c$$

where V_c is the critical volume. Substitute the value of m into equation (5) and solve for n

$$\frac{RT_c}{(V_c^2 - 2mV_c + m^2} = \frac{n}{T_c^{\frac{1}{2}}} \frac{2}{V_c^3}$$

or

$$n = \frac{RT_c^{3/2} V_c^3}{2V_c^2 - \frac{4}{3} V^2 + \frac{2}{9} V^2}$$

$$= \frac{RT_c^{3/2} V_c^3}{V_c^2 (2 - \frac{4}{3} + \frac{2}{9})}$$

$$= \frac{RT_c^{3/2} V_c^3}{V_c^2 (\frac{8}{9})}$$

$$= \frac{9RT_c^{3/2} V_c}{8} \tag{7}$$

Equation (2) becomes at the critical point

$$P_c = \frac{RT_c}{V_c - m} - \frac{n}{V_c^2 T_c^{\frac{1}{2}}}$$

where P_c is the critical pressure

$$P_c = \frac{RT_c}{V_c - m} - \frac{9/8 \; RT^{3/2} V_c}{V_c^2 T_c^{\frac{1}{2}}}$$

$$= \frac{3}{2} \frac{RT_c}{V_c} - \frac{9}{8} \frac{RT_c}{V_c}$$

$$= \frac{3}{8} \frac{RT_c}{V_c}$$

or

$$\frac{P_c V_c}{RT_c} = \frac{3}{8} \tag{8}$$

CO_2 has a molecular weight of 44 g mol^{-1}

$$V = \left(6.948\ \frac{(\mathrm{dm})^3}{\mathrm{kg}}\right)\left(\frac{10^3\,\mathrm{cm}^3}{(\mathrm{dm})^3}\right)\left(\frac{0.044\ \mathrm{kg}}{\mathrm{mol}}\right)$$

$$= 3.057 \times 10^2\ \mathrm{cm}^3/\mathrm{mol}\ .$$

From equation (8)

$$V_c = \frac{3}{8}\ \frac{RT_c}{P_c}$$

$$= \frac{3}{8} \times \frac{(82.05\ \mathrm{cm}^3\mathrm{atm}/{}^\circ\mathrm{K}^{-1}\ \mathrm{mol}^{-1})(304.2^\circ\ \mathrm{K})}{72.9\ \mathrm{atm}}$$

$$= 128.3\ \mathrm{cm}^3\ \mathrm{mol}^{-1}$$

Remember that

$$m = V_c/3$$

$$= \frac{128.3\ \mathrm{cm}^3\ \mathrm{mol}^{-1}}{3}$$

$$= 42.79\ \mathrm{cm}^3\ \mathrm{mol}^{-1}\ .$$

From equation (7)

$$n = \frac{(9)(82.05\ \mathrm{cm}^3\mathrm{atm}\ {}^\circ\mathrm{K}^{-1}\ \mathrm{mol}^{-1})\ (304.2^\circ\ \mathrm{K})^{3/2}(128.3\ \mathrm{cm}^3\ \mathrm{mol}^{-1})}{8}$$

$$= 6.28 \times 10^7\ \frac{\mathrm{cm}^6\ \mathrm{atm}\ \mathrm{K}^{\frac{1}{2}}}{\mathrm{mol}^2}$$

Solving for P using equation (2) gives

$$P = \left[\frac{(82.05\ \mathrm{cm}^3\mathrm{atm}\ \mathrm{K}^{-1}\mathrm{mol}^{-1})(373^\circ\ \mathrm{K})}{(3.057 \times 10^2\mathrm{cm}^3/\mathrm{mol}) - (42.79\ \mathrm{cm}^3/\mathrm{mol})}\right]$$

$$- \left[\frac{6.28 \times 10^7\mathrm{cm}^6\mathrm{atm}\ \mathrm{K}^{\frac{1}{2}}/\mathrm{mol}^2}{(3.057 \times 10^2\mathrm{cm}^3/\mathrm{mol})^2(373^\circ\ \mathrm{K})^{\frac{1}{2}}}\right]$$

$$= 81.57\ \mathrm{atm}\ .$$

By definition the compressibility factor Z is given as

$$Z = \frac{PV}{RT}$$

$$= \frac{(81.57\ \mathrm{atm})(3.057 \times 10^2\ \mathrm{cm}^3/\mathrm{mol})}{(82.05\ \mathrm{cm}^3\ \mathrm{atm}\ {}^\circ\mathrm{K}^{-1}\ \mathrm{mol}^{-1})(373^\circ\ \mathrm{K})}$$

$$= 0.815.$$

CHAPTER 2

FIRST LAW OF THERMODYNAMICS

HEAT CAPACITY

• PROBLEM 2-1

(a) Derive the expression $\left(\frac{\partial E}{\partial T}\right)_P = C_P - P\left(\frac{\partial V}{\partial T}\right)_P$

(b) Calculate $(C_P - C_V)$ for Al at 25°C.

Density of Al = 2.702×10^3 kg m^{-3}

Mass of Al = 26.98×10^{-3} kg mol^{-1}

$\alpha = 69 \times 10^{-6}$ K^{-1}

$\beta = 1.34 \times 10^{-6}$ atm^{-1}

Solution: (a) The internal energy, E, is a function of temperature and volume. That is

$$E = f(T,V)$$

$$dE = \left(\frac{\partial E}{\partial T}\right)_V dT + \left(\frac{\partial E}{\partial V}\right)_T dV$$

Divide by dT to obtain,

$$\left(\frac{\partial E}{\partial T}\right)_P = \left(\frac{\partial E}{\partial T}\right)_V + \left(\frac{\partial E}{\partial V}\right)_T \left(\frac{\partial V}{\partial T}\right)_P \qquad (1)$$

By definition, the heat capacity at constant pressure,

$C_P = \left(\frac{\partial H}{\partial T}\right)_P$ and the heat capacity at constant volume,

$$C_V = \left(\frac{\partial E}{\partial T}\right)_V$$

$\therefore$ Equation (1) becomes

$$\left(\frac{\partial E}{\partial T}\right)_P = C_V + \left(\frac{\partial E}{\partial V}\right)_T \left(\frac{\partial V}{\partial T}\right)_P \tag{2}$$

Now,

$$C_P - C_V = \left(\frac{\partial H}{\partial T}\right)_P - \left(\frac{\partial E}{\partial T}\right)_V \tag{3}$$

But, $H = E + PV$

Therefore,

$$\left(\frac{\partial H}{\partial T}\right)_P = \left(\frac{\partial E}{\partial T}\right)_P + P\left(\frac{\partial V}{\partial T}\right)_P$$

Substituting this into equation (3) changes it to

$$C_P - C_V = \left(\frac{\partial E}{\partial T}\right)_P + P\left(\frac{\partial V}{\partial T}\right)_P - \left(\frac{\partial E}{\partial T}\right)_V \tag{4}$$

$$C_P - C_V = \left(\frac{\partial E}{\partial T}\right)_V + \left(\frac{\partial E}{\partial V}\right)_T \left(\frac{\partial V}{\partial T}\right)_P + P\left(\frac{\partial V}{\partial T}\right)_P - \left(\frac{\partial V}{\partial T}\right)_V$$

$$= \left(\frac{\partial V}{\partial T}\right)_P \left[\left(\frac{\partial E}{\partial V}\right)_T + P\right]$$

Solving for C_V gives

$$C_V = C_P - \left[P + \left(\frac{\partial E}{\partial V}\right)_T\right] \left(\frac{\partial V}{\partial T}\right)_P \tag{5}$$

Using equation (5), equation (2) can be written as

$$\left(\frac{\partial E}{\partial T}\right)_P = C_P - \left[P + \left(\frac{\partial E}{\partial V}\right)_T\right] \left(\frac{\partial V}{\partial T}\right)_P + \left(\frac{\partial E}{\partial V}\right)_T \left(\frac{\partial V}{\partial T}\right)_P$$

$$= C_P - P\left(\frac{\partial V}{\partial T}\right)_P - \left(\frac{\partial E}{\partial V}\right)_T \left(\frac{\partial V}{\partial T}\right)_P + \left(\frac{\partial E}{\partial V}\right)_T \left(\frac{\partial V}{\partial T}\right)_P$$

Hence,

$$\left(\frac{\partial E}{\partial T}\right)_P = C_P - P\left(\frac{\partial V}{\partial T}\right)_P$$

(b) Since

$$E = f(V,T)$$

$$dE = \left(\frac{\partial E}{\partial T}\right)_V dT + \left(\frac{\partial E}{\partial V}\right)_T dV$$

where E = internal energy

V = volume

and T = temperature

f means "a function of".

But $dq = dE + PdV$

where q = heat and P = pressure

$$\therefore \quad dq = \left(\frac{\partial E}{\partial T}\right)_V dT + \left[P + \left(\frac{\partial E}{\partial V}\right)_T\right] dV \qquad (6)$$

By definition,

$$C_V = \left(\frac{\partial E}{\partial T}\right)_V \quad \text{and} \quad C_P = \left(\frac{\partial q}{\partial T}\right)_P$$

Divide equation (6) through by dT,

$$\left(\frac{dq}{dT}\right)_P = \left(\frac{\partial E}{\partial T}\right)_V + \left[P + \left(\frac{\partial E}{\partial V}\right)_T\right]\left(\frac{\partial V}{\partial T}\right)_P$$

$$C_P = C_V + \left[P + \left(\frac{\partial E}{\partial V}\right)_T\right]\left(\frac{\partial V}{\partial T}\right)_P$$

$$\text{or} \quad C_P - C_V = \left[P + \left(\frac{\partial E}{\partial V}\right)_T\right]\left(\frac{\partial V}{\partial T}\right)_P \qquad (7)$$

For an ideal gas,

$$\left(\frac{\partial E}{\partial V}\right)_T = 0 \quad \text{and} \quad \left(\frac{\partial V}{\partial T}\right)_P = \frac{R}{P}$$

$$C_P - C_V = [P + 0]\frac{R}{P} = \frac{PR}{P} \quad \text{or} \quad C_P - C_V = R$$

One unit of R = liter atm K^{-1} mol^{-1}

$$\text{liter} = \text{volume} = \frac{\text{mass}}{\text{density}} = \frac{m}{\rho}$$

K is given by α and atm is given by β

$$\therefore \quad C_P - C_V = R = \frac{\alpha^2 VT}{\beta} \qquad (8)$$

Substituting the respective values into equation (8) gives

$$\text{Volume} = \frac{26.98 \times 10^{-3}\ \frac{kg}{mole}}{2.702 \times 10^3\ \frac{kg}{m^3}}$$

$$C_P - C_V = \frac{(69 \times 10^{-6}\ K^{-1})^2}{(1.34 \times 10^{-6}\ \text{atm}^{-1})} \frac{\left(26.98 \times 10^{-3}\ \frac{\text{kg}}{\text{mole}}\right)(298°K)}{\left(2.702 \times 10^{-3}\ \frac{\text{kg}}{\text{m}^3}\right)}$$

$$= 10.57 \times 10^{-6}\ \frac{\text{m}^3\ \text{atm}}{\text{mole K}}$$

$$= 10.57 \times 10^{-6}\ \text{m}^3\ \text{atm mol}^{-1}\ \text{K}^{-1}$$

To convert the answer from m^3atm to Joules use the ratio of the different values for the gas constant R.

Thus,

$$(10.57(10^{-6})\text{m}^3\text{atm mol}^{-1}\text{K}^{-1}) \times \frac{8.31441\ \text{J K}^{-1}\text{mol}^{-1}}{(8.20575(10^{-2})\text{dm}^3\text{atm mol}^{-1}\text{K}^{-1})}$$

$$\times \frac{(10\ \text{dm})^3}{\text{m}^3} = C_P - C_V$$

$$\therefore\ C_P - C_V = 1.07\text{J mol}^{-1}\ \text{K}^{-1}$$

• PROBLEM 2-2

Calculate $C_P - C_V$ for water at 25°C given that the coefficient of thermal expansion of water is $257.05 \times 10^{-6}K^{-1}$ and the compressibility is 45.24×10^{-6} bar^{-1}. The density of water is 0.997075×10^3kg m^{-3}.

Solution: The difference between the heat capacities, $C_P - C_V$ is given by

$$C_P - C_V = \frac{\alpha^2 VT}{\beta} \quad \text{where} \tag{1}$$

α = coefficient of thermal expansion

β = compressibility factor

V = volume

and T = temperature

1 bar = 0.987 atm

Substituting the respective values into their appropriate places, equation (1) becomes

$$C_p - C_V =$$

$$\left[\frac{\left(257.05 \times 10^{-6}K^{-1}\right)^2\left(18.015 \times 10^{-3}kg\ mol^{-1}\right)}{\left(45.24 \times 10^{-6}\ bar^{-1}\right)\left(0.987\ atm\ bar^{-1}\right)^{-1}}\right.$$

$$\left.\times\left(\left(0.997075 \times 10^3\ kg\ m^{-3}\right)^{-1}\left(298\ K\right)\right)\right]$$

$$= 7.76 \times 10^{-6} m^3\ atm\ mol^{-1}K^{-1}$$

$$= 0.786\ J\ mol^{-1}K^{-1}$$

• PROBLEM 2-3

Use the first law of thermodynamics and other relevant definitions to derive the following expression for C_V

$$C_V = -\left(\frac{\partial E}{\partial V}\right)_T \left(\frac{\partial V}{\partial T}\right)_E$$

Solution: The temperature rise, dT, of a system by 1 degree due to the heat absorbed when a small amount of heat, dq, is added to the system is called the heat capacity, C.

That is,

$$C = \frac{dq}{dT}$$

But dq = dE + PdV

where dE = small change in Internal Energy

P = Pressure

dV = small change in volume

$$\therefore \quad C = \frac{dE + PdV}{dT} \qquad (1)$$

Here, there is a need to find the heat capacity, C at constant volume. That is dV = 0 in equation (1) .

$$\therefore \quad C_V = \left(\frac{\partial E}{\partial T}\right)_V$$

Note that the subscript V refers to constant volume.

Thus, the internal energy, E is a function of both the volume and the temperature. This dependence can be written as

$$E = f(V,T)$$

where V = volume and T = Temperature. The f means "a function of"
Differentiating yields

$$dE = \left(\frac{\partial E}{\partial T}\right)_V dT + \left(\frac{\partial E}{\partial V}\right)_T dV$$

Divide through by dT and keep E constant

$$0 = \left(\frac{\partial E}{\partial T}\right)_V + \left(\frac{\partial E}{\partial V}\right)_T \left(\frac{\partial V}{\partial T}\right)_E$$

$$\left(\frac{\partial E}{\partial T}\right)_V = - \left(\frac{\partial E}{\partial V}\right)_T \left(\frac{\partial V}{\partial T}\right)_E$$

$$C_V = - \left(\frac{\partial E}{\partial V}\right)_T \left(\frac{\partial V}{\partial T}\right)_E$$

• PROBLEM 2-4

Show that the heat capacity at constant volume, C_V , for an ideal diatomic gas is given by:

$$C_V = \frac{5}{2} R + \frac{R\ x^2 e^x}{(e^x - 1)^2}$$

Solution: Thermodynamic quantities of molecules like C_V are made up of additive terms from contributions of translational, rotational, vibrational and electronic modes of the molecule. To fully describe translational modes, 3 coordinates are needed. From the equipartition principle of statistical molecule, a diatomic molecule has three degrees of translational freedom and each degree of freedom contributes $\frac{1}{2}$ RT to the translational energy. Thus,

$$E_{trans} = (3/2)RT$$

That is, each translational freedom contributes $\frac{1}{2}$ R to C_V . For the 3 translational degrees of freedom,

$$\frac{1}{2} RT + \frac{1}{2} RT + \frac{1}{2} RT = (3/2)RT$$

is contributed to C_V .

There are two rotational degrees of freedom for a diatomic molecule and each degree of freedom contributes $\frac{1}{2}$ RT to C_V

$$\therefore \quad \frac{1}{2}RT + \frac{1}{2}RT = RT$$

Thus, the rotational freedom contributes RT to C_V .

The vibrational mode contributes

$$RT \frac{x}{e^x - 1} \quad \text{to } C_V$$

where $x = \frac{h\nu}{kT}$

P = Planck's constant

ν = frequency

k = Boltzmann's constant

From quantum mechanics, the vibrational mode is quantized and the occupation of vibrational energy levels depends on temperature.

The total contribution to C_V from translational, rotational and vibrational modes of a diatomic molecule is therefore

$$C_V = d/dT \left(E_{translation} + E_{rotation} + E \quad vibration\right)$$

$$\frac{d}{dT}\left(3/2 \; RT + RT + RT \frac{x}{e^x - 1}\right)$$

$$= d/dT \; [(5/2)RT + RT \; x/(e^x - 1)]$$

$$\therefore \quad C_V = \frac{5}{2}R + \frac{Rx^2e^x}{(e^x - 1)^2}$$

Note that $dE = C_V dT$, by definition

and $C_V = \frac{dE}{dT}$

where $E = E_{trans} + E_{rot} + E_{vib}$

Recall that x is also a function of temperature. Therefore, x is differentiated with respect to T.

• PROBLEM 2-5

At 20°C ΔH for the reaction of one mole of NaCl with sufficient water to give a solution containing 12% NaCl by weight is 774.6 cal. At 25°C ΔH for the same reaction is 700.8 cal. Calculate the heat capacity of the solution in cal/deg-g given the following:

C_p of solid NaCl = 12 cal/deg-mole

C_p for water = 18 cal/deg-mole .

Solution: One can write the reaction equation using a basis of 100 g of solution. 12% of NaCl by weight in the solution is given, which means that there is 88% by weight of water since this is a binary solution.

$$12 \text{ g NaCl} + 88 \text{ g } H_2O = 100 \text{ g solution} \quad (1)$$

Writing in terms of mole fractions gives

$$\left(12 \text{ g NaCl}\right)\left(\frac{1 \text{ mole NaCl}}{58.2 \text{ g NaCl}}\right) = 0.205 \text{ moles NaCl} \quad .$$

ΔC_p is defined as the change in ΔH per degree. Thus from 20°C to 25°C temperature increase is 5°C. ΔC_p is then the change in ΔH between 20°C and 25°C divided by 5. That is

$$\Delta C_p = \frac{\Delta H}{\Delta T}$$

$$\text{or} \quad \Delta C_p = \frac{(700.8 - 774.6)\text{cal}}{5}$$

$$= -14.7 \text{ cal/degree per mole} \; .$$

Now defining ΔC_p to be change in ΔH per 12 g or 0.205 mole

$$\Delta C_p = -3.01$$

From equation (1),

$$C_{p(\text{solution})} - .205 \; C_p\text{NaCl} - 4.89 \text{ moles } C_p \; H_2O = -3.01$$

$$\therefore \; C_p(\text{soln}) - .205 \; (12 \text{ cal/deg-mole}) - 4.89 \text{ moles } (18 \text{ cal/deg mole}) = -3.01$$

$$C_p(\text{soln}) = 87 \text{ cal/deg}$$

$$= 0.87 \text{ cal/deg-g}$$

• PROBLEM 2-6

Consider the following reaction at 25°C

$$C(s) + 2H_2O\,(g) = CO_2(g) + 2H_2(g)$$

Calculate the heat capacity at constant pressure, C_P, for each of the substances in the reaction. For $H_2O(g)$, assume the contribution to C_P from the vibrational mode is 20%.

Solution: For C(s), assume Dulong and Petit's law. Therefore, the value of C_P is approximately 6 cal $K^{-1}mol^{-1}$.
For $H_2O(g)$, assuming 20% of vibrational contribution to C_P,

$$C_P = R + \left(\frac{3R}{2}\right)_{(trans)} + \left(\frac{3R}{2}\right)_{(rot)} + 0.2\ (3R)_{(vib)}$$

$$= 4.6R$$

$$= (4.6)(1.987 \text{ cal mol}^{-1}\ {}^\circ K^{-1})$$

$$= 9.1 \text{ cal } {}^\circ K^{-1} mol^{-1}$$

For $CO_2(g)$: This is a linear molecule.

$$\therefore\ C_P = R + \left(\frac{3R}{2}\right)_{(trans)} + (2R/2)_{(rot)} + 0.2(4R)_{(vib)}$$

$$= 4.3R$$

$$= 8.5 \text{ cal } {}^\circ K^{-1} mol^{-1}$$

for $H_2(g)$:

$$C_P = R + (3R/2)_{(trans)} + (2R/2)_{(rot)} + 0.2(R)_{(vib)}$$

$$= 3.7R$$

$$= 7.3 \text{ cal } {}^\circ K^{-1} mol^{-1}$$

• PROBLEM 2-7

Calculate ΔH when 1 mole of Al is heated from 25° to 100°C, given that $a = 4.94$ cal $mol^{-1}\ K^{-1}$

$b = 2.96 \times 10^{-3}$ cal $mol^{-1}\ K^{-2}$

Solution: The change in enthalpy of a reaction at constant pressure is given by

$$\Delta H = \int_{T_1}^{T_2} C_P\, dT$$

where $C_p = a + bT + CT^2 + dT^3 + \ldots$ (1)

In any given problem, the best available data is used. Since only the a and b values are given, Equation (1) is truncated to $C_p = a + bT$. For our purposes, this approximation is good enough.

Therefore,

$$\Delta H = \int_{T_1}^{T_2} (a + bT)\,dT \tag{2}$$

Integrating equation (2) yields

$$= a(T_2 - T_1) + \frac{1}{2} b\left(T_2^2 - T_1^2\right)$$

$$= \left(\frac{4.94 \text{ cal}}{\text{mol } ^\circ\text{K}}\right)\left(\frac{4.184 \text{ J mol}}{1 \text{ cal}}\right)(373 - 298)\,^\circ\text{K}$$

$$+ \frac{1}{2}\left(\frac{2.96 \times 10^{-3} \text{ cal}}{\text{mol}^{-1}\ ^\circ\text{K}^2}\right)\left(\frac{4.184 \text{ J mol}}{1 \text{ cal}}\right)\left((373)^2 - (298)^2\right)^\circ\text{K}^2$$

$$= 1565.8 + 311.63$$

or $\Delta H = 1877.43\text{J}$

• PROBLEM 2-8

Calculate the heat absorbed, ΔH at constant pressure when one mole of $H_2(g)$ is heated from 0°C or 273°K to 100°C or 373°K. The heat capacity at constant pressure is

$$C_p = 6.9469 - 0.1999 \times 10^{-3}T + 4.808 \times 10^{-7}T^2 \text{ cal K}^{-1}\text{mol}^{-1}$$

Solution: The heat absorbed is given by $dH = C_p dT$. This equation is integrated between the temperature limits of 273°K and 373°K: That is

$$\Delta H = H_{T_2} - H_{T_1} = \int_{T_1}^{T_2} C_p\,dT$$

Using the C_p expression and integrating yields

$$\Delta H = \int_{273}^{373} (6.9469 - 0.1999 \times 10^{-3}T + 4.808 \times 10^{-7}T^2)$$

$$= 6.9469\ (373-273) - \frac{0.1999 \times 10^{-3}}{2} [(373)^2 - (273)^2]$$

$$+ \frac{4.808 \times 10^{-7}}{3} [(373)^3 - (273)^3]$$

$$= (694.69 - 6.49 + 5.06) \text{ cal mol}^{-1}$$

$$= 693.26 \text{ cal mol}^{-1} \frac{4.184 \text{ J}}{1 \text{ cal}}$$

$$\Delta H = 2900.7 \text{ J mol}^{-1}$$

• PROBLEM 2-9

One mole of an ideal diatomic gas is heated from 0°C to 100°C. Calculate ΔH, excluding vibrational contributions. Compare your answer with the calculated ΔH of 2900.7J mol^{-1} for H_2 .

Solution: In calculating the heat absorbed at constant pressure when the temperature is increased from 0°C to 100°C the equation

$$dH = C_P dT$$

is integrated between 0°C and 100°C.

$$\therefore \quad \Delta H = \int_{0°}^{100°C} C_P dT = \int_{273}^{373} C_P dT$$

The total contribution to C_V from translational and rotational motion of a diatomic gas, excluding the vibrational contributions is

$$E_{trans} = (3/2)R$$

$$E_{rot} = R$$

$$\therefore \quad C_V = (3/2)R + R$$

or $\quad C_V = (5/2)R.$

But $C_P - C_V = R$. Therefore, $C_P = C_V + R$

$$= \left(\frac{5}{2}\right)R + R$$

$$= (7/2)R$$

$$\therefore \quad \Delta H = \int_{273°K}^{373°K} \left(\frac{7}{2}\right)R\ dT$$

$$= \frac{7}{2} R(T_2 - T_1)$$

$$= \frac{7}{2} \frac{8.314\ J}{mol\ °K} (373 - 273°K)$$

$$\Delta H = 2909.9 J\ mol^{-1}$$

The above value is in agreement with the calculated value of 2900.7J mol^{-1} for 1 mole of H_2.

• PROBLEM 2-10

The empirical formula for a hypothetical gas is ABA. What can be said about the structure of the gas if the ratio of heat capacities $\frac{C_P}{C_V}$ is 1.38?

Solution: Given: $$\frac{C_P}{C_V} = 1.38 \quad (1)$$

If it is assumed that the gas is ideal, then

$$C_P - C_V = R$$

or $$C_P = C_V + R .$$

Substituting for C_P in equation (1) gives

$$\frac{C_V + R}{C_V} = 1.38$$

or $$C_V + R = 1.38\ C_V . \quad (2)$$

Rearranging equation (2) yields

$$0.38\ C_V = R$$

and solving for C_V gives

$$C_V = (1/.38)R$$

or

$$C_V = 2.63R \quad (2)$$

From the literature it is found that $C_V = 2.5R$ for a linear triatomic gas excluding the vibrational contributions and $C_V = 3.0\ R$ for a non linear triatomic gas excluding the vibrational contribution. Since C_V in (2) is closer to 2.5R it can be concluded that the triatomic gas ABA is linear. The difference between the two C_V's; 2.63R - 2.5R = 0.13R can be assumed to be due to vibrational contributions.

• PROBLEM 2-11

An ideal gas X contains n atoms per molecule. Assuming that at 0°C the vibrational contribution to heat capacity C_P is negligible then C_P for X(g) and for $N_2(g)$ is the same. Also the equipartition value of C_P for X(g) minus the equipartition values of C_P for $N_2(g)$ = 6 cal/deg-mole. What can be said about the structure of X?

Solution: Three coordinates must be known in order to properly describe the translational motion of a molecule. Thus, according to the principle of equipartition, a molecule has three degrees of translational freedom and each degree of freedom contributes (1/2) RT to the translational energy. The corresponding contribution to the heat capacity of the gas is (1/2) R per molecule. A molecule containing n atoms has 3n degrees of freedom and 3 coordinates are required to locate the molecule in space. A linear molecule requires two coordinates for the specification of its rotation. In the problem it is stated that N_2 is linear. Its heat capacity at 0°C, excluding vibrational contributions, is made up of R (for C_P) + (3R/2) (trans) + (2R/2) (rot). This means that N_2 has two degrees of freedom. Since C_P for N_2 is the same as C_P for X at 0°C, then X must also be linear.

However, it is stated that 6 cal/deg-mole equipartition difference exists between C_P for X(g) and C_P for $N_2(g)$. This means three additional vibrational degrees of freedom of X than N_2 or 1 more atom for X. Thus X is a linear triatomic molecule.

• PROBLEM 2-12

Two 1.00 kg pieces of iron, one at 99°C and the other at 25°C, are in contact with each other. The heat flow between the two pieces of iron is given by $q = mC_P\Delta T$ where $C_P = 444\ J\ kg^{-1}K^{-1}$. Calculate the final temperature and the amount of heat transferred between the two pieces of iron.

Solution: When the two pieces of iron are placed together heat will flow from the hotter piece to the cooler piece until a stage is reached when the two pieces are in thermal equilibrium. At this point they have the same temperature and the heat transfer from the hotter piece, q_h , is the same as the heat transfer to cooler piece q_c. This is a statement of the "zeroth law".

Thus at equilibirum;

$$q_h = - q_c \tag{1}$$

$$q = mC_P \Delta T$$

$$\therefore \quad m_h C_P (T_f - T_h) = - m_c C_P (T_f - T_c)$$

where T_f is the final temperature at equilibrium. T_h and T_c are temperatures of the hotter and cooler pieces respectively. C_P can be removed because it is the same for both sides.

$$\therefore \quad m_h (T_f - T_h) = - m_c (T_f - T_c)$$

$$1.00 \text{ kg } (T_f - 99°C) = - 1.00 \text{ kg } (T_f - 25°C)$$

$$1.00\ T_f - 99°C = - 1.00\ T_f + 25°C$$

$$2.00\ T_f = (99 + 25)°C$$

$$T_f = 62°C = 335°K$$

The amount of heat transfered after equilibrium is calculated using $T_f = 62°C$ at equilibrium:

Thus, using the relation

$$q_h = - q_c = mC_P \Delta T ,$$

$$q_h = (1 \text{ kg})(444 \text{ J kg}^{-1}\text{K}^{-1})(62-99) = - 16.4 \text{ kJ}$$

• PROBLEM 2-13

(a) The ratio $C_P/C_V = \gamma$ for an ideal ozone gas is 1.15. Show whether ozone is linear or nonlinear.

(b) Calculate the composition of a lead-silver alloy given that the heat capacity at constant volume,

$$C_V = 0.0383 \text{ cal/deg-g}.$$

The atomic weights of lead and silver are 207 and 107 respectively.

Solution: The heat capacity C_V is made up of contributions due to translational, rotational and vibrational motions. If ozone is linear, then the equipartition C_V would be

$$(3R/2)(\text{trans.}) + R(\text{rot.}) + 4R(\text{vib}) = 6.5R .$$

Given: $\gamma = \dfrac{C_P}{C_V}$

But $C_P - C_V = R$

$$\therefore \quad C_P = R + C_V = R + 6.5R = 7.5R$$

and

$$\gamma = \frac{C_P}{C_V} = \frac{7.5R}{6.5R} = 1.15$$

If, however, ozone is non-linear then

$$C_V = (3/2)R\ (\text{trans}) \quad \frac{3}{2}R(\text{rot}) + 3R(\text{vib})$$

$$= 6R$$

Now, $C_P = R + C_V = R + 6R = 7R$

and

$$\gamma = \frac{C_P}{C_V} = \frac{7R}{6R} = 1.166$$

Since the γ computation of the linear molecule corresponds to the value of the γ given, the molecule is linear.

b) Using the fact that the product of the specific heat and the atomic weight of an element is a constant = 6 cal/deg-mole,

$$(C_V)(\text{M.Wt.}) = 6\ \text{cal/deg-mole}$$

$$\therefore \quad \text{M.Wt} = \frac{6\ \text{cal deg}^{-1}\ \text{mole}^{-1}}{0.0383\ \text{cal deg}^{-1} - \text{gm}^{-1}}$$

$$= 157\ \frac{\text{gm}}{\text{mole}}$$

This is the molecular weight of the alloy made up of lead and silver. The mole fraction of lead in the alloy = X_{Pb} and that of silver is X_{Ag} .

$$\therefore \quad 157\ \text{g/mole} = X_{Pb}(207) + X_{Ag}(107) \qquad (1)$$

But $X_{Pb} + X_{Ag} = 1$ (2)

Therefore $X_{Pb} = 1 - X_{Ag}$. Substituting this into equation (1) yields

$$157 = (1-X_{Ag})(207) + X_{Ag}(107)$$

$$= 207 - 207\ X_{Ag} + X_{Ag}\ 107 = 207 - 100\ X_{Ag}$$

$$\therefore \quad 157 - 207 = -100\ X_{Ag}$$

$$-50 = -100\, X_{Ag}$$

or $$X_{Ag} = \frac{1}{2} = 0.5$$

using equation (2),

$$X_{Pb} + X_{Ag} = 1$$

$$X_{Pb} + 0.5 = 1$$

$$\therefore \quad X_{Pb} = 1 - 0.5 = 0.5$$

• PROBLEM 2-14

One mole of ideal gas at 300 K is expanded adiabatically and reversibly from 20 to 1 atm. What is the final temperature of the gas, assuming $C_V = \frac{3}{2} R$ per mole?

Solution: From the first law of thermodynamics,

$$dE = Q - W \tag{1}$$

For reversible adiabatic expansion of gas, one can write $Q = 0$ and $W = \int P dV$

For ideal gas $dE = C_V dT$. Then, equation (1) can be written as

$$C_V dT = - PdV \tag{2}$$

Now from the ideal gas law,

$$PV = nRT$$

Since n = 1 mole.

$$PV = RT \tag{3}$$

Differentiating equation (3) yields

$$PdV + VdP = RdT \tag{4}$$

Combining equations (2) and (4) gives

$$- C_V dT + VdP = RdT$$

or

$$RdT + C_V dT = VdP$$

$$(R + C_V)\, dT = VdP$$

But $C_P - C_V = R$

Therefore,

$$C_p dT = VdP$$

Using ideal gas law gives

$$C_p dT = \frac{RT}{P} dP$$

or

$$C_P \frac{dT}{T} = R \frac{dP}{p} \tag{5}$$

Integrating equation (5) gives

$$C_P \ln \frac{T_2}{T_1} = R \ln \frac{P_2}{P_1} \tag{6}$$

Now, $C_P = R + C_V = R + (3/2)R = (5/2)R$

$T_1 = 300°K$

$P_1 = 20$ atm.

$P_2 = 1$ atm.

Substitution of these values into equation (6) gives

$$\frac{5}{2} R \ln \frac{T_2}{300} = R \ln \frac{1}{20}$$

$$\ln T_2 - \ln 300 = (2/5) \ln \frac{1}{20}$$

$$\ln T_2 = - 1.198 + 5.704$$

$$= 4.506$$

or $T_2 = 90.5°K$.

THERMOCHEMISTRY

• PROBLEM 2-15

Using the data shown in the following table for sulfur trioxide, sulfur dioxide, and oxygen, develop an equation for the standard enthalpy change as a function of temperature for the reaction

$$SO_2(g) + \frac{1}{2} O_2(g) \rightarrow SO_3(g)$$

and calculate ΔH° for the reaction at 600°C.

Substance	$(\Delta H_f^\circ)_{291}$ (cal mol^{-1})	C_P (cal K^{-1}mol^{-1})	Temperature Range (K)
$SO_3(g)$	-93,900	$12.65 + 6.40 \times 3^{-3}\ T$	(273 - 900)
$SO_2(g)$	-70,970	$11.40 + 1.714 \times 10^{-3}\ T - 2.045 \times 10^5\ T^{-2}$	(273 - 2000)
$O_2(g)$		$7.52 + 0.81 \times 10^{-3}\ T - 9 \times 10^4\ T^{-2}$	(273 - 2000)

Solution: The temperature dependence of enthalpies of a reaction is given by

$$\Delta H_T - \Delta H_{291} = \int_{291}^{T} \Delta C_P dT$$

or

$$\Delta H_T = \Delta H_{291} + \int_{291}^{T} \Delta C_P dT \qquad (1)$$

where

$$\Delta C_P = \sum_{\text{products}} nC_P - \sum_{\text{reactants}} nC_P$$

If the heat capacities of the products and reactants are expressed as a function of temperature by equations of the form

$$C_P = a + BT + CT^{-2}$$

then equation (1) becomes,

$$\Delta H_T = \Delta H_{291} + \Delta a(T - 291) + \frac{\Delta B}{2}(T^2 - 291^2) - \Delta C\ (T^{-1} - 291^{-1})$$

If all the constant terms in this equation are collected and lumped together in a constant designated as ΔH_o, the result is

$$\Delta H_T = \Delta H_o + aT + \frac{\Delta B}{2} T^2 - \Delta CT^{-1} \qquad (2)$$

where

$$\Delta a = \sum_{\text{products}} na - \sum_{\text{reactants}} na$$

with similar definitions for ΔB and ΔC. Using the given data, Δa, ΔB, and ΔC can be calculated as follows.

$$\Delta a = 12.65 - 11.40 - 1/2(7.52) = -2.51$$

$$\Delta B = 6.40 \times 10^{-3} - 1.714 \times 10^{-3} - 1/2(0.81 \times 10^{-3})$$

$$= 4.281 \times 10^{-3}$$

$$\Delta C = -(-2.045 \times 10^{5}) - 1/2\ (-9 \times 10^{4}) = 2.495 \times 10^{5}$$

Substituting for Δa, ΔB and ΔC in equation (2) gives

$$\Delta H_T = \Delta H_o + (-2.51)T + \frac{4.281 \times 10^{-3}}{2} T^2 - 2.495 \times 10^5\ T^{-1}$$

The constant ΔH_o may be calculated if the standard heat of reaction is known at a single temperature, e.g., 291°K. Using Hess's law, calculate the enthalpy of the reaction at 291°K.

$$\Delta H^\circ_{291} = \sum_P \nu_P\ (\Delta H^\circ_f)_{291} - \sum_R \nu_R (\Delta H^\circ_f)_{291}$$

$$= -93{,}900 - (-70{,}970)$$

$$= -22{,}930 \text{ cal.}$$

This allows the calculation of the constant ΔH_o :

$$-22{,}930 = \Delta H_o - (2.51)(291) + \frac{4.281 \times 10^{-3}}{2} (291)^2$$

$$+ 2.495 \times 10^5 (291)^{-1} \quad \text{from which}$$

$$\Delta H_o = -21{,}523.4 \text{ cal}$$

Therefore, the equation giving the dependence of ΔH° on temperature is

$$\Delta H^\circ_T = -21{,}523.4 - 2.51T + 2.14 \times 10^{-3} T^2 - 2.495 \times 10^5 T^{-1}$$

From this equation, we get for ΔH° at a temperature of 600°C (873°K)

$$\Delta H^\circ_{873} = -21{,}523.4 - 2.51(873) + 2.14 \times 10^{-3}(873)^2$$

$$- 2.495 \times 10^5 \times (873)^{-1}$$

$$= -22{,}369.4 \text{ cal.}$$

$$= -93.59 \text{ kJ}.$$

• PROBLEM 2-16

Calculate the change in enthalpy involved in heating 1 kg of aluminum from 0°C to 800°C, if t_{mp} = 658°C, ΔH_{fusion} = 86.6 kcal kg^{-1} , $(C_p)_s = 0.218 + 0.48 \times 10^{-4}\,t$ (kcal $°C^{-1}$ kg^{-1}) for solid Al, and $(\bar{C}_p)_l = 0.259$ (kcal K^{-1} kg^{-1}) for liquid Al (1 kcal = 4.184 kJ).

Solution: The enthalpy change in changing the temperature of a substance is given by

$$\Delta H = \sum_{i}^{\text{phases}} \int C_{P,i}\,dT + \sum_{j}^{\text{transitions}} \Delta H_T(\text{transition, j}) \qquad (1)$$

Now the desired process can be represented as a series of three steps, as illustrated in Fig. 1.

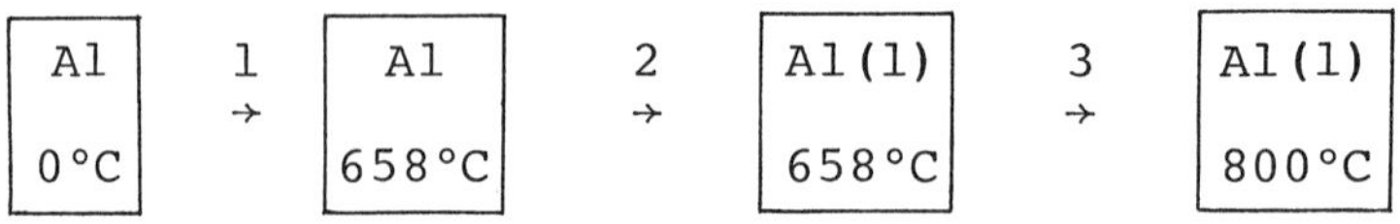

Fig. 1

For this process, equation (1) becomes,

$$\Delta H = \Delta H_1 + \Delta H_2 + \Delta H_3$$

$$\Delta H = \int_{273}^{931} (C_p)_s\, dT + \Delta H_{931}\,(\text{fusion}) + \int_{931}^{1073} (C_p)_l\, dT$$

Substitute the numerical data for $(C_p)_s$, $(C_p)_l$, and ΔH_{931} (fusion) into the above equation to obtain

$$\Delta H = \int_{273}^{931} (0.218 + 0.48 \times 10^{-4} t)\,dT + 86.6 + \int_{931}^{1073} 0.259\, dT$$

In the above equation, t is the temperature in °C while T is the absolute temperature (T = t + 273). Therefore t = T - 273. In order to perform the integration, substitute t = T - 273. Thus,

$$\Delta H = \int_{273}^{931} [0.218 + 0.48 \times 10^{-4}\,(T - 273)]\, dT$$

$$+ 86.6 + \int_{931}^{1073} 0.259\, dT$$

or

$$\Delta H = \int_{273}^{931} [0.218 + 0.48 \times 10^{-4} T - 0.48 \times 273 \times 10^{-4}] \, dT$$

$$+ 86.6 + \int_{931}^{1073} 0.259 \, dT$$

Integrating yields,

$$\Delta H = \left(0.218 T + 0.48 \times 10^{-4} \frac{T^2}{2} - 0.48 \times 10^{-4} \times 273 T\right) \Bigg|_{273}^{931}$$

$$+ 86.6 + 0.259 T \Bigg|_{931}^{1073}$$

$$= 0.218(931-273) + \frac{0.48 \times 10^{-4}}{2} (931^2 - 273^2)$$

$$- 0.48 \times 10^{-4} \times 273(931 - 273) + 86.6$$

$$+ 0.259 (1073 - 931)$$

$$= 143.444 + 19.0135 - 8.622 + 86.6 + 36.778$$

$$\therefore \quad \Delta H = 277.3 \frac{\text{kcal}}{\text{kg}} \times 1 \text{ kg} = 277.3 \text{ kcal}$$

or $\Delta H = 1160.2$ kJ

• PROBLEM 2-17

Calculate the heat of formation of $CH_4(g)$ in the reaction:

$$C(\text{graphite}) + 2H_2(g) = CH_4(g) \,,$$

using the reactions below and their given $\Delta H°$ values:

$CH_4(g) + 2O_2(g) = CO_2(g) + 2H_2O(l)$	$\Delta H° = -212.80$ kcal mole^{-1}
$C(\text{graphite}) + O_2(g) = CO_2(g)$	$\Delta H° = -94.05$ kcal mole^{-1}
$H_2(g) + 1/2\ O_2(g) = H_2O(l)$	$\Delta H° = -68.32$ kcal mole^{-1}

Solution: Enthalpy is a thermodynamic property of every substance, and at a given temperature and pressure, it is the same regardless of how the substance was produced. Thus, this makes it possible to calculate the enthalpy changes for reactions that cannot be studied directly. In this problem, it is not practical to measure directly the heat formed when C (graphite) burns with H_2 (gas) to produce CH_4 (gas). But the given series of reactions can be arranged with known ΔH_f° values such that when they are added up, they produce the reaction C (graphite) + $2H_2$ (g) = CH_4 (g). Then the ΔH° for this reaction will be equal to the sum of the ΔH_f° values for the individual reactions. ΔH° is the enthalpy of change for the reaction in which a mole of the substance is formed from elements each in its standard state of 25°C = 298°K and 1 atm. Thus for all elements in their standard states, ΔH° is zero.

ΔH_f° is the ΔH° for a reaction in which one mole of a compound is produced from its elements, both product and reactants being in their standard state of 25°C = 298°K and 1 atm. Thus the enthalpy of any substance in its standard state is equal to ΔH_f° .

∴ Arrange the three given reactions with known ΔH_f° values, such that when added up, they give the desired reaction. CH_4(g) is to be on the right, so, the first reaction shall be reversed along with the sign of its ΔH_f° . Also, multiply the third reaction by 2, since $2H_2$(g) is needed. The three reaction equations thus become

	ΔH_f° (kcal $mole^{-1}$)
$CO_2(g) + 2H_2O(l) = 2O_2(g) + CH_4(g)$	+ 212.80
$C(graphite) + O_2(g) = CO_2(g)$	- 94.05
$2H_2(g) + O_2(g) = 2H_2O(l)$	- 136.64

Total: $CO_2(g) + 2H_2O(l) + C(graphite) + O_2(g) + 2H_2(g) + O_2(g)$

$= 2O_2(g) + CH_4(g) + CO_2(g) + 2H_2O(l)$

$= 212 - 94.05 - 136.64$ kcal $mole^{-1}$

∴ (graphite) + $2H_2(g) = CH_4(g)$; $\Delta H^\circ = \Delta H_f^\circ = -17.89$ kcal $mole^{-1}$

• PROBLEM 2-18

Given the reaction

$$CO(g) + H_2O(g) = CO_2(g) + H_2(g) \quad \Delta H_{298°K} = -10 \text{ kcal}$$

Calculate ΔH at 1000°K.

The heat capacities are

$C_p(CO) = 6.60 + 1.0 \times 10^{-3}T$

$C_p(H_2) = 6.6 + 1.0 \times 10^{-3}T$

$C_p(H_2O) = 7.3 + 2.0 \times 10^{-3}T$

$C_p(CO_2) = 7.3 + 3.0 \times 10^{-3}T$

Solution: The equation

$$\Delta H_{T_2} = \Delta H_{298°K} + \int_{T_1}^{T_2} \Delta C_p dT \qquad (1)$$

is to be used

where ΔH = Enthalpy change

ΔC_p = Heat Capacity change

$$\Delta C_p = \sum_{\text{products}} C_p - \sum_{\text{reactants}} C_p$$

That is,

$$\Delta C_p = \sum (C_p(CO_2) + C_p(H_2) - C_p(CO) - C_p(H_2O))$$

Therefore,

$$\begin{aligned} \Delta C_p &= 7.3 + 3.0 \times 10^{-3}T \\ &+ 6.6 + 1.0 \times 10^{-3}T \\ &- 6.60 + 1.0 \times 10^{-3}T \\ &- 7.3 + 2.0 \times 10^{-3}T \end{aligned}$$

$$\Delta C_p = 0 + 10^{-3}T$$

From equation (1),

$$\Delta H_{1000°K} = \Delta H_{298°K} + \int_{298}^{1000} (10^{-3}T)dT$$

$$= \Delta H_{298°K} + \frac{10^{-3}}{2}(T_2^2 - T_1^2)$$

$$= -10 \text{ kcal} + \frac{10^{-3}}{2}(1000^2 - 298^2)$$

$$= -10 \text{ kcal} + 0.46$$

$$\therefore \quad \Delta H_{1000°K} = -9.54 \text{ kcal}$$

• PROBLEM 2-19

At a constant pressure and a temperature of -10°C, water freezes. Calculate the heat evolved in the process.

$$H_2O\ (\ell) = H_2O(s)$$

Given the following:

$$\Delta H_{273} = -79.7 \text{ cal g}^{-1},$$

$$C_{P,H_2O(\ell)} = 1.00 \text{ cal K}^{-1}\text{g}^{-1}$$

and

$$C_{P,H_2O(s)} = 0.49 \text{ cal K}^{-1}\text{g}^{-1}$$

Solution: The enthalpy change of a reaction at a certain temperature T_2 is given by

$$\Delta H_{T_2} = \Delta H_{T_1} + \int_{T_1}^{T_2} \Delta C_P dT ,$$

if the enthalpy of reaction at temperature T_1 is known.

C_P is the heat capacity at constant pressure. If C_P is considered to be independent of temperature,

$$\text{then,} \quad \Delta H_{T_2} = \Delta H_{T_1} + \Delta C_P \int_{T_1}^{T_2} dT$$

Integration yields

$$\Delta H_{T_2} = \Delta H_{T_1} + \Delta C_P (T_2 - T_1)$$

$$= \Delta H_{T_1} + [C_{P,H_2O(s)} - C_{P,H_2O(\ell)}](T_2 - T_1)$$

$$\Delta H_{263} = \Delta H_{273} + (0.49-1)(263-273)$$

$$= \Delta H_{273} + (0.49-1)(-10)$$

$$= -79.7 \frac{cal}{g} + \left(-0.51 \frac{cal}{g°K}\right)(10°K)$$

$$\therefore \quad \Delta H_{263} = -74.6 \text{ cal } g^{-1}$$

• PROBLEM 2-20

For the reaction

$$4C_2H_5Cl(g) + 13O_2(g) = 2\ Cl_2(g) + 8\ CO_2(g) + 10\ H_2O(g)\ ,$$

$$\Delta H_{298°K} = -1229.6 \text{ kcal} .$$

Also, the heat of combustion per mole of C_2H_6 (g) to CO_2 (g) and H_2O (g) = -341 kcal, the heat of formation per mole of H_2O (g) = -57.8 kcal and the heat of formation per mole of HCl (g) = -2.1 kcal. For the reaction

$$C_2H_6(g) + Cl_2(g) = C_2H_5Cl(g) + HCl(g)$$

a) Calculate $\Delta H_{298°K}$

b) Calculate $\Delta H_{398°K}$ for the first reaction assuming $\Delta C_p = -10$ cal/deg

c) Calculate $\Delta E_{298°K}$ for the first reaction

Solution: a) The desired reaction is

$$C_2H_6(g) + Cl_2(g) = C_2H_5Cl(g) + HCl(g)$$

Since C_2H_5Cl(g) is needed on the right of the desired equation, the first reaction is reversed and the sign of ΔH is changed.

$$10H_2O + 8CO_2 + 2Cl_2 = 13O_2 + 4C_2H_5Cl \qquad (1)$$

with $\Delta H_1 = 1229.6$ kcal.

Next, the combustion of C_2H_6 is added since it appears in the desired equation

$$4C_2H_6 + 14O_2 = 8CO_2 + 12H_2O \qquad (2)$$

with $\Delta H_2 = -4(341) = -1364$ kcal.

Cl_2(g) is also needed and an HCl. Therefore, the formation of HCl is added

$$2Cl_2(g) + 2H_2(g) = 4HCl(g) \qquad (3)$$

$$\Delta H_3 = -21 \times 4 = -84 \text{ kcal}$$

Finally, the formation of water is added to make the required equation complete. Then cancel out terms that are not needed.

$$2H_2O(g) = O_2(g) + 2H_2(g) \qquad (4)$$

with $\Delta H_4 = 2(57.8) = 115.6$

Adding equations (1) through (4) together and cancelling out unwanted terms yields

$10H_2O + 8CO_2 + 2Cl_2 = 13O_2 + 4C_2H_5Cl$	$\Delta H_1 = 1229.6$ kcal
$4C_2H_6 + 14O_2 = 8CO_2 + 12H_2O$	$\Delta H_2 = -1364$ kcal
$2Cl_2 + 2H_2 = 4HCl$	$\Delta H_3 = -84$ kcal
$2H_2O = O_2 + 2H_2$	$\Delta H_4 = 115.6$ kcal
$4C_2H_6 + 4Cl_2 = 4C_2H_5Cl + 4HCl$	$\Delta H = (1229.6-1364 -84+115.6)$ kcal

$$\therefore \quad \Delta H = -103 \text{ kcal}$$

b) $$\Delta H_T = \Delta H_{298°K} + \int_{T_1}^{T_2} \Delta C_p dT$$

Assuming that ΔC_p is a constant, then

$$\Delta H_T = \Delta H_{298°K} + \Delta C_p \Delta T$$

$$\therefore \quad \Delta H_{398°K} = \Delta H_{298°K} + \Delta C_p (T_2 - T_1)$$

where $T_1 = 298°K$

and $T_2 = 398°K$

Substituting the respective values into the above equation gives

$$\Delta H_{398°K} = -1229.6 - \frac{10 \text{ cal}}{\text{deg}} \frac{1 \text{ kcal}}{1000 \text{ cal}} (100 \text{ deg})$$

The 1000 cal in the denominator is a conversion factor.

$$\therefore \quad \Delta H_{398°K} = -1230.6 \text{ kcal}$$

c) $\Delta E = \Delta H - \Delta(PV)$

But $PV = nRT$, $\Delta(PV) = \Delta(nRT) = (\Delta n)RT$,

since R, T are constant

$$\therefore \quad \Delta E = \Delta H - \Delta nRT$$

$$= -1229.6 - 3 \text{ mol } RT$$

$$\Delta E = -1231.4 \text{ kcal}$$

• PROBLEM 2-21

Calculate the heat of combustion of hydrogen gas at 1500°K, given that ΔH° for the reaction

$$2H_2(g) + O_2(g) = 2H_2O(g)$$

is -115,595.8 cal at 25°C = 298°K.

Solution: To calculate the enthalpy of the combustion at 1500°K, make use of the equation

$$\Delta H^\circ_T = \Delta H^\circ_{298} + \int_{T_1}^{T_2} \Delta C_P dT$$

$$\Delta H^\circ_{1500} = \Delta H^\circ_{298} + \int_{298}^{1500} \left(2\, C_{P,H_2O} - C_{P,O_2} - 2C_{P,H_2}\right) dT$$

C_P is often expressed as a function of temperature.

$$\therefore \quad C_P = a + bT + CT^2$$

where the parameters a, b, and C are empirical constants and their values can be found in table of constants.

$$2C_{P,H_2O} = 2[a + bT + CT^2]$$

$$= 2[7.1873 + 2.3733 \times 10^{-3}T + 2.084 \times 10^{-7}T^2]$$

$$= 14.3746 + 4.7466 \times 10^{-3}T + 4.168 \times 10^{-7}T^2$$

$$C_{P,O_2} = [a + bT + CT^2]$$

$$= [6.0954 + 3.2533 \times 10^{-3}T - 10.171 \times 10^{-7}T^2]$$

$$2C_{P,H_2} = 2[a+bT + cT^2]$$

$$= 2[6.949-0.1999 \times 10^{-3}T + 4.808 \times 10^{-7} T^2]$$

$$= 13.8938 - 0.3998 \times 10^{-3}T + 9.616 \times 10^{-7}T^2]$$

$$(2C_{P,H_2O} - C_{P,O_2} - 2C_{P,H_2}) = (-5.6146 + 1.8931 \times 10^{-3}T + 4.723 \times 10^{-7}T^2)$$

$$\therefore \Delta H^\circ_{1500} = \Delta H^\circ_{298} + \int_{298}^{1500} (-5.6146 + 1.8931 \times 10^{-3}T + 4.723 \times 10^{-7}T^2)\,dT$$

$$= -115{,}595.8 \text{ cal} - 5.6146\,(1500-298) + \frac{1.8931 \times 10^{-3}}{2}(1500^2 - 298^2) + \frac{4.723 \times 10^{-7}}{3}(1500^3 - 298^3)$$

$$\Delta H^\circ_{1500} = -119{,}767 \text{ cal}$$

• PROBLEM 2-22

The standard enthalpy of the hydrogenation of propene in the reaction $CH_2{:}CH.CH_3 + H_2 \rightarrow CH_3.CH_2.CH_3$ is -124 kJ mol^{-1}. The standard enthalpy of the oxidation of propane in the reaction $CH_3.CH_2.CH_3 + 5O_2 \rightarrow 3CO_2 + 4H_2O$ is -2222 kJmol^{-1}. Find the standard enthalpy of the combustion reaction of propene.

Solution: The enthalpy of the reaction

$$C_3H_6(g) + \frac{9}{2} O_2(g) \rightarrow 3CO_2(g) + 3H_2O(\ell) \qquad (1)$$

is required. The reactions given are:

$$C_3H_6(g) + H_2(g) \rightarrow C_3H_8(g) \qquad \Delta H^\circ = -124 \text{ kJ mole}^{-1} \qquad (2)$$

$$C_3H_8(g) + 5O_2(g) \rightarrow 3CO_2(g) + 4H_2O(\ell)$$

$$\Delta H^\circ = -2222 \text{ kJ mol}^{-1} \qquad (3)$$

Surveying the equations (2) and (3), observe that the following substances are to be eliminated to obtain the desired equation (1): $C_3H_8(g)$, and $H_2(g)$. From the standard heats of formation,

$$H_2(g) + 1/2\ O_2(g) \rightarrow H_2O(\ell) \quad \Delta H^\circ = -286 \text{ kJ mole}^{-1} \qquad (4)$$

Arrange equations (2), (3) and (4) as follows, with the substances to be retained placed on the left or right depending on where they appeared in the desired equation.

$$C_3H_6(g) + H_2(g) \rightarrow C_3H_8(g) \quad \Delta H^\circ = -124 \text{ kJ mol}^{-1}$$

$$C_3H_8(g) + 5O_2(g) \rightarrow 3CO_2(g) + 4H_2O(\ell) \quad \Delta H^\circ = -2222 \text{ kJ mol}^{-1}$$

$$H_2O(\ell) \rightarrow H_2(g) + 1/2\ O_2(g) \quad \Delta H^\circ = +286 \text{ kJ mol}^{-1}$$

Addition of these three equations yields

$$C_3H_6(g) + \frac{9}{2} O_2 \rightarrow 3CO_2(g) + 3H_2O(\ell),$$

$$\Delta H^\circ = (-124 - 2222 + 286) = -2068 \text{ kJ mol}^{-1}$$

Hence, the standard enthalpy of the combustion reaction of propene, is -2068 kJ mol^{-1}.

In general, the enthalpies of the reaction may be found by adding and substracting the appropriate reactions and using Hess's law. Thermochemical equations can be manipulated in the same way as algebraic equations.

• PROBLEM 2-23

Calculate the heat, ΔH° at 1000°K for the reaction:

$$H_2(g) + Cl_2(g) = 2HCl(g)$$

given that $\Delta H^\circ_{298} = -44.124$ kcal. The heat capacity data for the reaction is given as

$$C_P^\circ = 6.9469 - 0.1999 \times 10^{-3}T + 4.808 \times 10^{-7}T^2 \text{ for } H_2(g)$$

$$C_P^\circ = 7.5755 + 2.4244 \times 10^{-3}T - 9.650 \times 10^{-7}T^2 \text{ for } Cl_2(g)$$

$$C_P^\circ = 6.7319 + 0.4325 \times 10^{-3}T + 3.697 \times 10^{-7}T^2 \text{ for } HCl(g)$$

Solution: To calculate ΔH° for a reaction at another temperature when one temperature is known, and the values of C_P for the reactants and products given, use the formula

$$\Delta H^\circ_T = \Delta H^\circ_{298} + \int_{T_1}^{T_2} \Delta C_P dT$$

$$= \Delta H^\circ_{298} + \int_{298}^{1000} (2C_{P,HCl} - C_{P,H_2} - C_{P,Cl_2})\,dT$$

$$C_{P,HCl} = 2[a + bT + CT^2 + ...]$$

$$C_{P,H_2} = [a + bT + CT^2 + ...]$$

$$C_{P,Cl_2} = [a + bT + CT^2 + ...]$$

$$\Delta a = 2a_{HCl} - a_{H_2} - a_{Cl_2}$$

$$= 2(6.7319) - 6.9469 - 7.5755$$

$$= 1.0586$$

$$\Delta b = 2b_{HCl} - b_{H_2} - b_{Cl_2}$$

$$= 2(0.4325 \times 10^{-3}) + 0.1999 \times 10^{-3} - 2.4244 \times 10^{-3}$$

$$= -1.3595 \times 10^{-3}$$

$$\Delta C = 2C_{HCl} - C_{H_2} - C_{Cl_2}$$

$$= 2(3.697 \times 10^{-7}) - 4.808 \times 10^{-7} + 9.650 \times 10^{-7}$$

$$= 12.236 \times 10^{-7}$$

$$\Delta H^\circ_T = \Delta H^\circ_{298} + \int_{T_1}^{T_2} \Delta C_P\,dT$$

$$= \Delta H^\circ_{298} + \int_{T_1}^{T_2} \left(\Delta a + \Delta bT + \Delta CT^2\right) dT$$

$$= \Delta H^\circ_{298} + [\Delta aT + \frac{\Delta b}{2} T^2 + \frac{\Delta C}{3} T^3] \Big|_{T_1}^{T_2}$$

$$= \Delta H^\circ_{298} + \Delta a(T_2 - T_1) + \frac{\Delta b}{2} (T_2^2 - T_1^2) + \frac{\Delta C}{3} (T_2^3 - T_1^3)$$

$$\Delta H^\circ_{1000} = -44.124 + 1.0586(1000-298)$$

$$- \frac{1.3595 \times 10^{-3}}{2} (1000^2 - 298^2)$$

$$+ \left((12.236 \times 10^{-7})/3\right)(1000^3 - 298^3)$$

$$\therefore \quad \Delta H^\circ_{1000} = -182.435 \text{ kJ}$$

Note that the values for the constants a, b and C can be found in literatures or Handbooks if they are not given.

• PROBLEM 2-24

Predict the heat of fusion for LiCl at 883°K given the following:

$$Li(liq) + \frac{1}{2}Cl_2(g) = LiCl(liq) \qquad \Delta H^\circ_{883} = -92.347 \frac{\text{koal}}{\text{mole}}$$

$$Li(liq) + \frac{1}{2}Cl_2(g) = LiCl(s) \qquad \Delta H^\circ_{883} = -97.105 \frac{\text{kcal}}{\text{mole}}$$

Solution: Hess's law states that if a series of reactions having known ΔH values can be arranged in such a way that when added up, they produce a desired reaction, the ΔH value for the desired reaction will be equal to the sum of the ΔH values for the individual reactions. The formation of LiCl(liq) from LiCl(s) illustrates the law. The heat of formation is the enthalphy change for a chemical reaction in which a compound is produced from its elements, both products and reactants being in their natural states.

By definition,

$$\Delta H^\circ_T(\text{reaction}) = \sum_i^{\text{Products}} n_i \Delta H^\circ_T(\text{formation}, i) - \sum_j^{\text{reactants}} n_j \Delta H^\circ_T(\text{formation}, j)$$

where n_i and n_j are the number of moles of products and reactants respectively

∴ For the reaction

$$LiCl(s) = LiCl(liq)$$

and using the equation above,

$$\Delta H^\circ_{883} = (1)(-92.374) - (1)(-97.105)$$

$$= (4.731 \text{ kcal})\left(\frac{4.184 \times 10^3 J}{1 kcal}\right)\left(\frac{1 kJ}{1000 J}\right)$$

$$\Delta H^\circ_{883} = 19.795 kJ$$

Consider the formation of ethylcyclohexane (C_8H_{16})

$$C_8H_{10}(\ell) + 3H_2(g) = C_8H_{16} \qquad \Delta H_{298°K} = -48.3 \text{ kcal}$$

and $C_8H_8(\ell) + 4H_2(g) = C_8H_{16} \qquad \Delta H_{298°K} = -74.65$ kcal .

Given that at 298°K, the heats of combustion of C_8H_{16} to water vapor and CO_2 is -1238.23 kcal/mole, and the heats of formation of water vapor and CO_2 are, -58.32 and -94.05 kcal/mole respectively, calculate (a) heat of hydrogenation of styrene to ethylbenzene. (b) the heat of formation of ethylbenzene.

Solution: a) The hydrogenation of styrene to ethylbenzene is represented by equations

$$C_8H_{10} + 3H_2 = C_8H_{16} \quad (1) \quad \Delta H_{298°K} = 48.3 \text{ kcal}$$

and

$$C_8H_8 + 4H_2 = C_8H_{16} \quad (2) \quad \Delta H_{298°K} = -74.65 \text{ kcal} .$$

Subtracting equation (1) from equation (2), the required hydrogenation equation can be written as:

$$C_8H_8 + 4H_2 - C_8H_{16} - C_8H_{10} - 3H_2 + C_8H_{16} = 0$$

Therefore,

$$C_8H_8 + H_2 = C_8H_{10}$$

where C_8H_8 = styrene and C_8H_{10} = ethylbenzene
Also, subtracting their enthalpy changes yields

$$\Delta H = -74.65 - (-48.3)$$

$$\Delta H = -26.4 \text{ kcal}$$

b) The combustion of C_8H_{16} can be written as:

$$C_8H_{16} + 12O_2 = 8CO_2 + 8H_2O \qquad \Delta H_{C(298)} = -1238.23 \text{ kcal}$$

$$\therefore \quad \Delta H_{C(298)} = -1238.23 = \left(8H_{CO_2} + 8H_{H_2O}\right) - H_{C_8H_{16}}$$

That is,

$$\sum\left(H_{products} - H_{reactant}\right) .$$

H is the heat of formation.

$$\therefore \quad H_{(C_8H_{16})} = 1238.23 + 8(-94.05) + 8(-58.32)$$

$$= (1238.23 - 752.4 - 466.6)\text{kcal}$$

$$H_{(C_8H_{16})} = 19.27 \text{ kcal}$$

From equation (1) the heat of formation of C_8H_{16} can be written as

$$\Delta H_{298°K} = -48.3 = H_{(C_8H_{16})} - H_{(C_8H_{10})}$$

$$\therefore \quad H_{(C_8H_{10})} = 48.3 + H_{(C_8H_{16})}$$

$$= (48.3 + 19.3)\text{kcal}$$

$$H_{(C_8H_{10})} = 67.6 \text{ kcal}$$

• PROBLEM 2-26

Cyclopropane $(CH_2)_3$ was burned to carbon dioxide and liquid water, as represented by the equation

$$(CH_2)_3 + \frac{9}{2} O_2(g) = 3CO_2(g) + 3H_2O(\ell)$$

The heats of combustion of $(CH_2)_3$, carbon and H_2 are, -500.0, -94.0 and -68.0 kcal/mole respectively. The heat of formation of $CH_3CH = CH_2$ is 4.9 kcal/mole. Calculate

a) the heat of formation, ΔH of cyclopropane $(CH_2)_3$

b) the heat of isomerization of $(CH_2)_3$ to propylene.

Solution:

$$(CH_2)_3 + \frac{9}{2} O_2 = 3CO_2 + 3H_2O$$

Heat of combustion is the amount of heat liberated per mole of the substance burned. For an organic compound like $(CH_2)_3$, the heat of formation may be calculated from the heat of combustion

$$\therefore \quad \Delta H_c = -500\text{kcal/mole} = \left(3\Delta H_{CO_2} + 3\Delta H_{H_2O} - \Delta H_{(CH_2)_3}\right)$$

where ΔH = heat of formation.

The heat of formation of CO_2 is the same as the heat of

combustion of carbon. Also, the heat of formation of H_2O is the same as the heat of combustion of H_2 .

$$\therefore \quad \Delta H_{(CH_2)_3} = 500 + \left(3\Delta H_{CO_2} + 3\Delta H_{H_2O}\right)$$

$$= 500 + (-282 - 204)\text{kcal}$$

$$\Delta H_{(CH_2)_3} = 14 \text{ kcal}$$

b) Cyclopropane isomerizes to propylene according to the equation

$$(CH_2)_3 \rightarrow CH_3CH = CH_2$$

$$\therefore \quad \Delta H_{\text{isomerization}} = \Delta H_{(CH_3CH = CH_2)} - \Delta H_{(CH_2)_3}$$

$$= (4.9 - 14.0)\text{kcal}$$

$$\Delta H_{(\text{isomerization})} = -9.1 \text{ kcal}$$

• PROBLEM 2-27

For the reaction

$$C(s) + 2\ H_2O(g) = CO_2(g) + 2H_2(g)$$

calculate ΔH and ΔE at 25°C,given the following data: heat of formation at 25°C:

$$H_2O(g) = -57.8 \text{ kcal}, \ CH_4(g) = -17.9 \text{ kcal}.$$

Also, the heat of combustion of CH_4 at 25°C to CO_2 and $H_2O(g)$ is -192.2 kcal.

Solution: Hess's law states that at a given temperature and pressure, the overall heat of a chemical reaction is the same, regardless of the intermediate steps involved. Thus if a series of reactions having known ΔH values can be arranged in such a way that when added up to produce the desired reaction, the ΔH value for the desired reaction will be equal to the sum of the ΔH values for the individual reactions. For the above reaction since the process that involve C(s) is the heat of formation of CH_4 , write equations involving the heat of formation of $CH_4(g)$ and $H_2O(g)$ and the heat of combustion of $CH_4(g)$. Thus

$$C(s) + 2H_2(g) = CH_4(g) \qquad (1)\ \Delta H = -17.9 \text{ kcal}$$

$$CH_4(g) + 2O_2(g) = CO_2(g) + 2H_2O(g) \qquad (2)\ \Delta H = -192.2$$

$$4H_2O(g) = 4H_2(g) + 2O_2(g) \qquad (2)\ \Delta H = 4(57.8)$$

Adding and cancelling the undesired terms, the above three equations become

$$C(s) + 2H_2 - CH_4 + CH_4 + 2O_2 - CO_2 - 2H_2O + 4H_2O - 4H_2 - 2O_2 =$$

$$C + 2H_2 - CO_2 - 2H_2O + 4H_2O - 4H_2 \ .$$

Therefore,

$$C(s) + 2H_2O(g) = CO_2(g) + 2H_2(g) \quad ,$$

which is the desired reaction

$$\Delta H = (-17.9) + (-192.2) + (4 \times 57.8)$$

$$\Delta H = 21.3 \text{ kcal}$$

Note that the third equation above was reversed, thus the sign of ΔH also changed. From the first law of thermodynamics:

$$\Delta E = q - w \qquad (1)$$

where ΔE is the energy change, q is the heat added to a system and w is work done by the system.

Equation (1) can also be written as

$$\Delta E = \Delta H - \Delta(PV) \qquad (2)$$

from the ideal gas law $PV = nRT$.

Thus equation (2) becomes

$$\Delta E = \Delta H - \Delta nRT$$

$$= 21.3 \text{ kcal} - (1 \text{ mole})\left(\frac{1.98 \text{ cal}}{\text{mol } °\text{K}}\right)\left(\frac{1 \text{ kcal}}{1000 \text{ cal}}\right)(298°\text{K})$$

$$\Delta E = 20.7 \text{ kcal}$$

• PROBLEM 2-28

The isomer of $C_2H_5OH(\ell)$ is $CH_3\text{-}O\text{-}CH_3(g)$. Given that, at 25°C, the heat of formation of $C_2H_5OH(\ell)$ = -66 kcal/mole, the heat of combustion of the isomeric $CH_3\text{-}O\text{-}CH_3(g)$ to $CO_2(g)$ and $H_2O(\ell)$ = -348 kcal/mole, the heat of formation of $H_2O(\ell)$ = -68 kcal/mole and the heat of combustion of carbon to $CO_2(g)$ = -94 kcal/mole. Calculate a) $\Delta H_{298°K}$ for the reaction and b) $\Delta E_{298°K}$ for the reaction assuming $\Delta H_{298°K}$ in part a) = -10 kcal.

Solution: The desired reaction is obtained by adding up a number of reactions. The desired ΔH value will be the sum of the ΔH values for the individual reactions.

For the formation of C_2H_5OH, the reaction equation is

$$C_2H_5OH(\ell) = 2C(s) + 3H_2(g) + \frac{1}{2} O_2(g) \quad (1)$$

with ΔH = 66 kcal. Notice that ΔH is positive because the equation is reversed.

For CH_3-O-CH_3 ,

$$2CO_2(g) + 3H_2O(\ell) = CH_3\text{-O-}CH_3(g) + 3O_2(\ell) \quad (2)$$

with ΔH = 348 kcal.

Equation (2) is also reversed. So, ΔH is positive.

$$2C(s) + 2O_2(g) = 2CO_2(g) \quad (3)$$

ΔH_3 = -94 x 2 = -188 kcal.

$$3H_2(g) + 3/2\ O_2(g) = 3H_2O(\ell) \quad (4)$$

ΔH_4 = -68 x 3 = -204 kcal.

Adding up equations (1), (2), (3) and (4) and elminating terms that are not needed yield

$$C_2H_5OH = CH_3\text{-O-}CH_3(g)$$

with ΔH = (66 + 348 - 188-204) kcal

= 22 kcal

b) $\Delta E = \Delta H - \Delta PV$

But $PV = nRT$

$\therefore \quad \Delta E = \Delta H - \Delta nRT$

Here ΔnRT = (1 mole)(1.987 cal/mole °K)(298°K)

$$\therefore \quad \Delta E = -10 - (1 \text{ mole})\left(\frac{1.987 \text{ cal}}{\text{mol °K}}\right)(298\text{°K})\left(\frac{1 \text{ kcal}}{1000 \text{ cal}}\right)$$

Observe that the last term is a conversion factor.

$\Delta E = -10 - 0.6$

$\Delta E = -10.6$ kcal

(a) The standard enthalpy of combustion (ΔH°_c) of crystalline benzoic acid, C_6H_5COOH, to $CO_2(g)$ and H_2O (ℓ) is -771.72 kcal $mole^{-1}$ at 25°C. Find ΔH° and ΔE° of formation of benzoic acid from its elements at 25°C. (b) Find ΔH° of formation of crystalline benzoic acid at 100°C. Assume that the following heat capacities are constant over the temperature range involved:

	$C_6H_5COOH(c)$	C (graphite)	$H_2(g)$	$O_2(g)$
$\bar{C}^\circ_p$, cal $°K^{-1} mole^{-1}$	35.1	2.0	4.9	5.0

Solution: a) The combustion reaction is

$$C_6H_5COOH + \frac{15}{2} O_2(g) \rightarrow 7CO_2(g) + 3H_2O(\ell)$$

$$\Delta H^\circ = -771.72 \text{ kcal}$$

Now from the Hess law,

$$\Delta H^\circ_T \text{ (reaction)} = \sum_{\text{product}} n\Delta H^\circ_T \text{ (formation)}$$

$$- \sum_{\text{reactants}} n\Delta H^\circ_T \text{ (formation)}$$

The heat of formation of O_2 , CO_2 and H_2O are as follows: O_2 = 0 (this is because the heat of formation for an element in its naturally occurring physical state is zero)

$$CO_2 = -94.0518 \text{ kcal}$$

$$H_2O = -68.3174 \text{ kcal.}$$

Let x be the heat of formation of benzoic acid

Then,

$$-771.72 = 7(-94.0518) + 3(-68.3174) - x - \frac{15}{2}(0)$$

from which

$$x = -91.59 \text{ kcal.}$$

Thus the ΔH° of formation for crystalline benzoic acid is -91.59 kcal.

Now

$$\Delta H^\circ = \Delta E^\circ + (\Delta n_{gas})RT \quad (1)$$

where Δn_{gas} is the difference between the number of moles of gaseous products and the number of moles of gaseous reactants.

The formation reaction of benzoic acid is

$$7C\ (\text{graphite}) + 3H_2(g) + O_2(g) \rightarrow C_6H_5COOH(c)$$

In this reaction, $\Delta n_{gas} = -3 - 1 = -4$.

Then equation (1) becomes,

$$91590(\text{cal}) = \Delta E° + (-4)(1.987)(298)$$

from which

$$\Delta E° = 93958.5 \text{ cal}$$

or

$$\Delta E° = 93.958 \text{ kcal}.$$

b) The standard heat of formation as a function of temperature can be represented by the equation

$$\Delta H_T = \Delta H_{298} + \int_{298}^{T} \Delta C_P dT$$

Since the heat capacities are constant over the temperature range involved, the above equation can be rewritten as

$$\Delta H_T = \Delta H_{298} + \Delta C_P \int_{298}^{T} dT$$

or $$\Delta H_T = \Delta H_{298} + \Delta C_P (T-298). \qquad (2)$$

But,

$$\Delta C_P = \sum_{\text{products}} nC_P - \sum_{\text{reactants}} nC_P$$

$$= 35.1 - 7(2.0) - 3(4.9) - 5.0$$

$$= 1.4 \text{ cal°K}^{-1} = 0.0014 \text{ kcal°K}^{-1}$$

Therefore, from equation (2),

$\Delta H°_T$ at 100°C (373°K), is

$$\Delta H°_T = -91.59 + 0.0014\ (373-298)$$

$$= -91.49 \text{ kcal}.$$

For the reaction: $H_2(g) + Br_2(g) = 2HBr(g)$, the heat of formation of HBr(g) at 25°C is -9kcal/mole. a) What is the heat of formation of HBr(g) at 125°C assuming a constant heat capacity, C_P of 7 cal/deg-mole for all diatomic gases? b) calculate the final temperature inside an insulated bomb, if 1 mole of $H_2(g)$ and 99 moles of $Br_2(g)$ are exploded initially at 25°C inside the bomb.

Solution: Heat of formation ΔH is a function of temperature and pressure only. By definition,

$$\Delta H = \Delta H_{products} - \Delta H_{reactants} .$$

The variation of ΔH with temperature at constant pressure is

$$\left(\frac{\partial(\Delta H)}{\partial T}\right)_P = \left(\frac{\partial H_{products}}{\partial T}\right)_P - \left(\frac{\partial H_{reactants}}{\partial T}\right)_P$$

$$\left(\frac{\partial(\Delta H)}{\partial T}\right)_P = n\, C_{P_{products}} - n\, C_{P_{reactants}}$$

$$= \Delta C_P$$

$$\therefore \left(\frac{\partial(\Delta H)}{\partial T}\right)_P = \Delta C_P$$

The problem indicates that ΔC_P is a constant, thus integrating between 25°C = 298°K and 125°C = 398°K gives

$$\int_{\Delta H_1}^{\Delta H_2} d(\Delta H) = \int_{T_1}^{T_2} \Delta C_P dT$$

$$\int_{\Delta H_{298°K}}^{\Delta H_{398°K}} d(\Delta H) = \int_{298}^{398} \Delta C_P dT$$

$$\Delta H_{398} - \Delta H_{298} = \Delta C_P\ (398\text{-}298°K)$$

Consequently,

$$\Delta H_{398°K} = \Delta H_{298°K} + \Delta C_P\ (100°K) \qquad (1)$$

In the reaction equation, the molecules are all diatomic and are the same number on both sides. Therefore,

$$\Delta C_P = 0$$

Therefore, equation (1) becomes

$$\Delta H_{398°K} = \Delta H_{298°K} + 0$$

$$= -9 \text{ kcal}$$

$$\Delta H_{398°K} = -9 \text{ kcal}$$

b) The total number of diatomic gas after the reaction = 100 moles: -- 2 moles of HBr and 98 moles of Br_2

$$\therefore \quad C_V = n(C_P - R)$$

$$\therefore \quad C_V = 100(7 - 1.987)$$

$$\cong 500 \text{ cal/deg}$$

From the first law of thermodynamics

$$\Delta H = \Delta E + w$$

$$\Delta H = \Delta E + \int_{V_1}^{V_2} P dV$$

At constant volume $dV = 0$

$$\therefore \quad \Delta H = \Delta E = -9000 \text{ cal}$$

$$\Delta E_2 = C_V(T_2 - T_1)$$

$$\therefore \quad 9000 \text{ cal} = 500 \frac{\text{cal}}{\text{deg}} (T_2 - 25°C)$$

$$500\ T_2 = 21500$$

$$T_2 = 43°C$$

• PROBLEM 2-31

The following molar heat capacities are given in calories per degree Kelvin per mole (cal $K^{-1}mole^{-1}$).

$$CH_4(g): \quad C_P = 7.5 + 5 \times 10^{-3}T$$

$$O_2(g): \quad C_P = 6.5 + 1 \times 10^{-3}T$$

$N_2(g)$: $C_P = 6.5 + 1 \times 10^{-3}T$

$H_2O(g)$: $C_P = 8.15 + 5 \times 10^{-4}T$

$CO_2(g)$: $C_P = 7.7 + 5.3 \times 10^{-3}T$

Calculate the final adiabatic reaction temperature of the reaction

$$CH_4(g) + 2\,O_2(g) = CO_2(g) + 2\,H_2O(g) \qquad \Delta H^\circ_{298} = -165.2 \text{ kcal}$$

if the reactants, $CH_4(g)$ and air, respectively, are heated to 200°C before burning. Assume that 100% of the methane reacts.

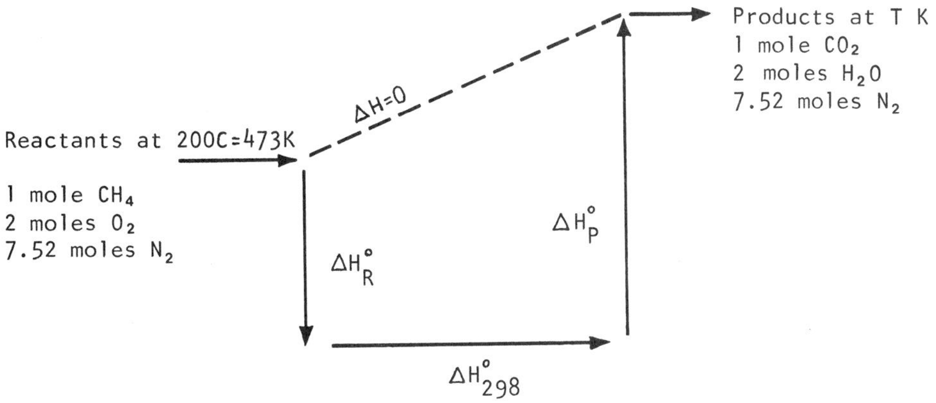

Solution: For the adiabatic process, Q = 0. With the usual assumptions that the kinetic- and potential-energy terms are negligible and that there is no shaft work, the over-all energy balance for this process reduces to

$$\Delta H = 0$$

One mole of methane burned will be taken as a basis. The reaction is

$$CH_4(g) + 2\,O_2(g) = CO_2(g) + 2\,H_2O(g) \qquad \Delta H^\circ_{298} = -165.2 \text{ kcal.}$$

Thus, from the above reactions:

Number of moles of reactants:	Number of moles of products:
$CH_4(g) = 1$	$CO_2(g) = 1$
$O_2(g) = 2$	$H_2O(g) = 2$

The approximate contents of the air are 79% N_2 and 21% O_2. Since there are 2 moles of O_2 in this reaction, the corresponding number of moles of N_2 will be

$N_2(g) = \frac{2 \times 0.79}{0.21} = 7.52$	$N_2(g) = 7.52$

The final temperature of the products T°K is unknown. For the purpose of calculations, to proceed from the reactants at 200°C (473°K) to the products at T°K, any convenient path between the initial and final states may be used. Since data are available for the standard heats of reaction at 25°C, the most convenient path is the one which includes the reactions at 25°C (298°K). This is shown schematically in the accompanying diagram.

The dashed line represents the actual path for which the enthalpy change is, $\Delta H = 0$.

Since the enthalpy change must be the same regardless of the path considered,

$$\Delta H = \Delta H_R^\circ + \Delta H_{298}^\circ + \Delta H_P^\circ = 0 \qquad (1)$$

But

$$\Delta H_R^\circ = \sum_{\text{reactants}} \left(n \int_{473}^{293} C_P \, dT\right)$$

$$= - n_{CH_4} \int_{473}^{293} C_{P(CH_4)} \, dT + n_{O_2} \int_{473}^{293} C_{P(O_2)} \, dT$$

$$+ n_{N_2} \int_{473}^{293} C_P(N_2) \, dT$$

Substitution of given data yields

$$\Delta H_R^\circ = (1) \int_{473}^{293} \left(7.5 + 5 \times 10^{-3} T\right) dT$$

$$+ (2) \int_{473}^{293} \left(6.5 + 1 \times 10^{-3} T\right) dT$$

$$+ (7.52) \int_{473}^{293} \left(6.5 + 1 \times 10^{-3} T\right) dT$$

Now,

$$\Delta H^\circ_{298} = -165.2 \text{ kcal} = -165{,}200 \text{ cal.}$$

and

$$\Delta H^\circ_P = \sum_{\text{products}} \left(n \int_{298}^{T} C_P \right) dT$$

$$= n_{CO_2} \int_{298}^{T} C_{P(CO_2)}\, dT + n_{H_2O} \int_{298}^{T} C_{P(H_2O)}\, dT$$

$$+ n_{N_2} \int_{298}^{T} C_{P(N_2)}\, dT$$

or

$$\Delta H^\circ_P = (1)\int_{298}^{T} (7.7 + 5.3 \times 10^{-3}T)\,dT + (2)\int_{298}^{T} (8.15 + 5 \times 10^{-4}T)\,dT$$

$$+ 7.52 \int_{298}^{T} (6.5 + 1 \times 10^{-3}T)\,dT$$

Substituting the values of ΔH°_R, ΔH°_{298} and ΔH°_P into equation (1) yields

$$\int_{473}^{293} (7.5 + 5 \times 10^{-3}T)\,dT + 2 \int_{473}^{293} (6.5 + 10^{-3}T)\,dT$$

$$+ 7.52 \int_{473}^{293} (6.5 + 10^{-3}T)\,dT + (-165{,}200)$$

$$+ \int_{298}^{T} (7.7 + 5.3 \times 10^{-3}T)\,dT + 2 \int_{298}^{T} (8.15 + 5 \times 10^{-4}T)\,dT$$

$$+ 7.52 \int_{298}^{T} (6.5 + 10^{-3}T)\,dT = 0$$

Integration yields

$$7.5(293-473) + \frac{5 \times 10^{-3}}{2}(293^2 - 473^2) + 2 \times 6.5(293-473)$$

$$+ \frac{2 \times 10^{-3}}{2}(293^2 - 473^2) + 7.52 \times 6.5(293-473)$$

$$+ \frac{7.52 \times 10^{-3}}{2}(293^2 - 473^2)$$

$$- 165{,}200 + 7.7(T - 298) + \frac{5.3 \times 10^{-3}}{2}(T^2 - 298^2)$$

$$+ 2 \times 8.15(T - 298) + \frac{2 \times 5 \times 10^{-4}}{2}(T^2 - 298^2)$$

$$+ 7.52 \times 6.5(T - 298) + \frac{7.52 \times 10^{-3}}{2}(T^2 - 298^2) = 0$$

Simplify to obtain,

$$- 1350 - 344.7 - 2340 - 137.88 - 8798.4 - 518.43$$

$$- 165{,}200 + 7.7T - 2294.6 + 0.00265T^2 - 235.33$$

$$+ 16.3T - 4857.4 + 0.0005T^2 - 44.4 + 48.88T$$

$$- 14566.24 + 0.00376T^2 - 333.9 = 0$$

$$- 201021.28 + 72.88T + 0.00691T^2 = 0$$

Rearrangements results in a quadratic equation of the form

$$6.91 \times 10^{-3}T^2 + 72.88T - 201{,}021.28 = 0$$

This equation can be solved by using the "almighty" quadratic formula. That is

$$T = \frac{-b \pm \sqrt{b^2 - 4ac}}{2a}$$

where $a = 6.91 \times 10^{-3}$

$b = 72.88$

$c = -201021.28$

Substituting these values into the formula gives

$$T = \frac{-72.88 \pm \sqrt{(72.88)^2 + (4 \times 6.91 \times 10^{-3} \times 201021.28)}}{(2 \times 6.91 \times 10^{-3})}$$

$$= \frac{-72.88 \pm \sqrt{5311.49 + 5556.23}}{0.01382}$$

$$= \frac{-72.88 \pm \sqrt{10867.72}}{0.01382}$$

$$= \frac{-72.88 \pm 104.25}{0.01382}$$

Observe that there are two possible values for T; But the negative one will be discarded because this is a heating process. The two values are

$$\frac{-72.88 + 104.25}{0.01382} = 2269 \text{ K}$$

and

$$\frac{-72.88 - 104.25}{0.01382} = -12817 \text{ K}$$

Thus, the solution of this equation is T = 2269 K and consequently, the final adiabatic reaction temperature of the reaction is 2269 K.

• PROBLEM 2-32

At 298°K, the heats of formation of $CO_2(g)$, $C_2H_4O_2(\ell)$ (acetic acid) and $H_2O(g)$ are -94.0 kcal, -116.4 kcal and -57.8 kcal respectively. In the combustion of $CH_4(g)$ to give $CO_2(g)$ and $H_2O(g)$ the heat of combustion of $CH_4(g)$ = -192.7 kcal. Also, the heat of vaporization of water at 100°C = 9.4 kcal/mole. The C_P values in cal/mole deg of $C_2H_4O(g)$ (acetaldehyde), $CO(g)$, $H_2O(g)$, $CH_4(g)$, $H_2O(\ell)$ are 12.5, 7.5, 7.3, 9.0 and 18.0 respectively.

With the above information calculate a) heat of formation of liquid water, $H_2O(\ell)$, at 298°K, b) $\Delta H_{298°K}$ for the reaction $C_2H_4O_2(\ell) = CH_4(g) + CO_2(g)$, c) the temperature at which ΔH for the reaction $C_2H_4O(g) = CH_4(g) + CO_2(g)$ should be zero. Assume $\Delta H_{298°K} = -4.0$ kcal.

Solution: a) The heat of formation of $H_2O(g)$ is given to be -57.8 kcal. But the heat of formation of $H_2O(\ell)$ is less negative by the molar heat of vaporization of H_2O at 373°K given in the problem as 9.4 kcal/mole. Thus the heat of formation of $H_2O(\ell)$ at 298°K is (-57.8 + 9.4) kcal

$$= -48.4 \text{ kcal}$$

b) The desired equation is

$$C_2H_4O_2(\ell) = CH_4(g) + CO_2(g)$$

A series of equations, with known ΔH values are to be written such that when added up and terms cancelled out, the result will give the desired equation. The ΔH value will be the summation of the ΔH values for the series of equations written. In the desired equation, $C_2H_4O_2$ is needed on the left; But the ΔH of its formation is given, which means $C_2H_4O_2$ is on the right. So beginning with the reverse of its formation and changing the sign of the ΔH, the desired equation and its ΔH value become

$$C_2H_4O_2 = 2C(s) + 2H_2 + O_2 \qquad (1)$$

and

$$\Delta H = 116.4 \text{ kcal.}$$

Since CH_4 is present in the desired equation, the reverse of its combustion is also added. That is,

$$CO_2 + 2H_2O = CH_4 + 2O_2 \qquad (2)$$

with $\Delta H = 192.7$ kcal.

CO_2 is also needed in the desired equation; As a result, add an equation of the formation of CO_2 as follows:

$$2C(s) + 2O_2 = 2CO_2 \qquad (3)$$

with $\Delta H = 2(-94.0) = -188$ kcal.

Add the formation of H_2O. This will cancel out the H_2O on the left of reaction (2). That is,

$$2H_2 + O_2 = 2H_2O \qquad (4)$$

with $\Delta H = 2(-57.8) = -115.6$ kcal.

Adding up equations (1) through (4), and subtracting terms that are not needed give

$$C_2H_4O_2 = 2C(s) + 2H_2 + O_2 \qquad \Delta H_1 = 116.4 \text{ kcal}$$

$$CO_2 + 2H_2O = CH_4 + 2O_2 \qquad \Delta H_2 = 192.7 \text{ kcal}$$

$$2C(s) + 2O_2 = 2CO_2 \qquad \Delta H_3 = -188 \text{ kcal}$$

$$2H_2 + O_2 = 2H_2O \qquad \Delta H_4 = -115.6 \text{ kcal}$$

Total: $C_2H_4O_2 = CH_4 + CO_2$ $\qquad \Delta H = (116.4 + 192.7 - 188 - 115.6)$ kcal

$$\therefore \quad \Delta H = 5.5 \text{ kcal} .$$

Make sure the total is the desired equation.

c) To calculate the value of ΔH at another temperature when ΔH is known at some reference temperature, use the relation

$$\Delta H_T = \Delta H_{298°K} + \int_{T_1}^{T_2} \Delta C_P dT .$$

If ΔC_P is independent of temperature between T_1 and T_2 then write

$$\Delta H_T = \Delta H_{298°K} + \Delta C_P \int_{T_1}^{T_2} dT$$

Integrating the above equation gives

$$\Delta H_T = \Delta H_{298°K} + \Delta C_P (\Delta T)$$

$$\therefore \quad \Delta T = \frac{\Delta H_T - \Delta H_{298°K}}{\Delta C_P} \qquad (5)$$

The given reaction is

$$C_2H_4O(g) = CH_4(g) + CO(g)$$

$$\Delta H_{298°K} = -4.0 \text{ kcal} = -4000 \text{ cal}$$

$$\Delta C_P = nC_{P_{(CH_4)}} + nC_{P_{(CO)}} - nC_{P_{(C_2H_4O)}}$$

$$= \big((1)9.0 + (1)7.5 - (1)12.5\big) \text{ cal/deg K-mole}$$

$$= 4.0 \text{ cal/deg}$$

The temperature at which $\Delta H_T = 0$ is found by substituting 0 for ΔH_T in equation (5).

$$\therefore \quad \Delta T = \frac{0 + 4000 \text{ cal}}{4 \text{ cal deg}^{-1}}$$

$$\Delta T = 1000°$$

$$(T - 298) = 1000$$

or $$T = 1000° + 298°K$$

$$T = 1298°K = 1025°C$$

• PROBLEM 2-33

Calculate the internal energy change for the reaction

$$\frac{1}{2} N_2(g) + \frac{1}{2} O_2(g) + \frac{1}{2} Cl_2(g) = NOCl(g)$$

at 25°C given that the gases are ideal. The enthalpy ΔH, for the formation of NOCl (g) is 12.57 kcal mol^{-1} at 25°C.

Solution: From the first law

$$\Delta E = \Delta H - \Delta(PV)$$

The work done against the atmosphere is $(n_b - n_a)RT$:

where n_{b_g} = number of moles of gaseous products

n_{a_g} = number of moles of gaseous reactants

$$\therefore \quad \Delta E = \Delta H - (n_{b_g} - n_{a_g})RT \qquad (1)$$

$$(n_{b_g} - n_{a_g}) = \Delta n_g = n_{NOCl} - \frac{1}{2} n_{N_2} - \frac{1}{2} n_{O_2} - \frac{1}{2} n_{Cl_2}$$

$$= 1 - \frac{1}{2} - \frac{1}{2} - \frac{1}{2}$$

$$= -\tfrac{1}{2} \text{ mole}$$

Substituting this into equation (1) gives

$$\Delta E = (12.57 \text{ kcal})\left(\frac{4.184 \text{ kJ}}{1 \text{ kcal}}\right) - \left(-\frac{1}{2} \text{ mole}\right)\left(\frac{8.314 \times 10^{-3} \text{ kJ}}{1 \text{ mole °K}}\right)(298°K)$$

$$= (52.59 + 1.24) \text{ kJ}$$

or

$$\Delta E = 53.83 \text{ kJ}$$

Calculate the energy change, ΔE, for the reaction

$$H_2(g) + \frac{1}{2} O_2(g) = H_2O(liq) \quad (1)$$

Given that the heat of combustion of $H_2(g)$ at 1 atm and 25°C is -68.32 kcal mol^{-1}. Pressure is constant and water has a density of 1.00×10^3 kg m^{-3} .

Solution: The first law written for a constant pressure calorimeter is

$$\Delta E = \Delta H - P(\Delta V)$$

Calculate the PV contribution of the liquid phase and that of the gaseous phase. The work done against the atmosphere in the constant pressure calorimeter is $P(\Delta V)$ where $P(\Delta V)$ = the PV contribution of the liquid phase

$$\therefore \quad P(\Delta V) = P\left(\frac{\text{mass of liquid water}}{\text{Density of water}}\right) - n_{H_2}RT - n_{O_2}RT$$

or

$$P(\Delta V) = 1 \text{ atm}\left(\frac{18.0 \times 10^{-3}\text{kg}}{1 \text{ mol } H_2O}\right)\left(\frac{1 \text{ m}^3}{1.00 \times 10^3\text{kg}}\right)\left(\frac{101{,}325 \text{ J}}{1 \text{ m}^3 \text{ atm}}\right)(1 \text{ mol})$$

$$- (1 \text{ mol } H_2)RT - \left(\frac{1}{2} \text{ mol } O_2\right)RT$$

$$= 1.82\text{J} - \frac{3}{2} \text{ mol RT}$$

$$\Delta E = \Delta H - P(\Delta V)$$

For reaction (1), ΔH = -68.32 kcal.

Therefore,

$$\Delta E = (-68.32 \text{ kcal})\left(\frac{4.184\text{kJ}}{1 \text{ kcal}}\right) - (1.82\text{J})\left(\frac{1\text{kJ}}{10^3\text{J}}\right)$$

$$- \left(\frac{3}{2} \text{ mol}\right)\left(\frac{8.314 \times 10^{-3}\text{kJ}}{\text{mole °K}}\right)(298\text{°K})$$

$$= [285.9 - (-3.7)]\text{kJ}$$

$$= -282.2 \text{ kJ}$$

For the following gaseous reaction at 25°C:

$$H_2(g) + 10O_2(g) = H_2O(g) + \text{excess } O_2(g)$$

Calculate a) ΔE at 25°C, b) $\Delta H_{498°K}$, c) the maximum temperature in an adiabatic explosion of the mixture with reactants initially at 25°C inside a sealed bomb, given that the heat of formation of $H_2O(g)$ = -58 kcal,

$$C_{P_{(H_2)}} = C_{P_{(O_2)}} = 6.5 \text{ cal °K}^{-1}\text{mol}^{-1}$$

and $C_{P_{(H_2O(g))}} = 7.5 \text{ cal°K}^{-1}\text{mol}^{-1}$

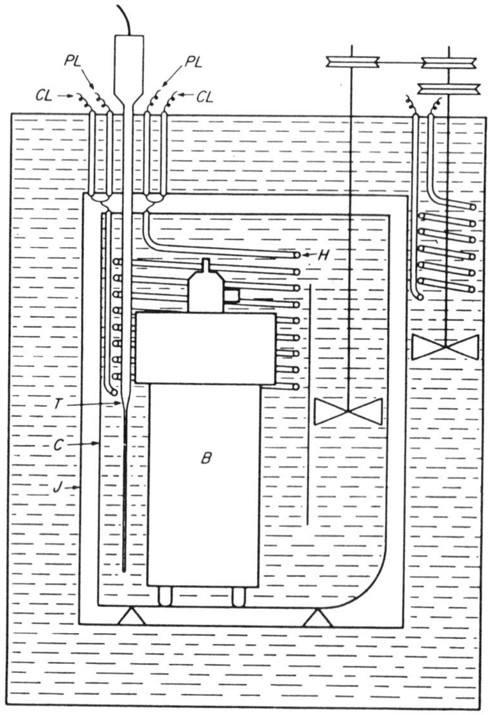

Bomb calorimeter used at National Bureau of Standards. (*B*, bomb; *H*, heater; *C*, calorimeter vessel; *T*, resistance thermometer; *J*, jacket; *PL*, potential leads; *CL*, current leads.

Solution: a) From the first law of thermodynamics

$$\Delta E = \Delta H - \Delta PV$$

But $\quad PV = nRT$

$$\therefore \quad \Delta E = \Delta H - \Delta n_g RT$$

where n_g is the number of moles of gaseous products.

Here $n_g = - 1/2$

The balanced equation is $H_2(g) + \frac{1}{2} O_2(g) = H_2O(g)$.

$$\Delta n = 1 - \left(1 + \frac{1}{2}\right) = - \frac{1}{2}$$

It is this equation which tells us the relative change in the number of moles. Anything that doesn't react doesn't change the relative number of moles.

$$\therefore \quad \Delta E = -58 \text{ kcal} - (-\tfrac{1}{2} \text{ mole})\left(\frac{1.98 \text{ cal}}{\text{mol °K}}\right)(298\text{°K})\left(\frac{1 \text{ kcal}}{1000 \text{ cal}}\right)$$

$$\Delta E = -57.7 \text{ kcal}$$

b) Here, make use of the fact that

$$\Delta H_T = \Delta H_{298} + \int_{T_1}^{T_2} \Delta C_P dT$$

$$\Delta H_{498} = \Delta H_{298} + \Delta C_P \int_{T_1}^{T_2} dT$$

Integration gives

$$\Delta H_{498} = \Delta H_{298} + \Delta C_P (T_2 - T_1)$$

$$\Delta C_P = nC_{P_{H_2O}} - [nC_{P_{H_2}} + nC_{P_{O_2}}]$$

$$= 1 \text{ mole} \left(7.5 \frac{\text{cal}}{\text{°K mole}}\right) - [1(6.5) + \frac{1}{2}(6.5)] = -2.25 \frac{\text{cal}}{\text{mole}}$$

$$= -58 \text{ kcal} + \left(\frac{-2.25 \text{ cal}}{\text{°K mole}}\right)\left(\frac{1 \text{ kcal}}{1000 \text{ cal}}\right)(498-298)\text{°K}$$

$$\Delta H_{498} = -58.45 \text{ kcal}$$

c) The maximum temperature is that obtained from ΔE for heating the product. By definition

$$\Delta E = nC_V \Delta T$$

C_V is calculated from C_P as follows. For $H_2O(g)$ $C_P = 7.5$ cal mol^{-1} deg K^{-1}. $C_V = C_P - R = 7.5$ cal mol^{-1} K^{-1} $- 1.98$ cal mol^{-1} K^{-1} $= 5.5$ cal mol^{-1} K^{-1} . There is 1 mole of $H_2O(g)$, so $C_V = 5.5$ cal K^{-1}. Initially, there are 10 moles of O_2. However, $\frac{1}{2}$ mole reacts so the number of moles of excess O_2 is 9.5. C_P for O_2 is 6.5 cal mol^{-1} K^{-1}. Therefore, C_V for O_2 is $C_P - R = 6.5$ cal mol^{-1} K^{-1} - 1.98 cal mol^{-1} K^{-1} = 4.5 cal mol^{-1} K^{-1}. Finally, C_V for O_2 is multiplied by the number of moles of O_2 which yields $C_V = 4.5$ cal mol^{-1} K^{-1} x 9.5 mol = 42.75 cal K^{-1}.

$$\therefore \quad 57700 = (5.5 + 9.5 \times 4.5)\Delta T = 69.2\Delta T$$

$$\therefore \quad \Delta T = 1200°C \text{ and}$$

$$T = 1225°C$$

WORK

• PROBLEM 2-36

Derive a mathematical expression, involving only constants and readily measurable physical properties, for the work done on the surroundings when a gas that has the equation of state

$$PV = nRT - n^2a/V$$

expands reversibly from V_i to V_f at constant temperature.

Solution: If n moles of an ideal gas expand reversibly from volume V_i to volume V_f at constant temperature then

$$w = \int_{V_i}^{V_f} P_{ex}\, dV = \int_{V_i}^{V_f} P dV ,$$

since P_{ex} and P differ infinitesimally. V is volume, P is pressure and w is work. Dividing the given equation of state by V gives

$$P = \frac{nRT}{V} - \frac{n^2a}{V^2} \qquad (1)$$

Since the work done on the surroundings is defined as

$$\int_{V_i}^{V_f} P dV$$

and the expression for P is given by equation (1), the integral becomes

$$w = \int_{V_i}^{V_f} \left(\frac{nRT}{V} - \frac{n^2 a}{V^2}\right) dV$$

where

$$\left(\frac{nRT}{V} - \frac{n^2 a}{V^2}\right) = P$$

or

$$w = \int_{V_i}^{V_f} \frac{nRT}{V}\, dV - \int_{V_i}^{V_f} \frac{n^2 a}{V^2}\, dV \tag{2}$$

Observe that n, R, T and a in equation (2) are constants. Therefore, the integral can be rewritten as

$$w = nRT \int_{V_i}^{V_f} \frac{dV}{V} - n^2 a \int_{V_i}^{V_f} \frac{dV}{V^2} \tag{3}$$

Performing the integral in equation (3) yields

$$w = nRT[\ln V]\Big|_{V_i}^{V_f} - n^2 a \left(-\frac{1}{V}\right)\Big/_{V_i}^{V_f}$$

$$\therefore \quad w = nRT \ln \frac{V_f}{V_i} + n^2 a \left(\frac{1}{V_f} - \frac{1}{V_i}\right)$$

• PROBLEM 2-37

Calculate the maximum work obtainable by (a) the isothermal expansion, and (b) the adiabatic expansion of 2 moles of nitrogen, assumed ideal, initially at 25°C, from 10 liters to 20 liters. Assume $\bar{C}_V = (5/2)R$.

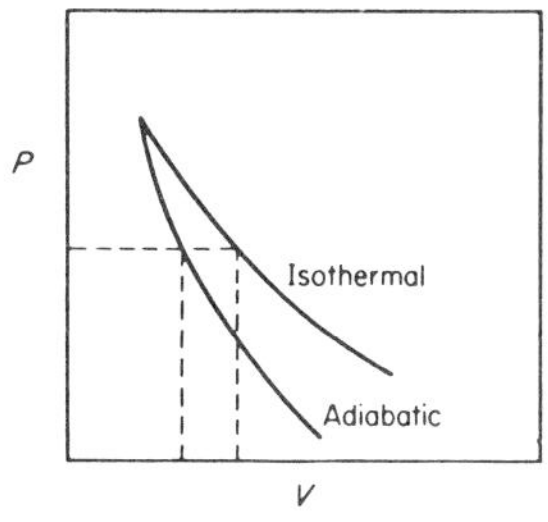

Solution: a) For a given change in state, the work w is a maximum when the change is carried out reversibly. Then when a gas is expanded reversibly, the work performed is

$$\int_{V_1}^{V_2} P_{ex}\, dV$$

For an ideal gas at a constant temperature T and reversible expansion, the external pressure must be equal to the ideal gas pressure P = nRT/V. Thus,

$$w_{max} = \int_{V_1}^{V_2} \frac{nRT}{V}\, dV \qquad (1)$$

Integrating equation (1) yields

$$w_{max} = nRT \ln \frac{V_2}{V_1}$$

Substitution of the numerical data yields

$$w_{max} = 2 \times 1.987 \times (273 + 25) \ln \frac{20}{10}$$

$$= 822 \text{ cal.}$$

b) From the first law of thermodynamics,

$$\Delta E = Q - w$$

Since the process is adiabatic, Q = 0. Hence,

$$- w_{max} = \Delta E \qquad (2)$$

For an ideal gas, ΔE is given by

$$\Delta E = nC_V dT = nC_V(T_2 - T_1)$$

To compute maximum work, the final temperature of the process is needed. The final temperature can be obtained as follows. For reversible adiabatic process, and an ideal gas,

$$w = P_{ex} dV = PdV = \frac{nRT}{V}\, dV$$

Thus equation (2) becomes,

$$nC_V dT = - \frac{nRT}{V}\, dV$$

Divide both sides by n to obtain

$$\bar{C}_V \, dT = -\frac{RT}{V} \, dV$$

where $\bar{C}_V$ is for one mole.

Rearranging and integrating gives

$$\bar{C}_V \frac{dT}{T} = -\frac{R}{V} \, dV$$

$$\int_{T_1}^{T_2} \bar{C}_V \frac{dT}{T} = -\int_{V_1}^{V_2} \frac{R}{V} \, dV$$

$$\int_{T_1}^{T_2} \bar{C}_V \, d \ln T = -\int_{V_1}^{V_2} R \, d\ln V$$

or

$$\bar{C}_V \ln \frac{T_2}{T_1} = -R \ln \frac{V_2}{V_1}$$

$$\ln \frac{T_2}{T_1} = -\frac{R}{\bar{C}_V} \ln \frac{V_2}{V_1}$$

Substituting the numerical data, into the above equation gives

$$\ln\left(\frac{T_2}{298}\right) = -\left(\frac{2}{5}\right) \ln \left(\frac{20}{10}\right) .$$

Recall that $\ln\left(\frac{a}{b}\right) = \ln a - \ln b$. Therefore,

$$\ln T_2 - \ln (298) = -(2/5) \ln \frac{20}{10}$$

or

$$\ln T_2 = -(2/5) \ln \frac{20}{10} + \ln 298 = -0.28 + 5.70$$

$$= 5.42$$

From which $T_2 = e^{5.4} = 226.5°K$

Now,

$$w_{max} = -\Delta E$$

$$= n\bar{C}_V (T_2 - T_1)$$

$$= 2 \times 5/2 \times 1.987 \ (298-226.5)$$

$$= 715 \text{ cal}$$

• PROBLEM 2-38

A horizontal piston-and-cylinder arrangement is placed in contact with a constant-temperature bath. The piston slides in the cylinder with negligible friction, and an external force holds it in place against an initial gas pressure of 200 psia. The initial gas volume is 1 ft^3. The external force on the piston is to be reduced gradually, allowing the gas to expand, until its volume doubles. Under these conditions it has been determined that the volume of the gas is related to its pressure in such a way that the product PV is constant. Calculate the work done by the gas in moving the external force.

How much work would be done if the external force were suddenly reduced to half its initial value instead of being gradually reduced?

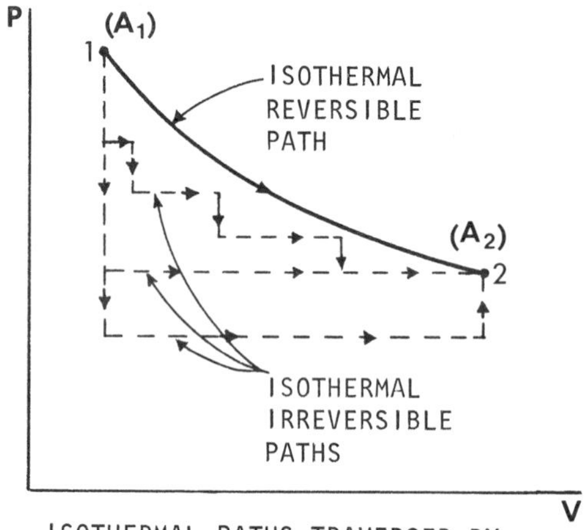

ISOTHERMAL PATHS TRAVERSED BY A SYSTEM BETWEEM STATE(1) AND STATE(2). THE MAXIMUM PATH IS THE REVERSIBLE ONE.

Solution: The process, carried out as first described, is a reversible one. Therefore,

$$W = \int_{V_1}^{V_2} PdV$$

Applying Boyle's law $\left[PV = K \text{ (a constant) or } P = \frac{K}{V}\right]$

gives

$$W = \int_{V_1}^{V_2} \frac{K}{V}\, dV$$

$$= K \ln \frac{V_2}{V_1} \qquad (1)$$

But

$$K = PV = P_1V_1 = 200 \frac{\text{lbs}}{(\text{inch})^2} (144) \frac{(\text{in})^2}{(\text{ft})^2} (1 \text{ ft}^3)$$

$$= 28{,}800 \text{ ft-lb}_f. ,$$

$$V_1 = 1 \text{ ft}^3 \text{ and } V_2 = 2 \text{ ft}^3$$

Therefore, equation (1) becomes

$$W = 28{,}800 \ln \frac{2}{1}$$

$$= 19{,}930 \text{ ft-lb}_f .$$

The final pressure will be

$$P_2 = \frac{K}{V_2} = \frac{28{,}800}{2} = 14{,}400 \text{ lb/sq ft}$$

or

$$P_2 = 100 \text{ psia}$$

In the second case the force exerted is constant and equivalent to a pressure of 100 psia. After half the initial force has been removed, the gas will undergo a sudden expansion. Eventually the system will return to an equilibrium condition identical with the final state attained in the reversible process. Thus ΔV will be the same as before, and the net work accomplished will equal the equivalent external pressure times the volume change, or

$$W = (100) \frac{\text{lb}}{\text{in}^2} (144) \frac{\text{in}^2}{\text{ft}^2} (2-1) \text{ ft}^3$$

$$= 14{,}400 \text{ ft-lb.}$$

This process is clearly irreversible, and it demonstrates the fact that an irreversible process accomplishes less work than a reversible process for the same change in state.

Compared to the reversible process, the irreversible expansion is said to have an efficiency of

$$\frac{14{,}000}{19{,}930} = 0.723 \text{ or } 72.3\%$$

• PROBLEM 2-39

Calculate the work done a) at 25°C, b) at 100°C, when 100 g of nitrogen at a pressure of 760 torr is expanded reversibly and isothermally to a pressure of 100 torr.

Solution: In expanding a gas reversibily from volume, V_1 to volume V_2 , the work done is given by

$$W_{rev} = \int_{V_1}^{V_2} PdV \qquad (1)$$

Assuming that nitrogen is ideal,

$$P = \frac{nRT}{V}$$

where n = number of moles

R = gas constant

and T = temperature

Combining the $P = \frac{nRT}{V}$ and equation (1) yields

$$W_{rev} = \int_{V_1}^{V_2} \frac{nRT}{V}\, dV$$

Since this is an isothermal expansion,

$$W_{rev} = +\, nRT \int_{V_1}^{V_2} \frac{dV}{V}$$

$$= +\, nRT \ln \frac{V_2}{V_1} \qquad (2)$$

Using the Boyle's law $P_1V_1 = P_2V_2$, equation (2) can be rewritten in the form

$$W_{rev} = + nRT \ln \frac{P_1}{P_2} ,$$

where

$$\frac{P_1}{P_2} = \frac{V_2}{V_1}$$

a) Converting the mass to moles gives

$$100g\ N_2 \left(\frac{1\ \text{mole}}{28g\ N_2}\right) = 3.57\ \text{moles}\ N_2$$

Therefore,

$$W_{rev} = + (3.57\ \text{moles}) \left(\frac{1.987\ \text{cal}}{°K\ \text{mole}}\right) (298\ °K)\ \ln \left(\frac{760}{100}\right)$$

or $\quad W_{rev} = + 4287$ cal

b) $\quad T = 100°C = 373°K$

$$\therefore \quad W_{rev} = + (3.57\ \text{moles}) \left(\frac{1.987\ \text{cal}}{°K\ \text{mole}}\right) (373°K)\ \ln \left(\frac{760}{100}\right)$$

$$W_{rev} = + 5366\ \text{cal}$$

• PROBLEM 2-40

Calculate the work done when 18.0g of liquid water are vaporized at 100°C against a constant external pressure of 1.00 atm, given that

$$\Delta H_{vap}(H_2O) = 9.7\ \text{kcal mole}^{-1}$$

$$\Delta H_{fus}(H_2O) = 1.4\ \text{kcal mole}^{-1}$$

$$R = 0.0820\ \text{liter atm mole}^{-1}\ \text{deg}^{-1}$$

$$= 1.99\ \text{cal mole}^{-1}\ \text{deg}^{-1}$$

Density of $H_2O(\ell)$ = 1.00g cm^{-3} and molecular wt of water = 18.0 g mol^{-1}

Solution: The work done by a system on the surrounding at constant temperature is given by the expression

$$W = \int_{V_i}^{V_f} PdV \qquad (1)$$

where V_f = final volume (or V_g)

V_i = initial volume (or V_ℓ)

The subscripts g and ℓ stand for gas and liquid respectively.

Since this is a constant pressure process, Charle's law applies. This can be used to find V_f before using equation (1). It is defined as

$$V_1 = KT_1 \text{ and } V_f = KT_f$$

where K = constant.

Dividing V_1 by V_f gives

$$\frac{V_1}{V_f} = \frac{KT_1}{KT_f}$$

or

$$V_f = \frac{V_1 T_f}{T_1} \quad . \tag{2}$$

Here V_1 = 22.4 liters

T_f = 100°C = 373°K

T_1 = 273°K

Using these values in equation (2) gives

$$V_f = \frac{(22.4 \text{ liters})(373°K)}{273°K}$$

$$= 30.6 \text{ liters}$$

Note that V_f is taken to be the volume of the gas after vaporization. V_1 is not the volume of liquid. It is the volume of the gas at STP.

To find the volume of liquid, V_i , convert the 18.0g sample to volume. Since the density of water is 1.00g cm^{-3} ,

$$V_\ell = V_i = \frac{\text{mass}}{\text{density}} = \frac{18.0g}{1.00g\ cm^{-3}}$$

$$\therefore \quad V_i = 18.0\ cm^3$$

Because $V_f = V_g$ is in liters,

$$V_i = 18.0\ cm^3 \times \frac{1\ \text{liter}}{1000\ cm^3}$$

or $\quad V_i = 0.018$ liter.

Now, using equation (1) gives

$$W = \int_{V_i}^{V_f} PdV = \int_{0.018}^{30.6} PdV \qquad (3)$$

Equation (3) can be written in the form

$$W = P\int_{0.018}^{30.6} dV$$

because P is constant and is equal to 1 atm. Therefore,

$$W = P\Delta V = 1\ (30.6 - 0.018)$$

$$= 30.582 \text{ liters atm.}$$

Converting this to calories using the value of R given yields

$$W = 30.582 \text{ liter atm} \times \frac{1.99 \text{ cal}}{0.0820 \text{ liter atm}}$$

$\therefore \quad W = 742.17$ cal

• PROBLEM 2-41

> The valve on a cylinder containing initially 10 liters of an ideal gas at 25 atm and 25°C is opened to the atmosphere, where the pressure is 760 torr and the temperature is 25°C. Assuming that the process is isothermal, how much work in liter atmospheres is done on the atmosphere by the action of expanding gas?

Solution: The work done by the system on the surroundings is given by

$$W = \int_{V_i}^{V_f} P_{ex}\, dV$$

Since the gas is expanded against a constant external pressure of 760 torr, the above equation becomes,

$$W = P_{ex} \int_{V_i}^{V_f} dV$$

or

$$W = P_{ex} [V_f - V_i] \quad (1)$$

V_f is the final volume and V_i is the initial volume.

To obtain the final volume of the gas, Boyle's law can be used. For isothermal process,

$$P_1V_1 = P_2V_2$$

or

$$V_2 = \frac{P_1V_1}{P_2}$$

where

P_1 = initial pressure = 25 atm

V_1 = initial volume of gas = 10 liters

P_2 = finial pressure = 1 atm.

Hence,

$$V_2 = \frac{25 \times 10}{1} = 250 \text{ liters.}$$

Substituting the values of V_2 and P_{ext} into equation (1) gives

$$W = 760 \text{ (torr)} [250-10] \text{ (liter)}$$

or $W = 1 \text{ (atm)} [250-10] \text{ (liter)}$

$= 240$ liter-atm.

• PROBLEM 2-42

Calculate the temperature change of 1 mole of a monatomic gas contained in a piston. q = 50J and w = 100J.

Solution: The kinetic energy of a monatomic ideal gas is given by

$$\Delta E = (3/2) R\Delta T \quad (1)$$

But $\Delta E = q-w$ from the first law.

$$\therefore \quad \Delta E = 50J - 100J$$

$$= -50J$$

Rearranging equation (1) to solve for ΔT gives

$$\Delta T = \frac{\Delta E}{(3/2)R} \tag{2}$$

Substituting the respective values into equation (2) yields

$$\Delta T = \frac{-50 J\,mol^{-1}}{(3/2)(8.314 J\ mol^{-1}\ K^{-1})}$$

or $\Delta T = -4.0°K$

• PROBLEM 2-43

1 mole of an ideal gas is expanded reversibly and isothermally from 0°C and 1 atm. Calculate the final volume occupied by the gas if the heat absorbed during the process is q = 1000 cal. The external pressure over the system is 1 atm.

Solution: The energy of an ideal gas cannot change for an isothermal process. Therefore, the first law of thermodynamics can be written as

$$0 = dQ = dw$$

or $Q = w.$

The total work obtained in expanding the gas reversibly from the initial volume to the final volume is equal to the integral of the pressure times the differential of the volume:

That is:

$$w = q = \int_{V_i}^{V_2} PdV \tag{1}$$

where V_1 = initial volume.

Assume that V_1 is 22.4 liters. This is because 1 mole of an ideal gas at standard temp of 0°C and pressure of 1 atm occupies 22.4 liters.

V_2 = final volume

The pressure in equation (1) is a constant at 1 atm.

$$\therefore \quad q = P(V_2 - V_1)$$

$$(1000\ cal)\left(\frac{4.184J}{cal}\right)(101{,}325J\ m^{-3}\ atm^{-1})^{-1}$$

$$= (1.00\ atm)(V_2 - 22.4\ \ell) \tag{2}$$

[The conversions between m^3 and liters can be found by

$$1 \text{ ml} = 1 \text{cm}^3 \text{ and}$$

$$1\ell = 1000 \text{ ml} = 1000 \text{ cm}^3 = 1 \text{ dm}^3 \text{ and } 1 \text{ m}^3 = 1000 \text{ dm}^3]$$

From equation (2),

$$V_2 = 41.3 + 22.4$$

or $$V_2 = 63.7 \text{ liters}$$

• PROBLEM 2-44

1 mole of an ideal gas is expanded reversibly and isothermally from 0°C and 1 atm. Calculate the final volume occupied by the gas if the heat absorbed during the process is q = 1000 cal.

Solution: From the first law of thermodynamics,

$$dE = dQ - dw$$

For an isothermal process, dE = 0. Hence

$$0 = dQ - dw$$

or $$Q = w$$

The total work obtained in expanding the gas reversibly from the initial volume to the final volume is equal to the integral of the pressure times the differential of the volume. Thus

$$w = q = \int_{V_1}^{V_2} PdV$$

where

V_1 = initial volume

V_2 = final volume

1 mole of an ideal gas at standard temperature and pressure occupies 22.4 liters

$$\therefore \quad V_1 = 22.4 \ \ell$$

Since the expansion process above is carried out reversibly at constant temperature, P is given by

$$P = \frac{nRT}{V}$$

$$\therefore \quad q = n\,RT \int_{V_1}^{V_2} \frac{dV}{V}$$

$$\int_{V_1}^{V_2} \frac{dV}{V} = \ln V \Big|_{V_1}^{V_2} = \ln V_2 - \ln V_1$$

But ln a - ln b = ln a/b .

$$\therefore \quad \ln V_2 - \ln V_1 = \ln \frac{V_2}{V_1}$$

and

$$q = n\,RT\,\ln \frac{V_2}{V_1}$$

$$(1000\text{ cal})\left(\frac{4.184\text{J}}{1\text{ cal}}\right) = (1.00\text{ mol})\left(\frac{8.314\text{J}}{\text{mol }^\circ\text{K}}\right)(298^\circ\text{K})\ \ln \frac{V_2}{22.4}$$

$$\ln \frac{V_2}{22.4} = 1.689$$

$$\ln V_2 - \ln 22.4 = 1.689$$

$$\ln V_2 = 1.689 + \ln 22.4$$

$$\ln V_2 = 1.689 + 3.11$$

$$\ln V_2 = 4.799$$

Taking exponents of both sides,

$$V_2 = e^{4.799}$$

or $\quad V_2 = 121.\ 2$ liters

• PROBLEM 2-45

What can you say about the following statements if one has an adiabatic process in which there is no heat transfer between the system and the surroundings, either because the system is well insulated or because the process occurs very rapidly?

1. $q = +w$

2. $q = 0$

3. $\Delta E = q$

4. $\Delta E = w$

5. $P\Delta V = 0$

Solution: In an adiabatic system there is no heat flow into or out of the system, thus $q = 0$

1. This statement gives q to be +w but this can only happen when $\Delta E = 0$ since for instance $\Delta E = q - w$ for isothermal expansion of an ideal gas.

2. Statement (2) is correct since $q = 0$ for the process.

3. This statement indicates $\Delta E = q$, but this can only happen, as in the case when one expands a gas into a vacuum, when $w = 0$.

4. Since $\Delta E = q - w$, ΔE will be equal to w only when $q = 2w$ so that

$$\Delta E = 2w - w = w$$

5. $\Delta E = q - w$

$$= q - P\Delta V$$

Thus for $P\Delta V$ to be zero, ΔE must be equal to q such that

$$\Delta E = \Delta E - P\Delta V$$

$$\therefore \ P\Delta V = 0$$

• PROBLEM 2-46

From the following five statements, indicate which ones are correct when an ideal gas is allowed to escape reversibly and isothermally into a vacuum. [Hint: What is the average kinetic energy of an ideal gas?]

1. $W = 0$, $\Delta E = q =$ a positive number

2. $w = P\Delta V + V\Delta P$

3. $w = P\Delta V$, $\Delta E = 0$, $q = -P\Delta V$ and is a negative number

4. $\Delta E = 0$, $q = -w =$ a positive number

5. $w = 0$, $q = 0$, $\Delta E = 0$

Solution: When a system does work, it is pushing against an external pressure which is the pressure concerned with here. But in a vacuum, according to the problem statement, the external pressure is zero, thus w is zero even if the pressure does not remain constant.

The average kinetic energy for an ideal gas is directly proportional to the thermodynamic temperature and is given by

$$\overline{E}_K = (3/2)RT.$$

This problem is an isothermal process, thus temperature does not change and as such ΔE is zero. Looking now at the five statements:

1. ΔE must be zero and not a positive number. There is no transfer of heat. Thus q = 0.

2. This is an incorrect expression for work. Instead, it is an expression for Δ(PV) since

$$\Delta(PV) = P\Delta V + V\Delta P$$

$$= w + V\Delta P$$

3. In this statement w has a finite value which contrasts with work done in a vacuum.

4. This statement also has a finite value for w.

5. This is a correct statement.

• PROBLEM 2-47

Calculate the heat transfered when 100J of work is done on a system consisting of 1 mole of an ideal gas. At constant temperature, ΔE = 0 for the expansion of an ideal gas.

Solution: A statement of the first law of thermodynamics is expressed as

$$\Delta E = q - w$$

where ΔE = change in internal energy of the system

q = quantity of heat

w = work done

In this problem, work is done on the system and so w is negative. (Note that we are adopting the convention that work done on the system is negative.) Since ΔE = 0 for an isothermal expansion of an ideal gas,

$$\Delta E = 0 = q - w$$

$$\therefore \quad q = w$$

or $\quad q = -100J$

As a result, 100J of heat must be transfered from the system to maintain isothermal conditions.

• PROBLEM 2-48

What is ΔE, q, w and ΔH for the reversible compression of two moles of an ideal gas at 25°C from 1.00 atm to 100.0 atm?

Solution: The internal energy of an ideal gas does not change with the distance between molecules because there is no interaction between them. At constant temperature the internal energy is independent of volume also. Since the energy is not changed, the enthalpy will not change.

$$\therefore \quad \Delta E = \Delta H = 0$$

and $q = w = \int_{V_1}^{V_2} PdV$.

But $P = \frac{nRT}{V}$

Therefore,

$$q = w = \int_{V_1}^{V_2} PdV = \int_{V_1}^{V_2} \frac{nRT}{V} dV .$$

$$q = nRT \int_{V_1}^{V_2} \frac{dV}{V} .$$

The nRT term is outside the integral because it is a constant (independent of the volume).

Solving the integral,

$$q = nRT \ln V \Big|_{V_1}^{V_2}$$

$$= nRT (\ln V_2 - \ln V_1)$$

But $\ln a - \ln b = \ln(a/b)$

$$\therefore \quad q = nRT(\ln V_2 - \ln V_1) = nRT \ln \frac{V_2}{V_1}$$

At constant temperature, Boyle's law states that

$$P_1V_1 = P_2V_2$$

or $$\frac{V_2}{V_1} = \frac{P_1}{P_2}$$

$$\therefore \quad q = w = nRT \ln \frac{P_1}{P_2}$$

$$= (2.00 \text{ mol})(8.314\text{J mol}^{-1} \text{ K}^{-1})(298°\text{K}) \ln \frac{1.00}{100.0}$$

$$= -22800\text{J} = -22.8\text{kJ}$$

• PROBLEM 2-49

1 mole of a monatomic ideal gas at 25°C is compressed adiabatically and reversibly from 0.1000 m^3 to 0.0100 m^3. Calculate q, w, ΔH and ΔE for the process.

Solution: From the first law of thermodynamics:

$$\Delta E = q - w \qquad (1)$$

where ΔE = change in internal energy of system

q = heat added to system

w = work done by system on its surroundings

In an adiabatic process there is no exchange of heat between a system and its surroundings, thus q = 0.

From equation (1),

$$\Delta E = 0 - w$$

or $$\Delta E = - w \qquad (2)$$

Work done on the system is negative. Consequently, the internal energy of the gas is negative and it increases by dE for a small decrease in the volume V. From equation (2),

$$PdV = -dE.$$

But

$$C_V = \left(\frac{\partial E}{\partial T}\right)_V$$

$$\therefore \quad dE = nC_V dT$$

and $$PdV = -dE$$

$$= -\ nC_V dT \qquad (3)$$

For an ideal gas, $P = \frac{nRT}{V}$.

Substituting for P in equation (3) gives

$$\frac{nRT\ dV}{V} = -\ nC_V dT$$

$$\frac{dV}{V} = \frac{-\ n\ C_V dT}{nRT}$$

$$\frac{dV}{V} = -\ \frac{C_V}{R}\ \frac{dT}{T} \qquad (4)$$

Considering C_V constant and integrating equation (4) gives

$$\int_{V_1}^{V_2} \frac{dV}{V} = -\ \frac{C_V}{R} \int_{T_1}^{T_2} \frac{dT}{T}$$

$$\ln V \Big|_{V_1}^{V_2} = \frac{-C_V}{R} \ln T \Big|_{T_1}^{T_2}$$

$$\ln V_2 - \ln V_1 = \frac{-C_V}{R}\left(\ln T_2 - \ln T_1\right)$$

But ln a - ln b = ln a/b

$$\therefore \qquad \ln V_2 - \ln V_1 = \ln \frac{V_2}{V_1}$$

and $\ln T_2 - \ln T_1 = \ln \frac{T_2}{T_1}$

Hence,

$$\ln \frac{V_2}{V_1} = -\ \frac{C_V}{R} \ln \frac{T_2}{T_1} \qquad (5)$$

Rearranging equation (5) and taking exponents give

$$V_1 T_1^{(C_V/R)} = V_2 T_2^{(C_V/R)} \qquad (6)$$

For the above problem we can use equation (6) to calculate the final temperature for the process. Thus

$$V_1 T_1^{(C_V/R)} = V_2 T_2^{(C_V/R)}$$

$$(0.1000\ m^3)(298)^{C_V/R} = (0.0100)(T_2^{C_V/R})$$

For a monatomic gas $C_V = (3/2)R$

$$\therefore \quad (0.1000\ m^3)(298)^{3/2} = (0.0100)(T_2^{3/2})$$

$$T_2^{3/2} = (298)^{3/2}(10)$$

$$(3/2)\log T_2 = (2/3)\log 298 + \log 10.0$$

$$\frac{3}{2}\log T_2 = (3/2)(2.474) + 1.000$$

$$= 4.711$$

$$\therefore \quad \log T_2 = 3.140$$

$$\text{or} \quad T_2 = 1383K$$

From equation (2) $\quad \Delta E = -w$

$$= \int_{T_1}^{T_2} n\, C_V\, dT$$

$$= n(3/2)\ R\Delta T$$

The (3/2) is included because C_V for a monatomic gas is $C_V = (3/2)R$

$$\therefore \quad \Delta E = (1.00\ mol)(3/2)\left(\frac{8.314J}{mol\ {}^\circ K}\right)(1383{}^\circ K - 298{}^\circ K)$$

$$\Delta E = 13.6kJ$$

$$\Delta H = \int_{T_1}^{T_2} nC_P\, dT$$

For a monatomic gas C_P is given by

$$C_P = \frac{5}{2} R$$

$$\therefore \quad \Delta H = \int_{298}^{298} n\, C_P\, dT$$

$$= n\left(\frac{5}{2}\right) R\Delta T$$

where $R = 8.314\text{J mol}^{-1}\text{ K}^{-1}$

$n = 1$

and $\Delta T = 1383 - 298.$

$$\therefore \quad \Delta H = 22600\text{J} = 22.6\text{kJ}$$

• PROBLEM 2-50

1 mole of water at 100°C and 1.00 atm is converted to steam. Calculate q, w and ΔE for the conversion, given that $\Delta H = 970.3 \text{ Btu lb}^{-1}$. 1 lb of liquid occupies 0.016719 ft^3 and 1 lb of gas occupies 26.799 ft^3.

Solution: The enthalpy H is given by

$$H = E + PV$$

$$\therefore \quad \Delta H = \Delta E + \Delta(PV)$$

The conversion of water is done under a constant pressure of 1 atm. Thus

$$\Delta H = \Delta E + P(\Delta V) \tag{1}$$

But under constant pressure conditions

$$P(\Delta V) = w$$

and $\Delta E = q - w$

$$\therefore \quad \Delta H = q - w + w$$

$$\Delta H = q$$

For the above problem

$$\Delta H = q = \left(\frac{970.3 \text{ Btu}}{\text{lb}}\right)\left(\frac{1054.35\text{J}}{\text{Btu}}\right)\left(\frac{1 \text{ lb}}{0.45359 \text{ kg}}\right)\left(\frac{18.015 \times 10^{-3} \text{ kg}}{\text{mol}}\right)$$

$$= 40631.3\text{J mol}^{-1}$$

$$= 40.63\text{kJ mol}^{-1}.$$

$$w = \int_{V_1}^{V_2} PdV$$

or

$$W = P\int_{V_1}^{V_2} dV\ , \qquad \text{since P is constant.}$$

Performing the integration gives

$$W = P(V_2 - V_1)$$

$$= (1.00\ \text{atm})(26.799 - 0.016719)\text{ft}^3 \left(\frac{28.316\ \ell}{\text{ft}^3}\right) x$$

$$\left(\frac{101{,}325\text{J}}{\text{m}^3\ \text{atm}}\right)\left(\frac{\text{lb}}{0.45359\ \text{kg}}\right)\left(\frac{18.015 \times 10^{-3}\ \text{kg}}{\text{mol}}\right)$$

$$= 3.05\text{kJ mol}^{-1}$$

From equation (1),

$$\Delta H = \Delta E + P(\Delta V)$$

$$= \Delta E + w$$

$$\therefore \quad \Delta E = \Delta H - w$$

$$= (40.63 - 3.05)\ \text{kJ mol}^{-1}$$

or $\quad \Delta E = 37.58\text{kJ mol}^{-1}$

• PROBLEM 2-51

> At 760 torr, 100 grams of benzene is vaporized at its boiling point of 80.2°C. Calculate a) W_{rev}, b) q, c) ΔH, d) ΔE. The heat of vaporization is 94.4 $\frac{\text{cal}}{\text{g}}$.

Solution: 1 mole of benzene (C_6H_6) = 78 g. That is, the molecular weight of C_6H_6 = 72+6 = 78 g mol^{-1}.

$$\therefore \quad 100\ \text{g}\ C_6H_6 = 100\ \text{g}\ C_6H_6 \frac{1\ \text{mole}\ C_6H_6}{78\ \text{g}\ C_6H_6}$$

$$= 1.28\ \text{mole}\ C_6H_6$$

$T = 80.2°C = 353.2°K$

$$W_{(rev)} = - nRT$$

for 1 mole,

$$W_{rev} = - (1.987 \text{ cal } K^{-1} \text{ mol}^{-1})(353.2°K)$$

$$= - 701.8 \text{ cal/mol for 1 mole } C_6H_6$$

and for 1.28 mole, $W_{rev} = - (701.8 \text{ cal mol}^{-1})(1.28 \text{ mol})$

$$W_{rev} = -898 \text{ cal}$$

b) The heat of vaporization per gram of the benzene is 94.4 cal.

$\therefore$ For 100g, $q = 94.4 \text{ cal} \times 100$

$$q = 9440 \text{ cal}$$

c) $q = H_2 - H_1 = \Delta H$

where H is the enthalpy

$$\therefore \quad \Delta H = q$$

$$\Delta H = 9440 \text{ cal}$$

d) $$\Delta E = q + w$$

where E is the internal energy and w is the work

$$\Delta E = (9440 - 898) \text{ cal}$$

$$\Delta E = 8542 \text{ cal}$$

• PROBLEM 2-52

1 mole of a diatomic ideal gas at 25°C is compressed adiabatically and reversibly from 0.1000 m^3 to 0.0100 m^3, calculate q, w, ΔH and ΔE for the process, excluding vibrational contributions.

Solution: $\Delta E = q - W$ from first law.

q = 0 because in an adiabatic process there is no exchange of heat between the surroundings and the system.

For a diatomic gas $C_V = (5/2)R$, excluding vibrational contributions. Using the formula that

$$V_1 T_1^{(C_V/R)} = V_2 T_2^{(C_V/R)}$$

$(0.1000\ m^3)(298)^{5/2} = (0.0100)(T_2^{5/2})$, T_2 can be computed as follows:

$$T_2^{5/2} = (298)^{5/2}(10.0).$$

Taking the log of both sides gives

$$(5/2)\log T_2 = (5/2)\log 298 + \log 10.0$$

$$\frac{5}{2}\log T_2 = (5/2)(2.474) + 1.000$$

$$= 7.185$$

$$\therefore \quad \log T_2 = 2.874$$

$$T_2 = 748\ °K$$

But $\Delta E = -w$

$$= \int_{T_1}^{T_2} n\ C_V\ dT$$

$$= n\left(\frac{5}{2}\right)R\Delta T$$

$$\therefore \quad \Delta E = (1.00\ mol)(5/2)\left(\frac{8.314J}{mol\ °K}\right)\left(748°K - 298°K\right)$$

or $\Delta E = 9.35kJ$.

$$\Delta H = \int_{T_1}^{T_2} n\ C_P\ dT$$

$$\Delta H = \int_{298}^{748} n\ C_P\ dT = n\ C_P\ \Delta T$$

But $C_P - C_V = R$

$$\therefore \quad C_P = C_V + R = (5/2)R + R = (7/2)R$$

$$\therefore \quad \Delta H = n\left(\frac{7}{2}\right)(R)(748 - 298)$$

$$= 13.09kJ$$

• PROBLEM 2-53

Two moles of an ideal gas at 25°C undergoes an isothermal compression from 1.00 atm to 100.0 atm. Calculate ΔE, q, w and ΔH for the process. The external pressure over the system is 500.0 atm.

Solution: This is a constant temperature process and the internal energy of an ideal gas depends only on temperature. Since the temperature is not changing, the internal energy of the process will then remain constant

$$\therefore \quad \Delta E = 0$$

The only work done in the process is pressure volume work. The work is done by the atmosphere.

Since this is a constant temperature process,

$$\Delta H = 0$$

$$\text{and } q = w = \int_{V_1}^{V_2} P_{ext}\, dV = P_{ext}\,(V_2 - V_1).$$

It is the external pressure, P_{ext}, that is doing the Pressure-Volume work during compression. The initial and final pressures are internal pressures which are only used to calculate the initial and final volumes. Remember that the equation of state PV = nRT is used for the internal gas states. The two are only equal when the work done is reversible work.

From the ideal gas law,

$$P_{int}V = nRT$$

or

$$V = \frac{nRT}{P_{int}} \tag{1}$$

Using equation (1) yields

$$V_1 = \frac{(2.00\text{ mol})(0.0821\ell\text{-atm K}^{-1}\text{ mol}^{-1})(298°\text{K})}{1.00\text{ atm}}$$

$$= 48.9 \text{ liters}$$

$$V_2 = \frac{(2.00\text{ mol})(0.0821\ell\text{-atm K}^{-1}\text{ mol}^{-1})(298°\text{K})}{100\text{ atm}}$$

$$= 0.489 \text{ liters}$$

Substituting these values into the equation

$$q = w = P_{ext}(V_2 - V_1)$$

gives

$$q = w = (500.0\ \text{atm})(0.489\ell - 48.9\ell)\left(\frac{101325\text{J}}{\text{m}^3\ \text{atm}}\right)$$

$$\therefore \quad q = w = -2.45\text{MJ}$$

CHAPTER 3

SECOND LAW OF THERMODYNAMICS

CARNOT CYCLE

• PROBLEM 3-1

A carnot engine using 1 mole of an ideal diatomic gas is operating between 500°C and 0°C. A sketch of the process is shown. If V_1 and V_2 are given as 0.0100 m^3 and 0.1000 m^3 respectively, calculate V_3, V_4, q, ω and ΔE for steps 1 through 4 and also q, ω, and ΔE for the overall process.

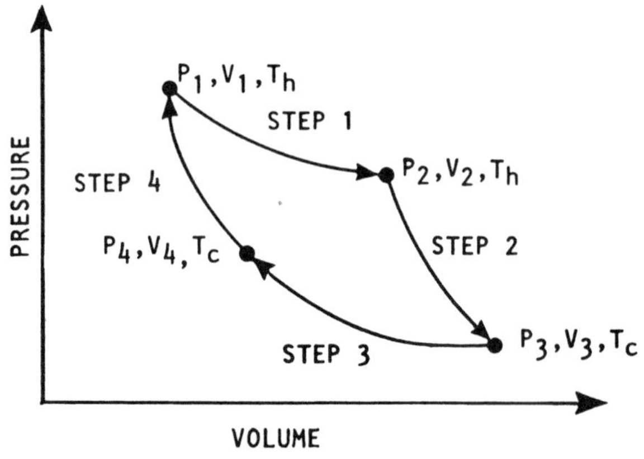

Solution: A carnot engine is an idealized heat engine that follows the cyclic process of the diagram. The process consist of four steps, two isothermal and two adiabatic and yields the maximum work that one can obtain from a quantity of heat absorbed at a higher temperature and given out at a lower temperature. Step 1 is a reversible isothermal expansion from volume V_1 to volume V_2 at T_h. Step 2 indicates a reversible adiabatic expansion from V_2 to V_3 with a temperature change from T_h to T_c. Step 3 is another isothermal change but this time through compression from V_3 to V_4 at temperature T_c and step 4 is a reversible adiabatic compression from V_4 to V_1 with a temperature change from T_c to T_h.

Consider steps 2 and 4 for a small increase and decrease respectively in volume dV at a pressure P. The work done by the gas is PdV. The internal energy of the gas, E decreases by an amount, ΔE since the PdV work is accomplished using the internal energy of the gas.

Thus $$PdV = -dE$$

But $$dE = nC_V dT$$

where n = number of moles of the gas

C_V = heat capacity at constant volume

$$\therefore PdV = -nC_V dT \tag{1}$$

Also using the ideal gas law

$$P = \frac{nRT}{V}$$

Equation (1) now becomes

$$\frac{nRTdV}{V} = -nC_V dT$$

or

$$\frac{dV}{V} = -\frac{C_V}{R}\left(\frac{dT}{T}\right) \tag{2}$$

Since C_V is a constant then (2) for step 4 can be integrated using the limits V_1 at T_h and V_4 at T_c,

$$\int_{V_4}^{V_1} \frac{dV}{V} = -\frac{C_V}{R}\int_{T_c}^{T_h} \frac{dT}{T}$$

$$\ln\left(\frac{V_1}{V_4}\right) = -\frac{C_V}{R}\ln\left(\frac{T_h}{T_c}\right) \tag{3}$$

Taking exponents and rearranging equation (3),

$$V_1 T_h^{C_V/R} = V_4 T_c^{C_V/R} \tag{4}$$

Similarly $$V_2 T_h^{C_V/R} = V_3 T_c^{C_V/R} \tag{5}$$

For the above problem a diatomic ideal gas is used and C_V for such a gas is

$$C_V = (5/2)R$$

Using equation (5),

$$V_3 = V_2\left(\frac{T_h}{T_c}\right)^{C_V/R}$$

$$\therefore\ V_3 = \left(0.1000\ m^3\right)\left(\frac{773°K}{273°K}\right)^{5/2}$$

$$V_3 = 1.349m^3$$

Dividing equation (4) by equation (5) then

$$V_4 = V_3\left(\frac{V_1}{V_2}\right)$$

$$= \left(1.349m^3\right)\left(\frac{0.0100}{0.1000}\right)$$

$$V_4 = 0.1349m^3$$

From the first law of thermodynamics

$$\Delta E = q - \omega \tag{6}$$

where ΔE is the increase in the internal energy of the system. q is the heat added to system and ω is the work done by the system. Since we are only interested in the PdV work then

$$d\omega = PdV$$

$$\therefore\ \omega = \int_{V_1}^{V_2} PdV$$

Equation (6) becomes

$$\Delta E = q - \int_{V_1}^{V_2} PdV \tag{7}$$

For isothermal processes of an ideal gas $\Delta E = 0$ since ΔE depends only on temperature and the temperature is constant. Equation (7) thus becomes:

$$0 = q - \int_{V_1}^{V_2} PdV$$

and

$$q = \omega = \int_{V_1}^{V_2} PdV \tag{8}$$

But $$P = \frac{nRT}{V}$$

Equation (8) becomes

$$q = \omega = \int_{V_1}^{V_2} \frac{nRTdV}{V}$$

$$= nRT \int_{V_1}^{V_2} \frac{dV}{V}$$

$$q = \omega = nRT\ell n\frac{V_2}{V_1} \qquad (9)$$

For adiabatic reversible processes of an ideal gas, there is no exchange of heat between the system and its surroundings. Thus q = 0. Equation (6) becomes

$$\Delta E = -\omega \qquad (10)$$

Step 1: Isothermal reversible expansion at T_h

$$\Delta E_{(1)} = 0$$

From equation (9)

$$q_{(1)} = \omega_{(1)} = nRT_h \ \ell n \ \frac{V_2}{V_1}$$

$$= (1.00 \text{ mol}) \left(\frac{8.314J}{\text{mol } °K}\right) (773°K) \left(\frac{1kJ}{1000J}\right) \ell n \left(\frac{0.1000}{0.0100}\right)$$

$$q_{(1)} = \omega_{(1)} = 14.80 \text{ kJ}$$

Step 2: Adiabatic reversible compression from T_h to T_c

$$q_{(2)} = 0$$

From equation (10)

$$\Delta E_{(2)} = -\omega_{(2)}$$

$$= +n \int_{T_h}^{T_c} C_V dT$$

$$= +nC_V(T_c - T_h)$$

$$\Delta E_{(2)} = +n\frac{5}{2}R(T_c - T_h)$$

$$= (1.00 \text{ mol})\left(\frac{5}{2}\right)\left(\frac{8.314 J}{\text{mol °K}}\right)(272°K - 773°K)\left(\frac{1 kJ}{1000 J}\right)$$

$$\Delta E_{(2)} = -\omega_{(2)} = -10.39 \text{ kJ}$$

Step 3: Isothermal reversible compression at T_1

$$\Delta E_{(3)} = 0$$

From equation (9)

$$q_{(3)} = \omega_{(3)} = nRT_c \; \ell n \frac{V_4}{V_3}$$

$$= (1.00 \text{ mol})\left(\frac{8.314 J}{\text{mol °K}}\right)(273°K)\left(\frac{1 kJ}{1000 J}\right)\ell n\left(\frac{0.1345}{1.345}\right)$$

$$q_{(3)} = \omega_{(3)} = -5.23 \text{ kJ}$$

Step 4: Adiabatic reversible compression from T_c to T_h

$$q_{(4)} = 0$$

From equation (10)

$$\Delta E_{(4)} = -\omega_{(4)}$$

$$= +nC_V(T_h - T_c)$$

$$= +n \frac{5}{2} R(T_h - T_c)$$

$$= (1.00 \text{ mol})\left(\frac{5}{2}\right)\left(\frac{8.314 J}{\text{mol °K}}\right)(773°K - 273°K)\left(\frac{1 kJ}{1000 J}\right)$$

$$\Delta E_{(4)} = -\omega_{(4)} = 10.39 \text{ kJ}$$

For the overall process

$$\Delta E_{overall} = \Delta E_{(1)} + \Delta E_{(2)} + \Delta E_{(3)} + \Delta E_{(4)}$$

$$= 0 + (-10.39) + 0 + 10.39$$

$$\Delta E_{overall} = 0$$

$$q_{overall} = \omega_{overall} = q_{(1)} + q_{(2)} + q_{(3)} + q_{(4)}$$

$$= 14.80 + 0 + (-5.23) + 0$$

$$q_{overall} = \omega_{overall} = 9.57 \text{ kJ}$$

• **PROBLEM 3-2**

On an entropy, S versus temperature, T diagram, draw the paths corresponding to the four steps for a carnot cycle operating reversibly with an ideal gas between temperatures T_1 and T_2. Show, using arrows, the direction along each path and label each step starting first with an isothermal expansion at T_2.

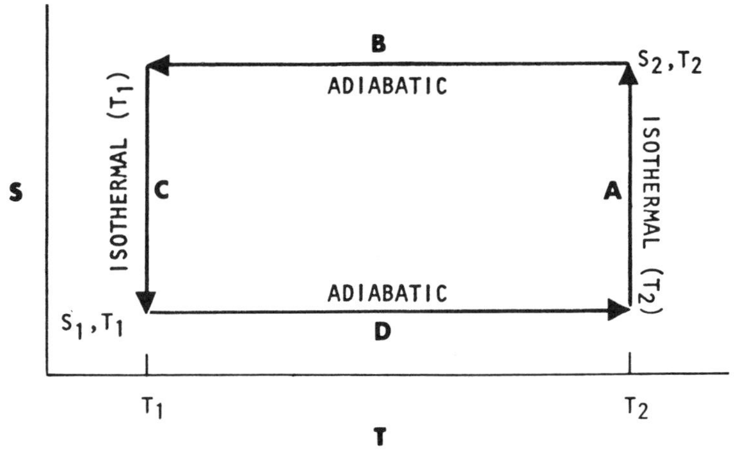

Solution: Usually the four steps of a carnot cycle are given in terms of a P - V diagram. In terms of an S - T diagram we can draw the following
The diagram shows the carnot cycle consisting of four steps, two isothermal and two adiabatic.

Step A represents an isothermal expansion at temperature T_2. Step B represents an adiabatic expansion at T_2. Step C is an isothermal compression at T_1 and Step D represents an adiabatic compression at T_2. Remember the expression that relates volume and entropy for an isothermal process is $\Delta S = R \ln\left(\frac{V_2}{V_3}\right)$.

COMBINED FIRST AND SECOND LAWS

• **PROBLEM 3-3**

For any gas that obeys van der Waals equation of state, show that $\left(\frac{\partial U}{\partial V}\right)_T = \frac{a}{V^2}$

Solution: The combined first and second laws of thermodynamics state that

$$dU = TdS - PdV.$$

This can be obtained by starting with the first law,

$$\Delta U = q - w$$

From the second law,

$$\Delta S = \frac{q}{T}.$$

$$\therefore dq = TdS.$$

From the first law

$$dU = dq - dw.$$

But $$dw = +PdV$$

$$\therefore dU = dq - dw = TdS - PdV. \qquad (1)$$

where U = internal energy

T = temperature

S = entropy

V = volume

P = pressure

q = amount of heat

w = work

If equation (1) is differentiated partially with respect to V and keeping T constant, it becomes

$$\left(\frac{\partial U}{\partial V}\right)_T = T\left(\frac{\partial S}{\partial V}\right)_T - P.$$

By the Maxwell relation,

$$\left(\frac{\partial S}{\partial V}\right)_T = \left(\frac{\partial P}{\partial T}\right)_V.$$

The above equation yields

$$\left(\frac{\partial U}{\partial V}\right)_T = T\left(\frac{\partial P}{\partial T}\right)_V - P. \qquad (2)$$

The van der Waals equation of state is

$$\left(P + \frac{a}{V^2}\right)(V - b) = RT \quad \text{for 1 mole.}$$

From this, $\left(\frac{\partial P}{\partial T}\right)_V = \frac{R}{V - b}$

But from rearranging the equation of state,

$$\frac{R}{V - b} = \left(P + \frac{a}{V^2}\right)\frac{1}{T} .$$

Therefore $\left(\frac{\partial U}{\partial V}\right)_T = T\left(P + \frac{a}{V^2}\right)\frac{1}{T} - P$

$$= P + \frac{a}{V^2} - P$$

$$\left(\frac{\partial U}{\partial V}\right)_T = \frac{a}{V^2}$$

• PROBLEM 3-4

A strip of rubber may be regarded as thermodynamically analogous to a confined gas. Stretching the rubber corresponds to compressing the gas. The work done on the rubber is $-dw = f\ dl$, where f is the contractile force exerted by the rubber and l its length.
(a) Define analogues of the Helmholtz and Gibbs free energies (A and G) for a strip of rubber.
(b) Show that for a process at constant T, $-dw \geq dA$, and that for a process at constant T and f, $-dw_{useful} \geq dG$. Formulate your own definition of w_{useful}. State the general thermodynamic principles from which your proofs begin.
(c) Obtain an equation for $(\partial U/\partial l)_T$ in terms of any or all of the quantities T, f, l, and their derivatives with respect to each other.
(d) An ideal rubber is one for which $(\partial U/\partial l)_T = 0$. Show what implications can be drawn about the equation of state (f - l - T relation) for an ideal rubber.

Solution: a) By definition $A = U - TS$ (1)

and $G = U + PV - TS$ (2)

where A = Helmholtz free energy,
U = internal energy,
T = temperature,
S = entropy,
G = Gibbs free energy,
P = pressure
and V = volume

Comparing equations (1) and (2), $G = A + PV$ since $A = U - TS$.

If it is assumed that P - V work is done, the PV term in the Gibbs free energy equation can be redefined using the given relation $-dw = fdl$.

Integrating both sides, $-\int dw = \int fdl$.

$$\therefore \quad -w = fl.$$

But $$w = PV = -fl$$

$$\therefore G = A - fl.$$

b) From the first law, $\Delta U = q - w$

$$\therefore dU = dq - dw$$

$$\therefore -dw = dU - dq \qquad (3)$$

From equation (1) $$A = U - TS$$

$$\therefore dA = dU - [TdS + SdT]$$

But $SdT = 0$ at constant temperature.

Therefore $$dA = dU - TdS \qquad (4)$$

According to the second law, $dS \geq dq/T$. The $>$ sign stands for an irreversible process and the $=$ sign stands for a reversible process. From this relation, $dq \geq TdS$. Comparing equations (3) and (4),

$$dU_{(3)} = dU_{(4)}$$

and $$dq_{(3)} \geq TdS_{(4)}$$

$$\therefore -dw = dU - dq \geq dU - TdS = dA$$

$$\therefore -dw \geq dA.$$

Note that this is at constant temperature.

$$W_U = W_{useful} = w + \int fdl = w + f\Delta l$$

$$\therefore dW_U = dw + fdl$$

or $$-dW_U = -dw - fdl.$$

Since $$-dw \geq dA,$$

$$-dW_U = -dw - fdl \geq dA - fdl = dG$$

c) If there is no work other than fdl,

$$dU = TdS + fdl$$

$$dA = dU - TdS = TdS + fdl - TdS - SdT$$

$$\therefore dA = fdl - SdT$$

$$\therefore -\left(\frac{\partial S}{\partial l}\right)_T = \left(\frac{\partial f}{\partial T}\right)_l.$$

Therefore $\left(\frac{\partial U}{\partial l}\right)_T = T\left(\frac{\partial S}{\partial l}\right)_T + f = -T\left(\frac{\partial f}{\partial T}\right)_l + f.$

d) $\left(\frac{\partial U}{\partial l}\right)_T = -T\left(\frac{\partial f}{\partial T}\right)_l + f = 0$ or $\left(\frac{\partial f}{\partial T}\right)_l = \frac{f}{T}$

Therefore $$\left(\frac{\partial \ln f}{\partial \ln T}\right)_l = 1.$$

Rearranging and integrating both sides, the expression becomes $\ln f = \ln T + \ln C(l)$ where $C(l)$ = arbitrary function of l.

$$\therefore\ f = T\,C(l).$$

As a result, f must be directly proportional to T at constant l.

• PROBLEM 3-5

One gram of liquid water at 100°C is initially at 1.00 atm pressure and is confined to a volume in which no vapor is present. A valve is then opened and the water evaporates into an evacuated space of such volume that the final pressure is 0.10 atm. The entire apparatus is in a heat reservoir at 100°C. ΔH for the vaporization of H_2O is 540 cal g^{-1} at 100°C. Assume that the vapor is an ideal gas and that the volume of the liquid is negligible as compared to the volume of the vapor. Find q and ΔS for (a) the water, (b) the reservoir, and (c) the universe. (d) Describe a reversible process by which the water could be brought to the same final state. Show in what way the final state of the universe after this reversible process would differ from its state after the actual process.

Solution: a) From the first law, $\Delta E = q - w$ where E = internal energy, q = quantity of heat and w = work done. Since this is a constant volume process, w = 0. Therefore

$$\Delta E = q.$$

But $\Delta E = \Delta H - \Delta(PV) = \Delta H - RT(\Delta n_{gas})$.

Here H = enthalpy, R = gas constant, P = pressure, V = volume, T = temperature and n = number of moles.

$$q = \Delta E = \Delta H - \Delta(PV) = \Delta H - RT(\Delta n_{gas})$$

$$= 540 \text{ cal } g^{-1} \times 1g - \left[1.987 \text{ cal/mole K} \times 373K \times \frac{1g}{18g/\text{mole}}\right]$$

$$= 498.82 \text{ cal}$$

To find ΔS, two steps are involved; the first is vaporizing to gas at 1 atm and the second is expanding from 1 atm to 0.10 atm.

For the first step:

$$\Delta S = \frac{\Delta H}{T} \quad \text{by definition.}$$

$$\therefore \quad \Delta S = \frac{540 \text{ cal g}^{-1}}{373°K} = 1.448 \text{ cal g}^{-1} \text{ deg}^{-1}$$

$$\Delta S = 1.448 \text{ cal g}^{-1} \text{ K}^{-1} \times 1g = 1.44 \text{ cal K}^{-1}$$

For the second step:

$$\Delta S = nR \, \ln\left(\frac{P_1}{P_2}\right)$$

$$\therefore \quad \Delta S = \frac{1g}{18g/\text{mole}} \times 1.987 \frac{\text{cal}}{\text{mole°K}} \times \ln\left(\frac{1}{.10}\right)$$

$$= 0.254 \text{ cal deg}^{-1}$$

$$\therefore \quad \Delta S_{total} = 1.448 + 0.254 = 1.702 \text{ cal deg}^{-1}$$

Note that these are the q and ΔS for water.

b) For the reservoir:

The quantity of heat released by the reservoir is equal to the quantity of heat absorbed by the water for evaporation. Therefore, $q_r = -q_w$ where the subscripts r and w refer to the reservoir and water respectively.

$$\therefore \quad q_r = -q_w = -498.82 \text{ cal}$$

For the reservoir, w = 0 and ΔE = q. The change in the state of the reservoir, determined only by its energy, is the same whether the process is reversible or irreversible. Therefore $\Delta S = \frac{q}{T}$ both for the reversible and irreversible processes.

$$\Delta S_r = \frac{q}{T} = -\frac{498.82}{373} = -1.337 \text{ cal deg}^{-1}$$

c) For the universe:

For the universe, $q_u = 0$.

$$\Delta S_u = \Delta S_w + \Delta S_r$$

$$= 1.702 + (-1.337)$$

$$\therefore \quad \Delta S_u = 0.365 \text{ cal deg}^{-1}$$

d) The same final state can be attained through a reversible process by

1) allowing the water to evaporate isothermally at 100°C and reversibly against a constant opposing pressure of 1 atm.

2) allowing the water to evaporate isothermally at 100°C and reversibly against an opposing pressure equal to its own pressure.

In the reversible process the evaporating and expanding water does work in, for example, lifting a weight, and this work is stored in the surroundings available for use in the reverse process if desired. In the irreversible process the water did no work and the possibility of obtaining work from it has been lost. Correspondingly less heat was withdrawn from the reservoir in the irreversible process.

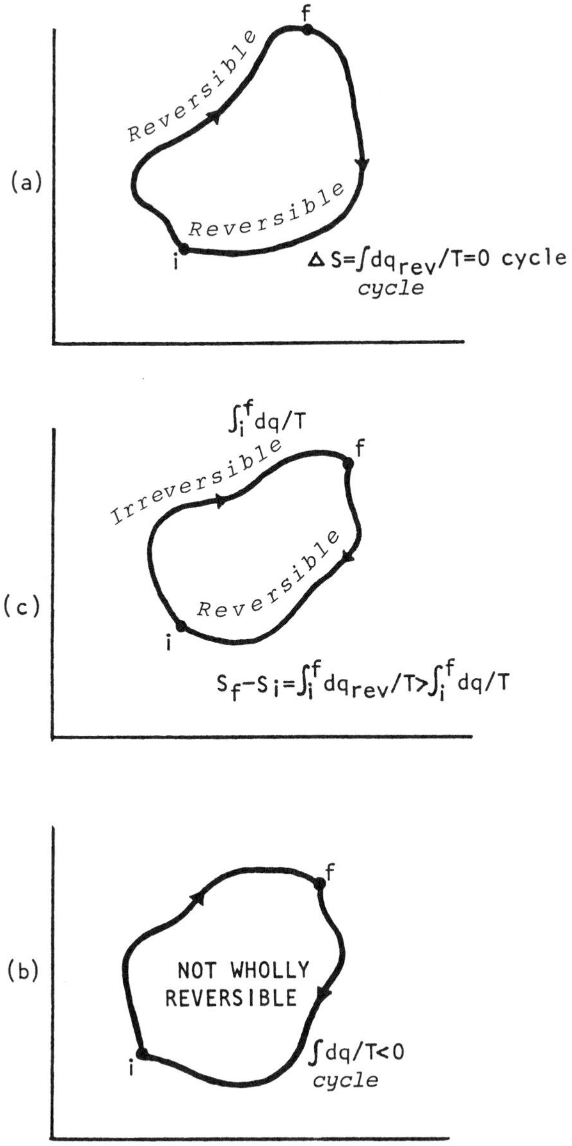

HEAT ABSORPTION AND ENTROPY CHANGES ON THREE TYPES OF CYCLE.

• PROBLEM 3-6

Let the reversible work done by a magnetic induction B in increasing the magnetization M of a paramagnetic solid be dw = BdM. Also, let two heat capacities C_M and C_B be defined for magnetic systems by analogy with C_V and C_P.

a) Prove that

$$C_B - C_M = -T\left(\frac{\partial M}{\partial T}\right)_B \left(\frac{\partial B}{\partial T}\right)_M$$

b) At moderate temperatures and fields, paramagnetic solids follow the Curie equation $M = \frac{\tau B}{T}$, where τ = constant. In this case, show that $C_B - C_M = M^2/\tau$.

c) If the Curie constant for gadolinium sulfate is 15.7 cm^3 K mol^{-1}, calculate the work done on 1 mole of this salt when it is reversibly magnetized by raising the field from 0 to 1.0 tesla at 300°K. Note that 1 tesla = 10^4 Gauss.

Solution: a) Define $C_B = T\left(\frac{\partial S}{\partial T}\right)_B$ and $C_M = T\left(\frac{\partial S}{\partial T}\right)_M$ where S = entropy. If S is taken to be a function of T and B; that is S = f(T,B), then

$$dS = \left(\frac{\partial S}{\partial T}\right)_B dT + \left(\frac{\partial S}{\partial B}\right)_T dB \qquad (1)$$

Also $$\left(\frac{\partial S}{\partial T}\right)_M = \left(\frac{\partial S}{\partial T}\right)_B + \left(\frac{\partial S}{\partial B}\right)_T \left(\frac{\partial B}{\partial T}\right)_M \qquad (2)$$

$$C_B - C_M = T\left(\frac{\partial S}{\partial T}\right)_B - T\left(\frac{\partial S}{\partial T}\right)_M .$$

But $\left(\frac{\partial S}{\partial T}\right)_M$ is given by equation (2). Therefore

$$C_B - C_M = T\left(\frac{\partial S}{\partial T}\right)_B - T\left[\left(\frac{\partial S}{\partial T}\right)_B + \left(\frac{\partial S}{\partial B}\right)_T \left(\frac{\partial B}{\partial T}\right)_M\right]$$

$$= T\left(\frac{\partial S}{\partial T}\right)_B - T\left(\frac{\partial S}{\partial T}\right)_B - T\left(\frac{\partial S}{\partial B}\right)_T \left(\frac{\partial B}{\partial T}\right)_M$$

But at constant pressure, $\left(\frac{\partial S}{\partial B}\right)_T = \left(\frac{\partial M}{\partial T}\right)_B$. Therefore

$$C_B - C_M = -T\left(\frac{\partial S}{\partial B}\right)_T \left(\frac{\partial B}{\partial T}\right)_M = -T\left(\frac{\partial M}{\partial T}\right)_B \left(\frac{\partial B}{\partial T}\right)_M \qquad (3)$$

b) The Curie equation is

$$M = \frac{\tau B}{T}. \tag{4}$$

From this equation, $\left(\frac{\partial M}{\partial T}\right)_B = -\frac{\tau B}{T^2}$ (5)

Solve for B in equation (4) $B = \frac{MT}{\tau}.$ (5a)

Therefore $\left(\frac{\partial B}{\partial T}\right)_M = \frac{M}{\tau}.$ (6)

Substitute equations (5) and (6) in equation (3);

$$C_B - C_M = -T\left(-\frac{\tau B}{T^2}\right)\left(\frac{M}{\tau}\right) = \frac{BM}{T} \tag{7}$$

But $B = \frac{MT}{\tau}$ from equation (5a). Putting this into (7),

$$C_B - C_M = \frac{BM}{T} = \frac{M}{T}\left(\frac{MT}{\tau}\right) = \frac{M^2}{\tau}$$

c) From the first law's definition of work, the magnetic work can be defined to be

$$W = \int B dM$$

But $B = \frac{MT}{\tau}.$

Therefore $w = \int_{M_1}^{M_2} \frac{MT}{\tau} dM$

B_1 is given to be 0 tesla and B_2 is given to be 1.0 tesla $= 10^4$ Gauss.

$$w = \frac{TM^2}{2\tau}\Bigg|_{M_1}^{M_2} \tag{8}$$

But $M = \frac{B\tau}{T}$ and $M^2 = \frac{B^2\tau^2}{T^2}$

Substituting this into equation (8),

$$w = \frac{T}{2}\,\frac{B^2\tau^2}{T^2}\,\frac{1}{\tau}\Bigg|_{B_1}^{B_2} = \frac{B^2}{2}\,\frac{\tau}{T}\Bigg|_0^{10^4}$$

$$w = \frac{(10^4)^2(15.7)}{2(300)} = 2.62 \times 10^6 \text{ ergs at } 300°K$$

EFFICIENCY OF HEAT ENGINES

• PROBLEM 3-7

An imaginary ideal-gas heat engine operates on the following cycle: (1) increase in pressure of gas at constant volume V_2 from P_2 to P_1; (2) adiabatic expansion from (P_1, V_2) to (P_2, V_1); (3) decrease in volume of gas at constant pressure P_2 from V_1 to V_2. Draw the cycle on a PV diagram and show that the thermal efficiency is

$$\varepsilon = 1 - \gamma \frac{(V_1/V_2) - 1}{(P_1/P_2) - 1}$$

where $\gamma = C_P/C_V$ and heat capacities are assumed to be independent of temperature.

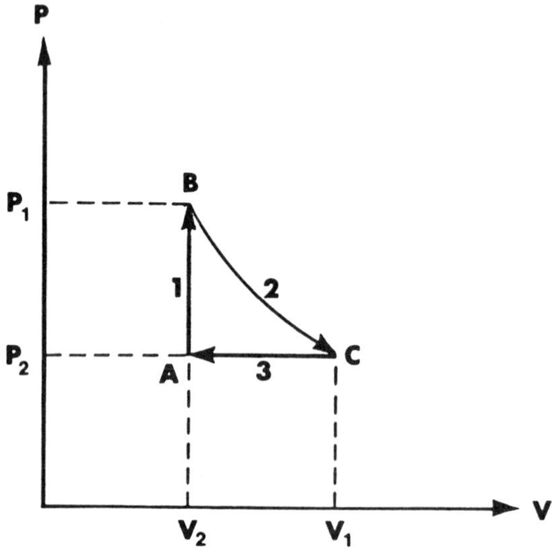

Fig. 1

Solution: The three stages of the cycle are drawn on a PV diagram shown in figure 1.
From the first law,

$$\Delta U = q - w$$

where U = internal energy, q = amount of heat and w = work.
But $\Delta U = 0$

$$\therefore \quad q - w = 0 \quad \text{or} \quad q = +w. \tag{1}$$

$$q = q_1 + q_2 + q_3 \tag{2}$$

For an adiabatic expansion, $q = 0$. Therefore, $q_2 = 0$.
From equations (1) and (2)

$$q = q_1 + q_3$$

$$= +w$$

The thermal efficiency, $\varepsilon = \frac{+w}{q_1}$

But $\quad +w = q_1 + q_3$

$$= \frac{q_1 + q_3}{q_1}$$

By definition, $q = C_V(T_{final} - T_{initial})$ where

C_V = Heat capacity at constant volume.

For step 1;

$$q_1 = C_V(T_B - T_A).$$

Also, since this is at constant volume,

$$P_1T_A = P_2T_B \quad \text{or} \quad \frac{P_2}{P_1} = \frac{T_A}{T_B}.$$

From step 2, $dU = C_V dT$ by definition.

This is equal to $-P_x dV$ where $P_x = P - dP$ for a reversible process. That is

$$dU = C_V dT = -P_x dV.$$

Also, for a reversible expansion, $P_x = P - dP = \frac{RT}{V}$. Therefore

$$dU = C_V dT = -\frac{RT}{V}\,dV. \qquad (3)$$

By rearranging and integrating, equation (3) becomes

$$C_V \frac{dT}{T} = -R\frac{dV}{V}$$

and

$$\int_{T_B}^{T_C} C_V \frac{dT}{T} = -R\int_{V_2}^{V_1} \frac{dV}{V}$$

Therefore,

$$C_V \ln T\Big|_{T_B}^{T_C} = -R \ln V\Big|_{V_2}^{V_1}$$

(Take note of the appropriate limits.)

$$C_V[\ln T_C - \ln T_B] = -R[\ln V_1 - \ln V_2]$$

$$\therefore \quad C_V \ln \frac{T_C}{T_B} = - R \ln \frac{V_1}{V_2}$$

But $$R = C_P - C_V$$

$$\therefore \quad C_V \ln \frac{T_C}{T_B} = - (C_P - C_V) \ln \frac{V_1}{V_2}$$

or $$\ln \frac{T_C}{T_B} = - \frac{(C_P - C_V)}{C_V} \ln \frac{V_1}{V_2} \qquad (4)$$

Let $\frac{C_P}{C_V} = \gamma$. Therefore $- \frac{(C_P - C_V)}{C_V} = - \frac{C_P}{C_V} + \frac{C_V}{C_V} = 1 - \gamma$

If the exponents of both sides of equation (4) are taken, it becomes

$$\frac{T_C}{T_B} = \left(\frac{V_1}{V_2}\right)^{1-\gamma}$$

Also $$\frac{P_1}{P_2} = \left(\frac{V_1}{V_2}\right)^{\gamma} \quad \text{or} \quad P_1 V_2^{\gamma} = P_2 V_1^{\gamma} .$$

For step 3, $q_3 = C_P(T_A - T_C)$. There is work done on the system in step 3 of cycle. This is given by $P_2(V_2 - V_1)$. However, when calculating efficiency, it is only work done by the system that matters. Therefore,

$$\varepsilon = \frac{+w}{q_1} = \frac{q_1 + q_3}{q_1} = \frac{C_V\left(T_B - T_A\right) + C_P\left(T_A - T_C\right)}{C_V(T_B - T_A)}$$

Rearranging this and substituting the appropriate parameters from the preceeding derivations into their appropirate places, the expression for ε becomes

$$\varepsilon = 1 - \gamma \left[\frac{T_C - T_A}{T_B - T_A}\right]$$

or $$\varepsilon = 1 - \gamma \left[\frac{\frac{T_C}{T_B} - \frac{T_A}{T_B}}{1 - \frac{T_A}{T_B}}\right]$$

$$= 1 - \gamma \left[\frac{\left(\frac{V_1}{V_2}\right)^{1-\gamma} - \frac{P_2}{P_1}}{1 - \frac{P_2}{P_1}} \right]$$

$$= 1 - \gamma \left[\frac{\left(\frac{V_1}{V_2}\right)\left(\frac{V_2}{V_1}\right)^{\gamma}\left(\frac{P_1}{P_2}\right) - 1}{\left(\frac{P_1}{P_2}\right) - 1} \right]$$

$$\varepsilon = 1 - \gamma \left[\frac{\left(\frac{V_1}{V_2}\right) - 1}{\left(\frac{P_1}{P_2}\right) - 1} \right]$$

ENTROPY

• PROBLEM 3-8

For the following reaction at 25°C

$$CuO(s) + H_2(g) \rightarrow Cu(s) + H_2O(g)$$

Values of S°, the absolute entropies for the substances are:

CuO(s)	=	10.4 cal/mole
$H_2(g)$	=	31.2 cal/mole
Cu(s)	=	8.0 cal/g-atm
$H_2O(g)$	=	45.1 cal/mole

Assuming standard conditions find out if the reaction will proceed spontaneously.

Solution: Entropy change is often used to predict the spontaneity of a reaction. A process will occur spontaneously if there is an increase in entropy i.e. ΔS° is positive.

$$\Delta S° = S°_{(products)} - S°_{(reactants)}$$

For the above reaction

$$\Delta S° = S°_{Cu(s)} + S°_{H_2O(g)} - S°_{CuO(s)} - S°_{H_2(g)}$$

$$= (8 + 45.1 - 10.4 - 31.2) \text{ cal/deg-mole}$$

$= +11.5$ cal/deg-mole

$\Delta S°$ is positive thus this is a spontaneous reaction.

• PROBLEM 3-9

At 368°K 1 mole of sulfur changes from the monoclinic to the rhombic solid state. ΔH for the transition = -96.01 cal mol^{-1}. Calculate the entropy changes if the surroundings is an ice-water bath at 0°C.

Solution: The total change of entropy for the phase transition is given by summing ΔS for the system and surroundings, thus:

$$\Delta S(\text{universe}) = \Delta S(\text{system}) + \Delta S(\text{surroundings})$$

For a system undergoing transition

$$\Delta S(\text{system}) = \frac{\Delta H}{T}$$

$$= \frac{\left(-96.01\ \frac{\text{cal}}{\text{mol}}\right)(1.00\ \text{mol})\left(\frac{4.184\ \text{J}}{1\ \text{cal}}\right)}{368°\text{K}}$$

$$= -1.092\ \frac{\text{Joules}}{°\text{K}}$$

$\Delta S(\text{surroundings}) = \frac{q}{T}$ where q = heat transfer. The surrounding is at 0°C = 273°K and the heat transferred to it is the 96.01 cal mol^{-1} given up from the transition

$$\therefore\quad \Delta S(\text{surroundings}) = \left(96\ \frac{\text{cal}}{\text{mol}}\right)(1\ \text{mol})\left(\frac{4.184\ \text{J}}{1\ \text{cal}}\right)\Big/273°\text{K}$$

$$\Delta S(\text{surroundings}) = 1.471\frac{\text{J}}{°\text{K}}$$

$$\therefore\quad \Delta S(\text{universe}) = (-1.092) + 1.471)\frac{\text{J}}{°\text{K}}$$

$$\Delta S(\text{universe}) = 0.379\frac{\text{J}}{°\text{K}}$$

• PROBLEM 3-10

For the reaction

$$Ag(s) + \tfrac{1}{2}Cl_2(g) = AgCl(liq)$$

Metz and Seifert gave the voltage, $\varepsilon°$, of the electrochemical cell as

$$\varepsilon° = 0.9081 - 0.2801X + 0.110X^2$$

where X = (T - 728.2)10^{-3}K. Calculate the value of ΔS° at 1000K given that

$$\Delta S° = nF \frac{d\varepsilon°}{dT}$$

where $n = 1$

and $F = 9.648456 \times 10^{4}$ C mol^{-1}

<u>Solution</u>: It is stated that

$$\Delta S_T^\circ = nF \frac{d\varepsilon°}{dT}.$$

Using the chain rule method of differentiation from calculus, $\frac{d\varepsilon°}{dT}$ can be written as

$$\frac{d\varepsilon°}{dT} = \frac{d\varepsilon°}{dX}\frac{dX}{dT}$$

$$\therefore \quad \Delta S_T^\circ = nF \frac{d\varepsilon°}{dX}\frac{dX}{dT}$$

$$\varepsilon° = 0.9081 - 0.280X + 0.110X^2$$

$$\frac{d\varepsilon°}{dX} = -0.280 + 2(0.110X)$$

$$= -0.280 + 0.220X$$

$$X = (T - 728.2)10^{-3}K$$

$$\therefore \quad \frac{dX}{dT} = 10^{-3}$$

$$\therefore \quad \Delta S_T^\circ = 1\ mol\left(\frac{9.648456\times 10^{4}C}{mol}\right)\left(\frac{As}{C}\right)\left(\frac{J}{AsV}\right)(-0.280+0.220X)\left(10^{-3}\ \frac{V}{°K}\right)$$

$$\Delta S_T^\circ = (-27.02 + 21.23X)JK^{-1}$$

where A = amperes, S = seconds, J = Joules and V = volts.

$$\Delta S_{1000}^\circ(\text{reaction}) = -27.02 + 21.23(T - 728.2)10^{-3}$$

$$= -27.02 + 21.23(1000 - 728.2)10^{-3}$$

$$= -27.02 + 5.77$$

$$\Delta S_{1000}^\circ(\text{reaction}) = -21.25\ J/K$$

For the reaction;

$$C_2H_5OH(liq) + HI_{(g)} = C_2H_5I(liq) + H_2O(liq),$$

$$S^\circ_{298[C_2H_5OH(liq)]} = 38.4 \text{ eu mol}^{-1}$$

$$S^\circ_{298[HI(g)]} = 49.351 \text{ eu mol}^{-1}$$

$$S^\circ_{298[C_2H_5I(liq)]} = 50.6 \text{ eu mol}^{-1}$$

$$S^\circ_{298[H_2O(liq)]} = 16.71 \text{ eu mol}^{-1}.$$

The eu unit is equivalent to the units of cal K^{-1}.

In order to change the rate of reaction the process was run at 60°C = 333°K.

$$C^\circ_{P[C_2H_5OH(liq)]} = 26.64 \text{ cal mol}^{-1} \text{ K}^{-1}$$

$$C^\circ_{P[HI(g)]} = 6.969 \text{ cal mol}^{-1} \text{ K}^{-1}$$

$$C^\circ_{P[C_2H_5I(liq)]} = 27.5 \text{ cal mol}^{-1} \text{ K}^{-1}$$

$$C^\circ_{P[H_2O(liq)]} = 17.995 \text{ cal mol}^{-1} \text{ K}^{-1}.$$

Calculate S°_{333} for this reaction.

Solution: ΔS°_T for a chemical reaction is given by

$$\Delta S^\circ_{T(\text{reaction})} = \underset{\text{products}}{\sum_i n_i S^\circ_{T,i}} - \underset{\text{reactants}}{\sum_j n_j S^\circ_{T,j}}$$

where n_i and n_j are the stoichiometric coefficients of the balanced reaction equation. Thus

$$\Delta S^\circ_{298(\text{reaction})} = [(1)S^\circ_{298,(C_2H_5I)} + (1)S^\circ_{298,(H_2O)}]$$

$$- [(1)S^\circ_{298,C_2H_5OH} + (1)S^\circ_{298,HI}]$$

$$= [(1)(50.6) + (1)(16.71)]$$

$$- [(1)(38.4) + (1)(49.351)]$$

$$= -20.4 \text{ eu}$$

But $$\Delta S^\circ_{T(\text{reaction})} = \Delta S^\circ_{298(\text{reaction})} + \int_{298°K}^{T} \frac{\Delta C^\circ_P}{T}\, dT \qquad (1)$$

$$\therefore \Delta S^\circ_{T(\text{reaction})} = \Delta S^\circ_{298(\text{reaction})} + 2.303\ \Delta C^\circ_P \log \frac{T_2}{T_1}$$

$$\Delta C^\circ_P = \sum_{i\,(\text{products})} n_i C^\circ_{P,i} - \sum_{j\,(\text{reactants})} n_j C^\circ_{P,j}$$

where n_i and n_j are stoichiometric coefficients of the products and reactants respectively.

$$\therefore \Delta C^\circ_P = [(1)(27.5) + (1)(17.995)]$$

$$- [(1)(26.64) + (1)(6.969)]$$

$$= 11.9 \text{ cal K}^{-1}$$

Substituting this value for ΔC°_P into equation (1),

$$\Delta S^\circ_{333(\text{reaction})} = -20.4 + \int_{298°K}^{333°K} \frac{11.9}{T}\, dT$$

$$= -20.4 + 2.303(11.9)\log \frac{333°K}{298°K}$$

$$\Delta S^\circ_{333(\text{reaction})} = -19.1 \text{ eu} = -79.9 \text{ EU}$$

• PROBLEM 3-12

Given the reaction $H_{2(g)} + \frac{1}{2}O_{2(g)} = H_2O$ and

$$S^\circ_{298[H_2(g)]} = 31.208 \text{ eu mol}^{-1}$$

$$S^\circ_{298[O_2(g)]} = 49.003 \text{ eu mol}^{-1}$$

$$S^\circ_{298[H_2O(l)]} = 16.71 \text{ eu mol}^{-1}$$

$$S^\circ_{298[H_2O(g)]} = 45.104 \text{ eu mol}^{-1},$$

Compare the $\Delta S^\circ_{298(\text{formation})}$ of $H_2O(g)$ and $H_2O(\text{liq})$.

Solution: ΔS°_T for a chemical reaction is given by

$$\Delta S^\circ_{T(\text{reaction})} = \sum_{\substack{i \\ \text{products}}} n_i S^\circ_{T,i} - \sum_{\substack{j \\ \text{reactants}}} n_j S^\circ_{T,j}$$

where n_i and n_j are the stoichiometric coefficients of the balanced reaction equation. Thus for the given reaction,

$$\Delta S^\circ_{298} = \left[(1) S^\circ_{298,H_2O}\right] - \left[(1) S^\circ_{298,H_2(g)} + \left(\frac{1}{2}\right) S^\circ_{298,O_2(g)}\right]$$

a) $\therefore \Delta S^\circ_{298(\text{formation})}$ for $H_2O(g)$ is

$$\Delta S^\circ_{298} = [(1)(45.104)] - [(1)(31.208) + \left(\frac{1}{2}\right)(49.003)]$$

$$= -10.66 \text{ eu}$$

$$\therefore \Delta S^\circ_{298(\text{formation})} = -10.66 \text{ eu}$$

b) $\Delta S^\circ_{298(\text{formation})}$ for $H_2O(l)$ is

$$\Delta S^\circ_{298} = [(1)(16.71)] - [(1)(31.208) + \left(\frac{1}{2}\right)(49.003)]$$

$$= -39.00 \text{ eu}$$

$$\Delta S^\circ_{298(\text{formation})} = -39.00 \text{ eu}$$

Entropy is a measure of the amount of randomness in a material. For a), there are 1.5 moles of gaseous reactants to form 1 mole fo gaseous products indicating a decrease in the randomness. For b), 1.5 moles of gaseous reactants form 1 mole of liquid product indicating a large decrease in randomness as compared to a.

• PROBLEM 3-13

1 mole of solid aluminum expands isothermally from 100.0 atm to 1.0 atm. Calculate ΔS(system) for the process given that $\alpha \equiv \frac{1}{V}\left(\frac{\partial V}{\partial T}\right)_P = 69 \times 10^{-6} K^{-1}$ and density, $d = 2.702 \times 10^3 \text{ kg m}^{-3}$

Solution: ΔS for the isothermal expansion of a system is given by

$$\Delta S(\text{system}) = -\int_{P_1}^{P_2} \left(\frac{\partial V}{\partial T}\right)_P dP$$

α = compressibility is given by

$$\alpha = \frac{1}{V}\left(\frac{\partial V}{\partial T}\right)_P$$

$$\therefore \Delta S(\text{system}) = -\alpha V \int_{P_1}^{P_2} dP$$

$$= -\alpha V(P_2 - P_1)$$

1 mole solid aluminum = 26.9815×10^{-3} kg

$\therefore \Delta S(\text{system}) =$

$$-(69 \times 10^{-6} K^{-1})(1 \text{ mol})\left[\frac{26.9815 \times 10^{-3} \text{kg mol}^{-1}}{2.702 \times 10^{3} \text{ kg m}^{-3}}\right](1.0-100.0)\text{atm}$$

$$\left(101{,}325 \text{ J m}^{-3} \text{ atm}^{-1}\right)$$

$$\Delta S(\text{system}) = 6.91 \times 10^{-3} \frac{\text{Joules}}{°K}$$

• PROBLEM 3-14

1 mole of $O_{2(g)}$ at 298 °K is cooled to O_2(liq) at 90.19 °K. The cooling is carried out reversibly and irreversibly by placing the sample in liquid hydrogen at 13.96 °K. Calculate the values of the entropy changes for the process given that ΔH(vaporization) = 1630 cal mol^{-1} at 90.19 °K and C_P = (7/2)R for the gas.

Solution: ΔS(universe) = ΔS(system) + ΔS(surroundings). The process can be considered as consisting of two separate stages. The first being cooling the gas at constant pressure to liquid and the second being compressing the liquid.

For the reversible process

$$\Delta S(\text{system}) = \int_{T_1}^{T_2} \frac{C_P}{T} dT + \frac{-\Delta H(\text{vaporization})}{T_{bp}}$$

$$= \int_{298°K}^{90.19°K} \frac{C_P}{T} dT + \frac{-\Delta H(\text{vaporization})}{T}$$

$$= (1.00 \text{ mol})\left(\frac{7}{2}\right)\left(\frac{8.314 \text{ J}}{\text{mol °K}}\right) \ln\left(\frac{90.19°K}{298°K}\right)$$

$$+ \frac{(1 \text{ mol})\left(-1630 \frac{\text{cal}}{\text{mol}}\right)\left(\frac{4.184 \text{ J}}{\text{cal}}\right)}{90.19 \text{ °K}}$$

$$= \left(-34 + (-75.62)\right)$$

$$\Delta S(\text{system}) = (-110.40) \frac{\text{Joules}}{\text{°K}}$$

$$\therefore \Delta S(\text{surroundings}) = 110.40 \frac{\text{Joules}}{\text{°K}}$$

ΔS(universe) for the reversible process, using ΔS(universe) = ΔS(system) + ΔS(surroundings), is

$$\Delta S(\text{universe}) = 0 + 0$$

$$= 0$$

For the irreversible process, q for the surroundings is

$$q = -\int_{298 \text{ K}}^{90.19 \text{ K}} C_p dT + \Delta H(\text{vaporization})$$

$$= -(1.00 \text{ mol})\left(\frac{7}{2}\right)\left(8.314 \text{ J mol}^{-1} \text{ K}^{-1}\right)(90.19 \text{ K} - 298 \text{ K})$$

$$+ (1.00 \text{ mol})\left(1630 \text{ cal mol}^{-1}\right)\left(4.184 \text{ J cal}^{-1}\right)$$

$$= 12.87 \text{ kJ}$$

using ΔS = q/T,

$$\therefore \Delta S(\text{surroundings}) = \frac{12,870}{13.96} = 922 \frac{\text{J}}{\text{°K}} \quad \text{and}$$

$$\Delta S(\text{universe}) = 922 + (-110.40) = 812 \frac{\text{J}}{\text{°K}}$$

• PROBLEM 3-15

1 mole of an ideal gas is compressed isothermally. If compression is done reversibly and irreversibly from 1.00 atm to 5.00 atm against an external pressure of 100.0 atm, calculate the entropy changes for both processes.

Solution: The entropy of a system can be defined as:

$$dS = \frac{dq_{\text{reversible}}}{T}$$

$$\Delta S = \int \frac{dq_{\text{rev}}}{T} \tag{1}$$

$$\Delta S(\text{universe}) = \Delta S(\text{system}) + \Delta S(\text{surroundings}) \tag{2}$$

From equation (1), ΔS(system) can only be determined using the reversible process. This is because the entropy change is determined by the reversible heat and not by the heat actually absorbed. For the irreversible process one must look for a reversible step, that has the same end states as the actual process

(ΔS(universe) > 0 for an irreversible process)

$$\Delta S(\text{system}) = \frac{dq_{rev}}{T}$$

$$= nR \ \ln \frac{V_2}{V_1} \text{ at const T}$$

From ideal gas law

$$PV = nRT$$

$$\therefore \quad V = \frac{nRT}{P}$$

$$V_1 = \frac{(1.00 \text{ mol})\left(\frac{0.0821 \text{ dm}^3 \text{ atm}}{°\text{K mol}}\right)(298 \ °\text{K})}{1 \text{ atm}}$$

$$= 24.5 \text{ dm}^3$$

$$V_2 = \frac{(1.00 \text{ mol})\left(\frac{0.0821 \text{ dm}^3 \text{ atm}}{°\text{K mol}}\right)(298 \ °\text{K})}{5 \text{ atm}}$$

$$= 4.9 \text{ dm}^3$$

$$\therefore \Delta S(\text{system}) = (1.00 \text{ mol})\left(\frac{8.314 \text{ J}}{\text{mol } °\text{K}}\right) \ln \frac{4.9}{24.5}$$

$$= -13.38 \text{ EU}$$

For an isothermal process, one can also use the equation, $\Delta S = nR \ \ln\left(\frac{P_1}{P_2}\right)$. Hence, after substitution yields

$$\Delta S = 1 \text{ mole}\left(\frac{8.314 \text{ J}}{\text{mole } °\text{K}}\right) \ln\left(\frac{1 \text{ atm}}{5 \text{ atm}}\right)$$

$$= 13.38 \text{ J K}^{-1}$$

For the reversible process

$$\Delta S(\text{surroundings}) = 13.38 \text{ EU}$$

∴ ΔS(universe) for the reversible process using equation (2) is

$$\Delta S(\text{universe}) = -13.38 + 13.38 \text{ EU}$$

$$= 0$$

For the irreversible process ΔS(system) is still the same as in the reversible system because ΔS is determined by the reversible heat and not by the heat that is actually absorbed.

$$\therefore \ \Delta S(\text{system}) = -13.38 \text{ EU}$$

$$\Delta S(\text{surroundings}) = \frac{q}{T}$$

$$= \frac{P\Delta V}{T}$$

This equation used comes about as follows. Since, this is an isothermal compression, $\Delta E = q - w = 0$ and $q = w$. Also, since this is an isobaric compression the work done is given by $P\Delta V$. Hence,

$$\Delta S(\text{surroundings}) = \frac{q}{T} = \frac{P\Delta V}{T}$$

$$= \frac{(100.0 \text{ atm})(24.5 \text{ dm}^3 - 4.9 \text{dm}^3)(101{,}325 \text{ J m}^{-3}\text{atm}^{-1})}{298°\text{K}}$$

$$= 666 \text{ J °K}^{-1}$$

$$\Delta S(\text{universe}) = 666 \text{ J°K}^{-1} + -13.38 \text{ J°K}^{-1}$$

$$= 653 \text{ J°K}^{-1}$$

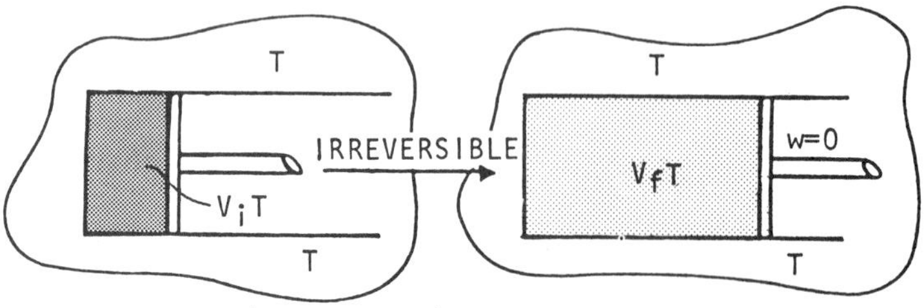

$\Delta S^{sys} = nR \ln(V_f/V_i)$; $\Delta S^{surr} = 0$; $\Delta S = nR \ln(V_f/V_i) > 0$

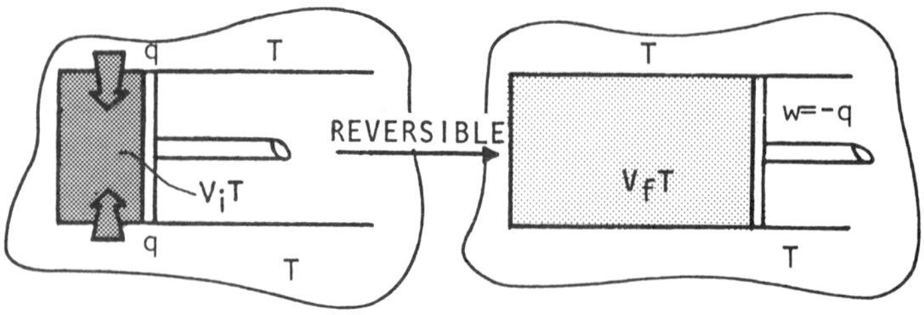

$\Delta S^{sys} = nR \ln(V_f/V_i)$; $\Delta S^{surr} = -nR \ln(V_f/V_i)$; $\Delta S = 0$

CALCULATING THE ENTROPY CHANGES IN IRREVERSIBLE AND REVERSIBLE EXPANSION OF AN IDEAL GAS($P_{ex}=0$ IN THE FORMER).

What is the change in entropy when argon at 25 °C and 1 atm pressure is expanded isothermally from 500 cm^3 to 1000cm^3 and simultaneously heated to a temperature of 100 °C?

Solution: In this problem, two steps are required to take the sample from the initial state of 500 cm^3 and 25 °C to a final state of 1000 cm^3 and 100 °C. The first step involves an isothermal expansion from the initial volume to the final volume. The second step involves a constant volume heating from the initial temperature to the final temperature.

For the first step, the entropy change is

$$\Delta S_1 = nR \ \ell n\left(\frac{V_2}{V_1}\right)$$

where
ΔS = Entropy change
n = number of moles
R = gas constant
V_2 = final volume
V_1 = initial volume.

For the second step, the entropy change is

$$\Delta S_2 = \int_{T_1}^{T_2} \frac{\left(dq_{rev}\right)_V}{T} = \int_{T_1}^{T_2} \frac{dU}{T} = \int_{T_1}^{T_2} C_V \frac{dT}{T}$$

$$= C_V \ \ell n \ T\Big|_{T_1}^{T_2} = C_V(\ell n \ T_2 - \ell n \ T_1) = C_V \ \ell n \frac{T_2}{T_1}$$

where
C_V = Heat capacity at constant volume
T_2 = final temperature
T_1 = initial temperature

C_V for argon = 12.6 JK^{-1} mol^{-1}. Therefore,

$$\Delta S_{total} = \Delta S_1 + \Delta S_2$$

where ΔS_{total} = total entropy change.

$$\therefore \Delta S_{total} = nR \ \ell n\left(\frac{V_2}{V_1}\right) + n \ C_V \ \ell n\left(\frac{T_2}{T_1}\right). \qquad (1)$$

The number of moles, n can be calculated from the relation $P_1V_1 = nRT_1$. Upon rearranging,

$$n = \frac{P_1V_1}{RT_1}$$

$$n = \frac{(1\ \text{atm})(0.5\ \text{dm}^3)}{(0.082\ \text{atm dm}^3\ \text{K}^{-1}\ \text{mol}^{-1})(298\ °\text{K})}$$

$$\therefore \quad n = 0.020\ \text{mol.}$$

Substituting the respective values into equation (1),

$$\Delta S_{total} = \left[(0.020\ \text{mol})\left(8.31\ \text{JK}^{-1}\ \text{mol}^{-1}\right)\ell n\left(\frac{1000}{500}\right)\right]$$

$$+ \left[(0.020\ \text{mol})\left(12.6\ \text{JK}^{-1}\ \text{mol}^{-1}\right)\ell n\left(\frac{373}{298}\right)\right]$$

$$= 0.115\ \text{JK}^{-1} + 0.057\ \text{JK}^{-1}$$

$$\Delta S_{total} = 0.172\ \text{JK}^{-1}$$

• PROBLEM 3-17

Consider a sample of hydrogen confined to a cylinder fitted with a piston of 5 cm^2 cross-section. At room temperature 25°C, it exerts a pressure of 2 atm and it occupies 500 cm^3. What is the change of entropy of the gas when the piston is withdrawn isothermally through a length of 100 cm?

Solution: By definition,

$\Delta S = nR\ \ell n\left(\frac{V_2}{V_1}\right)$ at constant temperature, if the gas is assumed to be ideal

where ΔS = change of entropy of the gas
R = gas constant
V_2 = final volume
V_1 = initial volume
n = the number of moles.

Before the above equation can be used, n and V_2 must be known.

Since ideal behavior is assumed, n can be computed by the relation $PV = nRT$

where P = Pressure
T = Temperature

Upon rearranging,

$$n = \frac{PV}{RT} = \frac{(2)(5 \times 10^{-4}m^3)}{(0.082)(298°K)}$$

$$n = 0.0409 \text{ mol.}$$

Now to compute V_2: The problem indicates that the piston (of 5 cm^2 cross-sectional area) is moved through 100 cm. Therefore, the volume of that section is 5 × 100 = 500 cm^3. But, the gas already occupies 500 cm^3 before the piston is withdrawn isothermally through the length of 100 cm. Therefore, the final volume,

$$V_2 = 500 \text{ cm}^3 + 500 \text{ cm}^3 = 1000 \text{ cm}^3.$$

Substituting the respective values into $\Delta S = nR \ln\left(\frac{V_2}{V_1}\right)$,

$$\Delta S = (0.0409 \text{ mol})\left(8.31 \text{ JK}^{-1} \text{ mol}^{-1}\right) \ln\left(\frac{1000 \text{ cm}^3}{500 \text{ cm}^3}\right)$$

$$= [(0.0409)(8.31)]\text{JK}^{-1} \ln 2$$

$$\therefore \Delta S = 0.24 \text{ JK}^{-1}$$

Be careful about the usage of the units of entropy. Sometimes entropies are quoted in e.u., "entropy units" which means cal/deg/mol. Also note that 1 e.u. = 4.184 $JK^{-1}mol^{-1}$.

• PROBLEM 3-18

If the pressure and temperature at the center of the earth are 3×10^6 atm and 4000 °C respectively, estimate the change in the Gibbs function, ΔG of reaction on going from the crust to the core. Changes in volume, ΔV and entropy, ΔS are 1 cm^3 mol^{-1} and 2·1 J K^{-1} mol^{-1} respectively.

Solution: By definition,

$$\left(\frac{\partial \Delta G}{\partial P}\right)_T = \Delta V \quad \text{and} \quad \left(\frac{\partial \Delta G}{\partial T}\right)_P = -\Delta S.$$

(The parameters are defined in the problem). Using these definitions, an approximation can be made from

$$\Delta G(\text{core}) - \Delta G(\text{crust}) \sim \Delta V\left(P_{\text{core}} - P_{\text{crust}}\right) - \Delta S\left(T_{\text{core}} - T_{\text{crust}}\right)$$

where the symbol ∿ means approximate or asymptotically equal to.

Since $\Delta V = 1\ cm^3\ mol^{-1} = 1 \times 10^{-6}\ m^3\ mol^{-1}$ and the pressure at the center of the earth equals 3×10^6 atm,

$$\Delta V\left(P_{core} - P_{crust}\right) \sim \left(1\times10^{-6}m^3mol^{-1}\right)\left(3\times10^6\times1.013\times10^5Nm^{-2}\right)$$

$$= 3.039 \times 10^5\ J\ mol^{-1}$$

$$\sim 300\ kJ\ mol^{-1}$$

Also,

$$\Delta S\left(T_{core} - T_{crust}\right) \sim \left(2\cdot1\ JK^{-1}\ mol^{-1}\right) \times (4273\ °K - 298\ °K)$$

$$= 8347.5\ J\ mol^{-1}$$

$$\sim 8.3\ kJ\ mol^{-1}$$

Therefore, $\Delta G(core) - \Delta G(crust) \sim 300\ kJ\ mol^{-1} - 8.3\ kJ\ mol^{-1}$

$$= 291.7\ kJ\ mol^{-1}$$

• PROBLEM 3-19

Prove that

$$\left(\frac{\partial S}{\partial E}\right)_H = \frac{-C_P}{T[C_P(P\beta - 1) + PV\alpha(1 - T\alpha)]}$$

where

$$\alpha = \frac{1}{V}\left(\frac{\partial V}{T}\right)_P \quad \text{and} \quad \beta = -\frac{1}{V}\left(\frac{\partial V}{\partial P}\right)_T$$

Solution: If S is taken to be a function of E and H, that is, $S = f(E,H)$, then

$$dS = \left(\frac{\partial S}{\partial E}\right)_H dE + \left(\frac{\partial S}{\partial H}\right)_E dH$$

Therefore, $TdS = T\left(\frac{\partial S}{\partial E}\right)_H dE + T\left(\frac{\partial S}{\partial H}\right)_E dH.$

Here S = entropy, H = enthalpy, E = internal energy.

Now, let $X = T\left(\frac{\partial S}{\partial E}\right)_H$ and $Y = T\left(\frac{\partial S}{\partial H}\right)_E$. Then

$$TdS = XdE + YdH$$

But $$TdS = dE + PdV$$

$$\therefore \quad dE + PdV = XdE + YdH.$$

If E is taken to be a function of P and T, that is E = f(P,T), then

$$dE = \left(\frac{\partial E}{\partial P}\right)_T dP + \left(\frac{\partial E}{\partial T}\right)_P dT.$$

Similarly, if V = f(P,T), then

$$dV = \left(\frac{\partial V}{\partial P}\right)_T dP + \left(\frac{\partial V}{\partial T}\right)_P dT$$

or in terms of α and β,

$$dV = V(-\beta dP + \alpha dT).$$

Also, if H = f(P,T), then

$$dH = \left(\frac{\partial H}{\partial P}\right)_T dP + \left(\frac{\partial H}{\partial T}\right)_P dT.$$

But $\left(\frac{\partial H}{\partial T}\right)_P = C_P$ = Heat Capacity at constant pressure.

Therefore $dH = \left(\frac{\partial H}{\partial P}\right)_T dP + C_P dT$. Thus,

$$TdS = X\left[\left(\frac{\partial E}{\partial P}\right)_T dP + \left(\frac{\partial E}{\partial T}\right)_P dT\right] + Y\left[\left(\frac{\partial H}{\partial P}\right)_T dP + C_P dT\right].$$ Recall

that TdS = dE + PdV. Therefore

$$TdS = \left(\frac{\partial E}{\partial P}\right)_T dP + \left(\frac{\partial E}{\partial T}\right)_P dT - PV\beta dP + PV\alpha dT.$$

Equating the coefficients of dP and dT,

$$X\left(\frac{\partial E}{\partial P}\right)_T + Y\left(\frac{\partial H}{\partial P}\right)_T = \left(\frac{\partial E}{\partial P}\right)_T - PV\beta$$ and

$$X\left(\frac{\partial E}{\partial T}\right)_P + YC_P = \left(\frac{\partial E}{\partial T}\right)_P + PV\alpha.$$

Solving these equations for X,

$$X = \frac{\left[\left(\frac{\partial E}{\partial P}\right)_T - PV\beta\right]C_P - \left[\left(\frac{\partial E}{\partial T}\right)_P + PV\alpha\right]\left(\frac{\partial H}{\partial P}\right)_T}{\left(\frac{\partial E}{\partial P}\right)_T C_P - \left(\frac{\partial H}{\partial P}\right)_P \left(\frac{\partial E}{\partial T}\right)_P} \quad (1)$$

But $\left(\frac{\partial H}{\partial P}\right)_T = V - T\left(\frac{\partial V}{\partial T}\right)_P = V(1 - T\alpha)$, (2)

$$\left(\frac{\partial E}{\partial P}\right)_T = \left(\frac{\partial H}{\partial P}\right)_T - P\left(\frac{\partial V}{\partial P}\right)_T - V = V(1 - T\alpha) + PV\beta - V$$

$$= V(P\beta - T\alpha) \qquad (3)$$

and $$\left(\frac{\partial E}{\partial T}\right)_P = C_P - P\left(\frac{\partial V}{\partial T}\right)_P = C_P - PV\alpha \qquad (4)$$

Substitute equations (2), (3) and (4) in equation (1),

$$X = \frac{\left[[V(\beta P - T\alpha) - PV\beta]C_P - (C_P - PV\alpha + PV\alpha)V(1 - T\alpha)\right]}{V(\beta P - T\alpha)C_P - V(1 - T\alpha)(C_P - PV\alpha)}$$

Expanding and eliminating terms that are equal and have opposite signs,

$$X = \frac{-C_P}{C_P(\beta P - 1) + PV\alpha(1 - T\alpha)}$$

Recall that X was defined to be

$$T\left(\frac{\partial S}{\partial E}\right)_H .$$

Therefore $$T\left(\frac{\partial S}{\partial E}\right)_H = \frac{-C_P}{C_P(\beta P - 1) + PV\alpha(1 - T\alpha)}$$

or $$\left(\frac{\partial S}{\partial E}\right)_H = \frac{-C_P}{T[C_P(\beta P - 1) + PV\alpha(1 - T\alpha)]}$$

• PROBLEM 3-20

Two moles of an ideal monatomic gas initially at 1 atm and 300°K are put through the following cycle, all stages of which are reversible: (I) isothermal compression to 2 atm, (II) isobaric temperature increase to 400°K, (III) return to the initial state by the path P = a + bT, where a and b are constants. Sketch the cycle on a P-T plot and evaluate numerically ΔE and ΔS for the working substance for each stage of the cycle.

Solution: The diagramatic representation of the three steps of the cycle is as follows:
For the first step:
ΔE = 0 because it is an isothermal compression. E is the internal energy.

By definition,

$$\Delta E = \int_{T_1}^{T_2} nC_V dT$$

where n = number of moles and C_V = Heat Capacity at constant volume.

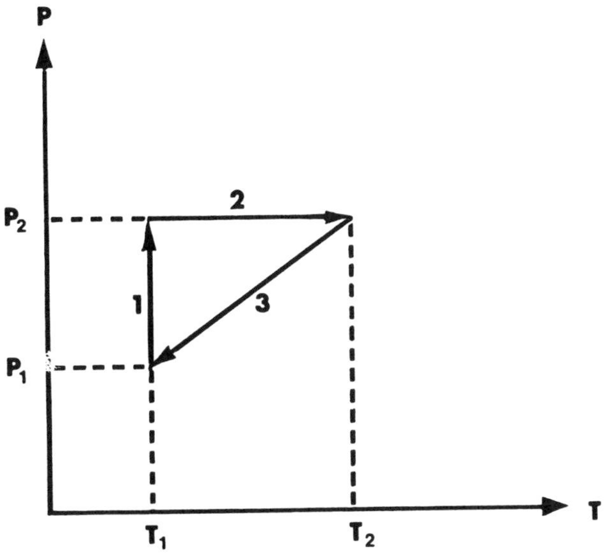

$$\therefore \Delta E_{(1)} = \int_{300}^{300} nC_V dT = 0$$

for the second step:

$$\Delta E_{(2)} = \int_{T_1}^{T_2} nC_V dT = \int_{300}^{400} nC_V dT$$

For a monatomic gas, $C_V = (3/2)\ R$.

$$\therefore \Delta E_{(2)} = \int_{300}^{400} (2)(3/2)(R)dT = 3RT\Big|_{300}^{400}$$

$$= 3R[400 - 300]$$

$$= [3 \times 1.987]100 = 596.1 \text{ cal.}$$

For step 3:

$$\Delta E_{(3)} = \int_{T_1}^{T_2} nC_V dT.$$

Here $T_1 = 400$ and $T_2 = 300$.

$$\therefore \Delta E_{(3)} = \int_{400}^{300} 2(3/2)(R)dT = 3R(300 - 400)$$

$$= -596.1 \text{ cal.}$$

To calculate ΔS: By definition,

$$TdS = dw + dE$$

where S = entropy, w = work and E = internal energy. Therefore

$$dS = \frac{dw + dE}{T} = P\,\frac{dV}{T} + \frac{nC_V dT}{T}$$

$$= \frac{nRTdV}{TV} + \frac{nC_V dT}{T}$$

By integrating between the limits of V_1 and V_2 and T_1 and T_2,

$$\Delta S = nR\,\ell n\left(\frac{V_2}{V_1}\right) + nC_V\,\ell n\left(\frac{T_2}{T_1}\right)$$

Using this expression,

$$\Delta S_1 = 2 \times 1.987 \times \ell n\left(\frac{1}{2}\right) + 2 \times \frac{3}{2}R \times \ell n\ 1.$$

$$\therefore \quad \Delta S_1 = -2.76 \text{ cal K}^{-1} + 0$$

$$= -2.76 \text{ cal K}^{-1}$$

$$\Delta S_2 = nR\,\ell n\left(\frac{V_2}{V_1}\right) + nC_V\,\ell n\left(\frac{T_2}{T_1}\right)$$

$$= 2 \times 1.987 \times \ell n\left(\frac{400}{300}\right) + 2 \times \frac{3}{2} \times 1.987 \times \ell n\left(\frac{400}{300}\right)$$

$$= 2.86 \text{ cal K}^{-1}$$

ΔS_{total} for the three steps = $\Delta S_1 + \Delta S_2 + \Delta S_3 = 0$. Therefore ΔS_3 can be found as follows:

$$\Delta S_3 = -\Delta S_1 - \Delta S_2 = 2.76 - 2.86$$

$$= -0.10 \text{ cal K}^{-1}$$

• PROBLEM 3-21

Use two simplified forms of the van der Waals equation of state, one is which b = 0 and the other with a = 0, to find an explicit expression for the fugacity of Ammonia in each case when the pressure is 10 atm. The van der Waals constants for NH_3 are a/dm^6 atm mol^{-2} = 4.170 and $100b/dm^3$ mol^{-1} = 3.707. Use these values to assess the contributions to the fugacity of the two aspects of non-ideality.

Solution: The van der Waals equation of state is given by

$$\left(P + \frac{n^2a}{V^2}\right)(V - nb) = nRT \tag{1}$$

where P = Pressure of the gas
n = Number of moles
V = Volume of the gas
T = Temperature of the gas
R = Gas constant
a and b = constants.

When a = 0, equation (1) becomes

$$P(V - nb) = nRT$$

$$\therefore \quad P = \frac{nRT}{V-nb}$$

For one mole, $P = \frac{RT}{V-b}$. (2)

When b = 0, the equation becomes

$$\left(P + \frac{n^2a}{V^2}\right)V = nRT$$

$$\therefore \quad P = \frac{nRT}{V} - \frac{n^2a}{V^2}$$

For one mole, $P = \frac{RT}{V} - \frac{a}{V^2}$ (3)

or $$V^2 - \frac{VRT}{P} + \frac{a}{P} = 0 \tag{4}$$

Solve for V in equation (4) (using the quadratic formula).

That is $V = \dfrac{-b \pm \sqrt{b^2 - 4ac}}{2a}$. Note that the a and b in the quadratic formula are just the coefficients of V^2 and V respectively.

Therefore, $$V = \frac{\frac{RT}{P} \pm \sqrt{\frac{R^2T^2}{P^2} - \frac{4a}{P}}}{2} \qquad (5)$$

Discarding the negative solution, equation (5) becomes

$$V = \frac{\frac{RT}{P} + \left[\frac{R^2T^2}{P^2} - \frac{4a}{P}\right]^{1/2}}{2} .$$

Upon rearranging,

$$V = \frac{RT}{2P}\left[1 + \left(1 - \frac{4aP}{R^2T^2}\right)^{1/2}\right] \qquad (6)$$

If deviation from ideality is small, the term $\dfrac{4aP}{R^2T^2}$ in equation (6) is small. Therefore, $\left(1 - \dfrac{4a}{R^2T^2}\right)^{1/2}$ can be approximated by $1 - \dfrac{2aP}{R^2T^2}$. (7)

$$\text{Now, fugacity } f = P \exp \int_0^P [(Z - 1)/P]dP \qquad (8)$$

where Z = compression factor. Because of the small deviation from ideality, this can be approximated by $1 - \dfrac{aP}{R^2T^2}$.

Therefore equation (8) becomes $P \exp\left(\dfrac{-aP}{R^2T^2}\right)$. (9)

Remember that this is for the condition, $b = 0$.

Recall that when $a = 0$, $P = \dfrac{RT}{V - b}$

$$\therefore \quad PV - Pb = RT$$

$$\text{and} \quad PV = RT + Pb$$

$$\therefore \quad V = \frac{RT}{P} + b$$

So, Z can be approximated by $1 + \frac{Pb}{RT}$. Therefore,

$$f = P \exp \int_0^P (b/RT)dP = P \exp(Pb/RT) \qquad (10)$$

Using the data given, equation (9) becomes

$$f = (10 \text{ atm}) \exp\left[\frac{-\left(4.17 \text{ dm}^6 \text{ atm mol}^{-2}\right)(10 \text{ atm})}{\left(0.082 \text{ dm}^3 \text{ atm K}^{-1} \text{ mol}^{-1}\right)^2 \left(298°K\right)^2}\right]$$

$$\therefore\ f = (10 \text{ atm})\exp(-0.0698) = 10\left(e^{-0.0698}\right)$$

$$f = (10)(0.93) = 9.3 \text{ atm}$$

Also equation (10) becomes

$$f = (10 \text{ atm})\exp\left[\frac{(0.037)(10)}{(0.082)(298)}\right]$$

$$\therefore\ f = (10)\exp(0.0151) = 10\left(e^{0.0151}\right)$$

$$\therefore\ f = (10)(1.02) = 10.2 \text{ atm.}$$

The results show that the effect of the constant a is to reduce the fugacity and that of constant b is to increase it. This agrees with the relation of these parameters to the attractive and repulsive interactions respectively.

FREE ENERGY

• PROBLEM 3-22

The molar volume of mercury at P = 0 and T = 273°K is 14.72 cm^3 mol^{-1}, and the compressibility is $\beta = 3.88 \times 10^{-11}$ m^2 N^{-1}. If β is assumed to be constant over the pressure range, calculate the free energy change for the compression of mercury from 0 to 3000 kg cm^{-2}.

Solution: At constant temperature, the compressibility factor is given by

$$\beta = -\frac{1}{V_0}\left(\frac{\partial V}{\partial P}\right)_T \qquad (1)$$

where V_0 = initial molar volume

$\frac{\partial V}{\partial P}$ = partial derivative of the molar volume with respect to P keeping T constant.

Also, dG = VdP at constant temperature, where G = free energy.

Solving for $\left(\frac{\partial V}{\partial P}\right)_T$, in equation (1)

$$\left(\frac{\partial V}{\partial P}\right)_T = -\beta V_0. \qquad (2)$$

The subscript T means at constant temperature.

Integrating equation (2), it becomes

$$\int \partial V = - \int \beta V_0 dP$$

$$\therefore \quad V = -\beta V_0 P + C \qquad (3)$$

where C is an integration constant.

Using the initial conditions P = 0 and $V = V_0$, equation (3) becomes

$$V_0 = -\beta V_0(0) + C$$

$$V_0 = 0 + C$$

$$\therefore \quad C = V_0$$

Substituting this value into equation (3),

$$V = -\beta V_0 P + V_0$$

$$V = V_0(-\beta P + 1) \quad \text{or} \quad V = V_0(1 - \beta P) \qquad (4)$$

Since an expression that relates V, P and β has been developed, the right hand side of equation (4) can replace V in the free energy equation. That is,

$$dG = VdP$$

$$dG = V_0(1 - \beta P)dP. \qquad (5)$$

Integrating this expression, equation (5) becomes

$$\Delta G = \int_{P_1}^{P_2} V_0(1 - \beta P)dP$$

Note that there are limits here, so an integration constant is not needed.

$$\therefore \Delta G = \int_{P_1}^{P_2} (V_0 - V_0\beta P)dP = V_0 P \Big|_{P_1}^{P_2} - V_0\beta \frac{P^2}{2}\Big|_{P_1}^{P_2}$$

$$\Delta G = V_0(P_2-P_1) - \frac{V_0\beta}{2}\left(P_2^2 - P_1^2\right) = V_0\left[\left(P_2-P_1\right) - \frac{\beta}{2}\left(P_2^2-P_1^2\right)\right]$$

Here $P_1 = 0$ and $P_2 = 3000$ kg cm^{-2} = 2.94×10^8 Nm^{-2}. The conversion is as follows:

$$3000 \frac{kg}{cm^3} \times \frac{(100\ cm)^2}{(m)^2} \times \frac{9.8m}{sec^2} = 2.94(10^8)\frac{N}{m^2}.$$ The reason for multiplying by "g" is the fact that pressure is force/area and what is given is mass/area. Hence, multiplication of the mass by an acceleration is necessary.

$$\therefore\ \Delta G = 14.72 \times 10^{-6} \frac{m^3}{mole}\left[2.94{\times}10^8 Nm^{-2} - \frac{3.88{\times}10^{-11}}{2}\left(2.94{\times}10^8\right)^2\right]$$

$$= 4300\ Nm/mole.$$

REFRIGERATION

• PROBLEM 3-23

A heat pump with a coefficient of performance given by

$$COP = -\frac{q_1}{w} = \frac{T_1}{T_2 - T_1} = 7.0$$

is used to pump an amount of heat q_1 at a temperature T_1, from the cold outdoors to the interior of a house at a temperature T_2. Calculate q_2/w, the ratio of the heat liberated at the higher temperature T_2 to the work done.

Solution: A heat pump is essentially a refrigerator operated in reverse; that is, it is used to heat a system at a higher temperature by pumping heat from the surroundings at a lower temperature. Thus a heat pump could be used to warm a house by pumping heat from the cold outdoors and delivering it to the warm interior of the house. The advantage of this method of heating is that the maximum efficiency of a refrigerator is much greater than that of other methods of heating.

$$COP = -\frac{q_1}{w} = \frac{T_1}{T_2 - T_1} \tag{1}$$

where q = quantity of heat
w = work done.

Here $w = q_1 + q_2$

or $q_1 = w - q_2$ (2)

Therefore using equations (1) and (2)

$$-\frac{q_1}{w} = \frac{-(w - q_2)}{w} = \frac{-w + q_2}{w}$$

But the problem indicates that $\frac{-q_1}{w} = 7.0$. Therefore

$$\frac{-q_1}{w} = 7.0 = \frac{-w + q_2}{w} = -\frac{w}{w} + \frac{q_2}{w}$$

or $\frac{-q_1}{w} = -1 + \frac{q_2}{w} = 7.0$

$$\therefore \quad \frac{q_2}{w} = 7.0 + 1 = 8.0$$

Consequently the heat pump will be 8 times as "efficient" as a 100% efficient resistor. That is it would produce 8 times as much heat as a 100% efficient resistor per caloric of energy input.

• PROBLEM 3-24

A cooling system is designed to maintain a refrigerator at -25°C in a room at ambient temperature +25°C. The heat transfer into the refrigerator is estimated as 10^4 J min^{-1}. If the unit is assumed to operate at 50% of its maximum thermodynamic efficiency, estimate its power requirement.

Solution: A perfect refrigerator that operates between the temperatures of T_c and T_h has a COP of $\frac{T_c}{T_h - T_c} = \frac{q_c}{w}$ where COP is the coefficient of performance. The subscripts c and h stand for "cold and hot sinks" respectively and q = amount of heat transfered.

$T_c = 248°K$ and $T_h = 298°K$.

$$COP = \frac{248}{298 - 248} = \frac{248}{50} = 4.96.$$

But $$COP = \frac{T_c}{T_h - T_c} = \frac{q_c}{w} = 4.96.$$

The values for q_c is given to be 10^4 J min^{-1}.

$$\therefore \quad \frac{q_c}{w} = \frac{10^4}{w} = 4.96$$

or $$w = \frac{10^4}{4.96} = 0.202 \times 10^4 \text{ J min}^{-1}$$

$$= 0.202 \times 10^4 \text{ J min}^{-1} \times \frac{1 \text{ min}}{60 \text{ sec}}$$

$$\therefore w = 0.00337 \times 10^4 \text{ J sec}^{-1}$$

$$= 33.7 \text{ J sec}^{-1}.$$

Recall that this is for a perfect refrigerator (with approximately 100% efficiency). Therefroe more power will be needed to operate anything less than 100% efficiency. At 50% efficiency, Power $= \frac{33.7}{0.5} = 67.4$ watts.

• PROBLEM 3-25

In regions with mild winters, heat pumps can be used for space heating in winter and cooling in summer. Assuming ideal thermodynamic efficiency for the pump, compare the cost of keeping a room at 25°C in winter and in summer when outside temperatures are 12 and 38°C, respectively. Suppose the heat pump were running 50% of the time when the outside temperature was 12°C. If the outside temperature fell to 0°C, could this heat pump maintain the inside at 25°C?

Solution: The quantity of heat added to the room is equal to the heat absorbed from the outside together with the work done by the pump.

The amount of work needed to add q_h cal to a room when the outside temperature is T_c can be found by the relation

$$\text{COP} = \frac{q_h}{w} = \frac{T_h}{T_h - T_c} \qquad (1)$$

where w = work

COP is the coefficient of performance of the pump. The subscripts h and c are used to represent "hot and cold" respectively. [Note that this relation is used because the problem indicates that an ideal thermodynamic efficiency for the pump should be assumed.]

Solve for W in equation (1)

$$WT_h = q_h(T_h - T_c)$$

$$\therefore \quad W = \frac{q_h(T_h - T_c)}{T_h} \qquad (2)$$

If $q_h = 100$ cal is chosen as a basis for the calculation, then equation (2) becomes

$$W = \frac{100(T_h - T_c)}{T_h} .$$

Here $T_h = 25°C = 298°K$ and $T_c = 12°C = 285°K$.

$$\therefore \quad W = \frac{100(298 - 285)}{298} = 4.362 \text{ cal.}$$

This is the amount of work required to keep a room at 25°C when the outside temperature is 12°C in the winter. In the summer, the requirement is that 100 cal should be absorbed from the room and discharged at the higher temperature outside. Again,

$$W = \frac{q_c(T_h - T_c)}{T_c} .$$

Note that q_c is now 100 cal instead of q_h.

$T_h = 38°C = 311°K$ and $T_c = 25°C = 298°K$

$$\therefore \quad W = \frac{100(311 - 298)}{298} = 4.362 \text{ cal}$$

Since the same amount of work is required for both cases, SUMMER COST = WINTER COST.

If the pump ran 50% of the time to deliver 4.362 cal, then $\frac{4.362}{0.5} = 8.724$ cal would be delivered in the same time running continuously.

• PROBLEM 3-26

What is the amount of work required

a) to freeze 100g of water at 0°C when the temperature of the surroundings is 25°C?
b) to withdraw the same amount of heat from a body at 10^{-5}°K when the surroundings is 1°K?

Assume perfect thermodynamic efficiency.

Solution: For a perfect refrigerator operating between the temperatures of T_c and T_h, the

$$COP = \frac{T_c}{T_h - T_c}$$

where COP = coefficient of performance.

The subscripts c and h stand for "cold and hot sinks" respectively.

The amount of work required is given by

$$w = \frac{q}{COP} \tag{1}$$

where q = amount of heat.

The amount of heat needed in order to freeze water is the number of moles of water multiplied by enthalpy of fusion; given by $n\Delta H_{fusion}$ where n = number of moles. For water

$$\Delta H_{fusion} = 6.01 \text{ kJ mol}^{-1}.$$

Since 100 g of water is to be frozen,

$$n = \frac{\text{weight}}{\text{molecular weight}} = \frac{100\text{g}}{18\text{g mol}^{-1}} = 5.6 \text{ mol}.$$

Therefore, the amount of heat, $q = n\Delta H_{fusion}$.

$$q = (5.6 \text{ mol})(6.01 \text{ kJ mol}^{-1})$$

$$q = 33.6 \text{ kJ}$$

a) Here $T_h = 298°K$, $T_c = 273°K$

$$\therefore \quad COP = \frac{T_c}{T_h - T_c} = \frac{273}{298 - 273} = 10.92.$$

From equation (1), $w = \frac{q}{COP} = \frac{33.6 \text{ kJ}}{10.92}$

$$\therefore w = 3.07 \text{ kJ}.$$

b) Here $T_h = 1°K$, $T_c = 10^{-5}°K$

$$\therefore \quad COP = \frac{T_c}{T_h - T_c} = \frac{10^{-5}}{1 - 10^{-5}}.$$

Since the denominator is very close to 1, the COP value is approximately 10^{-5}. Again from equation (1),

$$w = \frac{q}{COP} = \frac{33.6\text{kJ}}{10^{-5}} = 33.6 \times 10^5 \text{ kJ}.$$

CHAPTER 4

STATISTICAL THERMODYNAMICS

ENSEMBLE

• PROBLEM 4-1

(a) Show that the partition function appropriate to an isothermal-isobaric ensemble is

$$\Delta(N,P,T) = \sum\sum \Omega(N,V,E)e^{-E/kT}e^{-PV/kT}$$

(b) Derive the principal thermodynamic connection formulas for this ensemble.

Solution: An ensemble is a (mental) collection of a very large number of systems, each constructed to be a replica on a thermodynamic level of the actual thermodynamic system whose properties are being investigated. For example, consider a system of pressure P that contains N molecules of a single component and is immersed in a large heat bath at a temperature T. In this case, the ensemble consist of π systems, all of which are constructed to duplicate the thermodynamic state (N,P,T) and the environment of the original system. Define:

H_i = enthalpy measured from system i

$\bar{N} = \sum n_i$, where n_i is the number of systems with enthalpy H_i

$\bar{H} = \sum n_i H_i$

The constraints are

$$\phi_i = \sum n_i - \bar{N} = 0$$

i) $\alpha' d\phi_1 = \sum \alpha dn_i = 0$

where the parameter α is called the Lagrange multiplier

$$\phi_2 = \sum n_i H_i - \bar{H} = 0.$$

ii) $\beta d\phi_2 = \sum \beta H_i dn_i = 0.$

For each value of N, there will be a different set of energy states. Let the number of states associated with the distribution n = $\Omega(n)$. Then

$$\Omega(n) = \frac{\bar{N}!}{\prod_i n_i} \tag{1}$$

Let the total number of states over all n = C. Then,

$$C = \sum_n \Omega(n) \tag{2}$$

and the probability $\omega(n)$, of a given distribution is given by

$$\omega(n) = \frac{\Omega(n)}{C} \ . \tag{3}$$

Since the most probable distribution set is desired, maximize ω using equations (1) and (3):

$$\ln \omega(n) = \ln \bar{N}! - \sum_i \ln n_i! - \ln C.$$

Using Stirling's approximation

$$\ln \omega(n) = N \ln \bar{N} - \bar{N} - \sum_i n_i \ln n_i + \sum n_i - \ln C.$$

But $\bar{N} = \sum n_i$,

$$\therefore \quad \ln \omega(n) = N \ln \bar{N} - \sum_i n_i \ln n_i - \ln C.$$

$$\frac{d \ln \omega(n)}{dn} = -\sum_i (n_i \frac{dn_i}{n_i} + dn_i \ln n_i)$$

$$= -\sum_i (1 + \ln n_i) dn_i$$

Apply Lagrange's method of undetermined multipliers;

$$\sum_i (-1 - \ln n_i - \alpha' - \beta H_i) dn_i = 0.$$

Thus, $(1 + \alpha') + \ln n_i + \beta H_i = 0.$

Let $\alpha = 1 + \alpha'$ then

$$\ln n_i = -\alpha - \beta H_i$$

or

$$n_i = e^{-\alpha} e^{-\beta H_i} \ . \tag{4}$$

Recall that $\sum n_i = \bar{N}$. Therefore,

$$\bar{N} = \sum_i e^{-\alpha} e^{-\beta H_i}$$

$$= e^{-\alpha} \sum_i e^{-\beta H_i} \qquad (5)$$

Let the probability of the system having enthalpy of H_i in the maximum distribution n be P_i

$$\therefore \quad P_i = \frac{n_i}{\bar{N}}$$

From equations (4) and (5)

$$P_i = \frac{e^{-\alpha} e^{-\beta H_i}}{e^{-\alpha} \sum_i e^{-\beta H_i}}$$

$$= \frac{e^{-\beta H_i}}{\sum e^{-\beta H_i}}$$

$$= \frac{e^{-\beta H_i}}{\Delta} \qquad (6)$$

where Δ is the partition function. Now

$$\bar{H} = \sum_i P_i H_i \qquad (7)$$

$$\therefore \quad \bar{H} = \frac{\sum_i H_i e^{-\beta H_i}}{\sum_i e^{-\beta H_i}}$$

$$= \frac{\sum H_i e^{-\beta H_i}}{\Delta}$$

Differentiate equation (7) to obtain

$$d\bar{H} = \sum_i P_i dH_i + \sum_i H_i dP_i \qquad (8)$$

From the combined first and second laws of thermodynamics

$$dH_i = TdS + V_i dP \qquad (9)$$

But $$\left(\frac{\partial H_i}{\partial P}\right)_N = V_i$$

$$\therefore \quad dH_i = \left(\frac{\partial H_i}{\partial P}\right)_N dP = V_i dP \tag{10}$$

Also, from equation (6)

$$\ell n\ P_i + \ell n\ \Delta = -\beta H_i$$

Rearranging this to solve for H_i yields

$$H_i = -\frac{1}{\beta}(\ell n\ P_i + \ell n\ \Delta) \tag{11}$$

Using the expressions for dH_i and H_i in equation (8) gives

$$d\bar{H} = \sum_i P_i V_i dP - \sum_i \frac{1}{\beta}(\ell n\ P_i + \ell n\ \Delta) dP_i$$

$$= \bar{V}dP - \sum_i \frac{1}{\beta}\ \ell n\ P_i\ dP_i - \frac{1}{\beta}\ \ell n\ \Delta \sum dP_i$$

$$= \bar{V}dP - \sum_i \frac{1}{\beta}\ \ell n\ P_i\ dP_i - 0$$

But $$d\left(\sum P_i\ \ell n\ P_i\right) = \sum_i P_i \frac{dP_i}{P_i} + \sum_i dP_i\ \ell n\ P_i$$

$$= 0 + \sum_i dP_i\ \ell n\ P_i$$

$$= \sum_i dP_i\ \ell n\ P_i$$

$$\therefore \quad d\bar{H} = -\frac{1}{\beta}\ d\left(P_i\ \ell n\ P_i\right) + \bar{V}dP \tag{12}$$

and from equation (9)

$$dH = TdS + VdP$$

Comparing equations (9) and (12) imply that

$$TdS = -\frac{1}{\beta}\ d\left(P_i\ \ell n\ P_i\right)$$

From the cannonical ensemble, β is defined as

$$\beta = \frac{1}{kT}.$$

But $$\Delta = \sum_i e^{-\beta H_i}$$

$$\therefore \quad \Delta = \sum_i e^{-E_i/kT} e^{-PV/kT}$$

Summing over all levels yields

$$\Delta = \sum_E \sum_V \Omega(N,V,E) e^{-E/kT} e^{-PV/kT}$$

(b) The derivation of the thermodynamic functions are as follows

$$dS = -kd\left(\sum_i P_i \ \ell n \ P_i\right)$$

$$= -kd\left[\frac{\sum_i e^{-\beta H_i}}{\Delta} \ \ell n \left(\frac{e^{-\beta H_i}}{\Delta}\right)\right]$$

$$= \frac{1}{\beta T} \ d\left[\frac{\sum_i e^{-\beta H_i}}{\Delta}(+\beta H_i + \ell n \ \Delta)\right]$$

$$S = \frac{1}{T} \frac{\sum_i H_i e^{-\beta H_i}}{\Delta} + \frac{1}{\beta T} \frac{\ell n \ \Delta \sum_i e^{-\beta H_i}}{\Delta}$$

$$= \frac{\bar{H}}{T} + k \ \ell n \ \Delta \quad . \tag{13}$$

$$G = H - TS$$

or $$S = \frac{H}{T} - \frac{G}{T} \tag{14}$$

From equation (13)

$$\frac{-G}{T} = k \ \ell n \ \Delta$$

or $$G = -kT \ \ell n \ \Delta(N,P,T)$$

$$dG = -SdT + VdP + \mu dN$$

and $$\left(\frac{\partial G}{\partial T}\right)_{P,N} = S$$

$$\left(\frac{\partial G}{\partial P}\right)_{T,N} = V$$

$$\left(\frac{\partial G}{\partial N}\right)_{T,P} = \mu$$

$$\therefore \quad S = k \frac{\partial}{\partial T}\left(T \ln \Delta(N,P,T)\right)_{P,N}$$

$$= k\left[T\left(\frac{\partial \ln \Delta(N,P,T)}{\partial T}\right)_{P,N} + \ln \Delta\right]$$

$$= kT\left(\frac{\partial \ln \Delta}{\partial T}\right)_{P,N} + k \ln \Delta$$

From equation (14)

$$H = kT^2\left(\frac{\partial \ln \Delta}{\partial T}\right)_{P,N}$$

PARTITION FUNCTION

• PROBLEM 4-2

Data for monatomic fluorine at 1000 °K are as follows:

Term symbol	Wave numbers $\bar{\nu} = \varepsilon/hc/(cm^{-1})$	Electronic degeneracy, g_{el}
$P_{3/2}$	0.0	4
$P_{1/2}$	404.0	2
$P_{5/2}$	102,406.5	6

Calculate the fraction of fluorine atoms in each of the first three electronic levels.

Solution: The electronic partition function of the fluorine atom is calculated using the relation;

$$Q_{elec} = \sum g_j e^{-\varepsilon_{elec,j}/kT}$$

$$= g_0 + g_1 e^{-\varepsilon_{elec,1}/kT} + g_2 e^{-\varepsilon_{elec,2}/kT} + \ldots$$

where $\varepsilon_{elec,j}$ is the electronic energy of level j taken relative to the ground state, and g_j is the degeneracy number. Using the given data,

$$Q_{elec.} = g_0 e^{-\varepsilon_{0,el}/kT} + g_1 e^{-\varepsilon_{1,el}/kT} + g_2 e^{-\varepsilon_{2,el}/kT} + \ldots$$

$$= 4e^{-(\varepsilon_{0,el}/hc)(hc/kT)} + 2e^{-(\varepsilon_{1,el}/hc)(hc/kT)}$$

$$+ 6e^{-(\varepsilon_{2,el}/hc)(hc/kT)} + \ldots$$

Computing the hc/kT term gives

$$\frac{hc}{kT} = \frac{(6.63\times10^{-34}\text{J s})(3.0\times10^{10}\text{ cm s}^{-1})}{(1.38\times10^{-23}\text{JK}^{-1})(1000\ °\text{K})}$$

$$= 1.44 \times 10^{-3}\text{ cm}$$

From the table in the problem set, $\varepsilon_{0,el}/hc = 0.0$, $\varepsilon_{1,el}/hc = 404\text{ cm}^{-1}$ and $\varepsilon_{2,el}/hc = 102{,}406.5\text{ cm}^{-1}$. Therefore,

$$Q_{elec} = 4e^0 + 2e^{-(404\text{ cm}^{-1})(1.44\times10^{-3}\text{cm})}$$

$$+ 6e^{-(102{,}406.5\text{ cm}^{-1})(1.44\times10^{-3}\text{ cm})}$$

$$= 4e^0 + 2e^{-0.5817} + 6e^{-147.47}$$

$$= 4 + 1.117 + 5.404 \times 10^{-64}$$

$$\simeq 5.117.$$

The Maxwell-Boltzman distribution law is used to calculate the fraction of fluorine atoms in each of the first three electronic levels. This law is given by

$$\frac{n_j}{N} = \frac{g_{elec,j}e^{-\varepsilon_{elec,j}/kT}}{Q_{elec}} \qquad (2)$$

For the ground level, equation (2) is

$$\frac{n_0}{N} = \frac{g_{elec,0}e^{-\varepsilon_{elec,0}/kT}}{Q_{elec}}$$

$$= \frac{4e^0}{5.117}$$

$$= \frac{4}{5.117}$$

$$= 0.782$$

For the first level

$$\frac{n_1}{N} = \frac{g_{elec,1}e^{-(\varepsilon_{elec,1}/hc)(hc/kT)}}{Q_{elec}}$$

$$= \frac{2e^{-(404/1.44\times10^{-3})}}{5.117}$$

$$= \frac{2e^{-0.5817}}{5.117}$$

$$= \frac{2(0.558)}{5.117}$$

$$= 0.218.$$

For the second electronic level

$$\frac{n_2}{N} = \frac{g_{elec,2}e^{-(\varepsilon_{elec,2}/hc)(hc/kT)}}{Q_{elec}}$$

$$= \frac{6e^{-(102,406.5\ cm^{-1})(1.44\times10^{-3}\ cm)}}{Q_{elec}}$$

$$= \frac{6e^{-147.47}}{5.117}$$

$$\simeq 0$$

Apparently, the fraction of fluorine atoms in the second electronic level is very small and so can be neglected, by approximating it to be zero.

• PROBLEM 4-3

Calculate the molecular translational partition functions in a volume of 1 cm^3 at 298 °K for the following molecules a) H_2, b) CH_4, c) C_8H_{18}.

Solution: The molecular translational partition function is given by

$$q_{trans.} = \left[\frac{2\pi mkT}{h^2}\right]^{3/2} V$$

where h is Planck's constant, m is the mass of the molecule and V is the volume. Taking the mass out of the square bracket, gives

$$q_{trans.} = \left[\frac{2\pi kT}{h^2}\right]^{3/2} Vm^{3/2}$$

$$= \left[\frac{2\pi(1.38\times10^{-23}JK^{-1})(298°K)}{(6.63\times10^{-34}J\ Sec)^2}\right]^{3/2} (1\ cm^3)\left(\frac{1\ m}{100\ cm}\right)^3 m^{3/2}$$

$$= 1.42 \times 10^{64}\left(J^{-1}S^{-2}\right)^{3/2} m^{3/2}(\text{meters})^3 \qquad (1)$$

a) For H_2:

$$\text{Mass per molecule of } H_2 = \frac{(2.016 \text{ g mol}^{-1})\left(\frac{1 \text{ kg}}{1000 \text{ g}}\right)}{6.02 \times 10^{23} \text{ mol}^{-1}}$$

$$= 3.348 \times 10^{-27} \text{ kg}$$

From equation (1)

$$q_{trans.} = 1.42 \times 10^{64}\left(J^{-1}S^{-2}\right)^{3/2}\left(3.348 \times 10^{-27} \text{ kg}\right)^{3/2}$$

$$= 2.750 \times 10^{24}\left(J^{-1}S^{-2}\right)^{3/2} \text{kg}^{3/2}(\text{met})^3$$

$$= 2.750 \times 10^{24}\left[\frac{\sec^2}{\text{kg}(\text{met})^2}\ \frac{1}{\sec^2}\right]^{3/2} \text{kg}^{3/2}(\text{met})^3$$

$$= 2.750 \times 10^{24} \text{ kg}^{-2/3} \text{ met}^{-3} \text{ kg}^{3/2} \text{ met}^3$$

$$= 2.750 \times 10^{24}$$

b) For CH_4:

$$\text{mass per molecule of } CH_4 = \frac{(16.04 \text{ g mol}^{-1})\left(\frac{1 \text{ kg}}{1000 \text{ g}}\right)}{6.02 \times 10^{23} \text{ mol}^{-1}}$$

$$= 2.664 \times 10^{-26} \text{ kg}$$

$$\therefore\ q_{trans.} = (1.42 \times 10^{64})\left(2.664 \times 10^{-26}\right)^{3/2}$$

$$= 6.175 \times 10^{25}$$

c) For C_8H_{18}:

$$\text{Mass per molecule of } C_8H_{18} = \frac{(114.22 \text{ g mol}^{-1})\left(\frac{1\text{kg}}{1000 \text{ g}}\right)}{6.02 \times 10^{23} \text{ mol}^{-1}}$$

$$= 1.897 \times 10^{-25} \text{ kg}$$

$$\therefore\ q_{trans.} = (1.42 \times 10^{64})\left(1.897 \times 10^{-25}\right)^{3/2}$$

$$= 1.173 \times 10^{27}$$

Two molecules $^{14}N_2$ and $^{14}N^{15}N$ have the same internuclear distance given as 0.1095 nm. Evaluate the molar rotational partition function at 298°K for both molecules.

Solution: The molar partition function, Q and the molecular partition function, q are related to each other by the equation

$$Q = q^N \tag{1}$$

where N is the Avogadro number. Taking the $\ln$ of both sides changes equation (1) to

$$\ln Q = N \ln q \tag{2}$$

The molecular rotational partition function is given as

$$q_{rot.} = \frac{8\pi^2 IkT}{\sigma h^2} \tag{3}$$

where I is the moment of inertia about the center of mass, h is the Planck's constant and σ, the symmetry number, is equal to the number of indistinguishable positions into which the molecule can be turned by simple rigid rotation. σ takes the values 1 for heteronuclear diatomics and 2 for homonuclear diatomics.

The moment of inertia is calculated using the internuclear distance given by the relation

$$I = \mu r^2$$

where r is the internuclear distance and μ is the reduced mass given as

$$\mu = \frac{m_1 m_2}{m_1 + m_2}$$

m_1 and m_2 are the masses of atoms 1 and 2 of the molecule. Therefore,

$$I = \frac{m_1 m_2}{m_1 + m_2} r^2$$

a) $^{14}N_2$: Here m_1 and m_2 are the same atoms. Therefore,

$$I = \frac{m^2}{2m} r^2$$

$$= \frac{\left[(14.007 \text{ g mol}^{-1})\left(\frac{1 \text{ kg}}{1000 \text{ g}}\right)\right]^2 \left[(0.1095 \text{ nm})\left(\frac{10^{-9} \text{ m}}{1 \text{ nm}}\right)\right]^2}{2(14.007 \text{ g mol}^{-1})\left(\frac{1 \text{ kg}}{1000 \text{ g}}\right)\left(6.02 \times 10^{23} \text{ mol}^{-1}\right)}$$

$= 1.393 \times 10^{-46}$ kg·m^2.

The symmetry number, σ for $^{14}N_2$ = 2. Therefore, using equation (3) gives

$$q_{rot.} = \frac{8\pi^2(1.393\times10^{-46}\ kg.m^2)(1.38\times10^{-23} J\ K^{-1})(298°K)}{2(6.63 \times 10^{-34}\ J\ S)^2}$$

$$= 51.44\ \frac{J\ kg\ m^2}{J^2\ sec^2} = 51.44\ \frac{J^2}{J^2}$$

$$= 51.44.$$

The molar rotational partition function is thus given by

$$\ell n\ Q_{rot.} = N\ \ell n\ 51.44$$

$$= (6.02 \times 10^{23}\ mol^{-1})\ell n\ 51.44$$

$$= 2.37 \times 10^{24}$$

$$\therefore\ Q_{rot.} = e^{2.37\times10^{24}}$$

b) For $^{14}N^{15}N$,

$$I = \frac{m_1 m_2}{m_1 + m_2}\ r^2 = \mu r^2$$

$$= \frac{(14.007\times10^{-3}\ kg\ mol^{-1})(15.004\times10^{-3}\ kg\ mol^{-1})(0.1095\times10^{-9}\ m)^2}{(29.011 \times 10^{-3})(6.02 \times 10^{23})}$$

$$= 1.44 \times 10^{-46}\ kg\ m^2$$

For this molecule, σ = 1

$$\therefore\ q_{rot.} = \frac{8\pi^2(1.44\times10^{-46}\ kg\ m^2)(1.38\times10^{-23}\ J\ K^{-1})(298\ °K)}{(1)(6.63 \times 10^{-34}\ J\ S)^2}$$

$$= 106.37$$

The molar rotational partition function is thus

$$\ell n\ Q_{rot.} = N\ \ell n\ 106.37$$

$$= (6.02 \times 10^{23}\ mol^{-1})\ell n\ 106.37$$

$$= 2.81(10^{24})$$

and $$Q = e^{2.81\times10^{24}}.$$

The degeneracies of the singlet (paired electron spins) or triplet (unpaired spins) levels of a certain molecule are 1 and 3, respectively. The energy of the singlet state is greater than that of the triplet by a factor ε. a) Write the electronic factor in the partition function of the molecule. Indicate the approximations made. b) Given that the factor $\varepsilon = 1.38 \times 10^{-14}$ erg and $T = 100°K$, calculate the ratio of the population of the singlet level to the population of the triplet level.

Solution: a) The electronic partition function of the molecule is given by the relation

$$Q_{elec} = \sum_i g_i e^{-\varepsilon_{elec,j}/kT}$$

$$= g_0 + g_1 e^{-\varepsilon_{elec,1}/kT}$$

$$+ g_2 e^{-\varepsilon_{elec,2}/kT} + \ldots$$

For every level i with $\varepsilon_i > \varepsilon$, assume that
$g_i e^{-\varepsilon_i/kT} << e^{-\varepsilon/kT}$,

$$\therefore \quad Q_{elec} = 3 + e^{-\varepsilon/kT}$$

b) The ratio of the population of the singlet level to the population of the triplet level is given by

$$\frac{N_{singlet}}{N_{triplet}} = \frac{e^{-\varepsilon/kT}}{3}$$

$$= \frac{1}{3}\exp\left\{\frac{-1.38\times10^{-14}\text{ erg}}{(1.38\times10^{-16}\text{ erg °K}^{-1})(100\text{K})}\right\}$$

$$= \frac{1}{3}e^{-1}$$

$$= \frac{1}{3}(0.3678)$$

$$= 0.123$$

In an imperfect gas with a distribution of various sized physical clusters, there is an association-dissociation equilibrium between all the clusters which are unstable. Consider Band's approximation and that you can treat the system as a Dalton's law vapor. Now, let the canonical partition function for the system (ensemble) be

$$Q = \prod_{g=1}^{N} F_g$$

where N = number of species and

$$F_g = \frac{1}{m_g^*!} J_g^{m_g^*}$$

J_g is the complete partition function for a cluster with g monomers, m_g^* is the most probable distribution of cluster sizes and

$$J_1 = \frac{VZ_1}{\Lambda^3} e^{-U/kT}$$

where Λ is the thermal de Broglie wavelength. Z_1 is the partition function corresponding to the rotational and other degrees of freedom of the monomer. U is the potential energy in the absence of these degrees of freedom. Show that

$$m_g^* = J_g e^{g\mu/kT}$$

where μ = the chemical potential of a monomer in the vapor, k is the Boltzmann constant and T is the temperature.

Solution: By definition

$$\frac{-\mu_g}{kT} = \frac{\partial \ln Q}{\partial m_g} = \frac{\partial \ln F_g}{\partial m_g}$$

But

$$F_g = \frac{1}{m_g^*!} J_g^{m_g^*}$$

Taking the ℓn of both sides yields

$$\ln F_g = -m_g^* \ln m_g^* + m_g^* + m_g^* \ln J_g \qquad (1)$$

Differentiating equation (1) with respect to m_g gives

$$\frac{\partial \ln F_g}{\partial m_g^*} = -1 - \ln m_g^* + 1 + \ln J_g .$$

Also $$m_g^* = J_g \, e^{g\mu/kT}$$

Taking $\ln$ gives

$$\ln m_g^* = \ln J_g + \frac{\mu g}{kT}$$

or $$\frac{-\mu g}{kT} = \ln J_g - \ln m_g^*$$

from which

$$\ln m_g^* = J_g \, e^{\mu g/kT} .$$

Since the system is being treated as Dalton's law vapor,

$$\mu g = g\mu_1 = g\mu$$

and $$m_g^* = J_g \, e^{g\mu/kT}$$

• PROBLEM 4-7

Using the Euler-Maclaurin summation formula

$$\sum_{n=a}^{\infty} f(n) = \int_a^{\infty} f(x)dx + \frac{1}{2}f(a) - \frac{1}{12}f'(a) + \frac{1}{720}f'''(a) + \ldots,$$

evaluate the rotational partition function at high temperatures.

Solution: The rotational partition function for a diatomic molecule is given by

$$q_{rot.}(T) = \sum_{J=0}^{\infty} (2J + 1)e^{-\beta\bar{B}J(J+1)/kT}$$

where J = the rotational quantum number.

Let $\beta\bar{B}/k = \Theta$

$$\therefore \quad q_{rot.}(T) = \sum_{J=0}^{\infty} (2J + 1)e^{-\Theta_{rot}J(J+1)/T} \qquad (1)$$

The Euler-Maclaurin summation formula is

$$\sum_{J=0}^{\infty} f(J) = q_{rot} = \frac{1}{\sigma}\int_0^{\infty} f(x)dx + \frac{1}{2}f(0) - \frac{1}{12}f'(0)$$

$$+ \frac{1}{720}f'''(0) + \ldots \qquad (2)$$

where $f(J) = (2J + 1)e^{-J(J+1)\Theta_{rot}/T}$ (3)

and σ is symmetry number.

Let $a = \frac{\Theta_{rot}}{T}$. Take the ℓn of both sides of equation (3) and differentiate it to obtain

$$\ell n\ f(J) = \ell n(2J + 1) - a(J^2 + J)$$

$$\ell n\ f'(J) = 2 - a(2J + 1)a.$$

Then $\frac{f'(J)}{f(J)} = \frac{2}{2J + 1} - \frac{a(2J + 1)a}{a(J^2 + J)}$

$$\therefore\ f'(J) = \left[\frac{2}{2J+1} - \frac{(2J+1)a}{J^2+J}\right]\left[(2J+1)e^{-(J^2+J)a}\right]$$

$$= \left[2 - a(2J + 1)^2\right]e^{-(J^2+J)a}.$$

Taking natural logarithm

$$\ell n\ f'(J) = \ell n\left[2 - a(2J+1)^2\right]\ell n\ e^{-(J^2+J)a}$$

$$= \ell n\left[2 - a(2J+1)^2\right] - (J^2+J)a$$

$$\frac{f''(J)}{f'(J)} = \left[\frac{-4a(2J+1)}{2-a(2J+1)^2} - (2J+1)a\right]\left[2-a(2J+1)^2\ e^{-(J^2+J)a}\right]$$

$$\therefore\ f''(J) = \left[-4a(2J+1) - (2J+1)a\left[2-a(2J+1)^2\right]e^{-(J^2+J)a}\right]$$

$$= \left[-4a(2J+1) - 2a(2J+1) + a^2(2J+1)^3\right]e^{-(J^2+J)a}$$

$$= \left[a^2(2J+1)^3 - 6a(2J+1)\right]e^{-(J^2+J)a}$$

Taking ℓn of both sides

$$\ell n\ f''(J) = \ell n\left[a^2(2J+1)^3 - 6a(2J+1)\right]\ell n\ e^{-(J^2+J)a}$$

$$= \ell n\left[a^2(2J+1)^3 - 6a(2J+1)\right] - (J^2+J)a$$

Evaluating the third derivative

$$\frac{f'''(J)}{f''(J)} = \frac{a^3 3(2J+1)^2 \times 2 - 6a \times 2}{a^2(2J+1)^3 - 6a(2J+1)} - (2J+1)a$$

$$f'''(J) = \left[6a^2(2J+1)^2 - 12a - a^3(2J+1)^4 + 6a^2(2J+1)^2\right]e^{-(J^2+J)a}$$

$$\therefore \quad f'''(J) = \left[-a^3(2J+1)^4 + 12a^2(2J+1)^2 - 12a\right]e^{-(J^2+J)a}$$

The terms under the Euler-Maclaurin summation formula will now be evaluated. Let J = x. Thus

$$\int_0^\infty f(x)dx = \int_0^\infty (2x+1)e^{-(x^2+x)a}\,dx.$$

Let $U = x^2 + x$

$dU = (2x+1)dx$

$$\therefore \quad \int_0^\infty f(x)dx = \int_0^\infty e^{-aU}\,dU$$

$$= -\frac{1}{a}\int_0^\infty (-a)e^{-aU}\,dU$$

$$= -\frac{1}{a}e^{-aU}\Big|_{U=0}^{U=\infty}$$

$$= \frac{1}{a}$$

Also $f(0) = (1)e^0$

$= 1$

$f'(0) = \left[2 - a(1^2)\right]e^0$

$= 2 - a$

$f'''(0) = [-a^3 + 12a^2 - 12a]$

$= a[-a^2 + 12a - 12].$

Therefore from eqn (2)

$$\sum_{J=0}^{\infty} f(J) = q_r = \frac{1}{\sigma}\left[\frac{1}{a} + \frac{1}{2}(1) - \frac{1}{12}(2-a) + \frac{a}{720}(-a^2+12a-12)\right]$$

$$= \frac{1}{\sigma}\left[\frac{1}{a} + \frac{1}{2} - \frac{1}{6} + \frac{a}{12} - \frac{a^3}{720} + \frac{12a^2}{720} - \frac{12a}{720} + \ldots\right]$$

$$= \frac{1}{\sigma}\left[\frac{1}{a} + \frac{1}{3} + \frac{48a}{720} + \frac{a^2}{60} - \frac{a^3}{720} + \ldots\right]$$

$$= \frac{1}{\sigma}\left[\frac{1}{a} + \frac{1}{3} + \frac{1a}{15} + \frac{a^2}{60} - \frac{a^3}{720} + \ldots\right]$$

$$= \frac{1}{\sigma a}\left[1 + \frac{a}{3} + \frac{a^2}{15} + \frac{a^3}{60} - \frac{a^4}{720} + \ldots\right]$$

But $\quad a = \frac{\Theta_{rot}}{T}$

Therefore,

$$q_{rot} = \frac{T}{\sigma\Theta_{rot}}\left[1 + \frac{1}{3}\left(\frac{\Theta_{rot}}{T}\right) + \frac{1}{15}\left(\frac{\Theta_{rot}}{T}\right)^2 + \frac{1}{60}\left(\frac{\Theta_{rot}}{T}\right)^3 - \frac{1}{720}\left(\frac{\Theta_{rot}}{T}\right)^4 + \ldots\right]$$

For $T >> \Theta_{rot}$, then $q_{rot} = \frac{T}{\sigma\Theta_{rot}}$, which is the classical high temperature result.

THERMODYNAMIC FUNCTIONS

• PROBLEM 4-8

Calculate a) the rotational partition function q_{rot}, b) the entropy contribution from rotation and c) the rotational contribution to the heat capacity at constant volume, C_{Vr} for HD gas at 96 °K. Take Θ_r = 64 °K. d) What is the value of E in cal mole^{-1} deg^{-1} for HD at 96 °K ? e) Find the fraction of HD molecules in each of the first four rotational energy levels at 32 °K, 96 °K and 256 °K. The value of θ_{vib} is 6100 °K.

Solution: a) At low temperatures, a direct summation must be carried out in order to calculate $q_r(T)$

$$q_r(T) = \sum_{J=0}^{\infty} (2J + 1)e^{-J(J+1)\Theta_r/T} \qquad (1)$$

where Θ_r is the characteristic temperature given by

$$\Theta_r = \frac{h^2}{8\pi^2 Ik}.$$

I is the moment of inertia about the center of mass, and J is the rotational quantum number. Expanding equation (1) gives

$$q_r = 1 + 3e^{-2\Theta/T} + 5e^{-6\Theta/T} + 7e^{-12\Theta/T} + 9e^{-20\Theta/T} + \ldots$$

$$= 1 + 0.790 + 0.092 + 0.002 + 0.000015$$

$$= 1.884$$

b) $E_r = NkT^2\left(\frac{\partial \ \ell n \ q_r}{\partial T}\right)$

Let $q_r = x$. Therefore,

$$NkT^2 \frac{\partial \ \ell n \ q_r}{\partial T} = NkT^2 \frac{1}{x}\frac{dx}{dT}$$

$$= \frac{NkT^2}{q_r}\left[\frac{6\Theta_r}{T^2}e^{-2\Theta_r/T} + \frac{30\Theta_r}{T^2}e^{-6\Theta_r/T} + \frac{84\Theta_r}{T^2}e^{-12\Theta_r/T}\right]$$

$$= \frac{R}{q_r}\left(6\Theta_r e^{-2\Theta_r/T} + 30\Theta_r e^{-6\Theta_r/T} + 84\Theta_r e^{-12\Theta_r/T}\right) \qquad (2)$$

$$R = 1.987 \text{ cal/mole °K}$$

$$q_r = 1.884$$

$$\Theta_r = 64 \text{ °K}$$

Substitute these values into equation (2) and solve for E_r.

As a result, $E_r = 145.7$ cal/mole

c) $C_{Vr} = \left(\frac{\partial E}{\partial T}\right)_V$

$$= Rq_r\left(\frac{12\Theta_r^2}{T^2}e^{-2\Theta/T} + 180\,\frac{\Theta^2}{T^2}e^{-6\Theta/T} + 1008\,\frac{\Theta^2}{T^2}e^{-12\Theta/T}\right)$$

$$- R\left(6\Theta_r e^{-2\Theta_r/T} + 30\Theta_r e^{-6\Theta_r/T} + 84\Theta e^{-12\Theta_r/T}\right)$$

$$\left(6\,\frac{\Theta_r}{T^2}e^{-2\Theta_r/T} + 30\,\frac{\Theta_r}{T^2}e^{-6\Theta_r/T} + 84\,\frac{\Theta_r}{T^2}e^{-12\Theta_r/T}\right)/q_r^2$$

$$= \frac{1}{q_r^2}\left[Rq_r \frac{\Theta_r^2}{T^2}\left(12e^{-2\Theta_r/T} + 180e^{-6\Theta_r/T} + 1008e^{-12\Theta_r/T}\right)\right.$$

$$\left. - \frac{R\Theta_r^2}{T^2}\left(6e^{-2\Theta_r/T} + 30e^{-6\Theta_r/T} + 84e^{-12\Theta_r/T}\right)^2\right]$$

$$= \frac{11.3106 - 1.9068}{q^2}$$

$$= 2.65 \text{ cal/deg mole}$$

d) $E_{total} = E_{trans} + E_{rot} + E_{V_i} + E_{elec.}$ (3)

$$E_{trans.} = (3/2)NkT$$

$$= \frac{3}{2}\left(6.02\times10^{23} \text{ mole}^{-1}\right)\left(1.38\times10^{-16} \text{ erg deg}^{-1}\right)$$

$$\left(\frac{1 \text{ cal}}{4.18\times10^7 \text{ erg}}\right)(96\ °\text{K})$$

$$= 286.2 \text{ cal mole}^{-1}$$

$$E_{rot} = 145.7 \text{ cal mole}^{-1}$$

$$E_{Vi} = Nk\left(\frac{\Theta_{Vi}}{2} + \frac{\Theta_{Vi}}{\left(e^{\Theta_{Vi}/T} - 1\right)}\right)$$

The value of $\Theta_{Vi} = 6100\ °K$

$$\therefore \quad E_{Vi} = 1.987 \text{ cal mole } °\text{K}^{-1}(3050\ °\text{K})$$

$$= 6060.35 \text{ cal mole}^{-1}.$$

$$E_{elec} \simeq 0.$$

Using the above values in equation (3) gives

$$E_{tot} = (286.2 + 145.7 + 6060.35)\text{cal mole}^{-1}$$

$$= 6492.3 \text{ cal mole}^{-1}.$$

e) Fraction of HD molecules in each of the first four rotational energy levels is estimated using the Boltzmann distribution and it is given by

$$P(\varepsilon)d\varepsilon = \frac{\omega_j e^{-\varepsilon_j/kT}}{q} \qquad j = 1, \ldots, 4$$

$$= \frac{(2J+1)e^{-J(J+1)\Theta_r/T}}{q(T)}$$

The following results are tabulated as

	T = 32 °K	96 °K	256 °K
J = 0	0.948	0.531	0.230
J = 1	0.052	0.420	0.419
J = 2		0.049	0.257
J = 3			0.080

T(°K)	q(T) (°K)
32	1.055
96	1.884
256	4.345

• PROBLEM 4-9

The experimental value of the entropy of xenon as determined from calorimetric data is $S^o_{298} = 170.29 \pm 1.2 JK^{-1} mol^{-1}$ a) Calculate the entropy of xenon at 298 °K and compare with the experimental value. b) Determine the values of the thermodynamic function C^0_p, $\left(\frac{H^o}{T}\right)$ and $\left(\frac{G^o}{T}\right)$, respectively.

Solution: Xenon is a monoatomic gas, and thus $q_{rot} = q_{vib} = 1$. At low temperatures $q_{elect.}$ is also equal to 1. Therefore, if $q_{nucl.}$ can be neglected, the thermodynamic properties of xenon results from translational motion only.

Thus for 1 mole of gas,

$$Q_{trans.} = \left(\frac{1}{N!}\right) q^N_{trans} = \left(\frac{1}{N!}\right)\left[\frac{V(2\pi mkT)^{3/2}}{h^3}\right]^N$$

and $\ell n\ Q_{trans.} = -N\ \ell n\ N + N\ \ell n\ e + N\ \ell n\ q_{trans}$

$$= N\ \ell n\left[\frac{Ve}{Nh^3}(2\pi mkT)^{3/2}\right] \qquad (1)$$

For an ideal gas, $V = \frac{RT}{P}$. Substitute for V in equation (1) and differentiate with respect to T to get

$$\left[\frac{\partial \ln Q_{trans.}}{\partial T}\right]_P = \frac{5}{2}\frac{1}{T}$$

Therefore, $$H^o = RT^2\left(\frac{\partial \ln Q_{trans.}}{\partial T}\right)_P$$

$$= RT^2 \frac{5}{2}\frac{1}{T}$$

$$= \frac{5}{2}RT$$

$$= \frac{5}{2}(8.314J\ K^{-1}\ mol^{-1})(298\ °K)$$

$$= 6193.9J\ mol^{-1}.$$

The enthalpy function is thus given by

$$\left(\frac{H^o}{T}\right) = \frac{5}{2}R$$

$$= \frac{5}{2}(8.314J\ K^{-1}\ mol^{-1})$$

$$= 20.78J\ K^{-1}\ mol^{-1}.$$

The molar heat capacity function at constant pressure is given by

$$C_P^o = \left[\frac{\partial}{\partial T}(H^o)\right]_P$$

$$= \frac{\partial}{\partial T}\left(\frac{5}{2}RT\right)$$

$$= \frac{5}{2}R$$

$$= 20.78J\ K^{-1}\ mol^{-1}.$$

The entropy of xenon at P = 1 and T = 298 °K is thus given by

$$S^o_{trans.} = R \ln\left[\frac{Ve^{5/2}}{h^3 N}(2\pi mkT)^{3/2}\right]$$

$$= 169.58J\ K^{-1}\ mol^{-1}.$$

This value of $S^o_{trans.}$ agrees reasonably with the experimental value. The Gibbs free energy function is given by

$$-\left(\frac{G}{T}\right)_{trans} = -\left(\frac{H^o}{T}\right)_{trans} + S^o_{trans}$$

$$= -\frac{5}{2}R + 169.58$$

$$= 148.80 J\ K^{-1}\ mol^{-1}$$

• PROBLEM 4-10

> For the $^{35}Cl_2$ molecule, the following data is available. The equilibrium internuclear distance = 1.988×10^{-8} cm. The reduced mass = $17.4894 g\ mol^{-1}$. The fundamental vibrational frequency = $1.6947 \times 10^{13} s^{-1}$. Neglecting the electronic contributions, calculate the a) molar heat capacity at constant pressure, b) enthalpy functions, c) Gibbs free energy function, d) and the entropy of $^{35}Cl_2$ at 25 °C and 1 atm.

Solution: The translational contributions to the thermodynamic functions of an ideal gas are as follows

Internal Energy:

$$\left(\frac{U^o - U^o_0}{T}\right)_{trans} = kT\left(\frac{\partial\ \ln\ Q_{trans}}{\partial T}\right)_{V,N} = \frac{3}{2}R$$

where U^o_0 is the internal energy at standard conditions, Q is the molar partition function and R is the gas constant.

a) In the same manner, the enthalpy function and the molar heat capacity are given by

$$\left(\frac{H^o - H^o_0}{T}\right)_{trans} = \left(C^o_P\right)_{trans} = \frac{3}{2}R + R$$

$$= \frac{3}{2}(8.314 J\ K^{-1}\ mol^{-1}) + (8.314 J\ K^{-1}\ mol^{-1})$$

$$= 20.78 J\ K^{-1}\ mol^{-1}.$$

b) The Gibbs free energy function is given by

$$\left(\frac{G^o - H^o_0}{T}\right)_{trans} = -R\ \ln\left(\frac{q_{trans}}{N}\right)$$

$$= -R\ \ln\left[\frac{V(2\pi mkT)^{3/2}}{Nh^3}\right]$$

where V for an ideal gas is given as V = RT/P. N is Avogadro's number and h is Plank's constant.

$$\therefore \quad \left(\frac{G^{o}-H_{0}^{o}}{T}\right)_{trans} = -141.00 \text{J K}^{-1} \text{mol}^{-1}.$$

The rotational contributions to the enthalpy functions and molar heat capacity are

$$\left(\frac{H^{o}-H_{0}^{o}}{T}\right)_{rot} = kT\left(\frac{\partial \ \ell n \ Q_{trans}}{\partial T}\right)_{N}$$

$$= \left(C_{P}^{o}\right)_{rot}$$

$$= R$$

$$= 8.314 \text{J K}^{-1} \text{mol}^{-1}$$

The rotational contribution to the Gibbs free energy function is given by

$$\left(\frac{G^{o}-H_{0}^{o}}{T}\right)_{rot} = -R \ \ell n\left(\frac{q_{rot}}{N}\right)$$

$$q_{rot} = \frac{8\pi^{2} IkT}{h^{2}}$$

where I is the moment of inertia given by $I = \mu r^{2}$. μ is the reduced mass of the $^{35}Cl_{2}$ molecule and r is the equilibrium internuclear distance which is 1.988×10^{-8} cm

$$\therefore \quad I = 17.4894 \text{ g mol}^{-1} \times (1.988 \times 10^{-8} \text{ cm})^{2}$$

$$= 6.912 \times 10^{-15} \text{ g cm}^{2} \text{ mol}^{-1}$$

$$q_{rot} = \frac{8\pi^{2}\left[6.912)10^{-15} \text{g cm}^{2}\text{mol}^{-1}\right]\left[\frac{1\text{kg}}{1000\text{g}}\right]\left[\frac{1\text{m}}{100\text{cm}}\right]^{2}\left[1.38\times10^{-23}\text{JK}^{-1}\right]\left[298\,^{\circ}\text{K}\right]}{(6.63 \times 10^{-34} \text{ J}\cdot\text{S})^{2}}$$

$$= \frac{8\pi^{2}(6.912 \ 10^{-22}\text{kg m}^{2}\text{mol}^{-1})(4.11\times10^{-21})}{4.396 \ 10^{-67} \text{ m}^{2} \text{ kg S}^{-2}\cdot\text{S}^{2}}$$

$$= 5.102 \times 10^{26} \text{ mol}^{-1}.$$

Therefore the Gibbs free energy function becomes

$$\left(\frac{G^{o}-H_{0}^{o}}{T}\right)_{rot} = -8.314\ J\ K^{-1}\ mol^{-1}\ \ell n\left(\frac{5.102 \times 10^{26}\ mol^{-1}}{6.02 \times 10^{23}\ mol^{-1}}\right)$$

$$= -56.06\ J\ K^{-1}\ mol^{-1}.$$

The vibrational contribution to the enthalpy function is given by

$$\left(\frac{H^{o}-H_{0}^{o}}{T}\right)_{vib} = R\frac{\Theta_{vib}/T}{\left(e^{\Theta_{vib}/T} - 1\right)} \qquad (1)$$

where Θ_{vib} is the characteristic temperature of vibration given by

$$\Theta_{vib} = \frac{h\nu}{k}$$

h is Planck's constant and ν is the fundamental vibrational frequency, in this case given as $1.6947 \times 10^{13}\ s^{-1}$. For $^{35}Cl_2$ the value of

$$\frac{\Theta_{vib}}{T} = 2.74$$

From equation (1),

$$\left(\frac{H^{o}-H_{0}^{o}}{T}\right)_{vib} = 8.314\ J\ K^{-1} mol^{-1}\left[\frac{2.74}{e^{2.74} - 1}\right]$$

$$= 8.314\ J\ K^{-1}\ mol^{-1}(0.189)$$

$$= 1.573\ J\ K^{-1}\ mol^{-1}$$

The vibrational contribution to the heat capacity is given as

$$C_{vib}^{o} = R\frac{\left(\Theta_{vib}/T\right)^{2}\ e^{\Theta_{vib}/T}}{\left(e^{\Theta_{vib}/T} - 1\right)^{2}}$$

$$= 8.314\ J\ K^{-1}\ mol^{-1}\left[\frac{(7.50)(15.48)}{209.87}\right]$$

$$= 8.314\ J\ K^{-1}\ mol^{-1}(0.554)$$

$$= 4.606\ J\ K^{-1}\ mol^{-1}$$

The vibrational contribution to the Gibbs free energy function is given as

$$G_{vib} = R \ln\left(1 - e^{-\Theta_{vib}/T}\right)$$

$$= 8.314 \text{ J K}^{-1} \text{ mol}^{-1} \ln(1 - e^{-2.74})$$

$$= 8.314 \text{ J K}^{-1} \text{ mol}^{-1} \ln(0.935)$$

$$= -0.555 \text{ J K}^{-1} \text{ mol}^{-1}$$

The total contributions to the thermodynamic functions are as follows;

$$C_P^o = \left(C_P^o\right)_{trans} + \left(C_P^o\right)_{rot} + \left(C_P^o\right)_{vib}$$

$$= (20.78 + 8.31 + 4.60) \text{J K}^{-1} \text{ mol}^{-1}$$

$$= 33.66 \text{ J K}^{-1} \text{ mol}^{-1}$$

$$\left(\frac{H^o - H_0^o}{T}\right) = \left(\frac{H^o - H_0^o}{T}\right)_{trans} + \left(\frac{H^o - H_0^o}{T}\right)_{rot} + \left(\frac{H^o - H_0^o}{T}\right)_{vib}$$

$$= (20.78 + 8.31 + 1.57) \text{J K}^{-1} \text{ mol}^{-1}$$

$$= 30.66 \text{ J K}^{-1} \text{ mol}^{-1}$$

$$\left(\frac{G^o - H_0^o}{T}\right) = \left(\frac{G^o - H_0^o}{T}\right)_{trans} + \left(\frac{G^o - H_0^o}{T}\right)_{rot} + \left(\frac{G^o - H_0^o}{T}\right)_{vib}$$

$$= (-141.00 + (-56.06) - 0.55) \text{J K}^{-1} \text{ mol}^{-1}$$

$$= -191.89 \text{ J K}^{-1} \text{ mol}^{-1}$$

d) The entropy is given in terms of the thermodynamic functions. Thus

$$S^o = \left(\frac{H^o - H_0^o}{T}\right) - \left(\frac{G^o - H_0^o}{T}\right)$$

$$= 30.66 + 191.89$$

$$= 222.55 \text{ J K}^{-1} \text{ mol}^{-1}.$$

• **PROBLEM 4-11**

Give an explanation of why the heat capacity of a solid or a liquid is usually greater than that of the same substance as a gas at the same temperature.

Solution: A gas molecule has 3 translational and 2 or 3 rotational degrees of freedom, each of which contributes $\frac{1}{2}R$ to the molar heat capacity at or above (or even considerably below) room temperature. In a solid these degrees of freedom become lattice vibrations, each of which contributes R to the heat capacity at any temperature such that $kT > h\nu$, where ν is the frequency of the vibration. Since the frequency of the lattice vibrations is low, this condition is well satisfied at or above room temperature. We thus expect the molar heat capacity of a solid to exceed that of a gas by approximately 5/2R if the molecules are linear, or 3R if they are nonlinear. Similar considerations apply to a liquid. The additional heat capacity may be greater if there are strong intermolecular forces, especially hydrogen bonds, which break with absorption of heat as the temperature increases.

• **PROBLEM 4-12**

Calculate the entropy, heat capacity at constant pressure in cal $mole^{-1}$ deg^{-1} and the chemical potential, μ in cal $mole^{-1}$ for N_2 and HBr at 25 °C and 1 atm pressure. In both cases, assume the value of the degeneracy, ω_{el} of the electronic ground state to be unity. The dissociation energy at 0 °K, D_0, for N_2 is $1.5639(10^{-11})$erg and for HBr is 5.7716×10^{-12} erg.

Solution: The translational, rotational, vibrational and electronic contributions to the entropy of an ideal diatomic gas is given (respectively) by

$$\frac{S}{Nk} = \ln\left\{\left[\frac{2\pi(m_1+m_2)kT}{h^2}\right]^{3/2} \frac{Ve^{5/2}}{N}\right\} + \ln\left(\frac{Te}{\sigma\theta_r}\right) + \frac{\theta_{vi}/T}{\left(e^{(\theta_{vi}/T)}-1\right)}$$

$$- \ln\left(1 - e^{-\theta_{vi}/T}\right) + \ln \omega_{el} \qquad (1)$$

where m_1, m_2 are the respective masses of the diatomic gas, σ is the symmetry number and it is a constant for unsymmetrical and symmetrical molecules, $\theta_{vi} = \frac{h\nu}{k}$ where ν is the frequency, and V is the volume.

Assume that this is an ideal gas problem. Therefore, the ideal gas equation can be used. That is,

$$PV = NkT$$

or

$$\frac{V}{N} = \frac{kT}{P} \tag{2}$$

$$\omega_{el} = 1$$

$$h = 6.63 \times 10^{-27} \text{ erg sec}$$

$$k = 1.38 \times 10^{-16} \text{ erg K}^{-1}$$

$$e = 2.718$$

$$N = 6.023 \times 10^{23} \text{ mole}^{-1}$$

For N_2: $\theta_{rot} = 2.86\ °K$

$$\theta_{vi} = 3340\ °K$$

$$m_1 + m_2 = 2m = \frac{28}{N}$$

$$= \frac{28 \text{ g mole}^{-1}}{6.023 \times 10^{23} \text{ mole}^{-1}}$$

$$= 4.65 \times 10^{-23} \text{ g}$$

$T = 298\ °K$ and $\sigma = 2$

Combining equations (1) and (2) yields

$$\frac{S}{Nk} = \ln\left\{\left[\frac{(2\pi)\times(4.65(10^{-23})\text{g}\times 1.38(10^{-16})\text{erg K}^{-1})\times 298\ °K}{(6.63(10^{-27})\text{erg sec})^2}\right]^{3/2}\right.$$

$$\times \left[\frac{1.38(10^{-16})\text{erg K}^{-1}\times 298\ °K\times(2.718)}{1 \text{ atm}}\right]^{5/2}$$

$$\left.\times \left[\frac{82.056 \text{ cm}^3 \text{ atm}/°K \text{ mol}}{8.31433\times 10^7 \text{erg}/°K \text{ mole}}\right]\right\} +$$

$$\ln\left[\frac{(298°K)(2.718)}{(2)(2.86°K)}\right] + \left[\frac{3340°K/298°K}{(e^{3340/298}-1)}\right] - \ln\left[1 - e^{-3340/298}\right] + \ln 1$$

$$= \ln\left\{\left[1.4291\times 10^{26}\left(\frac{\text{g erg}}{\text{erg}^2 \text{ sec}^2}\right)^{3/2}\right]\times\left[5.01\times 10^{-13}\left(\frac{\text{erg}}{\text{atm}}\right)\right]\right.$$

$$\times \left[9.869\times10^{-7}\left(\frac{cm^3\ atm}{erg}\right)\right]\Bigg\} + 4.953 + 1.52\times10^{-4} + 1.356\times10^{-5}$$

$$= \ln\left\{(1.4291\times10^{26})\times(5.01\times10^{-13})\times(9.869\times10^{-7})\left(\frac{g\ erg}{erg^2\ sec^2}\right)^{3/2}\right.$$

$$\left.\times\left(\frac{erg}{atm}\right)\quad\times\left(\frac{cm^3\ atm}{erg}\right)\right\} + 4.953 + 1.52\times10^{-4} + 1.356\times10^{5}$$

$$= \ln\left\{(7.066\times10^7)\left(\frac{g}{erg\ sec^2}\right)^{3/2}\left(\frac{erg}{atm}\right)\left(\frac{cm^3\ atm}{erg}\right)\right\} +$$

$$4.953 + 1.52\times10^{-4} + 1.356\times10^{-5}$$

$$= \ln\left\{(7.066\times10^7)\left(\frac{g}{erg\ sec^2}\right)^{3/2}(cm^3)\right\} + 4.953 + 1.52\times10^{-4}$$

$$+ 1.356\times10^{-5}$$

$$= \ln\left\{(7.066\times10^7)\left(\frac{g}{\frac{g\ cm^2}{sec^2}\ sec^2}\right)^{3/2}(cm^3)\right\} + 4.953 + 1.52\times10^{-4}$$

$$+ 1.356\times10^{-5}$$

$$= \ln\left\{(7.066\times10^7)\left(\frac{1}{cm^2}\right)^{3/2}(cm^3)\right\} + 4.953 + 1.52\times10^{-4} + 1.356\times10^{-5}$$

$$= \ln\left\{(7.066\times10^7)\left(\frac{1}{cm^3}\right)(cm^3)\right\} + 4.953 + 1.52\times10^{-4} + 1.356\times10^{-5}$$

$$= \ln\{7.066\times10^7\} + 4.953 + 1.52\times10^{-4} + 1.356\times10^{-5}$$

$$= 18.073 + 4.953 + 1.52\times10^{-4} + 1.356\times10^{-5}$$

$$= 23.03$$

$$\therefore\quad S = (23.03)(N)(k)$$

$$= 23.03\times6.023\times10^{23}\times1.38\times10^{-16}$$

$$= 191.42\times10^7\ \frac{erg}{°K\ mole}$$

$$= 191.42\times10^7\ \frac{erg}{°K\ mole}\times\frac{1.98717\ cal/°K\ mole}{8.31433\ erg/°K\ mole}$$

or $\quad S = 45.76$ cal/mole

For HBr: $\sigma = 1$

$$\theta_{rot} = 12.1$$

$$\theta_{vi} = 3700$$

$$m_1 + m_2 = \frac{81}{N}$$

Combining equations (1) and (2) yields

$$\frac{S}{Nk} = 19.669 + 4.204 + 5.03 \times 10^{-5} + 4.0 \times 10^{-6}$$

$$S = 47.43 \text{ cal mole}^{-1}$$

The translational, rotational and vibrational contributions to C_V are given respectively by

$$\frac{C_V}{Nk} = \frac{3}{2} + 1 + \left(\frac{\theta_{vi}}{T}\right)^2 \frac{e^{\theta_{vi}/T}}{\left(e^{\theta_{vi}/T}-1\right)^2}$$

$\therefore$ For N_2:

$$\frac{C_V}{Nk} = 2.500 + 0.0017$$

or $C_V = 2.5017(Nk)$

$$= 4.9709 \text{ cal mole}^{-1} \text{ °K}^{-1}$$

But $C_P = C_V + R$

$$= (4.9709 + 1.987)\text{cal mole}^{-1}\text{°K}^{-1}$$

$$= 6.958 \text{ cal mole}^{-1} \text{ °K}^{-1}$$

For HBr:

$$\frac{C_V}{Nk} = 2.5 + 0.006$$

$$= 2.5006$$

$$C_V = 2.5006(Nk)$$

$$= 4.9686 \text{ cal mole}^{-1} \text{ °K}^{-1}$$

$\therefore$ $C_P = C_V + R$

$= (4.9686 + 1.987) \text{cal mole}^{-1}\ ^\circ K^{-1}$

$= 6.956 \text{ cal mole}^{-1}\ ^\circ K^{-1}$

For an ideal gas, the chemical potential μ is given by

$$\mu(P,T) = \mu^\circ(T) + kT \ \ln \frac{P}{P^\circ} \tag{3}$$

where $\mu^\circ(T)$ is the standard chemical potential.

Divide equation (3) through by kT to obtain

$$\frac{\mu}{kT} = \frac{\mu^\circ(T)}{kT} + \ln \frac{P}{P^\circ}$$

If $P = P^\circ = 1$ atm, then $\mu = \mu^\circ$.

The translational, rotational, vibrational and electronic contributions to the chemical potential are given by

$$\frac{\mu^\circ(T)}{kT} = -\ln \left[\frac{2\pi(m_1+m_2)kT}{h^2}\right]^{3/2} \frac{kT}{P} - \ln \frac{T}{\sigma\theta_r} + \frac{\theta_{vi}}{2T}$$

$$+ \ln\left(1 - e^{-\theta_{vi}/T}\right) - \frac{De}{kT} \tag{4}$$

De is related to the dissociation energy of the diatomic molecule at 0 °K, by

$$D_0 = De - \frac{1}{2}h\nu$$

But $\qquad h\nu = k\,\theta_{vi}$

Therefore, $\qquad D_0 = De - \frac{1}{2}k\theta_{vi}.$

Using the D_0 data, De value can be obtained.

For N_2: $\qquad De = 1.587 \times 10^{-11}$ erg

and for HBr: $\quad De = 6.027 \times 10^{-12}$ erg

Making substitutions into equation (4) gives

For HBr:

$$\frac{\mu^\circ(T)}{kT} = -\ln\left\{\left[\frac{2\pi\times(81 \text{ g mol}^{-1})\times 1.38(10^{-16})\text{erg K}^{-1}\times 298\ ^\circ K}{6.023(10^{23})\text{mol}^{-1}\times\left(6.63(10^{-27})\text{erg sec}\right)^2}\right]^{3/2}\right.$$

$$\times \left[\frac{1.38(10^{-16})\text{erg K}^{-1}\times 298\ ^\circ K}{1 \text{ atm}}\right]$$

$$\times \left[\frac{82.055\ \text{cm}^3\ \text{atm K}^{-1}\ \text{mol}^{-1}}{8.31433(10^7)\text{erg K}^{-1}\ \text{mol}^{-1}}\right]\Bigg\}$$

$$- \ln \frac{298}{(1)(12.0)} + \frac{3700}{(2)(298)} + \ln\left(1-e^{-3700/298}\right) - \frac{6.027\times 10^{-12}}{(1.38\times 10^{-16})(298)}$$

$$= -\ln\left\{\left[7.0288(10^{26})\left(\frac{\text{g erg}}{\text{erg}^2\ \text{sec}^2}\right)^{3/2}\right]\right.$$

$$\times \left[4.1124(10^{-14})\left(\frac{\text{erg}}{\text{atm}}\right)\right]$$

$$\times \left.\left[9.869(10^{-7})\left(\frac{\text{cm}^3\ \text{atm}}{\text{erg}}\right)\right]\right\} - 3.204 + 6.208 - 4.05\times 10^{-6} - 146.557$$

$$= -\ln\left\{(7.0288\times 10^{26})\times(4.1124\times 10^{-14})\times(9.869\times 10^{-7})\right.$$

$$\times \left.\left(\frac{\text{g erg}}{\text{erg}^2\ \text{sec}^2}\right)^{3/2}\left(\frac{\text{erg}}{\text{atm}}\right)\left(\frac{\text{cm}^3\ \text{atm}}{\text{erg}}\right)\right\}$$

$$- 3.204 + 6.208 - 4.05\times 10^{-6} - 146.557$$

$$= -\ln\left\{2.857\times 10^7(\text{cm}^{-3})(\text{cm}^3)\right\} - 3.204 + 6.208 - 4.05\times 10^{-6} - 146.557$$

$$= -17.168 - 3.204 + 6.208 - 4.05\times 10^{-6} - 146.557$$

$$\therefore\ \frac{\mu°(T)}{kT} = -17.169 - 3.204 + 6.208 - 4.05\times 10^{-6} - 146.557$$

$$= -160.72$$

$$\mu°(T) = (-160.72)(kT)$$

$$= (-160.72)(1.38\times 10^{-16}\ \text{erg K}^{-1})(298\ °\text{K})$$

$$= -6.6095\times 10^{-12}\ \text{ergs}$$

$$= (-6.6095\times 10^{-12}\ \text{ergs})\left(\frac{10^{-7}\ \text{J}}{1\ \text{erg}}\right)\left(\frac{4.184\ \text{cal mole}^{-1}}{1\ \text{J}}\right)$$

$$= -2.765\times 10^{-18}\ \text{cal/mole}$$

Remember that the ln function can only be taken of a dimensionless number. Note also that the expression involved "mixed" units of atm and erg. Hence, a conversion using the gas constants was required.

Calculate the constant-pressure heat capacity, C_p and entropy, S of ideal gaseous fluoroform, CHF_3, at 25°C and 1 atm. The following data are available

C-H bond length: 1.096 Å

C-F bond length: 1.330Å

Each of the bond angles (F-C-F and F-C-H) is very close to the tetrahedral value of 109° 28'. The vibrational wave numbers are $\omega_1 = 3,035.6\ cm^{-1}$, $\omega_2 = 1,209\ cm^{-1}$, $\omega_3 = 703.2\ cm^{-1}$, $\omega_4(2) = 1,351.5\ cm^{-1}$, $\omega_5(2) = 1,152.4\ cm^{-1}$ and $\omega_6(2) = 509.4\ cm^{-1}$. The last three modes are doubly degenerate.

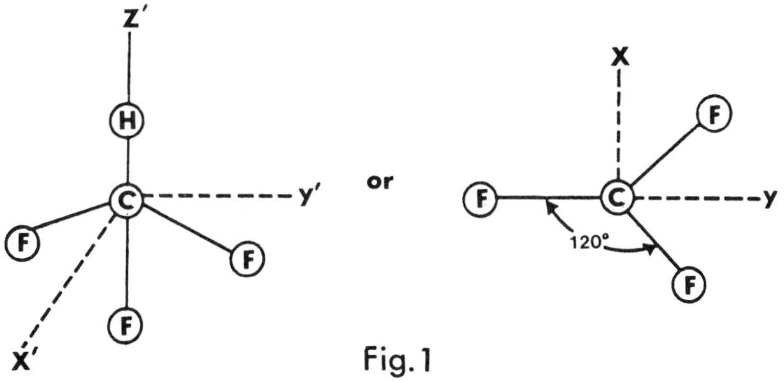

Fig. 1

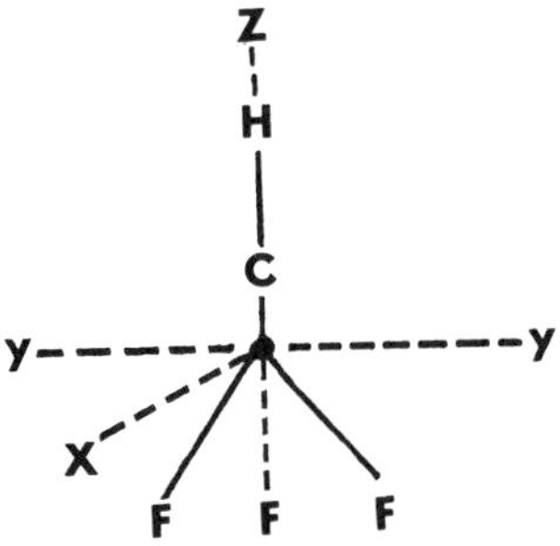

Fig. 3

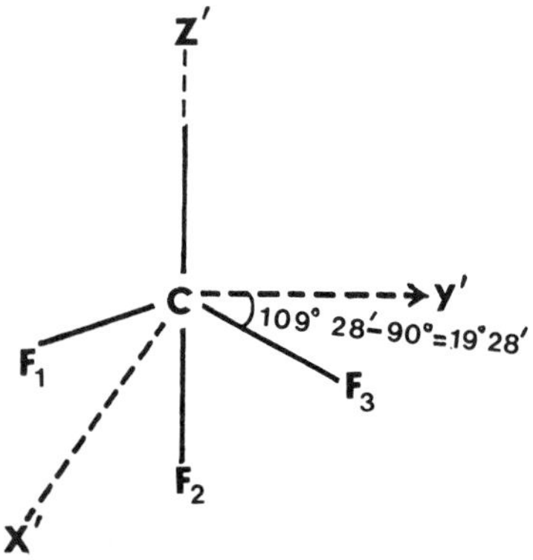

Fig. 2

Solution: Assume that the electronic contributions to entropy are negligible at the 25°C. Therefore the general partition function $Q = Q_t Q_r Q_v$. The fluoroform molecule has the structure shown in figure 1.

ROTATIONAL CONTRIBUTION:

The rotational contribution to heat capacity is given by

$$C_{P_{rot}} = (3/2)R$$

where R is the gas constant.

$$\therefore \quad C_{P_{rot}} = 3/2\ (1.987 \text{ cal mole}^{-1}\ {}^\circ K^{-1})$$

$$= 2.980 \text{ cal mole}^{-1}\ {}^\circ K^{-1}\ .$$

Find the entropy contribution by first calculating the principal moments of inertia. To do this, calculate the center of mass of the molecule.
Reducing the tetrahedral structure of the molecule as in fig. 2 to a linear molecule gives

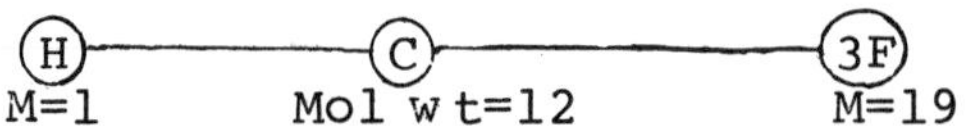

The molecule CHF_3 is a symmetric top and therefore the center of mass is located on the Z-axis and is given by Z'_{cm}

$$Z'_{cm} = \frac{1}{M} \sum_i m_i z_i .$$

Here, M is the molecular mass of CHF_3, m is the mass of the atoms and z_i is the perpendicular distance.

Therefore from the bond distances and angles

$$Z'_{cm} = \frac{1}{70 \text{ gm}} [(1.096\text{Å})(1.008) - (3 \times 19.00 \times 1.330 \sin 19°28')]$$

To convert 28' to its decimal degree equivalent use the relation $28 \text{ ft} \times \frac{1 \text{ degree}}{60 \text{ ft}} = .467$ degree. Hence 19°28' becomes 19.467°.

$$Z'_{cm} = -0.345\text{Å}$$

Now, construct the principal axes x,y,z parallel to x', y', z' and having their origin at the center of mass: The principal moments of inertia about the new principal axes are I_x, I_y, I_z. But $I_x = I_y$ because of the symmetry of the molecule. See Fig. (3).

Calculate the moment of inertia about the z and x axes;

$$I_z = \sum_i m_i (x_i^2 + y_i^2)$$

$$= \frac{19(1.330\text{ Å})^2}{6.023 \times 10^{23}} \times 10^{-16} \frac{\text{cm}^2}{\text{Å}^2} \times (2 \cos^2 19°28' \cos^2 60°$$

$$+ 2 \cos^2 19°28' \cos^2 30°$$

$$+ \cos^2 19°28')$$

$$149 \times 10^{-40} \text{ gm cm}^2$$

$$I_x = I_y = \sum_i m_i(y_i^2 + z_i^2)$$

$$= \frac{19}{6.023 \times 10^{23}} \times 10^{-16} \times [3(.345 - 1.330 \sin 19°28')^2$$

$$+ 2(1.330)^2 \cos^2 19°28' \cos^2 30°]$$

$$+ \frac{12.00}{6.023 \times 10^{23}} \times 10^{-16} \times (0.345)^2$$

$$+ \frac{1.008}{6.023 \times 10^{23}} \times 10^{-16} \times (1.096 + 0.345)^2$$

$$= 82 \times 10^{-40} \text{ g cm}^2$$

Therefore the entropy contribution per mole for rotation is given by

$$S_r = R \ln Q_{rot.} + C_{P_r}$$

$$= R \ln Q_{rot.} + (3/2)R \qquad (1)$$

where Q_{rot} is the rotational partition function given by

$$Q_{rot} = \frac{\pi^{1/2}}{\sigma}\left(\frac{8\pi^2 I_x kT}{h^2}\right)^{1/2}\left(\frac{8\pi^2 I_y kT}{h^2}\right)^{1/2}\left(\frac{8\pi^2 I_z kT}{h^2}\right)^{1/2} \qquad (2)$$

σ is the degree of freedom, I_x, I_y, I_z are the principle moments of inertia and h is Planck's constant.
For these molecules, $\sigma = 3$.
From equation (2)

$$Q_{rot} = \frac{\pi^{1/2}}{3}\left[\frac{8\pi^2(82\times10^{-40})(1.38\times10^{-16})(298°K)}{\left(6.626 \times 10^{-27}\right)^2}\right]$$

$$\left[\frac{8\pi^2(149\times10^{-40})(1.38\times10^{-16})(298°K)}{\left(6.626 \times 10^{-27}\right)^2}\right]^{1/2}$$

$$= 16030.5$$

From equation (1)

$$S_{rot} = 1.987 \text{ cal mole}^{-1} \text{ °K}^{-1} \ \ell n\ 16030.5$$

$$+ 3/2(1.987 \text{ cal mole}^{-1} \text{ °K}^{-1})$$

$$= 22.2 \text{ cal mole}^{-1} \text{ °K}^{-1}$$

TRANSLATIONAL CONTRIBUTION: The heat capacity contribution per mole is given by

$$C_{P_{(t)}} = \frac{5}{2}R$$

$$= \frac{5}{2}(1.987 \text{ cal mole}^{-1} \text{ °K}^{-1})$$

$$= 4.967 \text{ cal mole}^{-1} \text{ °K}^{-1}$$

Therefore, the entropy contribution per mole is given by

$$S_{trans} = R\ \ell n\ Q_{trans.} + \frac{5}{2}R \qquad (3)$$

But $$Q_{trans.} = \left(\frac{2\pi mkT}{h^2}\right)^{3/2} V$$

where V is the volume given by

$$V = \frac{RT}{PN}.$$

Consequently, equation (3) becomes

$$S_{trans} = R\ \ell n\left[\left(\frac{2\pi mkT}{h^2}\right)^{3/2} \frac{RT}{PN}\right] + \frac{5}{2}R \qquad (4)$$

$$= 1.987\ \ell n\left[\frac{2\pi(70)(1.38\times10^{-16})(298)}{(6.023\times10^{23})(6.626\times10^{-27})^2}\right]^{3/2}$$

$$\times \left[\frac{(82.05)(298)}{1(6.023\times10^{23})}\right] + \frac{5}{2}(1.987)$$

$$= 38.6 \text{ cal mole}^{-1} \text{ K}^{-1}$$

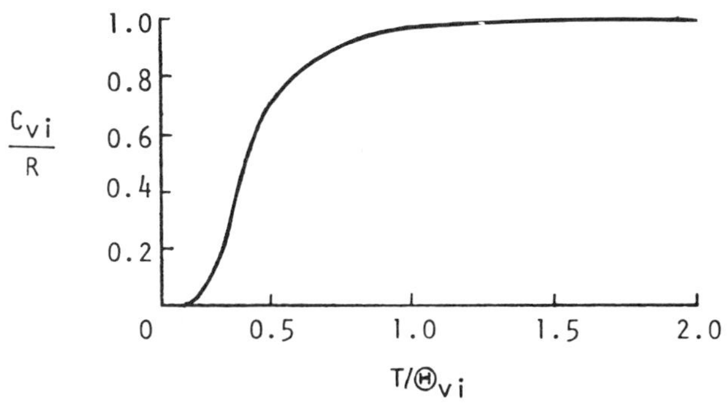

Vibrational contribution to heat capacity: as $T/\Theta_{vi} \to \infty, C_{vi} \to R$.

Fig. 4

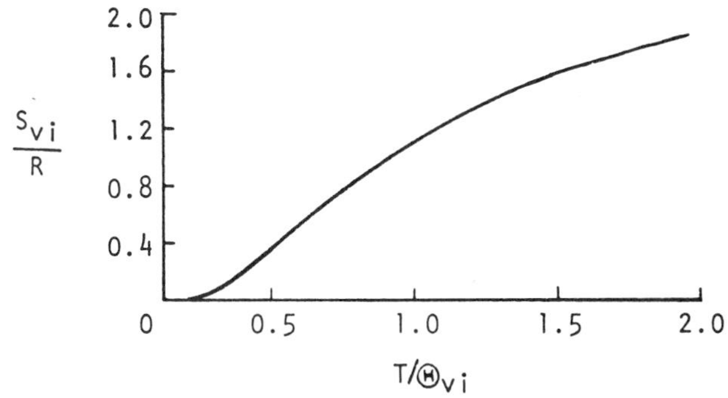

Vibrational contribution to entropy: as $T/\Theta_{vi} \to \infty, S_{vi} \to \infty$.

Fig. 5

VIBRATIONAL CONTRIBUTION: The entropy contribution is given by

$$S_{Vi} = \sum_{i=1}^{6} \left[\frac{Nk\ \Theta}{T\left(e^{\Theta_{vi}/T} - 1\right)} - Nk\left(\ell n\ 1 - e^{-\Theta_{vi}/T}\right) \right]$$

where Θ is the vibrational characteristic temperature given as

$$\Theta_{vib} = \frac{hc}{k}\omega_{vi} \qquad (5)$$

$$= 1.439\omega_{vi}$$

ω_{vi} represents the vibrational wave numbers.

Graphs of $\frac{C_{V_{trans}}}{R}$ vs $\frac{T}{\Theta_{vi}}$ and $\frac{S_{vi}}{R}$ vs $\frac{T}{\theta_{vi}}$ are plotted in fig. 4 and fig. 5 respectively and the entropy contribution S_{vt} and the specific contribution C_{V_i} can be calculated using the wave numbers.

From equation (5)

$$\Theta_{vi} = \frac{hc}{k}\omega_{vi}$$

For the first wave number

$$\Theta_{V_1} = \frac{hc}{k}\omega_1$$

$$= 1.44(3035.6)$$

$$= 4.37 \times 10^3$$

$$\therefore \quad \frac{T}{\Theta_{V_1}} = \frac{298}{4.37 \times 10^3}$$

$$= 0.068$$

$$\omega_2 = 1{,}209 \text{ cm}^{-1}$$

$$\Theta_{V_2} = 1.44(1209)$$

$$= 1740.9$$

$$\therefore \quad \frac{T}{\Theta_{V_2}} = \frac{298}{1740.9}$$

$$= 0.171$$

Similarly $\quad \frac{T}{\Theta_{V_3}} = 0.294$

$$\frac{T}{\Theta_{V_4}} = 0.154$$

$$\frac{T}{\Theta_{V_5}} = 0.180$$

and $\quad \frac{T}{\Theta_{V_6}} = 0.407.$

Now. using figs 4 and 5 and values of the reduced vibrational temperatures $\frac{T}{\Theta_{vi}}$, the different values of $C_{P_{vi}}$ and S_{Vi} the contributions to thermodynamic properties, can be read off the graph. They are tabulated as follows

$T^*_{vi} = \frac{T}{\Theta_{vi}}$	$\frac{C_{vi}}{R}$	$\frac{S_{vi}}{R}$
0.068	0	0
0.171	0.098	0.011
0.294	0.50	0.173
0.154	0.135	0.010
0.180	0.251	0.060
0.407	0.130	0.531
	1.114	0.786

T^*_{vi} is the reduced vibrational temperature. The total heat capacity and entropy are:

$$\text{Total } C_P = C_{P_{rot.}} + C_{P_{trans.}} + C_{Vi}$$

$$= (2.980 + 4.967 + 1.114) \text{ cal mole}^{-1}\ {}^\circ K^{-1}$$

$$= 9.06 \text{ cal mole}^{-1}\ {}^\circ K^{-1}$$

and $\text{Total } S = S_{rot.} + S_{trans.} + S_{vi}$

$$= (22.2 + 38.6 + 0.786) \text{ cal mole}^{-1}\ {}^\circ K^{-1}$$

$$= 61.58 \text{ cal mole}^{-1}\ {}^\circ K^{-1}$$

• PROBLEM 4-14

CO_2 is a linear molecule with moment of inertia, $I = 71.67 \times 10^{-40}$ g cm^2, and four degrees of vibrational freedom corresponding to wave numbers of $\bar{\nu}_1 = 2349$ cm^{-1}, $\bar{\nu}_2 = 1320$ cm^{-1} and $\bar{\nu}_3 = \bar{\nu}_4 = 667$ cm^{-1} (doubly degenerate). Assume that CO_2 is an ideal gas, calculate the heat capacity at constant volume, C_V, per mole of CO_2 at intervals of 200 °K from 0 to 1000 °K.

Solution: The heat capacity at constant volume is defined as

$$C_V = \left(\frac{\partial U}{\partial T}\right)_V \tag{1}$$

where U is the internal energy given by

$$U = NkT^2\left(\frac{\partial \ \ell n \ Q}{\partial T}\right)_V \tag{2}$$

N is the Avogadro's number and Q is the molar vibrational

partition function. But

$$Q_{vib} = \left(1 - e^{-hc\bar{\nu}/kT}\right)^{-1} \quad (3)$$

where h is Planck's constant, c is the speed of light and $\bar{\nu}$ is the wave number. Let

$$\theta = \frac{hc\bar{\nu}}{k} \quad (4)$$

then, equation (3) can be written as

$$Q_{vib} = \left(1 - e^{-\theta/T}\right)^{-1}$$

or $\quad \ell n\, Q_{vib} = -\ell n(1 - e^{-\theta/T}).$

Equation (2) then becomes

$$U = \frac{Nk\theta}{e^{\theta/T} - 1}$$

The expression for the heat capacity in equation (1) changes to

$$C_V = \frac{R\left(\frac{\theta}{T}\right)^2 e^{\theta/T}}{\left(e^{\theta/T} - 1\right)^2} \quad (5)$$

From equation (4),

$$\theta = \frac{(6.63\times10^{-34}\text{J s})(3\times10^{10}\text{ cm s}^{-1})\bar{\nu}}{(1.38\times10^{-23}\text{ J K}^{-1})}$$

$$= 1.438\text{ cm °K }\bar{\nu} \quad (6)$$

The heat capacity has contributions from the three modes of motion namely translational, rotational and vibrational modes, neglecting the electronic contributions. Therefore

$$C_V = C_{V,trans.} + C_{V,rot.} + C_{V,\,vib.}$$

$$= C_{V,trans.} + C_{V,rot.} + C_V(2349\text{ cm}^{-1}) + C_V(1320\text{ cm}^{-1})$$

$$+ 2C_V(667\text{ cm}^{-1}) \quad (7)$$

The translational contributions to the molar heat capacity is given by equations (1) and (2)

$$C_{V,trans.} = \left(\frac{\partial U_{trans.}}{\partial T}\right)_V$$

$$= \frac{\partial}{\partial T}\left[kT^2\left(\frac{\partial \ \ell n \ Q_{trans.}}{\partial T}\right)_V\right]$$

$$= \frac{\partial}{\partial T}\left(\frac{3}{2} RT\right)$$

$$= \frac{3}{2}R$$

$$= \frac{3}{2}\left(8.314 \text{ J } {}^\circ K^{-1}\right)$$

$$= 12.47 \text{ J}\cdot K^{-1}$$

The rotational contributions to the molar heat capacity is given by

$$C_{V,rot.} = \left(\frac{\partial \ U_{rot.}}{\partial T}\right)_V$$

But $$U_{rot.} = NkT^2\left(\frac{\partial \ \ell n \ q_{rot.}}{\partial T}\right)_N$$

and $$q_{rot.} = \frac{8\pi^2 IkT}{\sigma h^2} .$$

$$\therefore \quad U_{rot.} = RT^2\left\{\left[\frac{\partial \ \ell n\left(8\pi^2 Ik/\sigma h^2\right)}{\partial T}\right] + \frac{\partial \ \ell n \ T}{\partial T}\right\}$$

$$= RT^2 \ \frac{1}{T}$$

$$= RT$$

and $$C_{V,rot.} = \left(\frac{\partial (RT)}{\partial T}\right)_V$$

$$= R$$

$$= 8.314 \text{ J}\cdot K^{-1}$$

The four degrees of vibrational freedom in CO_2 will now be used in calculating q_{vib} at intervals of 200 °K from 0 to 1000 °K. For wave number $\bar{\nu}_1 = 2349 \text{ cm}^{-1}$ and from equation (6)

$$\theta = (1.438 \text{ cm °K})(2349 \text{ cm}^{-1})$$

$$= 3380 \text{ °K}$$

Using equation (5) with values of T = 0, 200, 400, 600, 800 and 1000 °K, the corresponding values of C_V are tabulated as follows:

T	0	200	400	600	800	1000
C_V $J \cdot K^{-1}$	0	1.09×10^{-4}	0.127	0.950	2.235	3.466

For wave number $\bar{\nu}_2 = 1320 \text{ cm}^{-1}$

$$\theta = (1.438 \text{ cm °K})(1320 \text{ cm}^{-1})$$

$$\theta = 1899 \text{ °K}$$

and the corresponding table is

T	0	200	400	600	800	1000
C_V $J \cdot K^{-1}$	0	0.0564	1.653	3.833	5.304	6.209

For wave number, $\bar{\nu}_3 = 667 \text{ cm}^{-1}$

$$\theta = (1.438 \text{ cm °K})(667 \text{ cm}^{-1})$$

$$= 959.7 \text{ °K}.$$

The corresponding table is

T, °K	0	200	400	600	800	1000
C_V $J \cdot K^{-1}$	0	1.604	5.225	6.746	7.384	7.705

Using equation (7)

at T = 200 °K ,

$$C_V = 12.47 + 8.314 + 1.09 \times 10^{-4} + 0.0564 + 2(1.604) \text{J K}^{-1}$$

$$= 24.04 \text{ J K}^{-1}.$$

At T = 400 °K ,

$$C_V = 12.47 + 8.314 + 0.127 + 1.653 + 2(5.225) \text{J K}^{-1}$$

$$= 33.07 \text{ J K}^{-1}$$

Similarly at T = 600 °K ,

$C_V = 39.06 \text{ J K}^{-1}$

At $T = 800\ °K$,

$C_V = 43.09 \text{ J K}^{-1}$

and at $T = 1000\ °K$

$C_V = 45.87 \text{ J K}^{-1}$

• PROBLEM 4-15

Consider an ideal monatomic gas at temperature T and volume V, show that the entropy of one mole of this gas is given by

$$S = R \ln\left[Q_i \frac{(2\pi mkT)^{3/2}}{N h^3} V\right] + \frac{5}{2}R$$

where Q_i represents the internal partition function. State all assumptions. This expression is known as the Sackur-Tetrode Equation.

Solution: The expression for the internal energy U measured from a ground state energy U_0, in terms of the partition function. Q is given on a molar basis by

$$U = RT^2\left(\frac{\partial \ln Q}{\partial T}\right)_{V,N} \qquad (1)$$

where N is the number of moles. Also, in terms of the partition function the Helmholtz free energy A, is given by

$$A = -kT \ln Q.$$

But $$A = U - TS$$

or $$TS = U - A$$

Thus, $$S = \frac{U - A}{T}$$

$$= \frac{kT^2\left(\frac{\partial \ln Q}{\partial T}\right)_{V,N} + kT \ln Q}{T}$$

$$= kT\left(\frac{\partial \ln Q}{\partial T}\right)_{V,N} + k \ln Q \qquad (2)$$

When molecules are in a crystal, they are said to be localized because they can be identified as a, b, ..., but if the molecules are in a gas they are not localized and are said to be indistinguishable and non localized. For localized molecules a, b, ..., their molecular partition functions are identical if the molecules are identical, and for N independent molecules the canonical ensemble partition function is given by

$$Q = q^N$$

where q is the molecular partition function. For non-localized molecules the partition function is given by

$$Q = \frac{1}{N!} q^N \tag{3}$$

But the molecular, partition function is given by

$$q = q_{trans.} Q_i$$

where Q_i = the internal partition function.
Also,

$$q_{trans.} = \frac{V}{\Lambda^3}$$

where $$\Lambda^3 = \left[\frac{h^2}{2\pi mkT}\right]^{3/2} \tag{4}$$

Therefore, from equation (2)

$$Q = \frac{1}{N!} \frac{V^N}{\Lambda^{3N}} Q_i^N(T).$$

Taking ℓn of both sides gives

$$\ell n\ Q = -N\ \ell n\ N + N + N\ \ell n\ V - 3N\ \ell n\ \Lambda + N\ \ell n\ Q_i(T)$$

From the above equation

$$\left(\frac{\partial\ \ell n\ Q}{\partial T}\right)_{V,N} = -3N \frac{\frac{\partial\Lambda}{\partial T}}{\Lambda} + \frac{N \frac{\partial}{\partial T}(Q_i)}{Q_i(T)} \tag{5}$$

From equation (3),

$$\Lambda = \frac{h}{\sqrt{2\pi mk}} T^{-1/2}$$

and $$\frac{\partial\Lambda}{\partial T} = -\frac{1}{2} \frac{h}{\sqrt{2\pi mk}} T^{-3/2}$$

$$= -\frac{1}{2} \frac{h}{\sqrt{2\pi mkT}} T^{-1}$$

$$= - \frac{1}{2}\Lambda T^{-1}.$$

From equation (4)

$$\left(\frac{\partial \ \ell n \ Q}{\partial T}\right)_{V,N} = \frac{3}{2}NT^{-1} + \frac{N\frac{\partial}{\partial T}(Q_i)_{V,N}}{Q_i(T)}$$

Therefore, equation (2) can now be written as

$$S = kT\left[\frac{3}{2}\frac{N}{T} + N\frac{\frac{\partial}{\partial T}(Q_i)}{Q_i}\right] + k \ [-N \ \ell n \ N + N + N \ \ell n \ V$$

$$-3N \ \ \ell n \ V + N \ \ell n \ Q_i]$$

$$= \frac{3}{2}R + \frac{RT\frac{\partial}{\partial T}(Q_i)}{Q_i} - R \ \ell n \ N + R + R \ \ell n \ V - 3R \ \ell n \ \Lambda^3$$

$$+ R \ \ell n \ Q_i$$

$$= \frac{5}{2}R + R \ \ell n\left[\frac{VQ_i}{N\Lambda^3}\right] + \frac{RT\frac{\partial}{\partial T}(Q_i)}{Q_i}$$

$$= R \ \ell n\left[Q_i\frac{(2\pi mkT)^{3/2}}{Nh^3}V\right] + \frac{5}{2}R + \frac{RT\frac{\partial}{\partial T}Q_i}{Q_i}$$

The last term $\frac{RT\frac{\partial}{\partial T}(Q_i)}{Q_i}$ is assumed to be negligible

$$\therefore \quad S = R \ \ell n\left[Q_i\frac{(2\pi mkT)^{3/2}}{Nh^3}V\right] + \frac{5}{2}R$$

The following assumptions were made in deriving the expression for S.

a) $\frac{\partial}{\partial T}Q_i$ is small.

b) The translational partition function is classical.

Spectroscopic studies give the moments of inertia of water molecule as $I_A = 1.022 \times 10^{-40}$ g cm^2, $I_B = 1.918 \times 10^{-40}$ g cm^2, $I_C = 2.940 \times 10^{-40}$ g cm^2 and the vibrational frequencies as $V_1 = 3657$ cm^{-1}, $V_2 = 1595$ cm^{-1} and $V_3 = 3756$ cm^{-1}. Calculate the entropy of water vapor at a temperature of 25 °C and a pressure of 1 atm, given that the symmetry number of the molecule is 2 and assuming ideal gas conditions. Discuss why the calorimetric value of entropy $\frac{S}{R} = 22.29 \pm 0.03$ is less than the calculated value.

Solution: The molar partition function for an assembly of independent indistinguishable molecules is given by

$$Q = \frac{q^N}{N!}$$

where q is the individual molecular partition function given in terms of the translational, rotational, vibrational and electronic contributions. That is

$$q = q_{trans.} q_{rot.} q_{vi.} q_{elec.}$$

Also $$Q = Q_{trans.} Q_{rot.} Q_{vi.} Q_{elec.}$$

The molar translational contribution to entropy is given by

$$S_{trans.} = Nk \,\ell n \left[\frac{V}{N\Lambda^3}\right] + \frac{5}{2} Nk \tag{1}$$

where $$\Lambda = \frac{h}{(2\pi mkT)^{1/2}} \tag{2}$$

h is the Planck's constant and m is mass of the water molecule given by

$$m = \frac{M}{N}$$

$$= \frac{18 \text{ gm mole}^{-1}}{6.02\times 10^{23} \text{ mole}^{-1}}$$

$$= 2.99 \times 10^{-23} \text{ gm}$$

Since ideality is assumed,

$$V = \frac{RT}{P}$$

$$= \frac{(8.314 \text{ N m °K}^{-1}\text{mole}^{-1})(298 \text{ °K})}{101325 \text{ N m}^{-2}}$$

$$= (0.02445 \text{ m}^3)\left(\frac{100 \text{ cm}}{1 \text{ m}}\right)^3$$

$$= 2.445 \times 10^4 \text{ cm}^3 \text{ mole}^{-1}$$

From equation (2),

$$\Lambda = \frac{6.63 \times 10^{-27} \text{ erg sec}}{\left[2\pi(2.990\times10^{-23} \text{ g})(1.38\times10^{-16} \text{ erg °K}^{-1})(298 \text{ °K})\right]^{1/2}}$$

$$= 2.38 \times 10^{-9} \frac{\text{erg sec}}{(\text{g erg})^{1/2}} = 2.38 \times 10^{-9} \frac{\text{erg sec}}{\left(\text{g} \frac{\text{g cm}^2}{\text{sec}^2}\right)^{1/2}}$$

$$= 2.38 \times 10^{-9} \frac{\frac{\text{g cm}^2}{\text{sec}^2}\text{sec}}{\text{g} \frac{\text{cm}}{\text{sec}}}$$

$$= 2.38 \times 10^{-9} \text{ cm.}$$

From equation (1)

$$\frac{S_{trans.}}{Nk} = \frac{S_{trans.}}{R} = \ell n\left[\frac{2.445\times10^4 \text{ cm}^3 \text{ mole}^{-1}}{(6.02\times10^{23} \text{ mole}^{-1})(2.38\times10^{-9} \text{ cm})^3}\right] + \frac{5}{2}$$

$$= 14.915 + \frac{5}{2}$$

$$= 17.415$$

The rotational contribution to entropy is given by

$$\frac{S_{rot}}{R} = \ell n\, Q_{rot} + \frac{3}{2} \tag{3}$$

where $$Q_{rot} = \frac{\pi^{1/2}}{\sigma}\left(\frac{T^3}{\theta_A\theta_B\theta_C}\right)^{1/2} \tag{4}$$

Here σ is the symmetry number and θ is the characteristic temperature. For substance A,

$$\theta_A = \frac{h^2}{8\pi^2 k\, I_A}$$

where I is moment of inertia

$$\therefore \theta_A = \frac{(6.63 \times 10^{-27} \text{ ergsec})^2}{8\pi^2(1.38\times10^{-16} \text{ erg °K}^{-1})(1.022\times10^{-40} \text{ g cm}^2)}$$

$$= 39.4 \text{ °K.}$$

For substance B,

$$\theta_B = \frac{h^2}{8\pi^2 k\ I_B}$$

$$= \frac{(6.63\times10^{-27} \text{ ergsec})^2}{8\pi^2(1.38\times10^{-16} \text{ erg °K}^{-1})(1.918\times10^{-40} \text{ g cm}^2)}$$

$$= 20.99 \text{ °K.}$$

Similarly,

$$\theta_C = \frac{h^2}{8\pi^2 k\ I_C}$$

$$= \frac{(6.63 \times 10^{-27} \text{ ergsec})^2}{8\pi^2(1.38\times10^{-16} \text{ erg °K}^{-1})(2.940\times10^{-40} \text{ g cm}^2)}$$

$$= 13.69 \text{ °K}$$

From equation (4) with $\sigma = 2$,

$$Q_{rot} = \frac{\pi^{1/2}}{2}\left[\frac{(298 \text{ °K})^3}{(39.4)(20.99)(13.69)}\right]^{1/2}$$

$$= 42.85$$

From equation (3)

$$\frac{S_{rot}}{R} = \ell n\ 42.85 + \frac{3}{2}$$

$$= 5.258$$

The vibrational contribution to entropy is given by

$$\frac{S_{vi}}{R} = \sum_{i=1}^{3} \frac{\theta_i/T}{e^{\theta_i/T}-1} - \ell n\left(1 - e^{-\theta_i/T}\right) \qquad (5)$$

where $\theta_i = \frac{h\nu_i}{k}$,

and ν is the frequency given by

$$\nu_i = cVi$$

where c is the speed of light and Vi is the vibrational frequency. Therefore

$$\theta_i = \frac{hcVi}{k}$$

$$= \frac{(6.63\times 10^{-27}\text{ erg sec})(3\times 10^{10}\text{ cm s}^{-1})}{1.38 \times 10^{-16}\text{ ergs }^\circ K^{-1}} Vi$$

$$= 1.438 \text{ cm }^\circ K\, Vi$$

$V_1 = 3657\text{ cm}^{-1}$, $V_2 = 1595\text{ cm}^{-1}$ and $V_3 = 3756\text{ cm}^{-1}$

$$\therefore \quad \theta_1 = 1.438\ (3657\text{ cm}^{-1})$$

$$= 5261.7\ ^\circ K.$$

Similarly,

$$\theta_2 = 2294.9$$

and $$\theta_3 = 5404.1$$

From equation (5)

$$\frac{S_{Vi}}{R} = \sum_{i=1}^{3} \frac{\theta_i/T}{e^{\theta_i/T}-1} - \ell n\left(1 - e^{-\theta_i/T}\right)$$

$$= \frac{\theta_1/T}{e^{\theta_1/T}-1} - \ell n\left(1 - e^{-\theta_1/T}\right) + \frac{\theta_2/T}{e^{\theta_2/T}-1} - \ell n\left(1 - e^{-\theta_2/T}\right)$$

$$+ \frac{\theta_3/T}{e^{\theta_3/T}-1} - \ell n\left(1 - e^{-\theta_3/T}\right)$$

$\frac{\theta_1}{T} = \frac{5261.7\ ^\circ K}{298\ ^\circ K} = 17.657$, $\quad \frac{\theta_2}{T} = \frac{2294.9\ ^\circ K}{298\ ^\circ K} = 7.701$

$$\frac{\theta_3}{T} = \frac{5404.1\ ^\circ K}{298\ ^\circ K} = 18.135$$

$$\frac{S_{Vi}}{R} = 4.004\times 10^{-7} + 3.3937\times 10^{-3} + 2.5462\times 10^{-7}$$

$$\frac{S_{Vi}}{R} = 0.004$$

Assume $\frac{S_{elec.}}{R} \simeq 0$

Therefore $\frac{S_{total}}{R} = 1/R \left[S_{trans.} + S_{rot.} + S_{Vi} \right]$

$$= (17.415 + 5.258 + 0.004)$$

$$= 22.677.$$

The argument for the difference between the calculated and calorimetric values of entropy is as follows.

Ice has oxygen atoms tetrahedrally situated with a hydrogen atom in between each O-O position of the tetrahedron. Each water molecule has two hydrogens and therefore two possible orientations with respect to the rest of the crystal. With N molecules, there are 2^{2N} possible configurations. However only a few are acceptable with respect to possible species.

1 way for 4H to be close to O => $(OH_4)^{+2}$

4 ways for 3H to be close to O => $(OH_3)^{+}$

6 ways for 2H to be close to O => OH_2

4 ways for 1H to be close to O => OH^{-}

1 way for no H to be close to O => O^{-2}

16 total ways but only six yield for H_2O molecule.

Therefore, fraction of ways acceptable $= \frac{6}{16} = \frac{3}{8}$ and total acceptable ways $= \frac{3^{2N}}{8} \times 2^{2N}$

$$= \left(\frac{3}{2}\right)^{N}$$

$$= \Omega$$

But from Boltzmann's formula

$$S = kN \ln \Omega$$

and $\frac{S}{R} = \ln \frac{3}{2}$

$$= 0.41$$

Therefore the calorimetric value with correction is

$$\frac{S}{R} = (22.29 \pm 0.03) + 0.41$$

$$= 22.70 \pm 0.03$$

and $$\frac{S}{R} = 22.68$$

which is now comparable with the calculated value.

• PROBLEM 4-17

In the vapor state the atoms of thallium have a doublet ground state of energy separation $S_{1/2} - S_{3/2}$ equal to $\varepsilon/k = 11{,}200$ °K. Calculate the entropy of thallium vapor at 877 °K and 1 atm. Compare it with the value of 203 ± 1 J mole^{-1} K^{-1} obtained by integrating the calorimetric data and reducing the value to the standard atmospheric pressure. $\omega_{e_1} = 2$ and $\omega_{e_2} = 4$.

Solution: If N molecules in a gas could be identified, they could be arranged N! ways between the N different microstates that they happen to occupy. Therefore, the canonical ensemble partition function calculated, which assumes that the molecules are distinguishable, yields too large a value by a factor of N!. Consequently, for non-localized subsystems,

$$Q = \frac{1}{N!} q^N$$

where Q = molar partition function and $q = q_{trans} q_{elec.}$ = individual molecular partition function. By definition,

$$q_{trans} = \frac{V}{\Lambda^3}$$

where $$\Lambda = \frac{h}{(2\pi mkT)^{1/2}}$$

$$= \frac{(6.63 \times 10^{-27} \text{ erg sec})}{\left[2\pi\left(\frac{204.37 \text{ g mole}^{-1}}{6.02\times10^{23} \text{ mole}^{-1}}\right)(1.38\times10^{-16} \text{ erg °K}^{-1})(877 \text{ °K})\right]^{1/2}}$$

$= 4.124 \times 10^{-10}$ cm.

From the ideal gas law

$$V = \frac{RT}{P}$$

$$= \frac{(8.314\ \mathrm{N\,m}\ {}^{\circ}\mathrm{K}^{-1}\ \mathrm{mole}^{-1})(298\ {}^{\circ}\mathrm{K})}{101325\ \mathrm{N\,m}^{-2}} \left(\frac{100\ \mathrm{cm}}{1\ \mathrm{m}}\right)^3$$

$$= 7.198 \times 10^4\ \mathrm{cm}^3/\mathrm{mole}$$

$$q_{elec} = \omega_{e_1} + \omega_{e_2}\, e^{-\varepsilon_{e_2}/kT}$$

where ω_e = the degeneracy of the electronic ground state.

$$q_{elec} = 2 + 4e^{-11200/877}$$

$$= 2 + 0.00001137$$

$$\simeq 2.$$

The expression for the molar entropy is given by

$$S = Nk\ \ln\left[\frac{Ve^{5/2}\Omega e_1}{\Lambda^3 N}\right]$$

where $\Omega e_1 = 2$ = the first fold degenerate of the electronic ground state, normally the only electronic state thermally accessible.

$$\therefore\quad S = 8.317\times10^7\ \frac{\mathrm{erg}}{\mathrm{mole}\ {}^{\circ}\mathrm{K}} \quad \times$$

$$\ln\left[\frac{(7.198\times10^4\ \mathrm{cm}^3\ \mathrm{mole}^{-1})e^{5/2}(2)}{(4.124\times10^{-10}\ \mathrm{cm})^3(6.02\times10^{23}\ \mathrm{mole}^{-1})}\right]$$

$$= 2.03 \times 10^9\ \mathrm{erg}\quad \mathrm{mole}^{-1}\ {}^{\circ}\mathrm{K}^{-1}$$

$$= 203.3\ \mathrm{J}\ \mathrm{mole}^{-1}\ {}^{\circ}\mathrm{K}^{-1}$$

This result is within the experimental error of the calorimetric data (203 $\pm$ 1 J mole^{-1} °K^{-1}).

• PROBLEM 4-18

Consider the reaction

$$I_2 \rightarrow 2I$$

at 1000 °K and 1 atm. The fundamental vibration frequency $\bar{\nu}$ of I_2 is 214.4 cm^{-1}, and the internuclear distance is 0.2667 nm. Calculate the equilibrium constant K_P for the reaction if the ground state of I is a doublet $^2P_{3/2,1/2}$ with a separation of 7603 cm^{-1}. The dissociation energy of I_2 is 1.542 eV.

Solution: For the dissociation of $I_2(g)$ into $2I(g)$, the equilibrium constant expression can be written in the form

$$K_P = \frac{[q°(I)]^2}{[q°(I_2)]N} \exp(-\Delta\varepsilon_0°/kT) \qquad (1)$$

where q° is the partition function given by

$$q° = q_{trans.} q_{rot.} q_{vi.} q_{elec.}$$

$$\therefore \quad K_P = \frac{[q_{trans.}(I)]^2}{[q_{trans.}(I_2)]N} q_{rot} q_{vi} q_{elec} \exp(-\Delta\varepsilon_0/kT) \qquad (2)$$

The translational partition function is

$$\frac{[q_{trans}(I)]^2}{[q_{trans}(I_2)]N} = \left(\frac{2\pi kT}{h^2}\right)^{3/2} \frac{m_I^3}{m_{I_2}^{3/2}} \frac{RT}{PN} \qquad (3)$$

where h = Planck's constant, m is the mass and N is Avogadro's number. The mass of I_2 is twice the mass of I. Therefore,

$$m_{I_2} = 2m_I$$

or $\quad m_I = \frac{1}{2} m_{I_2}$

$$= \frac{\frac{1}{2}(253.8 \text{ g mol}^{-1})}{6.02 \times 10^{23} \text{ mol}^{-1}}$$

$$= 2.108 \times 10^{-22} \text{ g}$$

$$m_{I_2} = 2(2.108 \times 10^{-22}\ g)$$

$$= 4.216 \times 10^{-22}\ g$$

Using equation (3) gives

$$q_{trans} = \left[\frac{2\pi(1.38\times10^{-16}\ erg/°K)(1000\ °K)}{(6.63 \times 10^{-27}\ ergsec)^2}\right]^{3/2}$$

$$\times \left[\frac{(2.108\times10^{-22}\ g)^3}{(4.216\times10^{-22}\ g)^{3/2}}\right]\left[\frac{(82.06\ cc\ atm\ K^{-1})(1000\ °K)}{(1\ atm)(6.02\times10^{23}\ mol^{-1})}\right]$$

$$= (2.77 \times 10^{60})(1.082 \times 10^{-33})(1.363 \times 10^{-19})$$

$$= 4.085 \times 10^{8}$$

The rotational partition function of I_2 is given by

$$q_{rot} = \frac{8\pi^2 IkT}{\sigma h^2} \qquad (4)$$

where σ is the symmetry number, which is 2 for a homonuclear molecule. I is the moment of inertia given by

$$I = \mu r^2$$

where μ is the reduced mass and r is the internuclear distance, given here as 0.2667 nm.

$$\therefore \quad I = \left(\frac{m_1 m_2}{m_1 + m_2}\right) r^2$$

$$= \left(\frac{m_{I_2}^2}{2m_{I_2}}\right) r^2$$

$$= \left[\frac{(4.216\times10^{-22}\ g)^2}{2(4.216\times10^{-22}\ g)}\right]\left[(0.2667\ nm)^2\left(\frac{10^{-9}\ m}{1\ nm}\right)^2 \times \left(\frac{100\ cm}{1\ m}\right)^2\right]$$

$$= 1.499 \times 10^{-37}\ g\ cm^2$$

Using equation (4) yields

$$q_{rot} = \frac{8\pi^2(1.499\times10^{-37}\text{ g cm}^2)(1.38\times10^{-16}\text{ erg/°K})(1000\text{ °K})}{2\left(6.63\times10^{-27}\text{ erg sec}\right)^2}$$

$$= 1.8579 \times 10^4.$$

The vibration partion function of I_2 is given by

$$q_{vi} = \left(1 - e^{-hc\bar{\nu}/kT}\right)^{-1} \qquad (5)$$

where $\bar{\nu}$ is the fundamental vibration frequency and c is the speed of light.

$$e^{-hc\bar{\nu}/kT}$$

$$= \exp\left\{\left[\frac{(-6.63\times10^{-27}\text{ erg sec})(3\times10^{10}\text{ cm sec}^{-1})}{(1.38\times10^{-16}\text{ erg °K}^{-1})(1000\text{ °K})}\right] \times \left[214.4\text{ cm}^{-1}\right]\right\}$$

$$= 0.7342$$

Now, equation (5) becomes

$$q_{vib} = (1 - 0.7342)^{-1}$$

$$= 3.762$$

The electronic partition function of a molecule (or an atom) is given by the relation

$$q_{elec.} = g_0 e^{-\varepsilon_0/kT} + g_1 e^{-\varepsilon_1/kT} + g_2 e^{-\varepsilon_2/kT} + \ldots \qquad (6)$$

where g_j is the electronic degeneracy and ε_j is the electronic energy of level j taken relative to the ground level. The ground state of I is a doublet $({}^2P_{3/2,1/2})$ spearated by 7603 cm^{-1}. Thus for the term symbol ${}^2P_{3/2}$, the corresponding degeneracy is 4 and for the term symbol ${}^2P_{1/2}$, the degeneracy is 2.

From equation (6)

$$q_{elec.} = 4e^{-(\varepsilon_0/hc)(hc/kT)} + 2e^{-(\varepsilon_1/hc)(hc/kT)}$$

$$\frac{hc}{kT} = \frac{(6.63\times10^{-27}\text{ erg sec})(3\times10^{10}\text{ cm s}^{-1})}{(1.38\times10^{-16}\text{ erg °K}^{-1})(1000\text{ °K})}$$

$$= 1.44 \times 10^{-3}\text{ cm}$$

Given that the ground state has a separation of 7603 cm^{-1},

$\varepsilon/hc = 0$ for the term symbol $^2P_{3/2}$ corresponding to the degeneracy number of 4, and $\varepsilon/hc = 7603\ cm^{-1}$ for the term symbol $^2P_{1/2}$ corresponding to the degeneracy number 2. Thus,

$$q_{elec}(I) = 4e^0 + 2e^{-(7603\ cm^{-1})(1.44\times10^{-3}\ cm)}$$

$$= 4 + 2e^{-10.94}$$

$$= 4 + 3.5 \times 10^{-5}$$

$$= 4.000035$$

and $$q_{elec}(I)^2 = (4.000035)^2$$

$$= 16.00028$$

Finally, the dissociation energy term of equation (2) is

$$\exp(-\Delta\varepsilon_0/kT)$$

where $\Delta\varepsilon_0$ is the energy of dissociation of I_2 given in the literature as 1.542 eV.

$$\therefore \quad \frac{\Delta\varepsilon_0}{kT} = \frac{1.542\ eV\left(\frac{1.602\times10^{-19} J}{1\ eV}\right)\left(\frac{10^7\ ergs}{1\ J}\right)}{(1.38 \times 10^{-16}\ erg\ °K^{-1})(1000\ °K)}$$

$$= 17.90$$

and $$e^{-17.90} = 1.68 \times 10^{-8}$$

The equilibrium constant expression can be written as

$$K_P = \frac{(q_{trans}q_{elec})^2_I}{(q_{trans}q_{rot}q_{vib})_{I_2}} \exp(-\Delta\varepsilon_0/kT)$$

$$= \frac{(4.085\times10^8)(16.00028)}{(18579)(3.762)} 1.68 \times 10^{-8}$$

$$= 1.571 \times 10^{-3}$$

Figure 1 shows the potential energy curve for the dissociation reaction

$$N_2(g) \rightarrow 2N(g)$$

N_2 and N have degeneracy numbers in the electronic ground levels of one and four respectively. Calculate the equilibrium constant for the dissociation reaction at 5000 °K assuming the rigid rotor and harmonic oscillator approximation. The ground state of N is a doublet denoted by $^2P_{3/2,1/2}$ with a separation of $3.8854(10^4)\text{cm}^{-1}$.

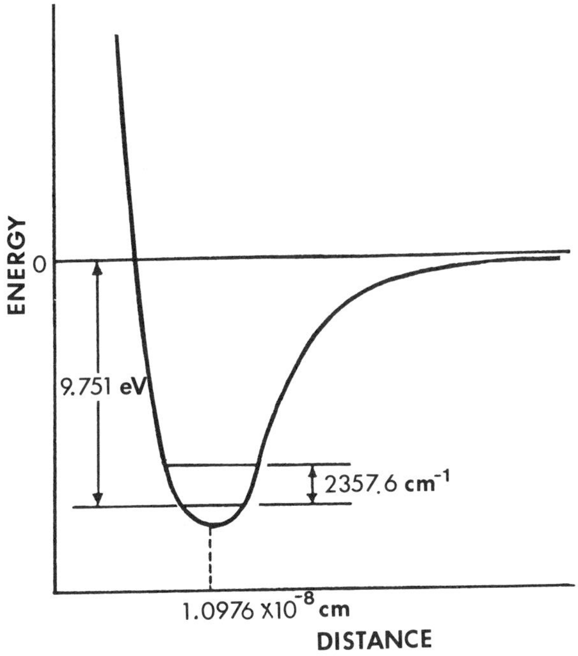

Fig. 1

Solution: From figure 1, the energy of dissociation of N_2 is $\Delta E_0 = 9.751$ eV. The fundamental vibration frequency $\bar{\nu} = 2357.6\ \text{cm}^{-1}$, and the internuclear distance is 1.0976×10^{-8} cm. The equilibrium constant expression for the reaction has the form

$$K_P = \left[\frac{\left(\frac{q}{N}\right)^2_{N(g)}}{\left(\frac{q}{N}\right)_{N_2(g)}}\right] e^{-\Delta\varepsilon_0/RT} \qquad (1)$$

where q is the partition function given by

$$q = q_{trans.} \times q_{rot.} \times q_{vi.} \times q_{elec.}$$

From equation (1)

$$K_P = \left[\frac{\left(\frac{q_{trans}}{N}\right)_{N\,(g)}}{\left(\frac{q_{trans}}{N}\right)_{N_2\,(g)}}\right] \times q_{rot.} \times q_{vi.} \times q_{elec.} \times e^{-\Delta\varepsilon_0/RT}$$

$$= \frac{\left[\frac{\left(2\pi m_N kT\right)^{3/2} RT}{Nh^3 P}\right]^2}{\left[\frac{\left(2\pi m_{N_2} kT\right)^{3/2}}{Nh^3 P}\right]} \left(\frac{h^2\sigma}{8\pi^2 IkT}\right)_{N_2\,(g)} \left(1 - e^{-\theta_{vi}/T}\right)_{N_2\,(g)}$$

$$\times \left(q_{elec}\right)^2_{N\,(g)} \times e^{-\Delta\varepsilon_0/RT} \qquad (2)$$

where $\theta_{vi} = \frac{hc\bar{\nu}}{k}$

here c is the speed of light and $\bar{\nu}$ is the vibration frequency. σ is the symmetry number and N is the Avogadro's number.

From equation (2)

$$q_{trans} = \frac{[(2\pi mkT)^{3/2} RT/Nh^3 P]^2_{N(g)}}{[2\pi mkT)^{3/2} RT/Nh^3 P]_{N_2(g)}} \qquad (3)$$

$$m_{N(g)} = \frac{1}{2} m_{N_2(g)} = \frac{14 \text{ g mole}^{-1}}{6.02\times10^{23} \text{ mole}^{-1}}$$

$$= 2.33 \quad 10^{-23} \text{ g}$$

$$q_{trans} = 8.393 \times 10^8$$

$$q_{rot} = \left(\frac{h^2\sigma}{8\pi^2 IkT}\right)_{N_2\,(g)} \qquad (4)$$

where I = moment of inertia given by

$$I = \mu r_e^2$$

where μ is the reduced mass and r is the internuclear distance

$$\therefore \qquad I = \left(\frac{m_1 m_2}{m_1 + m_2}\right) r_e^2$$

$$= \frac{\left(\frac{14.008 \text{ g mole}^{-1}}{6.023\times10^{23} \text{ mole}^{-1}}\right)^2}{\left(\frac{28.016 \text{ g mole}^{-1}}{6.023\times10^{23} \text{ mole}^{-1}}\right)} \times (1.098\times10^{-8} \text{ cm})^2$$

$$= 1.402 \times 10^{-39} \text{ g cm}^2$$

Substitution of these values into equation (4) gives

$$q_{rot} = 1.150 \times 10^{-3}$$

$$q_{vi} = \left(1 - e^{-\theta_{vi}/T}\right)_{N_2(g)}$$

$$\frac{\theta_{vi}}{T} = \frac{h\bar{\nu}}{kT}$$

$$= \frac{hc\bar{\nu}}{kT}$$

$$= 6.7915 \times 10^{-1}$$

$$q_{vi} = .4923$$

$e^{-\Delta\varepsilon_0/RT}$ is computed as follows:

$$\Delta\varepsilon_0 = 9.751 \frac{\text{eV}}{\text{molec}} \times 6.023(10^{23}) \frac{\text{molec}}{\text{mole}} \times \frac{1.602(10^{-19})\frac{\text{J}}{\text{eV}}}{4.184 \text{ J/cal}}$$

$$= 225{,}023 \text{ cal/mole}$$

$$\frac{\Delta\varepsilon_0}{RT} = \frac{225023 \text{ cal/mole}}{1.987 \text{ cal/°K mole} \times 5000 \text{ °K}} = 22.650$$

$$e^{-\Delta\varepsilon_0/RT} = 1.457 \times 10^{-10}$$

q_{elec} is calculated as follows:

$$q_{elec} = g_0 e^{-\varepsilon_0/kT} + g_1 e^{-\varepsilon_1/kT} + g_2 e^{-\varepsilon_2/kT} + \ldots$$

where g_j is the electronic degeneracy and ε_j is the electronic energy of level j taken relative to the ground level. The ground state of N is a doublet ($^2P_{3/2,1/2}$) separated by 7603 cm^{-1}. Thus, the first term has a degeneracy of 4 while the second term has a degeneracy of 2. Hence

$q_{elec} = 4e^{-(\varepsilon_0/hc)(hc/kT)} + 2e^{-(\varepsilon_1/hc)(hc/kT)}$. Given that the ground state has a separation of 7603 cm^{-1}, $\varepsilon_0 = 0$, while $\varepsilon_1/hc = 7603\ cm^{-1}$. Therefore

$q_{elec} = 4e^0 + 2e^{-(3.8854(10^4)cm^{-1})(hc/kT)}$. Now

$$\frac{hc}{kT} = \frac{(6.63\times10^{-27})\text{ erg sec} \times (3\times10^{10})\text{cm sec}^{-1}}{(1.38\times10^{-16})\text{erg K}^{-1} \times 5000\ °K}$$

$$= 2.882(10^{-4})\text{cm}$$

$$q_{elec} = 4 + 2.74 \times 10^{-5} \simeq 4$$

From equation (2)

$$K_p = (8.393\times10^8)(1.150\times10^{-3})\times(0.4923)\times16\times(1.457\times10^{-10})$$

$$= 1.108 \times 10^{-3}\text{ atm.}$$

• PROBLEM 4-20

Calculate the equilibrium constant for the reaction at 300°K

$$H_2 + D_2 \rightleftarrows 2HD$$

using the following data

	H_2	HD	D_2
Fundamental vibration $\bar{\nu}$ (cm^{-1})	4371	3785	3092
Moment of inertia I($g\cdot cm^2\times10^{40}$)	0.458	0.613	0.919

Solution: The expression for the equilibrium constant in terms of partition functions is given by

$$K_P = \frac{[Q°(HD)]^2}{[Q°(H_2)][Q°(D_2)]}\exp(-\Delta\varepsilon_0°/kT) \qquad (1)$$

The translational partition function is given by

$$Q_{trans.} = \frac{Q_{trans}(HD)^2}{Q_{trans}(H_2)Q_{trans}(D_2)}$$

$$= \frac{\left[\dfrac{(2\pi m_{HD}kT)^{3/2}}{h^3}V\right]^2}{\left(\dfrac{(2\pi m_{H_2}kT)^{3/2}V}{h^3}\right)\left(\dfrac{(2\pi m_{D_2}kT)^{3/2}V}{h^3}\right)}$$

$$= \frac{(m_{HD})^3}{(m_{H_2}m_{D_2})^{3/2}} = \frac{(1 + 2)^3}{[(2\times 1)(2\times 2)]^{3/2}}$$

$$= \frac{(3)^3}{(2\times 4)^{3/2}} = \frac{27}{(8)^{3/2}} = \frac{27}{\left(8^3\right)^{1/2}}$$

or $Q_{trans.} = 1.193.$

The rotational partition function

$$Q_{rot.} = \frac{Q_{rot.}(HD)^2}{Q_{rot.}(H_2)Q_{rot}(D_2)}$$

$$= \frac{\left[\dfrac{8\pi^2 kT\ I_{HD}}{h^2\sigma_{HD}}\right]^2}{\left(\dfrac{8\pi^2 kT\ I_{H_2}}{h^2\sigma_{H_2}}\right)\left(\dfrac{8\pi^2 kT\ I_{D_2}}{h^2\sigma_{D_2}}\right)}$$

$$= \frac{(I/\sigma)^2_{HD}}{(I/\sigma)_{H_2}(I/\sigma)_{D_2}}$$

where I = the moment of inertia and σ is the symmetry number, which is 1 for HD, 2 for H_2 and 2 for D_2.

$$Q_{rot.} = \frac{(.613/1)^2}{(.458/2)(.919/2)} = \frac{(.3758)}{(.229)\ (.4595)}$$

or $Q_{rot.} = 3.57.$

The vibrational partition function

$$Q_{vib.} = \left(1 - e^{-hc\bar{\nu}/kT}\right)^{-1}$$

$$\frac{hc\bar{\nu}}{kT} \text{ for HD} = \frac{(6.63\times10^{-34}\text{ J s})(3\times10^{8}\text{m s}^{-1})(3785\text{ cm}^{-1})(\frac{100\text{ cm}}{1\text{ m}})}{(1.38\times10^{-23}\text{ J K}^{-1})(300\text{ °K})}$$

$$= 18.183$$

$$\frac{hc\bar{\nu}}{kT} \text{ for } H_2 = \frac{(6.63\times10^{-34}\text{J s})(3\times10^{8}\text{m s}^{-1})(4371\text{cm}^{-1})(\frac{100\text{ cm}}{1\text{ m}})}{(1.38\times10^{-23}\text{ J K}^{-1})(300\text{ °K})}$$

$$= 20.998$$

$$\frac{hc\bar{\nu}}{kT} \text{ for } D_2 = \frac{(6.63\times10^{-34}\text{J s})(3\times10^{8}\text{m s}^{-1})(3092\text{cm}^{-1})(\frac{100\text{ cm}}{1\text{ m}})}{(1.38\times10^{-23}\text{ J K}^{-1})(300\text{ °K})}$$

$$= 14.85$$

$\therefore\ Q_{vib.} = \left(1 - e^{-hc\bar{\nu}/kT}\right)^{-1}$ is essentially unity for each molecule.

The dissociation energy term,

$$\frac{\Delta\varepsilon_0^\circ}{kT} = \frac{\frac{1}{2}hc\left[2\bar{\nu}_{HD} - \bar{\nu}_{H_2} - \bar{\nu}_{D_2}\right]}{kT}$$

$$= \frac{\frac{1}{2}hc[2(3785\text{ cm}^{-1}) - 4371\text{ cm}^{-1} - 3092\text{ cm}^{-1}]}{(1.38\times10^{-23}\text{ J K}^{-1})(300\text{ °K})}$$

$$= \frac{\frac{1}{2}hc(107\text{ cm}^{-1})(\frac{100\text{ cm}}{1\text{ m}})}{(1.38\times10^{-23}\text{J K}^{-1})(300\text{ °K})}$$

$$= \frac{\frac{1}{2}(6.63\times10^{-34}\text{J s})(3\times10^{8}\text{m s}^{-1})(10900)}{(1.38\times10^{-23}\text{ J K}^{-1})(300\text{ °K})}$$

$$= .2570$$

$$e^{-0.2570} = .7734$$

Therefore, from the relation

$$K_p = Q_{trans.}Q_{rot.}Q_{vib.}\exp^{(-\Delta\varepsilon_0^\circ/kT)}$$

$$K_p = (1.193)(3.57)(.7734)$$

or $$K_p = 3.29$$

For the dissociation reaction

$$Cl_2(g) \rightleftarrows 2Cl(g)$$

at 1200 °K, calculate the equilibrium constant K_P by statistical thermodynamics. The equilibrium internuclear distance is 0.199 nm, the fundamental vibration frequency of Cl_2 is at $\bar{\nu} = 565\ cm^{-1}$, and the energy of dissociation of Cl_2 is 2.48 eV.

Solution: The equilibrium constant K_P of a chemical reaction can be calculated from the partition functions, Q of the reactants and products by using the relation

$$\Delta G° = -RT\ \ell n\ K_P \tag{1}$$

Using the expression for Helmholtz free energy, partition functions and Stirling formula, equation (1) becomes

$$\Delta G° = -RT\ \ell n(Q°/L) \tag{2}$$

where L = the Avogadro's number and Q° = the partition function of an ideal gas in the standard state, and is given by

$$Q° = Q_{int}\frac{(2\pi mkT)^{3/2}}{h^3}(RT) \tag{3}$$

Here, Q_{int} indicates the product of the rotational, vibrational and electronic contributions to Q°.

For the general reaction

$$aA + bB \rightleftarrows cC + dD,$$

Equation (2) gives

$$\Delta G° = -RT\ \ell n\frac{(Q°_C/L)^c(Q°_D/L)^d}{(Q°_A/L)^a(Q°_B/L)^b}\exp(-\Delta\varepsilon^{\circ}_0/kT)$$

where $\exp(-\Delta\varepsilon^{\circ}_0/kT)$ = the dissociation energy term.

The equilibrium constant expression is then

$$K_P = \frac{(Q°_C/L)^c(Q°_D/L)^d}{(Q°_A/L)^a(Q°_B/L)^b}\exp(-\Delta\varepsilon^{\circ}_0/kT)$$

Now, write the K_P expression for the dissociation reaction $Cl_2 \rightleftarrows 2Cl$ as

$$K_P = \frac{[Q°(Cl)]^2}{[Q°(Cl_2)]L} \exp(-\Delta\varepsilon_0^\circ/kT) \tag{4}$$

From Equation (3)

$$K_P = \left(\frac{2\pi kT}{h^2}\right)^{3/2} \frac{m_{Cl}^3}{m_{Cl_2}^{3/2}} \left(\frac{RT}{PL}\right) Q_{rot} Q_{vib} Q_{electronic}$$

But, $m_{Cl} = \frac{1}{2} m_{Cl_2}$

$$= \frac{35.5 \text{ g mole}^{-1}}{6.02\times10^{23} \text{ mole}^{-1}}$$

$$= 5.89 \times 10^{-23} \text{ g}$$

$R = 82.06$ cc atm K^{-1}.

Take note of the units of R.

Thus the translational partition function

$$Q_{trans} = \left(\frac{2\pi kT}{h^2}\right)^{3/2} \frac{m_{Cl}^3}{m_{Cl_2}^{3/2}} \frac{RT}{PL}$$

$$= \left[2\pi \frac{(1.38\times10^{-16} \text{ erg K}^{-1})(1200°K)}{(6.63\times10^{-27} \text{ erg sec})^2}\right]^{3/2}$$

$$\times \frac{(5.89\times10^{-23})^3}{\left(2(5.89\ 10^{-23})\right)^{3/2}} \frac{(82.06 \text{ cc atm K}^{-1} \text{ mole}^{-1})(1200°K)}{(1 \text{ atm})6.02\times10^{23} \text{ mole}^{-1}}$$

$$Q_{trans} = 9.298 \times 10^7$$

The rotational partition function,

$$Q_{rot.} = \frac{8\pi^2 IkT}{\sigma h^2}$$

where h = the Planck's constnat, σ is the symmetry number = 2 for a homonuclear molecule. I is the moment of inertia given by

$$I = \mu r^2$$

$$= \frac{m_1 m_2}{m_1+m_2} r^2$$

Observe that the molecule is homonuclear.

$$\therefore \quad I = \frac{m^2}{2m} r^2$$

$$= \frac{1}{2} m_{Cl} r^2$$

r is the interatomic distance

$$\therefore \quad I = 116.5 \times 10^{-40} \text{ g cm}^2$$

Consequently,

$$Q_{rot.} = \frac{8\pi^2 (116.5\times 10^{-40} \text{ g cm}^2)(1.38\times 10^{-16} \text{ erg K}^{-1})(1200°K)}{2(6.63 \times 10^{-27} \text{erg s})^2}$$

$$= 1732.7.$$

The vibrational partition function,

$$Q_{vib} = \left(1 - e^{-hc\tilde{\nu}_0/kT}\right)^{-1}$$

where c = the speed of light and $\tilde{\nu}_0$ is the fundamental vibrational frequency. The term

$$\frac{hc\tilde{\nu}_0}{kT} = \frac{(6.63\times 10^{-34} \text{J s})(3\times 10^8 \text{m s}^{-1})(565 \text{ cm}^{-1})\left(\frac{100 \text{ cm}}{1 \text{ m}}\right)}{(1.38 \times 10^{-23} \text{J K}^{-1})(1200 °K)}$$

$$= .67861.$$

$$\therefore \quad Q_{vib} = \left(1 - e^{-.67861}\right)^{-1}$$

or $\quad Q_{vib} = 2.030.$

The electronic partition function

$$Q_{elect.} = 4 + g(e^{-\varepsilon/kT})$$

where g = the statistical weight of the degenerate level and is equal to the number of superimposed levels. The ground state of Cl_2 is singly degenerate and the ground state of Cl is a doublet $(^2P_{3/2,1/2})$, separated by 881 cm^{-1}

$$\therefore \quad Q_{elect.}(Cl) = 4 + 2 \exp(-\varepsilon/kT)$$

$$\varepsilon/kT = (\varepsilon/hc)\ (hc/kT)$$

$$\frac{hc}{kT} = \frac{6.63\times10^{-27}\text{ erg sec}\times3\times10^{10}\text{ cm/sec}}{1.38\times10^{-16}\text{ erg/°K}\times1200\text{°K}} = 1.20 \times 10^{-3}\text{ cm}$$

$$\varepsilon/kT = 881\text{ cm}^{-1} \times 1.20 \times 10^{-3}\text{ cm} = 1.056$$

$$\therefore\ Q_{elect}(Cl) = 4 + 2e^{-1.056}$$

$$= 4.696$$

$$Q_{elect.}(Cl)^2 = 22.05$$

The dissociation energy term

$$\frac{\Delta\varepsilon_0^\circ}{kT} = \frac{(2.48\text{ eV})\left(\frac{1.602\ 10^{-19}\text{ J}}{\text{eV}}\right)}{(1.38\times10^{-23}\text{ J°K}^{-1})(1200\text{ °K})}$$

$$= 23.90$$

$$e^{-23.90} = 4.17 \times 10^{-11}$$

From (4)

$$K_p = \frac{(Q_{trans.}Q_{elec.})^2_{Cl}}{(Q_{trans.}Q_{rot.}Q_{vib.})_{Cl_2}}\exp(-\Delta\varepsilon_0^\circ/kT)$$

$$= \frac{9.298\times10^7\times22.05\times4.17\times10^{-11}}{1,732.7\times2.032}$$

$$K_p = 2.43 \times 10^{-5}$$

GIBB'S PARADOX

• PROBLEM 4-22

What is Gibb's Paradox? Explain its significance.

Solution: The Gibb's Paradox is the problem of a discontinuity of the entropy function upon the mixing of two gases as they change from distinguishable to indistinguishable gases.

The problem gave rise to the $\frac{1}{N!}$ term for indistinguishable particle in the molar ensemble partition function Q, given by

$$Q = \frac{q^N}{N!}$$

If two non reactive ideal gases, 1 and 2, are mixed to form an ideal mixture such that there is no heat transfer or any work done at constant temperature and pressure, then the associated entropy changes are given by

$$\Delta S_1 = n_1 R \ln \frac{V}{V_1} \tag{1}$$

$$\Delta S_2 = n_2 R \ln \frac{V}{V_2} \tag{2}$$

after an independent, isothermal expansion to the final volume V. V is the total volume and n_1, n_2 are the moles of gases 1 and 2. But these expansions occur independently and thus, the total entropy change can be written as

$$\Delta S_{mix} = \Delta S_1 + \Delta S_2 \tag{3}$$

Substituting equations (1) and (2) into equation (3) and using the fact that $\frac{V_1}{V} = \frac{n_1}{n} = x_1$ and $\frac{V_2}{V} = \frac{n_2}{n} = x_2$, then the entropy of mixing becomes

$$\Delta S_{mix} = -R(n_1 \ln x_1 + n_2 \ln x_2) \tag{4}$$

x_1 and x_2 are the mole fractions of gases 1 and 2 respectively. Dividing equation (4) by n, the total number of moles, gives

$$\Delta \bar{S}_{mix} = -R(x_1 \ln x_1 + x_2 \ln x_2) \tag{5}$$

where $\Delta \bar{S}_{mix}$ = entropy of mixing per mole of mixture.

Gibb's Paradox arises if gases 1 and 2 are homogeneous. In this case equations (4) or (5) would still represent the entropy of mixing but this is a paradoxical result because from a thermodynamic point of view, when molecules of the two identical gases are mixed together, it is not easy (or almost impossible), to distinguish between the initial and final states of the system.

This indistinguishability of the molecules is taken into account by the factor $\frac{1}{N!}$ in the expression for the molar partition function for a homogeneous binary gas mixture. This expression is given by

$$Q = \frac{q_1^{N_1} q_2^{N_2}}{N_1! N_2!}$$

where q_1 and q_2 are the molecular partition functions of gases 1 and 2.

The entropy of an ideal gas is given by

$$S = kT\left(\frac{\partial \ \ell n \ Q}{\partial T}\right)_{V,N} + k \ \ell n \ Q$$

where $Q = q^N$ for distinguishable molecules, or $Q = \frac{1}{N!}q^N$ for indistinguishable molecules.

From Boltzmann's formula

$$S = k \ \ell n \ \Omega \tag{6}$$

where $\Omega(V,N,E)$ represents the quantum degeneracy of the thermodynamic system specified by the variables V, N, E. Equation (6) implies that the larger the number of quantum states available to a system, the higher will be its entropy. Therefore the mixing of identical gases does not increase the number of states, but the mixing of non identical gases increases Ω. Since with N molecules, the total number of permutations of identical molecules is N!, then $\frac{1}{N!}$ is the correction for homogeneous gases.

DISTRIBUTION FUNCTION

• PROBLEM 4-23

What is the superposition approximation? Give a physical and a mathematical description. In what context is it used?, and when does it fail?

Solution: The superposition principle can be written as

$$g_3(r) = g(r_{12})g(r_{23})g(r_{13})$$

where $g_3(r)$ is a three particle distribution function and by definition

$$g_3(r) = \frac{f_3}{\rho^3}.$$

f_3 is proportional to the probability of particles located at positions $d\underline{r}_1$, $d\underline{r}_2$, $d\underline{r}_3$.

The superposition approximation indicates that the three-body problem is related to the three separate two-body (g_2) radial distribution function by a simple product. The approximation is used in connection with the Yvon, Born and Green (YBG) equation,

$$\frac{\partial g(r_{12})}{\partial r_1} + g(r_{12})\frac{\partial \phi(r_{12})}{\partial r_1} + \rho \int \frac{\partial \phi(r_{13})}{\partial r_1} g_3(r)dr_3 = 0,$$

to determine the equation of state of fluids. This approximation fails at high densities.

Every unit area of a dilute monomolecular film on the surface of a liquid contains N identical molecules each of mass m. Answer the questions below, expressing them in terms of mass m, number of molecules N, T, and universal constants; assume that each molecule moves independently of one another and of the solvent molecules. a) Determine the two-dimensional speed distribution function f(v) for these molecules, normalized so that

$$\int_0^\infty f(v)dv = 1$$

b) Calculate the average velocities $\bar{v}$, $\overline{v^2}$, $\overline{v^3}$. c) A line segment is placed on the edge of the surface layer. Calculate the number of collisions, per unit length per unit time, with the line. d) Calculate the average kinetic energy of those molecules escaping through a small gap in the partition.

Solution: a) The two dimensional speed distribution function is given by

$$f(v) = \left(Ce^{-mv^2/2kT}\right)v \qquad (1)$$

where m is the mass of the molecules, v is the speed and k is the Boltzmann constant. The constant C is determined by the normalization condition,

$$\int_0^\infty f(v)dv = 1 \qquad (2)$$

since the possible values of v run from 0 to ∞. A distribution function obeying equation (2) is said to be normalized. Substituting equation (1) into equation (2) yields

$$\int_0^\infty Ce^{-mv^2/2kT} \quad vdv = 1$$

or $$C\int_0^\infty e^{-mv^2/2kT}\, vdv = 1 \qquad (3)$$

The integration is performed as follows: Let $x = v^2$, then $dx = 2vdv$ and $\frac{1}{2}dx = vdv$. Also let $a = \frac{m}{2kT}$. Therefore, the equation becomes

$$\frac{1}{2}C \int_0^{\infty} e^{-ax}dx = 1.$$

It is now in a familiar standard form and easily integrated to yield $\frac{C}{2}\left(-\frac{1}{a}\right)e^{-ax}\Big|_0^{\infty} = 1$. After replacing a by $\frac{m}{2kT}$ the equation becomes

$$-\frac{kT}{m}C\ e^{-mv^2/2kT}\Big|_0^{\infty} = 1$$

$$-C\frac{kT}{m}(0) + C\frac{kT}{m} = 1$$

$$C\frac{kT}{m} = 1$$

and $$C = \frac{m}{kT}$$

From equation (1), the normalized two dimensional speed distribution functinn becomes

$$f(v) = \frac{m}{kT} e^{-mv^2/2kT}\ vdv$$

b) (i) The mean speed $\bar{v}$ is given by

$$\bar{v} = C\int_0^{\infty} vf(v)dv$$

$$= \frac{m}{kT}\int_0^{\infty}\left(e^{-mv^2/2kT}\right)v^2dv$$

$$= \frac{m}{kT}\cdot\frac{\sqrt{\pi}}{4}\left(\frac{2kT}{m}\right)^{3/2}$$

$$= \left(\frac{\pi kT}{2m}\right)^{1/2}$$

(ii) $$\overline{v^2} = C\int_0^{\infty} v^2 f(v)dv$$

$$= \frac{m}{kT}\int_0^{\infty} e^{-mv^2/2kT}\ v^3dv$$

$$= \frac{m}{kT}\cdot\frac{1}{2}\left(\frac{2kT}{m}\right)^2$$

$$= \frac{2kT}{m}$$

(iii) $$\overline{v^3} = C\int_0^\infty v^3 f(v)dv$$

$$= \frac{m}{kT}\int_0^\infty e^{-mv^2/2kT}\, v^4 dv$$

$$= \frac{m}{kT}\,\frac{3\sqrt{\pi}}{8}\left(\frac{2kT}{m}\right)^{5/2}$$

$$= 3\sqrt{\frac{\pi}{2}}\left(\frac{kT}{m}\right)^{3/2}$$

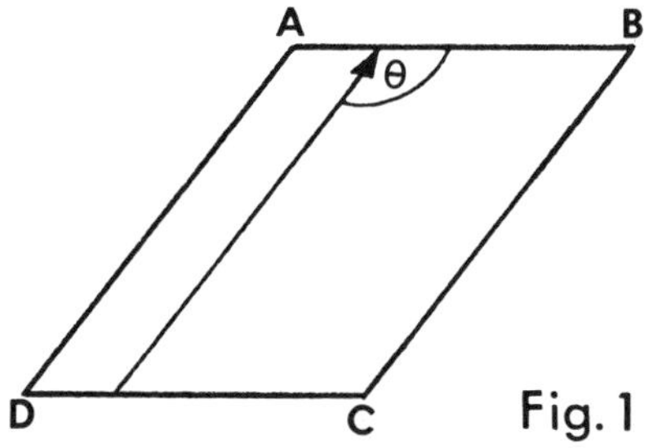

Fig. 1

c) Fig. 1 shows a line segment AB which contains molecules. The molecules have speeds between v and v + dv and a velocity vector between angles θ and θ + dθ. They collide if they are in the area ABCD.

$$\overline{AD} = v.$$

This area is given by

$$(\overline{AB})(\overline{AD})\sin\theta$$

and since there is a unit line segment the area becomes

$$v \sin\theta.$$

As a result, the number of molecules in this area is Nv sin θ. The number of molecules in the range v, v + dv and θ, θ + dθ is given by

$$Nv\sin\theta\cdot\frac{m}{kT}e^{-mv^2/2kT}\, vdv\,\frac{d\theta}{2\pi}$$

$$= \frac{Nm\sin\theta\, d\theta\, e^{-mv^2/2kT}\, v^2\, dv}{2\pi kT} \qquad (3)$$

Equation (3) gives the number of collisions in the given v and θ range. To obtain the total number of collisions Z, integrate equation (3) as follows:

$$Z = \frac{Nm}{2\pi kT}\int_0^{\pi} \sin\theta\, d\theta \int_0^{\infty} e^{-mv^2/2kT}\, v^2 dv$$

$$= N\left(\frac{kT}{2\pi m}\right)^{1/2}$$

d) The number of molecules colliding with the gap is equal to the number of molecules escaping, since any molecule striking the gap will escape. Therefore the average kinetic energy of the escaping molecules $\bar{\varepsilon}$, is equal to the total kinetic energy E, divided by the number of molecules colliding with the gap. That is,

$$\bar{\varepsilon} = \frac{E}{Z} \tag{4}$$

But $E = \frac{1}{2}mv^2 Z$

$$= \frac{Nm}{2\pi kT}\cdot\frac{1}{2}mv^2 \int_0^{\pi} \sin\theta\, d\theta \int_0^{\infty} e^{-mv^2/2kT}\, v^2\, dv$$

$$= \frac{Nm}{2\pi kT}\cdot\frac{1}{2}m \int_0^{\pi} \sin\theta\, d\theta \int_0^{\infty} e^{-mv^2/2kT}\, v^4\, dv$$

$$= \frac{3N}{\sqrt{\pi m}}\left(\frac{kT}{2}\right)^{3/2}$$

From equation (4)

$$\bar{\varepsilon} = \frac{\frac{3N}{\sqrt{\pi m}}\left(\frac{kT}{2}\right)^{3/2}}{N\left(\frac{kT}{2\pi m}\right)^{1/2}}$$

$$= \frac{3kT}{2}$$

DISTRIBUTION LAW

• PROBLEM 4-25

A set of ideal gas molecules, each of mass m, are restricted to two dimensions. The distribution law for each component of velocity is given by

$$\frac{dN_{v_x}}{N_{total}} = A\ e^{(-mv_x^2/2kT)}\ dv_x$$

a) Show that the distribution law with respect to speed v, is given by

$$\frac{dN_v}{N_{total}} = 2\pi A^2 e^{-mv^2/2kT}\ vdv$$

and evaluate the constant A.
b) Determine the average speed $\bar{v}$ of the molecules, in terms of mass m of the molecules, temperature T, and universal constants.

Solution: a) These molecules are confined to two dimensions, thus the probability of locating a molecule with velocity, v_x in the x-direction, is given by

$$\frac{dN_{v_x}}{N_{total}} = A\ e^{-mv_x^2/2kT}\ dv_x \tag{1}$$

Likewise for molecules with velocity, v_y in the y-direction,

$$\frac{dN_{v_y}}{N_{total}} = A\ e^{-mv_y^2/2kT}\ dv_y \tag{2}$$

Now the probability of simultaneously finding a molecule with velocity v_x, between v_x and $v_x + dv_x$ and with velocity v_y, between v_y and $v_y + dv_y$ is the product of the separate probabilities. Therefore,

$$\frac{dN_{v_x v_y}}{N_{total}} = \left(\frac{dN_{v_x}}{N_{total}}\right)\left(\frac{dN_{v_y}}{N_{total}}\right)$$

$$= \left(A\ e^{-mv_x^2/2kT}\ dv_x\right)\left(A\ e^{-mv_y^2/2kT}\ dv_y\right)$$

$$= A^2 \exp\left[-m\left(\frac{v_x^2 + v_y^2}{2kT}\right)\right] dv_x\ dv_y$$

$$= A^2 e^{-mv^2/2kT} v\, dv\, d\theta \tag{3}$$

Equation (3) is written in polar coordinates in velocity space, where θ is the angle such that $\tan \theta = \frac{v_y}{v_x}$ and v^2 replaces $v_x^2 + v_y^2$. The distribution law with respect to speed v (that is, the number of molecules with speeds between v and v + dv) is obtained by integrating equation (3) at all angles θ. Therefore,

$$\frac{dN_v}{N_{total}} = \int_0^{2\pi} A^2 e^{-mv^2/2kT} v\, dv\, d\theta$$

$$= A^2 e^{-mv^2/2kT} v\, dv \int_0^{2\pi} d\theta$$

$$= 2\pi A^2 e^{-mv^2/2kT} v\, dv \tag{4}$$

The constant A is determined by using the normalization condition given by

$$\int_{v=0}^{\infty} \frac{dN_v}{N_{total}} = 1$$

$$\therefore \quad \int_0^{\infty} 2\pi A^2 e^{-mv^2/2kT} vdv = 1$$

$$\text{or} \quad 2\pi A^2 \int_0^{\infty} e^{-mv^2/2kT} vdv = 1 \tag{5}$$

Let $\quad U = -\frac{mv^2}{2kT}$

Then, $\quad dU = -\frac{m}{2kT} 2v\, dv$

$$= -\frac{m}{kT} v\, dv$$

Eqn (5) becomes

$$-\frac{kT}{m} 2\pi A^2 \int_0^{\infty} e^U\, dU = 1$$

$$- \frac{kT}{m} 2\pi A^2 \; e^U \Big|_0^\infty = 1 \qquad (6)$$

Substituting $U = - \frac{mv^2}{2kT}$ back into equation (6) yields

$$- \frac{kT}{m} 2\pi A^2 e^{-mv^2/2kT} \Big|_0^\infty = 1$$

$$- \frac{kT}{m} 0 + \frac{kT}{m} 2\pi A^2 = 1$$

$$2\pi A^2 \; \frac{kT}{m} = 1$$

$$\therefore \qquad A^2 = \frac{m}{2\pi kT}$$

Alternatively, to solve for A^2, each of the separate integrals could be solved for A and this answer squared. Eqn. (4) then becomes

$$\frac{dN_v}{N_{total}} = 2\pi \left(\frac{m}{2\pi kT}\right) e^{-mv^2/2kT} \; v \; dv$$

$$= \frac{m}{kT} \; e^{-mv^2/2kT} \; v \; dv$$

b) The average speed $\bar{v}$ is given by

$$\bar{v} = \int_0^\infty v \; \frac{dN_v}{N_{total}}$$

$$= \frac{m}{kT} \int_0^\infty e^{-mv^2/2kT} \; v^2 \; dv$$

$$= \frac{m}{kT} \int_0^\infty v \; e^{-mv^2/2kT} \; v \; dv$$

$$= \frac{m}{kT} \int_0^\infty x \; e^{-mx^2/2kT} \; x \; dx \qquad (7)$$

Integrate by parts using

$$\int udv = uv - \int vdu \qquad (8)$$

From equation (7),

Let U = x and $dv = e^{-mx^2/2kT} x\,dx$

$\therefore$ dU = dx and $v = -\frac{2kT}{2m}e^{-mx^2/2kT}$

Using equation (8), equation (7) becomes

$$\bar{v} = \frac{m}{kT}\cdot\left(-x\frac{kT}{m}\right)e^{-mx^2/2kT}\Big|_0^\infty + \frac{m}{kT}\cdot\int_0^\infty \frac{kT}{m}e^{-mx^2/2kT}\,dx$$

$$= \frac{m}{kT}\cdot\left(-x\frac{kT}{m}\right)e^{-mx^2/2kT}\Big|_0^\infty + \frac{m}{kT}\cdot\frac{kT}{m}\int_0^\infty e^{-mx^2/2kT}\,dx$$

$$= 0 + \int_0^\infty e^{-mx^2/2kT}\,dx$$

$$= \frac{1}{2}\sqrt{\frac{\pi}{\frac{m}{2kT}}} \qquad \text{in polar coordinates.}$$

$$= \frac{\sqrt{\pi}}{2\sqrt{\frac{m}{2kT}}}$$

$$= \frac{\sqrt{\pi}}{\sqrt{\frac{4m}{2kT}}}$$

$$= \frac{\sqrt{\pi}}{\sqrt{\frac{2m}{kT}}}$$

$$= \left(\frac{\pi kT}{2m}\right)^{1/2}$$

BOLTZMANN'S CONSTANT

• PROBLEM 4-26

In one of the experiments on gravitational sedimentation equilibrium, the number of gamboge particles in water at 20°C were monitored. (Gamboge is a yellow pigment not soluble in water.) The following data was obtained:

Height in μm:	0	25	50	75	100
Mean no. of particles:	203	166	136	112	91

Assuming that the gamboge particles had a mean volume equal to 9.78×10^{-21} m^3 and a density equal to 1351 kg/m^3, calculate the Boltzmann constant.

Solution: Gravitational sedimentation implies that the downward velocity, V_G due to gravitational forces alone equals the upward velocity V_D due to diffusion alone.

Let component 1 = water
and component 2 = particle

The gravitational downward force = $m_2 g$. The bouyant diffusional upward force = $m_2 \frac{1}{\rho_2} \rho_1 g$. g is the acceleration due to gravity and ρ is the density. Another upward force is that due to Stoke's law, given by

$$f = 6\pi\mu a V_G$$

where a is the radius and μ is the coefficient of viscosity of the medium.

At equilibrium, the forces balance

$$\text{and } \Delta F = 0 = -m_2 g\left(1 - \frac{\rho_1}{\rho_2}\right) - 6\pi\mu a V_G$$

$$\text{or} \quad V_G = \frac{m_2 g\left(1 - \rho_1/\rho_2\right)}{6\pi\mu a}$$

$$= \frac{m_2 g'}{6\pi\mu a} \tag{1}$$

where $g' = g(1 - \rho_1/\rho_2)$.

Determination of V_D:

The rate of diffusion is the upward z-direction is given by

$$j_z = CV_D = -\mathscr{D}_{12} \frac{dC}{dZ} \tag{2}$$

where C is the concentration and $\mathscr{D}$ is the diffusion coefficient given by

$$\mathscr{D}_{12} = \frac{kT}{6\pi\mu a}$$

$$\text{Therefore,} \quad V_D = -\frac{kT}{6\pi\mu a} \frac{dC}{CdZ} \tag{3}$$

At equilibrium $V_G = V_D$ and equation (3) becomes

$$\frac{dC}{C} = -\frac{m_2 g'}{kT}\, dZ$$

Integration yields

$$\ell n\, C = \frac{-m_2 g' Z}{kT} + \bar{C}$$

From which

$$C = C_0 \exp\left[-\frac{m_2 g' Z}{kT}\right] \qquad (4)$$

where $C = C_0$ at $Z = 0$.

Equation (4) is the familiar Boltzmann's equation and it indicates that the equilibrium distribution of the particles obeys this equation. The Boltzmann's constant can then be determined from the equation. To do this, plot ℓn C vs h, where h is the height in the z-direction. From equation (4)

$$\ell n\, C = \ell n\, C_0 - \frac{m_2 g' h}{kT}$$

By using a linear regression calculation, or by graphically plotting the data, the slope can be found. Using linear regression calculation the formula for the slope is given by:

$$\text{Slope} = \frac{\sum x \sum y - n \sum xy}{(\sum x)^2 - n \sum x^2}$$

The letter n refers to the number of data item which in this case equals 5. Since the plot involves ℓn C versus h, the x in the above equation will the h and the y the ℓn C term. The following table represents our data.

h(μm)	0	25	50	75	100
C(mean number of particles)	203	166	136	112	91
ℓn C	5.313	5.112	4.913	4.718	4.511

$\sum x = 0+25+50+75+100 = 250$ μm, $(\sum x)^2 = 62500 (\mu m)^2$, $\sum y = 24.567$,

$$\sum xy = x_1y_1+x_2y_2+x_3y_3+x_4y_4+x_5y_5 = 0+127.8+245.65+353.85+451.1$$
$$= 117.84 \mu m$$

$$\sum x^2 = x_1^2+x_2^2+x_3^2+x_4^2+x_5^2 = 0+625+2500+5625+10{,}000 = 18750 (\mu m)^2$$

$$\text{Slope} = \frac{((250)(24.567) - 5(1178.4))\mu m}{(62500 - 5(18750))(\mu m)^2} = -7.99(10^{-3})\frac{1}{\mu m}$$

$$\text{Slope} = \frac{-m_2 g'}{kT} = -7.99 \times 10^{-3}\ \frac{1}{\mu m}$$

$$\therefore \quad k = \frac{m_2 g'}{(7.99 \times 10^{-3}) \frac{1}{\mu m} T} \qquad (5)$$

$$m_2 = V_2 \rho_2$$

$$= (9.78 \times 10^{-21}\ m^3)(1351\,kg\ m^{-3})$$

$$= 1.321 \times 10^{-17}\ kg$$

$$g' = g\left(1 - \frac{\rho_1}{\rho_2}\right)$$

$$= 9.78\ \frac{m}{sec^2}\left(1 - \frac{998.230}{1351}\right)$$

$$= 2.55\ m\ sec^{-2}$$

Using these values in equation (5) yields

$$k = \frac{(1.321\times 10^{-17}\ kg)(2.55\ m\ s^{-2})}{(7.99\times 10^{-3}\ \mu m)\left(\frac{10^6\ \mu m}{1\ m}\right)(293\ °K)}$$

$$= 1.44 \times 10^{-23}\ J/°K$$

or $k = 1.44 \times 10^{-16}$ ergs/°K

KINETIC ENERGY

• PROBLEM 4-27

Molecules of a gas are crossing a given plane of unit area in unit time. Show that the average total kinetic energy of the molecules is 2kT.

Solution: Let the number of particles in the gas be N, and their velocity be v. Also, let the number of molecules with velocities between v and v + dv be dN. The number of particles emerging across the plane is dN' and is proportional to dN. The emitted beam has a mean square velocity of $\overline{v'^2}$ and is given by

$$\overline{v'^2} = \frac{\int_0^\infty v^2 dN'}{\int_0^\infty dN'}$$

$$= \frac{\int_0^\infty v^3 dN}{\int_0^\infty v dN} \qquad (1)$$

Of particular interest are the fraction of the molecules having a speed in the range v to v + dv, independent of the direction. If the origins of the velocity vectors of all the molecules in a sample of the gas are brought to the origin of a coordinate system, molecules having speed vectors ending in a spherical shell of radius v around the origin with thickness dv are wanted. The volume of this shell is $4\pi v^2 dv$, and thus the fraction of the molecules with velocities v in the range v to v + dv is given by

$$f(v)dv = \left(\frac{m}{2\pi kT}\right)^{3/2} e^{-mv^2/2kT} \, 4\pi v^2 dv$$

which is the Maxwell equation. Substituting the Maxwell equation into equation (1) gives

$$\overline{v'^2} = \frac{4\pi N_0 \left(\frac{m}{2\pi kT}\right)^{3/2} \int_0^\infty v^5 \exp\left[-\frac{mv^2}{2kT}\right] dv}{4\pi N_0 \left(\frac{m}{2\pi kT}\right)^{3/2} \int_0^\infty v^3 \exp\left[-\frac{mv^2}{2kT}\right] dv}$$

$$= \frac{\int_0^\infty v^5 \exp\left[-\frac{mv^2}{2kT}\right] dv}{\int_0^\infty v^3 \exp\left[-\frac{mv^2}{2kT}\right] dv}$$

$$= \frac{\left[\frac{8k^3T^3}{m^3}\right]}{\left[\frac{2k^2T^2}{m^2}\right]}$$

$$= \frac{4kT}{m}$$

Kinetic energy is given by

$$E = \frac{1}{2}m\,\overline{v'^2}$$

$$= \frac{1}{2}m\left(\frac{4kT}{m}\right)$$

$$= 2kT .$$

CHAPTER 5

THIRD LAW OF THERMODYNAMICS

THIRD LAW ENTROPY

• PROBLEM 5-1

Explain the following statements in statistical terms:
(a) The entropy change in a chemical reaction usually approaches zero as the temperature approaches $0^\circ K$.

(b) The reaction $2C(\text{graphite}) + O_2(\text{crystal}) \rightarrow 2CO(\text{crystal})$ is an exception to this rule.

Solution: a) In statistical terms, the entropy of a chemical reaction is given by $S = k \ln W$ where k = some constant.

W = probability that every particle is in a given volume (container) or the number of detailed molecular states corresponding to the given gross (macroscopic) state.

Usually at $0^\circ K$, $W = 1$ for every reactant and product. Therefore,

$$S_{\text{reactant}} = k \ln W = k \ln 1 = 0$$

$$S_{\text{product}} = k \ln W = k \ln 1 = 0$$

By definition $\Delta S = \Sigma S_{\text{product}} - \Sigma S_{\text{reactant}}$

$$\Delta S \text{ at } 0 K = 0 - 0 = 0 .$$

b) Using the same procedure as in part a), $W = 1$ for C and O_2. Consequently, $S = 0$ for each. However, in the case of CO, the dipole moment is so small that the orientation of the molecules (CO or OC) in the crystal is almost random. this is so, even at 0 K. Therefore W is greater than 1 and consequently, S for the CO molecules is greater than 1. Thus, $\Delta S = \left[\Sigma S_{\text{product}} - \Sigma S_{\text{reactant}}\right]$ must be greater than zero for this particular reaction.

• PROBLEM 5-2

A thermodynamic study was made of the propeller-shaped molecule triptycene ($C_{20}H_{14}$; 9, 10-benzeno-9, 10-dihydroanthracene) by measurements of the heat capacity C_P from 10 to 550K. The compound melts at 527.18K with $\Delta H_m = 7236$ cal·mol^{-1}. The molar heat capacities were as follows.

Solid

T.K	10	20	30	40	50	60	70	80
cal.K^{-1}.mol^{-1}	0.863	4.303	7.731	10.649	13.17	15.40	17.43	19.33
	90	100	120	140	160	180	200	
	21.16	22.98	26.67	30.55	34.63	38.91	43.37	
	220	240	260	280	298.15	320		
	48.01	52.83	57.79	62.88	67.56	73.16		
	350	400	450	500	527.18			
	80.67	92.53	103.85	113.98	119.38			

Liquid

	527.18	530	550
	130.86	130.90	133.45

Calculate the third-law entropy S_1 for triptycene at 298.15K and for the liquid at 550K in units of J·K^{-1}mol^{-1}. 1 cal = 4.1840 J.

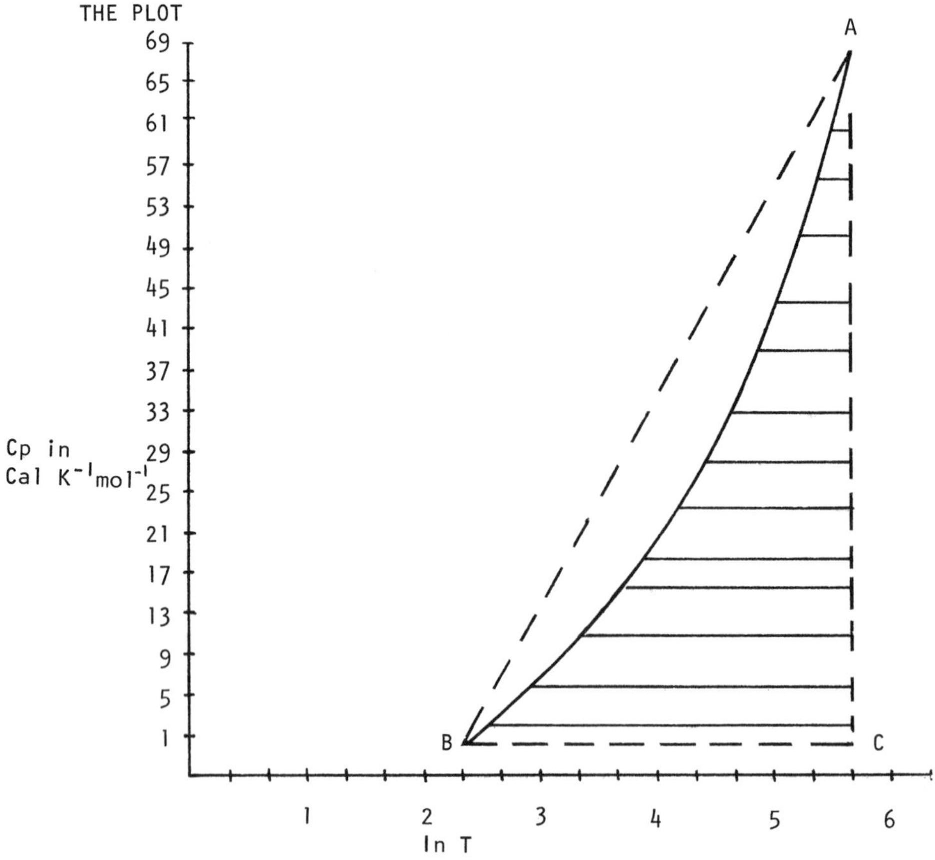

Solution: This problem can be solved in a number of steps. The first part, which involves the calculation of the third-law entropy at 298.15°K,

$$S_{298.15} = \Delta S_{0\to10} + \Delta S_{10\to298.15} ,$$

can be solved in two steps and the second part, which involves finding the entropy of the liquid at 550°K,

$$S_{550} = S_{298.15} + \Delta S_{298.15\to527.18} + \Delta S_f + \Delta S_{527.18\to550},$$

where $\Delta S_f = \frac{\Delta H_f}{T}$ and ΔH is the change in enthalpy, can be solved in four steps (including the final answer for the first part).

Solving the first part:

$\Delta S_{0\to10}$ can be obtained by using the Debye 3rd power law. That is, $C_p = AT^3$ where C_p = heat capacity at constant pressure and A = constant. By definition,

$$\Delta S = \int_{T_1}^{T_2} \frac{C_p}{T} dT \qquad (1)$$

Substituting the C_p expression into equation (1), it becomes

$$\Delta S = \int_0^{10} \frac{AT^3}{T} dT .$$

$$\Delta S_{0\to10} = \int_0^{10} AT^2 dt = \frac{AT^3}{3}\Big|_0^{10} = \left(\frac{AT^3}{3} \text{ at } 10^\circ K\right) - 0 .$$

Note that the answer is 1/3 C_p at 10°K because $AT^3 = C_p$. The C_p value at 10°K is obtained from the table and it is equal to 0.863.

$\Delta S_{0\to10}$ = 1/3 (0.863) = 0.288 cal $K^{-1}mol^{-1}$. The second step of the first part can be obtained by a graphical integration. That is, plot C_p vs. ln T and $\Delta S_{10\to298.15}$ is the area under the curve. From the table the C_p values and their corresponding ln T values are as follows:

C_p :	0.863	4.303	7.731	10.649	13.17	
ln T:	2.303	2.996	3.401	3.689	3.912	
C_p :	15.40	17.43	19.33	21.16	22.98	26.67
ln T :	4.094	4.248	4.382	4.499	4.605	4.787
C_p :	30.55	34.63	38.91	43.37	48.01	52.83
ln T:	4.942	5.075	5.193	5.298	5.394	5.481
C_p :	57.79	62.88	67.56			
ln T:	5.561	5.635	5.698			

The area under consideration is approximately the shaded portion. If the shaded portion is approximated to be about 2.9/5 of triangle

ABC, then its area is 2.9/5 (area of triangle). That is

$$\frac{2.9}{5} [113.2] \approx 65.$$

This is in cal $K^{-1}mol^{-1}$. But 1 cal = 4.1840 J

$$S_{298.15} = \Delta S_{0\to10} + \Delta S_{10\to298.15}$$

$$= [0.288 + 65]\ 4.184$$

$$= 272.9\ J\ K^{-1}mol^{-1}.$$

Solving the second part:

$$S_{550} = S_{298.15} + \Delta S_{298.15\to527.18} + \Delta S_f + \Delta S_{527.18\to550}$$

Using the method of graphical integration,

$$\Delta S_{298.15\to527.18} \approx 224\ J\ K^{-1}mol^{-1}$$

and

$$\Delta S_{527.18\to550} \approx 22.2\ J\ K^{-1}mol^{-1}.$$

Now,

$$\Delta S_f = \frac{\Delta H_f}{T} = \frac{(7236)(4.1840)}{527.18}$$

$$\Delta S_f = 57.3\ J\ K^{-1}mol^{-1}$$

$$S_{550} = 272.9 + 224 + 57.3 + 22.2$$

$$= 576.4\ J\ K^{-1}mol^{-1}.$$

• PROBLEM 5-3

At 300°K, the compound A is crystalline; the element B and the compound AB_2 are ideal gases. B is crystalline below 100°K and it sublimes (its vapor pressure becomes 1 atm) at this temperature, with the enthalpy of sublimation equal to 2000 cal $mole^{-1}$. For B(c) below 100°K the heat capacity is given approximately by the equation

$$\overline{C^\circ_p} = 2.50 \times 10^{-4}T^3 - 2.40 \times 10^{-10}T^6\ cal^\circ K^{-1}mole^{-1}$$

Above 100°K, $\overline{C^\circ_p}$ = 6.00 cal°$K^{-1}mole^{-1}$ for B(g). Enthalpies of formation and third-law entropies for the compounds at 300°K are as follows:

	$\overline{H^\circ_{300}}$	$\overline{S^\circ_{300}}$
A(c)	-10kcal $mole^{-1}$	15 cal°$K^{-1}mole^{-1}$
AB_2(g)	-41	55

(a) Find the standard third-law entropy of B(g) at 300°K.

(b) Find ΔG^0 and K_p for the reaction
$A(c) + 2B(g) = AB_2(g)$.

(c) 1.00 mole each of B and of AB_2 are introduced into a container in which solid A is present. At equilibrium, 1.10 mole of AB_2 is present and solid A is still present. The vapor pressure of A is negligible. What is the total pressure at equilibrium?

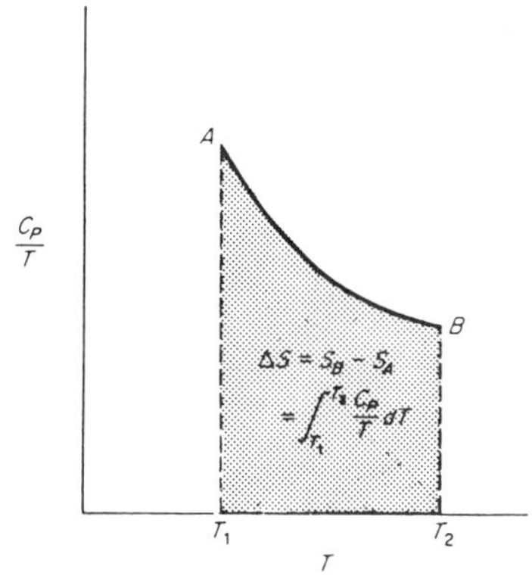

Graphical evaluation of the entropy change with temperature. Data on the heat capacity C_P of substance as a function of T allows one to calculate ΔS by this integration procedure.

Solution: a) This part of the problem involves the enumeration of three entropies. These are

$$\Delta S_{0\to100}\ ,\ \Delta S_{\text{sublimation}} \text{ and } \Delta S_{100\to300}\ .$$

By definition,

$$\Delta S_{T_1\to T_2} = \int_{T_1}^{T_2} \frac{C_p}{T}\, dT \qquad (1)$$

where C_p = heat capacity and T = temperture.

$$\Delta S_{\text{sublimation}} = \frac{\Delta H_{\text{sublimation}}}{T}$$

where $\Delta H_{\text{sublimation}}$ = enthalpy of sublimation. Using equation (1),

$$\Delta S_{0\to100} = \int_0^{100} \frac{C_p}{T}\, dT\ .$$

Below 100°K, C_p is given to be $2.50 \times 10^{-4}\, T^3 - 2.40 \times 10^{-10} T^6 \text{cal K}^{-1}\text{mol}^{-1}$

Therefore,

$$\Delta S_{0\to100} = \int_0^{100} \frac{2.50\times10^{-4}T^3 - 2.40\times10^{-10}T^6}{T}\, dT$$

$$= \int_0^{100} 2.50\times10^{-4}T^2 - 2.40\times10^{-10}T^5\, dT$$

$$= 2.50 \times 10^{-4} \frac{T^3}{3}\Big|_0^{100} - 2.40 \times 10^{-10} \frac{T^6}{6}\Big|_0^{100}$$

$$= 2.50 \times 10^{-4} \times \frac{(100)^3}{3} - 2.40 \times 10^{-10} \times \frac{(100)^6}{6}$$

$$= \frac{2.50\times(10)^6}{10^4 \times 3} - \frac{2.40}{10^{10}} \times \frac{(10)^{12}}{6} = 83.33 - 40$$

$$= 43.33 \text{ cal mol}^{-1}\,°K^{-1} .$$

Also, $\Delta S_{100\to300} = \int_{100}^{300} \frac{C_p}{T}\,dT = 6\int_{100}^{300} \frac{dT}{T} = 6[\ln 300 - \ln 100]$

$$= 6(1.099)$$

$$\Delta S_{100\to300} = 6.594 \text{ cal mol}^{-1}K^{-1}$$

$$\Delta S_{sublimation} = \frac{\Delta H_{sublimation}}{T}$$

$$= \frac{2000 \text{ cal mol}^{-1}}{100°K}$$

$$\Delta S_{sublimation} = 20 \text{ cal mol}^{-1}K^{-1}$$

Therefore $S_{300} = \Delta S_{0\to100} + \Delta S_{sublimation} + \Delta S_{100\to300}$

$$= 43.33 + 20 + 6.594$$

$$= 69.924 \text{ cal mol}^{-1}K^{-1}$$

b) For the reaction

$$A(c) + 2B(g) \rightleftarrows AB_2(g)$$

$$\Delta H_{300} = \Sigma H_{products} - \Sigma H_{reactants} \quad \text{at} \quad 300°K \qquad (2)$$

$$\Delta S_{300} = \Sigma S_{products} - \Sigma S_{reactants} \quad \text{at} \quad 300°K \qquad (3)$$

Using the data given, and equations (2) and (3)

$$\Delta H_{300} = -41 - (-10) = -31 \text{ kcal mol}^{-1}$$

and

$$\Delta S_{300} = 55 - (15 + 2\times69.924) = -99.8 \text{ cal K}^{-1}\text{mol}^{-1}.$$

By definition, change in Gibbs free energy is

$$\Delta G_{300} = \Delta H_{300} - T\Delta S_{300}$$

$$= -31 \times 10^3 - 300(-99.8)$$

$$= -31000 + 29940$$

$$\Delta G_{300} = -1060 \text{ cal mol}^{-1}$$

The thermodynamic equilibrium constant is given by

$$\ln K_p = -\frac{\Delta G}{RT}$$

where R = gas constant.

$$\ln K_p = \frac{+\,1060}{(1.987)(300)} = 1.778$$

$$K_p = e^{1.778} = 5.92$$

c) $K_p = \frac{P_{AB_2}}{P_B^2}$ where P_i = partial pressure of the ith specimen.

From the reaction, $n_{AB_2} = 1 + x = 1.10$ moles. Here n = number of moles and x = amount present initially. i.e.,

$$\begin{array}{ccc} AB_2 & \rightleftarrows & A + 2B \\ x & & 2x \\ 1 + x & & 1 - 2x \end{array}$$

But $n_{AB_2} = 1 + x = 1.10$,

$\therefore \quad x = 1.10 - 1 = 0.10$ mole .

Also $n_B = 1 - 2x = 1 - 0.20 = 0.80$ mole and $n_{total} = 1.10 + 0.80 = 1.90$ moles.

$$P_{AB_2} = \frac{n_{AB_2}}{n_{total}} P \quad \text{where } P = \text{total pressure}$$

$$P_{AB_2} = \frac{1.10}{1.90} P$$

and

$$P_B = \frac{n_B}{n_{total}} P = \frac{0.80}{1.90} P$$

$$K_p = \frac{P_{AB_2}}{P_B^2} = \left[\frac{1.10}{1.90} P\right] \Big/ \left[\frac{0.80}{1.90} P\right]^2 = 5.92$$

Therefore, P = 0.55 atm.

• PROBLEM 5-4

Between 0 and 60°K the heat capacity of Ag(s) is given approximately by the following expression: $\bar{C}_p\left(\text{cal mole}^{-1}\text{deg}^{-1}\right) \pm 0.1 = -0.023T + 2.5\left(10^{-3}\right)T^2 - 1.9\left(10^{-5}\right)T^3$. (a) About how much more entropy has a mole of Ag(s) at 60°K than at 0°K? (b) If, according to the third law, $S_{Ag(s)}$ is assigned a value of zero at 0°K what is its value at 60°K?

Solution: The increase in entropy of a system due to an increase in temperature can be calculated since the temperature change can be carried out in a reversible manner. Since the heating is carried out at constant pressure, the heat absorbed in each infinitesimal step is equal to the heat capacity multiplied by the differential increase in temperature, dT. Therefore, the increase in entropy

$$dS = \frac{C_p \, dT}{T} \qquad (1)$$

or

$$\left(\frac{\partial S}{\partial T}\right)_p = \frac{C_p}{T} \quad \text{where } S = \text{entropy.}$$

Integrating equation (1) between T_1 and T_2 gives

$$\int_{S_1}^{S_2} dS = \int_{T_1}^{T_2} \frac{C_p dT}{T} \qquad (2)$$

Here S_2 = entropy at 60°K and S_1 = entropy at 0°K.
Therefore,

$$\Delta S = S_2 - S_1 = \int_0^{60} \frac{C_p}{T} dT \qquad (3)$$

Substitute the expression for C_p into equation (3)

$$\Delta S = S_2 - S_1 = \int_0^{60} \left[\frac{-0.023T + 0.0025T^2 - 0.000019T^3}{T}\right] dT$$

$$= -0.023T + \frac{0.0025}{2} T^2 - \frac{0.000019}{3} T^3 \Big|_0^{60}$$

$$= \left[(-0.023)(60) + 0.00125(60)^2 - \frac{0.000019}{3}(60)^3\right] - 0$$

$$= -1.38 + 4.5 - 1.368$$

$$\Delta S = 1.752 \text{ cal mol}^{-1}\text{K}^{-1} .$$

b) $\Delta S = S_2 - S_1 = 1.752$. If $S_1 = 0$, then

$$S_2 = 1.752 + 0 = 1.752 \text{ cal mol}^{-1}\text{K}^{-1}$$

• PROBLEM 5-5

The heat capacity of uranium metal is 0.727 cal $\deg^{-1}$ mole^{-1} at 20°K. Calculate the standard absolute entropy of this substance in cal°K^{-1}mole at 20°K.

<u>Solution</u>: From the Debye 3rd power law $C_p = AT^3$ where C_p = heat capacity, A = constant and T = temperature. By definition,

$$\Delta S_{T_1 \to T_2} = \int_{T_1}^{T_2} \frac{C_p}{T} dT$$

where S = entropy.

$T_1 = 0°K$ in this case and

$T_2 = 20°K$.

Therefore $$\Delta S_{0\to 20} = \int_0^{20} \frac{C_p}{T} dT = \int_0^{20} \frac{AT^3}{T} dT$$

$$= \int_0^{20} AT^2 dT = \frac{AT^3}{3} \Big|_0^{20}$$

$$= \frac{1}{3} AT^3 \Big|_0^{20} = \left(\frac{1}{3} C_p \text{ at } 20^\circ K\right) - 0$$

$$\Delta S = \frac{1}{3}(0.727) = 0.2423 \text{ cal mol}^{-1}K^{-1}.$$

MOLAR ENTROPY

• PROBLEM 5-6

On the basis of the following data calculate the molar entropy of ethylene oxide gas at the boiling point. Graphical integrations are required. Use the Debye T^3 law below 15°K.

T, °K	$\bar{C}_p$, cal mole^{-1} °K^{-1}	T, °K	$\bar{C}_p$, cal mole^{-1} °K^{-1}
15	0.60	160.65	19.80
20	1.43	170	19.66
25	2.34	180	19.55
30	3.30	190	19.49
35	4.26	200	19.47
40	5.21	210	19.50
45	6.02	220	19.56
50	6.77	230	19.67
60	8.16	240	19.82
70	9.22	250	20.00
80	10.06	260	20.21
90	10.76	270	20.46
100	11.43	280	20.67
110	12.06	285	20.77
120	12.77		
130	13.58		
140	14.47		
150	15.39		
160	16.30		
160.65	16.35		

Melting point = 160.65°K

Boiling point = 283.66°K

Enthalpy of fusion = 1236.4 cal mole^{-1}

Enthalpy of vaporization = 6101 cal mole^{-1} at 1 atm

Solution: This problem involves a series of steps. They are

$\Delta S_{0\to15}$, $\Delta S_{15\to160.65}$, ΔS_{fusion}, $\Delta S_{160.65\to283.66}$ and ΔS_{vap}.

By definition, $\Delta S_{T_1\to T_2} = \int_{T_1}^{T_2} \frac{C_p}{T} dT$. Therefore, the area under the curve of a plot of C_p/T vs. T should give the desired ΔS, or C_p

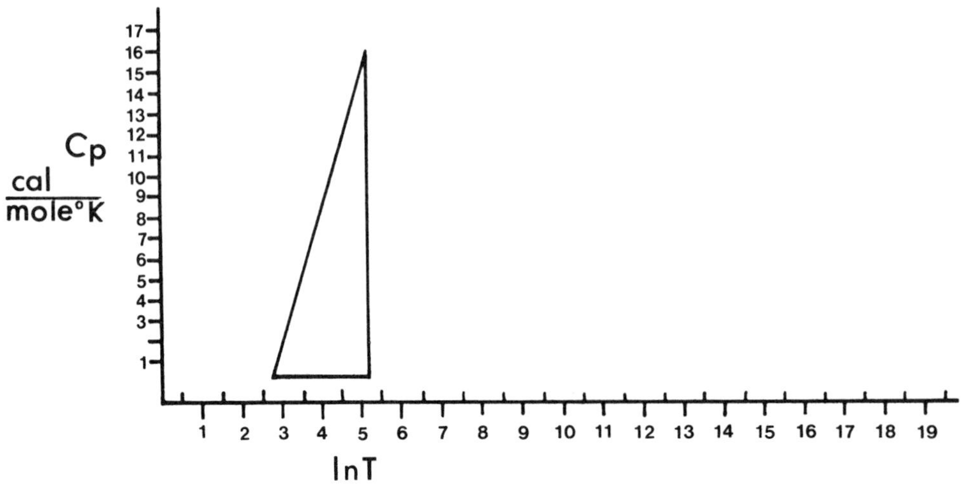

can be plotted again ln T.

ΔS_{fusion} is given by $\frac{\Delta H_{fusion}}{T}$ and ΔS_{vap} is given by $\frac{\Delta H_{vap}}{T}$.

$\Delta S_{0\to15}$ can be obtained by using the Debye 3rd power law. That is,

$C_p = AT^3$.

$$\Delta S_{0\to15} = \int_0^{15} \frac{C_p}{T}\,dT = \int_0^{15} \frac{AT^3}{T}\,dT = \int_0^{15} AT^2\,dT = \frac{AT^3}{3}\Big|_0^{15} = \left(\frac{AT^3}{3} \text{ at } 15^\circ K\right) - 0.$$

But AT^3 at $15^\circ K = C_p$ at $15^\circ K = 0.60$.

$\frac{1}{3} AT^3 = \frac{1}{3}(0.60) = 0.20$ cal $mol^{-1}K^{-1}$.

Plot of C_p against ln T should yield the following results.
The table below gives the value of C_p and the corresponding values of ln T.

$$\Delta S_{15\to160.65} = 16.55 \text{ cal mol}^{-1}K^{-1}$$

and

$$\Delta S_{160.65\to283.66} = 11.25 \text{ cal mol}^{-1}K^{-1}$$

$$\Delta S_{fusion} = \frac{\Delta H_{fusion}}{T} = \frac{1236.4}{160.65} = 7.70 \text{ cal mol}^{-1}K^{-1}$$

$$\Delta S_{vap} = \frac{\Delta H_{vap}}{T} = \frac{6101}{283.66} = 21.51 \text{ cal mol}^{-1}K^{-1}$$

$$S_{283.66} = 0.20 + 16.55 + 11.25 + 7.70 + 21.51$$

$$= 57.21 \text{ cal mol}^{-1}K^{-1}$$

The area of the graph which gives ΔS between $15^\circ K$ and $160.65^\circ K$ is approximately 16.55. Likewise, the area for the curve from $160.65^\circ K$ to $283.66^\circ K$ is 11.25.

C_p	.60	1.43	2.34	3.30	4.26	5.21	6.02	6.77	8.16	9.22	10.06	10.76	
lnT	2.708	2.996	3.219	3.401	3.555	3.689	3.807	3.912	4.094	4.248	4.382	4.500	
C_p	11.43	12.06	12.77	13.58	14.47	15.39	16.30	16.35	19.80	19.66	19.55	19.49	19.47
lnT	4.605	4.700	4.787	4.868	4.942	5.011	5.075	5.079	5.079	5.136	5.193	5.247	5.298
C_p	19.50	19.56	19.67	19.82	20.00	20.21	20.46	20.67	20.77				
lnT	5.347	5.394	5.438	5.481	5.521	5.561	5.598	5.635	5.652				

Calculate the standard molar entropy of gaseous platinum at 1000°K. Use only the following data, together with the assumption that Pt is an ideal monatomic gas with negligible electronic excitation below 1000°K.

T, °K	$\frac{\overline{G^\circ_T} - \overline{H^\circ_{298}}}{T}$, cal mole^{-1}°K^{-1}
298.15	-45.96
1000	-49.17

Solution: This problem can be solved in two ways. The first method is by using the expression

$$S_T = \frac{H_T - G_T}{T} = \frac{H_T - H_{298}}{T} - \frac{G_T - H_{298}}{T} . \tag{1}$$

where S = entropy

T = temperature

H = enthalpy

G = Gibb's free energy .

The other method is by using

$$S_T = S_{298} + \int_{T_1}^{T_2} \frac{C_p}{T}\, dT \tag{2}$$

where C_p = heat capacity at constant pressure. For an ideal monatomic gas,

$$C_p = C_v + R = \frac{5}{2} R .$$

C_v = heat capacity at constant volume.

R = gas constant. Using equation (1)

$$S_T = \frac{H_T - G_T}{T} = \frac{H_T - H_{298}}{T} - \frac{G_T - H_{298}}{T}$$

$$= \frac{H_{1000} - H_{298}}{1000} - \frac{G_{1000} - H_{298}}{1000} \tag{3}$$

At 1000°K, $\frac{G_{1000} - H_{298}}{1000}$ is given to be -49.17 cal mol^{-1}K^{-1},

and

$$H_{1000} - H_{298} = \Delta H = \int_{298}^{1000} C_p dT$$

$$= \int_{298}^{1000} \frac{5}{2} R\, dT = \frac{5}{2} R(1000 - 298) = \frac{5}{2} R(702)$$

$$H_{1000} - H_{298} = \frac{5}{2}(1.987)(702) = 3487.2 \text{ cal mol}^{-1}.$$

Therefore equation (3) becomes

$$S_{1000} = \frac{3487.2}{1000} - (-49.17) = 52.7 \text{ cal mol}^{-1}\text{K}^{-1}.$$

From equation (2) S_{298} is given to be $+45.96$ cal mol^{-1}K^{-1}.

Note that $S_{298} = -\frac{G_{298} - H_{298}}{298} = 45.96.$ Therefore,

$$S_{1000} = S_{298} + \int_{298}^{1000} \frac{C_p}{T}\,dT$$

$$= 45.96 + \frac{5}{2}R[\ln 1000 - \ln 298]$$

$$= 45.96 + \frac{5}{2}R[6.91 - 5.697]$$

$$= 45.96 + 6.02$$

$$= 51.98 \approx 52 \text{ cal mol}^{-1}\text{K}^{-1}$$

The two methods yield acceptable answers.

• PROBLEM 5-8

A certain substance has a molar heat capacity $\bar{C}_p$ given by the following equations:

$\bar{C}_p(s) = 4.0 \times 10^{-5}T^3, 0 < T < 50\,^\circ K$ in cal mole^{-1}K^{-1}

$\bar{C}_p(s) = 5.00,\ 50 \le T < 150\,^\circ K$ in cal mole^{-1}K^{-1}

$\bar{C}_p(liq) = 6.00,\ 50 < T < 400\,^\circ K$ in cal mole^{-1}K^{-1}

At the melting point, $150\,^\circ K$, $\Delta\bar{H}$ of fusion = 300 cal mole^{-1}.

(a) Calculate the third-law molar entropy of this substance in the liquid state at $300\,^\circ K$.

(b) Calculate the molar enthalpy of fusion, entropy of fusion, and Gibbs free energy of fusion at $100\,^\circ K$. Is the sign of $\Delta\bar{G}$ reasonable?

Solution: This is a constant pressure process. Therefore,

$$dS = \frac{C_p}{T}\,dT \tag{1}$$

where S = entropy

T = temperature.

Integrating equation (1) gives

$$\int_{S_1}^{S_2} dS = \int_{T_1}^{T_2} \frac{C_p}{T}\,dT$$

or

$$\Delta S = \int_{T_1}^{T_2} \frac{C_p}{T}\,dT \tag{2}$$

a) This involves the calculation of four entropies which are given by $\Delta S_{0\to 50}$, $\Delta S_{50\to 150}$, ΔS_{fusion} at $150\,^\circ K$ and $\Delta S_{150\to 300}$. It is so because the heat capacities are different at different temperature ranges.

$$\Delta S_{0\to 50} = \int_0^{50} \frac{C_p}{T}\,dT = \int_0^{50} \frac{4\times 10^{-5}T^3}{T}\,dT = \int_0^{50} 4\times 10^{-5}T^2 dT$$

$$\Delta S_{0\to 50} = 4\times 10^{-5}\,\frac{T^3}{3}\Big|_0^{50} = \frac{4\times 10^{-5}\times(50)^3}{3} = 1.67 \text{ cal K}^{-1}\text{mol}^{-1}$$

$$\Delta S_{50\to 150} = \int_{50}^{150} \frac{C_p}{T}\,dT = 5\int_{50}^{150} \frac{dT}{T} = 5[\ln 150 - \ln 50]$$

$$= 5[5.011 - 3.912]$$

$$= 5[1.099] = 5.49 \text{ cal mol}^{-1}\text{K}^{-1}\ .$$

$$\Delta S_{50\to 150} = 5.49 \text{ cal K}^{-1}\text{mol}^{-1}\ .$$

By definition,

$$\Delta S_{fusion} = \frac{\Delta H_{fusion}}{T} = \frac{300 \text{ cal mol}^{-1}}{150°K}$$

$$\Delta S_{fusion} = 2.00 \text{ cal K}^{-1}\text{mol}^{-1}$$

$$\Delta S_{150\to 300} = \int_{150}^{300} \frac{C_p}{T}\,dT = 6\int_{150}^{300} \frac{dT}{T} = 6[\ln 300 - \ln 150]$$

$$\Delta S_{150\to 300} = 6[5.704 - 5.011]$$

$$= 6[0.693] = 4.160 \text{ cal K}^{-1}\text{mol}^{-1}$$

$$S_{300} = \Delta S_{0\to 50} + \Delta S_{50\to 150} + \Delta S_{fusion} + \Delta S_{150\to 300}$$

$$= 1.67 + 5.49 + 2.00 + 4.160$$

$$= 13.32 \text{ cal K}^{-1}\text{mol}^{-1}$$

b) By definition,

1) $$\Delta H_{100} = \Delta H_{150} + \int_{150}^{100} \Delta C_p dT \qquad (3)$$

2) $$\Delta S_{100} = \Delta S_{150} + \int_{150}^{100} \frac{\Delta C_p}{T}\,dT \qquad (4)$$

3) $$\Delta G_{100} = \Delta H_{100} - T\Delta S_{100} \qquad (5)$$

Using equation (3),

$$\Delta H_{100} = 300 + \int_{150}^{100} \Delta C_p dT = 300 + 1.00[100 - 150]$$

$$\Delta H_{100} = 300 - 50 = 250 \text{ cal mol}^{-1}.$$

Equation (4) gives,

$$\Delta S_{100} = 2.00 + \int_{150}^{100} \frac{\Delta C_p}{T}\,dT = 2.00 + 1.00[\ln 100 - \ln 150]$$

$$= 2.00 - 0.41$$

$$= 1.59 \text{ cal K}^{-1}\text{mol}^{-1}\ .$$

Substituting ΔH_{100} and ΔS_{100} into equation (6) gives,

$$\Delta G_{100} = 250 - T\Delta S_{100} = 250 - (100)(1.59)$$
$$= 250 - 159 = 91 \text{ cal mol}^{-1} .$$

Note that $\Delta G_{100} > 0$. Since fusion is not spontaneous below the melting point (of 150°K), it is reasonable that ΔG is positive. Note that the thermodynamic criterion for spontaneity is ΔG be negative.

FREE ENERGY

• PROBLEM 5-9

What is the standard free energy for the oxidation of glucose given by the reaction

$$C_6H_{12}O_6(s) + 6O_2(g) = 6CO_2(g) + 6H_2O(\ell) ?$$

The standard free energy of formation of $C_6H_{12}O_6(s) = -218$ kcal mole^{-1}, for $CO_{2(g)}$, it is -94.0 kcal mole^{-1} and for $H_2O(\ell)$, it is -57.0 kcal mole^{-1}.

Solution: The standard free energy of reaction ΔG° is given by

$$\Delta G^\circ = \Sigma\, \Delta G^\circ_{f(\text{products})} - \Sigma\, \Delta G^\circ_{f(\text{reactants})}$$

where ΔG°_f is the standard free energy of formation. The standard heat of formation of an element in its standard state is zero.

$$\Delta G^\circ = [6(-94.0) + 6(-57.0)] - [-218 + 0]$$
$$\Delta G^\circ = -688 \text{ kcal mole}^{-1}$$

• PROBLEM 5-10

Iodine crystals sublime according to the reaction at 25°C.

$$I_2(s) \rightleftarrows I_2(g) .$$

Find the temperature at which solid iodine crystals and gaseous iodine will exist in equilibrium. Change in enthalpy for the reaction, $\Delta H = 9.41$ kcal/mole and ΔS, the change in entropy, $= 20.\bar{6}$ cal°K^{-1}mole^{-1}.

Solution: ΔG is related to ΔH and ΔS according to the equation

$$\Delta G = \Delta H - T\Delta S . \qquad (1)$$

where ΔG is maximum net energy at constant temperature and pressure available for doing useful work. The sign of ΔG is important because it determines the spontaniety of a reaction. At constant temperature and pressure if a reaction was represented as:

$$A + B \rightleftarrows C + D \qquad \Delta G = 0 \text{ (equilibrium)}$$

the reactants and products of the reaction will be in equilibrium if $\Delta G = 0$. From equation (1) when $\Delta G = 0$ we will then have a state of equilibrium.

$$\Delta G = \Delta H - T\Delta S$$

$$0 = \Delta H - T\Delta S$$

$$T\Delta S = \Delta H$$

$$T_{equil} = \frac{\Delta H}{\Delta S}$$

$$= \frac{9.41 \text{ kcal mole}^{-1}}{\left(20.6 \frac{\text{cal}}{\text{mole°K}}\right)\left(\frac{1 \text{ kcal}}{1000 \text{ cal}}\right)}$$

$$= 457°K$$

$$T_{equil} = 457°K - 273$$

$$T_{equil} = 184°C$$

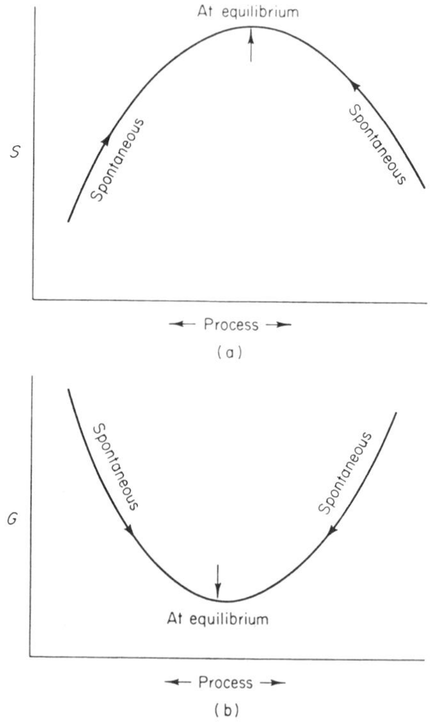

(a) For an isolated system S is a maximum at equilibrium. (b) For a system at constant T and P, G is a minimum at equilibrium.

• PROBLEM 5-11

By measurement of the equilibrium constant for the reaction $H_2O(liq) + CO(g) \rightleftarrows HCOOH(liq)$, the standard free energy of formation of formic acid from the elements is found to be -85,200 cal $mole^{-1}$ at 298°K.

The standard free energy of formation of formic acid from the elements at 298°K is -85,370 cal mole^{-1} by heat capacity measurements. How does the agreement between the two results offer experimental evidence for the validity of the third law of thermodynamics?

Solution: Both methods give results that are very close.

In the former method, the calculation of ΔG was not based on the assumption of the validity of the third law. However, in the latter case the third law was assumed to be valid. (That is, the calculation of ΔG was from the heat capacities).

The agreement between the two results is therefore an evidence that the third law is valid.

ENTHALPY

• PROBLEM 5-12

Use the following table to calculate the enthalpy of propane at 25°C and at one atm assuming the enthalpy of solid carbon and hydrogen gas to be zero at that temperature and pressure.

Bond	Energy	Bond	Energy
H-H	104.2	H-1	71.4
C-C	83.1	C-N	69.7
Cl-Cl	58.0	C-O	84.0
Br-Br	46.1	C-Cl	78.5
I-I	36.1	C-Br	65.9
C-H	98.8	C-I	57.4
N-H	93.4	O-O	33.2
O-H	110.6	N≡N	226
H-Cl	103.2	C=C	147
H-Br	87.5	C≡C	194

C=O 164 in formaldehyde
171 in other aldehydes
174 in ketones,

Resonance energy in kcal/g mole

Benzene ring	= 37
Naphthalene	= 75
Carboxylic acids	= 28
Esters	= 24

The heat of vaporization for carbon(s) to carbon(g) = 171.70 kcal/mole.

Solution: The formation reaction of propane from carbon and hydrogen is

$$3C(s) + 4H_2(g) = C_3H_8(g) .$$

The subscripts (s) and (g) represent solid and gas respectively.

Since the formation of propane takes place at constant pressure, the heat required would be the difference between that of the product and those of the reactants.

From the reaction, three carbons are vaporized and four H-H bonds are broken while two C-C bonds and eight C-H bonds are formed.

In the vaporization of a carbon atom, 171.70 kcal is required. Therefore, the vaporization of three carbon atoms would require 3(171.70) = 515.10 kcal.

From the table, the breaking of four H-H bonds would require 4(104.2) = 416.8 kcal. Therefore, total energy added = 931.9 kcal.

The energy released in the formation of the C_3H_8 molecule is

$$2(83.1) + 8(98.8) = 956.6 \text{ kcal}.$$

Hence the net energy = 931.9 - 956.6 = -24.7 kcal. Note that since the elements (C and H) were at the reference state, the enthalpy would be -24.7 kcal at 25°C.

ZERO POINT ENTROPY

• PROBLEM 5-13

Estimate the zero-point entropy of NO.

Solution: The solid state NO can exist in two orientations which have practically equal chances of existence. The orientations are NO NO and NO ON.

Consequently, the zero-point entropy = $k \ln 2^N$ where k = Boltzmann's constant and N = Avogadro's number.

But $k \ln 2^N = Nk \ln 2 = R \ln 2$

$$\text{Zero point entropy} = (1.987)(0.693)$$
$$= 1.38 \text{ cal mol}^{-1}\text{K}^{-1}.$$

CHAPTER 6

CHEMICAL EQUILIBRIUM

FREE ENERGY

• PROBLEM 6-1

Derive the expression

$$\ln K = \frac{-\Delta H^\circ}{RT} + C,$$

starting with the equation $\Delta G^\circ = -RT \ln K$. C is an integration constant.

Solution: $\Delta G^\circ = -RT \ln K$ (1)

Solve for $\ln K$

$$\ln K = \frac{-\Delta G^\circ}{RT}$$

$$\ln K = -\frac{1}{R}\left(\frac{\Delta G^\circ}{T}\right) \quad (2)$$

Differentiating equation (2) gives

$$\partial \ln K = -\frac{1}{R}\,\partial\left(\frac{\Delta G^\circ}{T}\right) \quad (3)$$

Equation (1) permits a thermodynamic treatment of the variation of K with temperature. For a constant pressure process the change in Gibbs free energy, dG with temperature is $dG = -SdT$. That is,

$$\left(\frac{\partial G}{\partial T}\right)_p = -S$$

or

$$\left[\frac{\partial(\Delta G^\circ)}{\partial T}\right] = -\Delta S^\circ .$$

By definition, $G = H - TS$

$$\therefore \quad \left[\frac{\partial(G/T)}{\partial T}\right]_p = -\frac{H}{T^2}$$

or

$$\left[\frac{\partial(\Delta G/T)}{\partial T}\right]_p = -\frac{\Delta H}{T^2}$$

and also

$$\left[\frac{\partial(\Delta G^\circ/T)}{\partial T}\right]_p = -\frac{\Delta H^\circ}{T^2}$$

Therefore, $$d\left(\frac{\Delta G^\circ}{T}\right) = \frac{-\Delta H^\circ dT}{T^2}$$

Substitute for $\partial\left(\frac{\Delta G^\circ}{T}\right)$ in equation (3)

$$d \ln K = -\frac{1}{R}\left(\frac{-\Delta H^\circ dT}{T^2}\right)$$

$$d \ln K = \frac{\Delta H^\circ dT}{RT^2}$$

Integrating the above equation leads to

$$\int d \ln K = \int \frac{\Delta H^\circ dT}{RT^2}$$

or $$\ln K = -\frac{\Delta H^\circ}{RT} + C$$

• PROBLEM 6-2

K_p has the value 10^{-5} for the equilibrium

$$CO_2(g) + H_2(g) = CO(g) + H_2O(g)$$

at 25°C, and ΔS°, the entropy change, is -10 cal/deg mole for the reaction as written (ΔH° and ΔS° do not change much with temperature.) One mole of CO, 2 moles of H_2, and 3 moles of CO_2 are introduced into a 5-liter flask at 25°C. Calculate (a) ΔG°, the free energy change, at 25°C, (b) the equilibrium pressure, (c) the moles of each species present at equilibrium, and (d) K_p at 100°C.

Solution: There are various expressions for K_p, one of which is

$$\ln K_p = -\frac{\Delta G^\circ}{RT} \tag{1}$$

$$\therefore \quad \Delta G^\circ = -RT \ln K_p$$

$$= -(1.98)(298)(\ln 10^{-5})$$

$$= 6.78 \text{ kcal/mole for the reaction as written.}$$

b) Using $PV = nRT$, we have $P = nRT/V$. Since there is no change in the number of moles, there will still be 6 moles of gas. Therefore, $n = 6$. Now

$$P = \frac{(6)(0.082)(298)}{5} = 29.323 \text{ atm}$$

c) Let x = number of moles of H_2O

What is present at equilibrium from what is introduced initially can be represented by

Initially	3 moles	2 moles	1 mole	0 moles
	$CO_2(g)$ +	$H_2(g)$ =	$CO(g)$ +	$H_2O(g)$
at equilibrium	(3-x)moles	(2-x)moles	(1+x)moles	(x)moles

This change comes about from the stoichiometry of the reaction where each mole of CO_2 and each mole of H_2 consumed produces a mole of CO and a mole of H_2O. Now the K_p expression is represented by:

$$K_p = \frac{P_{H_2O}\, P_{CO}}{P_{CO_2}\, P_{H_2}}$$ where P_i is the partial pressure of the respective gases. P_i = mole fraction of i x P_{tot} where P_{tot} is the total pressure = 29.3 atm.

The mole fraction of $i = \dfrac{\text{moles of } i}{\text{total number of moles}}$,

where total moles = 6 moles. Hence,

$$K_p = \frac{(x/6)\, P_{tot} \left(\frac{1+x}{6}\right) P_{tot}}{\left(\frac{3-x}{6}\right) P_{tot} \left(\frac{2-x}{6}\right) P_{tot}} = 10^{-5}$$

$$10^{-5} = \frac{x(1+x)}{(3-x)(2-x)} = \frac{x + x^2}{6-5x+x^2}$$

$$(x^2-5x+6)10^{-5} = x + x^2$$

$$\frac{x^2}{10^5} - \frac{5x}{10^5} + \frac{6}{10^5} - x - x^2 = 0$$

Approximately, $x = 6 \times 10^{-5}$. Therefore moles of CO_2, H_2, CO and H_2O are 3,2,1 and 6×10^{-5} respectively.

d) $\Delta H^\circ = \Delta G^\circ + T\Delta S^\circ$ (2)

Substituting values at 25°C = 298 °K into equation (2), we have $\Delta H^\circ = 6.78 + (298)(-10/1000)$.

$$\Delta H^\circ = 3.80 \text{ kcal/mole}.$$

Since the problem requires K_p at 100°C = 373°K, we first compute ΔG° at 373°K and then substitute its value into equation (1).

$$\begin{aligned} \Delta G^\circ_{373} &= \Delta H^\circ - T\Delta S^\circ \\ &= 3.80 - (373)(-10/1000) \\ &= 7.53 \text{ kcal/mole} \end{aligned}$$

Thus $$\ln K_p = \frac{-\Delta G^\circ}{RT} = -\frac{7.53 \text{ kcal/mole}}{(373^\circ K) \times 1.987 \times 10^{-3} \text{ kcal/mole}^\circ K}$$

$$\therefore \quad K_p = 3.86 \times 10^{-5}$$

• PROBLEM 6-3

Consider the water-gas reaction C(graphite) + H_2O(g) = CO(g) + H_2(g). Calculate ΔG° and the equilibrium constant at 1000 °K.

Solution: The enthalpy of reaction at temperature T is given by

$$\Delta H_T = \Delta H_0 + \int_0^T \Delta \bar{C}_p dT$$

where ΔH_0 is the hypothetical enthalpy of reaction at absolute zero, valid only in the temperature range where the empirical equations for $\bar{C}_p$ are valid. But $\Delta\bar{C}_p = \Delta\alpha + \Delta\beta T + \Delta\gamma T^2 + \ldots$ where α, β, γ are constants.

$$\therefore \quad \Delta H = \Delta H_0 + (\Delta\alpha)T + \tfrac{1}{2}(\Delta\beta)T^2 + \tfrac{1}{3}(\Delta\gamma)T^3 + \ldots \qquad (1)$$

From the Gibbs-Helmholtz equation

$$\left[\frac{\partial(\Delta G/T)}{\partial T}\right]_p = -\frac{\Delta H}{T^2} \qquad (2)$$

Substitute ΔH of equation (1) into equation (2). After integration the expression is

$$\Delta G = \Delta H_0 - (\Delta\alpha)T \ln T - \tfrac{1}{2}(\Delta\beta)T^2 - \frac{1}{6}(\Delta\gamma)T^3 + \ldots + IT \qquad (3)$$

where I = the integration constant.

$$C(\text{graphite}) + H_2O(g) = CO(g) + H_2(g)$$

$$\Delta G^\circ_{298} = \Delta G^\circ_{f,298}(CO,g) - \Delta G^\circ_{f,298}(H_2O,g)$$

$$= -32.8079 - (-54.6357)$$

$$= 21.8278 \text{ kcal mol}^{-1} .$$

Also from the values of $\Delta H_{f,298}$, determine ΔH°_{298} for the reaction. That is,

$$\Delta H^\circ_{298} = \Delta H^\circ_{f,298}(CO,g) - \Delta H^\circ_{f,298}(H_2O,g)$$

$$= -26.4157 - (-57.7979)$$

$$= 31.3822 \text{ kcal mole}^{-1}$$

The specific heats of the reactants and products in cal/mole K are

$$C(\text{graphite}),\ \bar{C}_p = 3.81 + 1.56 \times 10^{-3}T$$

$$H_2O(g),\ \bar{C}_p = 7.1873 + 2.3733 \times 10^{-3}T + 2.084 \times 10^{-7}T^2$$

$$CO(g),\ \bar{C}_p = 6.3424 + 1.8363 \times 10^{-3}T - 2.801 \times 10^{-7}T^2$$

$$H_2(g),\ \bar{C}_p = 6.9469 - 0.1999 \times 10^{-3}T + 4.808 \times 10^{-7}T^2$$

$$\therefore \Delta\bar{C}_p = \bar{C}_{p},H_2 + \bar{C}_p,CO - \bar{C}_p,H_2O - \bar{C}_p,\text{graphite}$$

$$= 6.9469 + 6.3424 - 7.1873 - 3.81 + (-0.1999\times10^{-3} + 1.8363\times10^{-3} - 2.3733 \times 10^{-3} - 1.56 \times 10^{-3})T + (4.808\times10^{-7} - 2.801\times10^{-7} - 2.084 \times 10^{-7})T^2$$

$$= 2.29 - 2.30 \times 10^{-3}T - 0.077 \times 10^{-7}T^2 .$$

Thus $\alpha = 2.29$, $\beta = -2.30 \times 10^{-3}$ and $\gamma = -0.077 \times 10^{-7}$.

From equation (1),

$$\Delta H_0 = \Delta H - (\Delta\alpha)T - \tfrac{1}{2}(\Delta\beta)T^2 - \tfrac{1}{3}(\Delta\gamma)T^3 + \ldots$$

$$= 31{,}382.2 - 2.29T - \tfrac{1}{2}(-2.30\times10^{-3})T^2 - \tfrac{1}{3}(-0.077\times10^{-7})T^3$$
$$= 31{,}382.2 - 2.29(298\,°K) - \tfrac{1}{2}(-2.30\times10^{-3})(298\,°K)^2 - \tfrac{1}{3}(-0.077\times10^{-7})(298\,°K)^3$$
$$= 31{,}382.2 - 682.42 + 1.0212\times10^2 + 6.7923\times10^{-2}$$
$$= 30{,}802 \text{ cal mol}^{-1}$$

Equation (3) then becomes

$$21{,}827.8 = 30{,}802 - 2.29(298 \ln 298) - \tfrac{1}{2}(-2.30\times10^{-3})(298)^2 - \frac{1}{6}(-0.077\times10^{-7})(298)^3 + 298\,I$$

$$21{,}827.8 = 30{,}802 - 3887.8105 + 1.0212\times10^2 + 3.3962\times10^{-2} + 298\,I$$

$$298\,I = -5.1885\times10^3 \text{ or } I = -17.4\,.$$

From equation (3)

$$\Delta G = 30{,}802 - 2.29T\ln T + 1.15\times10^{-3}T^2 + 0.0128\times10^{-7}T^3 - 17.4T \qquad (4)$$

At $T = 1000\,°K$ equation (4) gives

$$\Delta G°_{1000\,°K} = 30{,}802 - 2.29(1000 \ln 1000) + 1.15\times10^{-3}(1000)^2 + 0.0128\times10^{-7}(1000)^3 - 17.4(1000)$$

$$= 30{,}802 - 15818.76 + 1.15\times10^3 + 1.28 - 17400$$

or

$$\Delta G_{1000°K} = -1.2655 \times 10^3 \text{ cal mol}^{-1}.$$

The equilibrium constant is obtained from the relation

$$\Delta G°_{1000\,°K} = -RT \ln K_p = -1.2655 \times 10^3$$

$$\therefore \ln K_p = \frac{-1.2655\times10^3}{-RT}$$

$$= \frac{1.2655\times10^3 \text{ cal mol}^{-1}}{(1.987 \text{ cal mol}^{-1}\,°K^{-1})(1000\,°K)}$$

$$= 0.63689$$

and

$$K_p = e^{.63689}$$
$$= 1.89$$

• PROBLEM 6-4

K_p is 10^{-3} atm$^{\frac{1}{2}}$ at 2000°K and $\Delta S°$ is 21 cal/deg mole ($\Delta C_p = 0$) for the reaction:

$$CO_2 = CO + \tfrac{1}{2}\,O_2$$

(a) Calculate $\Delta G°$ at 2000°K.

(b) Calculate $\Delta G°$ at 298°K.

(c) Calculate the degree of dissociation of CO_2 if the equilibrium mixture is brought to 2000°K and 2 atm total pressure. Assume $\Delta H°$ and $\Delta S°$ do not change with temperature.

Solution: a) By definition, $\Delta G^\circ = -RT \ln K_p$. (1)

At 2000°K, $\Delta G^\circ = -(R)(2000) \ln 10^{-3}$

$= (-1.98)(2000) \ln 10^{-3}$

$= (-1.98)(2000)(-6.91)$

$\Delta G^\circ = 27354.7$ cal/mole

$= 27.4$ kcal/mole

It may seem odd that K_p has units since we are taking the natural log(ln) of it in finding the free energy. This may be distressing to the more observant student. The following explanation should clear matters up. Remember that $\Delta G = G - G^\circ = nRT \ln (P/P^\circ)$ where G° is the free energy in the standard state which is when $P^\circ = 1$ atm. Consider K_p in an equilibrium expression such as $K_p = P^2_{product}/P_{reactant}$ where the P's represent partial pressures. These partial pressures are actually ratios of these pressures to the standard pressure of 1 atm (which is usually neglected.) Hence, K_p is unitless as would be expected from $\Delta G^\circ = -RT \ln K_p$. Please remember that atmospheres should be used as the pressure units in K_p (not N/m^2, etc.) due to the above explanation.

b) At 298°K,

$$\Delta G^\circ = \Delta H^\circ - T\,\Delta S^\circ \qquad (2)$$

Note that equation (2) is used to determine ΔG° at 298°K and not (1) since K_p is not known at 298°K. At 2000°K, $\Delta H^\circ = \Delta G^\circ_{2000} + T\,\Delta S^\circ = 27.4 + (2000)\frac{(21)}{1000} = 69.4$ kcal/mole. Therefore, using equation (2),

$$\Delta G^\circ_{298} = \Delta H^\circ - (298)\,\Delta S^\circ$$

$$= 69.4 - (298)\frac{(21)}{1000} = 69.4 - 6.3$$

$$= 63.1 \text{ kcal} .$$

c) In calculating the degree of dissociation, the equation used is

$$K_p = \frac{P_{CO}\,P^{\frac{1}{2}}_{O_2}}{P_{CO_2}}$$

where the P with subscripts denote partial pressures. This is equal to

$$K_p = \frac{\left(\frac{n_{CO}}{N}P\right)\left(\frac{n_{O_2}P}{N}\right)^{\frac{1}{2}}}{\frac{n_{CO_2}}{N}P}$$

where the n's with the subscripts denote the number of moles, P represents the total pressure, and N represents the total number of moles. This is equivalent to

$$K_p = \frac{n_{CO}\, n_{O_2}^{\frac{1}{2}}}{n_{CO_2}} \left(\frac{P}{N}\right)^{\frac{1}{2}} \tag{3}$$

Let n° denote the number of moles if there is complete undissociation and α, the degree of dissociation, then

$$n_{CO_2} = (1 - \alpha)n^\circ_{CO_2}$$

$$n_{CO} = \alpha\, n^\circ_{CO_2}$$

$$n_{O_2} = \tfrac{1}{2}\, \alpha\, n^\circ_{CO_2}$$

$$\therefore \quad N = (1 - \alpha)n^\circ_{CO_2} + \alpha\, n^\circ_{CO_2} + \tfrac{1}{2}\, \alpha\, n^\circ_{CO_2}$$

$$= (1 + \tfrac{1}{2}\, \alpha)n^\circ_{CO_2}$$

Now

$$K_p = 10^{-3} = \frac{(\frac{1}{2}\, \alpha)^{\frac{1}{2}}(\alpha)2^{\frac{1}{2}}}{(1 - \alpha)(1 + \frac{1}{2}\alpha)^{\frac{1}{2}}} = \frac{\left(\sqrt{\frac{1}{2}}\, \alpha^{3/2}\, \sqrt{2}\right)}{(1 - \alpha)(\sqrt{1 + \frac{1}{2}\, \alpha})} \tag{4}$$

Since K_p is very small, it can be approximated to be $\alpha^{3/2}$

$$\therefore \quad 0.001 = \alpha^{3/2}$$

and

$$\alpha = 0.01$$

<u>TEST</u>: If we substitute α back into (4), we have

$$K_p = \frac{\sqrt{\frac{1}{2}}(0.001)\ (\sqrt{2})}{(0.99)(\sqrt{1 + 0.005})}$$

$$= .00100759 \approx .001$$

which is close to the original K_p value of 10^{-3}. Note that α can be found explicitly as follows.

Square both sides of equation (4) to get

$$(.001)^2 = \frac{(\alpha/2)(\alpha^2)(2)}{(1-\alpha)^2(1 + \alpha/2)} = \frac{2\left(\alpha^3/2\right)}{(1-2\alpha + \alpha^2)(1 + \alpha/2)}$$

$$(0.000001)(1+\alpha/2 - 2\alpha - 2\alpha^2/2 + \alpha^2 + \alpha^3/2) = 2\alpha^3/2$$

$$(0.000001)(1 - 3/2\ \alpha - \alpha^3/2) = 0$$

$$0.000001 - 0.0000015\alpha - 0.9999995\alpha^3 = 0 \tag{5}$$

Solving this by trial and error for the value of α that will make the left hand side of (5) = 0, $\alpha \approx 0.01$.

• PROBLEM 6-5

PCl_5 vapor decomposes according to the reaction

$$PCl_5 \rightarrow PCl_3 + Cl_2 .$$

Calculate the degree of dissociation α and ΔG° for the reaction, given that the density of a partially dissociated sample of PCl_5 vapor was $4.800 g.dm^{-3}$ at 1 atm and 403°K.

Solution: $PCl_5 = PCl_3 + Cl_2$

	PCl_5	PCl_3	Cl_2
Number of moles present initially	1	0	0
Number of moles of gases at equilibrium	$1-\alpha$	α	α

$$n_{total} = 1 - \alpha + \alpha + \alpha$$

or

$$n_{total} = 1 + \alpha \qquad (1)$$

The density of the equilibrium mixture is given by

$$\rho = \frac{m}{V} = \frac{PM}{RT} \qquad (2)$$

where m is the mass in grams, and M is the molecular weight in grams mol^{-1}. Define ρ_u = density of undissociated PCl_5 and ρ_d = density of mixture. Suppose 1 mole of PCl_5 was started with, then $\rho_u = 1 + \alpha$ and $\rho_d = 1$. Consequently,

$$\frac{\rho_u}{\rho_d} = \frac{1+\alpha}{1} \qquad (3)$$

From equation (2),

$$\rho_u = \frac{(1 \text{ atm})(208.27 g \text{ mole}^{-1})}{(0.08206 \text{ dm}^3 \text{atm}° K^{-1} \text{mole}^{-1})(403° K)}$$

$$= 6.298 \text{ g.dm}^{-3}$$

From equation (3),

$$\rho_d + \alpha \rho_d = \rho_u$$

$$\therefore \quad \alpha = \frac{\rho_u - \rho_d}{\rho_d}$$

ρ_d is given as $4.800 g \ dm^{-3}$

Therefore, $\alpha = \frac{6.298 - 4.800}{4.800}$

or $\alpha = 0.312$

An alternative way to calculate the degree of dissociation, α, is as follows: at equilibrium, the density of the vapor is known. This reflects all the species present and hence is the average density, ρ_{av}. The average molecular weight, M_{av} can be calculated from

$$\rho_{av} = \frac{m}{v} = \frac{PM_{av}}{RT} .$$

Hence,

$$M_{av} = \frac{\rho_{av}RT}{P} = \frac{4.8g\ dm^{-3} \times .0821 dm^3 atm\ °K^{-1} mol^{-1} \times 403°K}{1\ atm}$$

$$= 158.74\ g/mole.$$

The molecular weights of PCl_5, PCl_3, and Cl_2 are 208.24 g/mole, 137.33 g/mole and 70.906 g/mole respectively, Now, the total mass in gms is constant and is equal to M_{av} times the total number of moles at equilibrium. This is equal to the sum of the molecular weight of each species times its number of moles at equilibrium. The equation which represents this is

$$(1 + \alpha)(158.74) = (1 - \alpha)(208.24) + (\alpha)(137.33) + \alpha(70.906).$$

Solving, it is found that $\alpha = .312$

The expression for the equilibrium constant is

$$K_p = \frac{P_{Cl_2} P_{Cl_3}}{P_{Cl_5}}$$

$$= \frac{\left(\frac{\alpha P}{1+\alpha}\right)\left(\frac{\alpha P}{1+\alpha}\right)}{\frac{1-\alpha}{1+\alpha} P}$$

$$= \frac{\left(\frac{\alpha P}{1+\alpha}\right)^2}{\left(\frac{1-\alpha}{1+\alpha}\right) P} = \frac{\alpha^2 P}{(1+\alpha)(1-\alpha)}$$

$$K_p = \frac{\alpha^2 P}{1 - \alpha^2}$$

Therefore, $$K_p = \frac{(0.312)^2 (1\ atm)}{1 - (0.312)^2}$$

or $$K_p = 0.107$$

By definition

$$\Delta G° = -RT \ln K_p$$

$$= -(8.314\ J\ K^{-1} mole^{-1})(403\ K)(1\ mole) \ln 0.107$$

$$= 7488\ J$$

or $$\Delta G° = 7.488\ kJ$$

• PROBLEM 6-6

a) Calculate $\Delta H°$, $\Delta G°$ and K_p at 25°C (298°K) for the following reaction

$$2Ag(s) + 2HCl(g) \rightleftarrows 2AgCl(s) + H_2(g),$$

given that $\Delta H°_{298}$ of formation of HCl(g) and AgCl(s) are -22.06

and -30.36 kcal mole^{-1} respectively and ΔG°_{298} are -22.77 and -26.22 kcal mole^{-1} respectively.

b) In a certain experiment, HCl is introduced at 25°C into an evacuated flask containing both silver and silver chloride until the pressure is 0.5 atm. After equilibrium has been attained and constant temperature and pressure have been maintained, calculate the partial pressures of HCl and H_2 in the equilibrium mixture. (Hint: consider the gases to be ideal and define the unknown to be a quantity expected to be small.)

c) Given that the heat capacities of Ag, AgCl, H_2 and HCl to be 6.01, 12.61, 6.80 and 7.09 cal°K^{-1}mole^{-1} respectively, and that they are constant in the temperature range of 0 and 50°C, express ΔH^0 as a function of temperature in the given temperature range.

d) Express log K_p in the same temperature range.

Solution: $2Ag(s) + 2HCl(g) \rightleftarrows 2AgCl(s) + H_2(g)$

$$\Delta H^\circ_{298} = 2\Delta H^\circ_{f,298}(AgCl,s) - 2\Delta H^\circ_{f,298}(HCl,g)$$
$$= 2(-30.36) - 2(-22.06)$$
$$= (-60.72 + 44.12) \text{ kcal}$$
$$= -16.60 \text{ kcal}$$

$$\Delta G^\circ_{298} = 2\Delta G^\circ_{f,298}(AgCl,s) - 2\Delta G^\circ_{f,298}(HCl,g)$$
$$= 2(-26.22) - 2(-22.77)$$
$$= (-52.44 + 45.54)\text{kcal}$$
$$= -6.90 \text{ kcal}$$

ΔG° can be expressed as $\Delta G^\circ_{298} = -RT \ln K_p$

$$\therefore \quad \ln K_p = \frac{\Delta G^\circ_{298}}{-RT}$$
$$= \frac{-6900 \text{ cal}}{-1.987 \text{ cal mol}^{-1}{}^\circ K^{-1}(298^\circ K)(\text{mol})}$$

or

$$\ln K_p = 11.65 .$$

Consequently,

$$K_p = 1.15 \times 10^5$$

b) $2Ag + 2HCl \rightleftarrows 2AgCl + H_2$

	HCl	H_2
# of moles present initially	n_0	0
# of moles present at equilibrium	$(1-2\alpha)\, n_0$	$\alpha\, n_0$

$$n_{total} = (1 - 2\alpha)n_0 + \alpha\, n_0$$
$$= (1 - \alpha)\, n_0$$

The equilibrium constant expression is

$$K_p = \frac{P_{H_2}}{P^2_{HCl}} = 1.15 \times 10^5 \qquad (1)$$

$$P_{H_2} = \left(\frac{\#\text{ moles } H_2}{n_{total}}\right) P_{total}$$

$$= \left(\frac{\alpha}{1 - \alpha}\right) 0.50 \text{ atm} \qquad (2)$$

Similarly

$$P_{HCl} = \left[\left(\frac{1 - 2\alpha}{1 - \alpha}\right) 0.50 \text{ atm}\right] \qquad (3)$$

From equation (1),

$$1.15 \times 10^5 = \frac{\left(\frac{\alpha}{1 - \alpha}\right) 0.5}{\frac{(1 - 2\alpha)(1 - 2\alpha)}{(1 - \alpha)(1 - \alpha)} \quad (0.50 \text{ atm})^2}$$

$$1.15 \times 10^5 = \frac{\alpha(1 - \alpha)}{(1 - 2\alpha)^2 (0.50 \text{ atm})} \qquad (4)$$

To solve equation (4) : let $\beta = 1 - 2\alpha$, then $\alpha = \frac{1}{2}(1 - \beta)$ and $1 - \alpha = \frac{1}{2}(1 + \beta)$. Equation (4) then becomes

$$1.15 \times 10^5 = \frac{\frac{1}{2}(1 - \beta)[\frac{1}{2}(1 + \beta)]}{\beta^2 (0.50)}$$

$$= \frac{\left(\frac{1}{2} - \frac{\beta}{2}\right)\left[\frac{1}{2} + \frac{\beta}{2}\right]}{\beta^2 (0.50)}$$

$$= \frac{\frac{1 - \beta}{2} \cdot \frac{1 + \beta}{2}}{\beta^2 (0.50)}$$

$$1.15 \times 10^5 = \frac{(1 - \beta)(1 + \beta)}{\beta^2 4(0.5)}$$

$$2.30 \times 10^5 = \frac{1 - \beta^2}{\beta^2}$$

$$2.30 \times 10^5 \beta^2 = 1 - \beta^2$$

$$\beta^2 (2.30 \times 10^5 + 1) = 1$$

$$\beta^2 = \frac{1}{2.30 \times 10^5}$$

$$\beta = 2.1 \times 10^{-3}$$

From equation (2),

$$P_{H_2} = \frac{\frac{1}{2}(1 - \beta)(0.50)}{\frac{1}{2}(1 + \beta)}$$

$$= \frac{\frac{1}{2}(1 - 2.1 \times 10^{-3})(0.50 \text{ atm})}{\frac{1}{2}(1 + 2.1 \times 10^{-3})}$$

$$= 0.50 \text{ atm.}$$

Also from equation (3),

$$P_{HCl} = \left[\frac{\beta(0.50)}{\frac{1}{2}(1+\beta)}\right]$$

$$= \frac{(2.1 \times 10^{-3})(0.50\text{ atm})}{\frac{1}{2}(1 + 2.1 \times 10^{-3})}$$

$$= 2.09 \times 10^{-3}\text{ atm}$$

c) $\Delta C^\circ_P = 2C_P,\text{ AgCl} + C^\circ_P,H_2 - 2C^\circ_P,\text{Ag} - 2C^\circ_P,\text{HCl}$

$= 2(12.61) + 6.80 - 2(6.01) - 2(7.09)\text{cal}^\circ K^{-1}\text{mole}^{-1}$

$= 25.22 + 6.80 - 12.02 - 14.18$

or $\Delta C^\circ_P = 5.82\text{ cal}^\circ K^{-1}\text{mole}^{-1}$.

But $\Delta H^\circ_T = \Delta H^\circ_{298} + \int_{298^\circ}^{T} \Delta C^\circ_P\, dT$

$= \Delta H^\circ_{298} + \Delta C^\circ_P \times 10^{-3}(T - 298)\text{kcal}$

$= -16.60 + 5.82 \times 10^{-3}(T - 298)\text{kcal}$

$= (-16.60 + 5.82 \times 10^{-3}T - 1.73)\text{kcal}$

$\Delta H^\circ_T = -18.33 + 5.82 \times 10^{-3}T\text{ kcal}$

d) The equilibrium constant can be written as

$$\log K_{p,T} = \log K_{p,298} + \frac{1}{2.303\,R}\int_{298^\circ}^{T} \frac{\Delta H^\circ_T}{T^2}dT$$

$$= 5.06 + \frac{1}{4.576 \times 10^{-3}} \times \left[18.33\left(\frac{1}{T} - \frac{1}{298}\right) + 5.82 \times 10^{-3}\ln\frac{T}{298}\right]$$

or $\log K_p,T = 5.06 + 218.53\left[\frac{18.33}{T} - 0.0615 + 5.82 \times 10^{-3}\ln\frac{T}{298}\right]$

$\log K_p,T = 5.06 + 218.53\left[\frac{18.33}{T} - .0615 + 1.3403(10^{-2})\log\frac{T}{298}\right]$

$= 5.06 + 218.53\left[\frac{18.33}{T} - .0615 + 1.3403(10^{-2})\log T - 1.3403(10^{-2})\log\frac{1}{298}\right]$

$= 5.06 + 218.53\left[\frac{18.33}{T} - .0615 + 1.3403(10^{-2})\log T - \left(-3.3162(10^{-2})\right)\right]$

$= 5.06 + 218.33\left[\frac{18.33}{T} - .0615 + 1.3403(10^{-2})\log T + 3.3162(10^{-2})\right]$

$= 5.06 + 218.53\left[\frac{18.33}{T} + 1.3403(10^{-2})\log T + -2.834(10^{-2})\right]$

$= 5.06 + \frac{4005.65}{T} + 2.929\log T + (-6.1931)$

$= -1.1331 + \frac{4005.65}{T} + 2.929\log T$

The following data are available for the reaction $COCl_2 = CO + Cl_2$

$T(^\circ K)$:	635.7	670.4	686.0	722.2	760.2
K_p (atm):	0.01950	0.04414	0.07575	0.1971	0.5183

Plot a graph of $\ln K_p$ versus $1/T$ and extrapolate to $298^\circ K$. Calculate ΔH°, ΔS° and ΔG° for the reaction at $298^\circ K$.

Solution: An expression for the variation of equilibrium constant, K_p, with temperature is derived by using the Gibbs-Helmholtz equation in the form

$$\left[\frac{\partial}{\partial T}\left(\frac{\Delta G}{T}\right)\right]_p = -\frac{\Delta H^\circ}{T^2}$$

since $-\Delta G^\circ = RT \ln K_p$,

$$\left[\frac{\partial}{\partial T}\left(\frac{\Delta G}{T}\right)\right]_p = \frac{\partial}{\partial T}\left(\frac{RT \ln K_p}{T}\right) = +\frac{\Delta H^\circ}{T^2}$$

Therefore,

$$\left(\frac{\partial \ln K_p}{\partial T}\right)_p = \frac{d \ln K_p}{dT}$$

$$= \frac{\Delta H^\circ}{RT^2}$$

or

$$d \ln K_p = \frac{\Delta H^\circ}{RT^2} dT$$

Integrating yields

$$\ln K_p = C - \frac{\Delta H^\circ}{RT} \qquad (1)$$

where C is an integration constant or

$$\ln\left(\frac{K_p, T_2}{K_p, T_1}\right) = -\frac{\Delta H^\circ}{R}\left(\frac{1}{T_2} - \frac{1}{T_1}\right)$$

if the limits are K_p, T_1 at T_1 and K_p, T_2 at T_2. Thus, if $\ln K_p$ is plotted against $1/T$, the slope of the curve at any point is equal to $-\Delta H^\circ/R$

$\ln K_p$	-3.937	-3.120	-2.580	-1.624	-0.657
1000/T	1.573	1.492	1.458	1.385	1.315

The graph of $\ln K_p$ vs $1/T$ is a straight line, indicating that ΔH° is constant for the reaction over the specified temperature range. ΔH° calculated from the slope is

$$\Delta H^\circ = 105.8 \text{ kJ}$$
$$= 25.29 \text{ kcal}$$

Since ΔH° is constant over the temperature range, the following formula can be used to determine K_p at $298^\circ K$.

$$\ln\left(\frac{K_p, T_2}{K_p, T_1}\right) = -\frac{\Delta H^\circ}{R}\left(\frac{1}{T_2} - \frac{1}{T_1}\right) .$$

$$\ln\left(\frac{K_p, 298}{.01950}\right) = \frac{-25290 \text{ cal}}{1.987\text{cal}/^\circ K}\left(\frac{1}{298} - \frac{1}{635.7}\right)$$

$$\ln(K_p, 298) - \ln(.0195) = \frac{-25290}{1.987}(.0178264)$$

$$\ln K_p, 298 = \ln(.0195) - 22.689$$

$$\ln K_{p,298} = -26.63$$

$$K_{p,298} = 2.7 \times 10^{-12}$$

Alternatively:

$$\ln K_{p,T} = C - \frac{\Delta H^\circ}{RT}$$

$$\ln(.0195) = C - \frac{25290 \text{ cal}}{1.987\text{cal/mole}^\circ K(\text{mol}) \times 635.7^\circ K}$$

$$\therefore \quad C = 16.0843$$

$$\ln K_{p,298} = C - \frac{\Delta H^\circ}{RT} = 16.0843 - \frac{25290}{1.987\text{cal/mole}^\circ K(\text{mole}) \times 298^\circ K}$$

$$= -26.63$$

or $\quad K_{p,298} = 2.7 \times 10^{-12}$

Consequently, $\Delta G^\circ_{298} = -RT \ln K_{p,298} = -1.987 \times 298 \times \ln(2.7 \times 10^{-12})$

$$\Delta G^\circ_{298} = 15773 \text{ cal}$$

Now

$$\Delta G^\circ_{298} = \Delta H^\circ_{298} - T\, \Delta S^\circ_{298}$$

$$\therefore \quad \frac{\Delta H^\circ_{298} - \Delta G^\circ_{298}}{T} = \Delta S^\circ_{298} = \frac{25290 \text{ cal} - 15773 \text{ cal}}{298^\circ K}$$

$$\Delta S^\circ_{298} = 31.936 \text{ cal}/^\circ K \times \frac{4.184 \text{ J}}{\text{cal}} = 133.6 \text{ J/K} .$$

• PROBLEM 6-8

a) The equation for the hydrogenation of ethylene may be written as

$$C_2H_4(g) + H_2(g) = C_2H_6(g) .$$

Calculate the heat of hydrogenation using free energies of formation.
b) Determine the equilibrium constant at $200^\circ C$. The following information are given: $\Delta G^\circ_{f,298}$ for the formation of $C_2H_4(g)$ and $C_2H_6(g)$

are 16.282 kcal mole^{-1} and -7.860 kcal mole^{-1} respectively. ΔH°_{298} for the combustion of $C_2H_4(g)$, $H_2(g)$ and $C_2H_6(g)$ are -337.23 kcal, -68.317 kcal and -372.82 kcal respectively.

Solution: a) $C_2H_4(g) + H_2(g) = C_2H_6(g)$ (1)

$$\Delta G^\circ_{298} = \Delta G^\circ_{f,298}(C_2H_6,g) - \Delta G^\circ_{f,298}(C_2H_4,g)$$

$$\Delta G^\circ_{298} = -7.860\ \frac{\text{kcal}}{\text{mole}}(1\text{ mole}) - 16.282\ \frac{\text{kcal}}{\text{mole}}(1\text{ mole})$$

$$= -24.142\text{ kcal}$$

b) The corresponding ΔH°_{298} can be obtained from the enthalpies of combustion. Reaction (1) may be written as

$$C_2H_4(g) + 3O_{2(g)} = 2CO_2(g) + 2H_2O(\ell) \quad \Delta H^\circ_{298} = -337.23\text{ kcal}$$

$$H_2(g) + \tfrac{1}{2}\,O_2(g) = H_2O(\ell) \quad \Delta H^\circ_{298} = -68.317\text{ kcal}$$

$$C_2H_6(g) + 3\tfrac{1}{2}\,O_2(g) = 2CO_2(g) + 3\,H_2O(\ell) \quad \Delta H^\circ_{298} = -372.82\text{ kcal}$$

Then, ΔH°_{298} for equation (1) must be

$$(-337.23) + (-68.32) - (-372.82) = -32.73\text{ kcal}\ .$$

That is, the summation of the ΔH°_{298} of the above reaction equals -32.7 kcal. Observe that for the three reactions to add up to reaction (1), the last of the three must be reversed and consequently, its ΔH°_{298} becomes +372.82 kcal.

In order to calculate K_p at 200°C, it is necessary to find its value at the standard states of 1 atm and 25°C. The free energy change when the reaction occurs, with the reactants and products in their standard states, is given by

$$\Delta G^\circ_{298} = -RT\ln K_p \quad (2)$$

or

$$\ln K_p = \frac{\Delta G^\circ_{298}}{-RT}$$

$$= \frac{-24{,}142\text{ cal mole}^{-1}}{(-1.987\text{ cal mole}^{-1}\cdot K^{-1})(298^\circ K)}$$

$$\ln K_p = 40.772$$

As a result,

$$K_p = 5.09 \times 10^{17}\text{ atm}^{-1}$$

Knowing that

$$\left[\frac{\partial(\Delta G^\circ/T)}{\partial T}\right]_p = -\frac{\Delta H^\circ}{T^2}\ ,$$

Substitute the expression for ΔG° from equation (2) to obtain

$$\frac{d(\ln K_p)}{dT} = \frac{\Delta H^\circ}{RT^2} \quad (3)$$

But $dT/T^2 = -d(1/T)$. Therefore, an alternative form of equation (3) is

$$\frac{d(\ln K_p)}{d(1/T)} = -\frac{\Delta H^\circ}{R} \quad (4)$$

Equation (4) indicates that a plot of $\ln K_p$ versus $1/T$ should be a straight line of slope equal to $-\Delta H^\circ/R$. Integrating equation (4) assuming ΔH° is independent of T gives

$$\ln K_p = -\frac{\Delta H^\circ}{RT} + C$$

where C = the integration constant or if the integration is carried out between T_1 and T_2;

$$\ln \frac{K_{p},T_2}{K_{p},T_1} = \frac{\Delta H^\circ}{R}\left(\frac{1}{T_1} - \frac{1}{T_2}\right) \quad (5)$$

Equation (5) is used to obtain K_p at 200°C. That is,

$$\ln \frac{K_{p,200^\circ C}}{K_{p,25^\circ C}} = -\frac{32{,}730 \text{ cal mole}^{-1}}{1.987 \text{ cal mole}^{-1}\,{}^\circ K^{-1}}\left(\frac{1}{298} - \frac{1}{473}\right)$$

$$= -20.45$$

and

$$K_{p,200^\circ C} = (1.31 \times 10^{-9})(5.09 \times 10^{17})$$

or

$$K_{p,200^\circ C} = 6.67 \times 10^{8} \text{ atm} .$$

• PROBLEM 6-9

Consider the following simultaneous reactions

$$2CO + 4H_2 = C_2H_5OH + H_2O$$

$$CO + 2H_2 = CH_3OH$$

at 300°C and 20 atm, calculate the equilibrium composition when the concentration of H_2 is twice the concentration of CO. K_y for the methanol reaction is 0.0413 and it is 28,700 for the ethanol reaction. K_a, the equilibrium constant, represents the equilibrium activities for the system under standard condition. It is a constant at constant temperature.

Solution: The free energy equation for the methanol reaction is

$$\Delta G° = -16986 + 15.44T\ln T + 1.98 \times 10^{-4} T^2 + 1.14 \times 10^{-6} T^3 - 50.7T.$$

When T = 573°K,

$$\Delta G°_{573} = -16986 + 15.44(573)\ln 573 + 1.98 \times 10^{-4}(573)^2 + 1.14 \times 10^{-6}(573)^3 - 50.70(573) = 10{,}494 \frac{\text{cal}}{\text{mol}}$$

By definition,

$$\Delta G° = -RT \ln K_a$$

$$10{,}494 = -\left(1.987 \frac{\text{cal}}{\text{mol°K}}\right)(573°\text{K}) \ln K_a$$

$$= -1138.6 \ln K_a$$

Therefore $\ln K_a = -9.217$

and $K_a = 1.0 \times 10^{-4}$

Define y = number of moles of methanol and $\frac{x}{2}$ = number of moles of ethanol at equilibrium. At equilibrium, for the reaction

$$2CO + 4H_2 = C_2H_5OH + H_2O,$$

Moles: $1 - x - y$ $\quad 2 - 2x - 2y$ $\quad \frac{x}{2}$ $\quad \frac{x}{2}$

and for the reaction

$$CO + 2H_2 = CH_3OH,$$

Moles: $1 - x - y$ $\quad 2 - 2x - 2y$ $\quad y$

Total moles at equilibrium $= 1 - x - y + 2 - 2x - 2y + y + \frac{x}{2} + \frac{x}{2}$

$$= 3 - 2x - 2y$$

For the methanol reaction

$$K_y = \frac{\left(\frac{y}{3-2x-2y}\right)}{\left(\frac{1-x-y}{3-2x-2y}\right)\left(\frac{2-2x-2y}{3-2x-2y}\right)^2}$$

$$K_y = \frac{y(3-2x-2y)^2}{(1-x-y)(2-2x-2y)^2}$$

Substituting in the given value of K_y gives

$$0.0413 = \frac{y(3-2x-2y)^2}{(1-x-y)(2-2x-2y)^2} \qquad (1)$$

For the ethanol reaction

$$K_y = \frac{\left(\frac{\frac{x}{2}}{3-2x-2y}\right)\left(\frac{\frac{x}{2}}{3-2x-2y}\right)}{\left(\frac{1-x-y}{3-2x-2y}\right)^2\left(\frac{2-2x-2y}{3-2x-2y}\right)^4} = \frac{\left(\frac{x}{2}\right)\left(\frac{x}{2}\right)(3-2x-2y)^4}{(1-x-y)^2(2-2x-2y)^4}$$

Substituting in the given value of K_y gives

$$28{,}700 = \frac{\left(\frac{x}{2}\right)\left(\frac{x}{2}\right)(3-2x-2y)^4}{(1-x-y)^2(2-2x-2y)^4} \qquad (2)$$

Equations (1) and (2) will now be solved simultaneously for y.

From equation (1) set 0.0413 = a and square both sides of the equation.

$$a^2 = \left[\frac{y(3-2x-2y)^2}{(2-2x-2y)^2(1-x-y)}\right]^2 = \frac{y^2(3-2x-2y)^4}{(2-2x-2y)^4(1-x-y)^2}$$

$$\therefore\ a^2 = \frac{y^2}{(1-x-y)^2}\ \frac{(3-2x-2y)^4}{(2-2x-2y)^4} \qquad (3)$$

From equation (2) set 28,700 = b to give

$$b = \frac{\left(\frac{x}{2}\right)\left(\frac{x}{2}\right)(3-2x-2y)^4}{(1-x-y)^2(2-2x-2y)^4}$$

$$\frac{b(1-x-y)^2}{\left(\frac{x}{2}\right)\left(\frac{x}{2}\right)} = \frac{(3-2x-2y)^4}{(2-2x-2y)^4}$$

$$\frac{b(1-x-y)^2}{\frac{x^2}{4}} = \frac{(3-2x-2y)^4}{(2-2x-2y)^4}$$

$$\frac{4b(1-x-y)^2}{x^2} = \frac{(3-2x-2y)^4}{(2-2x-2y)^4} \qquad (4)$$

Substituting equation (4) into equation (3) gives

$$a^2 = \frac{y^2}{(1-x-y)^2} \times \frac{4b(1-x-y)^2}{x^2} = \frac{4by^2}{x^2}$$

or $\quad a^2x^2 = 4by^2$

from which $y^2 = \frac{a^2x^2}{4b}$

and $y = ax\sqrt{\frac{1}{4b}}$

But $a = 0.0413$ and $b = 28{,}700$

$$\therefore\ y = (0.0413x)\left(\sqrt{\frac{1}{4(28700)}}\right)$$

or $y \cong 1.2 \times 10^{-4}x$ (5)

Substituting y in equation (5) into equation (1) and solving for x gives

$$0.0413 = \frac{1.2\times10^{-4}x[3-2x-2(1.2\times10^{-4}x)]^2}{[1-x-(1.2\times10^{-4}x)][2-2x-2(1.2\times10^{-4}x)]^2} \quad (6)$$

A good approximation at this point is to assume that $1.2\times10^{-4}x$ is very much less than x. Hence equation (6) becomes

$$0.0413 = \frac{1.2\times10^{-4}x(3-2x)^2}{(1-x)(2-2x)^2}$$

Solving for x gives

$x = 0.902$

Substituting for x in equation (5) gives

$y = 1.2\times10^{-4}(0.902) = 1.08\times10^{-4}$

The equilibrium compositions are calculated as follows:

Total moles of reactants at equilibrium is

$= 3 - 2x - 2y$

$= 3 - 2(0.902) - 2(1.08\times10^{-4})$

$= 3 - 1.804 - 2.16\times10^{-4}$

$= 1.196$

Moles of CO $= 1 - x - y$

$= 1 - (0.902) - (1.08\times10^{-4})$

$= 0.098$

$$\text{Mole \% of CO} = \frac{\text{moles of CO}}{\text{Total moles of reactants at equilibrium}} \times 100$$

$$= \frac{0.098}{1.196} \times 100 = 8.20\%$$

$$\text{Moles of } H_2 = 2 - 2x - 2y$$

$$= 2 - 2(0.902) - 2(1.08\times10^{-4})$$

$$= 0.196$$

$$\text{Mole \% of } H_2 = \frac{0.196}{1.196} \times 100\%$$

$$= 16.38\%$$

$$\text{Moles of } C_2H_5OH = \text{moles of } H_2O = \frac{x}{2}$$

$$= \frac{0.902}{2}$$

$$= 0.451$$

$$\text{Mole \% of } C_2H_5OH = \text{mole \% of } C_2H_5OH$$

$$= \frac{0.451}{1.196} \times 100\%$$

$$= 37.70\%$$

$$\text{Moles of } CH_3OH = y$$

$$= 1.08 \times 10^{-4}$$

$$\text{Mole \% of } CH_3OH = \frac{1.08\times10^{-4}}{1.196} \times 100\%$$

$$= 0.009\%$$

EQUILIBRIUM CONSTANTS

• PROBLEM 6-10

At a temperature of 1482.53°K and 10.0 atm the equilibrium composition of sodium vapor contains 71.30 weight percent sodium monomer (Na,g), and 28.70 weight percent sodium dimer (Na_2,g). Use the above data to calculate K_p for the reaction

$$2Na(g) \rightleftarrows Na_2(g)$$

Solution: One of the expressions for the equilibrium constant, K_p is in terms of partial pressures. For the reaction

$$2Na(g) \rightleftarrows Na_2(g),$$

$$K_p = \frac{P_{Na_2}}{P_{Na}^2} . \qquad (1)$$

P_{Na_2} and P_{Na} are the partial pressures of Na_2 and Na respectively. Equation (1) can also be written as

$$K_p = \frac{P_{Na_2}}{P_{Na}^2} = \frac{X_{Na_2} P_{total}}{(X_{Na} P_{total})^2} \qquad (2)$$

where X_{Na_2} and X_{Na} = the mole fractions of Na_2 and Na respectively. Assume for the purposes of solving the problem that there are 100 gm of the mixture. The 71.30 weight percent Na would correspond to 71.30 gm and the 28.70 weight percent Na_2 would correspond to 28.70 gm.

$$\text{Moles of Na(g)} = (71.30 \text{ g Na})\left(\frac{1 \text{ mole Na}}{22.990 \text{ g Na}}\right)$$

$$= 3.101 \text{ moles Na}$$

$$\text{Moles of } Na_2(g) = (28.70 \text{ g } Na_2)\left(\frac{1 \text{ mole } Na_2}{45.980 \text{ g } Na_2}\right)$$

$$= 0.624 \text{ mole } Na_2$$

$$\text{Total number of moles} = (3.101 + 0.624)$$

$$= 3.725 \text{ moles}$$

$$\text{Mole fraction of Na(g)}, X_{Na}, = \frac{\text{moles of Na(g)}}{\text{total number of moles}} = \frac{3.101}{3.725} = 0.832$$

$$\text{Mole fraction of } Na_2(g), X_{Na_2} = \frac{\text{moles of } Na_2(g)}{\text{total moles}} = \frac{0.624}{3.725} = 0.167$$

The student should not believe that the assumption of 100 gm was vital to solving the problem. Any amount could have been chosen. The choice of 100 gm was made for convenience. For instance, assume that the total amount of the mixture was 200 gm. Then 71.30 weight percent of Na would be equal to (.7130)(200 gm) = 142.6 gm and the 28.70 weight percent of Na_2 would be equal to (.2870)(200 gm) = 57.4 gm. The number of moles of Na would then be 142.6 g/22.99 g/mole = 6.203 moles. The number of moles of Na_2 would be 57.4 g/45.98 g/mole = 1.248 moles. The total number of moles are then 7.451. The mole fraction of Na is then 6.203/7.451 = .832 and that of Na_2 is 1.248/7.451 = .167 which is the same as before.

From equation (2),

$$K_p = \frac{(0.167)(10 \text{ atm})}{[(0.832)(10 \text{ atm})]^2}$$

$$K_p = 0.024$$

ΔG° is 300 cal at 40°C for the reaction:

$$2NO_2 = N_2O_4$$

(a) Calculate K_p for this reaction at 40°C.

(b) The density of an equilibrium mixture of NO_2 and N_2O_4 gases is found to be 5.85 g/liter at 40°C and a certain pressure. Using the value in (a) for K_p, calculate the degree of dissociation of the N_2O_4, the average molecular weight of the mixture, and the total pressure of the mixture.

Solution: a) Looking at the data given in the problem, the best formula for calculating K_p is $\Delta G^\circ = -RT \ln K_p$ or

$$\ln K_p = -\frac{\Delta G^\circ}{RT} \qquad (1)$$

where ΔG° = free energy change, R = gas constant and T = temperature.

Here,
$$\Delta G^\circ = 300 \text{ cal}$$
$$R = 1.98 \text{ cal mole}^{-1}\text{degree}^{-1}$$
$$T = 40^\circ C = (40 + 273)^\circ K = 313^\circ K$$

Substituting these values into equation (1), gives

$$\ln K_p = -\frac{300}{(1.98)(313)} = -0.484$$

$$\therefore \quad K_p = e^{-0.484} = 0.62$$

or

$$2.303 \log K_p = -\frac{300}{(1.98)(313)}$$

$$\log K_p = -\frac{300}{(1.98)(313)(2.303)} = -0.21$$

or
$$K_p = 0.62 .$$

b) From the ideal gas law,

$$PM = \rho RT \qquad (2)$$

where
P = Pressure
M = Average molecular weight
ρ = Density = 5.85 g/liter
R = Gas constant = 0.082
T = Temperature = 313

Therefore $PM = (5.85)(0.082)(313) = 150$ g atm/mole . Let n° denote the number of moles if the N_2O_4 were completely undissociated and α, the degree of dissociation. Then $n_{N_2O_4} = (1 - \alpha)n^\circ$, $n_{NO_2} = 2\alpha n^\circ$ and $N = (1 + \alpha)n^\circ$. The average molecular weight M is:

$M = 46N_{NO_2} + 92N_{N_2O_4}$ where N_{NO_2} = mole fraction of $NO_2 = \dfrac{2\alpha n^\circ}{(1+\alpha)n^\circ}$

or $N_{N_2O_4}$ = mole fraction of $N_2O_4 = \dfrac{(1-\alpha)n^\circ}{(1+\alpha)n^\circ}$

$M = 46\dfrac{2\alpha}{1+\alpha} + 92\dfrac{1-\alpha}{1+\alpha} = 92/(1+\alpha)$. Since $P = 150/M$, we find $P = (1+\alpha)(150/92)$. Finally, the equilibrium constant is

$$K_p = \frac{n_{N_2O_4}}{n^2_{NO_2}} \frac{N}{P} = (1-\alpha)(1+\alpha)/4\alpha^2 P$$

or

$$0.62 = 92(1-\alpha)/150 \times 4\alpha^2$$

Then $(1-\alpha)/\alpha^2 = 4.04$. Use the formula $\alpha = \dfrac{-b \pm \sqrt{b^2 - 4ac}}{2a}$ to solve for α

$$\therefore \quad \alpha = \frac{-1 \pm \sqrt{1 + 16.16}}{8.08}$$

Picking the positive value for α gives $\alpha = 0.39$. M is then $92/1.39 = 66$, and $P = 150/66 = 2.27$ atm.

• PROBLEM 6-12

Four and four-tenths grams of CO_2 are introduced into a 1-liter flask containing excess solid carbon, at 1000°C, so that the equilibrium

$$CO_2(g) + C(s) = 2CO(g)$$

is reached. The gas density at equilibrium corresponds to an average molecular weight of 36.

(a) Calculate the equilibrium pressure and the value of K_p.

(b) If, now, an additional amount of He (inert) is introduced until the total pressure is doubled, the equilibrium amount of CO will be (increased, decreased, unchanged, insufficient information to tell). If, instead, the volume of the flask were doubled, with He introduced to maintain the same total pressure, the equilibrium amount of CO would (increase, decrease, be unchanged, insufficient data to tell).

(c) If in (a) there where actually 1.2 g of C(s) present, how many moles of CO_2 would have to be introduced so that at equilibrium only a trace of carbon remained?

(d) If the K_p for the equilibrium doubles with a 10°C increase in temperature, what is ΔH° for the reaction?

Solution: (a) From the definition of average molecular weight,

$$36 = 44N_{CO_2} + 28N_{CO} \qquad (1)$$

where

$$N_{CO_2} = \text{mole fraction of } CO_2$$

$$N_{CO} = \text{mole fraction of } CO \text{ .}$$

The summation of the mole fractions must be unity, that is

$$N_{CO_2} + N_{CO} = 1 \qquad (2)$$

Therefore solving equations (1) and (2) simultaneously gives

$$44N_{CO_2} + 28N_{CO} = 36$$

$$N_{CO_2} + N_{CO} = 1$$

or

$$N_{CO_2} = 1 - N_{CO}$$

If $N_{CO_2} = 1 - N_{CO}$ is substituted into equation (1), it (equation (1)) becomes $44(1 - N_{CO}) + 28N_{CO} = 36$

$$44 - 44N_{CO} + 28N_{CO} = 36$$

$$-44N_{CO} + 28N_{CO} = 36 - 44 = -8$$

$$-16N_{CO} = -8$$

$$N_{CO} = \tfrac{1}{2} \text{ .}$$

Now substituting the value for N_{CO} into equation (2), we have

$$N_{CO_2} + \tfrac{1}{2} = 1$$

or

$$N_{CO_2} = 1 - \tfrac{1}{2} = \tfrac{1}{2} \text{ .}$$

N_{CO_2} can also be found by substituting $N_{CO} = \frac{1}{2}$ into equation (1).

That is

$$(44)N_{CO_2} + (28)(\tfrac{1}{2}) = 36$$

$$44N_{CO_2} = 36 - 14 = 22$$

or

$$N_{CO_2} = 22/44 = \tfrac{1}{2} \text{ .}$$

The initial 4.4 g correspond to 0.1 mole of CO_2. That is, number of moles = weight/molecular weight. The molecular weight of $CO_2 = 12 + 32 = 44$. Therefore, the number of moles = 4.4/44 = 0.1. If x denotes the moles of CO formed, $0.1 - x/2$ = moles CO_2 remaining and $0.1 + x/2$ the total moles. Hence $\frac{1}{2} = x/(0.1 + x/2)$ or $x = 0.0667$ and the total moles are 0.133. The total pressure is then $P = nRT/v$ or $P = 0.133 \times 0.082 \times 1273/1$ or $P = 13.9$ atm, and $P_{CO_2} = P_{CO} = 6.95$ atm and $K_p = (6.95)^2/6.95 = 6.95$ atm. i.e., $K_p = P^2_{CO}/P_{CO_2}$.

(b) Introducing inert gas at constant volume will not change the equilibrium partial pressures and hence will not change the position of equilibrium. Doing so at constant total pressure, however, dilutes the mixture, and the equilibrium will shift in the direction of forming more CO.

(c) The moles of CO formed must be 0.2 since the 0.1 mole of carbon is to be essentially used up. P_{CO} is then 0.2 x 0.082 x 1273/1 = 20.9, and, from the equilibrium constant, P_{CO_2} must be $(20.9)^2/6.95 = 62.9$ atm, so there must be 62.9 x 1/0.082 x 1273 or 0.602 moles of CO_2 present. The total moles of CO_2 required will then be 0.1 + 0.602 or 0.702.

(d) From the van't Hoff equation, $2.303 \log(K_2/K_1) = -\Delta H^\circ/R\ (1/T_2 - 1/T_1)$.

$$\log 2 = \frac{-\Delta H^\circ}{1.98\ \text{cal}/^\circ K \times 2.303}(1/1283 - 1/1273) .$$

(Note that $K_2/K_1 = 2$ because K_p is doubled).

Note also that $(1/T_2 - 1/T_1) = ((T_1 - T_2)/T_2T_1)$. Hence $\log(2) = \frac{-\Delta H^\circ}{1.98 \times 2.303}\left(\frac{1}{1283} - \frac{1}{1273}\right)$ is equal to $\log(2) = \frac{-\Delta H^\circ}{1.987 \times 2.303}\left(\frac{1273 - 1283}{(1273)(1283)}\right)$

$$= \frac{\Delta H^\circ}{2.303 \times 1.987\text{cal}/^\circ K}\left(\frac{1283 - 1273}{(1273) \times (1283)}\right)$$

or

$$\Delta H^\circ = 0.3 \times 1.98\text{cal}/^\circ K \times 2.3 \times 1283 \times 1273/10 = 2.24 \times 10^5 \text{cal}$$
$$= 224 \text{ kcal} .$$

• PROBLEM 6-13

Calculate K_p for the reaction

$$S(s) + 2CO(g) = SO_2(g) + 2C(s) .$$

At the temperature in question, two atmospheres of CO are introduced into a vessel containing excess solid sulfur, and a final equilibrium pressure of 1.03 atm is observed.

Solution: For this reaction,

$$K_p = \frac{P_{SO_2}}{P^2_{CO}} \quad (1)$$

Let α = fraction of CO reacted (degree of dissociation). Then

$$P_{SO_2} = 2\left(\frac{\alpha}{2}\right) = \alpha$$

and

$$P_{CO} = 2(1 - \alpha) .$$

But total pressure, $P = 1.03 = P_{SO_2} + P_{CO}$

$$\therefore \quad 1.03 = 2\left(\frac{\alpha}{2}\right) + 2(1 - \alpha)$$

$$1.03 = \alpha + 2 - 2\alpha$$

$$-0.97 = -\alpha$$

or $$\alpha = 0.97$$

Now, using equation (1) yields

$$K_p = \frac{\alpha}{(2(1-\alpha))^2} = \frac{0.97}{(2(0.03))^2} = \frac{0.97}{0.0036}$$

$$K_p = 269.44 \text{ atm}^{-1} .$$

• PROBLEM 6-14

Gaseous COF_2 is passed over a catalyst at 1000°C and comes to equilibrium according to the equation:

$$2COF_2 = CO_2 + CF_4$$

The pressure is maintained at 10 atm. A sample of the equilibrium mixture is quickly cooled (which stops any shift in concentrations) and analysis shows that, out of 500 cc (STP) of the mixture, there are 300 cc (STP) of combined COF_2 and CO_2. (This is done by passing the mixture through barium hydroxide solution, which absorbs COF_2 and CO_2 but not CF_4).

(a) Calculate K_p for the equilibrium.

(b) If K_p increases by 1% per degree around 1000°C, calculate $\Delta H°$, $\Delta S°$, and $\Delta G°$ at this temperature.

Solution: a) The analysis shows that there are 300 cc COF_2 and CO_2 conbined, thus there are 500 - 300 = 200 cc (at STP) of CF_4. There is 200 cc (STP) of CO_2 since this is formed in equimolar amounts. There are then 100 cc (STP) of COF_2.

The ratio of $CF_4 : CO_2 : COF_2$ is 2:2:1 because of the 200: 200: 100. Therefore use this ratio to find out the individual mole fraction. Since the mole fractions must add up to unity, they (mole fractions) are (2/5) x 1 = 0.4, (2/5) x 1 = 0.4 and (1/5) x 1 = 0.2 for CF_4, CO_2 and COF_2 respectively. Now that the mole fractions are known and the total pressure is unchanged, the respective partial pressures can be computed by the equation $P_i = x_i P$ where

P_i = Partial pressure of substance i

x_i = Mole fraction of substance i

P = Total pressure = 10 atm in this problem.

Therefore $P_{CF_4} = (0.4)(10) = 4$ atm

$$P_{CO_2} = (0.4)(10) = 4 \text{ atm}$$

$$P_{COF_2} = (0.2)(10) = 2 \text{ atm}$$

By definition,

$$K_p = \frac{P_{CF_4} P_{CO_2}}{P^2_{COF_2}} = \frac{(4)(4)}{(2)^2} = 4 \text{ atm}$$

(b) We use the equation: $d \ln K_p/dT = \Delta H^\circ/RT^2$, where $d \ln K_p/dT$ is simply the fractional change in K_p per degree and is equal to 0.01, i.e., 1% increase/degree. Then $\Delta H^\circ = 0.01 \times 1.98 \times 10^{-3} \times 1273^2 = 32.1$ kcal. Also $\Delta G^\circ = -RT \ln K_p = -1.98 \times 10^{-3} \times 1273 \times 2.3 \log 4 = -3.49$ kcal. Therefore, $\Delta S^\circ = (\Delta H^\circ - \Delta G^\circ)/T = 27.96$ cal/deg.

• PROBLEM 6-15

Ferrous sulfate undergoes a thermal decomposition as follows:

$$2FeSO_4(s) = Fe_2O_3(s) + SO_2(g) + SO_3(g)$$

At 929°K the total gas pressure is 0.9 atm with both solids present.

(a) Calculate K_p for this temperature.

(b) Calculate the equilibrium total pressure that will be obtained if excess ferrous sulfate is placed in a flask at 929°K, which contains an initial SO_2 pressure of 0.6 atm.

<u>Solution</u>: a) In this problem, $K_p = P_{SO_2} P_{SO_3}$. (1)

P_{FeSO_4} and $P_{Fe_2O_3}$ are both unity since they are solids and do not affect the equilibrium constant of the reaction.

The reaction equation shows that each gas is formed in equal amounts, therefore their mole fractions are 0.5 each. Their partial pressures are given by the relation $P_i = x_i P$ where

P_i = partial pressure of the ith species

x_i = mole fraction of the ith species

P = total pressure

Therefore P_{SO_2}, P_{SO_3}, are 0.5P each, or (0.5)(0.9) = 0.45 atm each.

Substituting these values into equation (1) gives $K_p = (0.45)(0.45) = 0.203 \text{ atm}^2$.

b) Now, the new SO_2 partial pressure is equal to P_{SO_2} obtained in part (a) + 0.6. But P_{SO_2} from part (a) = P_{SO_3}. Therefore, new

SO_2 partial pressure = $P_{SO_3} + 0.6$. From equation (1),

$$K_p = \left(P_{SO_3} + 0.6\right)\left(P_{SO_3}\right)$$

$$0.203 = P^2_{SO_3} + 0.6P_{SO_3}$$

$$\therefore \quad P^2_{SO_3} + 0.6P_{SO_3} - 0.203 = 0$$

Using the quadratic " almighty" formula, we get

$$P_{SO_3} = \frac{-b \pm \sqrt{b^2 - 4ac}}{2a}$$

$$= \frac{-0.6 \pm \sqrt{0.36 + 0.812}}{2}$$

$$= \frac{-0.6 \pm 1.083}{2}$$

There are two possible answers which are

$$P_{SO_3} = \frac{-0.6 + 1.083}{2} = 0.241$$

and $P_{SO_3} = \dfrac{-0.6 - 1.083}{2} = -0.842$. But P_{SO_3} cannot be negative.

Therefore, $P_{SO_3} = 0.241$ atm. The new $P_{SO_2} = P_{SO_3} + 0.6 = 0.24 + 0.6$ $= 0.841$ atm. Total pressure, $P = P_{SO_3} + P_{SO_2}$

$$= 0.241 + 0.841$$

$$= 1.082 \text{ atm.}$$

• PROBLEM 6-16

In a study of the equilibrium, $H_2 + I_2 = 2HI$, a certain number of moles x of HI are formed when 1 mole of H_2 and 3 moles of I_2 are introduced into a flask of volume V at temperature T. On introducing 2 additional moles of H_2, the amount of HI formed is found to be 2x. Calculate K_p.

Solution: Let n = number of moles at equilibrium, then

$$n_{HI} = x$$

$$n_{H_2} = 1 - x/2$$

and $$n_{I_2} = 3 - x/2$$

Now, if $n_{HI} = 2x$,

$$n_{H_2} = 2 + (1 - 2x/2) = 3 - x$$

and $$n_{I_2} = 3 - 2x/2 = 3 - x \ .$$

Since there are an equal number of moles of gaseous species on both sides of the equation, $K_p = K_n$, hence

$$\frac{x^2}{(1 - x/2)(3 - x/2)} = \frac{(2x)^2}{(3 - x)^2}$$

Solving for x yields

$$x^2(3 - x)^2 = (2x)^2(1 - x/2)(3 - x/2)$$
$$x^2\left(9 - 6x + x^2\right) = 4x^2(3 - 2x + x^2/4)$$
$$9 - 6x + x^2 = 4(3 - 2x + x^2/4)$$

$$\therefore \quad \frac{9 - 6x + x^2}{3 - 2x + x^2/4} = 4$$

$$9 - 6x + x^2 = 12 - 8x + x^2$$
$$9 - 6x + x^2 - 12 + 8x - x^2 = 0$$
$$-3 + 2x = 0$$

or x = 1.5. Now,

$$K_p = \frac{(1.5)^2}{(1 - 1.5/2)(3 - 1.5/2)} = \frac{2.25}{(.25)(2.25)} = \frac{1}{.25} = 4 \ .$$

• PROBLEM 6-17

A 2-liter flask maintained at 700°K contains 0.1 mole of CO and a catalyst for the reaction

$$CO(g) + 2H_2(g) = CH_3OH(g)$$

Hydrogen is introduced until the equilibrium total pressure is 7 atm, at which point 0.06 moles of methanol are formed.

(a) Calculate K_p in atm^{-2}

(b) What would the final pressure be were the same amounts of CO and H_2 used but with no catalyst present so that no reaction occurs?

Solution: Using the equation PV = nRT

where
P = total pressure
V = volume
n = final total moles
R = gas constant
T = temperature

We can solve for n, the final total moles. This value will enable us to compute the individual moles and finally K_p .

$$n = \frac{PV}{RT} = \frac{(7)(2)}{(0.082)(700)} = 0.244 \text{ moles.}$$

In this problem, 0.06 moles of methanol are formed. So the number of moles of CO and H_2 are 0.244 - 0.06 = 0.184. However, the number of moles of the CO must be 0.1 - 0.06 = 0.04, so the number of moles of H_2 must be 0.184 - 0.04 = 0.144. Therefore, the equilibrium constant

$$K_p = \frac{(0.06)(0.244)^2}{(0.04)(0.144)^2(7)^2} = 0.088 \text{ atm}^{-2}$$

(b) Had no reaction occurred, the moles of CO would remain 0.1, and the moles of H_2 would be 0.144 plus twice the moles of methanol in (a), or 0.144 + 0.12 = 0.264. The total moles are then 0.364 and

$$P = \frac{nRT}{V} = \frac{(0.364)(0.082)(700)}{2}$$
$$= 10.45 \text{ atm.}$$

• PROBLEM 6-18

One and one-tenth grams of NOBr is placed in an evacuated 1-liter flask at -55°C. The flask is then warmed to 0°C, at which temperature the contents are gaseous and exert a pressure of 0.3 atm. On further warming to 25°C, the equilibrium total pressure rises to 0.35 atm. At both 0°C and 25°C the equilibrium

$$2NOBr = 2NO + Br_2$$

is present. Calculate K_p for the reaction at 0°C, and ΔH°. The atomic weight of Br is 80.

Solution: Number of moles NOBr = $\frac{\text{weight NOBr}}{\text{molecular weight NOBr}}$. The molecular weight of NOBr = 14 + 16 + 80 = 110 gm/mol. Therefore, the 1.1 grams of NOBr correspond to (1.1/110) moles of NOBr = 0.01 moles. Now, if α denotes the degree of dissociation, at equilibrium,

n_{NOBr} = number of moles of NOBr = $(1 - \alpha)(0.01)$

n_{NO} = number of moles of NO = 0.01α

n_{Br_2} = number of moles of Br_2 = $0.01\alpha/2 = 0.005\alpha$

$$N = \text{total number of moles} = (1 - \alpha)(0.01) + 0.01\alpha + 0.005\alpha$$
$$= 0.01 - 0.01\alpha + 0.01\alpha + 0.005\alpha$$
$$= 0.01 + 0.005\alpha = 0.01(1 + 0.5\alpha)$$
$$= 0.01(1 + \alpha/2)\ .$$

By definition, PV = NRT where P = pressure
V = volume
R = gas constant
T = temperature

Therefore $$N = \frac{PV}{RT} = \frac{(0.3)(1)}{(0.082)(273)} = 0.0134\ .$$ Hence

$$0.01(1 + \alpha/2) = 0.0134$$

$$\therefore \quad 1 + \alpha/2 = \frac{0.0134}{0.01} = 1.34$$

and $$\alpha/2 = 1.34 - 1 = 0.34$$

or $$\alpha = (2)(0.34) = 0.68$$

$$K_p = \frac{n_{NO}^2 \, n_{Br_2}}{n_{NOBr}^2} \frac{P}{N} \qquad (1)$$

From the calculations above,

$$n_{NO}^2 = [(0.01)0.68]^2 = 0.00004624$$

$$n_{Br_2} = 0.005\alpha = (0.005)(0.68) = 0.0034$$

$$n_{NOBr}^2 = [(1 - \alpha)(0.01)]^2 = [(0.32)(0.01)]^2 = 0.00001024$$

$$N = 0.01(1 + \alpha/2) = (0.01)(1 + 0.34) = 0.0134$$

Substituting these values into equation (1), gives

$$K_p = \frac{(0.00004624)(0.0034)}{(0.00001024)} \frac{0.3}{0.0134}$$

$$K_p = \frac{0.4624}{0.1024} \frac{(0.0034)(0.3)}{(0.0134)}$$

$$K_p = 0.344 \text{ atm}$$

The above calculations was done at $0^\circ C = 273^\circ K$. Repeating it for $25^\circ C = 298^\circ K$ and 0.35 atm, yields

$$N = \frac{PV}{RT} = \frac{(0.35)(1)}{(0.082)(298)} = 0.0143 \text{ mole} .$$

Therefore $$0.0143 = (1 + \alpha/2)(0.01)$$

$$0.43 = \alpha/2$$

or $$\alpha = 0.86 .$$

Using the new values and equation (1), $K_p = 3.97$ atm.

Consequently,

$$\ln \frac{K_{P2}}{K_{P1}} = -\frac{\Delta H^\circ}{R}\left(\frac{1}{T_2} - \frac{1}{T_1}\right)$$

$$\ln \frac{3.97}{0.344} = -\frac{\Delta H^\circ}{1.98}\left(\frac{1}{298} - \frac{1}{273}\right)$$

$$2.446 = \frac{-\Delta H^\circ}{1.98}(0.00336 - 0.00366)$$

$$2.446 = \Delta H^\circ (0.000155)$$

$$\Delta H^\circ = 15780.6 \text{ cal}$$

or $$\Delta H^\circ = 15.780 \text{ kcal.}$$

• PROBLEM 6-19

The reaction,

$$Fe_3O_4(s) + CO(g) \rightleftarrows 3FeO(s) + CO_2(g)$$

took place at $600^\circ C$ with an equilibrium constant of 1.15. Determine the amount of each substance at equilibrium if there were 1 mole of Fe_3O_4, 2 moles of CO, 0.5 moles of FeO and 0.3 moles of CO_2 originally present in the mixture, and then heated at a constant total pressure of 5.00 atm to a temperature of 600°C.

Solution: Let y = number of moles of each species present initially

$$Fe_3O_4(s) + CO(g) \rightleftarrows 3FeO(s) + CO_2(g)$$

	$Fe_3O_4(s)$	$CO(g)$	$3FeO(s)$	$CO_2(g)$
initial number of moles	1	2	.5	.3
number of moles reacting	y	y	3y	y
number of moles at equilibrium	(1 - y)	(2 - y)	(0.5+3y)	(0.3+y)

$$K_p = \frac{P_{CO_2}}{P_{CO}} = 1.15 \quad (1)$$

Total number of moles of gas = 2.3.

Therefore,

$$P_{CO_2} = \left(\frac{0.3 + y}{2.3}\right)\left(5.00 \text{ atm}\right) \quad (2)$$

$$P_{CO} = \left(\frac{2 - y}{2.3}\right)\left(5.00 \text{ atm}\right) \quad (3)$$

Substitute equations (2) and (3) into (1) to obtain

$$K_p = \frac{(0.3+y)/2.3}{(2-y)/2.3} = 1.15 \ .$$

Solving for y yields

$$\frac{(0.3+y)/2.3}{(2-y)/2.3} = 1.15$$

$$\frac{0.3+y}{2-y} = 1.15$$

$$0.3+y = 2.3 - 1.15y$$

$$2.15y = 2.0$$

or

$$y = 0.93$$

At equilibrium then,

number of moles of CO_2 = 0.3 + y = 1.23

number of moles of CO = 2 - y = 1.07

number of moles of Fe_3O_4 = 1 - y = 0.07

number of moles of FeO = 0.5 + 3y = 3.29

• PROBLEM 6-20

K_p has the value 10^{-6} atm^3 and 10^{-4} atm^3 at 25°C and 50°C, respectively, for the reaction:

$$CuSO_4 \cdot 3H_2O(s) = CuSO_4(s) + 3H_2O(g)$$

(a) What is the minimum number of moles of water vapor that

must be introduced into a 2-liter flask at 25°C in order to completely convert 0.01 mole of $CuSO_4$ to the trihydrate. Show your calculations.

(b) Calculate ΔH° for the reaction.

Solution: a) From the reaction, $K_p = P^3_{H_2O}$. Therefore, the H_2O pressure at equilibrium at 25°C is given by

$$P_{H_2O} = \sqrt[3]{K_p} = \left(K_p\right)^{\frac{1}{3}} = \left(10^{-6}\right)^{\frac{1}{3}}$$

$$= 10^{-2} \text{ atm} .$$

Using $PV = nRT$ to solve for n where P = pressure, V = volume, n = number of mole, R = gas constant and T = temperature, yields

$$n = \frac{PV}{RT} = \frac{(10^{-2})(2)}{(0.082)(298)}$$

$$\therefore \quad n = 0.00082 \text{ mole}$$

These are the number of moles that correspond to the equilibrium pressure of the water vapor. In addition, for every mole of $CuSO_4(s)$ that gets converted to the trihydrate, 3 moles of water vapor gets converted to the hydrate (from the stoichiometry of the reaction). Hence to convert .01 moles of $CuSO_4(s)$ to $CuSO_4 \cdot H_2O(s)$, .03 moles of $H_2O(g)$ are needed. Therefore, the total number of moles of $H_2O(g)$ that must be introduced into the 2 liter flask are .03 + .00082 = .03082 moles.

b) Using the van't Hoff equation,

$$\ln\left(\frac{K_{T_2}}{K_{T_1}}\right) = \frac{\Delta H^\circ}{R}\left(\frac{1}{T_1} - \frac{1}{T_2}\right)$$

where $\quad K_{T_2} = K_p$ at $T_2 \cdot \left(T_2 = 50^\circ C = 323^\circ K\right)$

$\quad K_{T_1} = K_p$ at $T_1 \cdot \left(T_1 = 25^\circ C = 298^\circ K\right)$

Now

$$\ln\left(\frac{10^{-4}}{10^{-6}}\right) = \frac{\Delta H^\circ}{1.98}\left(\frac{1}{298} - \frac{1}{323}\right)$$

$$\ln\left(10^2\right) = \frac{\Delta H^\circ}{1.98}(0.00336 - 0.00310)$$

or

$$2.303\log(10^2) = \Delta H^\circ (0.000131)$$

$$2.303(2) = \Delta H^\circ (0.000131)$$

$$4.606 = \Delta H^\circ (0.000131)$$

from which

$$\Delta H^\circ = \frac{4.606}{0.000131} = 35160 \text{ cal}$$

$$= 35.2 \text{ kcal}$$

• PROBLEM 6-21

In the ammonia synthesis reaction,

$$N_2(g) + 3H_2(g) \rightarrow 2NH_3(g),$$

all the gases involved are ideal. Prove that the maximum concentration of ammonia at equilibrium is attained when the ratio of H_2 to N_2 is 3:1 .

Solution: $N_2 + 3H_2 \rightarrow 2NH_3$. The equilibrium constant expression for this reaction is

$$K_p = \frac{P^2_{NH_3}}{P_{N_2}P^3_{H_2}} \tag{1}$$

The total pressure

$$P = P_{N_2} + P_{H_2} + P_{NH_3} \tag{2}$$

Define $y = \frac{P_{H_2}}{P_{N_2}}$. Then $P_{H_2} = yP_{N_2}$. From equation (2)

$$P_{total} = P_{N_2} + yP_{N_2} + P_{NH_3}$$

$$P_{total} = P_{N_2}(y + 1) + P_{NH_3}$$

$$\therefore \quad P_{N_2} = \frac{P_{total} - P_{NH_3}}{y + 1}$$

From equation (1)

$$K_p = \frac{P^2_{NH_3}}{\left(y^3P^3_{N_2}\right)\left(P_{N_2}\right)}$$

$$= \frac{P^2_{NH_3}}{y^3P^4_{N_2}}$$

$$K_p = \frac{P^2_{NH_3}}{y^3\left(\frac{P-P_{NH_3}}{y+1}\right)^4}$$

or

$$K_p\left[y^3\left(\frac{P - P_{NH_3}}{y + 1}\right)^4\right] = P^2_{NH_3} \tag{3}$$

Taking natural logarithm of both sides of equation (3) gives

$$\ln K_p + 3 \ln y + 4 \ln(P-P_{NH_3}) - 4 \ln(y+1) = 2 \ln P_{NH_3} .$$

Differentiate P_{NH_3} with respect to y at constant temperature and total pressure, to obtain

$$\frac{3}{y} + \frac{4}{P-P_{NH_3}}\left(\frac{-dP_{NH_3}}{dy}\right)_{P,T} - \frac{4}{y+1} = \frac{2}{P_{NH_3}}\left(\frac{dP_{NH_3}}{dy}\right)_{P,T} \quad (4)$$

To get the maximum value of P_{NH_3}, set the term $\left(dP_{NH_3}/dy\right)_{P,T}$ in equation (4) equal to zero to get

$$\frac{3}{y} - \frac{4}{y+1} = \frac{3-y}{y(y+1)} = 0$$

$$\therefore \quad y = 3 = P_{H_2}/P_{N_2} .$$

or $\quad 3P_{N_2} = P_{H_2}$

• PROBLEM 6-22

Consider the following reaction

$$3H_2(g) + N_2(g) = 2NH_3(g)$$

in which a mixture of hydrogen and nitrogen in a 3:1 mole ratio is passed over a catalyst at 400°C. Calculate the total pressure if the mole fraction of ammonia in the equilibrium mixture is to be 10%, and $K_p = 0.00164\ \text{atm}^{-2}$.

Solution: Define y = number of moles of ammonia present in a sample of equilibrium mixture, consisting of three moles of hydrogen and one mole of nitrogen

	$3H_2$	+ N_2	= $2NH_3$
number of moles present initially	3	1	0
number of moles present at equilibrium	3-(3/2)y	1 - ½y	y

Therefore,

$$n_{total} = 3 - (3/2)y + 1 - \tfrac{1}{2}y + y$$

or

$$n_{total} = 4 - y \quad (1)$$

Since the mole fraction of ammonia in the mixture is to be 0.1, then,

$$\frac{n_{NH_3}}{n_{total}} = 0.1$$

or

$$\frac{y}{4-y} = 0.1 .$$

Solving for y gives

$$y = 4/11 = n_{NH_3} .$$

From equation (1),

$$n_{total} = 4 - 4/11$$

$$n_{total} = 40/11$$

$$n_{H_2} = 3 - (3/2)y$$

$$= 3 - (3/2)(4/11)$$

$$n_{H_2} = 27/11$$

and

$$n_{N_2} = 1 - \tfrac{1}{2} y$$

$$= 1 - \tfrac{1}{2}(4/11)$$

$$n_{N_2} = 9/11 .$$

Writing the K_p term for the reaction yields

$$K_p = \frac{P^2_{NH_3}}{P^3_{H_2} P_{N_2}}$$

$$K_p = \frac{n^2_{NH_3}}{n^3_{H_2} n_{N_2}} \left(\frac{n_{total}}{P_{total}}\right)^2$$

But $K_p = 0.00164 \text{ atm}^{-2}$

$$K_p = 0.00164 \text{ atm}^{-2} = \frac{n^2_{NH_3}}{n^3_{H_2} n_{N_2}} \frac{n^2_{total}}{P^2_{total}}$$

or

$$0.00164 = \frac{(4/11)^2}{(27/11)^3(9/11)} \frac{(40/11)^2}{P^2}$$

$$0.00164 = \frac{0.132}{(14.788)(0.818)} \frac{13.223}{P^2}$$

$$0.00164 = \frac{0.144}{P^2}$$

Solve for P^2 and hence, P to obtain

$$P^2 = \frac{0.144}{0.00164}$$

$$P^2 = 87.80$$

$$P = 9.4 \text{ atm.}$$

• PROBLEM 6-23

For the reaction

$$N_2O_4(g) \rightleftarrows 2NO_2(g) \quad \text{at } 300^\circ K,$$

K_p is 0.174. Calculate the apparent molecular weight of an equilibrium mixture of N_2O_4 and NO_2 formed by the dissociation of 1 mole of pure N_2O_4 at a total pressure of 1 atm and a temperature of 300°K.

Solution:

	N_2O_4	$\rightleftarrows$	$2NO_2$
number of moles present initially:	1		0
number of moles present at equilibrium:	$(1-\alpha)$		2α

Observe that α is the degree of dissociation.

The total number of moles at equilibrium is

$$n_{total} = (1-\alpha) + 2\alpha$$

or

$$n_{total} = (1+\alpha)$$

The equilibrium constant expression is

$$K_p = \frac{P^2_{NO_2}}{P_{N_2O_4}}$$

$$= \frac{\left(X_{NO_2} \; P_{total}\right)^2}{\left(X_{N_2O_4} \; P_{total}\right)}$$

$$= \frac{\left[\left(\frac{2\alpha}{1+\alpha}\right)\right]^2 P^2_{total}}{\left(\frac{1-\alpha}{1+\alpha}\right) P_{total}} = 0.174$$

$$= \frac{4\alpha^2/[(1+\alpha)(1+\alpha)]}{(1-\alpha)/(1+\alpha)} P_{total} = 0.174$$

$$= \frac{4\alpha^2 \;(1)}{(1+\alpha)(1-\alpha)} = 0.174$$

$$K_p = \frac{4\alpha^2}{1-\alpha^2} = 0.174$$

$$4\alpha^2 = 0.174 - 0.174\alpha^2$$

$$4.174\alpha^2 = 0.174$$

$$\alpha = \sqrt{\frac{0.174}{4.174}}$$

$$\alpha = 0.204$$

$$\text{Mole fraction } NO_2,\ X_{NO_2} = \frac{\text{moles } NO_2}{\text{total moles}}$$

$$= \frac{2\alpha}{1 + \alpha}$$

$$= \frac{2(0.204)}{1 + (0.204)}$$

$$X_{NO_2} = 0.339$$

$$\text{Mole fraction } N_2O_4,\ N_2O_4 = \frac{1 - \alpha}{1 + \alpha}$$

$$= \frac{1 - (0.204)}{1 + (0.204)}$$

$$X_{N_2O_4} = 0.661$$

$\therefore$ The apparent molecular weight is

$$= \left(M_{NO_2}\right)\left(X_{NO_2}\right) + \left(M_{N_2O_4}\right)\left(X_{N_2O_4}\right)$$

$$= (46.0)(0.339) + (92.0)(0.661)$$

$$= 76.4 \text{ g mole}^{-1}$$

• PROBLEM 6-24

Consider the reaction

$$2SO_2(g) + O_2(g) \rightleftarrows 2SO_3(g) :$$

Initially 0.100 moles of SO_2 and 0.100 moles of SO_3 are present in a 2.00 liter flask at a temperature of 27°C. Equilibrium is attained at a pressure of 2.78 atm. Calculate
a) the mole fraction of O_2 at equilibrium;
b) K_p ;
c) the percent dissociation of SO_3 if 0.100 mole of SO_3 and no (zero) O_2 and no (zero) SO_2 were present initially in the flask.

Solution:

$$2SO_2(g) + O_2(g) \rightleftarrows 2SO_3(g) .$$

Define y as the number of moles of each species that react

	$2SO_2(g)$	+ $O_2(g)$	$\rightleftarrows$ $2SO_3(g)$
number of moles present initially	.1	0	.100
number of moles present at equilibrium	(0.100+2y)	y	(0.100-2y)

Total number of moles, $n_{total} = 0.100 + 2y + y + 0.100 - 2y$

or $$n_{total} = 0.200 + y \tag{1}$$

From the ideal gas law,

$$n = \frac{PV}{RT}$$

$$\therefore \quad n_{total} = \frac{(2.78\ \text{atm})(2.00\ \text{liters})}{(0.08206\text{liter atm}^\circ K^{-1}\text{mole}^{-1})(300^\circ K)}$$

$$n_{total} = 0.226\ \text{mole}$$

From equation (1),

$$n_{total} = 0.200 + y$$

or $$0.226 = 0.200 + y$$

Solving for y yields

$$y = 0.026\ \text{mole}$$

Mole fraction of $O_2, X_{O_2} = \dfrac{\text{mole of } O_2}{\text{total moles}}$

$$= \frac{0.026}{0.226}$$

or $$X_{O_2} = 0.115$$

b) K_p for the reaction is given in terms of partial pressures. That is,

$$K_p = \frac{P^2_{SO_3}}{P^2_{SO_2}\ P_{O_2}} = \frac{\left(X_{SO_3}\ P_{total}\right)^2}{\left(X_{SO_2}\ P_{total}\right)^2\left(X_{O_2}\ P_{total}\right)}$$

$$n_{SO_3} = 0.100 - 2y$$

$$= 0.100 - 2(0.026)$$

$$n_{SO_3} = 0.048$$

$$n_{SO_2} = 0.100 + 2y$$

$$= 0.100 + 2(0.026)$$

$$n_{SO_2} = 0.152$$

$$X_{SO_3} = \frac{0.048}{0.226}$$

$$= 0.212$$

$$X_{SO_2} = \frac{0.152}{0.226}$$

$$= 0.673$$

$$\therefore \quad K_p = \frac{\left[(0.212)(2.78)\right]^2}{\left[(0.673)(2.78)\right]^2\left[(0.115)(2.78)\right]}$$

$$= 0.31 .$$

c) $$2SO_2 + O_2 \rightleftarrows 2SO_3$$

	$2SO_2$	O_2	$2SO_3$
number of moles present at equilibrium	2y	y	(0.100-2y)

The equilibrium constant expression is

$$K_p = \frac{P^2_{SO_3}}{P^2_{SO_2}\, P_{O_2}} = \frac{n^2_{SO_3}}{n^2_{SO_2}\, n_{O_2}} \cdot \frac{V}{RT}$$

$$\therefore \quad \frac{n^2_{SO_3}}{n^2_{SO_2}\, n_{O_2}} = \frac{K_p RT}{V}$$

$$= \frac{0.31(0.08206 \text{ liter atm}^\circ K^{-1}\text{mole}^{-1})(300^\circ K)}{(2.00 \text{ liter})}$$

$$= 3.82$$

In terms of the number of moles present at equilibrium,

$$\frac{(0.100 - 2y)^2}{(2y)^2 y} = 3.82$$

or

$$\frac{(0.100 - 2y)^2}{y^3} = 15.28$$

A trial and error analysis is best used in solving this problem.

y	$(0.100\text{-}2y)^2/y^3$	Remark
0.025	160	y is too small
0.040	6.3	y is too large
0.036	16.79	
0.0365	14.99	interpolate
0.0363	15.70	

Obviously y must lie between 0 and 0.050, so first try the midpoint of this interval and other values as shown above. Consequently, fraction of SO_3 dissociated is approximately

$$\frac{2y}{0.100} = 0.73$$

$$= 73\% .$$

Observe that the value for y used is 0.0365.

For the reaction below K_p is 0.05 and ΔG° is 5.35 kcal at 900°K:

$$C_2H_6(g) = C_2H_4(g) + H_2(g)$$

If an initial mixture comprising 20 moles of C_2H_6 and 80 moles of N_2(inert) is passed over a dehydrogenation catalyst at 900°K, what is the equilibrium per cent composition of the effluent gas mixture? The total pressure is kept at 0.5 atm. Given that ΔS° is 32.3 cal/deg at 900°K, calculate ΔG° at 300°K (assume $\Delta C_p^\circ = 0$).

Solution: In this problem, the equilibrium constant can be defined as

$$K_p = \frac{\left(n_{C_2H_4}\right)\left(n_{H_2}\right)}{\left(n_{C_2H_6}\right)} \left(\frac{P}{N}\right)$$

where

$n_{C_2H_4}$ = number of moles of C_2H_4

n_{H_2} = number of moles of H_2

$n_{C_2H_6}$ = number of moles of C_2H_6

P = total pressure

$N = n_{C_2H_4} + n_{H_2} + n_{C_2H_6} + n_{N_2}$

If the number of moles of C_2H_4 is represented by x, that is $n_{C_2H_4} = x$, then $n_{H_2} = x$, $n_{C_2H_6} = 20 - x$ and $n_{N_2} = 80$. The total pressure, $P = 0.5$ atm and $N = x + x + (20 - x) + 80 = x + x + (20 - x) + 80$

$= 100 + x$

If these are substituted into the equation for K_p, the result is

$$K_p = \frac{(x)(x)}{(20-x)} \frac{0.5}{(100+x)}$$

But the value for K_p (given in the problem) is 0.05, therefore the expression becomes

$$K_p = \frac{x^2}{(20-x)} \frac{0.5}{(100+x)} = 0.05$$

or

$$K_p = \frac{0.5x^2}{2000-80x-x^2} = 0.05$$

Therefore $100 - 4x - 0.05x^2 = 0.5x^2$ and $0.55x^2 + 4x - 100 = 0$.

Using the quadratic formula,

$$x = \frac{-b \pm \sqrt{b^2 - 4ac}}{2a}$$

where $a = 0.55$, $b = 4$, $c = -100$. Substitute these values into the above formula. That is,

$$x = \frac{-4 \pm \sqrt{16 + 220}}{1.10} = \frac{-4 \pm 15.36}{1.10}$$

There exist two possible values for x which are $\frac{-4 + 15.36}{1.10}$ = 10.32 moles and

$$\frac{-4 - 15.36}{1.10} = -17.6 \text{ moles}$$

x cannot be negative, so the solution is $x = 10.32$ moles. Now, the various equilibrium per cent composition of the effluent gas mixture can be computed by computing the individual mole fraction of the gases. Since $x = 10.32$, $N = 100 + x = 110.32$.

Therefore, the mole fraction of $H_2 = 10.32/110.32 = 0.093$, that of $C_2H_4 = 10.3/110.32 = 0.093$, C_2H_6 has a mole fraction of $9.68/110.32 = 0.088$ and that of $N_2 = 80/110.32 = 0.72$. The percent compositions are 9.3% for C_2H_4 , 9.3% for H_2, 8.8% for C_2H_6 and 72% for N_2 . At 900°K, $\Delta H^\circ = \Delta G^\circ + T\,\Delta S^\circ = 5.35 + 900(32.5/1000) = 34.4$ kcal. Now at 300°K, $\Delta G^\circ = \Delta H^\circ - T\,\Delta S^\circ$. Since ΔC°_p is assumed to be zero, ΔH° and ΔS° will not change (will be constant). Therefore,

$$\Delta G^\circ = 34.4 - 300(32.5/1000) = 24.7 \text{ kcal.}$$

• PROBLEM 6-26

$$A_2 \rightleftarrows 2A$$

In the above reaction, A_2, which is an ideal gas, undergoes partial dissociation to the ideal gas A and the equilibrium constant, given in terms of partial pressures, is K. a) show that the degree of dissociation of A_2, α, is given by $\alpha = (1 + 4P/K)^{-\frac{1}{2}}$, where P = the total pressure of A_2 and A. b) Derive the equation of state for this gas mixture in terms of P, V, T, K and R, assuming i) that the gas mixture has a molecular weight of A_2, ii) that the gas mixture has a molecular weight of A.

Solution: a)

	A_2	$\rightleftarrows$	$2A$
number of moles present initially:	n_0		0
number of moles present at equilibrium:	$(1-\alpha)n_0$		$2\,\alpha\,n_0$

Therefore, $n_{total} = n_0(1 - \alpha) + 2\,\alpha\,n_0$ or $n_{total} = (1 + \alpha)n_0$.

The expression for K_p is

$$K_p = \frac{P_A^2}{P_{A_2}} \quad (1)$$

But,

$$P_A = \frac{2\alpha}{1 + \alpha} P$$

and

$$P_{A_2} = \frac{1 - \alpha}{1 + \alpha} P$$

Substitute the above expressions of P_A and P_{A_2} into equation (1) to obtain:

$$K_p = \frac{\frac{(2 \alpha P)^2}{(1+\alpha)(1+\alpha)}}{\frac{1 - \alpha}{1 + \alpha} P}$$

$$K_p = \frac{4\alpha^2 P}{(1+\alpha)(1-\alpha)}$$

or

$$K_p = \frac{4\alpha^2 P}{1 - \alpha^2}$$

Solving for α gives

$$K_p - K_p \alpha^2 = 4\alpha^2 P$$

$$4\alpha^2 P + K_p \alpha^2 = K_p$$

$$\alpha^2 (4P + K_p) = K_p$$

$$\alpha^2 = \frac{K_p}{4P+K_p}$$

Dividing both the numerator and the denominater of the right hand side by K_p yields $\alpha^2 = \dfrac{1}{\frac{4P}{K_p} + 1}$. Taking the square root of both sides gives

$$\alpha = \left(\frac{1}{\frac{4P}{K_p} + 1}\right)^{\frac{1}{2}} .$$

or

$$\alpha = (1 + 4P/K)^{-\frac{1}{2}}$$

where $K = K_p$.

b) From the ideal gas law $PV = nRT$ or $V = nRT/P$.

$$V = n_0(1 + \alpha) \; RT/P .$$

Assumption (i) : There are n_0 moles of gas

$$\therefore \quad \bar{V} = V/n_0$$

$$= (1 + \alpha) \; RT/P$$

$$\bar{V} = \left[1 + \left(\frac{1 + 4P}{K}\right)^{-\frac{1}{2}}\right] RT/P$$

Assumption (ii): There are $2n_0$ moles of gas

$$\therefore \quad \bar{V} = V/2n_0$$

$$= (1 + \alpha)\ RT/2P$$

$$\bar{V} = \left[1 + \left(\frac{1 + 4P}{K}\right)^{-\frac{1}{2}}\right] RT/2P\ .$$

GAS-SOLID EQUILIBRIUM

• PROBLEM 6-27

At 800°C the value of K_p for the decomposition of methane, according to the reaction

$$CH_4(g) = C(s) + 2H_2(g),$$

is 23 atm. Initially 3 moles of CH_4 were present in a 5-liter vessel. Calculate a) the number of moles of each species present at equilibrium. b) how much hydrogen gas should be introduced into the 5-liter vessel at 800°C in order to just convert 3 mole of carbon into methane.

<u>Solution</u>: $CH_4(g) = C(s) + 2H_2(g)$.

The expression for K_p is given by,

$$K_p = \frac{P^2_{H_2}}{P_{CH_4}} = 23 \qquad (1)$$

Define y = number of moles of H_2 present. Then, the number of moles of CH_4, $n_{CH_4} = 3 - \frac{1}{2}y$. Total number of moles, $n_{total} = y + 3 - \frac{1}{2}y$ or

$$n_{total} = 3 + \tfrac{1}{2}y \qquad (2a)$$

From (1),

$$K_p = \frac{P^2_{H_2}}{P_{CH_4}} \qquad (2)$$

$$K_p = \frac{\left[\left(n_{H_2}/n_{total}\right)P_{total}\right]^2}{\left[\left(n_{CH_4}/n_{total}\right)P_{total}\right]} = 23 \qquad (3)$$

But from the ideal gas law, $PV = n_{total}\ RT$ or

$$\frac{P}{n_{total}} = RT/V \qquad (4)$$

$$= \frac{(0.082\ \text{liter atm}°K^{-1}\text{mole}^{-1})(1073°K)}{5\ \text{liters}}$$

$$= 17.6\ \text{atm mole}^{-1}\ .$$

From equation (3),

$$K_p = \frac{n_{H_2}^2 \; P}{n_{CH_4} \; n_{total}}$$

$$23 = \frac{n_{H_2}^2}{n_{CH_4}} RT/V$$

$$23 = \frac{y^2}{3 - \frac{1}{2}y} \quad (17.6).$$

Solving for y gives

$$y = 1.68 \text{ .}$$

Thus from equation (2a),

$$n_{total} = 3 + \tfrac{1}{2}(1.68)$$
$$= 3.84$$

From equation (4),

$$P = 17.6 \; n_{total}$$
$$= 17.6(3.84)$$

or

$$P = 67.5 \text{ atm}$$

The number of moles of CH_4 at equilibrium $= 3 - \frac{1}{2}y = 3 - \frac{1}{2}(1.68)$ or $n_{CH_4} = 2.16$. Thus 0.84 mole has decomposed and n_C is therefore 0.84 mole .

b) When 3 moles of carbon is converted into methane, there will be 3 moles of methane. Consequently, the partial pressure of methane

$$P_{CH_4} = n_{CH_4}\left(P_{total}\right)$$
$$= 3(17.6)$$
$$= 52.8 \text{ atm .}$$

Since carbon is to have just disappeared, the hydrogen pressure will be the equilibrium pressure. That is,

$$K_p = \frac{P_{H_2}^2}{P_{CH_4}}$$

or

$$P_{H_2}^2 = K_p \; P_{CH_4}$$
$$= (23 \text{ atm})(52.8 \text{ atm})$$
$$= 1214.4 \text{ atm}^2$$
$$\therefore \quad P_{H_2} = 34.8 \text{ atm .}$$

Solving for n_{H_2} gives

$$n_{H_2} = \frac{P_{H_2}}{P_{total}}$$

$$= \frac{34.8 \text{ atm}}{17.6 \text{ atm mole}^{-1}}$$

or $$n_{H_2} = 1.98 \text{ mole} .$$

The total number of moles of hydrogen required is then 1.98 mole plus the number of moles required to convert the carbon to methane. That is, 6 additional mole, or a total of 7.98 moles.

• PROBLEM 6-28

$$A(g) + 2B(g) \rightleftarrows C(g) + D(s)$$

For the above reaction, A, B, and C are ideal gases and D is a solid of negligible volume and vapor pressure. Its $K_p = 1.0 \times 10^{-3}$. Initially A and B are introduced into a container until the partial pressure of each, before any reaction takes place, is 1.00 atm. Calculate the partial pressure of C at equilibrium,

a) When the volume of the container is held constant.

b) When the total pressure is held constant at 2.00 atm.

Solution:

	A	+	2B	$\rightleftarrows$	C	+	D(s)
number of moles present initially:	n_0		n_0		0		
number of moles present at equilibrium:	$(1-\alpha)n_0$		$(1-2\alpha)n_0$		$\alpha\, n_0$		

From the ideal gas law

$$PV = n_0RT$$

or

$$P = \frac{n_0RT}{V}$$

$$1.00 \text{ atm} = \frac{n_0RT}{V} .$$

a) The partial pressure of A, P_A, is given by

$$P_A = n_0(1 - \alpha)\ RT/V = (1 - \alpha)(1) = 1 - \alpha$$

$$P_B = n_0(1 - 2\alpha)\ RT/V = 1 - 2\alpha$$

$$P_C = n_0\alpha\ RT/V = \alpha .$$

The equilibrium constant expression is given by

$$K_p = \frac{P_C}{P_A\ P_B^2}$$

or

$$1.0 \times 10^{-3} = \frac{\alpha}{(1-\alpha)(1-2\alpha)^2}$$

Solve the quadratic equation for α. If 2α is assumed to be much less than 1, then $\alpha = 1.0 \times 10^{-3}$ atm. For an improved result, set $1 - \alpha = 0.999$ and $1 - 2\alpha = 0.998$. Therefore,

$$\alpha = 1.0 \times 10^{-3} \times 0.999 \times 0.996$$

$$\alpha = 0.995 \times 10^{-3} \text{ atm} = P_C$$

b) Total number of moles, n_{total} is

$$n_{total} = n_0(1 - \alpha) + (1 - 2\alpha)n_0 + \alpha\, n_0$$

$$= (2 - 2\alpha)n_0$$

$$P_{total} = 2.00 \text{ atm}$$

$$P_A = \left(\frac{\text{number of moles of A}}{\text{total moles}}\right) P_{total}$$

$$= \frac{1 - \alpha}{2 - 2\alpha} P$$

$$P_A = \left[\frac{1 - 0.995 \times 10^{-3}}{2 - 2(0.995 \times 10^{-3})}\right] 2.00 \text{ atm}$$

$$P_A = 1 \text{ atm}$$

$$P_B = \frac{1 - 2\alpha}{2 - 2\alpha} P$$

$$= \frac{1 - 2\alpha}{1 - \alpha}$$

$$P_C = \frac{\alpha}{2 - 2\alpha} P$$

$$P_C = \frac{\alpha}{1 - \alpha}$$

But $$K_p = \frac{P_C}{P_A\, P_B^2}$$

$$\therefore \quad 1.0 \times 10^{-3} = \frac{\alpha/(1 - \alpha)}{\left(\frac{1 - \alpha}{1 - \alpha}\right)\left(\frac{1 - 2\alpha}{1 - \alpha}\right)^2}$$

$$1.0 \times 10^{-3} = \frac{\alpha(1-\alpha)}{(1-2\alpha)^2}$$

If in solving for α, 2α is assumed to be much less than 1, then $\alpha = 1.0\ 10^{-3}$ atm. For a more refined result, set $1 - \alpha = .999$ and $1 - 2\alpha = .998$. Therefore,

$$\alpha = \frac{1.0 \times 10^{-3} \times 0.998^2}{0.999}$$

$$\alpha = 0.997 \times 10^{-3}$$

$$P_C = \alpha/1-\alpha$$

$$= \frac{0.997 \times 10^{-3}}{0.999}$$

or $$P_C = 0.998 \times 10^{-3}.$$

K_p is 0.05 atm^2 at 20°C for the reaction:

$$NH_4HS(s) = NH_3(g) + H_2S(g)$$

0.06 mole of solid NH_4HS are introduced into a 2.4 liter flask at 20°C.

(a) Calculate the per cent of the solid that will have decomposed into NH_3 and H_2S at equilibrium.

(b) Calculate the number of moles of ammonia that would have to be added to the flask to reduce the decomposition of the solid to 1%.

Solution: a) From the reaction, $K_p = P_{NH_3} P_{H_2S}$ (1)

where P_{NH_3} = partial pressure of NH_3

P_{H_2S} = partial pressure of H_2S

But $P_{NH_3} = P_{H_2S} = P/2$ at equilibrium. Therefore from (1)

$$K_p = 0.05 = (P/2)(P/2) = P^2/4$$

and

$$P^2 = 0.20$$

from which $P = \sqrt{0.20} = 0.447$ atm.

From PV = nRT,

$$n = PV/RT = \frac{(0.447)(2.4)}{(0.082)(293)}$$

$$= 0.0447 \text{ mole}$$

This represents the total moles. That is, $n_{NH_3} + n_{H_2S}$. Therefore,

$$n_{NH_3} = n_{H_2S} = 0.0447/2$$

$$= 0.0224$$

Since we started with 0.06 mole of solid NH_4HS, we have (0.06 - 0.0224) mole of solid remaining. That is

$$0.06 - 0.0224 = 0.0376 \text{ mole}$$

The per cent of solid that will have decomposed is $(0.0224/0.06) \times 100$

$$= 37.33\% .$$

b) If the decomposition is to be kept to 1%, the moles of H_2S present must be 0.0006, and $P_{H_2S} = 0.006$. From K_p, the pressure of NH_3 is then 0.05/0.006 or 8.33 atm. Therefore the moles of ammonia are

$$n = PV/RT = \frac{(8.33)(2.4)}{(0.082)(293)} = 0.833 .$$

CHAPTER 7

SOLUTIONS

ACTIVITY

• PROBLEM 7-1

In a certain binary solution, the activity a_1 of component 1 is given by the equation

$$R \ln a_1 = R \ln x_1 + Ax_2^2 + Bx_2^3$$

where x_1 and x_2 are the respective mole fractions and A and B are constants. Derive an expression for the activity of component 2 given that the equation is valid over the entire concentration range from pure liquid 1 to pure liquid 2.

Solution: $R \ln a_1 = R \ln x_1 + Ax_2^2 + Bx_2^3$

or $$\ln a_1 = \ln x_1 + \frac{Ax_2^2}{R} + \frac{Bx_2^3}{R} \qquad (1)$$

Differentiating equation (1) gives

$$d\ln a_1 = \frac{dx_1}{x_1} + \frac{2Ax_2 dx_2}{R} + \frac{3Bx_2^2 dx_2}{R}$$

One form of the Gibbs-Duhem equation is given as

$$x_1 d\ln a_1 + x_2 d\ln a_2 = 0 \qquad (2)$$

where x_1 and x_2 denote the mole fraction of components 1 (solvent) and 2. Equation (2) can also be written as

$$x_2 d\ln a_2 = -x_1 d\ln a_1$$

or $$d\ln a_2 = -\frac{x_1}{x_2} d\ln a_1$$

$$= -\frac{x_1}{x_2}\left[\frac{dx_1}{x_1} + \frac{2Ax_2 dx_2}{R} + \frac{3Bx_2^2 dx_2}{R}\right]$$

$$= -\frac{dx_1}{x_2} - \frac{2Ax_1dx_2}{R} - \frac{3Bx_1x_2dx_2}{R}$$

Now $x_1 + x_2 = 1$. So $dx_1 + dx_2 = 0$, or $dx_1 = -dx_2$. After the appropriate substitutions,

$$d\ell na_2 = \frac{dx_2}{x_2} + \frac{2Ax_1dx_1}{R} + \frac{3Bx_1(1-x_1)dx_1}{R}$$

$$(\ell na_2)_1^{x_2} = (\ell nx_2)_1^{x_2} + \left(\frac{Ax_1^2}{R}\right)_0^{x_1} + \left[\frac{3B}{R}\left(\frac{x_1^2}{2} - \frac{x_1^3}{3}\right)\right]_0^{x_1}$$

$$R\ell na_2 = R\ell nx_2 + Ax_1^2 + B\left(\frac{3}{2}x_1^2 - x_1^3\right)$$

ACTIVITY COEFFICIENT

• PROBLEM 7-2

Given an aqueous solution of NH_3 at 70°F (22.11°C), the partial pressure of water over the solution is 0.34 psi at 0.05 mole fraction. The partial pressure of NH_3 over the same solution is 0.83 psi. Calculate the activity coefficient of water, NH_3 and the activity of water and NH_3. The vapor pressure of pure water at 70°F is 18.77 torr, and Henry's constant, K_2 for NH_3 is 725 torr.

Solution:

Water: Activity coefficient, γ_i is defined as

$$\gamma_i = \frac{P_i}{x_iP_i^\circ}$$

where P_i = partial pressure of component i

P_i° = vapor pressure of component i

x_i = mole fraction of component i

$$\therefore \quad \gamma_{H_2O} = \frac{(0.34\text{ psi})\left(\frac{1\text{ atm}}{14.6960\text{ psi}}\right)\left(\frac{760\text{ torr}}{1\text{ atm}}\right)}{(0.95)\ (18.77\text{ torr})}$$

$$= 0.986$$

The activity, a_i of a nonelectrolyte is equal to the product of the activity coefficient and the mole fraction.

Thus $\quad a_i = \gamma_i x_i$

$$\therefore \quad a_{H_2O} = (0.986)(0.95) = 0.937$$

NH_3: Activity coefficient of NH_3 using Henry's law constant is defined as

$$\gamma_i = \frac{P_i}{K_i x_i}$$

where K_i is Henry's law constant

$$\therefore \gamma_{NH_3} = \frac{\left(0.83 \text{ psi}\right)\left(\dfrac{1 \text{ atm}}{14.6960 \text{ psi}}\right)\left(\dfrac{760 \text{ torr}}{1 \text{ atm}}\right)}{(0.05)\ (725 \text{ torr})}$$

$$= 1.18$$

$$a_{NH_3} = \gamma_{NH_3} x_{NH_3} = (1.18)(0.05) = 0.059$$

Note that the subscript 2 in K_2 refers to the Henry constant of the solute, in this case, NH_3.

• PROBLEM 7-3

In an ether-acetone solution containing 0.800 mole fraction ether at 30°C, the partial pressure of ether above the solution is 535 torr. That of acetone at the same concentration is 90 torr. Calculate the activity coefficient γ_1, γ_2 of ether and acetone respectively. If the vapor pressure of pure ether and acetone are 646 torr and 283 torr respectively and the actual vapor pressure of acetone is 148 torr at a 0.400 mole fraction, calculate Henry's law constant, K_2 for both conditions and the activity coefficient, γ_2 of acetone.

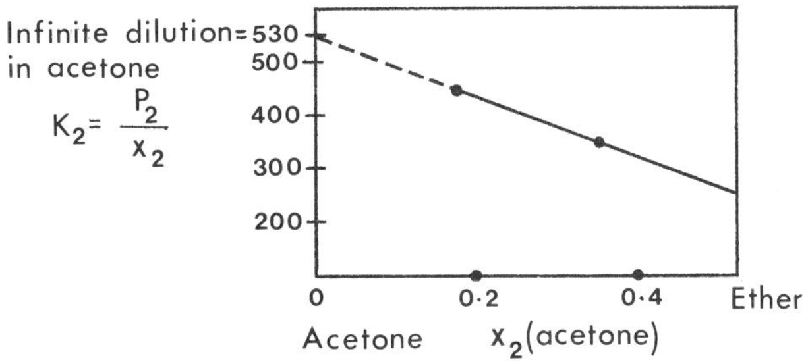

Fig. 1

Solution: Let x_i = mole fraction

Both ether and acetone are liquids and their activity coefficients approaches unity as their mole fraction also approaches unity.

Thus as $x_i \to 1$, $\gamma_i \to 1$

At equilibrium, the chemical potential, μ_i of the vapor phase of both ether and acetone are equal to the chemical potential, μ_i of the solution

$$\therefore \mu_{ether} = \mu_{soln}$$

and $\mu_{acetone} = \mu_{soln}$

Assuming the vapor phase is ideal, then

$$\mu_i = \mu_i^* + RT\ln\gamma_i x_i$$

and $\mu_i^\circ + RT\ln P_i = \mu_i^* + RT\ln\gamma_i x_i$

where μ_i° = chemical potential of pure component

μ_i^* = chemical potential in the standard state

P_i = partial pressure

Rearranging, $P_i = \gamma_i(x_i K_i)$

As $x_i \to 1$, $\gamma_i \to 1$,

Thus $P_i = \gamma_i(x_i P_i^\circ)$

where P_i° = vapor pressure of pure components

The activity coefficient is therefore given by

$$\gamma_i = \frac{P_i}{x_i P_i^\circ}$$

$$\gamma_{ether} = \frac{535\text{ torr}}{(0.800)(646\text{ torr})} = 1.04$$

and $$\gamma_{acetone} = \frac{90\text{ torr}}{(0.200)(283\text{ torr})} = 1.59$$

When a solution contains two volatile liquids such as this case it is not possible for each component to vary the mole fraction up to unity. What is done is to consider one component the solvent, in this case the ether, and determine its activity coefficient by the formula $\gamma_1 = \frac{P_1}{x_1 P_1^\circ}$. The other component is considered the solute, in this case acetone, and its activity coefficient is determined by the formula $\gamma_2 = \frac{P_2}{K_2 x_2}$. K_2 is Henry's Law constant determined when $x_2 = 0$.

To calculate K_2 (Henry's Law constant), using

$$K_2 = \frac{P_2}{x_2}, \qquad (1)$$

$$\therefore \quad K_{2\,(acetone)} = \frac{148\text{ torr}}{(0.400)} = 370$$

$$K_{2\,(\text{acetone})} = \frac{90 \text{ torr}}{(0.200)} = 450$$

If values of $\frac{P_2}{x_2}$ are plotted against x_2 as shown in figure 1 and K_2 extrapolated to infinite dilution in acetone, equation (1) gives K_2 = 530 torr.

$$\therefore \quad \gamma_{\text{acetone}} = \frac{P_i}{x_i K_2} = \frac{90 \text{ torr}}{(0.200)(530 \text{ torr})} = 0.85$$

IDEAL SOLUTIONS

• PROBLEM 7-4

> A mixture of the vapors of two liquids A and B which form ideal solutions is contained in a cylinder with a piston at constant temperature, T. The mixture contains 40 mole % A, with vapor pressures P°_A and P°_B given as 0.4 and 1.2 atm, respectively. The mixture is then slowly compressed. Calculate: (a) the total pressure at which the liquid first condenses and its composition; (b) the composition of that solution whose normal boiling point is T.

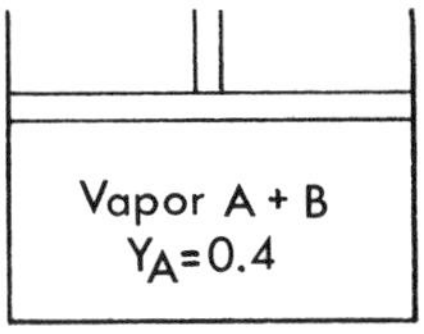

Fig. 1 Const T

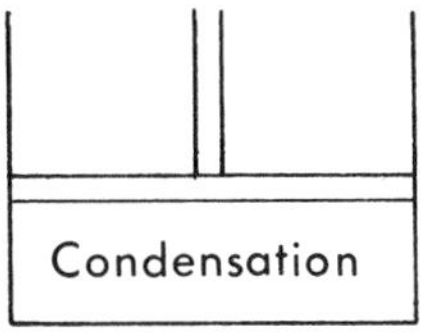

Fig. 2 Const T

Solution: a) The two liquids form ideal solutions thus they obey Raoults Law,

$$y_A = \frac{P_A}{P} = \frac{N_A P^\circ_A}{P} = \frac{N_A P^\circ_A}{P_A + P_B} = \frac{N_A P^\circ_A}{N_A P^\circ_A + N_B P^\circ_B}$$

where y_A = The vapor mole fraction in A

P_A = The partial pressure of A

P = The total pressure

N_A = The liquid mole fraction in A

P°_A = vapor pressure of A

In Fig. 1, before the system is compressed,

$$y_A = \frac{P_A}{P_{\text{total}}} = \frac{P^\circ_A N_A}{P^\circ_A N_A + P^\circ_B N_B} = 0.4$$

$$y_A = \frac{0.4N_A}{0.4N_A+1.2N_B}$$

$$y_A = \frac{0.4N_A}{1.2-0.8N_A}$$

$$\therefore \quad 0.4 = \frac{0.4N_A}{1.2-0.8N_A}$$

$$\therefore \quad N_A = 0.67$$

$$P_{total} = 1.2 - 0.8N_A \qquad (1)$$

$$P_{total} = 1.2 - 0.8 \times 0.67 = 0.67 \text{ atm}$$

b) A solution boils when total pressure, $P_{total} = 1$ atm
But from equation (1)

$$P_{total} = 1.2 - 0.8\ N_A$$

$$\therefore \quad 1 = 1.2 - 0.8\ N_A$$

$$N_A = \frac{1.2-1}{0.8}$$

$$N_A = 0.25$$

• PROBLEM 7-5

A certain solution of liquids A and B containing 25 mole % of A forms an ideal solution. The vapor above the solution in equilibrium with it contains 50 mole % of A, and the heat of vaporization of A and B are 5 kcal/mole and 7 kcal/mole respectively. Calculate a) the ratio of the vapor pressure of pure A to that of pure B. b) Calculate the same ratio at 100°C. Only set up the equations and put in numbers so that the desired ratio is the only unknown. Do not solve for the answer.

Solution: Since this is an ideal solution, according to Raoult's law, the mole fraction in the vapor phase is equal to the vapor pressure of the components above the solution. Thus we can write

$$\frac{y_A}{y_B} = \frac{P_A}{P_B} \qquad (1)$$

where y = mole fraction in the vapor phase. The vapor above the solution contains 50 mole % of A, thus the vapor must also contain 50 mole % of B, since $y_A + y_B = 1$.

$$y_A = y_B = 0.5 \qquad (2)$$

$$P_A = x_A P_A^\circ \qquad (3)$$

and $$P_B = x_B P_B^\circ \qquad (4)$$

substituting (2), (3), (4) in (1)

$$1 = \frac{0.25\, P_A^\circ}{0.75\, P_B^\circ}$$

P_A°, P_B° = vapor pressure of pure A and B

$$\therefore \quad \frac{P_A^\circ}{P_B^\circ} = \frac{1}{0.33} = 3$$

b) Using the Clausius-Clapeyron equation

$$\ell nP = -\frac{\Delta H_{vap}}{RT} + C$$

where P = vapor pressure

ΔH_{vap} = heat of vaporization

R = gas constant

and C = constant of integration

Integrating between limits yields for component A

$$\ell n \frac{P'_A}{P_A} = \ell n \frac{P'^\circ_A}{P_A^\circ} = \frac{\Delta H_A}{R}\left(\frac{1}{298^\circ K} - \frac{1}{373^\circ K}\right) \qquad (5)$$

where $100^\circ C = 373^\circ K$

and $25^\circ C = 298^\circ K$

For component B,

$$\ell n \frac{P'_B}{P_B} = \ell n \frac{P'^\circ_B}{P_B^\circ} = \frac{\Delta H_B}{R}\left(\frac{1}{298^\circ K} - \frac{1}{373^\circ K}\right) \qquad (6)$$

Subtracting (6) from (5),

$$\ell n \frac{G^{\circ\prime}}{G} = \frac{\Delta H_A - \Delta H_B}{R}\left(\frac{1}{298^\circ K} - \frac{1}{373^\circ K}\right) \qquad (7)$$

Here $$G = \frac{P_A^\circ}{P_B^\circ}$$

After substituting the values G = 3, the gas constant R, and the ΔH's, equation (7) becomes

$$\ln \frac{G^{\circ\prime}}{3} = \frac{5-7}{1.987\times 10^{-3}\ \frac{\text{kcal}}{{}^\circ K}} \left(\frac{1}{298} - \frac{1}{373}\right).$$

The desired equation is actually equation (7).

• PROBLEM 7-6

Fig. 1 shows a plot of P vs t of an ideal solution of liquids A and B. Using this graph, calculate the normal boiling point of: a) pure liquid A and B, b) a solution of $N_A = 0.25$ and c) a solution of $N_A = 0.75$ [give answer to b) and c) correct to a few degrees]. d) Estimate the vapor compositions for the solutions in b) and c) when at their normal boiling points, and construct a plot of the boiling-point diagram. e) Calculate the normal boiling points of mixtures b) and c) assuming that A and B are completely immiscible.

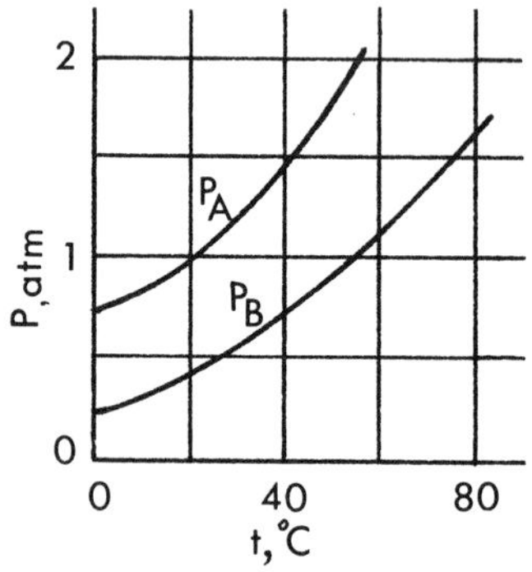

Fig. 1

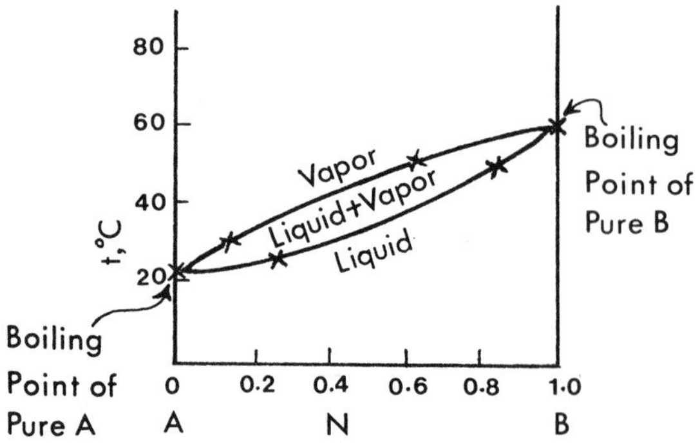

Fig. 2

Solution: a) The boiling point of a liquid at 1 atm pressure is called its normal boiling point. Thus from Fig. 1, the temperature corresponding to 1 atm for curves P_A and P_B are about 22°C and 58°C respectively.

b) Since this is an ideal solution, Raoult's law holds. Therefore

$$P_A = P_A^\circ N_A$$

and $$P_B = P_B^\circ N_B$$

$$P_{total} = P_A + P_B$$

The solution will boil when the total pressure, P_t, of the solution equals 1 atm.

Therefore $P_{total} = 1$ atm

and $$P_{total} = P_A + P_B$$

$$= N_A P_A^\circ + N_B P_B^\circ$$

$$\therefore \quad 1 \text{ atm} = N_A P_A^\circ + N_B P_B^\circ$$

where N_A and N_B are the concentration of liquid A and B respectively, in the solution. P_A° and P_B° are the vapor pressure of pure A and B. P_A and P_B are the partial pressures of components A and B respectively.

The above equations must be satisfied. Therefore

$$P_t = .25 P_A^\circ + .75 P_B^\circ$$

$$1 = .25 P_A^\circ + .75 P_B^\circ .$$

Using a trial and error substitution for various values of P_A° and P_B°, an approximate solution is found at 45°C where $P_A^\circ = 1.7$ and $P_B^\circ = 0.75$.

c) Here the equation is now

$$1 \text{ atm} = 0.75 P_A^\circ + 0.25 P_B^\circ \qquad (1)$$

By trial and error substitution of numerical values for P_A° and P_B°, a solution is at 27°C with $P_A^\circ = 1.2$ and $P_B^\circ = 0.5$.

d) The mole fraction of A, y_A, in the vapor phase is given by:

$$y_A = \frac{P_A}{P_{total}} = \frac{P_A^\circ N_A}{P_{total}}$$

$$\therefore \quad y_A = \frac{P_A}{1} = \frac{P_A^\circ N_A}{1}$$

$\therefore$ for solution b) $$y_A = \frac{(0.25)(1.7)}{1} = 0.42$$

For solution c) $$y_A = \frac{(0.75)(1.2)}{1} = 0.9$$

These values are plotted on Fig. 2 to provide the boiling-point plot.

e) A and B are now immiscible, and thus the equation becomes

$$1 \text{ atm} = P_A^\circ + P_B^\circ$$

Values for P_A° and P_B° are substituted into the equation until at approximately 10°C, a solution is found for which $P_A^o + P_B^o = 1$ atm. Thus the normal boiling point of the mixtures is 10°C.

• PROBLEM 7-7

a) The vapor pressure of a binary solution of liquids A and B at 80°C are 100 and 600 mm Hg respectively. Calculate several vapor compositions. On a plot of total vapor pressure of solutions at 80°C vs mole fractions, draw in a semiquantitative liquid and vapor-composition curve.
b) At 80°C, if one-third of the liquid of a solution containing 40 mole % B is evaporated in an evacuated container, calculate the compositions of the final liquid and vapor phases.
c) 1 mole of solution of mole fraction $N_B = 0.6$ is evaporated in an open container at constant temperature of 80°C until the total vapor pressure falls by 20%. Calculate final liquid composition and estimate the number of moles of liquid remaining after evaporation to this point.

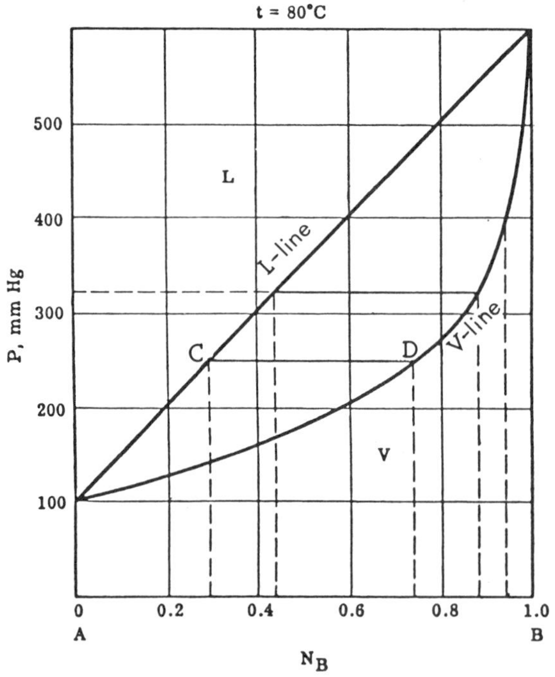

Fig. 1

Solution: a) The liquid-composition line (L-line) of a P vs N_B plot of figure 1 at constant temperature will be a straight line joining the two vapor pressures. Since the solution is ideal, Raoult's law applies. Therefore,

$$Y_B = \frac{P_B}{P_{total}} = \frac{P^\circ_B N_B}{P_{total}}$$

For $N_B = 0.2$, P_{total} from Fig. 1 = 200 mm Hg

$$\therefore \quad Y_B = \frac{P^\circ_B N_B}{P_{total}} = \frac{(600 \text{ mm Hg})(0.2)}{200 \text{ mm Hg}}$$

$$Y_B = 0.6$$

For $N_B = 0.4$, $P_{total} = 300$ mm Hg

$$\therefore \quad Y_B = \frac{(600 \text{ mm Hg})(0.4)}{300 \text{ mm Hg}}$$

$$Y_B = 0.80$$

For $N_B = 0.6$, $P_{total} = 400$ mm Hg

$$\therefore \quad Y_B = \frac{(600 \text{ mm Hg})(0.6)}{400 \text{ mm Hg}}$$

$$Y_B = 0.90$$

Using these three points the vapor composition curve can be drawn as in Fig. 1.

b) Since $N_B = 0.4$ and the problem indicates that 1/3 of the solution vaporizes, the correct tie line is the one which is of ratio 1:2 from the L-line to the V-line with a fulcrum at $N_B = 0.4$. This is called the Lever principle. This means that if the distance from the L-line to N_B equals 1 unit, that of N_B to V-line equals 3 units. This tie line gives a liquid-composition of 0.3 mole fraction and the vapor-composition of 0.75 mole fraction. It is shown in Fig. 1 as the CD line.

c) Initially, $N_B = 0.6$ mole fraction. The 0.6 composition crosses the L-line at a vapor pressure of 400 mm Hg. After evaporation, the vapor pressure falls by 20% of its initial value. The vapor pressure is now 80% of 400 mg Hg which is 320 mm Hg. Using this value of the vapor pressure the corresponding final liquid-composition is about $N_B = 0.45$.

Similarly from Fig. 1, the initial vapor-composition corresponding to 400 mm Hg is $Y_B^{initial} = 0.92$. The final vapor-composition corresponding to 320 mm Hg is $Y_B^{final} = 0.90$. Thus the average vapor composition

$Y_B^{av} = \frac{0.92 + 0.90}{2} = 0.91$. From Fig. 1, using the lever rule and the average vapor composition, the number of moles, n_ℓ, remaining after evaporation can be estimated as follows:

$$n_\ell = \frac{Y_B^{av} - N_B^{(400)}}{Y_B^{av} - N_B^{(320)}}$$

$$\therefore \qquad n_\ell = \frac{0.91 - 0.6}{0.91 - 0.45}$$

$$n_\ell = 0.67$$

• PROBLEM 7-8

An ideal isomeric (equal molecular weights and mole fractions) solution of liquids A and B is of composition N_A and has a vapor pressure of 650 mm Hg at 50°C. Half of the solution is then distilled (with no reflux) and collected as condensate. Calculate N_A, P_A°, and P_B° if the condensate has a composition of $N_A' = 0.60$ and the residual liquid has a composition of $N_A'' = 0.40$ and a vapor pressure of 600 mm Hg at 50°C.

Solution: Writing an overall mass (material) balance for component A:

Input of moles of A into distilling flash = Output of moles of A in the condensate.

$$\text{Input of A} = N_A$$

$$\text{Output of A} = N_A' + N_A''$$

Half of the Input was collected as condensate.

$$\therefore \quad \text{Output of A} = \frac{N_A' + N_A''}{2}$$

Since Input = Output,

$$N_A = \frac{N_A' + N_A''}{2} = \frac{0.6 + 0.4}{2}$$

$$N_A = 0.5$$

Using the vapor pressure balance on the system, P_A° and P_B° can be found.

Total vapor pressure of the original solution = total vapor pressure of the residual solution

Residual solution vapor pressure = $N_A P_A^\circ + N_B P_B^\circ$

Original solution vapor pressure = $N_A P_A^\circ + N_B P_B^\circ$

where N_A , N_B = composition of A and B

P_A° , P_B° = vapor pressure of pure A and B

$$\therefore \quad 650 = 0.5\ P_A^\circ + 0.5\ P_B^\circ \qquad (1)$$

$$600 = 0.4\ P_A^\circ + 0.6\ P_B^\circ \qquad (2)$$

Solving (1) and (2) simultaneously we find

$$P_A^\circ = 900 \text{ mm Hg}$$

and $P_B^\circ = 400$ mm Hg

• PROBLEM 7-9

In an ideal solution of liquids A and B, the vapor pressure of a mixture of 1 mole of A and 2 moles of B is 0.5 atm at 70°C. 3 moles of A is added to the solution at 70°C and the vapor pressure of the solution rises to 0.7 atm. a) Estimate graphically or calculate the values of P_A° and P_B°. b) Calculate what the vapor pressure would be if some of the vapor in equilibrium with the first solution were completely condensed.

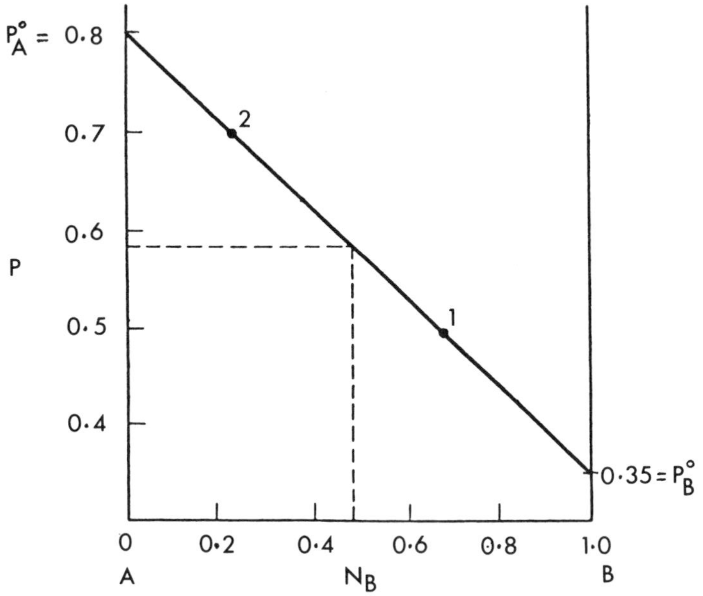

Fig. 1

Solution: Since this is an ideal solution, the plot of the total vapor pressure vs mole fraction is a straight line. In Fig. 1, the total pressure P is plotted against

N_B, the mole fraction of B.

Total original number of moles = 1 mole of A + 2 moles of B
= 3 moles

$$\therefore \quad N_A = \frac{1}{3} = 0.33$$

$$N_B = \frac{2}{3} = 0.67 \quad \text{or} \quad 1 - 0.33 = 0.67$$

After adding 3 moles of A

Total new number of moles = 4 moles of A + 2 moles of B

= 6 moles

$$\therefore \quad N_A = \frac{4}{6} = 0.67$$

$$N_B = \frac{2}{6} = 0.33 \quad \text{or} \quad 1 - 0.67 = 0.33$$

Thus using $N_B = 0.67$ at 0.5 atm point 1 on Fig. 1 is located; again when $N_B = 0.33$ at 0.7 atm point 2 is located. A straight line is drawn to connect these two points. If the line is extended on both sides to N_B = 0 and N_B = 1, the intercepts of the curve on both coordinates of Fig. 1 gives

$$P^\circ_A = 0.8 \text{ atm} \quad \text{and} \quad P^\circ_B = 0.35 \text{ atm}$$

b) The vapor composition that is in equilibrium with the first solution is obtained using Raoult's Law since this is an ideal solution.

$$\therefore \quad Y_A = \frac{P_A}{P_{total}} = \frac{P^\circ_A N_A}{P_{total}}$$

$$Y_A = \frac{0.8 \times 0.33}{0.5} = 0.53$$

From Fig. 1 and using $Y_A = 0.53$, P is estimated at about 0.58 atm.

• PROBLEM 7-10

A binary ideal solution of A and B consisting of 0.4 mole A and 0.6 mole of B is heated in a closed system at 1 atm to 50°C. The resulting composition of the solution is n_v moles of vapor of composition y_B and n_ℓ moles of liquid of composition N_B. After a partial condensation of the vapor at 50°C the vapor pressure of the condensate was 1.20 atm and a vapor of composition $y'_B = 0.85$ was in equilibrium with the condensate. Calculate a) y_B,

N_B b) n_v, n_ℓ and percent of B in the vapor phase.
c) Construct the liquid-vapor composition lines in the vapor pressure diagram and indicate values for P°_A and P°_B.

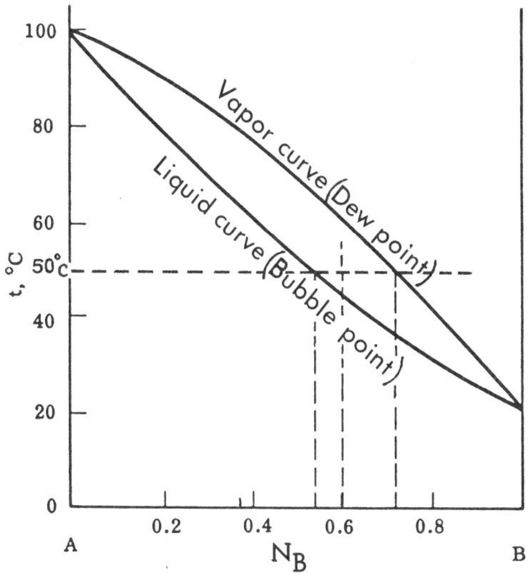

Fig. 1

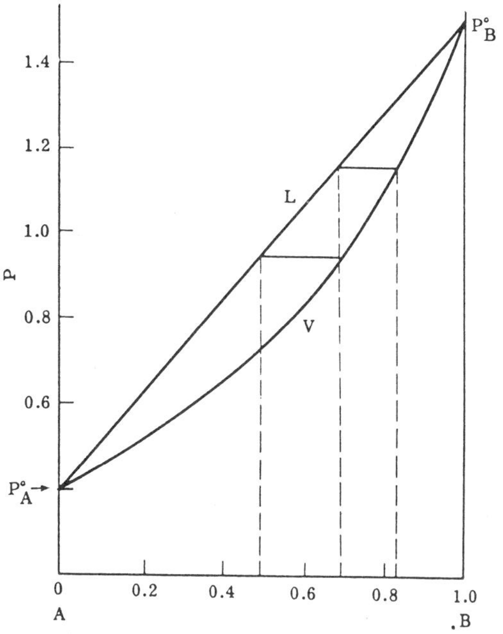

Fig. 2

Solution: a) Using the boiling point diagram of Fig. 1, estimation of y_B and N_B can be made using the vapor and liquid curves. At 50°C a tie line is drawn to bisect the vapor liquid curves. The starting solution contains 0.6 mole fraction of B, so using this composition a line is drawn from 0.6 mole fraction to intersect the tie-line. Where the tie line crosses the vapor-liquid curves gives $y_B = 0.70$ and $N_B = 0.53$.

b) To determine what the relative amount of liquid and vapor is in the vapor phase one uses the Lever rule. Consider a material balance on component B

n_ℓ = no. of moles of liquid

n_v = no. of moles of vapor

Referring to Fig. 1

$$n_v = \frac{0.6 - 0.53}{0.7 - 0.53} = 0.41$$

But $n_\ell + n_v = 1$

$\therefore \quad n_\ell = 1 - 0.41 = 0.59$

c) A plot of vapor pressure vs mole fraction at constant temperature for an ideal solution gives a straight line and the ends of this curve (where it crosses the coordinates of the plot) gives the vapor pressures P°_ℓ of the pure components of the liquids in solution. In order to plot this curve, the two points are given.

At 1 atm $n_v = 0.7$ and $n_\ell = 0.53$

At 1.2 atm $n_v = 0.85$ and $n_\ell = 0.70$

Now, these points can be plotted on the P_i vs N_i diagram as shown in Fig. 2. The intercepts of the coordinates gives $P^\circ_A \cong 0.4$ and $P^\circ_B \cong 1.5$.

• PROBLEM 7-11

The vapor pressure of two miscible liquids A and B at 50°C exhibit negative deviation from Raoult's Law:
a) Sketch the vapor pressure vs. composition diagram for 50°C. Label the total pressure line, the liquid-composition line and the vapor composition line.
b) Sketch the boiling-point diagram showing the vapor-composition lines.

Assume that B has a higher boiling point than A and be careful to sketch the correct shape for the lines.

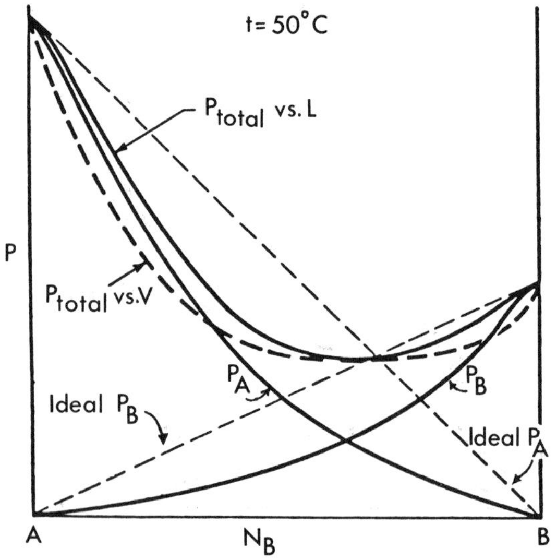

Fig. 1

Solution: A system is said to deviate negatively from Raoult's Law, when the total pressure of the system at equilibrium is less than the ideal value.

a) The total pressure line, liquid composition line and vapor composition line are all shown in Fig. 1. Note that component A has a higher vapor pressure at this temperature of 50°C because it has a lower boiling point. Also, the vapor pressure of the component present at higher

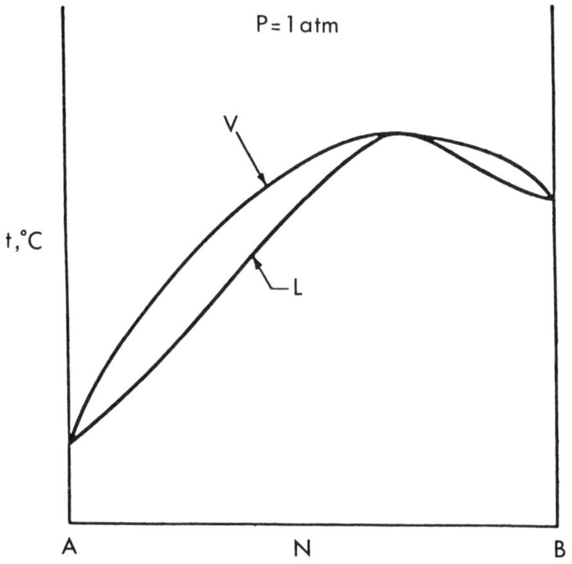

Fig. 2

concentration will approach the values given by Raoult's Law as its mole fraction approaches unity. Note also that the partial pressure curves must approach the Raoult's Law line as pure liquid is approached in composition.

b) The boiling point will be reached when the pressure is 1 atm. The vapor-composition line is indicated on the graph in Fig. 2. The boiling point graph is similar to the vapor pressure diagram of Fig. 1 if viewed upside down.

• PROBLEM 7-12

What can you say about the relationships of (a) the density and (b) the enthalpy of a solution to the densities and enthalpies of the pure component liquids A and B if both A and B form ideal solutions.

Solution: Density of a solution,

$$\rho_{soln} = \frac{\sum_i m_i}{\sum_i V_i}$$

where m_i = mass or weight of the component i in the solution

V_i = volume of the component i in the solution.

Since the two liquids A and B form ideal solution, the volume of the solution is additive.

That is $\sum_i V_i = n_i V_i$

where n_i = moles of component i

$\therefore \quad V_{soln} = n_A V_A + n_B V_B$

$\sum_i m_i = n_i M_i$

Mass of Soln = $n_A M_A + n_B M_B$

$$\therefore \quad \rho_{soln} = \frac{m}{V} = \frac{n_A M_A + n_B M_B}{n_A V_A + n_B V_B} \tag{1}$$

Since $\rho = \frac{m}{V}$, $\rho_A = \frac{m_A}{V_A}$ and $\rho_B = \frac{m_B}{V_B}$

Therefore, $m_A = \rho_A V_A$ or $V_A = \frac{m_A}{\rho_A}$

and $m_B = \rho_B V_B$ or $V_B = \frac{m_B}{\rho_B}$

If these values are substituted into equation (1), the relationship becomes

$$\rho_{soln} = \frac{n_A \rho_A V_A + n_B \rho_B V_B}{n_A V_A + n_B V_B} = \frac{n_A m_A + n_B m_B}{n_A \frac{m_A}{\rho_A} + n_B \frac{m_B}{\rho_B}}$$

Note that either one of the above equations is satisfactory.

The relationship of enthalpies, H, is

$$H_{soln} = n_A H_A + n_B H_B$$

NON IDEAL SOLUTIONS

• PROBLEM 7-13

The total vapor pressure, P, versus composition N (for a given temperature) of a non-ideal solution of liquids A and B is plotted in Fig. 1.

a) Sketch qualitatively P_A and P_B; the separate vapor pressure vs. component plots for each component.

b) Draw on Fig. 1 the vapor-composition line.

c) Indicate the boiling point of the system.

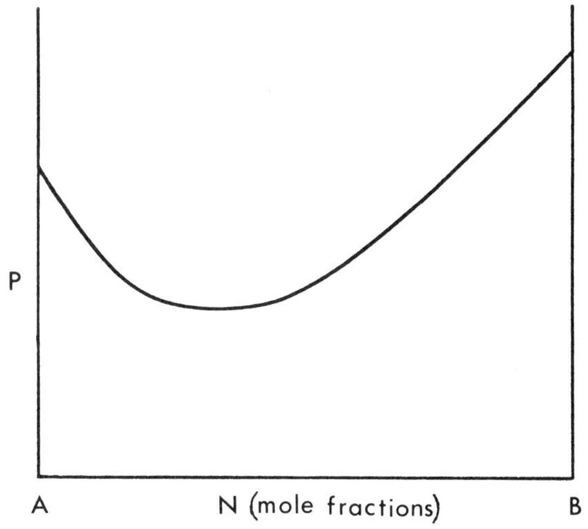

Fig. 1

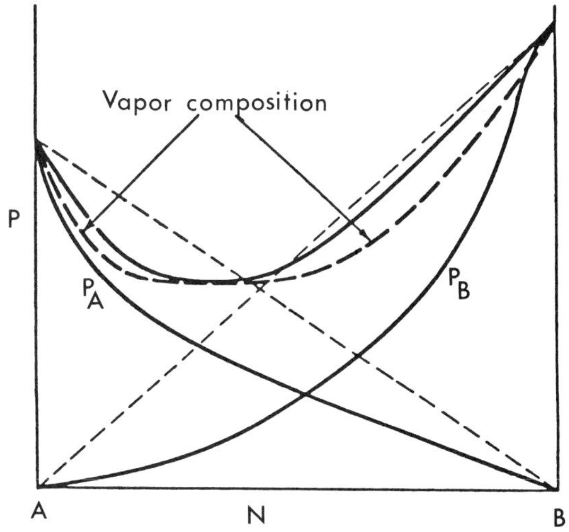

Fig. 2

<u>Solution</u>: The vapor pressure of a component in a non-ideal solution is not proportional to its concentration over the whole range of concentrations. There are negative deviations from Raoult's Law at higher concentrations.

a) The curves P_A and P_B are shown on Fig. 2.

b) The vapor-composition line has a minimum at the point it touches the liquid composition line. At this point the vapor and the liquid have the same composition. This point is called the azeotrope.

c) There is a maximum boiling point for the system, with the vapor line staying above the liquid composition line and touching it at the maximum. Component A will have a higher boiling point than component B.

• PROBLEM 7-14

The vapor pressure of two liquids A and B at 25°C are $P^\circ_A = 0.75$ atm and $P^\circ_B = 1.50$ atm respectively, and they form a non-ideal but regular solution. Liquid A has a mole fraction N_A of 0.50. Calculate the activity coefficient of A and the partial pressure, P_B of liquid B, given that the partial pressure, P_A , of A = 0.25 atm.

Solution: The vapor pressure of a component in a non-ideal solution is not directly proportional to its concentration over the whole range of concentrations.

The activity coefficient, f for component A using the ideal vapor pressure is given by

$$f_A = \frac{P_A}{N_A P^\circ_A}$$

where f_A = activity coefficient of component A

P_A = partial pressure of A

P°_A = vapor pressure of pure A

N_A, N_B = concentration of A and B respectively

Therefore,

$$f_A = \frac{0.25 \text{ atm}}{(0.5)(0.75 \text{ atm})} = 0.67$$

since $N_A + N_B = 1$

$\therefore \quad N_B = (1 - 0.5) = 0.5$

Using the formula

$$\log f_A = -\alpha N_B^2 ,$$

$$\log f_A = -\alpha (0.5)^2 = \log f_B$$

Thus $f_A = f_B = 0.67$

$$P_B = X_B P^\circ_B$$

$\therefore \quad P_B = (0.50)(1.5 \text{ atm}) = 0.75$ atm

• PROBLEM 7-15

In a binary solution, the two components form non-ideal solution. If one of the components exhibits negative deviation from ideality in its variation of partial pressures with composition, explain briefly why the other component will do likewise.

Solution: There are present in the solution intramolecular forces between component A or B and intermolecular forces between components A and B. Negative deviation from ideality arises when the intramolecular forces are less than the intermolecular forces, thus leading to association. When A is partially associated with B, B is similarly associated with A, therefore both partial pressures should show a negative deviation from ideality since we have a symmetrical situation.

• PROBLEM 7-16

A certain liquid solution contains two components 1 and 2. Component 1 follows Henry's law for the mole fraction range $0 \leq x_i \leq a$ at constant temperature (and low pressure). Show that component 2 must follow Raoult's law for the mole fraction range $(1 - a) \leq x_2 \leq 1$.

Solution: Henry's law is given by

$$P_1 = Kx_1 \tag{1}$$

where K is a constant at constant temperature and is called Henry's law constant. x_1 is the mole fraction of component 1 in the liquid phase and P_1 is the partial pressure of component 1.

From equation (1)

$$\ln P_1 = \ln K + \ln x_1$$

and

$$\frac{d(\ln P_1)}{dx_1} = \frac{1}{x_1} \tag{2}$$

By definition, the Gibbs-Duhem equation for a binary system under low pressure is given as

$$x_1 \frac{d(\ln P_1)}{dx_1} + (1-x_1)\frac{d(\ln P_1)}{dx_1} = 0 \tag{3}$$

Substituting equation (2) into equation (3) gives

$$1 + (1-x_1)\frac{d(\ln P_2)}{dx_1} = 0$$

and $d(\ln P_2) = d[\ln(1-x_1)] = d(\ln x_2) \quad (1-a) \leq x_2 \leq 1$ (4)

Integrating equation (4) yields

$$\ln P_2 = \ln x_2 + \ln C \tag{5}$$

where C is the constant of integration. The partial pressure of component 2 is its pure vapor pressure P_2' when $x_2 = 1$.

Therefore $C = P'_2$ and equation (5) becomes

$$\ln P_2 = \ln x_2 + \ln P'_2 = \ln P'_2 x_2$$

or $$P_2 = P'_2 x_2$$

which is Raoult's law, valid for the range $(1-a) \leq x_2 \leq 1$.

• PROBLEM 7-17

The Henry's law constant for the solubility of air in water is found to be as follows:

$t°C$	5	15
$H \times 10^{-4}$ atm	4.88	6.07

Extrapolate these data to obtain the solubility at 25°C.

<u>Solution</u>: Henry's law is defined as

$$P_1 = Hx_1 \quad (1)$$

where P_1 = partial pressure

x_1 = mole fraction

H = Henry's law constant

Rearranging equation (1) yields

$$H = \frac{P_1}{x_1}$$

$$H = P_1 x_1^{-1}$$

$$\ln H = \ln P_1 - \ln x_1 \quad (3)$$

Differentiate equation (3) with respect to T at constant P_1 gives

$$\left(\frac{\partial \ln H}{\partial T}\right)_{P_1} = -\left(\frac{\partial \ln x_1}{\partial T}\right)_{P_1} \quad (2)$$

But by definition $$\left(\frac{\partial \ln x_1}{\partial T}\right)_{P_1} = -\frac{(H''_1 - H'_1)}{RT^2} + \frac{\bar{H}'_1 - H'_1}{RT^2}$$

$$= \frac{-H''_1 + \bar{H}'_1}{RT^2}$$

where $H''_1 - H'_1$ = latent heat of vaporization

and $\bar{H}'_1 - H'_1$ = differential heat of solution.

R = gas constant

T = temperature

From equation (2)

$$\left(\frac{\partial \ell nH}{\partial T}\right)_{P_1} \quad \text{is also equal to} \quad -\left(\frac{\bar{H}_1' - H_1''}{RT^2}\right) \qquad (4)$$

If the $\left(\frac{\bar{H}_1' - H_1''}{R}\right)$ term in equation (4) is assumed to be a constant (because the latent heat is assumed to be constant over the temperature range), then equation (4) becomes

$$\left(\frac{\partial \ell nH}{\partial T}\right)_{P_1} = -\frac{C}{T^2} \qquad (5)$$

Integrating both sides with respect to T, equation (5) becomes

$$\ell nH = \frac{C}{T} + D \qquad (6)$$

where D is the integration constant.

The data give

t°C	T°K	$\frac{1}{T}$	$H\times 10^{-4}$	ℓnH
5°C	278	0.003597	4.88	10.795
15°C	288	0.003472	6.07	11.014

The constants in equation (6) can be found by using the two values of ℓnH.

That is, $$10.795 = \frac{C}{278} + D = \frac{C + 278D}{278} \qquad (7)$$

$$11.014 = \frac{C}{288} + D = \frac{C + 288D}{288} \qquad (8)$$

Subtracting equation (7) from equation (8) gives

$$(11.014 - 10.795) = \frac{C}{288} - \frac{C}{278} = 0.003472C - 0.003597C$$

$$= -0.000125C$$

$$0.219 = -0.000125C$$

$$\therefore \quad C = -1752.0$$

Substituting this into either equation (7) or (8),

$$D = 10.795 + \frac{1752.0}{278} = 17.097$$

Therefore equation (6) becomes

$$\ell nH = \frac{-1752.0}{T} + 17.097$$

At 25°C = 298°K,

$$\ell nH = \frac{-1752.0}{298} + 17.097 = -5.87919 + 17.097 = 11.218$$

or $H = e^{11.21} = 74444.2 = 7.44 \times 10^4$

• PROBLEM 7-18

The vapor pressure and partial vapor pressures of a mixture of acetone (propanone) and chloroform (trichloromethane) spanning the range from pure acetone to pure chloroform were measured at 35°C. The results were as follows:

x(chloroform)	0.00	0.20	0.40	0.60	0.80	1.00
p(chloroform)/mmHg	0	35	82	142	219	293
p(acetone)/mmHg	347	270	185	102	37	0

Confirm that the mixture conforms to Raoult's Law for the component in large excess, and to Henry's Law for the minor component. Find the Henry's Law constants.

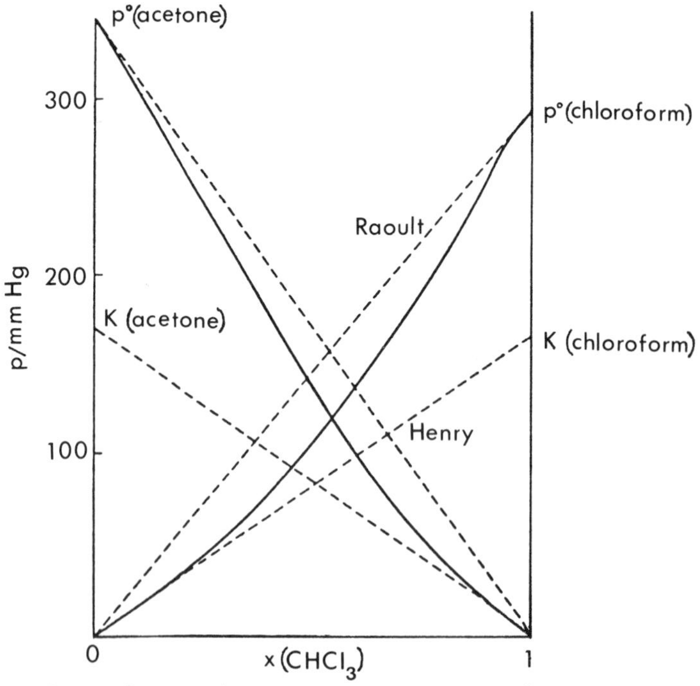

Experimental vapor pressures of an acetone/chloroform mixture.

Fig. 1

Solution: If a plot of the partial vapor pressures and

the total vapor pressure against mole fraction is drawn, then Raoult's Law can be tested by comparing the data with straight lines drawn according to $P_1 = x_1P_1^\circ$

where P_1 = partial pressure of component 1

x_1 = mole fraction of component 1

P_1° = vapor pressure of component 1

Also, Henry's Law can be tested by finding some value of K such that the line $P_1 = x_1K_1$ fits the data for small x_1.

K_1 = Henry's Law constant for component 1

Using the data given, the plot is shown in Fig. 1.

From the constructions, Henry's Law requires K (acetone) to be about 175 mmHg and that of chloroform to be about 165 mmHg.

• PROBLEM 7-19

Henry's Law constant for hydrogen gas in water is 5.34×10^7 torr and 2.75×10^6 torr in benzene. How much more soluble is hydrogen in benzene than in water?

Solution: Henry's Law constant K_2 is given by

$$K_2 = \frac{P_2}{x_2}$$ (valid in very dilute solution in the region where $x_2 \to 0$)

otherwise written as $K_2 = \lim_{x_2 \to 0} \frac{P_2}{x_2}$

where P_2 = partial pressure of hydrogen gas over the solution

x_2 = concentration or solubility

The subscript 2 indicates that the solute which is the component at lower concentration is being considered.

$$\therefore \quad K_{2\,(C_6H_6)}x_{2\,(C_6H_6)} = P_{2\,(C_6H_6)}$$

and $K_{2\,(H_2O)}x_{2\,(H_2O)} = P_{2\,(H_2O)}$

$$\therefore \quad K_{2\,(C_6H_6)}x_{2\,(C_6H_6)} = K_{2\,(H_2O)}x_{2\,(H_2O)} \qquad (1)$$

Taking the ratio of x_2 in the solvents as given by (1),

$$\frac{x_{2\,(C_6H_6)}}{x_{2\,(H_2O)}} = \frac{K_{2\,(H_2O)}}{K_{2\,(C_6H_6)}} = \frac{5.34\times10^7}{2.75\times10^6} = 19.4$$

H_2 is thus 19.4 times more soluble in benzene than in water.

• PROBLEM 7-20

Eqs. (a) and (b) relate the logarithm of the activity coefficients of the two components of the ethyl alcohol (1)-toluene(2) mixture to the concentration of the solution

$$\log \gamma_1 = \frac{1.0074x_2^2}{(1.3343x_1 + x_2)^2} \tag{a}$$

and

$$\log \gamma_2 = \frac{0.7550x_1^2}{(0.7495x_2 + x_1)^2} \tag{b}$$

The standard state to which these activity coefficients refer is the pure component, and the mole fraction concentration scale. Calculate: (a) the activity coefficients of both components referred to the standard state at infinite dilution and mole fraction concentration scale, γ_1^*, γ_2^*, (b) the activity coefficient of toluene(2) referred to the standard state at infinite dilution and molality concentration scale, $_m\gamma_2^*$.

Solution: a) By definition,

$$\mu_i = \mu_i^\circ + RT\ell n \frac{a_i}{a_i^\circ} \tag{1}$$

where μ_i° = chemical potential of component i at a standard state (a state that is usually chosen arbitrarily)

R = gas constant

T = temperature

a_i = activity in a given state

a_i° = activity in a standard state

In a standard state, the activity a_i° is always assigned a value of unity. As a result, equation (1) becomes

$$\mu_i = \mu_i^\circ + RT\ell n a_i \tag{2}$$

The activity of any substance is defined as

$$a_i = x_i\gamma_i$$

where x_i = mole fraction of component i

γ_i = activity coefficient of component i

Therefore, equation (2) can be written in the form

$$\mu_i = \mu_i^\circ + RT\ln x_i\gamma_i \tag{3}$$

Equation (3) is for the standard state referred to the pure component and mole fraction concentration scale.

For the standard state referred to infinite dilution and mole fraction concentration scale,

$$\mu_i = \mu_i^* + RT\ln x_i\gamma_i^* \tag{4}$$

where μ_i^* = chemical potential of component i referred to infinite dilution and mole fraction concentration scale

and γ_i^* = activity coefficient of component i referred to infinite dilution and mole fraction concentration scale.

Equations (3) and (4) show that the chemical potential, μ_i is independent of the selection of the standard state (that is, the left hand side of both equations are equal). Consequently,

$$\mu_i^\circ + RT\ln x_i\gamma_i = \mu_i^* + RT\ln x_i\gamma_i^* \tag{5}$$

for a certain concentration x_i.

Since this is a binary solution equation (5) takes the form

$$\mu_i^\circ + RT\ln\gamma_i^\infty = \mu_i^* \tag{6}$$

as $x_i \to 0$ (at infinite dilution), because $\gamma_i^* = 1$ and $\gamma_i = \gamma_i^\infty$ at infinite dilution.

Substituting equation (6) into equation (5) yields

$$\mu_i^\circ + RT\ln\gamma_i = \mu_i^\circ + RT\ln\gamma_i^\infty + RT\ln\gamma_i^*$$

$$= \mu_i^\circ + RT(\ln\gamma_i^\infty + \ln\gamma_i^*)$$

Therefore, $\ln\gamma_i = \dfrac{RT(\ln\gamma_i^\infty + \ln\gamma_i^*)}{RT}$

or $\ln\gamma_i = \ln\gamma_i^\infty + \ln\gamma_i^* = \ln\left(\gamma_i^\infty\gamma_i^*\right)$.

Consequently, $\gamma_i = \gamma_i^\infty\gamma_i^*$

$$\text{or} \quad \gamma_i^* = \frac{\gamma_i}{\gamma_i^\infty}\,. \tag{7}$$

Thus, the activity coefficients referred to the standard state at infinite dilution are simply given as a ratio of the activity coefficients referred to the pure component standard state at a given concentration, γ_i , and at infinite dilution, γ_i^{∞}.

From equation (a),

$$\ln\gamma_1^{\infty} = \left[\frac{1.0074x_2^2}{(0+x)^2}\right] \quad 2.303$$

But $x_2 = 1$ if $x_1 = 0$

$$\therefore \quad \ln\gamma_1^{\infty} = (1.0074)(2.303) = 2.32$$

and $\gamma_1^{\infty} = e^{2.32} = 10.173$

Similarly, equation (b) yields

$$\ln\gamma_2^{\infty} = (0.7550)(2.303) = 1.739$$

and $\gamma_2^{\infty} = e^{1.739} = 5.688$

Note the value 2.303 is multiplying the right hand side because $\ln$ is used instead of log. Using log directly will also give the same result.

The values of γ_1 and γ_2 calculated from equations (a) and (b) at various concentrations as well as γ_1^* and γ_2^* obtained from equation (7) are tabulated and shown in Fig. 1.

As expected from the definition of the infinite dilute standard state $\gamma_1^* \to 1$ as $x_1 \to 0$ and $\gamma_2^* \to 1$ as $x_2 \to 0$.

b) The chemical potential is independent of the chosen standard state, therefore, for component 2

$$\mu_2 = \mu_2^{*m} + RT\ln m^m\gamma_2^* = \mu_2^* + RT\ln x_2\gamma_2^* \qquad (8)$$

Recall that molality and mole fraction are related to each other by the equation

$$m = \frac{n_2}{w_1}(1000) = \frac{n_2}{M_1 n_1}(1000) = \frac{x_2}{x_1}\frac{1000}{M_1}$$

where m = molality

n = moles

w_1 = weight of component 1 (solvent)

M_1 = molecular weight of component 1

x = mole fraction

Using these relations, equation (8) becomes

$$\mu_2^{*m} + RT\ln m^m\gamma_2^* = \mu_2^* + RT\ln\frac{mx_1M_1}{1000}\gamma_2^*$$

$$= \mu_2^* + RT\ln\frac{M_1}{1000} + RT\ln m x_1 \gamma_2^* \qquad (9)$$

Remember as $x_2 \to 0$, $x_1 \to 1$.

Upon simplifying this yields

$$\mu_2^{*m} = \mu_2^* + RT\ln\frac{M_1}{1000} \qquad (10)$$

and $$^m\gamma_2^* = x_1\gamma_2^* \qquad (11)$$

The values of the activity coefficients of component 2 (toluene) referred to the infinite dilute standard state and molality concentration scale, $^m\gamma_2^*$ can be obtained by using equation (11). They are tabulated and shown in Fig. 1.

The results show that toluene behaves less ideally when molality concentration scale is employed.

• PROBLEM 7-21

J.J. Van Laar gave a useful semiempirical equation for the excess free enthalpy of solutions,

$$\Delta G^{ex} = \frac{b_{12}X_1X_2}{b_1X_1 + b_2X_2} \qquad (1)$$

where b_{12}, b_1, and b_2 are characteristic constants. Show that the Van Laar relation implies that

$$\sqrt{\frac{1}{\ln\gamma_1}} = \frac{\sqrt{A_{12}}}{B_{12}}\left(\frac{X_1}{X_2}\right) + \frac{1}{\sqrt{A_{12}}}$$

$$\frac{1}{\sqrt{\ln\gamma_2}} + \frac{\sqrt{B_{12}}}{A_{12}}\left(\frac{X_2}{X_1}\right) + \frac{1}{\sqrt{B_{12}}}$$

where $A_{12} = (b_{12}/b_2RT)$, $B_{12} = (b_{12}/b_1RT)$.

Solution: Since the problem requires relations between molal excess quantity, activity coefficients and mole fractions, it would be wise to begin with the Gibbs-Duhem equation of the form

$$\left(\frac{\partial\Delta G^{ex}}{\partial X_i}\right)_{T,P,X_j} = RT\ln\gamma_i \qquad (2)$$

where X_i = mole fraction of component i

R = gas constant

γ_i = activity coefficient of component i

T = temperature

The subscripts T, P, mean at constant temperature and pressure respectively while X_j means at constant mole fractions except that of the ith component.

Recall from differential calculus that if $y = \frac{u}{v}$ and $\frac{\partial y}{\partial x}$ is desired, then the relation

$$\frac{\partial y}{\partial x} = \frac{v\left(\frac{du}{dx}\right) - u\left(\frac{dv}{dx}\right)}{v^2} \quad \text{is used.}$$

Applying the same method to equation (1),

$$\left(\frac{\partial \Delta G^{ex}}{\partial X_1}\right)_{T,P,X_2} = \frac{(b_{12}X_2)[b_1X_1+b_2X_2] - (b_1)[b_{12}X_1X_2]}{(b_1X_1+b_2X_2)^2}$$

Clearly, $u = b_{12}X_1X_2$

and $v = b_1X_1 + b_2X_2$.

With further simplification,

$$\left(\frac{\partial \Delta G^{ex}}{\partial X_1}\right)_{T,P,X_2} = \frac{b_{12}b_1X_1X_2 + b_{12}b_2X_2^2}{(b_1X_1 + b_2X_2)^2}$$

$$- \frac{b_1b_{12}X_1X_2}{(b_1X_1 + b_2X_2)^2} = \frac{b_1b_{12}X_1X_2}{(b_1X_1 + b_2X_2)^2}$$

$$- \frac{b_1b_{12}X_1X_2}{(b_1X_1 + b_2X_2)^2} + \frac{b_1b_{12}X_2^2}{(b_1X_1 + b_2X_2)^2}$$

Since the first 2 terms cancel each other,

$$\left(\frac{\partial \Delta G^{ex}}{\partial X_1}\right)_{T,P,X_2} = \frac{b_2b_{12}X_2^2}{(b_1X_1 + b_2X_2)^2}$$

Thus, from equation (2),

$$RT\ln\gamma_1 = \frac{b_2b_{12}X_2^2}{(b_1X_1 + b_2X_2)^2}$$

or

$$\ln\gamma_1 = \frac{b_2b_{12}X_2^2}{RT(b_1X_1 + b_2X_2)^2} \qquad (3)$$

Taking the reciprocal of both sides, equation (3) becomes

$$\frac{1}{\ell n\gamma_1} = \frac{1}{\dfrac{[b_2 b_{12} X_2^2]}{RT[b_1X_1+b_2X_2]^2}} = \frac{RT(b_1X_1+b_2X_2)^2}{b_2 b_{12} X_2^2}$$

Taking the square root of both sides gives

$$\sqrt{\frac{1}{\ell n\gamma_1}} = \sqrt{\frac{RT(b_1X_1+b_2X_2)^2}{b_2 b_{12} X_2^2}}$$

Therefore, $$\frac{1}{\sqrt{\ell n\gamma_1}} = \left(\frac{RT}{b_{12}b_2}\right)^{1/2}\left(\frac{b_1X_1}{X_2}\right) + \left(\frac{RT}{b_{12}b_2}\right)^{1/2} b_2$$

$$= \left(\frac{b_{12}}{b_2RT}\right)^{1/2}\left(\frac{b_1RT}{b_{12}}\right)\frac{X_1}{X_2} + \left(\frac{RTb_2}{b_{12}}\right)^{1/2}$$

But let $A_{12} = \dfrac{b_{12}}{b_2RT}$

and $B_{12} = \dfrac{b_{12}}{b_1RT}$ or $\dfrac{1}{B_{12}} = \dfrac{b_1RT}{b_{12}}$

Consequently, $$\frac{1}{\sqrt{\ell n\gamma_1}} = \frac{\sqrt{A_{12}}}{B_{12}}\left(\frac{X_1}{X_2}\right) + \frac{1}{\sqrt{A_{12}}} .$$

b) Similarly,

$$RT\ell n\gamma_2 = \frac{b_{12}X_1^2 b_1}{(b_1X_1 + b_2X_2)^2}$$

or $$\ell n\gamma_2 = \frac{b_{12}b_1X_1^2}{RT(b_1X_1 + b_2X_2)^2}$$

Taking reciprocals and square roots yields

$$\frac{1}{\sqrt{\ell n\gamma_2}} = \sqrt{\frac{RT(b_1X_1 + b_2X_2)^2}{b_{12}b_1X_1^2}}$$

$$= \left(\frac{RT}{b_{12}b_1}\right)^{1/2}\left(\frac{b_2X_2}{X_1}\right) + \left(\frac{RT}{b_{12}b_1}\right)^{1/2} b_1$$

$$= \left(\frac{b_{12}}{b_1RT}\right)^{1/2}\left(\frac{b_2RT}{b_{12}}\right)\frac{X_2}{X_1} + \left(\frac{RTb_1}{b_{12}}\right)^{1/2}$$

$$\therefore \quad \frac{1}{\sqrt{\ln\gamma_2}} = \frac{\sqrt{B_{12}}}{A_{12}}\left(\frac{X_2}{X_1}\right) + \frac{1}{\sqrt{B_{12}}}$$

• PROBLEM 7-22

For an acetone(1)-methanol(2) system, the following boiling point and equilibrium composition of the liquid and vapor phase were measured at a pressure of 760 mm Hg:

x_1	y_1	t/(°C)	P_1^o/mm Hg	P_2^o/mm Hg
0.280	0.420	58.3	819	579

Calculate the activity coefficients of both components in a solution of $x_1 = 0.676$. The boiling point of this solution is 55.70°C at 760 mm Hg.

Solution: The activity coefficients as functions of the mole fraction are given by

$$\ln\gamma_1 = \frac{B_1}{RT} x_2^2 + \frac{C_1}{RT} x_2^3 \qquad \text{(a)}$$

and $$\ln\gamma_2 = \frac{(B_1 + \frac{3}{2}C_1)}{RT} x_1^2 - \frac{C_1}{RT} x_1^3 \qquad \text{(b)}$$

The equations (a) and (b) would be a matter of direct substitution if the constants B_1 and C_1 were known. So, this is not only a problem of computing the activity coefficients but the constants also.

The constants can be determined by using the given experimental data and the equation

$$\gamma_i = \frac{y_i P}{x_i P_i^o} \qquad (1)$$

where γ_i = activity coefficient of component i

y_i = composition of the vapor phase of component i

x_i = composition of the liquid phase of component i

P = total pressure = 760 mm Hg

P_i^o = vapor pressure of component i

$$\gamma_1 = \frac{y_1 P}{x_1 P_1^o} = \frac{(0.420)(760)}{(0.280)(819)} = \frac{319.2}{229.32}$$

$$\therefore \quad \gamma_1 = 1.3920$$

$$\gamma_2 = \frac{y_2 P}{x_2 P_2^\circ} = \frac{(1-y_1)P}{(1-x_1)P_2^\circ} = \frac{(0.580)(760)}{(0.720)(579)}$$

$$= \frac{440.8}{416.88}$$

$$\therefore \quad \gamma_2 = 1.0574$$

Note that these are not the required activity coefficients. Now from equations (a) and (b)

$$\ln 1.3920 = \frac{B_1}{RT}(0.720)^2 + \frac{C_1}{RT}(0.720)^3$$

and $\ln 1.0574 = \frac{(B_1+\frac{3}{2}C_1)}{RT}(0.280)^2 - \frac{C_1}{RT}(0.280)^3$

which becomes

$$0.3307 = \frac{B_1(0.5184)}{(R)(331.3)} + \frac{C_1(0.3732)}{(R)(331.3)} \qquad (2)$$

and $0.0558 = \frac{(B_1+\frac{3}{2}C_1)}{R(331.3)}(0.0784) - \frac{C_1(0.02195)}{R(331.3)} \qquad (3)$

In this case, R = 1.987.

Solving equations (2) and (3) simultaneously, gives

$$B_1 = 349.9$$

and $C_1 = 97.6$

Using these constants in equations (a) and (b) together with $x_1 = 0.676$ and $x_2 = 1-x_1 = 1-0.676 = 0.324$ gives

$\gamma_1 = 1.063$ and $\gamma_2 = 1.352$

• PROBLEM 7-23

The vapor pressures of C_2H_5OH and H_2O over solutions of these two at 20°C are as follows:

Weight percent C_2H_5OH	$P_{C_2H_5OH}$, torr	P_{H_2O}, torr
0	0	17.5
20.0	12.6	15.9
40.0	20.7	14.7
60.0	25.6	14.1
80.0	31.2	11.3
100	43.6	0

Find the activity and the activity coefficient of each

component in a solution of 40 percent C_2H_5OH by weight. Take the pure substance as the standard state for each component.

Solution: If the basis for the calculation is chosen to be 100 g of solution, then

weight of C_2H_5OH = 40 g

and weight of H_2O = 60 g

This is because the problem indicates that the solution is 40 percent C_2H_5OH by weight.

By definition, the activity a, is given by

$$a_{C_2H_5OH} = \frac{P_{C_2H_5OH}}{P^\circ_{C_2H_5OH}} \tag{1}$$

$$a_{H_2O} = \frac{P_{H_2O}}{P^\circ_{H_2O}} \tag{2}$$

and the activity coefficient, γ, given by

$$\gamma_{C_2H_5OH} = \frac{a_{C_2H_5OH}}{X_{C_2H_5OH}} \tag{3}$$

and $$\gamma_{H_2O} = \frac{a_{H_2O}}{X_{H_2O}} \tag{4}$$

where P = vapor pressure of the component for the mixture at that composition

P° = vapor pressure of the pure component

X = composition (or mole fraction)

The vapor pressure of the pure components C_2H_5OH and H_2O at 20°C are 43.6 torr and 17.5 torr respectively. $P^\circ_{C_2H_5OH}$ is found from the table when the weight percent of C_2H_5OH is 100, and that of $P^\circ_{H_2O}$ is found when the weight percent of H_2O is 100 (when the weight percent of C_2H_5OH is 0). From the given data, $P_{C_2H_5OH}$ at 40 weight percent = 20.7 torr and P_{H_2O} = 14.7 torr. Substituting these values into equations (1) and (2) yields

$$a_{C_2H_5OH} = \frac{P_{C_2H_5OH}}{P^\circ_{C_2H_5OH}} = \frac{20.7}{43.6} = 0.475$$

and $$a_{H_2O} = \frac{P_{H_2O}}{P^\circ_{H_2O}} = \frac{14.7}{17.5} = 0.840$$

Before equations (3) and (4) can be used, the compositions need to be known.

By definition,

$$X_{C_2H_5OH} = \frac{n_{C_2H_5OH}}{n_{C_2H_5OH}+n_{H_2O}} \tag{5}$$

and
$$X_{H_2O} = \frac{n_{H_2O}}{n_{H_2O}+n_{C_2H_5OH}} \tag{6}$$

where n = number of moles = $\frac{\text{weight}}{\text{molecular weight}}$. The molecular weights of C_2H_5OH and H_2O are 46 and 18 respectively.

Therefore, $n_{C_2H_5OH} = \frac{40}{46} = 0.8696$

$$n_{H_2O} = \frac{60}{18} = 3.3333.$$

Using these values in equations (5) and (6) gives

$$X_{C_2H_5OH} = \frac{0.8696}{0.8696 + 3.3333} = \frac{0.8696}{4.2029} = 0.207$$

$$X_{H_2O} = \frac{3.3333}{3.3333 + 0.8696} = \frac{3.3333}{4.2029} = 0.793$$

Therefore, equations (3) and (4) becomes

$$\gamma_{C_2H_5OH} = \frac{a_{C_2H_5OH}}{X_{C_2H_5OH}} = \frac{0.475}{0.207} = 2.30$$

and $\gamma_{H_2O} = \frac{a_{H_2O}}{X_{H_2O}} = \frac{0.840}{0.793} = 1.06$

• PROBLEM 7-24

From the data in the following table for the vapor pressure of water against the concentration of sugar (sucrose) at 25°C calculate the activity of the solvent and its activity coefficient. The total amount of water is 1 kg.

m(sucrose)/mol kg^{-1}	0.000	0.200	0.500	1.000	2.000
p(water)/mmHg	23.75	23.66	23.52	23.28	22.75

Solution: By definition,

$$a_i = \frac{P_i}{P_i^\circ} \quad (1)$$

and $$a_i = \gamma_i x_i \quad \text{or} \quad \gamma_i = \frac{a_i}{x_i} \quad (2)$$

where a_i = activity of component i

P_i = the component's vapor pressure for the mixture of interest at that composition

P_i° = vapor pressure of pure component i

γ_i = activity coefficient of component i

x_i = composition (or mole fraction) of component i

The given concentrations can be converted into mole fractions if the molecular weight is known. Fortunately, the molecular weight of water is known (18 g mol^{-1}). The mole fraction is related to the concentration by the equation

$$x_{water} = \frac{\dfrac{1000\text{ g}}{18\text{ g mol}^{-1}}}{\dfrac{1000\text{ g}}{18\text{ g mol}^{-1}} + m(\text{sucrose}) \times 1\text{ kg}} \quad (3)$$

Therefore, for the different concentration of sugar x_{water} can be computed directly by using equation (3). The respective results are

$\frac{m(\text{sucrose})}{\text{mol kg}^{-1}}$	0.000	0.200	0.400	1.000	2.000
x_{water}	1.000	0.996	0.993	0.982	0.965

These mean that when m(sucrose) is 0.000, equation (3) gives x_{water} = 1 and so on. It is obvious that water is the solvent in this problem. Therefore its activities and activity coefficients at the different concentrations can be computed by using equations (1) and (2). The complete results are tabulated below. Notice how the activity of the solvent (water) remains close to unity. This is because it is in large excess (very dilute solution).

The results are:

$\frac{m(\text{sucrose})}{\text{mol kg}^{-1}}$	0.000	0.200	0.400	1.000	2.000
x_{water}	1.000	0.996	0.993	0.982	0.965
a_{water}	1.000	0.996	0.990	0.980	0.958
γ_{water}	1.000	1.000	0.997	0.998	0.993

The activity coefficient γ_2 (on the mole fraction scale) of the solute in a certain dilute solution is given by $\gamma_2 = e^{AX_2^2}$, where A is a constant at constant temperature. Obtain an expression in terms of A and X_2 for the activity coefficient γ_1 (on the mole fraction scale) of the solvent in this solution.

Solution: Using the Gibbs-Duhem equation of the form $RT(X_1 d\ell n\gamma_1 + X_2 d\ell n\gamma_2) = 0$, it can be seen clearly that

$$X_1 d\ell n\gamma_1 + X_2 d\ell n\gamma_2 = 0$$

and that $X_1 d\ell n\gamma_1 = -X_2 d\ell n\gamma_2$ (1)

where X_1 = composition (or mole fraction) of component 1

X_2 = composition of component 2

γ_1 = activity coefficient of component 1

γ_2 = activity coefficient of component 2

But $\gamma_2 = e^{AX_2^2}$ and $\ell n\gamma_2 = AX_2^2$ by taking the natural logarithms of both sides. Differentiating,

$$d\ell n\gamma_2 = 2AX_2 dX_2 \qquad (2)$$

But $X_2 = 1 - X_1$

∴ Equation (2) becomes $d\ell n\gamma_2 = 2AX_2 dX_2 = -2A(1-X_1)dX_1$.

From equation (1)

$$d\ell n\gamma_1 = -\frac{X_2}{X_1} d\ell n\gamma_2.$$

Since $d\ell n\gamma_2 = -2A(1-X_1)dX_1$.

Therefore,
$$d\ell n\gamma_1 = -\frac{X_2}{X_1}\left[-2A(1-X_1)dX_1\right]$$

$$= -\frac{(1-X_1)}{X_1}\left[-2A(1-X_1)dX_1\right]$$

$$= 2A\left(\frac{1}{X_1} - 2 + X_1\right)dX_1$$

Integrating both sides gives

$$\ell n\gamma_1 = 2A\int_1^{X_1}\left(\frac{1}{X_1} - 2 + X_1\right)dX_1 = 2A\left[\ell nX_1 - 2X_1 + \tfrac{1}{2}X_1^2\right]_1^{X_1}$$

$$= 2A[\ell nX_1 - 2(X_1-1) + \frac{1}{2}(X_1^2-1)]$$

$$= 2A\left[\ell nX_1 - 2(X_1 - 1) + \frac{1}{2}\left[(X_1+1)(X_1-1)\right]\right]$$

$$\therefore \quad \ell n\gamma_1 = 2A\left[\ell n(1-X_2) + X_2 + \frac{1}{2}X_2^2\right]$$

• PROBLEM 7-26

Derive the expression for the elevation of the boiling point ΔT_b of a liquid A by addition of a nonvolatile solute at low molality m_B,

$$\Delta T_b = K_B m_B = \frac{RT_o^2 M_A}{(\Delta H_v)1000} m_B$$

where M_A is the molecular weight of solvent A, ΔH_v is its enthalpy of vaporization per mole, and T_o is its boiling point.

Solution: The liquid and vapor phases of the solvent are in equilibrium at the boiling point. Therefore,

$$\mu_A^v = \mu_A^\ell$$

where μ^ℓ = chemical potential of the liquid phase

and μ^v = chemical potential of the vapor phase

The quantity μ is also called the molar Gibbs function. By definition,

$$\mu_A^\ell = \mu_A^{o\ell} + RT\ell nX_A \qquad (1)$$

and

$$\mu_A^v = \mu_A^{ov} + RT\ell nX_A \qquad (2)$$

where $\mu_A^{o\ell}$ = chemical potential of pure liquid A, that is, μ_A^ℓ when $X_A = 1$ and X_A = mole fraction of A.

At the boiling point the pressure is 1 atm, so that $\mu_A^v = \mu_A^{ov}$, the chemical potential of pure A vapor at 1 atm. Therefore $(\mu_A^v = \mu_A^\ell)$ becomes

$$\mu_A^{ov} = \mu_A^{o\ell} + RT\ell nX_A \qquad (3)$$

Dividing equation (3) by T gives

$$\frac{\mu_A^{ov}}{T} = \frac{\mu_A^{o\ell}}{T} + R\ell nX_A$$

and differentiating with respect to T while keeping P constant gives

$$\left(\frac{\partial \frac{\mu_A^{\circ V}}{T}}{\partial T}\right)_P = \left(\frac{\partial \frac{\mu_A^{\circ \ell}}{T}}{\partial T}\right)_P + R\left(\frac{\partial \ln X_A}{\partial T}\right)_P$$

or

$$\left(\frac{\partial \frac{\mu_A^{\circ V}}{T}}{\partial T}\right)_P - \left(\frac{\partial \frac{\mu_A^{\circ \ell}}{T}}{\partial T}\right)_P = R\left(\frac{\partial \ln X_A}{\partial T}\right)_P \tag{4}$$

But $\left(\frac{\partial \frac{\mu}{T}}{\partial T}\right)_P = \frac{-H}{T^2}$

where H = enthalpy

Substituting this relation into equation (4) gives

$$-\frac{H_A^{\circ V}}{T^2} + \frac{H_A^{\circ \ell}}{T^2} = R\left(\frac{\partial \ln X_A}{\partial T}\right)_P$$

$$\therefore \quad -\left(\frac{H_A^{\circ V} - H_A^{\circ \ell}}{T^2}\right) = R\left(\frac{\partial \ln X_A}{\partial T}\right)_P$$

Since $(H_A^{\circ V} - H_A^{\circ}\ell)$ is the molar heat of vaporization then

$$-\frac{\Delta H_A^{\circ V}}{T^2} = R\left(\frac{\partial \ln X_A}{\partial T}\right)_P$$

or

$$\frac{-\Delta H_A^{\circ V}}{RT^2} = \left(\frac{\partial \ln X_A}{\partial T}\right)_P \tag{5}$$

If ΔH is taken as being constant over the temperature range, equation (5) can be integrated between the limits set by the pure solvent ($X_A = 1$, $T = T_o$) and the solution (X_A , T)

$$\int_{T_o}^{T} \frac{\Delta H_v}{RT^2}\, dT = -\int_{1}^{X_A} d\ln X_A$$

$$\therefore \quad -\ln X_A = \frac{\Delta H_v}{R}\left(\frac{1}{T_o} - \frac{1}{T}\right) = \frac{\Delta H_v}{R}\left(\frac{T-T_o}{TT_o}\right) \qquad (6)$$

When the boiling-point elevation is not large, the term TT_o in equation (6) can be replaced by T_o^2. If X_B = the mole fraction of solute, then the term $-\ln X_A$ can be written as $-\ln(1-X_B)$ and then expanded in a power series. Writing the boiling-point elevation, $T - T_o$, as ΔT_b, then equation (6) becomes

$$\frac{\Delta H_v \Delta T_b}{RT_o^2} = X_B + \frac{1}{2}X_B^2 + \frac{1}{3}X_B^3 + \ldots .$$

For dilute solutions, X_B is a small fraction whose higher powers may be neglected. Therefore,

$$\Delta T_b = \frac{X_B RT_o^2}{\Delta H_v}$$

$$X_B = \frac{n_B}{n_A+n_B}$$

but if $n_B \ll n_A$ then X_B can be approximated by $X_B \simeq \frac{n_B}{n_A}$ so ΔT_b becomes

$$\frac{RT_o^2}{\Delta H_v}\,\frac{n_B}{n_A}\,. \qquad (7)$$

Replacing n_B by m_B and n_A by $\frac{1000}{M_A}$, equation (7) becomes

$$\Delta T_b = \frac{RT_o^2 M_A m_B}{1000\Delta H_v} = K_B m_B$$

• PROBLEM 7-27

The law of osmotic pressure is $\pi\bar{V}_1 = X_2RT$, where $\bar{V}_1$ is the partial molar volume of the solvent and X_2 is the mole fraction of the solute. 10 g of a solute B were dissolved in 1000 g of a solvent A. The molecular weight of A is 100; its density is 1.00 g ml^{-1}. The observed osmotic pressure at 300°K was 0.50 atm. Find the molecular weight of B. Point out any approximations that you are obliged to introduce other than those used in deriving the given equation.

Solution: The assumption here is to take $\bar{V}_1$ to be the same as the molar volume of pure solvent A. By definition,

$$\text{molar volume} = \frac{\text{molecular weight}}{\text{density}} .$$

This is analogous to density $= \frac{\text{mass}}{\text{volume}}$ which can be rearranged to volume $= \frac{\text{mass}}{\text{density}}$ except that in the case of molar volume, mass is replaced by the molecular weight of the substance.

Therefore, $\bar{V}_1 = \frac{100 \text{ g mol}^{-1}}{1.00 \text{ g ml}^{-1}} = 100 \text{ ml mol}^{-1}$

The osmotic pressure, $\pi = \frac{X_2 RT}{\bar{V}_1}$.

Solving for X_2 gives,

$$X_2 = \frac{\pi \bar{V}_1}{RT} = \frac{(0.50 \text{ atm})(100 \text{ ml mol}^{-1})}{(82.06 \text{ ml atm K}^{-1})(300\text{K})} = \frac{50}{24618}$$

$$\therefore \quad X_2 = 2.03 \times 10^{-3}$$

Note that the subscript 1 stands for Solvent A and 2 stands for solvent B. From the definition of mole fraction,

$$X_2 = \frac{n_2}{n_2 + n_1}$$

where n_1 = moles of component 1

n_2 = moles of component 2

But the number of moles is defined as $\frac{\text{mass}}{\text{molecular weight}}$. If the molecular weight of B is taken to be M_2 ,

then $n_2 = \frac{10}{M_2}$

$$n_1 = \frac{1000}{100} = 10$$

and

$$X_2 = \frac{\frac{10}{M_2}}{\frac{10}{M_2} + 10} = \frac{1}{1 + M_2}$$

But $X_2 = 2.03 \times 10^{-3}$

$$\therefore \quad 2.03 \times 10^{-3} = \frac{1}{1 + M_2}$$

or $(1+M_2)(2.03\times10^{-3}) = 1$

$$2.03\times10^{-3} + 2.03\times10^{-3} M_2 = 1$$

$$\therefore \quad M_2 = \frac{1 - 2.03 \times 10^{-3}}{2.03 \times 10^{-3}} = \frac{1}{2.03 \times 10^{-3}} - 1$$

$$= 493 - 1$$

$$\therefore \quad M_2 = 492 \text{ g mol}^{-1}$$

• PROBLEM 7-28

> Iodine is added to a solution of water and carbon disulfide. The distribution coefficient, K_d, for I_2 between water and carbon disulfide is 410. After an amount of CS_2 equal to the water equilibrates with the aqueous phase, calculate the fraction of iodine remaining in the water phase.

Solution: Since the amount of substance or solute added is small, the distribution coefficient, K_d, is given by the ratio of the concentrations of the solute in the two phases.

$$\therefore \quad K_d = \frac{C'}{C} \tag{1}$$

where C' = concentration of I_2 in the CS_2 layer

and C = concentration of I_2 in the water layer

The fraction of I_2 in the two phases must sum up to unity, i.e.

$$n_2' + n_2 = 1 \tag{2}$$

where n_2' = fraction of I_2 in the CS_2 layer

n_2 = fraction of I_2 in the water layer

$$\therefore \quad C_2' = \frac{n_2'}{V'}$$

and $C_2 = \dfrac{n_2}{V}$

where v' and v are the volume CS_2 and water respectively.

From (1) $K_d = \dfrac{C_2'}{C_2} = \dfrac{n_2'/v'}{n_2/v} = 410$

But $v' = v \quad \therefore \quad \dfrac{n_2'}{n_2} = 410$ and $n_2' = 410n_2$

From (2) $n_2' + n_2 = 1$

$$\therefore \quad 410n_2 + n_2 = 1$$

$$411n_2 = 1$$

$$n_2 = \frac{1}{411}$$

$n_2 = 2.43 \times 10^{-3}$ of the original amount of I_2.

PARTIAL MOLAR QUANTITIES

• PROBLEM 7-29

Fig. 1 is a plot of average molar volume, V, for ethyl iodine-ethyl acetate system as a function of N_1, the mole fraction of ethyl iodine. Use Fig. 1 to obtain graphically or calculate the partial molar volumes $\bar{V}_1$ and $\bar{V}_2$ for ethyl iodine and ethyl acetate, respectively, for a system having a solution of composition $N_1 = 0.75$. (b) Calculate ΔV for the process: 3 ethyl iodine + ethyl acetate = solution.

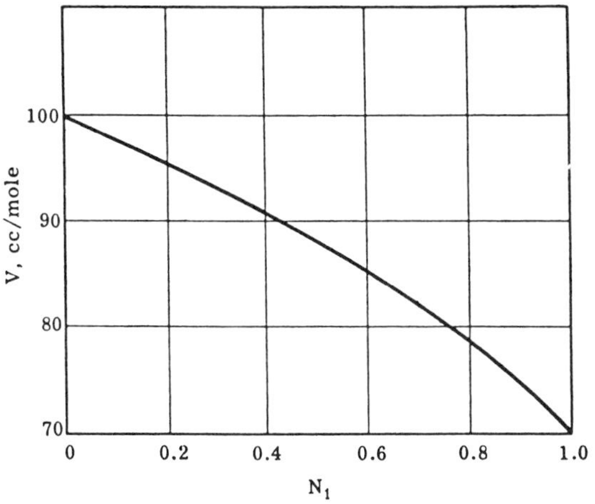

Fig. 1

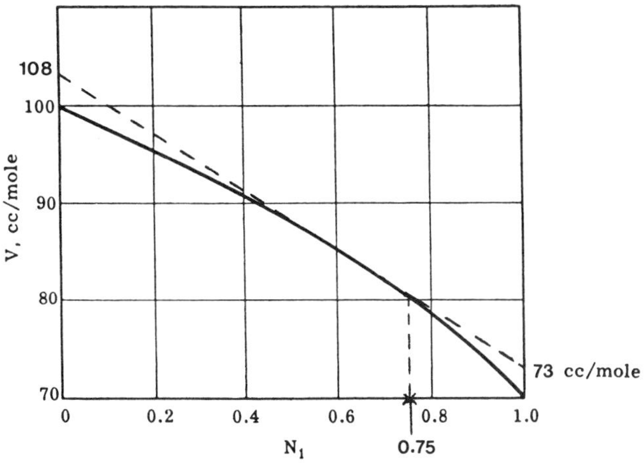

Fig. 2

Solution: The partial molar volume, $\bar{V}_i$, of a component i at constant temperature and pressure is defined as an infinitesimal increase in the volume of the system divided by the infinitesimal change in the number of moles, n_i, of this component which are added.

$$\therefore \qquad \bar{V}_i = \left(\frac{\partial V}{\partial n_i}\right)_{T,P,n_j \neq n_i}$$

$$\text{or} \qquad \bar{V}_i = \frac{V}{n}$$

One of the easiest way of obtaining $\bar{V}_i$ is by method of intercepts. From a plot of V vs. N_1 as in Fig. 2 the intercepts of the tangent line on the ordinates give the partial molar volumes. From Fig. 2 the intercepts

$\bar{V}_2$ = 108 cc/mole

$\bar{V}_1$ = 73 cc/mole

(b) 3 ethyl iodide + ethyl acetate = solution
the volumes are

$3 \times 70 + 100 = 4 \times$ volume of a solution of N_1

$= 0.75$ or $4 \times 81 = 324$cc

$\therefore \quad \Delta V = 324\text{cc} - 310\text{cc}$

$\Delta V = 14\text{cc}$

• PROBLEM 7-30

(a) A solution contains n_1 moles of component 1 and n_2 moles of component 2. Their molecular weights are M_1 and M_2, respectively. Obtain an expression for the partial molar volume $\bar{V}_2$ of component 2 in terms of n_1, n_2, the density ρ of the solution, the derivative(s) of ρ with respect to n_2 at constant n_1, and the molecular weights.

(b) Let X_1 and X_2 be the mole fractions of 1 and 2 in the solution. Show that

$$\bar{V}_2 = \frac{M_2}{\rho} - (M_1X_1 + M_2X_2)\frac{X_1}{\rho^2}\frac{d\rho}{dX_2}$$

(c) The density in g ml^{-1} of a water-methanol (CH_3OH) solution at 25°C is given by the equation

$$\rho = 0.9971 - 0.28930\ X_2 + 0.29907\ X_2^2 - 0.60876\ X_2^3 + 0.59438\ X_2^4 - 0.20581\ X_2^5$$

where X_2 is the mole fraction of methanol. Calculate $\bar{V}_2$ in a water-methanol solution at 25°C with $X_2 = 0.100$.

Solution: a) By definition,

$$\text{Density} = \frac{\text{mass}}{\text{volume}} \tag{1}$$

Rearranging equation (1) to get an expression for volume, it becomes

$$\text{Volume} = \frac{\text{mass}}{\text{density}} . \tag{2}$$

In order to get the mass, make use of the definition of moles, n_i. Thus,

$$n_1 = \frac{m_1}{M_1}$$

and $n_2 = \frac{m_2}{M_2}$ where m_1 = mass of component 1

m_2 = mass of component 2

Rearranging these give

$$m_1 = n_1M_1 \quad \text{and} \quad m_2 = n_2M_2 .$$

Therefore total mass = $m_1 + m_2 = n_1M_1 + n_2M_2$. Using these in equation (2),

$$V = \frac{\text{mass}}{\text{Density}} = \frac{n_1M_1 + n_2M_2}{\rho} . \tag{3}$$

Now, the partial molar volume $\bar{V}_2$ of component 2 is defined as the partial derivative of the total volume V with respect to the number of moles of component 2, holding those of component 1 constant. Mathematically, it is expressed as

$$\bar{V}_2 = \left(\frac{\partial V}{\partial n_2}\right)_{n_1} .$$

Rewriting equation (3) gives

$$V = (n_1M_1 + n_2M_2)\rho^{-1} \tag{4}$$

$$\text{Therefore } \bar{V}_2 = \left(\frac{\partial V}{\partial n_2}\right)_{n_1} = \frac{M_2}{\rho} - (n_1M_1 + n_2M_2)\frac{1}{\rho^2}\left(\frac{\partial \rho}{\partial n_2}\right)_{n_1} \tag{5}$$

b) Using the fact that $X_1 = \frac{n_1}{n_1+n_2}$ and $X_2 = \frac{n_2}{n_2+n_1}$

$$\left(\frac{\partial X_2}{\partial n_2}\right)_{n_1} = \frac{n_1}{(n_1+n_2)^2} .$$

By the mathematical relations, $\left(\frac{\partial \rho}{\partial n_2}\right)_{n_1} = \left(\frac{\partial X_2}{\partial n_2}\right)_{n_1} \frac{d\rho}{dX_2}$,

$$\left(\frac{\partial \rho}{\partial n_2}\right)_{n_1} = \frac{n_1}{(n_1+n_2)^2} \frac{d\rho}{dX_2}$$

Therefore, $\bar{V}_2 = \frac{M_2}{\rho} - (n_1M_1 + n_2M_2)\frac{n_1}{\rho^2(n_1+n_2)^2} \frac{d\rho}{dX_2}$

$$= \frac{M_2}{\rho} - (X_1M_1 + X_2M_2) \frac{X_1}{\rho^2} \frac{d\rho}{dX_2} \qquad (6)$$

c) From the given equation,

$$\frac{d\rho}{dX_2} = -0.28930 + 0.59814X_2 - 1.82628X_2^2 + 2.37752X_2^3 - 1.02905X_2^4$$

when $X_2 = 0.100$, $\frac{d\rho}{dX_2} = -0.24547$ g ml^{-1} by direct substitution.

Also, $\rho = 0.97061$ g ml^{-1}

$M_1 = 18$ g mol^{-1}, $M_2 = 32$ g mol^{-1} and

$X_1 = 1 - X_2 = 0.900$

Substitute these values into equation (6), to get

$$\bar{V}_2 = 37.56 \text{ ml mol}^{-1}$$

• PROBLEM 7-31

The partial molar volume V_2 of K_2SO_4 in water solutions at 298 K is given by

$$\bar{V}_2(\text{cm}^3) = 32.280 + 18.216m^{\frac{1}{2}} + 0.0222m$$

Obtain an equation for $\bar{V}_1$, the partial molar volume of H_2O. Take $\bar{V}_1^{\cdot} = 17.963$ cm^3·mol^{-2} for H_2O.

Solution: In a binary system, the partial molar volumes cannot vary independently of one another. If, for some reason, $\bar{V}_1$ increases, then $\bar{V}_2$ must decrease. This can be represented mathematically by

$$n_1 d\bar{V}_1 = -n_2 d\bar{V}_2 \qquad (1)$$

where n_1 = number of moles of component 1

and n_2 = number of moles of component 2.

Equation (1) is known as the Gibbs-Duhem Equation. $\bar{V}_2$ is given to be $32.280 + 18.216m^{1/2} + 0.0222m$. Therefore

$$d\bar{V}_2 = \frac{1}{2}(18.216m^{-\frac{1}{2}})dm + 0.0222dm$$

$$= (9.108m^{-\frac{1}{2}} + 0.0222)dm$$

where $m = \text{molality} = \frac{\text{g of solute}}{\text{1 kg of solvent}}$.

Replace n_2 by m and n_1 by $\frac{1000}{M_1}$ where M_1 = molecular weight of component 1 which is water. From equation (1)

$$d\bar{V}_1 = -\frac{n_2}{n_1}\,d\bar{V}_2 = -\frac{mM_1}{1000}(9.108m^{-1/2} + 0.0222)dm$$

$$= -\frac{M_1}{1000}(9.108m^{1/2} + 0.0222m)dm.$$

Integrating both sides with respect to m gives

$$\bar{V}_1 = -\frac{M_1}{1000}\int(9.108m^{1/2} + 0.0222m)dm + C \qquad (2)$$

where C is an integration constant.

$$\therefore \quad \bar{V}_1 = -\frac{M_1}{1000}(6.072m^{3/2} + 0.0111m^2) + C. \qquad (3)$$

Using the fact that $\bar{V}_1 = \bar{V}_1^\circ$ = initial partial molar volume of water (that is when m=0), equation (3) becomes

$$17.963 = 0 + C$$

$$\therefore \quad C = 17.963.$$

Since M_1 = molecular weight of H_2O = 18, equation (3) gives

$$\bar{V}_1 = -0.1094m^{3/2} - 0.0002m^2 + 17.963$$

which is the desired equation.

• PROBLEM 7-32

(a) Using the expression $V = 1002.94 + 16.40m + 2.140m^{3/2} + 0.0027m^{5/2}$ as a function of m for aqueous NaCl at 25°, find $\bar{V}_{NaCl}$ and $\bar{V}_{H_2O}$ in 1m solution.
(b) Given that the molar volumes of NaCl(s) and $H_2O(l)$ are 27.00 and 18.07 cm^3 $mole^{-1}$, respectively, find ΔV°_{298} for

(i) $\frac{1000}{18}$ $H_2O(l)$ + NaCl(s) → Solution (1m)

(ii) NaCl(s) → NaCl(1m)

(iii) $H_2O(l)$ → H_2O (1m)

Solution: By definition,

$$\bar{V}_{NaCl} = \frac{dV}{dm} = \left(\frac{\partial V}{\partial n_{NaCl}}\right)_{n_{H_2O}} \qquad \text{where}$$

n = number of moles

$\bar{V}$ = partial molar volume.

From the given V expression,

$$\bar{V}_{NaCl} = \frac{dV}{dm} = 16.40 + 3.210m^{1/2} + 0.0068m^{3/2} \qquad (1)$$

Since $\bar{V}_{NaCl}$ has been determined, $\bar{V}_{H_2O}$ can be found by the use of $V = n_1\bar{V}_1 + n_2\bar{V}_2$ where n_2 is replaced by m and n_1 by $\frac{1000}{M_1} = \frac{1000}{18} = 55.51$. Note that m = molality = $\frac{\text{moles of solute}}{\text{1 kg solvent}}$ and that M_1 = molecular weight of component 1, which is water in this case.

$$V = 1002.94 + 16.40m + 2.140m^{3/2} + 0.0027m^{\frac{1}{2}}$$

$$= 55.51\ \bar{V}_{H_2O} + m\bar{V}_{NaCl}.$$

Therefore, with the use of equation (1),

$$V = 55.51\bar{V}_{H_2O} + m(16.40+3.210m^{1/2}+0.0068m^{3/2})$$

from which $\bar{V}_{H_2O} = 18.07-1.928\times10^{-2}m^{3/2}-7.4\times10^{-5}m^{5/2}$ (2)

When m = 1, $\bar{V}_{NaCl}$ and $\bar{V}_{H_2O}$ can be obtained by direct substitution into equations (1) and (2). Thus

$$\bar{V}_{NaCl} = 19.61\ cm^3\ mol^{-1} \qquad \text{and}$$

$$\bar{V}_{H_2O} = 18.05\ cm^3\ mol^{-1}.$$

b) By definition,

(i) $\Delta V^\circ_{298} = V_{solution} - \left[n_1\bar{V}_{H_2O(l)} + n_2\bar{V}_{NaCl(s)}\right]$

But $n_1 = \frac{1000}{18}$ and $n_2 = m$

Therefore $\Delta V^\circ_{298} = V_{solution} - \left[\frac{1000}{18}\bar{V}_{H_2O(l)} + m\bar{V}_{NaCl(s)}\right]$

But $V_{solution} = 1002.94 + 16.40(1) + 2.140(1^{3/2}) + 0.0027(1^{5/2})$

Therefore, $V_{solution} = 1021.48\ cm^3$

so, $\Delta V^\circ_{298} = 1021.48 - [55.51(18.07) + 1(27.00)]$

$= -8.6\ cm^3$

(ii) Here, $\Delta V^\circ_{298} = \bar{V}_{NaCl(1m)} - \bar{V}_{NaCl(s)}$

The calculated $\bar{V}_{NaCl(1m)} = 19.61\ cm^3$

and $\bar{V}_{NaCl(s)}$ is given to be 27.00.

Note that there is a difference between NaCl(s) and NaCl(1m).

Therefore $\Delta V^\circ_{298} = 19.61 - 27.00 = -7.39\ cm^3$

(iii) $\Delta V^\circ_{298} = \bar{V}_{H_2O(1m)} - \bar{V}_{H_2O(l)} = 18.05 - 18.07$

$= -0.02\ cm^3$.

• PROBLEM 7-33

(a) When 1.158 moles of water are dissolved in 0.842 moles of ethanol the volume of the solution is 68.16 cm^3 at 25°. If $\bar{V}_{H_2O} = 16.98\ cm^3\ mole^{-1}$ in this solution find $\bar{V}_{C_2H_5OH}$. (b) Compare the partial molar volumes of the components with their molar volumes, if $H_2O(l)$ and $C_2H_5{\cdot}OH(l)$ have molecular weights of 18.02 and 46.07 g $mole^{-1}$, and densities of 0.9970 and 0.7852 g cm^{-3}, respectively, at this temperature.

Solution: a) Using the state function equation as applied to Volume,

$$V = n_1\bar{V}_1 + n_2\bar{V}_2 + n_3\bar{V}_3 + \ldots$$

where n_i = number of moles of component i

$\bar{V}_i$ = partial molar volume of component i

and V = volume of solution

Since this is a binary solution of water and ethanol,

$$V = n_{H_2O}\bar{V}_{H_2O} + n_{C_2H_5OH}\bar{V}_{C_2H_5OH}. \qquad (1)$$

Substituting the given values into equation (1), it becomes

$$68.16 = (1.158)(16.98) + (0.842)\left(\bar{V}_{C_2H_5OH}\right)$$

$$= 19.663 + 0.842\ \bar{V}_{C_2H_5OH}$$

$$\therefore \quad 48.497 = 0.842\ \bar{V}_{C_2H_5OH}$$

or $\bar{V}_{C_2H_5OH} = \frac{48.497}{0.842} = 57.60\ cm^3mol^{-1}$

b) By definition,

$$\text{molar volume} = \frac{\text{molecular weight}}{\text{density}} .$$

Therefore, molar volume of water $= \frac{18.02}{0.9970}$

$$= 18.074\ cm^3\ mol^{-1}$$

and that of ethanol $= \frac{46.07}{0.7852} = 58.673\ cm^3\ mol^{-1}$

In this case their molar volumes are greater than their partial molar volumes.

• PROBLEM 7-34

A corrupt barman attempts to prepare 100 cm^3 of some drink by mixing 30 cm^3 of ethanol with 70 cm^3 of water. Does he succeed? If not, what volumes should have been mixed in order to arrive at a mixture of the same strength but of the required volume?

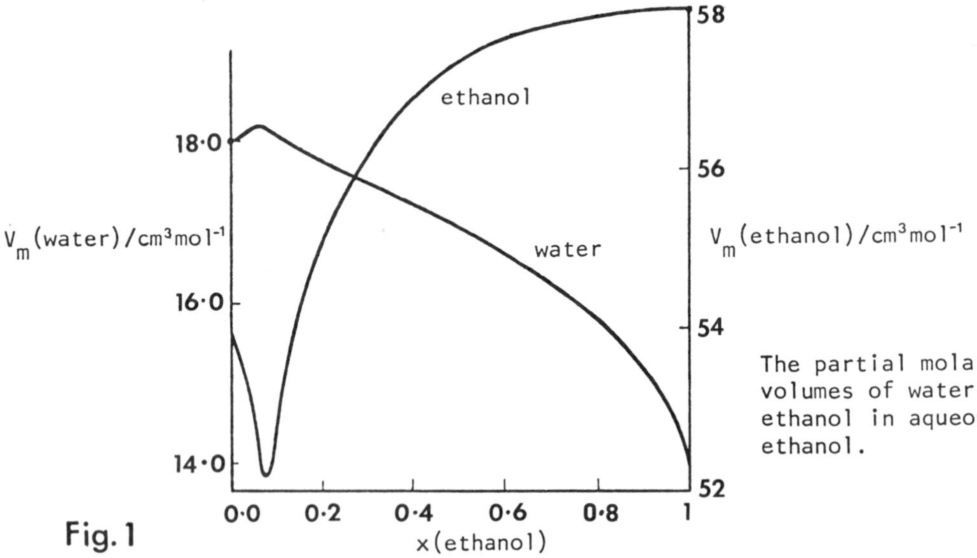

The partial molar volumes of water and ethanol in aqueous ethanol.

Fig. 1

Solution: Before this problem can be solved, it is important to know the number of moles of each liquid, their compositions in the mixture and their partial molar volumes at those compositions.

The compositions are obtained from the densities and molecular masses of the liquids while the partial molar volumes are obtained from Fig. 1 (the partial molar volumes of water and ethanol in aqueous ethanol.)

To find the number of moles of the liquids, the following relations can be used:

$$n = \text{number of moles} = \frac{\text{mass}}{\text{molecular weight}}\ .$$

But mass = Density × Volume.

$$\text{Therefore, } n = \frac{(\text{Density})(\text{Volume})}{\text{molecular weight}}\ .$$

For water,

$$n = \frac{(1\ \text{g cm}^{-3})(70\ \text{cm}^3)}{18\ \text{g mol}^{-1}} = 3.89\ \text{mol}$$

and for ethanol,

$$n = \frac{(0.785\ \text{g cm}^{-3})(30\ \text{cm}^3)}{46\ \text{g mol}^{-1}} = 0.51\ \text{mol}$$

From these figures, their compositions x (mole fractions) can be computed.

$$\text{Thus, x of water} = \frac{n_{H_2O}}{n_{H_2O} + n_{C_2H_5OH}} = \frac{3.89}{3.89 + 0.51} = 0.88$$

$$\text{and x of } C_2H_5OH = \frac{n_{C_2H_5OH}}{n_{C_2H_5OH} + n_{H_2O}} = \frac{0.51}{0.51 + 3.89} = 0.12$$

From Fig. 1 and using the aforecalculated molar compositions, the partial molar volumes can be obtained.

At the calculated composition, go up vertically until the curve is reached and get the volume by going horizontally to the left (in the case of water) and right (in the case of ethanol). In this case, these values happen to be 18.0 $cm^3\ mol^{-1}$ and 52.6 $cm^3\ mol^{-1}$ for water and ethanol respectively.

The total volume of the mixture is obtained from the expression

$$V = n_{H_2O}V_{H_2O} + n_{C_2H_5OH}V_{C_2H_5OH}$$

$$\text{Thus,} \quad V = (3.89\ \text{mol})(18\ \text{cm}^3\ \text{mol}^{-1}) + (52.6\ \text{cm}^3\text{mol}^{-1})$$

$$(0.51\ \text{mol}) = 96.8\ \text{cm}^3$$

A mixture of the same relative composition but of total volume, 100 cm^3 will have the same mole fractions of the components but a different overall amount of n.

Therefore,

$$100\ \text{cm}^3 = n[(0.88)(18.0) + (0.12)(52.6)]$$

$$\text{or} \quad n = \frac{100}{22.15} = 4.51\ \text{mol}.$$

The desired mixture should therefore contain 4.51 × 0.88 = 3.97 mol H_2O and 4.51 × 0.12 = 0.54 mol C_2H_5OH.

Their corresponding volumes are about 3.97 × 18.0 = 71.46 cm^3 for H_2O and 0.54 × 52.6 = 28.4 for C_2H_5OH.

PHASE EQUILIBRIA

• PROBLEM 7-35

The vapor-liquid equilibrium data of the system chloroform-ethanol at 45°C are listed in table 1.

x_1	y_1	$\frac{P}{(mmHg)}$	$\frac{P_1}{(mmHg)}$	$\frac{P_2}{(mmHg)}$
0.1260	0.3974	249.92	99.30	150.62
0.2569	0.6060	329.62	199.60	130.02
0.4015	0.7143	391.51	279.50	112.01
0.6283	0.7954	438.89	349.00	89.89
0.8206	0.8516	455.56	388.60	66.96
0.9557	0.9319	448.49	418.00	30.49

Table 1

Assuming ideal behavior of the vapor phase, prove the thermodynamic consistency of the experimental data.

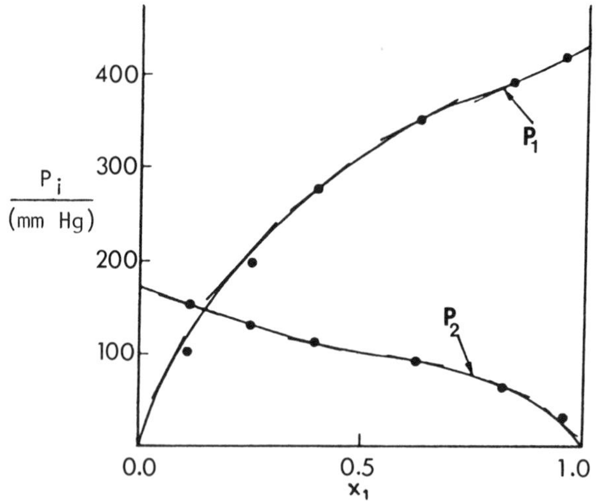

Variation of the partial pressure with composition: system, chloroform-ethanol at 45°C.

Fig. 1

Solution: The Gibbs-Duhem equation applies to this problem. When the vapor phase is assumed to be ideal (that is $f_i = P_i$), the Gibbs-Duhem equation can be written in the form

$$\Delta = \frac{x_1}{P_1}\frac{dP_1}{dx_1} - \frac{x_2}{P_2}\frac{dP_2}{dx_2}$$

where P_i = partial pressure of component i

f_i = fugacity of component i

x_i = mole fraction of component i

Δ = deviation (if any)

Note that the smaller Δ is the more consistent of the experimental data. To prove the consistency of this data, the slopes $\frac{dP_1}{dx_1}$, $\frac{dP_2}{x_2}$, P_1 and P_2, at the corresponding mole fractions must be known. The desired information can be obtained by plotting P_1 and P_2 against the mole fractions as shown below in Fig. 1. The slopes are computed for the given values of x_1. Then the Δ values can be computed. The respective values are tabulated in table 2.

$\frac{dP_1}{dx_1}$ $\frac{mmHg}{\text{mole fraction}}$	$\frac{dP_2}{dx_2}$	Δ
792	-176	-0.016
724	-140	+0.132
416	-118	-0.033
229	- 96	+0.015
176	-153	-0.038
290	-472	-0.023

Table 2

Since the Δ values are small, the data is thermodynamically consistent.

• PROBLEM 7-36

Fig. 1 shows the boiling point diagram for two miscible liquids. a) Show the composition of the first and last vapor, if 50 mole % solution is boiled in an open container. b) Find the liquid composition when half the solution is vaporized during heating in a closed system at 1 atm constant pressure. What is the temperature?

Solution: a) The composition of the liquid and vapor phases in equilibrium with each other are given by the ends of the horizontal lines called tie lines. One such line is line L of Fig. 2. The composition of the first vapor corresponding to 50 mole % solution is obtained using the top curve at about N_B = 0.1 at a temperature of about 68°C. The last vapor composition will correspond to the maximum boiling point at T_{bmax}. Thus N_B = 0.95.

b) The temperature corresponding to half vaporization in a closed system will be such that the system composition of 50 mole % bisects the tie line at point N. This

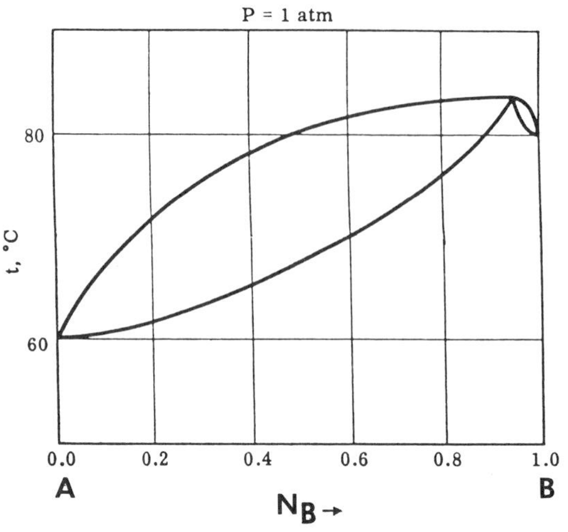

Fig. 1

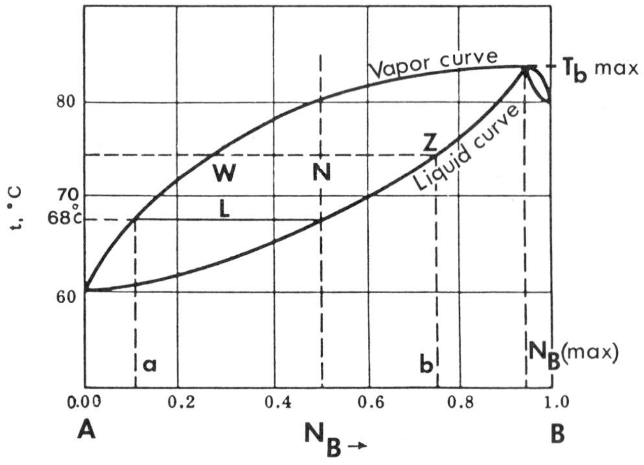

Fig. 2

means that distance WN = distance NZ. This occurs at about 75°C and the liquid composition corresponding to this point is $N_B = 0.75$.

• PROBLEM 7-37

Fig. 1 shows the boiling point plot for two liquids A and B. If a solution of mole fraction $N_B = 0.4$ is boiled openly in a beaker until $Y_B = 0.4$, show on the graph in Fig. 1 a) the temperature the solution first begins to boil; b) the composition of the first vapor coming off; c) the boiling point when the vapor reaches $Y_B = 0.4$; d) composition of final liquid.

In all cases give approximate numerical answers.

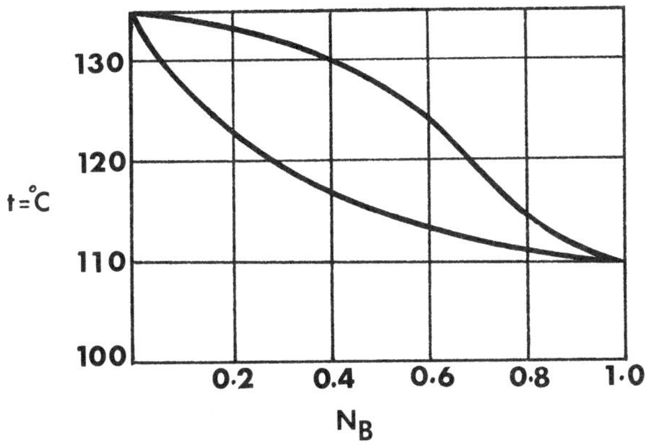

Fig. 1

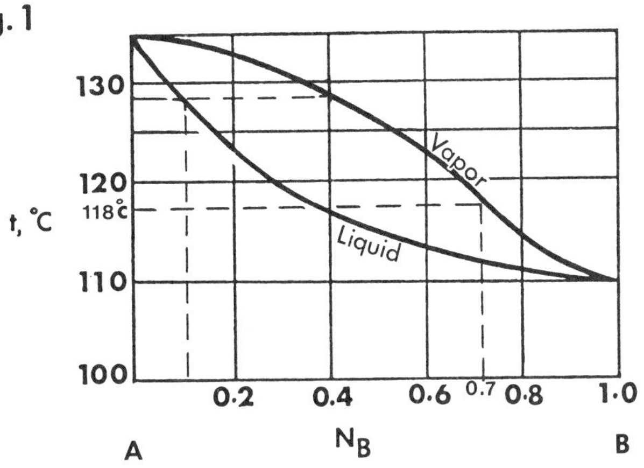

Fig. 2

Solution: a) The liquid begins to boil at a temperature given by the lower liquid curve. Thus at a composition of $N_B = 0.4$ the corresponding temperature using the lower curve is about 118°C.

b) The composition of the first vapor coming off is found using the top curve at $N_B = 0.4$. $\therefore$ $Y_B = 0.7$.

c) When the vapor reaches $Y_B = 0.4$, using the top curve at $N_B = 0.4$, the boiling point is about 126°C.

d) The composition of the final liquid is found using the lower curve at the boiling point of 126°C and it is estimated to be about $N_B = 0.12$. These are all shown in Fig. 2.

• PROBLEM 7-38

A 50 mole % solution of propyl alcohol and ethyl alcohol is distilled to the boiling point of 90°C. The vapor pressure of the condensate collected in a cooled receiver is 1066 mm Hg at that temperature. The vapor pressure of pure ethyl and propyl alcohols are 1190 and 574 mm Hg respectively, at 90°C. Calculate a) the mole fraction of ethyl alcohol in the boiling liquid; b) the mole fraction of ethyl alcohol in the distillate; c) the number of moles of ethyl alcohol that were distilled.

Assume ideal behavior of the solution and the vapors.

Solution: a) The solution will boil when the total pressure = 1 atm or 760 mm Hg. Since the behavior of both the solution and the vapors is ideal,

$$\text{Total Pressure, } P = \sum_i P_i$$

where P_i = partial pressure of component i.

$$\text{Therefore } P = P^\circ_{\substack{\text{ethyl}\\ \text{alcohol}}} X_{\substack{\text{ethyl}\\ \text{alcohol}}} + P^\circ_{\substack{\text{propyl}\\ \text{alcohol}}} X_{\substack{\text{propyl}\\ \text{alcohol}}} \quad (1)$$

where $P_{\substack{\text{ethyl}\\ \text{alcohol}}} = P^\circ_{\substack{\text{ethyl}\\ \text{alcohol}}} X_{\substack{\text{ethyl}\\ \text{alcohol}}}$

and X = mole fraction.

Note that $X_{\substack{\text{propyl}\\ \text{alcohol}}} = 1 - X_{\substack{\text{ethyl}\\ \text{alcohol}}}$.

Substituting given values into their appropriate places, equation (1) becomes

$$760 = 1190X_{\substack{\text{ethyl}\\ \text{alcohol}}} + 574(1-X_{\substack{\text{ethyl}\\ \text{alcohol}}})$$

$$760 = 1190X_E + 574 - 574X_E$$

$$\therefore \quad X_E = 0.30$$

b) Using the pressure in the distilling flask as the total pressure, equation (1) gives

$$1066 = 1190X_E + 574(1-X_E)$$

$$1066 = 1190X_E + 574 - 574X_E$$

$$X_E = 0.80$$

c) The moles of distillate in the receiver =

$$\frac{\text{moles of ethyl alcohol}}{\text{moles of propyl alcohol}}$$

Moles of ethyl alcohol by material balance on the distillation flask is given by number of moles put into the flask - number of moles taken out of the flask.

moles of ethyl alcohol = (0.5 - 0.3) = 0.2

moles of propyl alcohol = (0.8 - 0.3) = 0.5

$$\text{moles of distillate} = \frac{0.20}{0.50} = 0.40$$

The moles of ethyl alcohol in the distillate

$$= 0.40 \times 0.80 = 0.32.$$

• PROBLEM 7-39

Estimate the solubility of naphthalene in benzene at room temperature (25°C).

Solution: Since this is a matter of approximation, it is wise to assume ideal behavior. This problem wants an estimation of the number of moles of naphthalene (solute) that can form solution with some quantity of benzene (preferably 1000 g or 1 kg). So the problem is finding the molality of naphthalene (solute). This is defined as number of moles of solute per kg of solvent.

By definition,

$$\ln x_s = -\left[\frac{\Delta G_m(T)}{RT} - \frac{\Delta G_m(T^\circ)}{RT^\circ}\right] \qquad (1)$$

where x_s = mole fraction of solute

ΔG = Gibbs Free Energy. The subscript m stands for melt.

T = some temperature (which is equal to 25°C in this case)

T° = melting point temperature

R = gas constant

Since ideal behavior is assumed, the ΔS and ΔH will not change much over the temperature range. Therefore, equation (1) changes to

$$\ln x_s = -\left(\frac{\Delta H_m}{R}\right)\left(\frac{1}{T} - \frac{1}{T^\circ}\right) \qquad (2)$$

where ΔH = Enthalpy.

(Note that $\Delta G = \Delta H - T\Delta S$.)

Close to the melting point $T \sim T^\circ$; thus,

$$\ln x_s \approx \left(\frac{\Delta H_m}{RT^{\circ 2}}\right)\left(T - T^\circ\right) \qquad (3)$$

Taking the exponent of both sides of equation (3) gives

$$x_s = \exp\left[\frac{\Delta H_m}{RT^{\circ 2}}(T - T^\circ)\right]. \qquad (4)$$

In order to apply equation (4), the enthalpy of fusion of naphthalene and its melting point must be known. These can be found in the literatures. The enthalpy of fusion and melting point of naphthalene are 19.0 kJ mol^{-1} and 80.2°C respectively.

Using these values, equation (4) becomes

$$x_s = \exp\left[\frac{19.0\times10^3 J\ mol^{-1}\ (298-353.2)}{8.31\ JK^{-1}\ mol^{-1}\ (353.2K)^2}\right]$$

$$= \exp\left[\frac{19.0\times10^3(-55.2)}{8.31(353.2)^2}\right] = \exp(-1.01)$$

$$\therefore \quad x_s = 0.365$$

Recall that the mole fraction is related to the number of moles by

$$x_s = \frac{n_s}{\text{Total moles}} = \frac{n_s}{n_s + n} \tag{5}$$

where n_s = moles of solute

and n = moles of solvent

Rearranging equation (5) gives

$$n_s = \frac{x_s n}{1 - x_s} \tag{6}$$

Recall also that the basis of this calculation is 1000 g of benzene. Its molecular weight is 78 g mol^{-1}. Therefore,

$$n = \frac{\text{mass}}{\text{molecular weight}} = \frac{1000}{78} = 12.82 \text{ moles of benzene}$$

and equation (6) gives

$$n_s = \frac{(0.365)(12.82)}{(1 - 0.365)} = \frac{4.679}{0.635} = 7.37 \text{ moles of naphthalene.}$$

Therefore, the molality (concentration of solution) at 25°C is about

$$\frac{7.37 \text{ moles of solute}}{\text{kg of solvent}} .$$

SOLUBILITY

• PROBLEM 7-40

Find expressions for the change in solubility of a solid with temperature for the following cases: a) when the solubility is small; b) when the solubility is not small enough.

Solution: If a lump of solid is left in contact with a solvent it will dissolve until the solvent has become saturated. The saturated solution corresponds to the case in which the fugacity (or escaping tendency) of the pure solid is equal to the fugacity of the solute in the saturated solution. Let f'_2 represent the fugacity of the pure solid and f_2 its fugacity in a solution of mole fraction x_2.

At saturation maintaining equilibrium, the two fugacities can be equated. Thus, $f'_2 = f_2$. Taking the natural logarithm of both sides gives

$$\ell n f'_2 = \ell n f_2$$

Differentiating,

$$d\ell n f'_2 = d\ell n f_2 \qquad (1)$$

But f'_2 is a function of temperature only, while f_2 is a function of temperature and of concentration. The change in fugacity due to small change in pressure may be neglected. Thus keeping pressure constant and differentiating the left-hand side of equation (1) with respect to temperature alone gives

$$\left(\frac{\partial \ell n f'_2}{\partial T}\right)_P dT$$

Differentiating the right-hand side with respect to both temperature and concentration x_2 gives

$$\left(\frac{\partial \ell n f_2}{\partial T}\right)_{P,x_2} + \left(\frac{\partial \ell n f_2}{\partial x}\right)_{P,T} dx_2$$

Equation (1) thus becomes

$$\left(\frac{\partial \ell n f'_2}{\partial T}\right)_P dT = \left(\frac{\partial \ell n f_2}{\partial T}\right)_{P,x_2} dT + \left(\frac{\partial \ell n f_2}{\partial x_2}\right)_{P,T} dx_2 \qquad (2)$$

a) For the case when solubility is small meaning a dilute solution below solubility limit, the fugacity in the solution is equal to the mole fraction.

Thus $\quad f_2 = kx_2 \qquad (3)$

where k is an experimentally determined constant. Taking the natural logarithm of both sides of equation (3) gives,

$$\ell n f_2 = \ell n k + \ell n x_2$$

Differentiating with respect to x_2 at constant temperature and pressure gives

$$\left(\frac{\partial \ell n f_2}{\partial x_2}\right)_{P,T} = \frac{1}{x_2} \qquad (4)$$

The term $\left(\frac{\partial \ell n f_2}{\partial T}\right)_{P,x_2}$ is given by the expression

$$\left(\frac{\partial \ell n f_2}{\partial T}\right)_{P,x_2} = \frac{H_2^* - \bar{H}_2}{RT^2} \qquad (5)$$

Substituting equations (4) and (5) into equation (2) gives

$$\frac{H_2^* - H_2'}{RT^2}\, dT = \frac{H_2^* - \bar{H}_2}{RT^2}\, dT + \frac{1}{x_2}\, dx_2 .$$

Dividing all the terms by dT yields

$$\frac{H_2^* - H_2'}{RT^2} = \frac{H_2^* - \bar{H}_2}{RT^2} + \frac{1}{x_2}\frac{dx_2}{dT}$$

$$\frac{1}{x_2}\frac{dx_2}{dT} = \frac{\bar{H}_2 - H_2'}{RT^2}$$

$$\frac{d\ell n x_2}{dT} = \frac{\bar{H}_2 - H_2'}{RT^2} \qquad (6)$$

b) For the case when the solubility is not small enough equation (2) cannot be used and equation (6) does not hold. Instead, substitution of equation (5) alone into equation (2) gives

$$\left(\frac{\partial \ell n f_2}{\partial \ell n x_2}\right)_{P,T}\left(\frac{\partial \ell n x_2}{\partial T}\right) = \frac{\bar{H}_2 - H_2'}{RT^2}$$

for the case of large solubility.

• PROBLEM 7-41

The melting point of p-xylene is higher than that of m-xylene, and both form an ideal solution. Crystals of p-xylene precipitate out of the solution at a temperature lower than its melting point, and its solubility decreases with decreasing temperature. a) Assuming that the heat of fusion is constant, calculate the solubility of p-xylene at 220.3°K. b) Considering the difference in molal heat capacities between supercooled liquid and solid, ΔC_p, calculate again the solubility of p-xylene and compare the result with that obtained from part a. For p-xylene, T_f = 286.39°K, ΔH^F = 4090 cal/mol, ΔC_p = 3R = 5.96 cal/deg.mole and for m-xylene T_f = 219.5°K.

Solution: For the calculation of the solubility of solids in liquids, the relative activity of the solid must be estimated. The relative activity refers to the activity of the solid relative to that of the supercooled liquid at the temperature of interest.

From Clausius-Clapeyron equation the enthalpy of vaporization is given by

$$\frac{\Delta H_2^V}{RT^2} = \left(\frac{d\ell nP_2}{dT}\right)^V_{sat} \tag{1}$$

and the enthalpy of saturation by

$$\frac{\Delta H_2^S}{RT^2} = \left(\frac{d\ell nP_2}{dT}\right)^S_{sat} \tag{2}$$

The expression for the relative activity is given as

$$RT\ell n\left(\frac{f_2}{f_2^\circ}\right) = RT\ell na_2 \tag{3}$$

where f_2° is the fugacity of component 2 in the pure liquid state and the fugacity in the solution is represented by f_2.

When the vapor pressure is small, the ratio of the fugacities in equation (3) is equal to the ratio of the vapor pressures. Thus equation (3) becomes

$$RT\ell n\left(\frac{P_2}{P_2^\circ}\right) = RT\ell na_2 \tag{4}$$

Equations (2) and (3) thus become

$$\frac{d\ell na_2^S}{dT} = \frac{d\ell n\ P_2^S/P_2^\circ}{dT} = \frac{\Delta H_2^S - \Delta H_2^V}{RT^2}$$

$$= \frac{\Delta H_2^F}{RT^2} \tag{5}$$

where ΔH_2^S is the heat of sublimation, ΔH_2^V is the heat of vaporization, and ΔH_2^F the heat of fusion.

Integrating equation (5) over the range from the given arbitrary temperature T to the melting point T_f, with the assumption that the heat of fusion is constant, gives

$$\frac{d\ell na_2^S}{dT} = \int_{T_f}^{T} \frac{\Delta H_2^F}{RT^2}$$

$$d\ell na_2^S = \frac{\Delta H_2^F}{R}\int_{T_f}^{T} T^{-2}\,dT$$

$$\ell n a_2^S = -\frac{\Delta H_2^F}{R}\frac{1}{T}\Bigg|_{T_f}^{T} = \frac{-\Delta H_2^F}{R}\left(\frac{1}{T} - \frac{1}{T_f}\right)$$

$$\therefore \quad \ell n a_2^S = -\frac{\Delta H_2^F}{R}\left(\frac{T_f - T}{TT_f}\right) \tag{6}$$

a) From equation (6)

$$\ell n a_2^S = \ell n x_2 = \frac{\Delta H_2^F}{R}\left(\frac{T - T_f}{TT_f}\right)$$

$$= \frac{4090 \text{ cal/mol}}{1.987 \text{ cal/mol°K}}\left(\frac{220.3°K - 286.39°K}{(220.3°K)(286.39°K)}\right)$$

Therefore, $\ell n x_2 = -2.156$

$x_2 = 0.1158$

b) When the difference between the molal heat capacity of the liquid and the solid is known, the heat of fusion ΔH_2^F is given by

$$\Delta H_2^F(T) = \Delta H_2^F(T_f) - \Delta C_p(T_f - T) \tag{7}$$

where $\Delta C_p = C_p^\ell - C_p^S$

Substituting equation (7) into equation (5) and integrating gives:

$$\frac{d\ell n a_2^S}{dT} = \frac{\Delta H_2^F - \Delta C_p(T_f - T)}{RT^2}$$

$$= \frac{\Delta H_2^F}{RT^2} - \frac{\Delta C_p T_f}{RT^2} - \frac{\Delta C_p T}{RT^2}$$

$$d\ell n a_2^S = \frac{\Delta H_2^F}{RT^2}dT - \frac{\Delta C_p T_f}{RT^2}dT - \frac{\Delta C_p T}{RT^2}dT$$

$$= \frac{\Delta H_2^F}{R}\int_{T_f}^{T} T^{-2}dT - \frac{\Delta C_p}{R}\int_{T_f}^{T} T^{-2}dT - \frac{\Delta C_p}{R}\int_{T_f}^{T}\frac{1}{T}dT$$

$$\ell n a_2^S = -\frac{\Delta H_2^F}{R}\left[\frac{1}{T}\Bigg|_{T_f}^{T}\right] + \frac{\Delta C_p}{R}\left[\frac{1}{T}\Bigg|_{T_f}^{T}\right] - \frac{\Delta C_p}{R}\left[\ell n T\Bigg|_{T_f}^{T}\right]$$

$$= \frac{-\Delta H_2^F}{R}\left(\frac{1}{T}-\frac{1}{T_f}\right) + \frac{\Delta C_p}{R}\left(\frac{1}{T}-\frac{1}{T_f}\right) - \frac{\Delta C_p}{R}\left(\ell nT - \ell nT_f\right)$$

$$\therefore \quad \ell na_2^S = - \frac{\Delta H_2^F}{R}\left(\frac{T_f - T}{TT_f}\right) + \frac{\Delta C_p}{R}\left(\frac{T_f - T}{T}\right) - \frac{\Delta C_p}{R} \ell n \frac{T_f}{T} \tag{8}$$

Rearranging gives

$$\ell na_2^S = \ell nx_2 = \frac{(\Delta H_2^F - T_f \Delta C_p)(T - T_f)}{RTT_f} - \frac{\Delta C_p}{R} \ell n \frac{T_f}{T}$$

$$= \frac{[4090-(286.39)(5.96)][220.3-286.39]}{(1.987)(220.3)(286.39)} - 3\ell n \left(\frac{286.39}{220.3}\right)$$

$$= \frac{(4090-1706.88)(-66.09)}{125363.24} - 0.7871$$

$$\ell nx_2 = -2.043$$

$$\therefore \quad x_2 = 0.1296$$

It should be noted that ΔC_p varies with temperature and that considerably below the melting point, the value of a_2^S is subject to some uncertainty.

SOLUTION CONCENTRATIONS

• PROBLEM 7-42

13.00g NaOH (m.w. = 40.01 g mol^{-1}) and 87.00g H_2O are mixed to form a solution of density 1.1421×10^3 kg m^{-3}. Calculate a) wt % of NaOH, b) wt % of H_2O, c) the mass of the solvent, d) the mole fraction of NaOH, e) the mole fraction of H_2O, f) (g solute)$(dm^3 soln)^{-1}$, g) the molarity of the solution.

Solution: NaOH is the solute and H_2O is the solvent. By definition wt % of a solute in solution is given by

$$\frac{\text{grams solute}}{\text{grams solute + grams solvent}} \times 100\%$$

a) $$\text{Wt \% of NaOH} = \frac{(\text{g NaOH})}{(\text{g NaOH}) + (\text{g } H_2O)} \times 100\%$$

$$= \frac{13.00\text{g}}{(13.00\text{g})+(87.00\text{g})} \times 100\%$$

$$= 13.00\%$$

b) For wt % water, there is 100g of solution. So

wt % water = 100.00 - 13.00 = 87.00%

c) The number of moles of solute is given by

$$n_{NaOH} = \frac{13.00\not{g}}{(40.01\not{g}\ mol^{-1})} = 0.325 \text{ mole}$$

The number of moles of solvent is given by

$$n_{H_2O} = \frac{87.00\not{g}}{(18.015\not{g}\ mol^{-1})} = 4.83 \text{ mol}$$

Molality of the solution is defined as

$$\frac{\text{moles of solute}}{\text{kilograms of solvent}}$$

$$\text{Molality} = \frac{0.325 \text{ mol}}{(87.00\not{g}\ H_2O)\left(\frac{1kg\ H_2O}{1000\not{g}}\right)} = 3.73 \text{ m}$$

Since molality depends on moles of solute rather than grams, 13.00g NaOH is converted to moles. The molal concentration also gives an equivalence that will be useful in finding the mass of the solvent. The mass of the solvent is

$$13.00g\ NaOH \times \frac{1 \text{ mole NaOH}}{40.01g\ NaOH} \times \frac{1\ kg\ H_2O}{3.73 \text{ moles NaOH}}$$

$$= 8.700 \times 10^{-2} kg\ H_2O$$

d) Mole fraction, X is

$$\frac{\text{moles solute}}{\text{moles solute + moles solvent}} \text{ by definition.}$$

$$\text{Therefore,} \quad X_{NaOH} = \frac{0.325}{0.325 + 4.83} = 0.0631$$

The mole fractions of the solute and the solvent must sum up to 1. Thus the mole fraction

e) $X_{H_2O} = 1.0000 - 0.0631 = 0.9369$

or it can be obtained by using the definition of mole fraction. Therefore

$$X_{H_2O} = \frac{4.83}{4.83 + 0.325} = \frac{4.83}{5.155} = 0.9369$$

f) The volume of solution, V, using 100.00g basis is calculated using the fact that

Volume = mass ÷ density

$$\therefore \quad V = \frac{(100.00g)\ \frac{10^{-3}kg}{1g}}{1.1421\times10^{3}kg\ m^{-3}} = 87.56 \times 10^{-6}m^3$$

$$= 87.56 \times 10^{-3} dm^3 \text{ or } 87.56 \times 10^{-3} \text{ liters}$$

$$\therefore \quad (\text{g solute})(dm^3 \text{soln})^{-1} = (13.00\text{g NaOH})(87.56 \times 10^{-3} dm^3)^{-1}$$

$$= 148.5\text{g NaOH}(dm^3\text{soln})^{-1}$$

g) Molarity by definition is

$$C = \frac{\text{moles solute}}{\text{liters solution}} = \frac{0.325 \text{ mol NaOH}}{87.56 \times 10^{-3} \ dm^3} = 3.71M$$

• PROBLEM 7-43

How is 10 dm^3 (10 liters) of 3M acetic acid prepared from 17.4N commercial acetic acid?

Solution: In a normal acid-base reaction acetic acid dissociates according to the equation below:

$$HC_2H_3O_2 \rightarrow H^+ + C_2H_3O_2^-$$

There is only one replaceable hydrogen atom. Therefore the number of moles per liter of solution, H^+, is the same as the number of equivalents per liter of solution, H^+. This means that the molarity and normality of acetic acid are the same. Thus acetic acid is said to be a monoprotic acid.

Thus 17.4N = 17.4M

The volume of acetic acid that will be present in the 10 dm^3 of acid is given by

$$V = 10 \ dm^3 \left(\frac{3M}{17.4M}\right) = 1.72 \ dm^3$$

This volume of 17.4N acetic acid is diluted with enough water to make 10 dm^3 of solution.

• PROBLEM 7-44

How is 1 dm^3 of a 2.50 wt % Na_2CO_3 solution prepared from $Na_2CO_3 \cdot 10H_2O$ and water if the solution has a density of $1.0178 \times 10^3 kg \ m^{-3}$. The molecular weight of $Na_2CO_3 \cdot 10H_2O$ is 286.16g mol^{-1} and that of Na_2CO_3 is 106.00g mol^{-1}.

Solution: Essentially, this question is asking how many grams of Na_2CO_3 are in 1 dm^3 of 2.50 wt % Na_2CO_3.

First, with the use of appropriate conversion factors, the number of grams of solution in 1 dm^3 is found. Using the fact that g = (volume)(density)

$$\left(1\ dm^3\right)\left(\frac{10^{-3}m^3}{dm^3}\right)\left(1.0178\times10^3\frac{kg}{m^3}\right) = 1017.8\ g\ soln$$

Finding the weight of Na_2CO_3 dissolved in the 1017.8 g soln,

$$\left(1017.8g\right)\left(\frac{2.50}{100}\ Na_2CO_3\right) = 25.4g\ Na_2CO_3$$

and converting to moles, it becomes

$$\left(25.4g\ Na_2CO_3\right)\left(\frac{1\ mole\ Na_2CO_3}{106.00g\ Na_2CO_3}\right) = 0.240\ mol\ Na_2CO_3$$

Thus this is the amount of Na_2CO_3 present in 1 dm^3 of 2.50 wt % Na_2CO_3. To obtain this amount from $Na_2CO_3\cdot 10H_2O$, the mass of $Na_2CO_3\cdot 10H_2O$ needed is given by its molecular weight multiplied by the appropriate correction factor.

$$\left(286.16\ \frac{g\ Na_2CO_3\cdot 10H_2O}{mole\ Na_2CO_3\cdot 10H_2O}\right)\left(\frac{1\ mole\ Na_2CO_3\cdot 10H_2O}{mole\ Na_2CO_3}\right)$$

$$\times\ (.240\ mole\ Na_2CO_3) = 68.7g\ Na_2CO_3\cdot 10H_2O$$

Therefore, to prepare the solution, 68.7g of $Na_2CO_3\cdot 10H_2O$ is mixed with water in a volumetric flask, adding enough water to make up to 1 dm of solution (dilute to "the mark" as it is sometimes called).

CHAPTER 8

PHYSICAL EQUILIBRIUM

CLAUSIUS-CLAPEYRON EQUATION

• PROBLEM 8-1

The melting point of monoclinic sulfur at a pressure of 1 atm is 119.3°C. The change in volume during fusion is 41 cm^3kg^{-1} and ΔH_{fus} is 422 cal mol^{-1}. Find the melting point of sulfur when the pressure is raised to 1000 atm.

Solution: In a condensed system of one-component phase equilibrium, the Clapeyron equation is given by

$$\frac{dP}{dT} = \frac{\Delta H}{T\Delta V} \tag{1}$$

where P = Pressure
T = Temperature
H = enthalpy (of fusion in this case)

Rearranging equation (1), it becomes

$$dP = \frac{\Delta H}{\Delta V}\frac{dT}{T} \tag{2}$$

Assuming that $\frac{\Delta H}{\Delta V}$ is independent of both temperature and pressure, equation (2) can be integrated as follows

$$\int_{P_1}^{P_2} dP = \frac{\Delta H}{\Delta V}\int_{T_1}^{T_2} \frac{dT}{T}$$

$$P\Big|_{P_1}^{P_2} = \frac{\Delta H}{\Delta V}\, \ell n\, T\Big|_{T_1}^{T_2}$$

$$P_2 - P_1 = \frac{\Delta H}{\Delta V}\left[\ln T_2 - \ln T_1\right]$$

or
$$P_2 - P_1 = \frac{\Delta H}{\Delta V} \ln\left(T_2/T_1\right). \qquad (3)$$

Substituting all the known values into equation (3), T_2 can be computed. This is the temperature at which $P = P_2 = 1000$ atm. Thus,

$$1000 - 1 = \frac{422}{41} \ln\left(T_2/392\right). \qquad (4)$$

In order for the units to be consistent, equation (4) is rewritten in the form

$$(1000\text{-}1)\text{atm} = \frac{422\frac{\text{cal}}{\text{mole}} \times \frac{82.056\ \text{cm}^3\ \text{atm}/°\text{K mole}}{1.987\ \text{cal}/°\text{K mole}}}{41\frac{\text{cm}^3}{\text{kg}} \times \frac{1\ \text{kg}}{1000\text{g}} \times 32\frac{\text{g}}{\text{mole}}} \times \ln\frac{T_2}{392}$$

or after cancelling the appropriate units

$$1000 - 1 = \frac{422 \times 41.29 \times 1000}{32 \times 41} \ln\frac{T_2}{392}$$

Note that 41.29 is the conversion factor from calories to cubic centimeter determined from the ratio of the gas constants.

$$\therefore \quad \ln T_2 - \ln 392 = \frac{999 \times 32 \times 41}{1000 \times 41.29 \times 422} = 0.075$$

or
$$\ln T_2 = 0.075 + \ln 392$$
$$= 0.075 + 5.971$$
$$= 6.046$$

$$\therefore \quad T_2 = e^{6.046} = 423\ °\text{K}$$

or
$$423 - 273 = 150°\text{C}$$

• PROBLEM 8-2

The vapor pressure of lithium is given in the form of the following equation:

$$\ln p° = \frac{-3.29 \times 10^4\ °\text{R}}{T} + 14.05$$

where p is in psi and T is °R. The equation is applicable over a range of temperatures from 2500 to 2900°F. If the density of liquid and vapor are 25.6 lb_m/ft^3 and 0.092 lb_m/ft^3, respectively, at 2700°F, calculate the latent heat of vaporization at that temperature in Btu/lb_m.

Solution: The Clapeyron equation is given by

$$\frac{dP°}{dT} = \frac{\Delta H_{\ell v}}{T\Delta V} \qquad (1)$$

$\Delta H_{\ell v}$ = latent heat of vaporization

T = Temperature

ΔV = change in volume

P° = Vapor pressure

From the data, $\ell n\ P° = \frac{-3.29 \times 10^4}{T} + 14.05$, therefore,

$$P° = \exp\left[\frac{-3.29 \times 10^4 °R}{T} + 14.05\right] \qquad (2)$$

by taking the exponents of both sides. Now differentiating with respect to T,

$$\frac{dP°}{dT} = \frac{3.29 \times 10^4 °R}{T^2}\exp\left(\frac{-3.29 \times 10^4 °R}{T} + 14.05\right)$$

$$\text{or} \quad \frac{dP°}{dT} = \frac{P°}{T^2}(3.29 \times 10^4 °R) = \frac{\Delta H_{\ell v}}{T\Delta V}$$

$$\text{Therefore } \Delta H_{\ell v} = T\Delta V \frac{P°}{T^2}(3.29 \times 10^4 °R)$$

$$= \frac{P°}{T}\Delta V(3.29 \times 10^4 °R)$$

The Rankine scale is also known as the absolute Fahrenheit scale. The general equation to change °C to the absolute Kelvin scale is given by $°K = °C + k_1$. In this case, $k_1 = 273.15$. The general equation to change the Rankine scale to the aboslute Fahrenheit scale is given by $°R = °F + k_2$. It is now necessary to solve for k_2. This is done as follows: $°F = \frac{9}{5}°C + 32$ and $°C = °K - 273.15$. So $°F = \frac{9}{5}[°K - 273.15] + 32$. Now $°R = °F + k_2 = \frac{9}{5}[°K - 273.15] + 32 + k_2$. At $°K = 0$, $°R = 0$ and therefore $0 = \frac{9}{5}[0 - 273.15] + 32 + k_2$, $k_2 = -32 + \frac{9}{5}(273.15) = 459.7 = 460$. The conversion from Fahrenheit to Rankine scales is then given by $°R = °F + 460$. So 2700°F = 3160°R.

Solving for P° from equation (2) gives

$$P° = \exp\left[\frac{-3.29 \times 10^4 °R}{3160°R} + 14.05\right]$$

$$= \exp[-10.411 + 14.05]$$

$$= \exp[3.638]$$

$$\therefore \quad P° = e^{3.638} = 38 \text{ psi.}$$

Thus,

$$\Delta H_{\ell v} = \frac{(38 \text{ psi})\Delta V}{3160 \ °R}(3.29 \times 10^4) \qquad (3)$$

If a basis of 1 lb_m is chosen for the calculation; equation (3)

$$\text{becomes} \quad \Delta H_{\ell v} = \frac{38\frac{lb}{in^2}\left(\frac{1\ lb_m}{0.092\frac{lb_m}{ft^3}} - \frac{1\ lb_m}{25.6\frac{lb_m}{ft^3}}\right)\left(3.29 \times 10^4\right) °R}{3.160°R}$$

Use appropriate conversion factors.

(The student should be aware that there are two systems for which the pound (lb) has two different meanings. One is the metric system (hence the subscript m). This system is based on the fact that weights are derived from masses, i.e. weight = mass × acceleration due to gravity. The other system is the U.S. Customary system (avoirdupois). The pound in this system, lb_{avp}, is based on 16 ounces. Its equivalent in the metric system is 453.59 grams.

Note also that B.T.U.'s are units of energy. These units are equivalent to ones of force (weight) times a distance. Hence the lb in ftlb is assumed to be a metric pound even though there is no subscript). Hence,

$$\Delta H_{\ell v} = \frac{38\frac{lb}{in^2}(144\ in^2/ft^2)\left|\frac{1\ lb_m}{.092\frac{lb_m}{ft^3}} - \frac{1\ lb_m}{25.6\frac{lb_m}{ft^3}}\right|(3.29 \times 10^4)°R}{778\frac{lbft}{B.T.U.} \times 3160°R}$$

and after cancelling the appropriate units,

$$\Delta H_{\ell v} = \frac{(38)(144)\left[\frac{1}{0.092} - \frac{1}{25.6}\right]}{(778)(3160)}(3.29 \times 10^4)$$

$$= 7931 \text{ B.T.U.}$$

Remember 1 lb_m was assumed for the purpose of the calculation, so the answer is really per lb_m.

$$= 7931 \text{ Btu}/lb_m$$

This problem could also be solved by assuming that the vapor specific volume is much greater than that of the liquid and that the vapor behaves ideally. Then the Clapeyron equation will be in the form

$$\frac{d\,\ell n\,P^\circ}{dT} = \frac{\Delta H_{\ell v}}{RT^2} \tag{4}$$

From the expression given in the problem

$$\frac{d\,\ell n\,P^\circ}{dT} = \frac{3.29 \times 10^4}{T^2} \tag{5}$$

Equating (4) and (5)

$$\frac{\Delta H_{\ell v}}{RT^2} = \frac{3.29 \times 10^4}{T^2}$$

Therefore, $\Delta H_{\ell v} = \frac{RT^2}{T^2} = R \times 3.29(10^4)\,^\circ R$

$$= 1.987 \frac{BTU}{lb_{mole}\,^\circ R} \times 3.29\left(10^4\right)\,^\circ R$$

$$= 6.54(10^4)\,BTU/lb_{mole}.$$

Since the atomic weight = 6.94 lb/lb_{mole},

$$H_{\ell v} = \frac{6.54(10^4)\,BTU/lb_{mole}}{6.94\ lb/lb_{mole}} \simeq 9423\ BTU/lb$$

Note that the latter approach introduces a greater error. The accepted literature value at T = 3160°R is 8135 BTU/lb_m, which is about the same as the value from the former approach.

• PROBLEM 8-3

The vapor pressure of ethylene is given as a function of temperature by the equation

$$\log P = -\frac{834.13}{T} + 1.75 \log T - 8.375 \times 10^{-3} T + 5.32340$$

Calculate the enthalpy of vaporization of ethylene at its normal boiling point (-103.9°C).

Solution: From the expression for log P given in the problem,

$$\frac{d\,\ell n\ P}{dT} = \frac{2.303 \times 834.13}{T^2} + \frac{1.75}{T} - 8.375 \times 10^{-3} \times 2.303 \qquad (1)$$

Equation (1) is obtained by taking the derivative of log P with respect to T.

The Claussius-Clapeyron equation is given by

$$\frac{d\,\ell n\ P}{dT} = \frac{\Delta H_{vap}}{RT^2} \qquad (2)$$

where ΔH_{vap} = enthalpy of vaporization
R = gas constant
T = temperature

Substitute equation (1) into equation (2) to get

$$\frac{\Delta H_{vap}}{RT^2} = \frac{2.303 \times 834.13}{T^2} + \frac{1.75}{T} - 8.375 \times 10^{-3} \times 2.303$$

Solving for ΔH_{vap} gives,

$$\Delta H_{vap} = R\left[2.303 \times 834.13 + 1.75T - 8.375 \times 10^{-3} \times 2.303T^2\right].$$

Here $R = 8.314\ J\ mol^{-1}\ K^{-1}$. Using the temperature of $-103.9°C = 169.3°K$,

$$\Delta H_{vap} = 8.314[2.303 \times 834.13 + (1.75)(169.3) - 8.375 \times 10^{-3} \times 2.303 \times (169.3)^2]$$

$$= 8.314[1921 + 296.275 - 552.83]$$

$$= 8.314[2217.275 - 552.83]$$

$$= 8.314[1666.4]$$

$$= 13838\ J\ mol^{-1}$$

$$\therefore\ \Delta H_{vap} = 13.838\ kJ\ mol^{-1}$$

• PROBLEM 8-4

An equation for the temperature variation of the latent heat λ of a phase change along the equilibrium PT curve was derived by M. Planck as

$$\frac{d\lambda}{dT} = \Delta C_P + \frac{\lambda}{T} - \lambda\left(\frac{\partial\ \ln\ \Delta V}{\partial T}\right)_P$$

Derive the Planck equation, starting from

$$d\lambda = \left(\frac{\partial\lambda}{\partial T}\right)_P dT + \left(\frac{\partial\lambda}{\partial P}\right)_T dP$$

Solution: Starting from

$$d\lambda = \left(\frac{\partial\lambda}{\partial T}\right)_P dT + \left(\frac{\partial\lambda}{\partial P}\right)_T dP \qquad (1)$$

$\frac{d\lambda}{dT}$ can be obtained by dividing both sides of equation (1) by dT. That is

$$\frac{d\lambda}{dT} = \left(\frac{\partial\lambda}{\partial T}\right)_P \frac{dT}{dT} + \left(\frac{\partial\lambda}{\partial P}\right)_T \frac{dP}{dT} \qquad (2)$$

$$= \left(\frac{\partial\lambda}{\partial T}\right)_P + \left(\frac{\partial\lambda}{\partial P}\right)_T \frac{dP}{dT} \qquad (2a)$$

where T and P are temperature and pressure respectively. Using the Clapeyron equation,

$$\frac{dP}{dT} = \frac{\Delta H}{T\Delta V}$$

where ΔH = latent heat
ΔV = change in volume

But in this problem $\Delta H = \lambda$. Therefore,

$$\frac{dP}{dT} = \frac{\lambda}{T\Delta V}$$

Substituting this into equation (2a),

$$\frac{d\lambda}{dT} = \left(\frac{\partial\lambda}{\partial T}\right)_P + \left(\frac{\partial\lambda}{\partial P}\right)_T \frac{\lambda}{T\Delta V} \qquad (3)$$

[Note that the Clapeyron equation was chosen because of the variables involved in the problem. In the Clapeyron equation, there are: λ, ΔV, T and these are also in Planck's equation.] At constant pressure, dH is defined to be $\Delta C_P dT$. Therefore

$$d\lambda = \Delta C_P dT$$

or

$$\left(\frac{\partial\lambda}{\partial T}\right)_P = \Delta C_P$$

Substituting this into (3),

$$\frac{d\lambda}{dT} = \Delta C_P + \left(\frac{\partial\lambda}{\partial P}\right)_T \frac{\lambda}{T\Delta V} \qquad (3a)$$

Now using the relation

$$d(\Delta H) = Td(\Delta S) + \Delta V dP,$$

$$\left(\frac{\partial \lambda}{\partial P}\right)_T = \left(\frac{\partial \Delta H}{\partial P}\right)_T = T\left(\frac{\partial \Delta S}{\partial P}\right)_T + \Delta V$$

Putting this into equation (3a),

$$\frac{d\lambda}{dT} = \Delta C_P + \left(\frac{\partial \Delta S}{\partial P}\right)_T \frac{\lambda}{\Delta V} + \frac{\lambda}{T}$$

But, the Maxwell relation states that

$$\left(\frac{\partial \Delta S}{\partial P}\right)_T = -\left(\frac{\partial \Delta V}{\partial T}\right)_P .$$

Therefore $\dfrac{d\lambda}{dT} = \Delta C_P + \dfrac{\lambda}{T} - \left(\dfrac{\partial \Delta V}{\partial T}\right)_P \left(\dfrac{\lambda}{\Delta V}\right)$

or $\dfrac{d\lambda}{dT} = \Delta C_P + \dfrac{\lambda}{T} - \lambda\left(\dfrac{\partial \ln \Delta V}{\partial T}\right)_P$

COLLIGATIVE PROPERTIES

• PROBLEM 8-5

Calculate the vapor pressure of a solution of 20.0 grams of sucrose, $C_{12}H_{22}O_{11}$, in 40.0 grams of water at 34°C. The vapor pressure of water is 40.00 mm at 34°C.

Solution: Raoult's law states that at a given temperature, the partial pressure P_i of a component in solution is proportional to the mole fraction X_i as follows:

$$P_i = X_i P_i^o \qquad (1)$$

where P_i^o is the vapor pressure of pure component i.

Since the equation is not directly related to the weights of the substances, it is necessary to convert them (the weights) to moles by the relation,

$$n = \frac{\text{weight}}{\text{molecular weight}} \qquad (2)$$

where n = number of moles. The molecular weights of $C_{12}H_{22}O_{11}$ and H_2O are 342 g $C_{12}H_{22}O_{11}$/mole and 18 g H_2O/mole respectively. Therefore, their respective moles are

$$(20 \text{ g } C_{12}H_{22}O_{11}) \left(\frac{1 \text{ mole } C_{12}H_{22}O_{11}}{342 \text{ g } C_{12}H_{22}O_{11}}\right)$$

$$= 0.0584 \text{ mole } C_{12}H_{22}O_{11}$$

and $$(40 \text{ g } H_2O) \left(\frac{1 \text{ mole } H_2O}{18.0 \text{ g } H_2O}\right)$$

$$= 2.22 \text{ moles } H_2O.$$

Total moles in the solution = (0.0584 + 2.22)moles

= 2.28 moles

The mole fraction of water in the solution is

$$X_{H_2O} = \frac{n_{H_2O}}{n_{total}}$$

where X = mole fraction,

$$X_{H_2O} = \left(\frac{2.22 \text{ moles}}{2.28 \text{ moles}}\right)$$

$$X_{H_2O} = 0.974$$

Using Raoult's law to calculate the vapor pressure of the solution, equation (1) becomes

$$P_{sol} = X_{H_2O} P^o_{H_2O}$$

$$= (0.974)(40.00 \text{ mm})$$

$$P_{solution} = 39.0 \text{ mm}$$

• PROBLEM 8-6

NH_3 dissolves in water at 20°C to give a solution containing 0.040 mole fraction NH_3. The total vapor pressure of the solution is 50.00 mm Hg and the vapor pressure for water is 17.00 mm Hg at 20°C. Calculate a) the partial pressures of NH_3 and water using Henry's and Raoult's laws b) the total vapor pressure for a solution containing 0.05 mole fraction NH_3.

Solution: Raoult's law states that the partial pressure of a component in solution is equal to the vapor pressure of the pure component times the mole fracion of that component,

$$P_i = P_i^o X_i ,$$

where subscript i represents the ith component. For water

$$P_{H_2O} = P_{H_2O}^o X_{H_2O}$$

$$= (17.00 \text{ mm Hg})(1 - 0.04)$$

$$P_{H_2O} = 16.3 \text{ mm Hg}$$

Since this is a binary solution and the total vapor pressure of the solution is 50 mm Hg,

$$P_{NH_3} = (50 - 16.3) \text{mm Hg}$$

$$P_{NH_3} = 33.7 \text{ mm Hg}$$

Using Henry's law, the partial pressure of a component in solution is directly proportional to the mole fraction of that component.

$$P_i = K_i X_i$$

where K is Henry's constant.

$$K_i = \frac{P_i}{X_i}$$

$$\therefore K_{NH_3} = \frac{P_{NH_3}}{X_{NH_3}}$$

$$= \frac{33.7}{.04}$$

$$K_{NH_3} = 842.5$$

Now considering the 5 mole % solution: Using Raoult's law again,

$$P_{H_2O} = P_{H_2O}^o X_{H_2O}$$

$$= (17 \text{ mm Hg})(1 - 0.05)$$

$$P_{H_2O} = 16.2 \text{ mm Hg}$$

To calculate P_{NH_3} using this 5 mole % solution, Henry's law is used since the constant $K_{NH_3} = 842.5$ is known.

$$\therefore \quad P_{NH_3} = K_{NH_3} X_{NH_3}$$

$$= (842.5)(.05)$$

$$P_{NH_3} = 42.1 \text{ mm Hg}$$

The total vapor pressure for this 5 mole % solution is

$$P_{H_2O} + P_{NH_3} = (16.2 + 42.1) \text{mm Hg}$$

$$= 58.3 \text{ mm Hg}$$

• PROBLEM 8-7

At 25°C Henry's law constant for the solubility of oxygen gas in water is $K_2 = 3.30 \times 10^7$ torr. Calculate the solubility of oxygen under room temperature. Consider air to be 20% O_2 at room temperature.

Solution: Gases dissolve in liquids to form true solutions and according to Henry's law, the solubility of the gas in the liquid is directly proportional to the partial pressure of the gas above the liquid

$$\therefore \quad P_2 = X_2 K_2 \qquad (1)$$

where K_2 is Henry's constant.

Air contains 20% O_2, thus the mole fraction of O_2 in the air = 0.20. The partial pressure, P_2 can now be computed.

$$P_2 = (0.20)(760 \text{ torr})$$

$$= 152 \text{ torr}$$

Using equation (1),

$$X_2 = \frac{P_2}{K_2}$$

$$= \frac{152 \text{ torr}}{3.30 \times 10^7 \text{ torr}}$$

$$X_2 = 4.6 \times 10^{-6}$$

The value of X_2 indicates that this is a very dilute solution and thus the number of moles of n_2 in the solution is negligible. So, it is assumed that the total number of moles in the solution is n_1.

X_2 can also be written as

$$X_2 = \frac{n_2}{n_1 + n_2} \qquad (2)$$

where n_2 is the number of moles of O_2 in the water and n_1 is the number of moles of water. Since X_2 is dilute

$$n_1 + n_2 \cong n_1$$

∴ Equation (2) becomes

$$X_2 = \frac{n_2}{n_1} \qquad (3)$$

Using a basis of 100 g H_2O

$$n_1 \text{ for 100 g of water} = 5.55 \text{ mole}$$

From equation (3)

$$n_2 = X_2 n_1$$

$$= (4.6 \times 10^{-6})(5.55 \text{ mol})$$

$$n_2 = 2.6 \times 10^{-5} \text{ mol}$$

$$n_2 = \left(2.6 \times 10^{-5} \text{ mol } O_2\right)\left(\frac{32 \text{ g } O_2}{1 \text{ mol } O_2}\right)$$

$$n_2 = 8.3 \times 10^{-4} \text{ g } O_2 \text{ in 100 g } H_2O$$

or $$n_2 = 8.34 \times 10^{-6} \text{ g } O_2 \text{ in 1 g } H_2O$$

Figure 1 shows pressure versus mole fraction plot. Use the plot to calculate a) Henry's law constant for component A in the range where Henry's law, $P_A = K_A X_A$ is valid. b) the activity coefficient, f_A for $X_A = 0.6$ assuming that the pure liquid is the standard state of A. c) the activity coefficient, Y_A for $X_A = 0.6$ assuming the standard state to be hypothetical mole fraction unity.

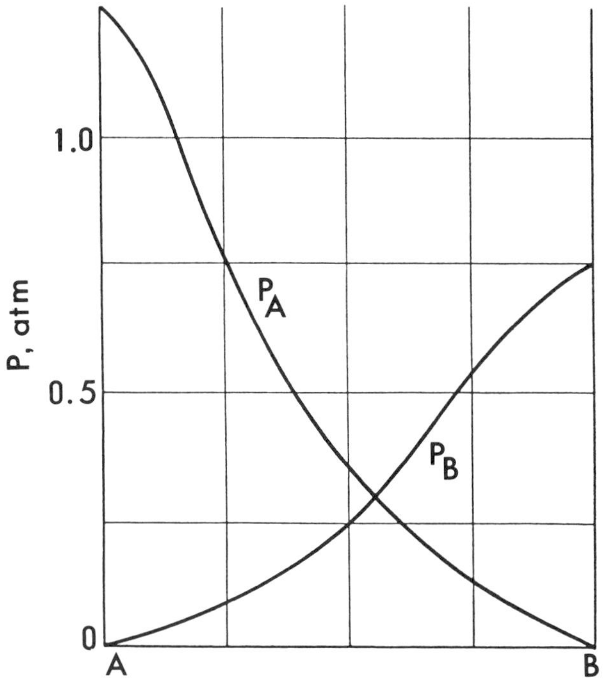

Fig. 1

Solution: Henry's law is written as

$$P_A = K_A X_A$$
$$\text{as } X_A \rightarrow 0$$

This indicates that P_A has a finite slope as $X_A \rightarrow 0$. The value of K_A as shown in figure 2 is the y-intercept at $X_A = 1$ of the straight line to which the P_A curve approaches as $X_A \rightarrow 0$. In other words, Henry's constant is obtained by drawing a tangent to the curve P_A at the lower section where X_A approaches unity. This tangent line is extended to the y-axis. This intercept occurs at 0.5 atm.

b) The activity coefficient of A, f_A assuming the standard state of A is the pure liquid, is given by

$$P_A = f_A X_A P_A^o \quad (1)$$

$$f_A = P_A/P_{A,ideal} \quad (2)$$

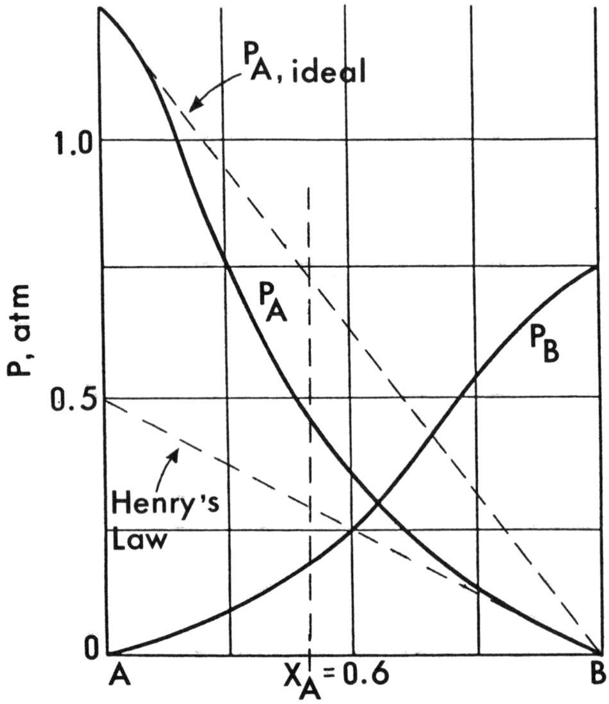

Fig. 2

From figure 2, $X_A = 0.6$ gives $P_A = 0.45$ and $P_{A,ideal} = 0.74$

$$\therefore \quad f_A = P_A/P_{A,ideal}$$

$$= 0.45/0.74$$

$$f_A = 0.61$$

c) Now, the activity coefficient of A, assuming that P_A^o is the hypothetical mole fraction unity, is given by $P_A = Y_A X_A K_A$ or $Y_A = P_A/P_{A,ideal}$. This means that the value of P_A^o will be read off the graph using the line labelled Henry's law. With $X_A = 0.6$, the intercept with Henry's law line is $0.30 = P_{A,ideal}$

$$\therefore \quad f_A = P_A/P_{A,ideal}$$

$$= \frac{0.45}{0.30}$$

$$f_A = 1.5$$

• PROBLEM 8-9

At -0.200°C, a solution of sucrose in water freezes. Given that the vapor pressure of pure water at 25°C is 23.506 mm Hg and the molal freezing point constant for water, K_f is 1.86°C/m, calculate the vapor pressure of this solution at 25°C. Assume there is 1 kg of solvent present.

Solution: The freezing point of a solution is lower than the freezing point of the pure solvent. The difference in their temperatures is called the freezing point depression, ΔT_F. ΔT_F is directly proportional to the molality (m) of the solution by the relation

$$\therefore \quad \Delta T_F = -K_F m \qquad (1)$$

where K_F is the molal freezing point constant

and m is the molality.

From Equation (1) the molality is given by:

$$m = \frac{\Delta T_F}{K_F}$$

$$= \frac{-(0.000°C - 0.200°C)}{1.86°C\text{-kg solvent/moles solute}}$$

$$m = 0.108 \frac{\text{moles solute}}{\text{kg solvent}}$$

The extent of vapor pressure lowering, ΔP, is given by $\Delta P = P°X_2$

$$\therefore \quad X_2 = \frac{\Delta P}{P°} \qquad (2)$$

Recall that the mole fraction of a component in solution is the ratio of its number of moles to the total moles present.

That is, $$X_2 = \frac{n_2}{n_1 + n_2}$$

But $n_2 = 0.108 \dfrac{\text{moles solute}}{\text{kg solvent}} \times 1 \text{ kg solvent} = .108$ moles solute

and $n_1 = \dfrac{1000 \text{ g } H_2O}{18 \text{ g/mole}} = 55.5$ moles solvent (H_2O)

$$\therefore \quad X_2 = \frac{0.108}{55.5 + 0.108}$$

$$X_2 = 0.00194$$

From Equation (2)

$$\frac{\Delta P}{P°} = 0.00194$$

$$\Delta P = (0.00194)(P°)$$

$$= (0.00194)(23.5 \text{ mm Hg})$$

$$\Delta P = 0.045 \text{ mm Hg}$$

$$\therefore \quad P = 23.506 - 0.045$$

or $$P = 23.461 \text{ mm Hg}$$

• PROBLEM 8-10

At 80°C an unknown solute dissolves in benzene to form a solution containing 1.25 wt.% of the solute. The vapor pressure of the solution is 752.4 mm Hg and its boiling point is 80.25°C compared to the normal boiling point of benzene which is 80.00°C. Determine a) the molecular weight of the solute assuming it is non volatile. b) the heat of vaporization (per gram) for benzene whose molecular weight is 78.

Solution: The vapor pressure of a liquid solvent is lowered whenever a solute dissolves in it, and the extent by which it is lowered is given by

$$\Delta P = P°X_2 \tag{1}$$

where ΔP is the extent of vapor pressure lowering. $P°$ is the vapor pressure of the pure solvent and X_2 is the mole fraction of the solute.

For this problem the vapor pressure of the solution after the solute has been added is 752.4 mm Hg. Thus the vapor pressure lowering, ΔP at 80°C is 760 - 752.4 mm Hg = 7.6 mm Hg.

From Equation (1)

$$X_2 = \frac{\Delta P}{P°}$$

$$= \frac{7.6 \text{ mm Hg}}{760 \text{ mm Hg}}$$

$$X_2 = 0.01$$

X_2 can also be written as

$$X_2 = \frac{n_2}{n_1 + n_2} \tag{2}$$

where n_2 is the number of moles of the solute in the solution and n_1 is the number of moles of the solvent, benzene. If we assume a basis of 100 g of benzene

$$n_1 = 100 \text{ g benzene}\left(\frac{1 \text{ mole benzene}}{78 \text{ g benzene}}\right)$$

$$n_1 = 1.28 \text{ moles benzene}$$

$\therefore$ From Equation (2)

$$0.01 = \frac{n_2}{1.28 + n_2}$$

$$0.0128 + 0.01n_2 = n_2$$

$$0.99n_2 = 0.0128$$

$$n_2 = 0.0129$$

This is the number of moles of the solute in the solution which corresponds to 1.25 g of solute.

$\therefore$ Molecular weight of solute $\cong$ 96.9

i.e, molecular weight of solute $\cong \dfrac{1.25}{0.0129}$

$= 96.9$

b) Assuming a dilute solution and making use of the boiling-point-elevation equation, h_f can be calculated from the equation

$$\Delta T = \left(\frac{RT_B^2}{1000h_f}\right)m$$

where h_f is the heat of vaporization and m is the molality

$\therefore$ 80.25°C - 80.00°C =

$$\frac{\left(1.987\dfrac{\text{cal}}{\text{mole°K}}\right)\left(353^2\text{°K}^2\right)\left(\dfrac{0.129 \text{ mol}}{\text{kg solvent}}\right)\left(\dfrac{1\text{°C}}{1\text{°K}}\right)}{\left(\dfrac{1000 \text{ g solvent}}{\text{kg solvent}}\right)h_f}$$

and $\qquad h_f = 128 \text{ cal/g}$

At 25°C, the vapor pressure of water is increased from 30 to 31 mm Hg against an external pressure of 10 atm. If the vapor pressure is to be maintained at 30 mm Hg for 1 liter (55.5 moles) of water at 25°C and 10 atm pressure, a) How much NaCl is to be added to the water? b) What is the osmotic pressure of this solution if NaCl forms an ideal solution with the water?

Solution: a) Here it could be assumed that the vapor pressure of the solution is that of the solvent because the vapor pressure of the solute can be assumed to be very negligible. Since this is an ideal solution, the vapor pressure of the solvent is given by Raoult's law

$$P_1 = X_1 P_1^o$$

$$P_1 = (1 - X_2) P_1^o \tag{1}$$

where subscript 1 indicates the solvent and subscript 2 indicates the solute.

From Equation (1) the effective mole fraction of the solute NaCl can be written as

$$X_2 = \frac{P_1^o - P_1}{P_1^o}$$

$$\therefore \quad X_2 = \frac{1}{31}$$

$$= 0.032$$

When NaCl dissociates in the solution it forms ions, Na^+ and Cl^- per formula weight. Thus the actual mole fraction of NaCl must be $\frac{0.032}{2} = 0.016$. The moles of solute (NaCl) to be added to 55.5 moles of water are given by

$$X_2 = \frac{n_2}{n_1 + n_2} \tag{2}$$

where n_2 = moles of NaCl

n_1 = moles of H_2O

$\therefore$ From Equation (2)

$$0.016 = \frac{n_2}{(55.5 \text{ moles} + n_2)}$$

$$0.888 + 0.016\, n_2 = n_2$$

$$n_2 = .904$$

b) The osmotic pressure is defined as the pressure difference across a membrane required to prevent flow across the membrane in either side. In this problem there is an external pressure of 10 atm and to maintain the vapor pressure at 30 mm Hg, the 10 atm pressure must be constant. Thus the osmotic pressure is 10 atm.

• PROBLEM 8-12

At 25°C 5.0 g of a non-volatile, C_6H_6O is added to 45.0 g C_6H_6. Determine how much the vapor pressure of C_6H_6 is lowered, given that at 25°C, the vapor pressure of C_6H_6 is 95 torr.

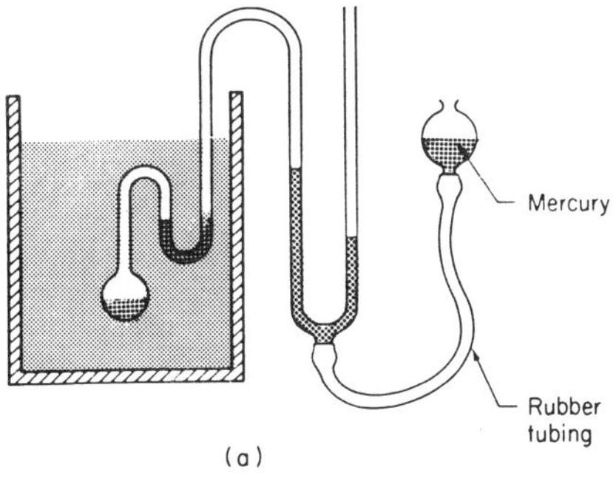

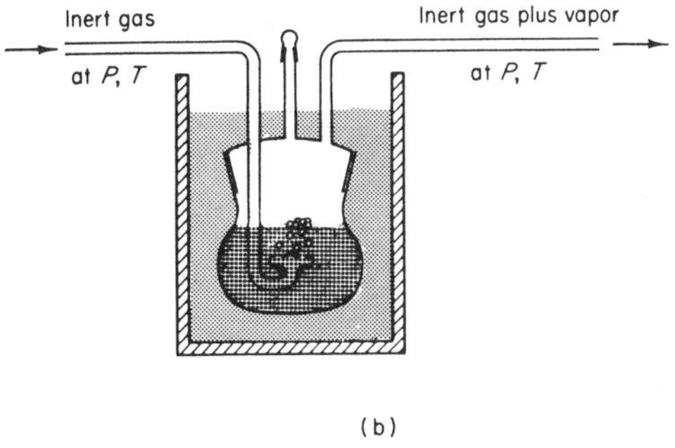

Vapor pressure determination. (a) The isotensiscope. (b) The evaporation method.

Solution: When a solute is dissolved in a solvent, the solute lowers the vapor pressure of the solvent. This vapor pressure lowering depends on both the vapor pressure of the solvent and the mole fraction of the solute in solution. This is the statement of Raoult's law. Thus

$$\Delta P_i = XP_i^o \qquad (1)$$

where ΔP_i is the vapor pressure lowering of solvent above the solution. X is the mole fraction of the solute and P_i^o is the vapor pressure of the pure solvent. ΔP must always be less than or equal to P°, since X in a solution is never greater than 1.00. For the above problem the grams of C_6H_6 and C_6H_6O are changed to moles so as to be able to determine the mole fraction. The number of moles of a substance is given by

$$n = \frac{W}{MW}$$

Therefore,

$$5.0 \text{ g } C_6H_6O \left(\frac{1 \text{ mole } C_6H_6O}{94 \text{ g } C_6H_6O}\right) = 0.053 \text{ mole } C_6H_6O$$

$$45.0 \text{ g } C_6H_6 \left(\frac{1 \text{ mole } C_6H_6}{78 \text{ g } C_6H_6}\right) = 0.577 \text{ moles } C_6H_6$$

The mole fraction of the solute, C_6H_6O, is

$$X_{C_6H_6O} = \frac{n_{C_6H_6O}}{n_{C_6H_6} + n_{C_6H_6O}}$$

$$\therefore \quad X_{C_6H_6O} = \frac{0.053 \text{ moles}}{(0.577 + 0.053)\text{moles}}$$

$$X_{C_6H_6O} = 0.084$$

Thus from Equation (1), the vapor pressure lowering ΔP is given by

$$\Delta P_{C_6H_6} = X_{C_6H_6O} P^o_{C_6H_6}$$

$$= (0.084)(95 \text{ torr})$$

$$\Delta P_{C_6H_6} = 8.0 \text{ torr}$$

The vapor pressure of C_6H_6 is thus lowered by 8.0 torr to become (95 - 8.0)torr = 87 torr.

• PROBLEM 8-13

At 20°C the vapor pressures of ethanol and methanol are 44.5 torr and 88.7 torr respectively. If 100 grams each of ethanol and methanol are mixed to form an ideal solution, calculate a) the mole fraction of methanol and ethanol in the solution. b) the partial pressures and total vapor pressure of the solution. c) the mole fraction of methanol in the vapor.

Solution: It is convenient to change the 100 grams each of

methanol and ethanol to moles since the problem is asking for mole fractions. The formula for ethanol is C_2H_5OH and that of methanol is CH_3OH. Therefore there are

$$100 \text{ g } C_2H_5OH \left(\frac{1 \text{ mole } C_2H_5OH}{46 \text{ g } C_2H_5OH}\right) = 2.17 \text{ moles } C_2H_5OH$$

and $$100 \text{ g } CH_3OH \left(\frac{1 \text{ mole } CH_3OH}{32 \text{ g } CH_3OH}\right) = 3.13 \text{ moles } CH_3OH$$

The total no. of moles of C_2H_5OH and CH_3OH are

$$(2.17 + 3.13) = 5.30 \text{ moles.}$$

a) The mole fraction of C_2H_5 is given by

$$X_{C_2H_5OH} = \frac{n_{C_2H_5OH}}{n_{C_2H_5OH} + n_{CH_3OH}}$$

where X is the mole fraction, n is the number of moles.

$$\therefore X_{C_2H_5OH} = \left(\frac{2.17 \text{ moles}}{5.30 \text{ moles}}\right)$$

$$X_{C_2H_5OH} = 0.41$$

$$X_{CH_3OH} = \frac{n_{CH_3OH}}{n_{C_2H_5OH} + n_{CH_3OH}}$$

$$= \left(\frac{3.13 \text{ moles}}{5.3 \text{ moles}}\right)$$

$$X_{CH_3OH} = 0.59$$

Note that the sum of mole fractions in a solution is equal to 1. So, X_{CH_3OH} could have been obtained by simply subtracting 0.41 from 1.00. That is $X_{CH_3OH} = 1 - 0.41 = 0.59$.

b) Ideal solutions obey Raoult's law given by $P_i = X_i P_i^o$

where P_i = partial pressure of component i

X_i = mole fraction of component i

P_i^o = vapor pressure of pure component i

$$\therefore P_{C_2H_5OH} = X_{C_2H_5OH} P^o_{C_2H_5OH}$$

$$= (0.41)(44.5 \text{ torr})$$

$$P_{C_2H_5OH} = 18.25 \text{ torr}$$

and $$P_{CH_3OH} = X_{CH_3OH}P^o_{CH_3OH}$$

$$= (0.59)(88.7 \text{ torr})$$

$$P_{CH_3OH} = 52.33 \text{ torr}$$

$$P_{total} = P_{C_2H_5OH} + P_{CH_3OH}$$

$$= (18.25 + 52.33)\text{torr}$$

$$P_{total} = 70.58 \text{ torr}$$

c) The mole fraction of CH_3OH in the vapor phase is equal to its pressure fraction in the vapor

$$X_{CH_3OH,vap} = \frac{P_{CH_3OH}}{P_{CH_3OH} + P_{C_2H_5OH}}$$

$$= \left(\frac{52.33 \text{ torr}}{70.58 \text{ torr}}\right)$$

$$X_{CH_3OH,vap} = 0.741$$

• **PROBLEM** 8-14

Consider the process

$$H_2O(\text{solution}, 25°C) = H_2O(\text{pure}, 25°C).$$

If the solution is NaCl of concentration m and has an osmotic pressure of 2.0 atm at 25°C, calculate ΔG_{298}, the free energy change for the process.

Solution: Here the NaCl is the solute because its mole fraction can be varied. For the above process, we consider the solution to be separated from a small amount of the pure solvent at the same temperature by means of a semipermeable membrane which is permeable only to solvent molecules. Then the excess pressure which must be placed on the solution to prevent any diffusion of solvent through the membrane is known as the Osmotic pressure. The diffusion arises because the solvent is at a lower chemical potential in the solution than it is in the pure liquid.

Let P be the pressure on the pure solvent and P' be the pressure on the solution. Then at equilibrium the Osmotic pressure

$$\pi \equiv P' - P.$$

For the process

$$H_2O(\text{solution}),\ G = G^o_{P'} + RT\ \ln P$$

and for

$$H_2O(\text{pure}),\ G = G^o_P + RT\ \ln P°$$

At equilibrium

$$G_P + RT\ \ln P° = G^o_{P'} + RT\ \ln P$$

$$\Delta G = RT\ \ln(P°/P) = G^o_P - G^o_{P'}$$

$$= \int_P^{P'} \bar{V}\ dP = \bar{V}(P' - P)$$

where $\bar{V}$ is the molar volume of the pure solvent. To a reasonably great extent, V remains constant

$$\therefore\quad RT\ \ln(P°/P) = \bar{V}(P' - P)$$

$$RT\ \ln(P°/P) = \bar{V}\pi$$

For water $\bar{V}$ = 18 cc

$$\therefore\quad \Delta G = RT\ \ln(P°/P) = 18\ \text{cc} \times 2\ \text{atm}$$

$$\Delta G = 36\ \text{cc - atm}$$

• PROBLEM 8-15

Determine the molar weight of 3.85 grams of a protein dissolved in 250 ml solvent whose Osmotic pressure is 10.4 mm Hg at 30°C.

Solution: The Osmotic pressure, π, of a solution is proportional to the molal concentration, m, of the solution. Thus,

$$\pi \propto m$$

or

$$\pi = mRT$$

where R is the gas constant and T is the absolute temperature.

But molality, m, is given by

$$m = \frac{n}{V}$$

where n is the number of moles of the solution and V is the volume of solvent

$$\therefore \quad \pi = \frac{n}{V}RT$$

or

$$\pi V = nRT \qquad (1)$$

n in Equation (1) is given by

$$n = \frac{g}{MW}$$

where MW is the molecular weight and g is the number of grams of molecule.

Substituting for n, Equation (1) becomes

$$\pi = \frac{g\ RT}{MW(V)}$$

and

$$MW = \frac{g\ RT}{\pi V}$$

$$= \left(\frac{3.85\text{ g protein}}{250\text{ m}\ell\text{ solution}}\right)\left(\frac{1000\text{ m}\ell}{1\ \ell}\right)\left(\frac{62.4\ \ell\text{mm Hg}}{°\text{K-mole}}\right)\left(\frac{303°\text{K}}{10.4\text{ mm Hg}}\right)$$

$$MW = 27{,}900\ \frac{\text{g protein}}{\text{mole}}$$

• PROBLEM 8-16

Sucrose has a moleuclar weight of 342 g/mole. At 0°C the Osmotic pressure of an aqueous solution of 1 gram of sucrose per 100 cm^3 solvent is 0.649 atm. Use the simple form of the Osmotic pressure equation to calculate the expected Osmotic pressure.

Solution: When a semipermeable membrane is used to separate a solution from the solvent, the Osmotic pressure is the difference of pressure across the membrane required to resist the flow from solvent to solution. It is proportional to the molal concentration by the relation

$$\pi \propto m$$

$$\pi = mRT$$

where m = molality.

A simple form of the Osmotic equation can be written as $\pi = \frac{nRT}{V}$ since m = number of moles, n, divided by the volume, V, of solvent.

$$n = (1\text{ g sucrose})\left(\frac{1\text{ mole sucrose}}{342\text{ g sucrose}}\right)$$

$$n = 0.002924\text{ mole}$$

$$V = 100\ cm^3 = .1\ liter$$

$$\therefore \quad \pi = \frac{nRT}{V}$$

$$\pi = \frac{(0.002924\ mol)\left[\frac{0.0821\ \ell\text{-atm}}{mole\ °K}\right](273°K)}{.1\ liter}$$

$$\pi = 0.655\ atm$$

• PROBLEM 8-17

35.0 grams of sugar, $C_{12}H_{22}O_{11}$ and 1 liter of solvent are mixed together. Calculate the Osmotic pressure of the resulting solution at 25 C.

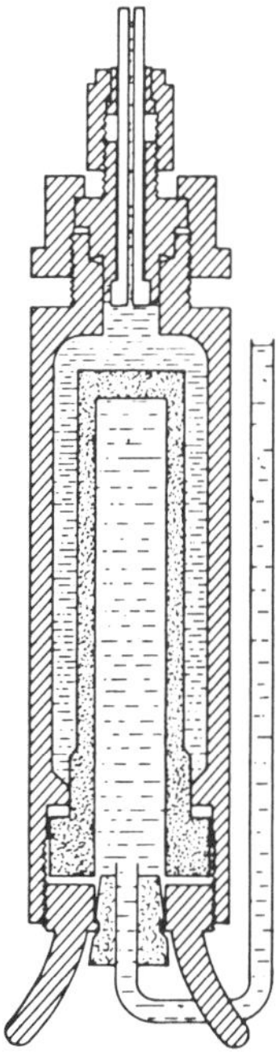

(a)

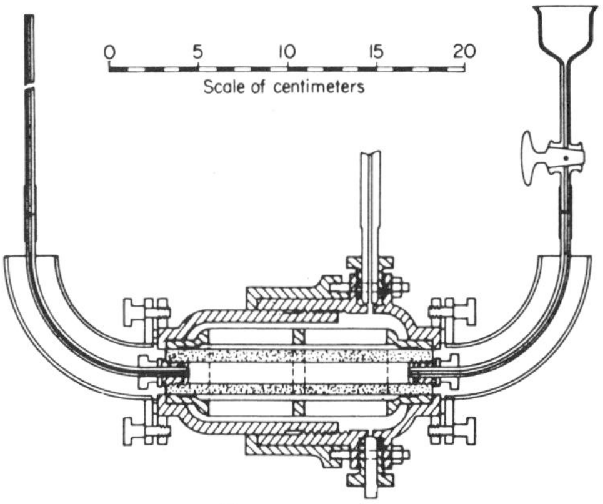

(b)

Apparatus for measurement of osmotic pressure: (a) The static method of Morse and Frazer. The semipermeable membrane is supported in the porous walls of a cylindrical cell. The interior of the cell is filled with pure solvent and the solution to be measured is placed in the volume surrounding the cell. (b) The dynamic method of Berkeley and Hartley. The internal cell contains pure solvent and the solution is outside the cell. Through the small-bore tubing that leads to the external chamber, hydrostatic pressure is applied until osmotic flow stops.

Solution: Osmotic pressure, π is proportional to molal concentration, m,

$$\therefore \quad \pi \propto m$$

$$\pi = mRT$$

But $m = \frac{n}{V}$ where n = no. of moles and V = volume of solvent.

$$\therefore \quad \pi = \frac{nRT}{V}$$

or $$\pi V = nRT$$

The number of moles n can be written as

$$n = \frac{\text{grams of substance}}{\text{molecular weight of substance}}$$

$$n = \frac{g}{MW}$$

$$\therefore \quad \pi V = \frac{gRT}{MW}$$

or

$$\pi = \frac{gRT}{V(MW)}$$

Molecular weight of $C_{12}H_{22}O_{11}$ = 342 grams/mole

$$\therefore \quad \pi = \left(\frac{35.0 \text{ g sugar}}{1 \text{ liter solution}}\right)\left(\frac{0.0821 \ \ell\text{-atm}}{\text{mole K}}\right)(298 \text{ K})\left(\frac{1 \text{ mole sugar}}{342 \text{ grams}}\right)$$

$$\pi = 2.50 \text{ atm}$$

• PROBLEM 8-18

Figure 1 is the apparatus for determining the Osmotic pressure of a solution. At equilibrium, the solvent molecules pass through the membrane raising the level of the solution to height, h. At this height, the Osmotic pressure of the solution is equal to the hydrostatic pressure. If the solution is ideal,

a) show that

$$RT \ \ell n(P/P°) = -Mgh$$

where P and P° are the vapor pressures of the solution and the pure solvent respectively. M is the molecular weight of the solvent. b) Discuss why the pressure of the gas decreases over a height as indicated in the equation above.

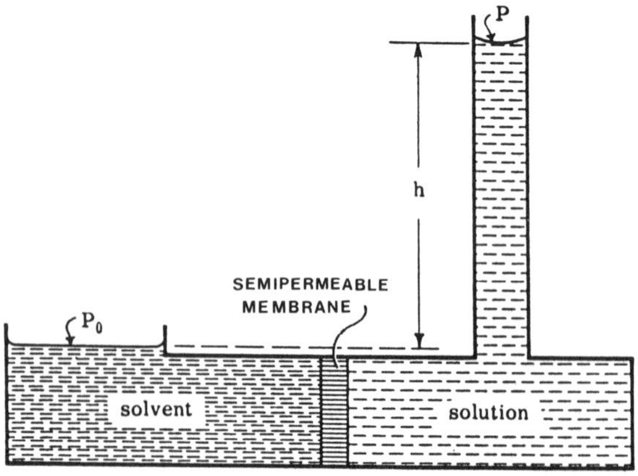

Fig. 1

Solution: Let P and P' be the pressures on the pure solvent and on the solution respectively. The Osmotic pressure at equilibrium is thus given by

$$\pi = P - P'$$

The chemical potentials of both the pure solvent and the solution at pressures P and P' are μ^*_P and $\mu^*_{P'} + RT \ln X$ respectively where X is the mole fraction of the solvent in the solution. At equilibrium, $\mu^*_P = \mu^*_{P'} + RT \ln X$

$$\therefore \quad RT \ln X = \mu^*_P - \mu^*_{P'}$$

$$= \int_{P'}^{P} \overline{V} dP = \overline{V}(P - P')$$

$$\therefore \quad RT \ln X = \overline{V}\pi \qquad (1)$$

at constant $\overline{V}$, where $\overline{V}$ is the molar volume of solvent.

In terms of vapor pressure, equation (1) becomes

$$RT \ln(P°/P) = \overline{V}\pi \qquad (2)$$

where π is the Osmotic pressure. At equilibrium, the Osmotic pressure equals the hydrostatic pressure

$$\therefore \quad \pi = P = \rho gh = \frac{Mgh}{\overline{V}}$$

where P is the hydrostatic pressure given by density times the acceleration due to gravity times the height of the solution in the tube.

With proper substitutions, Equation (2) becomes

$$RT \ln(P°/P) = Mgh$$

and so

$$RT \ln(P/P°) = -Mgh$$

b) The solvent molecules will be expected to evaporate at a pressure, P°, and condense on the solution at a pressure P, if the system is a closed system. This would be a violation of the first law of thermodynamics which states that for any form of energy that disappears, another form of energy will appear exactly equal to the amount that disappeared. This is not the case here. To prevent this, P° over the pure solvent must reduce to exactly P at a height h, which is what the given equation predicts.

• PROBLEM 8-19

Calculate the approximate molar weight of 35.0 grams of a nonelectrolyte in solution with 100 mℓ water. The boiling point of the solution is 102.16 C.

Solution: The same procedure that was followed in determining the approximate molar weight of an unknown solute using the freezing point depression also applies here. First, the concentration of the solution in grams of solute per kilogram of solvent is calculated, and then the molality of the solute is calculated using the boiling point elevation. The approximate molar weight is then obtained by dividing one concentration in terms of g solute/kg solvent by the other given by mole solute/kg solvent.

$$100 \text{ m}\ell \text{ } H_2O \times \frac{1 \text{ g}}{\text{m}\ell} \times \frac{1 \text{ kg}}{1000 \text{ g}} = .1 \text{ kg}$$

The concentration of the solution is

$$\frac{35.0 \text{ g solute}}{0.100 \text{ kg solvent}} = \frac{350 \text{ g solute}}{\text{kg solvent}}$$

To find the concentration in moles solute/kg solvent, we must calculate the molality, m given by the relation

$$m = \frac{\Delta T_B}{K_B}$$

where ΔT_B is the boiling point elevation and K_B is molal boiling point constant. The normal boiling point of water = 100°C and K_B for water is

$$0.52 \frac{°C - kg\ H_2O}{\text{moles solute}}$$

$$\therefore \quad m = \frac{(102.16 - 100.00)°C}{0.52°C - kg\ H_2O/\text{moles solute}}$$

$$= 4.15 \frac{\text{moles solute}}{kg\ H_2O}$$

The molar weight is given by dividing the first concentration by the second as follows:

$$\frac{350 \text{ g solute/kg } H_2O}{4.15 \text{ moles solute/kg } H_2O}$$

Therefore,

$$\text{Molar weight} = \frac{84 \text{ g solute}}{\text{mole solute}}$$

• PROBLEM 8-20

A nonvolatile benzoic acid dissolves in ethanol to form an ideal solution. Assuming there is no association or dissociation of the benzoic acid, calculate the solubility of the acid and the vapor pressure of the solution at 80°C given the following data.

Compound	Mol. wt	M.p; °C	Normal b.p	ΔH, cal/mole	
				Fusion	Vaporization
Benzoic acid	122	122	249°C	4,000	12,000
Ethanol	46	-114	80°C	2,000	9,500

Solution: Assuming that benzoic acid is the solute and ethanol is the solvent, this problem can be seen as the addition of a solute to a solvent. Consequently, it becomes a problem of freezing-point depression of ethanol by benzoic acid. An expression that relates the mole fraction or solubility to the freezing point depression is

$$-\ln X_2 = \frac{\Delta H_f (T_f - T)}{RTT_f}$$

where X_2 is the mole fraction of the acid

ΔH_f is the enthalpy of fusion of the acid

T_f is the freezing point of the acid

$$T_f = 122 + 273°K = 395°K$$

$$T = 80 + 273°K = 353°K$$

$$\Delta H_f = 4,000 \text{ cal/mole}$$

$$\therefore \quad -\ln X_2 = \frac{(4,000 \text{ cal mole}^{-1})(395°K - 353°K)}{(1.987 \text{ cal mole}^{-1} °K^{-1})(353°K)(395°K)}$$

$$X_2 = 0.55 \text{ mole fraction}$$

The solubility of benzoic acid is thus 0.55 mole fraction.

Since the problem says that the solution is ideal, the vapor pressure of the solution is given by Raoult's law.

$$P = X_1 P_1^o = (1 - X_2) P_1^o \qquad (2)$$

where subscript 1 refers to the solvent and subscript 2 to the nonvolatile solute. P is the vapor pressure of the solution. P_1^o is vapor pressure of pure solvent. The boiling point of ethanol at 80° is given. At the boiling point, the vapor pressure equals the atmospheric pressure

$$\therefore \quad P_1^o = 1 \text{ atm}$$

From Equation (2)

$$P = (1 - 0.55) 1 \text{ atm}$$

$$P = 0.45 \text{ atm}$$

Observe that as a result of adding the solute, the vapor pressure of solution is depressed.

• PROBLEM 8-21

At 25°C, sucrose and water form an ideal solution and the solubility of sucrose in the water is 6.2 molal. Calculate the heat of fusion of sucrose given that its molecular weight is 342, melting point is 200°C and the heat of fusion of water is 1400 cal/mole.

Solution: This problem can be considered a freezing point depression problem with sucrose as the solvent. The equation that relates the freezing point depression of a solution to the solubility is given by

$$-\ln X_s = \frac{\Delta H_f}{R} (1/T - 1/T_f) \tag{1}$$

where X_s is the mole fraction of sucrose. ΔH_f is the heat of fusion of sucrose. T_f is the melting point of sucrose. Solving for ΔH_f in equation (1), it becomes

$$\Delta H_f = -\left(\ln X_s\right)(R) \frac{TT_f}{T_f - T} \tag{2}$$

The mole fraction of a 6.2 molal solution can be calculated by the relation

$$X_S = \frac{n_S}{n_S + n_{H_2O}}$$

where n is the number of moles

$$X_S = \frac{6.2 \text{ moles/kg}}{(6.2 + 55.5)\text{moles/kg}}$$

$$X_S = 0.10$$

From Equation (2)

$$\Delta H_f = \left(-\ln 0.10 \text{ mol}\right)\left(\frac{1.987 \text{ cal}}{\text{mol °K}}\right)\left(298°\text{K}\right)\left(\frac{473}{175}\right)$$

or $$\Delta H_f = 3650 \text{ cal} = 3.65 \text{ kcal}$$

• PROBLEM 8-22

10.0 grams of urea, $CO(NH_2)_2$, is dissolved in 200 grams of water. What are the boiling and freezing points of the resulting solution?

Solution: Solutions containing non-volatile solutes have higher boiling points than the boiling points of the pure solvents. The difference between the boiling point of the solution and that of the pure solvent is known as the boiling point elevation, ΔT_B. On the contrary, solutions freeze at lower temperatures than the pure solvent. The difference between the temperatures is called the freezing point depression, ΔT_F. The boiling point elevation and the freezing point depression of any solution is directly proportional to the molality of the solution. Thus

$$\Delta T_B = K_B m \qquad (1)$$

$$\Delta T_F = K_F m \qquad (2)$$

where K_B and K_F are the molal boiling point constant and the molal freezing point constant respectively. m is the molality of the solute. For water

$$K_B = 0.52 \frac{°C - kg\ H_2O}{moles\ solute}$$

and

$$K_F = 1.86 \frac{°C - kg\ H_2O}{moles\ solute}.$$

Using equations (1) and (2), the elevation and depression temperatures can be determined. Add this difference to the normal boiling point of the solution and subtract it from the freezing point of the solvent. From Equation (1)

$$\Delta T_B = K_B m$$

$$\Delta T_B = \left(\frac{0.52°C - kg\ H_2O}{moles\ CO(NH_2)_2}\right)\left(\frac{10.0\ g\ CO(NH_2)_2}{0.200\ kg\ H_2O}\right)\left(\frac{1\ mole\ CO(NH_2)_2}{60.0\ g\ CO(NH_2)_2}\right)$$

$$\Delta T_B = 0.433°C$$

The normal boiling point of water is 100°C and, $\Delta T_B = 0.433°C$, meaning that the solution boils at 0.433°C higher than the normal boiling point. Therefore, the boiling point of the solution is 100°C + 0.433°C

$$T_B = 100.43°C$$

Using Equation (2), the freezing point of the solution can also be computed. Hence

$$\Delta T_F = K_F m$$

$$= \left(\frac{1.86°C - kg\ H_2O}{moles\ CO(NH_2)_2}\right)\left(\frac{10.0\ g\ CO(NH_2)_2}{0.200\ kg\ H_2O}\right)\left(\frac{1\ mole\ CO(NH_2)_2}{60.0\ g\ CO(NH_2)_2}\right)$$

$$\Delta T_F = 1.55°C$$

This means that the solution will freeze 1.55°C below the freezing point of the pure solvent which is 0.00°C. ∴ the freezing point of the solution = 0.00°C - 1.55°C.

$$T_F = -1.55°C.$$

• PROBLEM 8-23

> Calculate the freezing and boiling points of a solution containing 10 grams of $C_6H_{12}O_6$ and 40 grams of water.

Solution: In this problem, water is the solvent. When $C_6H_{12}O_6$ is added to the water, the resulting solution has a higher boiling point and a lower freezing point than that of the pure solvent. The difference between the boiling and freezing points of the solution and those of the pure solvent are the boiling point elevation, ΔT_B and the freezing point depression, ΔT_F respectively. ΔT_B and ΔT_F are directly proportional to the molality of the solution by the relations

$$\Delta T_B = K_B m$$

and $$\Delta T_F = K_F m$$

where K_B and K_F are the molal boiling point constant and the molal freezing point constant respectively. m is the molality of the solute. For water

$K_B = 0.52°C - kg\ H_2O/\text{mole solute}$ and

$$K_F = 1.86\ \frac{°C - kg\ H_2O}{\text{mole solute}}$$

But $\Delta T_B = K_B m$

$$= \left(\frac{0.52°C - kg\ H_2O}{\text{moles}\ C_6H_{12}O_6}\right)\left(\frac{10.0\ g\ C_6H_{12}O_6}{40.0\ g\ H_2O}\right)\left(\frac{10^3\ g\ H_2O}{1\ kg\ H_2O}\right)\left(\frac{1\ \text{mole}\ C_6H_{12}O_6}{180\ g\ C_6H_{12}O_6}\right)$$

$$\Delta T_B = 0.72°C$$

$$\therefore\ T_B = 100°C + 0.72°C$$

$$T_B = 100.72°C.$$

$$\Delta T_F = K_F m$$

$$= \left(\frac{1.86°C - kg\ H_2O}{\text{mole}\ C_6H_{12}O_6}\right)\left(\frac{10.0\ g\ C_6H_{12}O_6}{40.0\ g\ H_2O}\right)\left(\frac{10^3\ g\ H_2O}{1\ kg\ H_2O}\right)\left(\frac{1\ \text{mole}\ C_6H_{12}O_6}{180\ g\ C_6H_{12}O_6}\right)$$

$$\Delta T_F = 2.58°C$$

$$\therefore \quad T_F = 0.00°C - 2.58°C$$

$$T_F = -2.58°C.$$

• PROBLEM 8-24

A solution made up of 150 grams of benzene and 25.1 grams of a solute has a freezing point of -1.92°C. The freezing point of pure benzene is 5.50°C and the molal freezing point constant is 5.10. Determine the approximate molar weight of the solute.

Solution: The determination of the approximate molar weight of the unknown solute consist of first determining the concentration of the solution in grams of solute per kilogram of solvent. Then the freezing point of the solution can be determined. The molality of the solution can then be computed followed by the computation of the molar weight. The concentration of the solution is given by

$$\frac{\text{g of solute}}{\text{kg of solvent}} = \frac{25.1 \text{ g solute}}{0.150 \text{ kg benzene}} = 167 \frac{\text{g solute}}{\text{kg benzene}} \qquad (1)$$

The freezing point depression ΔT_F is

$$\Delta T_F = 5.50-(-1.92)$$

$$\Delta T_F = 7.42°C$$

Making use of this value of ΔT_F, the molality of the solute can be computed using the relation

$$\Delta T_F = K_F m.$$

where K_F is the molal freezing point constant and m is the molality

$$\therefore \quad m = \frac{\Delta T_F}{K_F}$$

$$= \frac{7.42°C}{5.10°C - \text{kg benzene/moles solute}}$$

$$m = 1.45 \frac{\text{moles solute}}{\text{kg benzene}} \qquad (2)$$

Now the quantity of the solute in a kg of benzene is known in both grams and moles given by Equations (1) and (2). If Equation (1) is divided by Equation (2), the result is g/mole of solute which is the molar weight of the solute

$$\therefore \quad \frac{167 \text{ g solute/kg benzene}}{1.45 \text{ mole solute/kg benzene}}$$

molar weight = 115 g solute/mole solute

FUGACITY

• PROBLEM 8-25

Carbon dioxide obeys the reduced Berthelot equation reasonably well

$$z = \frac{PV}{RT} = 1 + \frac{9}{128} \frac{PT_c}{P_c T}\left(1 - 6 \frac{T_c^2}{T^2}\right)$$

Given: T_c = 304.3 K and P_c = 73.0 atm, calculate the fugacity of carbon dioxide at a temperature of 150°C and pressure of 50 atm.

Solution: By definition, $d \ln f = d \ln P + \frac{1}{RT}\left(V - V_{id}\right) dP$. On substituting the solution for V from the given equation and using the relation $V_{id} = \frac{RT}{P}$ yields

$$d \ln f = d \ln P + \frac{9T_c}{128 P_c T}\left(1 - 6 \frac{T_c^2}{T^2}\right) dP \tag{1}$$

where
- f = fugacity
- P = pressure
- T_c = critical temperature or temperature at the critical point
- T = 150 C or, 423 K

Note that at a pressure approaching zero, the fugacity can be equated to the pressure, P.

Therefore, the integration of equation (1) gives

$$\ln f = \ln P + \frac{9 T_c}{128 P_c T}\left(1 - 6 \frac{T_c^2}{T^2}\right) P$$

Substituting the numerical values

$$\ln f = \ln 50 + \frac{(9)(304.3)}{(128)(73.0)(423)}\left(1 - \frac{6(304.3)^2}{(423)^2}\right) 50$$

$$= 3.91 + (0.0006929)(-2.105)50$$

and $\quad f = 46.4$ atm

• PROBLEM 8-26

Figure 1 shows the illustration of the law of rectilinear diameters in its simplest form. Show why this law is not compatible with Van der Waals statement that $V_c = 3b$.

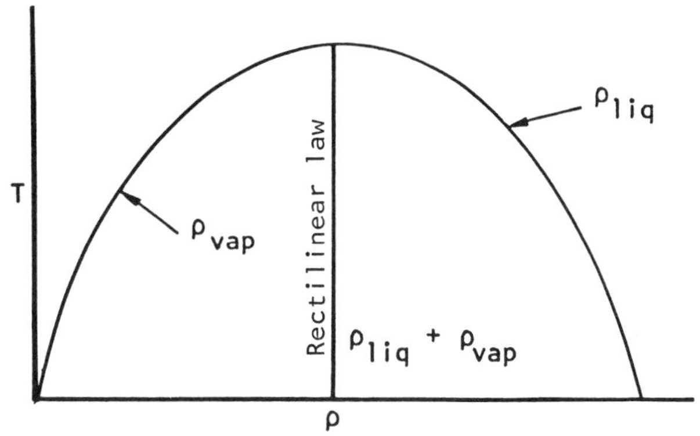

Fig. 1

Solution: The law of rectilinear diameters states that the sum of liquid and equilibrium vapor densities is a constant. This law implies that plots of the densities of a gas and a liquid will intersect at the critical point. For a liquid around its boiling point the vapor density is so small that this sum is essentially the liquid density. Thus at the critical temperature, the liquid and vapor densities are equal, and each must then be half the density of the liquid around its boiling point. That is, the critical volume is not three times that of the liquid, as predicted by Van der Waals. It is twice the volume of the liquid and hence only twice that of the volume of 1 mole of molecules (to which b is supposed to correspond).

• PROBLEM 8-27

Assume that data for the vapor pressures, P, and temperatures, T, of various liquids obeying the simple Clausius Clapeyron equation are available. The straight lines of $\ln P$ versus $\frac{1}{T}$ plotted for such liquids, as shown in figure 1 meet at $\frac{1}{T}$ equal to zero. Show that Trouton's rule requires this kind of behavior.

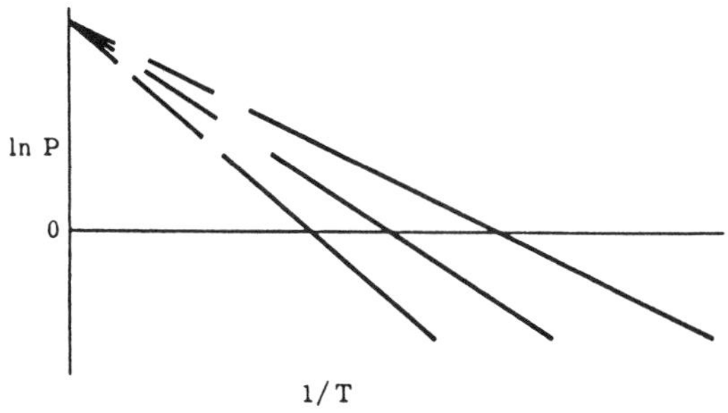

Fig. 1

Solution: Trouton's rule states that the ratio of the molar heat of vaporization of a liquid to its normal boiling point on the absolute scale is the same constant for all liquids. The value of this constant is usually taken as 21

$$\text{i.e.,} \quad \frac{\Delta H_{vap}}{T_b} = 21 = \text{constant}$$

where T_b = normal boiling point of the liquids

and ΔH = heat of vaporization of the liquids.

Alternatively, this rule states that when pressure, P = 1 atm, then

$$\frac{\Delta H}{T_b} = 21.$$

The simple Clausius-Clapeyron equation can be written as

$$\ell n\ P = -\frac{\Delta H}{RT} + \text{constant} \tag{1}$$

where R = gas constant.
When P = 1 atm,

Equation (1) becomes

$$\ell n\ 1 = -\frac{\Delta H}{RT} + \text{constant}$$

$$0 = -\frac{\Delta H}{RT} + \text{constant}$$

$$\therefore \quad \text{constant} = \frac{\Delta H}{RT}. \tag{2}$$

From Trouton's rule

$$21 = \frac{\Delta H}{T} \text{ when } P = 1 \text{ atm.}$$

Therefore, the constant from Equation (2) must be $\frac{21}{R}$. Hence Equation (1) can now be written as

$$\ell n\ P = -\frac{\Delta H}{RT} + \frac{21}{R}.$$

This means that all liquids are supposed to have a common intercept at $\frac{1}{T} = 0$ as required by Trouton's rule.

• PROBLEM 8-28

Pyridine, with a normal boiling point of 114°C has a vapor density of 2.5 g/liter and a liquid density of 0.8000 g/cc at this temperature. At a higher temperature, T', the liquid density becomes 0.7900 g/cc after it (the liquid) has expanded. Calculate a) the heat of vaporization of pyridine b) the boiling point of pyridine on a mountain top where atmospheric pressure is 740 mm Hg instead of the normal 760 mm Hg c) the vapor density of pyridine at temperature T'.

Solution: a) Since we are given the boiling point of pyridine and we desire ΔH_{vap} we can make use of Trouton's rule which states that

$$\frac{\Delta H_{vap}}{T_b} = \text{constant} = 21 \text{ cal mole}^{-1} \text{ K}^{-1}$$

where T_b is the normal boiling point and ΔH_{vap} is the heat of vaporization.

$$\therefore \quad \Delta H_{vap.} = 21(T_b)$$

$$= 21 \times 387°K$$

$$= 8127 \text{ cal}$$

$$\Delta H_{vap.} = 8.13 \text{ kcal}$$

b) We will use the Clausius Clapeyron equation here to calculate the boiling point of pyridine at the 740 mm Hg

$$\ell n \frac{P_2}{P_1} = \frac{\Delta H}{R}\left(\frac{1}{T_1} - \frac{1}{T_2}\right)$$

$$\ell n \frac{760}{740} = \left(\frac{8127 \text{ cal}}{1.987 \text{ cal°K}^{-1}}\right)\left(\frac{1}{T_1} - \frac{1}{387°K}\right)$$

$$0.027 = 4090\left(\frac{1}{T_1} - 0.00258\right)$$

Dividing both sides by 4090 and rearranging yields

$$\frac{1}{T_1} = \frac{0.027}{4090} + 0.00258$$

$$\frac{1}{T_1} = 0.00258$$

$$\therefore \quad T_1 = 386.6°K$$

c) The sum of the vapor and liquid densities is a constant. Thus at 114°C the density of vapor, d_{vap}, is 2.5 g/liter.

$$\text{Density of liquid, } d_{liq.}, = \left(0.800 \frac{g}{cc}\right)\left(\frac{1000 \text{ cc}}{1 \text{ liter}}\right)$$

$$= 800 \frac{g}{\text{liter}}$$

$\therefore$ Total density $= (d_{vap} + d_{liquid}) =$ constant

$$= (800 + 2.5) g/liter$$

$$= 802.5 \text{ g/liter}$$

$$\therefore \quad d_{vap} + d_{liquid} = 802.5 \text{ g/liter} \qquad (1)$$

At temperature T'

$$d_{liquid} = \left(0.7900 \frac{g}{cc}\right)\left(\frac{1000 \text{ cc}}{1 \text{ liter}}\right)$$

$$= 790 \text{ g/liter}$$

From Equation (1)

$$d_{vap.} + 790 \frac{g}{liter} = 802.5 \frac{g}{liter}$$

$$d_{vap} = (802.5 - 790) g/liter$$

$$d_{vap} = 12.5 \text{ g/liter}$$

• PROBLEM 8-29

> The critical temperature of a certain liquid of molecular weight 60 g/mole is 400 C. The normal melting point and the melting point at the triple point are, 15.000 C and 14.980 C respectively. (At the triple point the system is subjected only to its own low vapor pressure). Calculate a) ΔH_{vap}, b) ΔH_s, c) ΔH_f, d) the vapor pressure at the triple point, given that the solid and liquid densities of the liquid are 0.85 and 0.80 g/cc, respectively.

Solution: a) We can find ΔH_{vap} using Trouton's rule:

$$\frac{\Delta H_{vap}}{T_b} = 21 \text{ cal mole}^{-1} \text{ K}^{-1} \qquad (1)$$

T_b, the normal boiling point is about 2/3 of the critical temperature of 673°K.

$$\therefore \quad T_b = 2/3(673°K)$$

$$= 450°K$$

Substituting this value into Equation (1),

$$\frac{\Delta H_{vap}}{450} = 21 \text{ cal/°K mole}$$

$\therefore \qquad \Delta H_{vap} = 21(450°K)$ calories

$= 9450$ cal

$\Delta H_{vap} = 9.45$ kcal

b) We will now use Clapeyron equation which relates ΔH_{fusion} to the changes in pressure and temperature and is given by:

$$\frac{\Delta P}{\Delta T} = \frac{\Delta H_{fus.}}{T_{fus}\left(V_L - V_S\right)} \qquad (2)$$

where ΔH_{fus} is the heat of fusion V_L and V_S are the molar volumes of liquid and solid respectively.

$$V_L = \frac{\text{mass}}{\text{density}}$$

$$= \frac{60 \text{ g/mole}}{0.80 \text{ g/cc}}$$

$$= 75 \text{ cc/mole}$$

$$V_S = \frac{60 \text{ g/mole}}{0.85 \text{ g/cc}}$$

$$= 70.6 \text{ cc/mole}$$

$$\Delta V = V_L - V_S$$

$$= (75 - 70.6)\text{cc/mole}$$

$$\Delta V = 4.4 \text{ cc/mole.}$$

From equation (2)

$$\Delta H_{fus} = \frac{\Delta P(T)(\Delta V)}{\Delta T}$$

$$= \frac{(1 \text{ atm} - 0)(288 \text{ K})(4.4 \text{ cc/mole})}{(15.000 - 14.980)\,°C\left(\frac{1°K}{1°C}\right)}$$

$$= 6.3 \times 10^4 \text{ cc - atm}$$

$$= (6.3\times10^4 \text{cc-atm})\left(\frac{1\ \ell}{1000\text{cc}}\right)\left(\frac{1.987 \text{ cal mol}^{-1}\text{ K}^{-1}}{0.082\ell \text{ atm K}^{-1}\text{mol}^{-1}}\right)\left(\frac{1 \text{ kcal}}{1000 \text{ cal}}\right)$$

$$\Delta H_{fus} = 1.5 \text{ kcal}$$

c) $\Delta H_S = \Delta H_V + H_f$

where ΔH_S = heat of sublimation

$\therefore \quad \Delta H_S = (9.45 + 1.5)\text{kcal}$

$\Delta H_S = 10.95 \text{ kcal}$

d) We will now use the Clausius Clapeyron equation to calculate the vapor pressure at the triple point

$$\ln \frac{P_2}{P_1} = \frac{\Delta H_{vap}}{R}\left[\frac{1}{T_1} - \frac{1}{T_2}\right]$$

$$\ln \frac{760}{P_1} = \frac{9450 \text{ cal}}{1.987 \text{ cal°K}^{-1}}\left[\frac{1}{288} - \frac{1}{450}\right]$$

$$= 4755.9[0.00125]$$

$$\ln \frac{760}{P_1} = 5.9$$

$$\ln 760 - \ln P_1 = 5.9$$

$$\ln P_1 = 6.6 - 5.9$$

$$\ln P_1 = 0.73.$$

Taking the exponents of both sides,

$$P_1 = e^{0.73}$$

or $\quad P_1 = 2.08 \text{ mm Hg}$

• PROBLEM 8-30

Determine the heat of vaporization of acetonitrile with a normal boiling point of 80 C, given that acetonitrile has a vapor pressure which is changing at the rate of 0.030 atm/deg K around the boiling point.

Solution: The Clausius-Clapeyron equation relates the rate of changes of pressure and temperature to the heat of vaporization. Writing the equation in the form

$$\frac{dP}{dT} = \frac{P\Delta H_{vap}}{RT^2}, \tag{1}$$

ΔH_{vap} can easily be calculated. The problem states that

$$\frac{dP}{dT} = 0.030 \frac{\text{atm}}{\text{deg K}}$$

From Equation (1) therefore,

$$\Delta H_{vap} = \frac{dP}{dT}\frac{RT^2}{P_t}$$

At the boiling point $P_t = 1$ atm.

$$\therefore \quad \Delta H_{vap} = \left(0.030\ \frac{atm}{°K}\right)\frac{\left(1.987\ cal\ mole^{-1}\ °K^{-1}\right)(353°K)^2}{1\ atm}$$

$$= \left(7427.9\ cal\ mol^{-1}\right)\left(\frac{1\ kcal}{1000\ cal}\right)$$

$$= 7.4\ kcal\ mol^{-1}$$

An alternative, less precise, method yields a similar result. The procedure used is Trouton's Rule which states that

$\frac{\Delta H_{vap}}{T_b} = 21\ cal\ mole^{-1}\ K^{-1}$, where ΔH_{vap} is the heat of vaporization, and T_b is the normal boiling point temperature, in K. Hence, $\Delta H_{vap} = 21\ cal\ mole^{-1}\ K^{-1}(353\ K)$

$$= 7413\ cal/mole$$

$$= 7.4\ kcal\ mole^{-1}$$

• PROBLEM 8-31

Glacial acetic acid has a melting point of 16°C at a pressure of 1 atm. a) Calculate the melting point at its vapor pressure of 0 atm, given that the acid has a heat of fusion of 2700 cal/mole and a molecular weight of 60. Solid and liquid acetic acid have densities of 1.10 g/cc and 1.05 g/cc respectively. b) Calculate the heat of sublimation of solid acetic acid given that the acid has a normal boiling point of 118°C.

Solution: In this problem, the heat of fusion as well as the changes in pressure are given. So we can utilize the Clapeyron equation knowing how it relates changes in pressure and temperature to the ΔH_{fusion}.

a) The Clapeyron equation is

$$\frac{dP}{dT} = \frac{\Delta H_{fusion}}{T(V_L - V_S)} \qquad (1)$$

where V_L and V_S are the volumes of liquid and solid respectively. Equation (1) can also be written as

$$\frac{\Delta P}{\Delta T} = \frac{\Delta H_{fusion}}{T(\Delta V)} \qquad (2)$$

where $\Delta V = V_L - V_S$

From Equation (2),

$$\Delta T = \frac{\Delta P \; T\Delta V}{\Delta H_{fusion}} \tag{3}$$

$$\Delta P = (0 \text{ atm} - 1 \text{ atm}) = -1 \text{ atm}$$

$$T = 273 \text{ K} + 16 = 289°K$$

$$\Delta V = V_L - V_S$$

$$\text{Volume} = \frac{\text{mass}}{\text{density}}$$

$$\therefore \qquad V_L = \frac{60 \text{ g mole}^{-1}}{1.05 \text{ g cc}^{-1}} = 57.1 \frac{\text{cc}}{\text{mole}}$$

and $$V_S = \frac{60 \text{ g mole}^{-1}}{1.10 \text{ g cc}^{-1}} = 54.5 \frac{\text{cc}}{\text{mole}}$$

$$\therefore \qquad \Delta V = (57.1 - 54.5)\frac{\text{cc}}{\text{mole}}$$

$$= 2.6 \frac{\text{cc}}{\text{mole}}$$

From Equation (3) therefore,

$$\Delta T = \frac{(-1 \text{ atm})(289°K)\; 2.6\left(\frac{\text{cc}}{\text{mole}}\right)}{\left(2700\frac{\text{cal}}{\text{mole}}\right)\left(\frac{0.04129 \;\ell - \text{atm}}{\text{cal}}\right)\left(\frac{1000 \text{ cc}}{1\ell}\right)}$$

$$\Delta T = -0.007°K$$

Thus the melting point at 0°C is

$$T = 289°K - 0.007°K$$

$$T = 288.993°K = (288.993 - 273)°C$$

$$T = 15.993°C$$

b) We can calculate the heat of sublimation, ΔH_S, using the fact that

$$\Delta H_S = H_f + H_V$$

where ΔH_f and ΔH_V are respectively the heat of fusion and vaporization. The heat of fusion is given to be 2700 cal/mole, and to find the heat of vaporization, Trouton's rule can be used. This rule states that the molar entropy of vaporization for most liquids at their boiling points is approximately a constant at $21 \frac{\text{cal}}{\text{mole K}}$

$$\therefore \quad \Delta\bar{S}_{vap} = \frac{\Delta H_{vap}}{T_b} \approx 21 \frac{cal}{mole°K}$$

where T_b is the boiling point temperature and $\Delta\bar{S}_{vap}$ is the molar entropy of vaporization

$$\therefore \quad \Delta H_{vap} = \left(21 \frac{cal}{mole\ K}\right)(T_b)$$

$$= 21\left(\frac{cal}{mole\ K}\right)(391°K)$$

$$\Delta H_{vap} = 8200 \frac{cal}{mole}$$

$$\Delta H_S = \Delta H_f + \Delta H_V$$

$$= (2700 + 8200)\frac{cal}{mole}$$

$$\therefore \quad \Delta H_S = 10900 \text{ cal/mole}$$

• PROBLEM 8-32

At what temperature will water with a boiling point of 100°C and chloroform with a boiling point of 60°C, have the same vapor pressure. The heats of vaporization for water and chloroform are 12.0 kcal/mole and 7.0 kcal/mole respectively.

Solution: This problem can be solved by using the Clausius-Clapeyron equation. Clapeyron stated that when two phases of a pure substance are in equilibrium, then

$$V_V dP - V_L dP = S_V dT - S_L dT$$

$$(V_V - V_L)\,dP = (S_V - S_L)\,dT$$

$$\frac{dP}{dT} = \frac{S_V - S_L}{V_V - V_L}$$

$$\frac{dP}{dT} = \frac{\Delta S_{vap}}{V_V - V_L}$$

But $\quad \Delta S_{vaporization} = \frac{\Delta H_{vaporization}}{T}$

Therefore, $\frac{dP}{dT} = \frac{\Delta H_{vap}}{T(V_V - V_L)}$ which is the Clapeyron equation. Here ΔH_{vap} is the enthalpy of vaporization at temperature T and the equililbrium vapor pressure.

Clausius made the following assumptions on the Clapeyron equation: He assumed that the vapor phase was an ideal gas.

$$\therefore \quad V_V = \frac{RT}{P}$$

He also assumed that the liquid volume was negligible compared to the vapor volume

$$\therefore \quad V_V - V_L \cong V_V = \frac{RT}{P}$$

The Clapeyron equation then becomes

$$\frac{dP}{dT} = \frac{\Delta H_{vap}}{T\left(V_V - V_L\right)} = \frac{\Delta H_{vap}}{T\left(V_V\right)} = \frac{\Delta H_{vap}}{T\left(\frac{RT}{P}\right)}$$

$$\therefore \qquad \frac{dP}{dT} = \frac{\Delta H_{vap}\,P}{RT^2} \qquad (2)$$

This is the Clausius-Clapeyron equation. If we integrate Equation (2), taking ΔH_{vap} to be a constant, over a given temperature change in equilibrium, then the chemical potentials of the two phases are equal, at constant temperature and pressure.

Rearranging equation (2) yields

$$\frac{dP}{P} = \frac{\Delta H_{vap}}{RT^2}dT$$

$$\int_{P_1}^{P_2} d\ \ell n\ P = \frac{\Delta H_{vap}}{R}\int_{T_1}^{T_2} T^{-2}dT$$

$$\ell n\left(\frac{P_2}{P_1}\right) = \frac{\Delta H_{vap}}{R}\left[-T^{-1}\right]_{T_1}^{T_2}$$

$$\ell n\left(\frac{P_2}{P_1}\right) = \frac{\Delta H_{vap}}{R}\left[-\frac{1}{T_2} + \frac{1}{T_1}\right]$$

$$\ell n\left(\frac{P_2}{P_1}\right) = \frac{\Delta H_{vap}}{R}\left[\frac{1}{T_1} - \frac{1}{T_2}\right] \qquad (3)$$

P_1 can be taken to be 1 atm since all liquids boil when

their vapor pressure is equal to the total atmospheric pressure of 1 atm. Therefore Equation (3), for water, becomes

$$\ln\left(\frac{P_2}{1\text{ atm}}\right) = \frac{12{,}000\text{ cal mol}^{-1}}{R}\left[\frac{1}{373} - \frac{1}{T_2}\right]$$

and for chloroform

$$\ln\left(\frac{P_2}{1\text{ atm}}\right) = \frac{7000\text{ cal mol}^{-1}}{R}\left[\frac{1}{333} - \frac{1}{T_2}\right]$$

We want to find the temperature at which the water and chloroform will have the same vapor pressure, thus we can set the left-hand sides of the above two equations for water and chloroform equal. That is

$$\frac{12{,}000}{R}\left[\frac{1}{373} - \frac{1}{T_2}\right] = \frac{7000}{R}\left[\frac{1}{333} - \frac{1}{T_2}\right]$$

or $$12{,}000\left[\frac{1}{373} - \frac{1}{T_2}\right] = 7000\left[\frac{1}{333} - \frac{1}{T_2}\right]$$

solving now for T_2 we have

$$\frac{12{,}000}{373} - \frac{12{,}000}{T_2} = \frac{7000}{333} - \frac{7000}{T_2}$$

$$\frac{5000}{T_2} = 11.15$$

$$\therefore \quad T_2 = 448°K$$

• PROBLEM 8-33

At 46°C, the vapor pressure of liquid A is 50 mm Hg and at the same temperature, the vapor pressure of solid A is 0.50 mm less than that of the liquid. At 45°C the vapor pressure of the solid is 1 mm less than that of the liquid. If ΔH_V is 9.0 kcal, estimate a) the melting point of A; b) calculate the heat of sublimation of A; c) calculate the heat of fusion of A.

Solution: a) The vapor pressure of the solid and liquid are the same at the melting point. At 45°C, the difference between the vapor pressures of the liquid and solid is 1 mm. This difference is 0.5 mm at 46°C, thus at 47°C the vapor pressure difference should be close to zero. The melting point is therefore estimated to be 47°C.
b) We can calculate the heat of fusion of A using the Clausius-Clapeyron equation. First, we determine the heat of sublimation as follows,

$$\left(\frac{dP}{dT}\right)_{\text{sublimation}} = \frac{\Delta H_S P}{RT^2} \qquad (1)$$

In order to determine ΔH_S we must first calculate $\left(\frac{dP}{dT}\right)_{vap}$ for the vaporization of liquid to solid

$$\left(\frac{dP}{dT}\right)_{vap} = \frac{\Delta H_{vap}\ P}{RT^2} \qquad (2)$$

at 46°C, $$\left(\frac{dP}{dT}\right)_{vap} = \frac{(9000\ \text{cal})(50\ \text{mm Hg})}{\left(1.98\ \text{cal}\ °K^{-1}\right)\left(319^2 °K^2\right)}$$

or $$\left(\frac{dP}{dT}\right)_{vap} = 2.2\ \text{mm/deg}$$

At any given temperature the vapor pressure of the solid is increasing 0.5 mm/deg faster than is that of the liquid. Thus for the sublimation of the solid,

$$\left(\frac{dP}{dT}\right)_{sub.} = (2.2 + 0.5)\text{mm/deg}$$

or $$\left(\frac{dP}{dT}\right)_{sub.} = 2.7\ \text{mm/deg}$$

From Equation (1)

$$2.7 = \frac{\Delta H_S\ P}{RT^2}$$

From which

$$\Delta H_{sub.} = \frac{(2.7)RT^2}{P}$$

$$= \frac{\left(2.7\ \text{mm Hg}\ °K^{-1}\right)\left(1.98\ \text{cal}\ °K^{-1}\right)\left(320^2\ K^2\right)}{(50 + 2.7)\text{mm Hg}}$$

$$= \frac{\left(2.7\ \text{mm Hg}\ °K^{-1}\right)\left(1.98\ \text{cal}\ °K^{-1}\right)\left(102400\ °K^2\right)}{52.7\ \text{mm Hg}}$$

$$= \left(10387.6\ \text{cal}\right)\left(\frac{1\ \text{kcal}}{1000\ \text{cal}}\right)$$

$$= 10.38\ \text{kcal}$$

$$\therefore \quad \Delta H_{sub} = 10.38\ \text{kcal}$$

c) The heat of fusion is then given by

$$\Delta H_{fus.} = \Delta H_{sub} - \Delta H_{vap}$$

$$= (10.38 - 9) \text{ kcal}$$

$$\Delta H_{fus.} = 1.38 \text{ kcal}$$

• PROBLEM 8-34

Given that solid A does not float on liquid A, explain whether the melting point of the solid will be raised or lowered by pressure.

Solution: Here the Clapeyron equation applies. Thus,

$$\frac{dP}{dT} = \frac{\Delta H_f}{T(V_L - V_S)} = \frac{\Delta H_f}{T\Delta V} \quad (1)$$

where ΔH_f is heat of fusion for the process solid $\rightleftarrows$ liquid. V_S and V_L are the molar volume of solid and liquid respectively.

Since the solid does not float, it means that it is denser than the liquid. According to Equation (1), if the solid is denser, its molar volume is less than that of the liquid. Thus ΔV must be positive. This means that $\frac{\Delta H_f}{T\Delta V}$ must be positive and $\frac{dP}{dT}$ must also be positive. Thus the melting point is raised on application of pressure.

• PROBLEM 8-35

At 40°C the vapor pressures of two liquids A and B are 20 mm Hg and 40 mm Hg respectively. Liquid A has a normal boiling point of 120°C and that for liquid B is 140°C. Given that the heat of vaporization of A is 11.3 kcal/mole which of the following best describes the heat of vaporization of B(5.65 kcal/mole, 11.09 kcal/mole, 22.6 kcal/mole, less than 11.3 kcal/mole, greater than 11.09 kcal/mole, about the same, indeterminate because of insufficient data)?

Solution: There are two ways to approach this question. a) The Clausius-Clapeyron equation can be used to calculate the numerical values for ΔH_A and ΔH_B b) It can be answered qualitatively by comparing the boiling points and vapor pressures of both A and B.

a) The Clausius-Clapeyron equation is written as

$$\ln\left(\frac{P_2}{P_1}\right) = \frac{\Delta H_{vap}}{R}\left[\frac{1}{T_1} - \frac{1}{T_2}\right] \quad (1)$$

P_2 = 760 mm Hg since all liquids boil when their vapor pressures equal 760 mm Hg. Equation (1), written for 1 mole each of liquids A and B, becomes

$$\ln\left(\frac{760}{20}\right) = \left[\frac{\Delta H_A}{1.987 \text{ cal mol}^{-1}\cdot K^{-1}}\right]\left[\frac{1}{313} - \frac{1}{393}\right]$$

$$3.63 = \left[\frac{\Delta H_A}{1.987 \text{ cal}}\right]\left(6.5 \times 10^{-4}\right)$$

$$\Delta H_A = \frac{7.21}{6.5 \times 10^{-4}}$$

$$\Delta H_A = 11.09 \text{ kcal}$$

and for liquid B

$$\ln\left(\frac{760}{40}\right) = \left[\frac{\Delta H_B}{(1.987)}\right]\left[\frac{1}{313} - \frac{1}{413}\right]$$

$$2.94 = \frac{\Delta H_B}{1.987}(7.7 \times 10^{-4})$$

$$\Delta H_B = 7.58 \text{ kcal}$$

Apparently, ΔH_B is less than ΔH_A.

b) Qualitatively, at 40°C, the vapor pressure of A is less than that of B. At the normal boiling point of B, that is at 140°C, the vapor pressure of A must be greater than that of B since the boiling point of B is above the boiling point of A. The vapor pressure of A thus changes more rapidly with temperature than does that of B. Therefore the ΔH_{vap} of B must be less than that of A.

One should not attempt to use Trouton's Rule to solve this problem. Trouton's Rule which states that $\Delta H_{vap}/T_{bp}$ = 21 cal mole^{-1} K^{-1} would give as results ΔH^A_{vap} = 8.253 kcal mole^{-1} K^{-1} and H^B_{vap} = 8.673 kcal mole^{-1}K^{-1}. In fact H_{vap}/T_{bp} lies between 17 and 26 cal/mole K. This range of values is due to the fact that for each liquid ΔH_{vap} varies somewhat with temperature. The choice of 21 cal mole^{-1} K^{-1} is only an approximate average. It is best for nonpolar liquids. Therefore, since the liquids are unknown, it would be unwise to assume that ΔH_{vap} varies with temperature in the same manner for each liquid. Hence, the use of the value of 21 cal mole^{-1} K^{-1} is not appropriate and consequently Trouton's Rule should not be used.

Data for the vapor pressure, P of a liquid with a normal boiling point of 27°C is given. A plot of ℓn P vs. 1/T results in a straight line. Calculate the heat of vaporization of the liquid if the straight line extrapolated to infinite temperature yields a pressure of 10^5 atm.

Solution: The Clausius-Clapeyron equation is used to calculate the heat of vaporization, ΔH_{vap}, since it relates the changes in temperature and pressure to ΔH_{vap}. Assuming ideality of the vapor phase and neglecting the volume of the liquid in comparison to that of the vapor, Clausius-Clapeyron equation becomes

$$\frac{dP}{dT} = \frac{P\Delta H_{vap}}{RT^2}$$

Rearranging the above equation gives

$$\frac{dP}{P} = \frac{\Delta H_{vap}}{RT^2}\, dT$$

If ΔH_{vap} is assumed to be constant over the temperature and pressure ranges the above equation can be integrated as follows

$$\int d\ \ell n\ P = \frac{\Delta H_{vap}}{R} \int T^{-2}\, dT$$

$$\therefore \qquad \ell n\ P = -\frac{\Delta H_{vap}}{RT} + A \qquad (1)$$

where A is the integration constant. Using the information given in the problem, Equation (1) becomes

$$\ell n\ 10^5 = -\frac{\Delta H_{vap}}{RT} + A.$$

At the point where P = 10^5 atm, $\frac{1}{T}$ is essentially zero. $\frac{1}{T}$ is always zero on the ℓn P line (at any P and hence any ℓn P). Therefore

$$\ell n\ 10^5 = -\frac{\Delta H_{vap}}{R}(0) + A$$

$$= 0 + A = A$$

$$\therefore \qquad \ell n\ P = -\frac{\Delta H_{vap}}{RT} + \ell n\ 10^5$$

$$\ln P - \ln 10^5 = -\frac{\Delta H_{vap}}{RT}$$

$$\ln \frac{P}{10^5} = -\frac{\Delta H_{vap}}{RT}$$

Since the liquid will boil only when its vapor pressure equals 1 atm, then P = 1 atm

$$\therefore \quad \ln \frac{1}{10^5} = -\frac{\Delta H_{vap}}{RT}$$

$$-11.5 = -\frac{\Delta H_{vap}}{RT}$$

$$\Delta H_{vap} = 11.5(RT)$$

$$= 11.5\left(\frac{1.987\ \text{cal}}{\text{mol}\ °K}\right)(1\ \text{mol liquid})(300°K)$$

$$\Delta H_{vap} = 6855\ \text{cal} = 6.855\ \text{kcal}$$

• PROBLEM 8-37

At 25°C the vapor pressure of CCl_4 increases by 4% per degree. Calculate a) ΔH_V of CCl_4 b) the normal boiling point of CCl_4. List all assumptions and approximations involved in the derivation of the equation used to obtain ΔH_V.

Solution: a) The Clausius-Clapeyron equation will be used in the form

$$\frac{dP}{dT} = \frac{\Delta H_{vap}\ P}{RT^2} \tag{1}$$

to calculate ΔH_{vap}. Rewriting equation (1),

$$\left(\frac{dP/P}{dT}\right) = \frac{\Delta H_{vap}}{RT^2} \tag{2}$$

Given that P increases by 4% per degree, Equation (2) becomes

$$\left(\frac{dP/P}{dT}\right) = 0.04$$

and $$0.04 = \frac{\Delta H_{vap}}{RT^2}$$

$$\Delta H_{vap.} = 0.04(RT^2)$$

$$= (0.04\ °K^{-1})(1.98\ cal\ °K^{-1})(298^2\ °K^2)\left(\frac{1\ kcal}{1000\ cal}\right)$$

$$\Delta H_{vap.} = 7.03\ kcal$$

b) Trouton's rule gives the ratio of the molar heat of vaporization of a liquid to its normal boiling point to be a constant equal to 21 cal mol^{-1} K^{-1}.

$$\therefore \quad \frac{\Delta H_{vap}}{T_b} = 21$$

where T_b is the normal boiling point

$$\therefore \quad T_b = \frac{\Delta H_{vap}}{21}$$

$$= \frac{7030\ cal\ mol^{-1}}{31\ cal\ mol^{-1}\ K^{-1}}$$

$$T_b = 334.7\ °K$$

The assumptions made in deriving the equation for ΔH_V are as follows: 1) At temperatures not too near the critical, the molar volume, V_L of the liquid is small compared with the molar volume, V_g of the gas. Therefore V_L was neglected. 2) The vapor behaved like an ideal gas and thus the molar volume of the gas, V_g was given by

$$V_g = \frac{RT}{P}$$

3) There was equilibrium between liquid and vapor.
4) The first and second laws of thermodynamics were applicable.

• PROBLEM 8-38

For a certain liquid which obeys Trouton's rule, its vapor pressure increases by 15 mm Hg per degree at temperatures around its normal boiling point. Calculate the heat of vaporization and the normal boiling point of this liquid.

Solution: Clausius-Clapeyron equation, in the form

$$\left(\frac{dP}{dT}\right) = \frac{\Delta H_V P}{RT^2}, \qquad (1)$$

can be applied, where ΔH_V = heat of vaporization. Rearranging Equation (1), it becomes

$$\left(\frac{dP/P}{dT}\right) = \frac{\Delta H_V}{RT^2} \cdot \qquad (2)$$

Given that $\left(\frac{dP}{dT}\right)$ = 15 mm/deg and using P = 760 mm Hg, Equation (2) becomes

$$\frac{15/760}{1 \text{ deg}} = \frac{\Delta H_V}{RT^2}$$

$$0.019736 = \frac{\Delta H_V}{RT^2} \qquad (3)$$

Since this liquid obeys Trouton's rule,

$$\frac{\Delta H_V}{T_b} = 21 \qquad (4)$$

Substituting 21 for $\frac{\Delta H_V}{T_b}$ in Equation (3) gives

$$0.019736 = \frac{21}{RT_b}$$

$$\therefore \quad T_b = \frac{21 \text{ cal}}{(1.98 \text{ cal } °K^{-1})(0.019736)}$$

$$T_b = 537\ °K = (537 - 273)°C = 264\ °C.$$

Applying Trouton's rule (Equation (4)) again, the ΔH_V is given by

$$\frac{\Delta H_V}{T_b} = 21$$

$$\therefore \quad \Delta H_V = 21(T_b)$$

$$= 21 \text{ cal}(537\ °K)\left(\frac{1 \text{ kcal}}{1000 \text{ cal}}\right)$$

$$\Delta H_V = 11.2 \text{ kcal}$$

Fig. 1 illustrates a set up for measuring the surface tension of a liquid. A manometer, M, is connected to the tube, T, so that the difference in pressure between the gas in the tube and atmospheric pressure can be measured. Given that the radius of the bubble coming out of the end of the tube placed just inside the surface of the liquid is R and the radius of the tube is r, a) show that the gas pressure is a maximum when R = r. b) Calculate the surface tension of the liquid at 25°C when the maximum pressure difference is 0.30 mm Hg. The density of the liquid and mecury are 1.5 g/cc and 13.6 g/cc respectively and the radius of the tube is 0.10 cm.

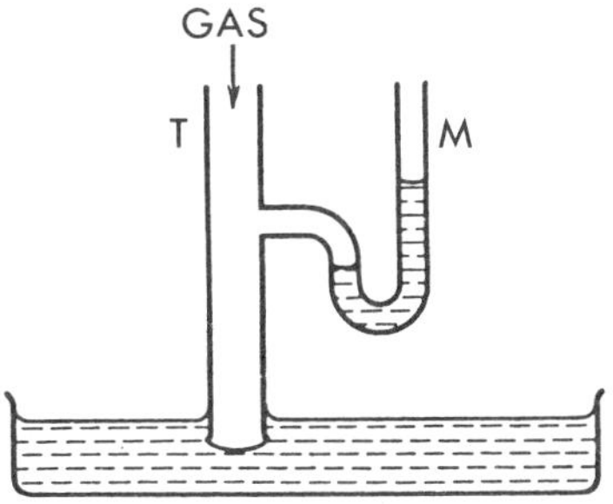

Fig. 1

Solution: Pressure is given by Laplace's equation

$$\Delta P = \frac{2\gamma}{R} \tag{1}$$

where γ is the surface tension and R is the radius of the bubble.

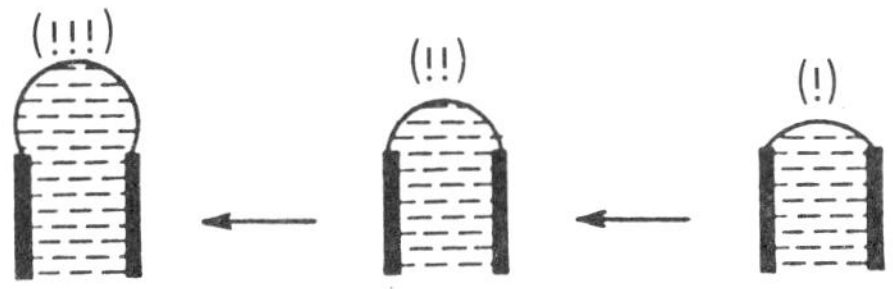

Fig. 2

Fig. 2 illustrates the stages in the formation of the bubble. As the gas pressure increases, the bubble starts forming as in Fig. 2 (i). The pressure will just be a maximum when the bubble is just hemispherical as in Fig. 2 (ii). At this point R = r.

We will now calculate the surface tension of the liquid using Equation (1) and to use this equation we must calculate, ΔP, the pressure exerted by the gas.

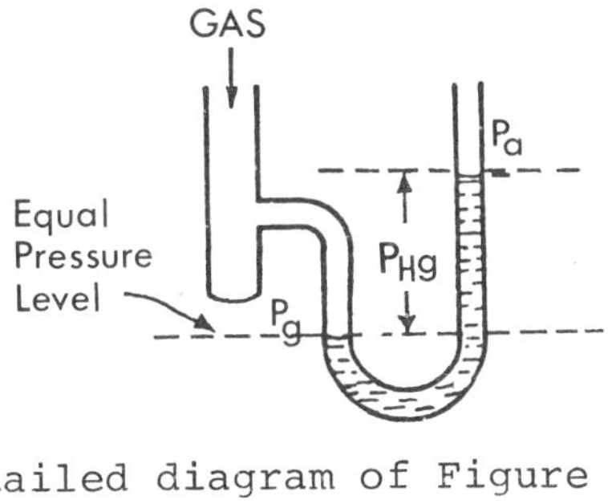

Fig. 3

Figure 3 is a detailed diagram of Figure 1 illustrating

the different pressures, where P_g = pressure of the gas, P_a = pressure of atmosphere and P_{Hg} is the pressure of mercury.

The difference between atmospheric and gas pressures is always equal to the difference in levels of mercury in the two legs of the manometer. So

$$h = 0.30 \text{ mm}$$

$$= 0.03 \text{ cm}.$$

But $$\Delta P = \rho_{Hg} gh$$

where ρ_{Hg} is the density of mercury, g is the acceleration due to gravity and h is the height of mercury.

$$\therefore \quad \Delta P = \frac{13.6 \text{ g}}{\text{cm}^3}\left(980 \frac{\text{cm}}{\text{sec}^2}\right)(0.03 \text{ cm})$$

$$= 400 \frac{\text{dynes}}{\text{cm}^2}$$

From Equation (1)

$$\gamma = \frac{(\Delta P) R}{2}$$

$$= \frac{\left(400 \frac{\text{dynes}}{\text{cm}^2}\right)(0.1 \text{ cm})}{2}$$

$$\gamma = 20 \text{ dynes/cm}.$$

• PROBLEM 8-40

The normal boiling point of benzophenone is 300°C. At 50°C its surface tension is estimated to be 45 ergs/cm^2. Calculate or estimate a) the heat of vaporization, b) the vapor pressure at 100°C c) the maximum bubble pressure of an air bubble blown in the liquid at 50°C using a 0.5 cm-diameter tube.

Solution: a) Since the normal boiling temperature is known, ΔH_V can be found using Trouton's rule. That is,

$$\frac{\Delta H_V}{T_b} = 21 \text{ cal mol}^{-1} \text{ K}^{-1}$$

$$\therefore \Delta H_V = 21(T_b)$$

$$= (21 \text{ cal °K}^{-1})(573 \text{ °K})\left(\frac{1 \text{ kcal}}{1000 \text{ cal}}\right)$$

$\therefore \Delta H_V = 12$ kcal

b) Now that we know ΔH_V, we can use the Clausius-Clapeyron equation to calculate the vapor pressure at 373°K

$$\therefore \quad \ln P_2 - \ln P_1 = \frac{\Delta H_V}{R}\left[\frac{1}{T_1} - \frac{1}{T_2}\right]$$

where P_2 refers to the vapor pressure at 373°K and T_2 is the temperature of 373°K

$$\therefore \quad \ln P_{373} - \ln P_{573} = \frac{12{,}000 \text{ cal}}{1.987 \text{ cal } °K^{-1}}\left(\frac{1}{573\ °K} - \frac{1}{373\ °K}\right) \quad (1)$$

The normal boiling point of benzophenone is 573°K and the vapor pressure at this boiling temperature is 1 atm. Thus $P_{573} = 1$ atm.

c) Substituting this into Equation (1),

$$\ln P_{373} - \ln 1 = \frac{12000}{1.987}\left(\frac{1}{573} - \frac{1}{373}\right)$$

$$= 6039.255(0.00175 - 0.00268)$$

$$= 6039.255(-0.000931)$$

$$\ln P_{373} - \ln 1 = -5.622$$

But $\quad \ln 1 = 0$

$$\therefore \quad \ln P_{373} = -5.622$$

Taking exponents of both sides,

$$P_{373} = e^{-5.622}$$

$$= 3.62(10^{-3})\text{atm.}$$

The surface tension of benzophenone is given to be 45 ergs cm^{-1}. Therefore the Laplace Equation can be used to find ΔP_{max}.

$\therefore \quad \Delta P = \frac{2\gamma}{R}$ where R is radius of the bubble. The ΔP is maximum when the bubble is just hemispherical. So, R = the radius of the tube, r.

$$\therefore \quad \Delta P_{max} = \frac{2\gamma}{r}$$

$$= \frac{2\left(\frac{45 \text{ ergs}}{\text{cm}^2}\text{cm}\right)}{0.25 \text{ cm}}$$

$$\Delta P_{max} = 360 \text{ dynes/cm}^2$$

The capillary rise for liquid A is 1.0 cm at 25°C. a) What will be the rise using the same capillary for liquid B given that liquid A has half the surface tension and twice the density of liquid B. b) How many times will the maximum bubble pressure for liquid B be greater than liquid A using the same tube for both liquids.

Solution: a) For most liquids that wet glass the height of a capillary rise is given by the relation

$$\rho gh = \frac{2\gamma}{r} \qquad (1)$$

where γ is the surface tension and h is the height of capillary rise. From Equation (1) then, h is proportional to $\frac{\gamma}{\rho}$ and the proportionality constant is $\frac{2}{gr}$ (since we are using the same capillary for both liquids). Therefore,

$$h_A \propto \frac{\gamma_A}{\rho_A}$$

but B has twice the surface tension and half the density of liquid A, so

$$h_B \propto \frac{2\gamma_A}{0.5\rho_A}$$

Combining h_A and h_B yields

$$h_B = 4h_A$$

b) The maximum bubble pressure, ΔP, is given by

$$\Delta P = \frac{2\gamma}{r}$$

$\Delta P_A = \frac{2\gamma_A}{r} = g\rho_A h_A$ and $\Delta P_B = \frac{2\gamma_B}{r} = g\rho_B h_B$. Now, the ratio of ΔP_A to ΔP_B is given by:

$$\frac{\Delta P_A}{\Delta P_B} = \frac{2\gamma_A/r}{2\gamma_B/r} = \frac{g\rho_A h_A}{g\rho_B h_B} = \frac{\rho_A h_A}{\rho_B h_B} .$$

It is known that $h_B = 4h_A$ and $\rho_A = 2\rho_B$. So, substituting these values in the expression yields:

$$\frac{\Delta P_A}{\Delta P_B} = \frac{\rho_A h_A}{\left(\frac{1}{2}\rho_A\right) 4h_A} = \frac{\rho_A h_A}{2\rho_A h_A} = \frac{1}{2}.$$

Hence $\Delta P_A = \frac{1}{2}\Delta P_B$ and ∴ the pressure will be twice as much for liquid B as for liquid A.

• PROBLEM 8-42

In figure 1, water which wets glass rises to a height, h, in a capillary tube placed in the water. Will the water spill over if the capillary tube is cut into half its length above the water surface? Use sketches to support your analysis.

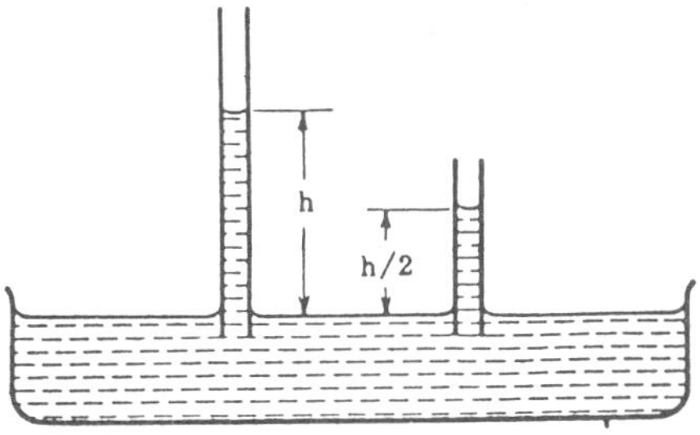

Fig. 1

Solution: In figure 2, both capillary tubes are shown. When the tube is cut in half as in Figure (ii) the miniscus will flatten out until its radius of curvature is half of what it was. Thus, there is a pressure drop across the meniscus which will equal the pressure drop along the column of the liquid; that is, the two pressures are in hydrostatic balance.

Hence, the liquid will not spill over when the tube is cut in half.

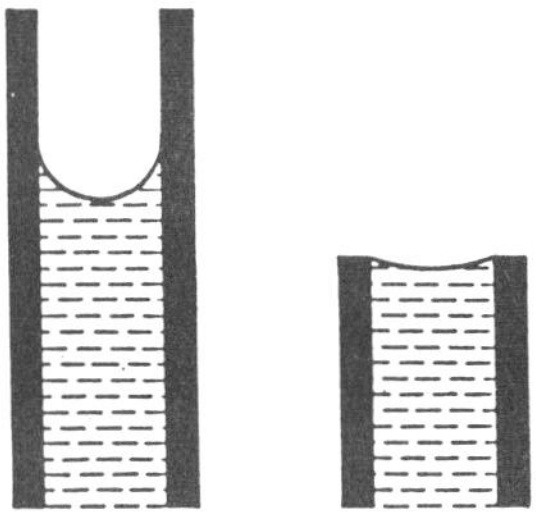

Fig. 2

• PROBLEM 8-43

In Figure 1, one end of an S-shaped capillary tube of uniform radius of 0.050 cm is immersed in a liquid whose surface tension and density are, 25 dynes/cm and 0.80 g/cc, respectively. Calculate or explain what the values of P_1, P_2, P_3, P_4 and P_5 must be, given that the external atmospheric pressure is 10^6 dynes/cm^2 and that the liquid wets the capillary tube.

Solution: Given that the liquid wets the capillary tube, a continous process of decreasing and increasing the free surface of the liquid will occur until the surface tension force acting upward is equal to the force due to the column of liquid in the capillary tube acting downward.

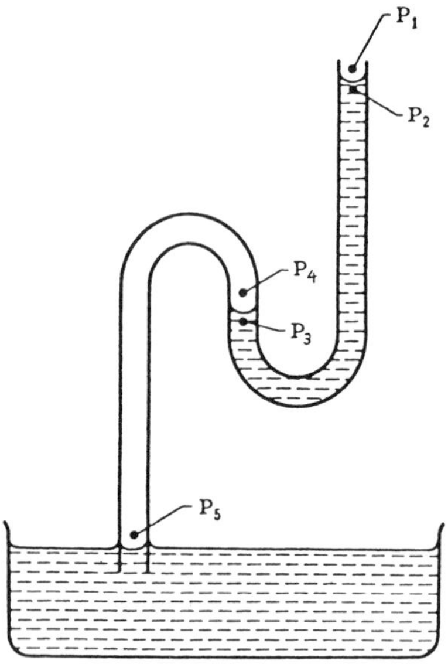

Fig. 1

$$\therefore \quad 2\pi r\gamma \cos\theta = \pi r^2 h\rho g$$

where r = radius of capillary tube

γ = surface tension

$h\rho g = \Delta P$

θ = contact angle with the vertical

$$\therefore \quad 2\pi r\gamma \cos\theta = \pi r^2 \Delta P$$

For most liquids that wet glass θ is approximately zero and thus $\cos\theta = 1$

$$\therefore \quad 2\pi r\gamma = \pi r^2 \Delta P$$

Solving for ΔP yields

$$\Delta P = \frac{2\pi r\gamma}{\pi r^2}$$

or $$\Delta P = \frac{2\gamma}{r}$$

$$= \frac{2(25 \text{ dynes cm}^{-1})}{0.050 \text{ cm}}$$

$$\Delta P = 1000 \text{ dynes/cm}^2$$

This is the pressure drop across the meniscus. P_1 is only the atmospheric pressure

$$P_1 = 10^6 \text{ dynes/cm}^2$$

We calculated $\Delta P = 1000$ dynes/cm^2

$$\Delta P = P_1 - P_2 = 1000 \text{ dynes/cm}^2$$

$$P_2 = P_1 - 1000$$

$$= (10^6 - 1000)\text{dynes/cm}^2$$

$$\therefore \quad P_2 = 0.999 \times 10^6 \text{ dynes/cm}^2.$$

P_5 which is just above the bottom meniscus is

1.001×10^6 dynes/cm^2. That is $(1000 + 10^6)$ dynes/cm^2. If the hydrostatic drop in air pressure along the capillary tube is neglected, then $P_5 = P_4$

$$\therefore \quad P_4 = 1.001 \times 10^6 \text{ dynes/cm}^2$$

$$P_4 - P_3 = \Delta P = 1000$$

$$\therefore \quad P_3 = P_4 - 1000$$

$$= (1.001 \times 10^6 - 1000)\text{dynes/cm}^2$$

$$P_3 = 1.000 \times 10^6 \text{ dynes/cm}^2$$

PHASE DIAGRAMS

• PROBLEM 8-44

The temperature-composition phase diagram for the 2-component system A-B at P = 1 atm is given. 200 g of a mixture of A and B boiling initially at 65°C is distilled until the boiling point of the residue remaining in the still reaches 75°C.

a) What is the composition of the residue?
b) What is the composition of the total distillate?
c) What is the weight of the total distillate?

Solution: The composition of the residue is obtained by using the lower (liquid) curve and that of the distillate is obtained by using the upper (vapor) curve.

a) The mixture boils initially at 65°C. The residue at this point is represented by the L composition of about 50% A and the distillate by the V composition of about 91% A.

Starting at the L curve and 65°C, trace the vertical

line of this composition (about 50% A) until the required temperature is reached (75°C in this case). Since the lower curve gives the information about the composition of the residue, the tie-line (horizontal line) at 75° isotherm indicates that the composition of the residue is 20% A.

b) The composition of the total distillate can be obtained by taking the average of composition of the distillate (measured from the V curve) at 65°C and 75°C.

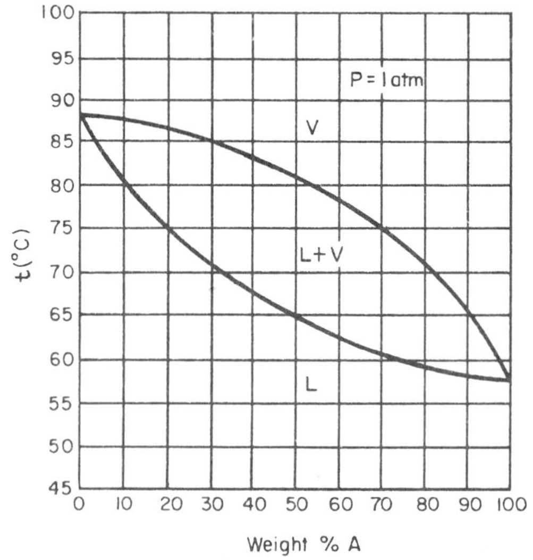

Composition of distillate at 65°C $\simeq$ 91%A

Composition of distillate at 75°C $\simeq$ 71%A

$$\text{Therefore composition of total distillate} = \frac{91 + 71}{2} = \frac{162}{2} = 81\%\text{A}$$

c) This can be calculated by using the overall material balance and also the component A balance. This will give two unknowns and two equations.

Let w_R = weight of residue

w_D = weight of distillate

By the overall balance,

$$w_R + w_D = 200 \qquad (1)$$

Recall that the initial mixture was at about 50%A. Therefore by the component A balance,

$$0.20\ w_R + 0.81\ w_D = 0.50(200) = 100 \qquad (2)$$

From Equation (1), $w_R = 200 - w_D$. Substituting for w_R in Equation (2),

$$0.20(200 - w_D) + 0.81\ w_D = 100$$

$$40 - .20\ w_D + .81\ w_D = 100$$

Therefore $0.61\ w_D = 60$

$$w_D = \frac{60}{0.61} = 98.36\ g.$$

• PROBLEM 8-45

The figure gives the boiling points of A-B mixtures at one atm. A liquid mixture consisting of 60 weight percent A and 40 weight percent B is placed in a closed container of variable volume. The pressure is kept constant at 1 atm, while the temperature and volume are so adjusted that one half the mixture (by weight) vaporizes. Estimate the temperature and the composition of each phase.

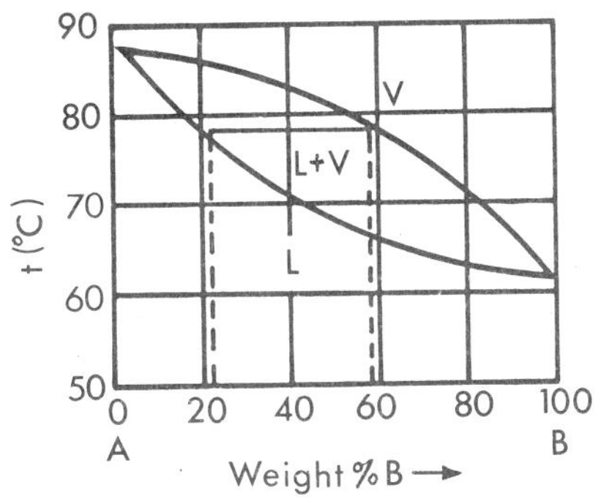

Solution: This can be solved by inspection. Since the mixture is 40% B, a vertical line at this composition is traced until the distance between the L line and this composition (40% B) is equal to the distance between this composition and the V line. This means that 1/2 of the mixture is vapor and 1/2 is liquid. The temperature is about 77°C.

A tie-line is constructed at this isotherm. The liquid composition is about 21% B and that of the vapor is about 59% B.

• PROBLEM 8-46

Figure 1 is a diagram for two substances that show partial miscibility with each other in the solid state. This type of diagram results from the ability of one substance to penetrate the empty spaces, etc., of the lattice of the other. There are limitations on this type of solubility and the maximum is indicated by the curved lines enclosing areas #1 and #4. Identify the phases present in the numbered areas.

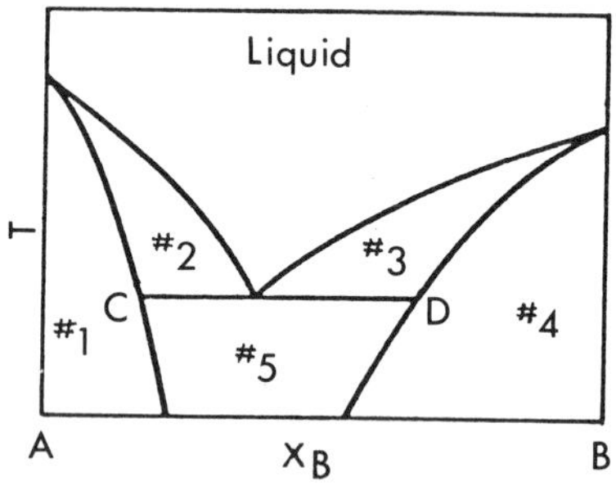

Solution: This is a T vs x_B plot where T = temperature and x_B = composition of component B. The points A and B represent pure A and pure B respectively. The horizontal line between points C and D is called a tie line. The composition of the liquid and solid phases in equilibrium with each other is given by the ends of the tie line. Thus the liquid and solid solution of component B in saturated component A are in equilibrium in area #2. Also the liquid and solid solution of component A in saturated component B are in equilibrium in area #3. In area #5, solid solution of B in saturated A and solid solution of A in saturated B are in equilibrium. Areas #1 and #4 are single phase regions. They consist of unsaturated solid solution of B in A and of A in B respectively.

• PROBLEM 8-47

Consider a liquid-liquid system containing 10.0 kg of A and 5.0 kg of B at a temperature such that two phases are present, one with $(\text{wt\% B})_1$ = 10.0% and the other with $(\text{wt\% B})_2$ = 40.0%. Calculate the masses of the two phases in equilibrium.

Solution: $(\text{wt\% B})_{AB}$ = weight % of component B in the A-B

$$\text{system} = \frac{5.0 \text{ kg}}{5.0 \text{ kg} + 10.0 \text{ kg}}$$

$$= .333 \text{ or } 33.3\%$$

The respective masses of these two phases can be determined by use of the relation

$$\frac{m_1}{m_2} = \frac{(\text{wt\% B})_2 - (\text{wt\% B})_{AB}}{(\text{wt\% B})_{AB} - (\text{wt\% B})_1} \quad (1)$$

where $(\text{wt\% B})_2$ = weight % of B in Phase 2

$(\text{wt\% B})_1$ = weight % of B in Phase 1

m_1 = mass of Phase 1

m_2 = mass of Phase 2

Also by material balance,

$$m_1 + m_2 = m_{AB} \quad (2)$$

Here m_{AB} = mass of A and B, which is = 15 kg. Now there are two equations and two unknowns. If the equations are solved simultaneously, we can find m_1 and m_2. Thus,

$$\frac{m_1}{m_2} = \frac{40.0 - 33.3}{33.3 - 10.0} = \frac{6.7}{23.3} = 0.288 \quad (1)$$

$$m_1 + m_2 = 15 \text{ kg} \quad (2)$$

In equation (1), $m_1 = (0.288)(m_2)$. If this is substituted in equation (2), we have

$$0.288m_2 + m_2 = 15 \text{ kg}$$

$$m_2(0.288 + 1) = 15 \text{ kg}$$

$$\therefore \quad m_2 = \frac{15 \text{ kg}}{1.288} = 11.646 \text{ kg.}$$

Using equation (2) and solving for m_1, we have $m_1 + 11.646 = 15$.

$$\therefore \quad m_1 = 15 - 11.646 = 3.354 \text{ kg.}$$

Note that the same answers would be found had the component A balance been used, where

$(\text{wt\% A})_{AB} = \frac{10}{10 + 5} = .67$ or 67%, $(\text{wt\% A})_2 = 100 - 40 = 60\%$,

$(\text{wt\% A})_1 = 100 - 10 = 90\%$ and $\frac{m_1}{m_2} = \frac{(\text{wt\% A})_2 - (\text{wt\% A})_{AB}}{(\text{wt\% A})_{AB} - (\text{wt\% A})_1}$

This together with equation (2) can now be used to get the same values for m_1 and m_2 as above.

• **PROBLEM 8-48**

Identify the areas labelled A, B. C in Figure 1 of a pure substance. (P denotes vapor pressure except for the line between areas A and B for which it denotes external pressure.)

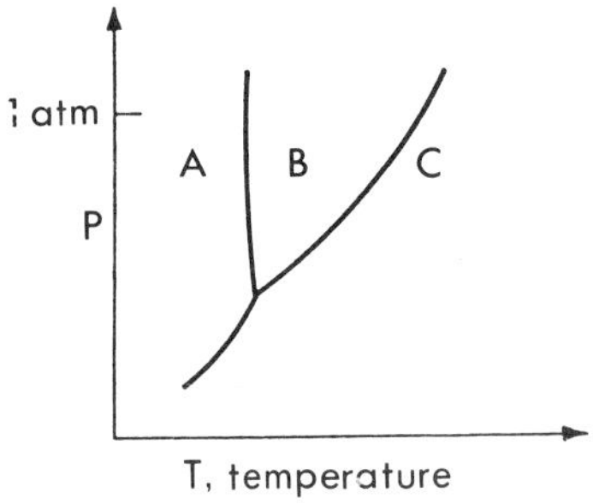

Fig. 1

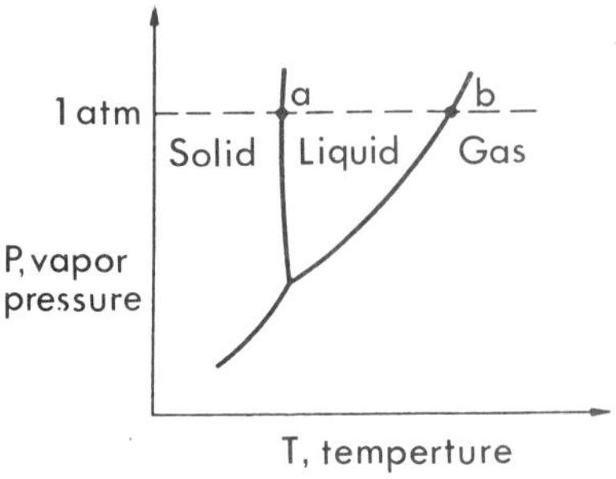

Fig. 2

Solution: If one maintains a constant pressure, say 1 atm, as indicated in Figure 2 and starting at a low temperature to a high temperature, the dashed line of Figure 2 is traced out. Because one is moving from a low to a high temperature, it is logical to say that areas A, B, C corresponds to solid phase, liquid phase and gas phase respectively. Point a indicates the freezing point of the substance and point b, the boiling point.

• **PROBLEM 8-49**

Consider the hypothetical phase diagram shown in Fig. 1. In such a diagram certain areas will be one-phase areas and others will be two-phase areas. The compositions of the phases in equilibrium in the two-phase areas will be determined by horizontal "tie lines." What would be the masses of the phases for a system containing 0.050 kg of A and 0.050 kg of B in equilibrium if $(\text{wt\% B})_1 = 30.0\%$ and $(\text{wt\% B})_2 = 85.5\%$?

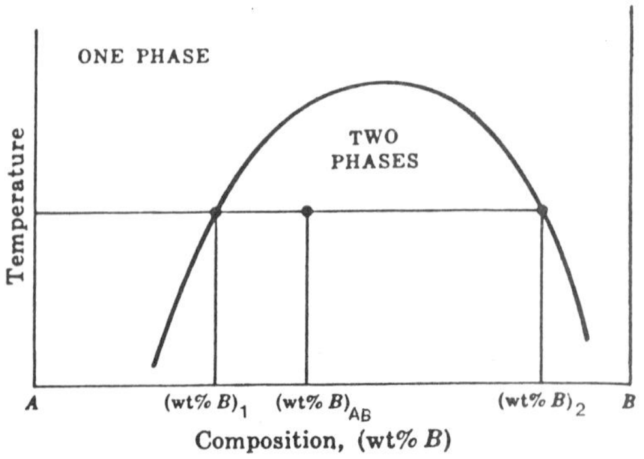

Fig. 1

Solution: By material balance,

$$m_1 + m_2 = m_{AB} \tag{1}$$

where m_1 = mass of Phase 1

m_2 = mass of Phase 2

m_{AB} = mass of components A and B, which is

0.050 kg + 0.050 kg = 0.100 kg.

Also, $\dfrac{(\text{wt\% B})_2 - (\text{wt\% B})_{AB}}{(\text{wt\% B})_{AB} - (\text{wt\% B})_1} = \dfrac{m_1}{m_2}$ by component B balance.

(This could be done for component A also). $(\text{wt\% B})_2$ = wt% B in Phase 2.

$(\text{wt\% B})_{AB}$ = wt% B in A-B system

$(\text{wt\% B})_1$ = wt% B in Phase 1

$$(\text{wt\% B})_{AB} = \frac{\text{wt. of B}}{\text{wt. of B + wt. of A}} = \frac{0.050}{0.050 + 0.050}$$

$$= 0.500 = 50.0\%$$

$$\therefore \quad \frac{m_1}{m_2} = \frac{85.5 - 50.0}{50.0 - 30.0} = \frac{35.5}{20.0} = 1.775$$

Now, there are two equations and two unknowns:

$$m_1 + m_2 = 0.100$$

$$\frac{m_1}{m_2} = 1.775$$

Upon solving them simultaneously,

m_1 = 0.064 kg and m_2 = 0.036 kg.

• PROBLEM 8-50

Describe the changes in the system shown in Fig. 1 as salt B is added to a solution of composition given by point 1.

Solution: The line between Point 1 and Vertex B represents addition of pure B to the solution of composition given by Point 1. As we add B to the solution, the system gets richer in B and less rich in A and C. If enough B is added for the bulk concentration to reach Point 2, solid B becomes a second phase in equilibirum with a solution phase of composition given by Point 2. If we add more B, the composition does not change but the relative amounts do, indicating saturation.

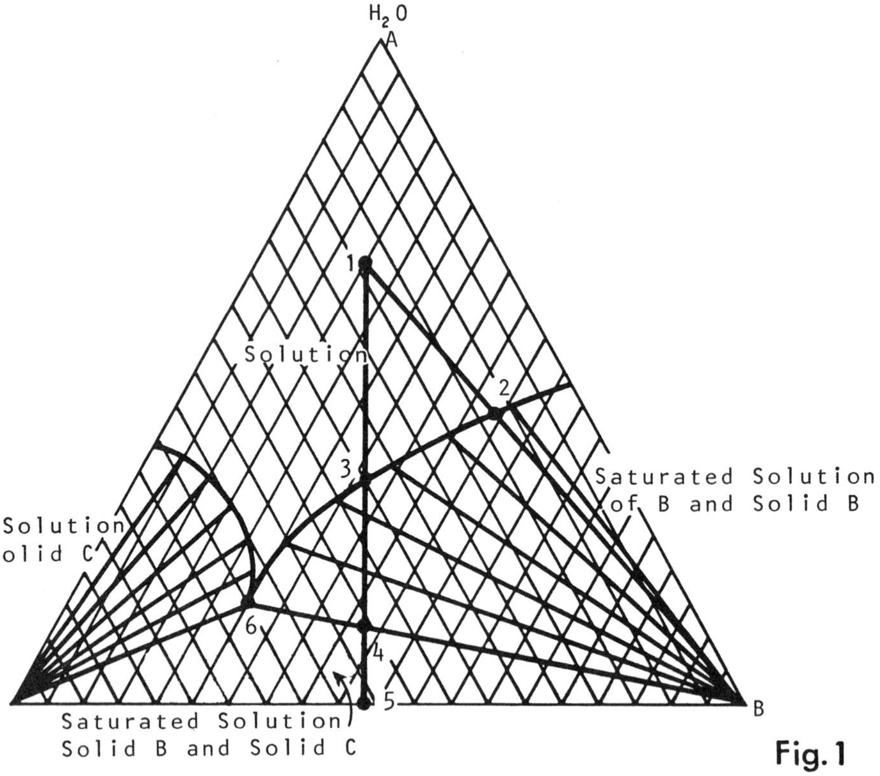

Fig. 1

PHASE EQUILIBRIUM

• PROBLEM 8-51

The system n-propanol-water under atmospheric pressure forms an azeotrope containing 43.2 mole % of 1-propanol. The boiling point of the azeotrope is 87.8°C. Using the van Laar equation and no additional equilibrium data, calculate the y-x equilibrium curve for this system and compare your results with those of the experimental data. $P^\circ_{H_2O} = 483$ mm Hg and $P^\circ_{prop} = 524$ mm Hg.

Solution: The azeotropic point is the point where both the compositions in the vapor and liquid phases are the same. That is, y = x, where y = composition of the vapor phase and x = composition of the liquid phase.

If the vapor phase is assumed to be an ideal gas, then

$$\gamma_1 = \frac{P}{P^\circ_1} \quad \text{and} \quad \gamma_2 = \frac{P}{P^\circ_2} \tag{1}$$

where γ_1 = activity coefficient of n-propanol

γ_2 = activity coefficient of water

P_1° = vapor pressure of n-propanol

P_2° = vapor pressure of water

P = total pressure

Using Equation (1) and a total pressure of 760 mm Hg,

$$\gamma_1 = \frac{760}{524} \quad \text{and} \quad \gamma_2 = \frac{760}{483}.$$

Therefore, $\gamma_1 = 1.451$

and $\gamma_2 = 1.575$

The Van Laar equation is

$$\ell n\ \gamma_1 = \frac{A_{12}}{\left[1 + \frac{A_{12}x_1}{B_{12}x_2}\right]^2}$$

and $$\ell n\ \gamma_2 = \frac{B_{12}}{\left[1 + \frac{B_{12}x_2}{A_{12}x_1}\right]^2}$$

where A_{12} and B_{12} are the Van Laar constants.

Since the activity coefficients have been calculated at $x_1 = 0.432$, the Van Laar constants can be solved for by solving the two equations. There are two unknowns, A_{12} and B_{12}. Therefore,

$$A_{12} = \ell n\ \gamma_1 \left[1 + \frac{x_2\ \ell n\ \gamma_2}{x_1\ \ell n\ \gamma_1}\right]^2$$

and $$B_{12} = \ell n\ \gamma_2 \left[1 + \frac{x_1\ \ell n\ \gamma_1}{x_2\ \ell n\ \gamma_2}\right]^2$$

Substituting the respective numerical values gives

$$A_{12} = (0.372)\left[1 + \frac{(0.568)(0.454)}{(0.432)(0.372)}\right]^2$$

$$= 2.523$$

and $$B_{12} = (0.455)\left[1 + \frac{(0.432)(0.372)}{(0.568)(0.454)}\right]^2$$

$$= 1.198$$

The compositions in the vapor and liquid phases are related to each other by

$$y_1 = \frac{\gamma_1 x_1 P_1^\circ}{P} \quad \text{and} \quad y_2 = \frac{\gamma_2 x_2 P_2^\circ}{P}$$

$$\therefore \quad \frac{y_1}{y_2} = \left(\frac{\gamma_1 x_1 P_1^\circ}{P}\right)\left(\frac{P}{\gamma_2 x_2 P_2^\circ}\right) = \frac{\gamma_1 x_1 P_1^\circ}{\gamma_2 x_2 P_2^\circ}$$

But $\quad y_2 = 1 - y_1 \quad$ and $\quad x_2 = 1 - x_1$

$$\therefore \quad \frac{y_1}{y_2} = \frac{y_1}{1 - y_1} = \frac{\gamma_1 x_1 P_1^\circ}{\gamma_2 (1 - x_1) P_2^\circ}$$

or

$$y_1 = \frac{(1-y_1)\gamma_1 x_1 P_1^\circ}{\gamma_2 (1-x_1) P_2^\circ} = \frac{1}{1 + \left(\frac{\gamma_2}{\gamma_1}\right)\left(\frac{P_2^\circ}{P_1^\circ}\right)\left(\frac{1}{x_1} - 1\right)} \tag{2}$$

The $\left(\frac{P_2^\circ}{P_1^\circ}\right)$ is very nearly constant over the temperature range; therefore the calculations are made easier. For example, $\left(\frac{P_2^\circ}{P_1^\circ}\right)$ at 87.8°C is 0.922 and at 97.8°C it is also 0.922. Now, using the constant value of $\frac{P_2^\circ}{P_1^\circ}$, x_1, γ_1 and γ_2 at a given temperature, y_1 is calculated. The two extremes are $x_1 = 0$ and $x_1 = 1$. Also, the temperature extremes are the boiling points of the substances. That is, temperatures are so chosen to be between the boiling points.

As an example, at the azeotrope $x_1 = 0.432$, $\gamma_1 = 1.451$, $\gamma_2 = 1.575$, $\frac{P_2^\circ}{P_1^\circ} = 0.922$. Therefore

$$y_1 = \frac{1}{1 + \left(\frac{\gamma_2}{\gamma_1}\right)\left(\frac{P_2^\circ}{P_1^\circ}\right)\left(\frac{1}{x_1} - 1\right)} = \frac{1}{1 + \left(\frac{1.575}{1.451}\right)(0.922)\left(\frac{1}{0.432} - 1\right)}$$

$$= \frac{1}{1 + (1.085)(.922)(1.3148)}$$

$$y_1 = 0.432$$

The values tabulated below are computed in a similar manner.

1-Propanol-Water System

x_1	γ_1	γ_2	y_1 Calculated	y_1 Experimental	Per Cent Error
0.00	12.6	1.000	0.000	0.000	0.0
0.10	5.22	1.044	0.376	0.372	+0.7
0.20	2.95	1.155	0.409	0.392	+4.3
0.30	2.00	1.311	0.415	0.404	+2.7
0.40	1.545	1.508	0.425	0.424	+0.2
0.432	1.451	1.575	0.432	0.432	0.0
0.50	1.297	1.737	0.447	0.452	-0.1
0.60	1.157	2.000	0.484	0.492	-0.2
0.70	1.074	2.290	0.542	0.551	-0.2
0.80	1.029	2.605	0.632	0.641	-0.1
0.90	1.006	2.940	0.769	0.778	-0.1
1.00	1.000	3.300	1.000	1.000	0.0

• **PROBLEM** 8-52

At 298 K, the standard heat of combustion of diamond is 395.3 $kJ \cdot mol^{-1}$, and that of graphite is 393.4 $kJ \cdot mol^{-1}$. The molar entropies are 2.439 and 5.694 $J \cdot K^{-1} \cdot mol^{-1}$, respectively. Find $\Delta G°$ for the transition graphite → diamond at 298 K and 1 atm. The densities are 3.513 $g \cdot cm^{-3}$ for diamond and 2.260$g \cdot cm^{-3}$ for graphite. Assuming densities and ΔH_s are independent of pressure, calculate the pressures at which diamond and graphite would be in equilibrium at 298 and 1300 K.

Solution: By definition,

$$\Delta G° = \Delta H°_{c(dia)} - \Delta H°_{c(gr)} - T\left(S°_{dia} - S°_{gr}\right)$$

where $\Delta G°$ = free energy change

ΔH_c = heat of combustion

S = entropy.

The subscripts gr and dia denote graphite and diamond respectively. Therefore $\Delta G°$ at 298°K is

$$\Delta G°_{298} = (395.3 - 393.4)\frac{kJ}{mole} - 298(2.439 - 5.694)10^{-3}\ \frac{kJ}{mole}$$

$$= 1.9 - (-969.99)(10^{-3}) = 1.9 + \frac{969.99}{10^3}$$

$$\therefore \quad \Delta G°_{298} = (1.9 + .9699)kJ/mole$$

$$= 2.870 \frac{kJ}{mole} = 2870 \text{ J/mole}$$

Using the relation $\Delta P = P_{eq} - P_1 = \frac{\Delta G_{eq}}{\Delta V} - \frac{\Delta G_1}{\Delta V}$,

$$P_{eq} = \frac{\Delta G_{eq} - \Delta G_1}{\Delta V} + P_1$$

where $P_1 = 1 \text{ atm} = 1.0133(10^5)\text{N/m}^2$ and

the subscript eq. means at equilibrium. But

$$\Delta V = \left(\frac{1}{\rho_{dia}} - \frac{1}{\rho_{gr}}\right) M \times 10^{-6}$$

Here ρ = density

$M = 12$ g/mole

$$P_{eq} = \frac{(0 - 2870)\text{J/mole}}{\left(\frac{1}{3.513 \text{ g/cm}^3} - \frac{1}{2.260 \text{ g/cm}^3}\right) \times 12 \frac{g}{mole}} + 1.0133 \times 10^5 \text{N/m}^2$$

$$= \frac{-2870 \text{ J/mole}}{\left(.2847 \frac{cm^3}{g} - .4425 \frac{cm^3}{g}\right) \times 12 \frac{g}{mole}} + 1.0133 \times 10^5 \text{N/m}^2$$

$$= \frac{-2870 \text{ J/mole}}{-1.894 \text{ cm}^3\text{/mole}} + 1.0133 \times 10^5 \text{ N/m}^2$$

$$= 1515.43 \text{ J/cm}^3 + 1.0133 \times 10^5 \text{ N/m}^2$$

But $1N = 1 \text{ kgm/sec}^2$ and $1J = 1 \text{ kgm}^2\text{/sec}^2$ so $1J = 1$ Nm. So

$$P_{eq} = \frac{1515.43 \text{ J}}{cm^3} \times \left(\frac{100 \text{ cm}}{m}\right)^3 + 1.0133(10^5)\text{N/m}^2$$

$$= 1.5154(10^9)\text{J/m}^3 + 1.0133(10^5)\text{N/m}^2$$

$$= 1.5154(10^9)\frac{Nm}{m^3} + 1.0133(10^5)\text{N/m}^2 = 1.5155(10^9)\text{N/m}^2$$

This is the P_{eq} at 298°K.

At 1300 K, $\Delta G°$ is found by using ΔC_p (as a function of temperature) to find $\Delta H°$ and then using the relation

$$\frac{\partial \frac{\Delta G°}{T}}{\partial T} = - \frac{\Delta H°}{T^2}$$

to calculate $\Delta G°$.

$$C_{P(dia)} = 9.056 + 12.815 \times 10^{-3}T - 5.4573 \times 10^{5}T^{-2} \qquad (1)$$

$$C_{P(gr)} = 11.193 + 10.965 \times 10^{-3}T - 4.8965 \times 10^{5}T^{-2} \qquad (2)$$

These expressions can be found in the literature. If (2) is subtracted from (1), then

$$\Delta C_P = -2.137 + 1.850 \times 10^{-3}T - 0.5608 \times 10^{5}T^{-2}.$$

By definition,

$$\Delta H° = \Delta H_0° + \int \Delta C_P \, dT$$

$$\Delta H° = \Delta H_0° + \int - 2.137 + 1.850(10^{-3})T - .5608(10^{5})T^{-2} \, dT$$

$$= \Delta H_0° + (-2.137T) + \frac{1.850(10^{-3})}{2}T^2 + \frac{.5608(10^5)}{T}$$

when T = 298.15°K, $\Delta H° = +395300 - 393400 = 1900$ J/mole

$$1900 \text{ J/mole} = \Delta H_0° + [-2.137(298.15)] + \frac{1.850(10^{-3})}{2}(298.15)^2$$

$$+ \frac{.5608(10^3)}{298.15}$$

$$1900 \text{ J/mole} = \Delta H_0° + (-366.83) \text{ J/mole}$$

$\Delta H_0° = 2267$ J/mole. This is the enthalpy of the reference state. Therefore,

$$\Delta H° = 2267 - 2.137T + 0.925 \times 10^{-3}T^2 + 0.5608 \times 10^{5}T^{-1}$$

Using $\dfrac{\partial \frac{\Delta G°}{T}}{\partial T} = -\dfrac{\Delta H°}{T^2}$,

$$\frac{\partial \frac{\Delta G°}{T}}{\partial T} = -2267T^{-2} + 2.137T^{-1} - 0.925 \times 10^{-3} - 0.5608 \times 10^{5}T^{-3}$$

Integrating both sides and multiplying by T yields

$$\Delta G° = 2267 + 2.137T \ln T - 0.925 \times 10^{-3}T^2 + 0.2804 \times 10^{5}T^{-1}$$

$$+ CT$$

where C is an integration constant. Using the condition $\Delta G° = 2870$ at 298°K,

$$C = -10.19$$

Therefore at 1300°K,

$$\Delta G° = 2267 + 2.137(1300)\ln 1300 - 0.925 \times 10^{-3}(1300)^2$$

$$+ \frac{0.2804 \times 10^5}{1300} + (-10.19)(1300)$$

$$= 2267 + 19919.3 - 1563.25 + 21.569 - 13247$$

$$= 7397.6 \text{ J/mole}$$

Now P_{eq} at 1300 K

$$= \frac{0 - 7397.6 \text{ J/mole}}{-1.894 \text{ cm}^3\text{/mole} \times \left(\frac{1 \text{ m}}{100 \text{ cm}}\right)^3} + 1.0133(10^5)\text{N/m}^2$$

$$= 3906(10^6)\text{N/m}^2 = 3.906(10^9)\text{N/m}^2$$

CHAPTER 9

ELECTROCHEMISTRY

CONDUCTANCE

• PROBLEM 9-1

A moving boundary experiment was performed at 25°C with 0.100 M KCl on the bottom and (initially) 0.0700 M NaCl on top. The transport numbers of K+ and Na+ in these solutions are 0.490 and 0.388, respectively. The boundary moved downward. The cross-sectional area of the tube was 0.100cm^2. The charge passed through was 96.5 coulombs.

(a) How far did the boundary move?

(b) While the current was flowing, what was the concentration of NaCl just above the boundary?

Solution: a) Suppose the boundary moves a distance D for the passage of Q coulombs, then by definition,

$$D = \frac{\text{volume swept out by boundary}}{\text{cross-sectional area of the tube}} . \tag{1}$$

Before this relation can be used, the volume swept out by the boundary needs to be known.

The number of equivalents transported is $\frac{Q}{F}$, of which $\frac{t_+ Q}{F}$ are carried by the positive ion. Here t_+ is the fraction of the current carried by the positive ion in solution and is called the transport or transference number of the positive ion. C is the concentration in equivalents per cm^3, thus the volume swept out by the boundary during the passage of Q coulombs is calculated by the relation

$$V = \frac{t_{K^+} Q/F}{C_{K^+}} \tag{2}$$

In equation (2) t_{K^+} = transport number of K^+

C_{K^+} = concentration of the K^+ ions in equivalents per cubic centimeter

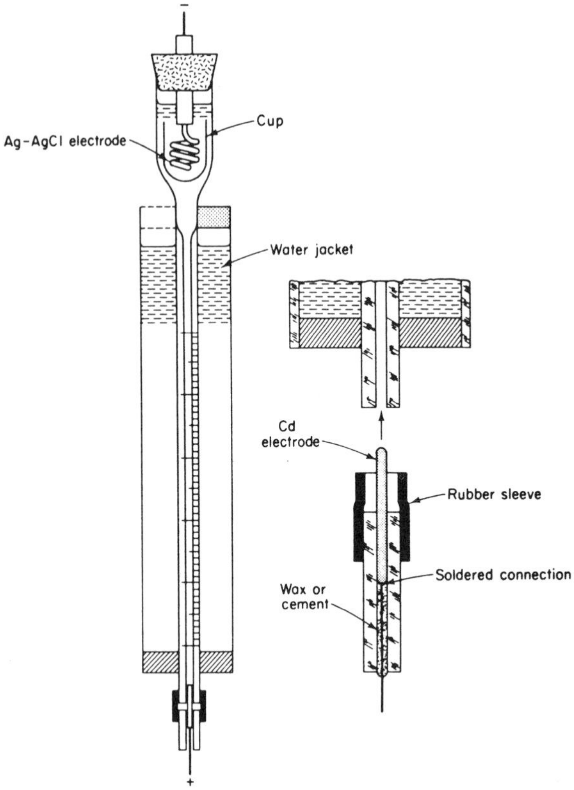

Cell for measurement of transference number by the moving boundary method.

As a result of fixing the units of C_{K^+}, its value is 1.00×10^{-4} eq cm^{-3}. This is obtained from 0.100 M KCl by the following

$$0.100\ \frac{\text{moles K}^+}{\ell} \times \frac{1\ \text{eq}}{\text{mole}} \times \frac{1\ell}{1000\text{ml}} \times \frac{1\ \text{ml}}{\text{cm}^3}\ .$$

F = Faraday's constant.

The Q/F term can be calculated as follows:

$$Q/F = \frac{96.5\ \text{coulombs}}{96500\ \text{coulombs Faraday}^{-1}}$$

$$= 1.00 \times 10^{-3}\ \text{Faraday} \times \frac{1\ \text{eq}}{\text{Faraday}} = 1\left(10^{-3}\right)\text{eq}.$$

Solving for V gives

$$V = \frac{(0.490)\left(1.00 \times 10^{-3}\right)\text{eq}}{\left(1.00 \times 10^{-4}\right)\ \frac{\text{eq}}{\text{cm}^3}}$$

$$= 4.90\ \text{cm}^3$$

If a = 0.100 cm^2 is the cross-sectional area of the tube, then the distance travelled by the boundary using equation (1) is

$$D = \frac{4.90\ cm^3}{0.100\ cm^2}$$

$$= 49.0\ cm$$

b) While the current was flowing, the distance travelled by the K^+ ions is the same as the distance travelled by the Na^+ ions. Therefore, D is the same for both of them. Likewise, the volume swept out by the boundary remains the same value.

Thus equation (1) gives

$$4.90 = \frac{t_{Na^+} Q/F}{C_{Na^+}}$$

Note also that the Q/F remains the same. t_{Na^+} is given to be 0.388. Therefore,

$$4.90 = \frac{(0.388)(1.00 \times 10^{-3})}{C_{Na^+}} ,$$

from which C_{Na^+} can be computed as follows:

$$C_{Na^+} = \frac{(0.388)(1.00 \times 10^{-3})}{4.90}$$

$$= 7.92 \times 10^{-5}\ eq\ cm^{-3}$$

or $$= 7.92 \times 10^{-2}\ mol\ liter^{-1} .$$

• PROBLEM 9-2

The moving boundary technique was used to determine t_+ in 0.0100 N HCl at 25° C. A current of 3.00 mA was passed through the cell having a cross-sectional area of 3.25 cm^2 for 45.0 min and the observed boundary moved 2.13 cm. Using these data, and given that $\Lambda = 412.00\ cm^2 mol^{-1} \Omega^{-1}$, find U_- (anionic mobility) and U_+ (cationic mobility).

Solution:

(1) $$U_+ = \frac{L}{t\left(\frac{dE}{dL}\right)} ,$$ (2) $$t_+ = \frac{U_+}{U_+ + U_-}$$

(3) $$\frac{dE}{dL} = \frac{I}{SK}$$ and (4) $$K = \Lambda 1000c$$

where

L = distance (in meters) that the moving boundary moves

t = time (in seconds)

t_+ = transference (transport) number

dE/dL = electric field strength

S = area

K = A constant

I = current (in amperes)

Λ = equivalent conductance

c = concentration

The above equations are being used because of the information (data) given in the problem. The dE/dL term cannot be calculated without knowing K. To get K equation (4) is used.

$$\Lambda = 412 \frac{cm^2}{mol\,\Omega} \times \frac{1\ mol}{eq} \times \frac{1\ m^2}{(100\ cm)^2} = .0412 \frac{m^2}{eq\ \Omega}.$$

The purpose of 1000 is to convert liters to cubic meters. Hence,

$$K = \Lambda(1000)(c) = .0412 \frac{m^2}{eq\ \Omega} \times 1000 \frac{\ell}{m^3} \times .01 \frac{eq}{\ell}$$

$$= .412\ \Omega^{-1}\ m^{-1}$$

Now, dE/dL can be calculated by using (3)

i.e., $dE/dL = I/SK$

$$= \frac{.003A}{(0.0003\ m^2)(0.412\ \Omega^{-1}\ m^{-1})} = 22.4V\ m^{-1}$$

Looking at both (1) and (2), it can be seen that there are three unknowns in (2) and one in (1). Since the unknown in (1) is one of the parameters in (2), U_+ is calculated first using (1) .

$$\text{Therefore } U_+ = \frac{L}{t\left(\frac{dE}{dT}\right)} = \frac{0.0213m}{(45 \times 60\ \frac{sec}{min})(22.4V\ m^{-1})}$$

$$= 0.000000352\ m^2V^{-1}sec^{-1}$$

$$= 3.52 \times 10^{-7} m^2V^{-1}\ sec^{-1}$$

To get t_+ , the expression

$$t_+ = \left[\frac{(F)(1000)c}{I}\right]\left(\frac{V}{t}\right) \text{is used}$$

where F = Faraday's constant

V = volume = (SL)

$$\therefore t_+ = \left[\frac{(96485)\frac{\text{coul}}{\text{eq}}(1000)\frac{\text{liter}}{\text{m}^3}(0.0100)\frac{\text{eq}}{\text{liter}}}{(0.003)\frac{\text{coul}}{\text{sec}}}\right]\left[\frac{(0.000325\ \text{m}^2)(0.0213\ \text{m})}{\left(45\ \text{min} \times 60\ \frac{\text{sec}}{\text{min}}\right)}\right]$$

$$= 0.825$$

Since U_- is the only unknown in (2) its value is found by substituting the values for U_+ and t_+ into the equation.

Therefore,

$$0.825 = \frac{3.52 \times 10^{-7}\ \text{m}^2\ \text{V}^{-1}\ \text{sec}^{-1}}{\left(3.52 \times 10^{-7}\right) + (U_-)}$$

$$\left(2.9 \times 10^{-7}\right) + \left(0.825U_-\right) = 3.52 \times 10^{-7}$$

$$0.825U_- = \left[\left(3.52 \times 10^{-7}\right) - \left(2.9 \times 10^{-7}\right)\right]$$

$$\therefore \quad U_- = 7.47 \times 10^{-8}\ \text{m}^2\ \text{V}^{-1}\ \text{sec}^{-1}$$

• PROBLEM 9-3

(a) A conductivity cell was calibrated using 0.01 N KCl ($k = 0.14087 \Omega^{-1} m^{-1}$) in the cell and the measured resistance was 688 Ω. Find the cell constant.

(b) A 0.0100 N $AgNO_3$ solution in the same cell had a resistance of 777 Ω. What is Λ?

Solution: (a) The cell constant, $L/S = kR$ (1)

where L = the distance between the electrodes

S = surface area of an electrode

k = specific conductance

R = resistance of the cell

$$L/S = (0.14087\ \Omega^{-1}\text{m}^{-1})(688\ \Omega) = 96.87\ \text{m}^{-1}$$

(b) $$\Lambda = \frac{k}{1000c} \tag{2}$$

where c = concentration expressed in terms of equivalents dm^{-3} of solution (N, normality).

Λ = the equivalent conductance.

Solving for k in (1)

$$k = \frac{L/S}{R} = \frac{96.87\ \text{m}^{-1}}{777\Omega} = 0.1247\ \Omega^{-1}\ \text{m}^{-1}$$

Now using the equation for Λ, in (2)

$$\Lambda = \frac{0.1247\ \Omega^{-1}\,m^{-1}}{(1000\ dm^3 m^{-3})(0.0100\ mol\ dm^{-3})}$$

$$= 0.01247\ \Omega^{-1} m^2\ mol^{-1}$$

• PROBLEM 9-4

Current was passed through a 0.100 N solution of KCl at 25°C. A silver coulometer in series with the KCl cell showed that 0.6136 g of Ag had been transferred from one electrode to the other during the electrolysis. The cathode portion weighing 117.51 g was drained and found to contain 0.56662% KCl. The anode portion weighing 121.45 g was drained and found to contain 0.57217% KCl. The middle portion of the Hittorf cell contained 0.74217% KCl. If inert electrodes were used, find t_+. Atomic weights: K = 39.1, Cl = 35.46, Ag = 107.868

Solution: The transference (transport) number,

$$t_+ = \frac{|N_o - N_f \pm N_e'|}{N_e}$$

where N_o = the original number of equivalents

N_f = the final number of equivalents present

N_e' = the number of equivalents involved in the electrode reaction (the positive sign is used if the equivalents are generated and the negative sign is used if they are removed)

N_e = the number of equivalents passed through the cell

The composition of the middle compartment is equal to the original composition of the anode and cathode compartments. Since 0.56662% KCl was found after draining the cathode portion, the amount of KCl after the electrolysis (draining) is

$$\left(117.51\ \text{gm Soln}\right)\left(0.56662\%\ \frac{\text{gm KCl}}{\text{gm Soln}}\right)$$

$$= (117.51)(0.0056662\ \text{gm KCl}) = 0.6658\ \text{gm KCl}.$$

Note the consistency of units. The amount of KCl is expressed in gm KCl to be consistent with the units given in the problem.

Initially there was 117.51 gm of KCl solution, so the amount of water after the electrolysis is

$$117.51\ \text{gm Soln} - 0.6658\ \text{gm KCl} = 116.84\ \text{gm}\ H_2O$$

Before electrolysis, there were $\left(\frac{116.84}{1-.0074217}\right) = 117.71$ gm Soln for 116.84 gm H_2O. For this amount of solution, there were (117.71)(.0074217) = .8736 gm KCl.

Thus,
$$N_o = \frac{0.8736 \text{ gm KCl}}{74.56 \text{ gm KCl/mol}} = 0.01172 \text{ mol}$$

$$N_f = \frac{0.6658 \text{ gm KCl}}{74.56 \text{ gm KCl/mol}} = 0.00893 \text{ mol}$$

$$N_e = \frac{0.6136 \text{ gm Ag}}{107.868 \text{ gm Ag/mol}} = 0.005688 \text{ mol}$$

$N_e' = 0$ because the cell is inert, and $= N_e$ if cell is not inert.

$$\therefore \quad t_+ = \frac{|0.01172 - (0.00893) \pm 0|}{0.005688} = 0.4905$$

• PROBLEM 9-5

The emf at 298 K of the concentration cell with transference,

$$H_2(1 \text{ atm}) | HCl(a = 0.0100) | HCl(a = 0.100) | H_2(1 \text{ atm})$$

is 0.0190 V. What is the average transference number of the H^+ ion?

Solution: From the given concentration cell, the reactions and their ion transfers are:

$$1/2\ H_2 \rightarrow H^+ (a_{\pm 2}) + e$$

$$t_+H^+(a_{\pm 2}) \rightarrow t_+H^+(a_{\pm 1})$$

$$t_-\ Cl^-(a_{\pm 1}) \rightarrow t_-Cl^-(a_{\pm 2})$$

$$H^+(a_{\pm 1}) + e \rightarrow 1/2\ H_2$$

overall: $t_-\ (H^+ + Cl^-)_1 \rightarrow t_-\ (H^+ + Cl^-)_2$

(Note that $t_- = 1 - t_+$)

Writing the Nernst equation for this reaction gives

$$E = E° - \left(\frac{RT}{nF}\right) \ln Q$$ where E = cell's emf, E° = standard emf and F = Faraday's Constant. Q is the reaction quotient.

Because this is a concentration cell, the electrode reactions are similar.

As a result, E° = 0 and the potential arises from the nonstandard conditions of the reactants and products.

For cells that have no liquid junction or have nearly eliminated the liquid junction,

$$E = -\frac{RT}{nF} \; t_i \; \ln Q \; .$$

Therefore, the reaction under consideration yields

$$E = -\frac{RT}{F}\left(2t_-\right)\ln\left(\frac{a_{\pm 2}}{a_{\pm 1}}\right) \qquad (1)$$

Here n = 1, $a_{\pm}$ = mean activity. Note that $Q = \dfrac{a_{\pm 2}}{a_{\pm 1}}$

Substituting the respective values into equation (1) yields

$$E = \left(2t_-\right)(0.05916)\log\left(\frac{0.100}{0.010}\right)$$

$$= (0.11832)t_-$$

But E is given to be 0.0190 volt

$$\therefore \qquad 0.0190 = (0.11832)t_-$$

$$\text{or} \qquad t_- = \frac{0.0190}{0.11832}$$

$$= 0.16058 \; .$$

Using the relation $t_+ + t_- = 1$,

t_+ can be computed.

Thus, $\quad t_+ = 1 - t_-$

or $\quad t_+ = 1 - 0.16058 = 0.83942$

• PROBLEM 9-6

Find the contributions of the conductivities of individual ions (ionic equivalent conductance λ_+ and λ_-) when Λ (equivalent conductance of electrolytic solution) = 0.0412 $m^2/(\Omega)(mol)$ and t_+ = 0.825.

Solution: By definition, $\quad \Lambda = \lambda_+ + \lambda_- \qquad (1)$

and $\quad \Lambda t_i = \lambda_i \;\; (i = +,-) \qquad (2)$

From (2), $\quad \lambda_+ = \left(0.0412 \; m^2/(\Omega)(mol)\right)(0.825)$

$$\lambda_+ = 0.03399 \; m^2/(\Omega)(mol)$$

Now using equation (1), $\lambda_- = \Lambda - \lambda_+$

$$= 0.0412 - 0.03399$$

$$= 0.00721 \ m^2/(\Omega)(mol)$$

t_+ = transference (transport) number

Ω = resistance unit

ELECTROCHEMICAL CELLS

• PROBLEM 9-7

Construct a diagram using the modules shown in figures a-f for the electrochemical cell given by Pt/Ag(s)/AgCl(s)/ Cl^-(0.1M)//Br^-(0.1 M)/Br_2(1 atm)/C(graph)/Pt.

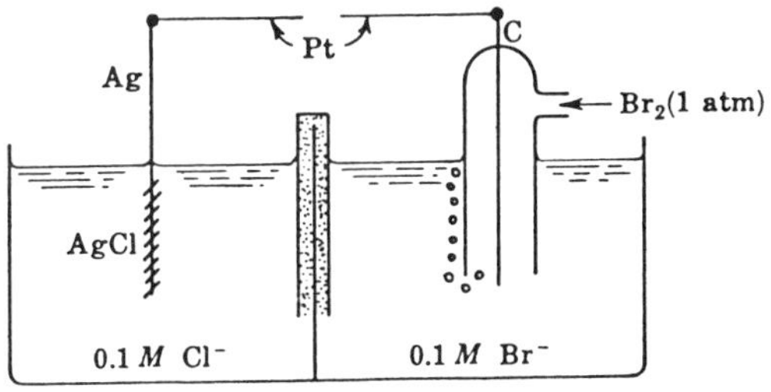

Fig. 1

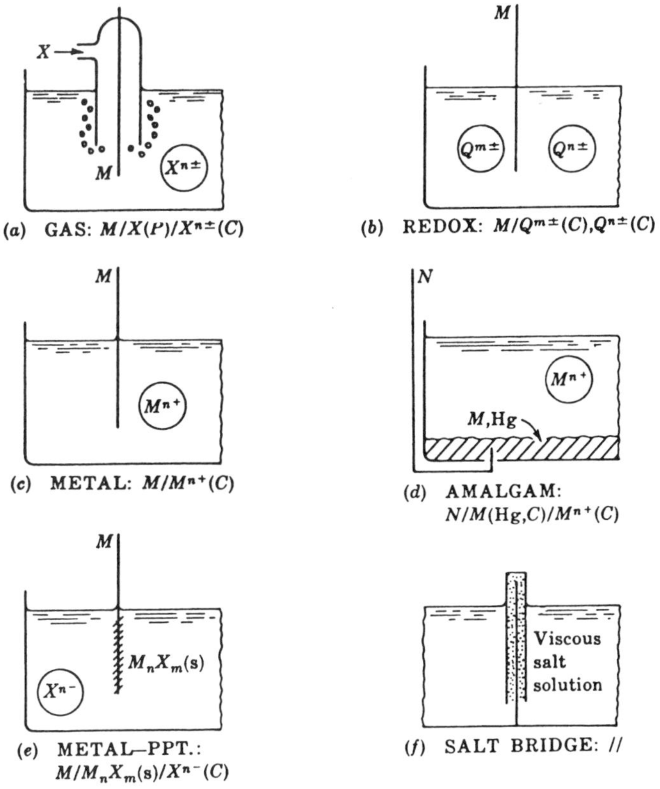

Solution: The Ag-AgCl anode will be represented by module (e), the salt bridge by module (f) and the Br_2 cathode by module (a). See figure 1 for the complete sketch.

In the six diagrams (modules) in the problem, note that different letters are used to represent different substances as follows:

X = gas = Br_2

M = metal = Ag

MX = metal and gas together = AgCl

M in (d) = metal = Hg for amalgamation.

• PROBLEM 9-8

A lead storage battery involves the two half-reactions

	Standard reduction Potential, E° (volts)
$PbSO_4(s) + 2e^- \rightleftarrows Pb + SO_4^{2-}$	-0.36
$PbO_2 + 4H^+ + SO_4^{2-} + 2e^- \rightleftarrows PbSO_4 + 2H_2O$	1.69

For a cell that duplicates the lead storage battery discharge reaction at unit concentrations, what is the overal reaction and potential in volts?

Solution: Since this is the discharge reaction, the reaction must be spontaneous, and the cell potential, E°, must be positive. If we reverse the first half-reaction and sum

	E°
$Pb + SO_4^{2-} \rightleftarrows PbSC_4(s) + 2e^-$	0.36
$PbO_2 + 4H^+ + SO_4^{2-} + 2e^- \rightleftarrows PbSO_4(s) + 2H_2O$	1.69
Sum: $Pb + PbO_2 + 2SO_4^{2-} + 4H^+ \rightleftarrows 2PbSO_4(s) + 2H_2O$	2.05

E° is positive and the overall reaction is the sum of the two half reactions.

Spontaneity calls for the reaction to proceed in the forward direction. The thermodynamic requirement for spontaneity is that $\Delta G = -nFE$ is negative. For ΔG to be negative, voltage (E=E°) must be positive.

• PROBLEM 9-9

During the charging of a lead storage cell, the following reaction takes place:

$$2PbSO_4(s) + 2H_2O(liq) = Pb(s) + PbO_2(s) + 2H_2SO_4(aq)$$

If ΔG°_{298}(formation) = -194.36 kcal mol^{-1} for $PbSO_4$(s), -56.687 kcal mol^{-1} for H_2O(liq), 0 for Pb(s), -51.95 kcal mol^{-1} for PbO_2(s) and -217.32 kcal mol^{-1} for H_2SO_4(aq, m=1), calculate ΔG°_{298}(reaction) and E°. Is this reaction spontaneous under standard conditions or is an outside source of energy required for it to proceed?

Solution: Using $\Delta G^\circ_{(reaction)} = \Sigma n_i \ \Delta G(i) - \Sigma n_j \ \Delta G(j)$

where i = products

j = reactants

n = number of moles

$$\therefore \quad \Delta G^\circ_{(reaction)} = [(1)(0) + (1)(-51.95) + (2)(-217.32)] - [(2)(-194.36) + (2)(-56.687)]$$

$$= 15.50 \text{ kcal} = (15.50)(4.186) = 64.9 \text{ kJ.}$$

$$\text{Now } E^\circ = \frac{-\Delta G^\circ_{(reaction)}}{nF}$$

where F = Faraday's Constant

Therefore

$$E^\circ = \frac{-64.9 \text{ kJ}}{(2 \text{ mol})\left(96.485 \text{ kJ mol}^{-1}V^{-1}\right)} = -0.336V$$

Since E° is negative, the reaction is not spontaneous as written. It can occur only if external power source is used. The reverse reaction would be spontaneous.

• PROBLEM 9-10

If 10.0 A were passed through a lead storage cell for 1.50 hr during a charging process, how much $PbSO_4$ would decompose?

Solution: The balanced equation is

$$2PbSO_4(s) + 2H_2O(liq) = Pb(s) + PbO_2(s) + 2SO_4^{2-}(aq) + 4H^+(aq) \quad (1)$$

The number of coulombs of electricity passed through the cell is given by

$$q = It$$

where I = current (in amperes)

t = time (in seconds)

$$\therefore \quad q = (10 \text{ A})\left(1.50 \text{ hr} \times \frac{3600 \text{ secs.}}{1 \text{ hr}}\right) = 54000 \text{ coulombs}$$

and this amount of electricity corresponds to

$$\frac{(54000 \text{ coulombs})}{(96485 \text{ coulombs/mol})} = 0.56 \text{ mol}$$

From the reaction equation of equation (1) the equivalent weight of $PbSO_4$ is equal to its molecular weight

$$= 303.25 \text{ gm/mol}$$

$$= 0.30325 \text{ kg/mol}$$

Recall that 0.56 mol corresponded to the quantity of electricity.

$\therefore$ the mass of $PbSO_4$(s) reacting is then,

$$(0.56 \text{ mol})(0.30325 \text{ kg/mol}) = 0.1697 \text{ kg.}$$

• PROBLEM 9-11

Given the two half-reactions, their standard reduction potentials (in volts) and the diagram below, what is the spontaneous reaction that occurs in the given cell and the voltage?

Half-reaction	Standard reduction potential, E° (volts)
$Cu^{2+} + 2e^- \leftrightarrows Cu$	0.34
$Zn^{2+} + 2e^- \leftrightarrows Zn$	-0.76

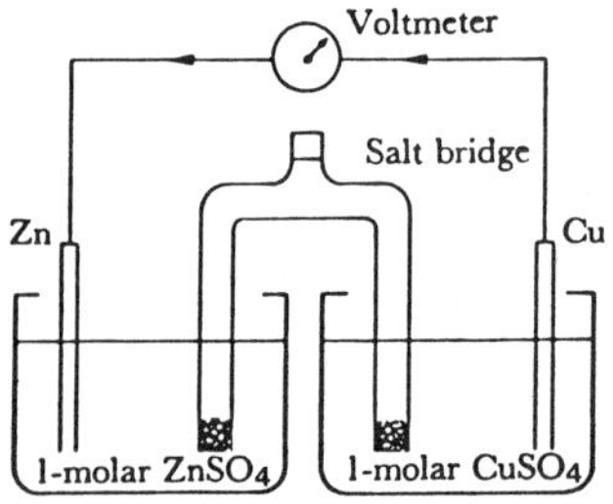

Solution: This is a trial and error problem because there are two possible overall reactions. That is:

Reactions	E°
$Cu^{2+} + 2e^- \leftrightarrows Cu$	0.34
$Zn \leftrightarrows Zn^{2+} + 2e^-$	0.76
$Cu^{2+} + Zn \leftrightarrows Cu + Zn^{2+}$	1.10 volts

The reaction can proceed as written or in the reverse sense. Q=1 since concentrations are equal. Therefore

$$E = E° - \frac{RT}{nF} \ln 1 = E° = 1.10 \text{ volts.}$$

Since E° is positive, the reaction is spontaneous and must go in the forward direction (as written).

• PROBLEM 9-12

The chemical reaction for the Daniell cell is

$$Zn(s) + Cu^{2+}(aq) = Zn^{2+}(aq) + Cu(s)$$

If $\Delta G_{25°C}$(formation) = 0 for Zn(s) and Cu(s), -35.14 kcal mol^{-1} for $Zn^{2+}(aq)$ and 15.66 kcal mol^{-1} for $Cu^{2+}(aq)$, calculate the cell potential under standard conditions. Is the reaction spontaneous?

Solution: $\Delta G°_{(reaction)} = -nFE°$. Therefore $E° = -\dfrac{\Delta G°_{(reaction)}}{nF}$ where

$\Delta G°_{(reaction)}$ = standard free energy change of reactions

F = Faraday's Constant = 96.485 kJ $mol^{-1}V^{-1}$

n = number of moles of electrons in the balanced reactions

E° = cell potential

By definition, $\Delta G°_{25°C}(reaction) = \Sigma n_i \Delta G°_{25°C}(products) - \Sigma n_j \Delta G°_{25°C}(reactants)$

where n_i and n_j = number of moles of products and reactants respectively.

$$\therefore \Delta G°_{25°C}(reaction) = [(1)(-35.14) + (1)(0)] - [(1)(0) + (1)(15.66)]$$

$$= -50.80 \text{ kcal} = (-50.80 \text{ kcal})(4.186 \text{ kJ/kcal})$$

$$= -212.6 \text{ kJ}.$$

Therefore

$$E° = \frac{-(-212.6 \text{ kJ})}{(2 \text{ mol})(96.485 \text{ kJ mol}^{-1}V^{-1})}$$

$$= +1.102V$$

Since the cell potential is positive, the reaction is spontaneous as written.

• PROBLEM 9-13

Find the cell potential for the cell whose

reaction equation is $Ni + Sn^{2+} \rightarrow Ni^{2+} + Sn$ if Conc. Ni^{2+} = 1.3 and Conc. $Sn^{2+} = 1.0 \times 10^{-4}$. Also predict the direction of the spontaneous reaction.

Solution: The two half reactions and their standard potentials are:

Reactions	E°
$N_i \rightarrow Ni^{2+} + 2e^-$	+0.25
$Sn^{2+} + 2e^- \rightarrow Sn$	-0.14
Sum: $Ni + Sn^{2+} \rightarrow Ni^{2+} + Sn$	E° = +0.11

$$E = E° - \frac{0.059157}{n} \log Q \qquad (1)$$

where

E = cell potential

E° = standard potential for the two half reactions.

$$Q = \frac{(\text{concentration } Ni^{2+})}{(\text{concentration } Sn^{2+})} = \frac{1.3}{1.0 \times 10^{-4}} = 1.3 \times 10^{4}$$

n = number of electrons transferred = 2

Substituting values of E° and Q into equation (1), gives

$$E = 0.11 - \frac{0.059157}{2} \log \left(1.3 \times 10^{4}\right)$$

$$= 0.11 - (0.0296)(4.11) = 0.11 - 0.12$$

$$= -0.01 \text{ volts.}$$

The cell potential is negative, thus the reaction is not spontaneous as written. The criterion of spontaneous reaction is that E be positive.

• PROBLEM 9-14

What is the electromotive force (emf) of a system when all concentrations are unity?

Solution: In the Nernst equation, $E = E° - \frac{RT}{nF} \ln Q$, where Q is the concentration quotient.

For example, if $aA + bB + ne^- \rightarrow cC + dD$ is the reaction in question,

$$Q = \frac{[C]^c [D]^d}{[A]^a [B]^b}$$

where $[C]^c$, $[D]^d$, $[A]^a$, $[B]^b$ are the concentrations of the species. The problem states that Q, the ratio of $[C]^c[D]^d$ to $[A]^a[B]^b$ is 1. Consequently, ln 1 = 0. Therefore, the Nernst equation becomes

$$E = E° - \frac{RT}{nF} \ln 1$$

$$E = E° - 0$$

or $E = E°$. Also $\Delta G = -nFE°$ since $E = E°$.

• PROBLEM 9-15

What is the electromotive force (emf) of a system when K, the equilibrium constant for the reaction = Q, the concentration quotient?

Solution: The Nernst equation is $E = E° - \frac{RT}{nF} \ln Q$ (1)

where E = emf,

n = number of moles of electrons transferred

and $E°$ = emf at the standard state concentrations.

K is fixed for any reaction and Q has the same form as K, but utilizes the actual concentrations of the different species in the reaction.

F = Faraday's constant.

Also, $\Delta G = - nFE$, where ΔG = free energy change.

When Q = K, the system is at equilibrium and the concentrations are equilibrium concentrations. For an equilibrium condition, $\Delta G = 0 = -nFE$. Therefore,

$$E = 0/-nF = 0.$$

Equation (1) becomes

$$0 = E° - \frac{RT}{nF} \ln Q$$

and

$$E° = \frac{RT}{nF} \ln K.$$

• PROBLEM 9-16

An electrochemical cell is to be designed by using a cell whose materials are of high performance, and can generate high power. $Li|LiCl$ (fused salt)$|Cl_2$ is to be used. What is the optimum ratio of Li weight to that of Cl_2? (atomic weights: Li = 6.94, Cl = 35.5)

Solution: The required reaction is $2Li + Cl_2 \rightarrow 2\ LiCl$.

The optimum ratio is one equivalent weight of Li to one equivalent weight of Cl. The respective equivalent weights are 6.94 and 35.5 for Li and Cl. Therefore, the ratio is

$$\frac{6.94}{35.5} = 0.196.$$

Note that the equivalent weight of Cl is not $2 \times 35.5 = 71.0$. This is because its equivalent weight is the weight of the material that will react with one gram of Li. 71.0 grams will react with $2 \times 6.94 = 13.88$ grams of Li.

• PROBLEM 9-17

What is E° for the cell

$Pt/Ag(s)/AgCl(s)/Cl^-(a=1)/Cl_2(1\ atm)/C(graph)/Pt$

if the standard half-cell reduction potentials are 0.2223 V for AgCl/Ag and 1.3583 V for Cl_2/Cl^-? Is the reaction spontaneous?

Solution: Since E° for the cell is required, the individual E° for the half reactions are added together.

Both reactions are supposed to be reduction reactions. Therefore, the one with the smaller protential can be taken to be the oxidation reaction. In that case, the E° sign changes.

The two reactions are:

$$AgCl(s) + e^- \rightarrow Ag(s) + Cl^-(a=1) \qquad (1)$$

and

$$Cl_2(1\ atm) + 2e^- \rightarrow 2Cl^-(a=1) \qquad (2)$$

E° value for the first reaction is given to be 0.2223 V and that of the second reaction is 1.3583 V.

But it has been stated that the reaction with the smaller reduction potential will be written as the oxidation reaction. Therefore, reaction (1) is reversed and the sign of its potential changes. That is,

$$Ag(s) + Cl^-(a=1) \rightarrow AgCl(s) + e^-$$

with an E° value of -0.2223 V.

Looking at both reactions, the first one contains an e^- and the second, a $2e^-$. Consequently, multiply the first by 2 and add to the second. The result is

$$2Ag(s) + Cl_2(1\ atm) \rightarrow 2AgCl(s).$$

Note that the potential is unaffected when multiplying reaction (1) by 2.

The cell potential is therefore (-0.2223) + (1.3583)

$\therefore$ E° for the cell = 1.1360 V.

A criterion for spontaneity (at standard conditions) is E° be positive. Therefore, the result indicates that the reaction is spontaneous.

• PROBLEM 9-18

What is E for the cell

$Ag/AgBr(s)/Br^-(a=0.34)$, $Fe^{3+}(a=0.1)$, $Fe^{2+}(a=0.02)/Pt$

if the standard half-cell reduction potentials are 0.0713 V for AgBr/Ag and 0.770 V for Fe^{3+}/Fe^{2+}?

Solution: In this problem, the Nernst equation applies. This is defined by

$$E = E° - \frac{RT}{nF} \ln Q \qquad (1)$$

where

E = overall cell potential

E° = standard cell potential

R = gas constant

n = number of equivalents (which is one in this problem)

F = Faraday's constant

Q = reaction quotient.

If the cell reactions are assumed to have taken place at 25°C = 298°K, then equation (1) becomes

$$E = E° - \frac{0.059157}{1} \log Q \qquad (2)$$

To get the cell's E° value, those of the two half cells are added up. Since the two half cell reactions are both reduction reactions, the one with the smaller reduction potential is written as an oxidation reaction. Consequently, its positive sign changes to negative. Thus, the two half reactions and their voltages are:

$$Ag(s) + Br^-(a=0.34) \rightarrow AgBr(s) + 1e^- \qquad E° = -0.0713\ V$$

$$Fe^{3+}(a=0.1) + 1e^- \rightarrow Fe^{2+}(a=0.02) \qquad E° = 0.770\ V$$

Adding the two above equations gives,

Total:

$$Ag(s) + Fe^{3+}(a=0.1) + Br^-(a=0.34) \longrightarrow AgBr(s) + Fe^{2+}(a=0.02)$$

$E° = 0.699$ V

Now that E° is obtained, Q has to be determined before equation (2) can be used.

The reaction quotient Q is defined by the ratio of the activities of the products to those of the reactants. That is

$$Q = \frac{a_{AgBr}\ a_{Fe^{2+}}}{a_{Ag}a_{Fe^{3+}}\ a_{Br^-}} \qquad (3)$$

where a = activity.

Observe that only the overall equation is used.

Since the activity of a solid is unity,

$a_{AgBr} = a_{Ag} = 1$ and equation (3) changes to

$$Q = \frac{a_{Fe^{2+}}}{a_{Fe^{3+}}\ a_{Br^-}}$$

$$= \frac{(0.02)}{(0.1)(0.34)}$$

$$\therefore \quad Q = 0.588$$

Now, using equation (2) gives

$$E = E° - 0.059157 \log 0.588$$

$$= E° - 0.059157\ (-0.2306)$$

But E° was found to be 0.699 V,

$$\therefore \quad E = 0.699 + 0.0136$$

$$= 0.7126 \text{ V}$$

• PROBLEM 9-19

Write the balanced cell reaction and calculate the emf at 298 K of the cell

$$Pt|Sn^{2+}(a=0.1000),\ Sn^{4+}(a=0.0100)||Fe^{3+}(a=0.200)|Fe$$

The standard electrode potentials are in the literature.

Solution: Before the overall cell reaction can be obtained,

first write the two half reactions and add them up.

The two reactions and their respective standard electrode potentials are:

		E° values
Reduction at right electrode:	$Fe^{3+} + 3e^- \rightarrow Fe$	-0.036 V
Oxidation at left electrode:	$Sn^{2+} \rightarrow 2e^- + Sn^{4+}$	0.15 V

Since the e^- does not balance in both equations, it can be eliminated only by multiplying the first equation by 3 and the second by 2 before adding them up. Note that the standard potentials are not affected.

Therefore, overall reaction = $3(Sn^{2+} \rightarrow Sn^{4+} + 2e^-)$ +

$2(Fe^{3+} + 3e^- \rightarrow Fe) = 3Sn^{2+} + 2Fe^{3+} \rightarrow 3Sn^{4+} + 2Fe$.

Adding the two half potentials gives

$$-0.036 + .15 = .114 \text{ V} = E°$$

for the cell.

The Nernst equation is

$$E_{cell} = E°_{cell} - \frac{RT}{nF} \ln Q$$

where n = number of equivalents = 6 in this problem because of the transfer of 6 electrons.

$$Q = \text{reaction quotient} = \frac{(a_{Sn^{4+}})^3}{(a_{Fe^{3+}})^2 (a_{Sn^{2+}})^3} \cdot a = \text{activity}$$

F = Faraday's constant.

At 25°C = 298°K,

$$E_{cell} = E°_{cell} - \frac{0.05916}{6} \log \frac{(0.0100)^3}{(0.2)^2(0.1)^3}$$

$$= .114 - 0.00986 \log 0.025$$

$$= .114 - 0.00986\ (-1.60206)$$

$$= .114 + 0.0157963 = .1298 \text{ V}$$

• PROBLEM 9-20

The emf of the cell, H_2 (1 atm)|HCl (0.01 m)|AgCl(c)|Ag is given by E (in volts) = $-0.096 + 1.90 \times 10^{-3}\ T - 3.041 \times 10^{-6}\ T^2$. Calculate ΔG, ΔS, ΔH, and ΔC_p for the cell reaction (state the reaction) at 298 K.

Solution: a) The cell reaction can be obtained by adding

up the two half reactions. That is,

$$(1/2\ H_2 \rightarrow H^+ + e^-) + (AgCl + e^- \rightarrow Ag + Cl^-) =$$

$$1/2\ H_2 + AgCl \rightarrow Ag + H^+ + Cl^- \tag{1}$$

The E value of a cell is related to the Gibbs free energy by

$$\Delta G = -\ nFE \tag{2}$$

where F = Faraday's constant.

Therefore,

$$\Delta G = -(1)\ \text{mole}\ (96500)\ \frac{\text{coul}}{\text{mole}}\ (-0.096V + 1.90 \times 10^{-3}\ V/°K\ T - 3.041 \times 10^{-6}\ V/°K^2\ T^2)\ \text{volt}$$

At 298°K,

$$\Delta G = -(1)(96500)[-0.096 + 1.90 \times 10^{-3}(298) - 3.041 \times 10^{-6}(298)^2]$$

$$= -96500\ [-0.096 + 0.5662 - 0.2700]$$

$$= -96500\ \frac{J}{V}\ (0.2002)\ V$$

$$= -19319.3\ J$$

b) The thermodynamic relationship between entropy, volume, temperature, free energy and pressure is given by

$$dG = VdP - SdT \tag{3}$$

At constant pressure, equation (3) becomes

$dG = -SdT$ from which

$$\left(\frac{\partial \Delta G}{\partial T}\right)_P = -\ \Delta S \tag{4}$$

From equation (2),

$$\left(\frac{\partial \Delta G}{\partial T}\right)_P = -\ nF\left(\frac{\partial E}{\partial T}\right)_P \tag{5}$$

where n = 1

The combination of equations (4) and (5) gives

$$\Delta S = F\left(\frac{\partial E}{\partial T}\right)_P \tag{6}$$

From the given E value,

$$\left(\frac{\partial E}{\partial T}\right)_P = 1.90 \times 10^{-3} - 6.082 \times 10^{-6}\, T \qquad (7)$$

At 298°K, equation (7) becomes

$$\left(\frac{\partial E}{\partial T}\right)_P = 1.90 \times 10^{-3} - 6.082 \times 10^{-6}\,(298)$$

$$= 0.0019 - 0.0018124$$

$$= 0.0000876\ \frac{V}{°K}$$

Substitute this value and the value of F in equation (6) and solve for ΔS to get

$$\Delta S = 96500\ \frac{J}{V}\ (0.0000876)\ \frac{V}{°K}$$

$$= 8.45\ J\ K^{-1}$$

c) Another thermodynamic relation is $\Delta H = \Delta G + T\Delta S$

But $\quad \Delta G = -19319.3\ J$

and $\quad \Delta S = 8.45\ J\ K^{-1}$

Therefore, at 298°K,

$$\Delta H = -19319.3\ J + (298\ K)(8.45\ J\ K^{-1})$$

$$= -19319.3\ J + 2518.1\ J$$

$$= -16801.2\ J$$

d) By definition,

$$\Delta C_P = \left(\frac{\partial \Delta H}{\partial T}\right)_P$$

where C_P = heat capacity at constant pressure.

Recall that $\Delta H = \Delta G + T\Delta S$

$$\therefore \quad \left(\frac{\partial \Delta H}{\partial T}\right)_P = \left(\frac{\partial \Delta G}{\partial T}\right)_P + \left(\frac{\partial (T\Delta S)}{\partial T}\right)_P$$

$$= \left(\frac{\partial \Delta G}{\partial T}\right)_P + \Delta S + T\left(\frac{\partial \Delta S}{\partial T}\right)_P \qquad (8)$$

From equation (4),

$$\left(\frac{\partial \Delta G}{\partial T}\right)_P = -\ \Delta S$$

Therefore equation (8) becomes

$$\left(\frac{\partial \Delta H}{\partial T}\right)_P = -\ \Delta S + \Delta S + T\left(\frac{\partial \Delta S}{\partial T}\right)_P$$

$$\therefore \qquad \Delta C_P = \left(\frac{\partial \Delta H}{\partial T}\right)_P = T\left(\frac{\partial \Delta S}{\partial T}\right)_P . \qquad (9)$$

But equation (6) gives,

$$\Delta S = F\left(\frac{\partial E}{\partial T}\right)_P$$

$$\therefore \qquad \left(\frac{\partial \Delta S}{\partial T}\right)_P = F\left(\frac{\partial^2 E}{\partial T^2}\right)_P \qquad (10)$$

Combining equations (9) and (10) gives

$$\Delta C_P = T\left(\frac{\partial \Delta S}{\partial T}\right)_P = T\,F\left(\frac{\partial^2 E}{\partial T^2}\right)_P \qquad (11)$$

From the given E value,

$$\frac{\partial^2 E}{\partial T^2} = -\ 6.082 \times 10^{-6}\ \frac{V}{°K^2}$$

$$\therefore \qquad \Delta C_P = TF\ (-6.082 \times 10^{-6}).$$

At 298°K,

$$\Delta C_P = (298°K)(96500)\ \frac{J}{V}\left(-6.082 \times 10^{-6}\right)\frac{V}{°K^2} = -174.9\ J\ K^{-1}$$

• PROBLEM 9-21

At 20°C the standard e.m.f. of the cell

$Hg|Hg_2Cl_2(s),\ HCl(aq)|H_2,Pt$

is 0.2692 V and at 30°C it is 0.2660 V. Find the values of ΔG°_m, ΔH°_m, and ΔS°_m at 25°C.

Solution: The two half reactions are

$$1/2\ Hg_2Cl_2(s) + e^- \rightarrow Hg(\ell) + Cl^-(aq)$$

and

$$1/2\ H_2(g) \rightarrow H^+(aq) + e^-$$

The overall cell reaction is obtained by adding up both equations. That is

$$1/2\ Hg_2Cl_2(s) + 1/2\ H_2(g) \rightarrow Hg(\ell) + Cl^-(aq) + H^+(aq).$$

By definition,

$$\Delta G°_m = -\ nFE°$$

where

$\Delta G°_m$ = Standard Gibbs free energy

n = number of equivalents (which is one in this case because there is only one electron transfer)

F = Faraday's constant

E° = Standard e.m.f.

At 20°C = 293°K

$$\Delta G°_m = -\left(9.649 \times 10^4 C\ mol^{-1}\right)\left(0.2692\ V\right)$$

$$= -25.98\ kJ\ mol^{-1}$$

and at 30°C = 303°K

$$\Delta G°_m = \left(9.649 \times 10^4\ C\ mol^{-1}\right)\left(0.2660\ V\right)$$

$$= -25.67\ kJ\ mol^{-1}$$

Since 25°C is the average of 20°C and 30°C, $\Delta G°_m$ will also be the average $\Delta G°_m$ value at 20°C and 30°C. That is, at 25°C = 298°K

$$\Delta G°_m = \frac{(-25.98) + (-25.67)}{2} = -\ \frac{51.65}{2}$$

$$= -25.825\ kJ\ mol^{-1}$$

From the above values, $\Delta S°_m$ can be approximated. By definition,

$$\Delta S°_m = -\left(\frac{\partial \Delta G°_m}{\partial T}\right)$$

But $$\left(\frac{\partial \Delta G°_m}{\partial T}\right)_{298°K} \sim \frac{-25.67 - (-25.98)}{(303 - 293)} = 31.00\ JK^{-1}\ mol^{-1}$$

Therefore

$$\Delta S°_m = -31.00 JK^{-1}\ mol^{-1}.$$

$$\Delta H°_m = \Delta G°_m + T\Delta S°_m$$

∴ At 298°K,

$$\Delta H°_m = -25.82 + (298)(-31.00)$$

$$= -35.06\ kJ\ mol^{-1}$$

• PROBLEM 9-22

Precise data for the cell Ag|AgCl|NaCl(4 m)|NaHg|NaCl (0.1 m)|AgCl|Ag are

T (°C)	15	20	25	30	35
E(V)	0.16265	0.18663	0.19044	0.19407	0.19755

Calculate ΔH for the cell reaction at 298°K.

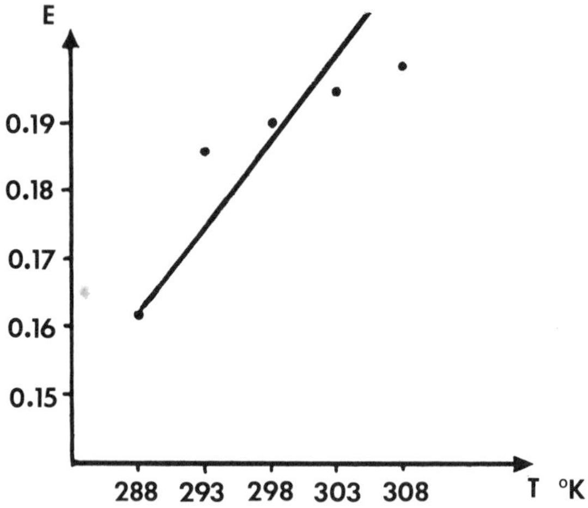

Solution: The thermodynamic definition of

ΔH is $\Delta H = \Delta G + T\Delta S$ (1)

where ΔH = ethalpy change

ΔG = Gibbs free energy change

T = Temperature

ΔS = entropy change.

The e.m.f. of a cell is related to the change in Gibbs free energy by

$$\Delta G = -\, nFE \qquad (2)$$

where n = the number of moles of electrons (equivalents) in the balanced reaction

F = Farady's constant

E = Voltage of the electrochemical cell.

From thermodynamic relations,

$$dG = VdP - SdT$$

where V = volume and P = pressure.

At constant P, $dG = -\, SdT$.

Therefore,

$$\left(\frac{\partial \Delta G}{\partial T}\right)_P = -\, \Delta S \qquad (3)$$

From equation (2), $\left(\frac{\partial \Delta G}{\partial T}\right)_P = - nF \left(\frac{\partial E}{\partial T}\right)_P$ (4)

Note that n and F are constants. Combining equations (3) and (4) yields

$$\Delta S = nF \left(\frac{\partial E}{\partial T}\right)_P \quad (5)$$

The $\frac{\partial E}{\partial T}$ term in equation (5) is the slope of the line obtained from the plot of E(V) versus T.

Using the given data, the plot is as follows.

The slope of this line is approximately 0.001745 VK^{-1}.

Therefore, equation (5) gives

$$\Delta S = (n \text{ eq})\left(96500 \frac{C}{eq}\right)(0.001745)\frac{V}{°K} = (1 \text{ eq})\left(96500 \frac{C}{eq}\right)$$

$$(0.001745)\frac{J/C}{°K}$$

$$= 168 \text{ J K}^{-1}$$

using equation (2) and the E(V) value at 25°C = 298°K yields

$$\Delta G = -(1 \text{ eq})\left(96500 \frac{C}{eq}\right)(0.19044) \text{ V} \times \frac{1J/C}{V}$$

$$= -18377.46 \text{ J}$$

Substitute for ΔG and ΔS in equation (1) and solving for ΔH gives

$$\Delta H = (-18377.46 \text{ J}) + (298°K)\left(168 \frac{J}{°K}\right)$$

$$= -18377.46 + 50064$$

$$= 31686.54 \text{ J}$$

• PROBLEM 9-23

One of the reactions important in the corrosion of iron in an acidic environment is Fe + 2HCl (aq) + 1/2 $O_2 \rightarrow$ $FeCl_2(aq) + H_2O$.

a) Which is the spontaneous direction of this reaction when the activity of the Fe^{2+} is unity and $a(H^+) = 1$?

b) At what activity of Fe^{2+} does iron cease dissolving in hydrochloric acid of $a(H^+) = 1$? Take temperature to be 25°C.

Solution: a) From the given equation, the cell reaction

may be written as

$$Fe + 2H^{+} + 2Cl^{-} + 2e^{-} + 1/2\ O_2 \rightleftarrows Fe^{2+} + 2Cl^{-} + 2e^{-} + H_2O$$

which becomes

$$Fe + 2H^{+} + 2e^{-} + 1/2\ O_2 \rightleftarrows Fe^{2+} + 2e^{-} + H_2O \qquad (1)$$

As a matter of convenience, it is advisable to write all reactions as though they involve single electron transfers. Therefore equation (1) can be reduced to

$$1/2\ Fe + H^{+} + e^{-} + 1/4\ O_2 \rightleftarrows 1/2\ Fe^{2+} + e^{-} + 1/2\ H_2O \qquad (2)$$

(this was done by merely dividing throughout by 2 so as to make the coefficients of e^{-} unity.)

The next step is to predict the direction of the reaction (to the right or to the left). Before this can be done, the standard electrode potential E° must be known. Since this can not be found directly, equation (2) needs to be broken down into two half reactions for which the standard electrode potentials are known. The addition of these potentials should give the desired potential.

The two half reactions and their standard potentials are

(reduction) $H^{+} + e^{-} + 1/4\ O_2 \rightleftarrows 1/2\ H_2O \qquad E° = 1.229\ V$

(oxidation) $1/2\ Fe \rightleftarrows 1/2\ Fe^{2+} + e^{-} \qquad E° = 0.440\ V$

Apparently, the addition of these half reactions is the overall reaction, therefore the desired $E°_{cell}$ value = 1.229 + 0.440

$$\therefore \quad E°_{cell} = 1.669\ V$$

Note that the second half reaction is written as a reduction reaction in most literatures, with a negative E° value. That is

$$1/2\ Fe^{2+} + e^{-} \rightleftarrows 1/2\ Fe \qquad E° = -0.440\ V.$$

Reversing the equation reverses the E° value. The criterion for spontaneous direction of a reaction is $E°_{cell}$ be positive; Since $E°_{cell} = +\ 1.669\ V$ is positive, the reaction is spontaneous as written. That is, it has the tendency to proceed to the right when the conditions are those specified.

b) This can be done by looking for the value of $a(Fe^{2+})$ for which $E_{oxidation} = E_{reduction}$. Using the Nernst equation,

$$E_{oxidation} = E°_{oxidation} - \frac{RT}{nF} \ln \left[\frac{1}{a(H^{+})}\right]$$

$$= E^\circ_{oxidation} + \frac{RT}{nF} \ln a\left(H^+\right)$$

Similarly,

$$E_{reduction} = E^\circ_{reduction} - \frac{RT}{nF} \ln a\left(Fe^{2+}\right)^{1/2},$$

where n = 1. Note that at $a\left(H^+\right) = 1$, $\frac{RT}{F} \ln a\left(H^+\right) = 0$

because ln 1 = 0. Therefore,

$$E_{oxidation} = E^\circ_{oxidation} .$$

Adding the two E values give

$$E_{total} = E_{oxidation} + E_{reduction} \qquad (3)$$

$$= E^\circ_{oxidation} + E^\circ_{reduction} - \frac{RT}{F} \ln a\left(Fe^{2+}\right)^{1/2}$$

$$= E^\circ_{oxidation} + E^\circ_{reduction} - (1/2)(0.05916) \log a\left(Fe^{2+}\right) \qquad (4)$$

But $E_{total} = 0$ when $E_{reduction} = - E_{oxidation}$.

Therefore, equation (4) gives

$$\log a\left(Fe^{2+}\right) = \left(E^\circ_{oxidation} + E^\circ_{reduction}\right) / (1/2)(0.05916)$$

$$= 1.669/(1/2)(0.05916)$$

$$= \frac{1.669}{0.02958} = 56.5 .$$

$$\therefore \quad a\left(Fe^{2+}\right) = 2.7 \times 10^{56}$$

• PROBLEM 9-24

The emf of the cell $H_2(P)|0.1\ m\ HCl|HgCl|Hg$ was measured as a function of P at 298 K.

P(atm)	1.0	37.9	51.6	110.2	286.6	731.8	1035.2
E(mV)	399.0	445.6	449.6	459.6	473.4	489.3	497.5

Calculate the fugacity coefficients ($\gamma = f/P$).

Solution: The two electrode reactions are,

$$1/2\ H_2(g) \rightarrow H^+ + e^- \qquad \text{(oxidation reaction)}$$

$$HgCl(s) + e^- \rightarrow Hg(s) + Cl^- \qquad \text{(reduction reaction)}$$

$$\text{OVERALL:} \quad 1/2\ H_2(g) + HgCl(s) \rightarrow Hg(s) + H^+ + Cl^-$$

For this reaction, the Nernst equation is written in the form

$$E = E^\circ - \frac{RT}{nF} \ln Q \tag{1}$$

where

E = cell's electromotive force (emf)

E° = standard potential

n = number of equivalents (which is one in this case)

Q = reaction quotient = $\dfrac{a_{HCl}}{a^{1/2}_{H_2(g)}}$.

Using the data at P = 1 atm as the standard (reference) state, E° can be calculated.

At moderate and low pressures,

$a_{H_2(g)} = P_{H_2(g)} = f_{H_2(g)}$ where f = fugacity.

Since P = 1 atm is low (and it's been chosen as the standard state), equation (1) can be rewritten in the form

$$E = E^\circ - \frac{RT}{F} \ln\left(\frac{a_{HCl}}{a^{1/2}_{H_2(g)}}\right) = E^\circ - \frac{RT}{F} \ln \frac{a_{HCl}}{f^{1/2}_{H_2(g)}} . \tag{2}$$

Remember that n=1; so it does not appear in the above equation.

Expanding equation (2) gives

$$E = E^\circ - [0.05916 \log a_{HCl} - 1/2(0.05916) \log f_{H_2}]$$

$$= E^\circ - 0.05916 \log a_{HCl} + 0.02958 \log f_{H_2} \tag{3}$$

Now, at P = 1 atm, f_{H_2} is assumed to be 1.00 and γ_{H_2} = 1.00 where γ = fugacity coefficient.

Therefore, equation (3) becomes

$$E = E^\circ - 0.05916 \log a_{HCl} + 0.02958 \log (1)$$

$$= E^\circ - 0.05916 \log a_{HCl} + 0$$

$$\therefore \quad E = E^\circ - 0.05916 \log a_{HCl} \tag{4}$$

But at P = 1 atm, E is given to be 399.0 mV = 0.399 V. Substituting for E in equation (4) gives

$$0.399 \text{ V} = E^\circ - 0.05916 \log a_{HCl} . \tag{5}$$

Note that everything on the right hand side of equation (5) appears in equation (3), therefore, that section of the equation can be replaced by 0.3990.

As a result of this manipulation, equation (3) becomes

$E = 0.3990 + 0.02958 \log f_{H_2}$.

Rearranging the above equation to solve for $\log f_{H_2}$ gives

$$\log f_{H_2} = \frac{E - 0.3990}{0.02958} \qquad (6)$$

Using equation (6) the fugacities at the different pressures can be computed by direct substitution of the given E values. Thus, at P = 37.9 atm,

$$\log f_{H_2} = \frac{0.4456 - 0.3990}{0.02958} = 1.5754$$

$$\therefore \quad f_{H_2} = 37.617$$

At P = 51.6 atm,

$$\log f_{H_2} = \frac{0.4496 - 0.3990}{0.02958} = 1.7106$$

$$\therefore \quad f_{H_2} = 51.359$$

Their corresponding fugacity coefficients are

$$\gamma = f/P = \frac{37.617}{37.9} = .9925$$

$$\gamma = f/P = \frac{51.359}{51.6} = .9953 \text{ respectively.}$$

Similar computations are done for the rest of the E values at their respective pressures.

• PROBLEM 9-25

What is the voltage at 25°C of the cell

$Pt/H_2(1\ atm)/HCl(0.5\ M)/HCl(1.0M)/H_2(1\ atm)/Pt$

if $t_+ = 0.83$?

Solution: This is a concentration cell as specified by the molar quantities in parenthesis. Concentration cells depend for their emf on a transfer of material from one electrode to the other as a result of concentration difference between the two. This difference in concentration, as in the above cell, arises from the solutions with which the electrodes are in contact. The cell has a liquid junction between the two HCl solutions of the same kind but different concentrations, resulting in a concentration cell with transference, t.

In the above cell, the concentration, (1.0M) of HCl in which the right electrode dips is greater than the concentration (0.5M) of the same HCl in which the left electrode dips. It can thus be assumed that the left electrode is negative. The reaction at the negative electrode will be

$$1/2\ H_2(1\ \text{atm}) = H^+(0.5M) + e^-$$

and that at the positive electrode will be

$$H^+(1.0M) + e^- = 1/2\ H_2(1\ \text{atm})$$

Adding the two reactions together gives the total reaction

$$H^+(1.0M) = H^+(0.5M)$$

By convention, current generated by the Cl^- is moving from the right to left electrode and the positive ions, H^+, is moving across the junction from left to right.

The voltage (E) of this concentration cell is given by

$$E = -\frac{RT}{nF} \ln\left(\frac{(0.5M)^{t_-}}{(1.0M)^{t_-}}\right) \tag{1}$$

where t_- is the transference (transport) number of the chloride ions (that is the ions to which the electrodes are not reversible). This voltage results from the fact that the overall process of the cell is given by

$$t_-\ HCl(1.0M) = t_-\ HCl(0.5M)$$

Since $t_+ + t_- = 1$, thus $t_- = 1 - t_+ = 0.17$. From (1)

$$E = -t_- \frac{RT}{nF} \ln\left(\frac{0.5M}{1.0M}\right)$$

In this problem, n=1 because only one mole is being transferred (see the net equation). Therefore,

$$E = -\frac{0.059157}{1}(0.17) \log \frac{0.5}{1.0}\ .$$

log (0.5/1.0) = - 0.30 and E = 0.0030 volts.

• PROBLEM 9-26

The following data refer to the cell $Zn(s)|ZnSO_4(aq)$, molality = $m|PbSO_4(s)\ |\ Pb$ at 25°C:

m	$\sqrt{m}$	$\frac{RT}{F}$ ln m (volts)	E(volts)
0.001000	0.03162	-0.17745	0.59714
0.005000	0.07071	-0.13611	0.56598

(a) Write the chemical equation for the cell process.

(b) Write the Nernst equation for this cell, in terms of m and the mean ionic activity coefficient $\gamma_\pm$ of $ZnSO_4$.

Assume that $PbSO_4$ is completely insoluble. m is the molality.

(c) By a process of linear extrapolation, either graphical or numerical, find E° for the cell.

(d) Find $\gamma_\pm$ in the 0.005 m solution from the emf data.

Solution: a) This problem can be solved by first writing the two half reactions, which are oxidation and reduction reactions. Then, they are added to give the desired overall cell reaction.

The oxidation reaction is written as

$$Zn(s) \rightarrow Zn^{2+}_{(aq)} + 2e^-$$

and the reduction reaction is

$$PbSO_4(s) + 2e^- \rightarrow Pb(s) + SO^{2-}_{4(aq)}$$

Adding these two reactions gives

$$Zn(s) + PbSO_4(s) \rightarrow Pb(s) + Zn^{2+}_{(aq)} + SO^{2-}_{4(aq)} \text{ ,}$$

which is the required overall reaction.

b) The Nernst equation is

$$E = E° - \frac{RT}{2F} \ln \left(a_{Zn^{2+}} a_{SO_4^{2-}}\right) \tag{1}$$

where E = the cell's emf

E° = standard emf

a = activity

F = Faraday's constant

T = temperature

But $a = \gamma m$ or $a_+ = \gamma_+ m$ and $a_- = \gamma_- m$

where γ = activity coefficient

m = molality

Therefore, equation (1) becomes

$$E = E^\circ - \frac{RT}{2F} \ln[(\gamma_+ m)(\gamma_- m)]$$

$$= E^\circ - \frac{RT}{2F} \ln (\gamma_\pm^2 m^2) \text{ where } \gamma_\pm^2 = \gamma_+\gamma_-$$

$$\therefore \quad E = E^\circ - \frac{RT}{F} \ln (\gamma_\pm m) \qquad (2)$$

c) Now let

$$E' = E + \frac{RT}{F} \ln m \qquad (3)$$

Substitute for E from equation (2)

$$\therefore \quad E' = E^\circ - \frac{RT}{F} \ln (\gamma_\pm m) + \frac{RT}{F} \ln m$$

$$= E^\circ - \frac{RT}{F} \ln \gamma_\pm - \frac{RT}{F} \ln m + \frac{RT}{F} \ln m$$

$$\therefore \quad E' = E^\circ - \frac{RT}{F} \ln \gamma_\pm \quad \text{from which}$$

$$E^\circ = \lim_{\text{as } m \to 0} E'$$

From the given data, E' can be calculated using equation (3). The results are

m	$\sqrt{m}$	$\frac{RT}{F} \ln m$	E	E'
0.001000	0.03162	-0.17745	0.59714	0.41969
0.005000	0.07071	-0.13611	0.56598	0.42987

According to the Debye-Hückel limiting law, $\ln \gamma_\pm$ should be proportional to $\sqrt{m}$. Therefore, E' should be a linear function of $\sqrt{m}$:

$$E' = E^\circ + K\sqrt{m} \qquad (4)$$

where K = proportionality constant.

Using the two values of E' and $\sqrt{m}$ from the table and equation (4), K and E° can be calculated by solving the resulting simultaneous equation.

$$0.41969 = E^\circ + K(0.03162)$$

$$0.42987 = E^\circ + K(0.07071)$$

$$0.01018 = K(0.03909)$$

$$\therefore \quad K = \frac{0.01018}{0.03909} = 0.2604$$

and $E° = 0.41146$ volts.

This could have been done graphically also. Plot E' vs $\sqrt{m}$. It should be a straight line. Extrapolate to $\sqrt{m} = 0$ to get E°.

d) Recall that

$$E' = E° - \frac{RT}{F} \ln \gamma_{\pm} \ .$$

At 25°C,

$$E' = E° - 0.059157 \log \gamma_{\pm} \ .$$

Therefore, $0.059157 \log \gamma_{\pm} = E° - E'$

$$= 0.41146 - 0.42987$$

$$= - 0.01841$$

or $\log \gamma_{\pm} = - \dfrac{0.01841}{0.05915} = - 0.3113$.

and $\gamma_{\pm} = 0.488$.

• PROBLEM 9-27

(a) For the reaction

$$2Ag(s) + PbSO_4(s) \rightarrow Pb(s) + 2Ag^+(aq) + SO_4^{2-}(aq)$$

$\Delta H°_{298} = 53.22$ kcal, $\Delta G°_{298} = 53.41$ kcal,

and $\Delta C°_{P,298} = -8.7$ cal $°K^{-1}$.

Find the equilibrium constant K as a function of temperature. Your expression should contain only T and actual numbers. Make any reasonable and necessary approximations.

(b) Devise a galvanic cell, or combination of cells, that can be used to determine K for the reaction of (a) at one temperature. Show what measurements would have to be made and how they would be used to calculate K. Illustrate with roughly drawn graphs when appropriate. Assume that $PbSO_4$ is completely insoluble in water and that Ag_2SO_4 is sufficiently soluble.

(c) Show how K would be changed if the activities of the ions were expressed on the "rational" (mole fraction) scale instead of the "practical" (molality) scale.

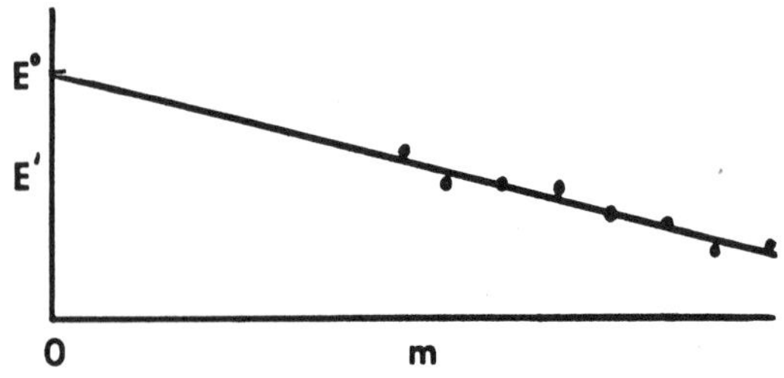

Fig.1

Solution: a) By definition,

$$\Delta G = \Delta G° + RT \ln K \text{ at constant T and P.} \tag{1}$$

where ΔG = Gibbs free energy of the reaction

$\Delta G°$ = Gibbs free energy at the standard (or reference) state

R = Gas constant

K = equilibrium constant

T = Temperature

P = Pressure

Also at constant Temperature and Pressure, $\Delta G = 0$.

Therefore, equation (1) becomes

$$0 = \Delta G°_{298} + RT \ln K_{298}$$

or $$-\Delta G°_{298} = RT \ln K_{298} \tag{2}$$

and $$\ln K_{298} = -\frac{\Delta G°_{298}}{RT} \tag{3}$$

If the numerical values are substituted into equation (3), it becomes

$$\ln K_{298} = -\frac{53.41 \times 1000}{(1.987)(298)} .$$

[The 1000 in the numerator is the conversion factor from kcal to cal.]

$$\therefore \quad \ln K_{298} = -90.2$$

If it is assumed that $\Delta C_P°$ is independent of Temperature, another relation can be written for the enthalpy as follows:

$$\Delta H_T° = \Delta H°_{298} + \int_{298}^{T} \Delta C_P° \, dT = \Delta H°_{298} + \Delta C_P° \int_{298}^{T} dT$$

where ΔH°_T = enthalpy change at Temperature T

ΔH°_{298} = enthalpy change at reference state (298°K in this case)

ΔC°_P = change in heat capacity at constant pressure.

Solving for ΔH°_T gives

$$\Delta H^\circ_T = 53.22 - 8.7 \int_{298}^{T} dT$$

$$= 53.22 - 8.7\ T \Big|_{298}^{T}$$

$$= 53.22 - 8.7(T-298) \qquad (4)$$

But the ΔH°_{298} is in kcal while the ΔC°_P term is in cal K^{-1}.

Therefore, equation (4) should be rewritten as

$$\Delta H^\circ_T = 53.22 - 8.7 \times 10^{-3}(T-298)$$

$$= 53.22 - 8.7 \times 10^{-3}T + (2592.6 \times 10^{-3})$$

$$= 53.22 - 8.7 \times 10^{-3}T + 2.5926$$

$$= 55.81 - 8.7 \times 10^{-3}T \text{ kcal}$$

Making use of the fact that

$$\ln K_T = \ln K_{298} + \ln K_{298 \to T}, \qquad (5)$$

the desired expression can be obtained. The subscripts mean at that temperature or temperature range, as the case may be.

Now the Gibbs-Helmholtz equation is

$$\left[\frac{\partial(\Delta G/T)}{\partial T}\right]_P = -\frac{\Delta H^\circ}{T^2} \qquad (6)$$

But $-\Delta G = RT \ln K$

and $$\frac{-\Delta G}{RT} = \ln K \qquad (7)$$

Using equations (6) and (7) gives

$$\left[\frac{\partial \ln K}{\partial T}\right]_P = \frac{\Delta H^\circ{}_T}{RT^2}$$

Integrating both sides yields

$$\int_{K \text{ at } 298}^{K \text{ at } T} d \ln K = \int_{298}^{T} \frac{\Delta H^\circ_T}{RT^2} dT$$

or

$$\ln K \Big|_{K \text{ at } 298}^{K \text{ at } T} = \int_{298}^{T} \frac{\Delta H^\circ_T}{RT^2} dT$$

Equation (5) then becomes

$$\ln K_T = \ln K_{298} + 1/R \int_{298}^{T} \frac{\Delta H^\circ_T}{T^2} dT \qquad (8)$$

But $\Delta H^\circ_T = 55.8 - 8.7 \times 10^{-3} T$ and $\ln K_{298} = -90.2$

Therefore, rewriting equation (8) gives

$$\ln K_T = -90.2 + \frac{1}{1.987 \times 10^{-3}} \int_{298}^{T} \left(\frac{55.8}{T^2} - \frac{8.7 \times 10^{-3}}{T} \right) dT$$

$$= -90.2 + 2.81 \times 10^4 \left(\frac{1}{298} - 1/T \right) - 4.4 \ln\left(\frac{T}{298} \right)$$

$$\therefore \quad \ln K_T = 28.8 - \frac{2.81 \times 10^4}{T} - 4.4 \ln T$$

b) It is easier to choose a cell for which the reaction is easily written by inspection. In that case, the cell

$Ag(s)|Ag_2SO_4(aq)|PbSO_4(s)|Pb(s)$ is suitable.

The cell reaction is

$$Ag(s) + PbSO_4(s) \rightarrow Ag^+_{(aq)} + SO^{2-}_{4(aq)} + Pb(s)$$

Balancing this reaction gives

$$2Ag(s) + PbSO_4(s) \rightarrow 2Ag^+(aq) + SO_4^{2-}(aq) + Pb(s).$$

For this reaction,

$$E = E^\circ - \frac{RT}{2F} \ln \left(a^2_{Ag+}\, a_{SO_4^{2-}} \right) \qquad (9)$$

where E = the cell's emf

$E°$ = the cell's standard emf

a = activity

F = the Faraday's constant.

Equation (9) is known as the Nernst Equation. It can also be written in the form

$$E = E° - \frac{3RT}{2F} \ln a_{\pm} \qquad (10)$$

where the $a_{\pm}$ = mean activity = $\left(a_+^2 a_-\right)^{1/(2+1)} = \left(a_+^2 a_-\right)^{1/3}$

But $a_{\pm} = \gamma_{\pm} m_{\pm} = \gamma_{\pm} \left(\sqrt[3]{4}\right) m$

where $\gamma_{\pm}$ = mean activity coefficient = $\left(\gamma_+^2 \gamma_-\right)^{1/3}$

and $m_{\pm}$ = mean ionic molality

$= \left(m_+^2 m_-\right)^{1/3} = \left[(2m)^2 (m)\right]^{1/3} = \left[(4m^2)(m)\right]^{1/3} = \left[4m^3\right]^{1/3}$

$= m\sqrt[3]{4}$

Also, the Debye-Hückel limiting law gives $\ln \gamma_{\pm} \approx - A\sqrt{m}$ where A is a known constant for any one temperature, solvent, and salt type.

Rewriting equation (10) gives

$$E = E° - \frac{3RT}{2F} \ln \left[\gamma_{\pm} (4)^{1/3} m\right]$$

Now let $E' = E + \frac{RT}{2F} (3 \ln m + \ln 4 - 3 A\sqrt{m})$

Therefore, $E' = E° - \frac{3RT}{2F} \left(\ln \gamma_{\pm} + A\sqrt{m}\right)$

Note that $\lim\limits_{m \to 0} E' = E°$

Measure E with a sequence of cells in which the molality m becomes smaller. A plot of E' vs m can be constructed. m=0 can be extrapolated. The rough graph is as shown in Fig.1.

At equilibrium, $\Delta G = -nFE = 0$, Hence $E=0$.

Finally using the relation $E = E° - \frac{RT}{2F} \ln K$,

then $\ln K = \frac{2FE°}{RT}$.

c) Recall that

$$K_m = a_{Ag+}^{(m)\,2} \, a_{SO_4^{2-}}^{(m)}$$

Therefore,

$$K_x = a_{Ag+}^{(x)2} \; a_{SO_4^{2-}}^{(x)}$$

where x = mole fraction.

$$\frac{a^{(x)}}{a^{(m)}} = \lim_{\substack{\text{as } m \to 0 \\ \text{and } x \to 0}} (x/m) = \frac{M_{H_2O}}{1000} = 0.018$$

where M_{H_2O} = Molecular weight of H_2O = 18 g mol^{-1}

Therefore,

$$\frac{K_x}{K_m} = (0.018)^3 = 5.83 \times 10^{-6} .$$

• PROBLEM 9-28

For the cell H_2(1 atm)|HCl|AgCl|Ag, E° = 0.2220 V at 298 K. If the measured E = 0.396 V, what is the pH of the HCl solution? Cite any approximations made.

Solution: The two half reactions are

$$1/2\ H_2 \rightarrow H^+ + e^- \qquad \text{(oxidation)}$$

$$AgCl + e^- \rightarrow Ag + Cl^- \qquad \text{(reduction)}$$

OVERALL: $1/2\ H_2 + AgCl \rightarrow Ag + H^+ + Cl^-$

Now, writing the Nernst equation for this overall reaction gives

$$E = E° - \frac{RT}{nF} \ln \left(\frac{a_{H+} \; a_{Cl-}}{a_{H_2}^{1/2}} \right) \qquad (1)$$

where E = cell e.m.f.

E° = standard potential

R = Gas Constant

T = Temperature

F = Faraday's constant

a = Activity

n = 1 (number of equivalents of electrons in the balanced reaction)

At 25°C = 298°K ,

$$\frac{RT}{F} \ln x = 0.05916 \log x.$$

Therefore, equation (1) becomes

$$E = E° - 0.05916 \log \left(\frac{a_{H+} \, a_{Cl-}}{a_{H_2}^{1/2}} \right)$$

$$= E° - 0.05916 \left[\log a_{H+} + \log a_{Cl-} - 1/2 \log a_{H_2} \right] \quad (2)$$

a_{H_2} can be approximated by P_{H_2} = 1 atm where P = pressure.

Therefore a_{H_2} = 1 and equation (2) becomes

$$E = E° - 0.05916 \left[\log a_{H+} + \log a_{Cl-} \right] \quad (3)$$

Since $a_{H+} = a_{Cl-}$, equation (3) can be written in the form

$$E = E° - (0.05916)(2) \log a_{H+} . \quad (4)$$

By definition, $pH = - \log a_{H+}$

Therefore, equation (4) becomes

$$E = E° + (0.05916)(2) \text{ pH} \quad (5)$$

Both values of E and E° are given to be 0.396 V and 0.2220 V respectively. Substitute these values into equation (5) to get

$$0.396 \text{ V} = 0.2220 \text{ V} + (0.05916)(2) \text{ pH}$$

or $0.396 - 0.2220 = + (0.05916)(2) \text{ pH}$

$$0.174 = 0.11832 \text{ pH}$$

$$\therefore \quad pH = \frac{0.174}{0.11832}$$

$$= 1.47$$

• PROBLEM 9-29

The ionization constant of lactic acid at 25°C is 1.4×10^{-4}. A buffer solution is prepared by adding 1.00 mole of lactic acid and 0.80 mole of sodium lactate to 1 kg of water. Assume that water is at unit activity and that the activity coefficient of each univalent ion is 0.65 throughout this problem.

(a) Find the pH (in the activity sense) of this solution at 25°C.

(b) Find the change in the pH of the solution resulting from the addition of 0.50 mole of sodium hydroxide to the quantity of solution containing 1 kg of water.

(c) Find the change in pH resulting from the addition of 0.50 mole of sodium hydroxide to 1 kg of pure water at 25°C.

Solution: a) The ionization or dissociation of an acidic solution is represented by the general equation,

$$HA \rightleftarrows H^+ + A^- \qquad (1)$$

Initially, there are 0 moles of H^+, 1.00 moles of lactic acid and .80 moles of sodium lactate. Since sodium lactate ionizes completely (it is a salt of a weak acid), there are .80 moles of lactate ions and .80 moles of sodium ions (which are spectator ions in the buffer preparation) in the initial mixture.

Let n represent the number of moles of H^+ at equilibrium, then the number of moles of A^- at equilibrium is 0.8 + n and that of HA = 1.0 - n.

By definition,

$$pH = -\log a_{H+} \qquad (2)$$

where a = activity.

Before equation (1) can be used, the a_{H+} term needs to be computed, and to do this,

K is defined to be $\dfrac{\gamma_{H+}\, m_{H+}\, \gamma_{A-}\, m_{A-}}{\gamma_{HA}\, m_{HA}}$

where γ = activity coefficient

m = molality

K = equilibrium ionization constant

Note that γm = a where a = activity.

γ_{HA} is given to be 1.

Therefore,

$$K = \frac{\gamma_{H+}\, m_{H+}\, \gamma_{A-}\, m_{A-}}{m_{HA}}$$

or

$$\frac{m_{H+}\, m_{A-}}{m_{HA}} = \frac{K}{\gamma_{H+}\, \gamma_{A-}} \qquad (3)$$

But $\gamma_{H+} = \gamma_{A-} = 0.65$; which makes equation (3)

$$\frac{m_{H+}\, m_{A-}}{m_{HA}} = \frac{K}{(0.65)^2} = \frac{K}{0.4225} .$$

$K = 1.4 \times 10^{-4}$, therefore,

$$\frac{m_{H+}\, m_{A-}}{m_{HA}} = \frac{1.4 \times 10^{-4}}{0.4225} = 0.00033$$

Recall that $m_{H+} = n$

$m_{A-} = 0.8 + n$

$m_{HA} = 1.0 - n$

Therefore,

$$\frac{m_{H+}\, m_{A-}}{m_{HA}} = \frac{n(0.8 + n)}{1.0 - n} = 0.00033 . \qquad (4)$$

[Note that m = molality is defined as

$$\frac{\text{the number of moles of solute}}{\text{1 kg of solvent}} .$$

Since the solution is prepared by using 1 kg of solvent, the individual number of moles in the solution are the values of the individual molalities. This is why $m_{H+} = n$, $m_{A-} = 0.8 + n$ and $m_{HA} = 1.0 - n$.]

The next step is to solve for n in equation (4).

Usually, n is assumed to be much less than unity (or close to zero) at equilibrium. So, equation (4) reduces to

$$\frac{n(0.8)}{1.0} = 0.00033 \qquad (5)$$

$$\therefore \quad n = \frac{0.00033}{0.8} = 0.0004125 \text{ mol kg}^{-1}$$

Note also that the expansion of equation (4) gives a quadratic equation which can be solved by using the quadratic formula. Expanding equation (4) gives

$$0.8\,n + n^2 = 0.00033 - 0.00033n.$$

$$\therefore \quad n^2 + 0.80033n - 0.00033 = 0$$

Using the formula,

$$n = \frac{-b \pm \sqrt{b^2 - 4ac}}{2a} = \frac{-0.80033 \pm \sqrt{0.64053 + 0.00132}}{2}$$

$$= \frac{-0.80033 \pm \sqrt{0.64185}}{2}$$

$$= \frac{-0.80033 \pm 0.8011554}{2}$$

The two possible answers here are

$$n = \frac{-0.80033 + 0.8011554}{2} = 0.0004127$$

and

$$n = \frac{-0.80033 - 0.8011554}{2} = -0.8007427$$

The two answers are mathematically correct but the second answer for n is not possible because of the negative sign.

So $n = 0.0004127 \quad \text{mol kg}^{-1}$,

observe that this result is very close to the result obtained when n was assumed to be very close to zero. Now that $n = m_{H+}$ has been computed, a_{H+} can be computed also by using the relation $a_{H+} = \gamma_{H+} m_{H+}$ and consequently, $pH = -\log a_{H+}$ can be computed. From the results,

$$a_{H+} = \gamma_{H+} m_{H+} = (0.65)(0.00041)$$

$$= 0.00027$$

$$pH = -\log a_{H+} = -\log 0.00027$$

$$= -(-3.57)$$

$$= 3.57$$

b) Adding 0.50 mole NaOH to the solution means that

$$m_{HA} = 1.0 - 0.5 = 0.5$$

and $m_{A-} = 0.8 + 0.5 = 1.3$

If m_{H+} is assumed to be y this time, then equation (3) gives

$$\frac{y(0.8 + 0.5)}{1.0 - 0.5} = 0.00033$$

or

$$\frac{y(1.3)}{0.5} = 0.00033; \text{ from which}$$

$$y = 0.000127 \simeq 0.00013 = m_{H+} .$$

Using the relation $a_{H+} = \gamma_{H+} m_{H+}$ gives

$$a_{H+} = (0.65)(0.00013) = 0.0000845 \text{ and}$$

$$pH = -\log a_{H+} = -\log 0.0000845$$

$$= -(-4.07)$$

$$= 4.07$$

c) Here m_{OH^-} is given to be 0.5 mol kg^{-1}.

$$\therefore \quad a_{OH^-} = \gamma_{OH^-} m_{OH^-} = (0.65)(0.5) = 0.325.$$

From this value $pOH = -\log a_{OH^-} = -\log 0.325.$

$$= -(-0.488)$$

$$= 0.488$$

By definition,

$$pH + pOH = -\log K_w = 14$$

where K_w = equilibrium constant of the ionization of water.

Therefore $pH = 14 - pOH = 14 - 0.488$

$$= 13.512.$$

• PROBLEM 9-30

The solubility of AgCl in water at 25°C is $10^{-4.895}$ mol dm^{-3}. By means of the Debye-Hückel theory, calculate $\Delta G°$ for the change: $AgCl(c) \rightarrow Ag^+ + Cl^-(aq)$. Calculate the solubility of AgCl in a solution of KNO_3 in which the ionic strength is $I = 0.010$ mol dm^{-3}.

Solution: a) The standard Gibbs free energy change is related to the solubility of any substance by

$$\Delta G° = -RT \ln K_{sp} \tag{1}$$

where $\Delta G°$ = standard Gibbs free energy

R = Gas constant

T = Temperature

K_{sp} = equilibrium solubility product constant

Before equation (1) can be solved, the K_{sp} value needs to be known.

This is defined as

$$K_{sp} = a_{Ag^+} a_{Cl^-} = \left(a_\pm\right)^{(1+1)} = \left(a_\pm\right)^2 \tag{2}$$

where a_{Ag^+} = activity of Ag^+ in the solution

a_{Cl^-} = activity of Cl^- in the solution

$a_\pm$ = mean activity

But $a_{\pm} = \gamma_{\pm} C_{\pm}$, where $\gamma_{\pm}$ = mean activity coefficient and $C_{\pm}$ = mean ionic molar concentration (or solubility of AgCl).

As a result,

$$K_{sp} = \left(\gamma_{\pm} C_{\pm}\right)^2 \tag{3}$$

$C_{\pm}$ is given to be $10^{-4.895}$ mol dm^{-3}. To calculate $\gamma_{\pm}$, the Debye-Hückel limiting law is used. This law states that

$$\log \gamma_{\pm} \simeq -0.509 |Z_+ Z_-| I^{1/2} \tag{4}$$

where Z = ionic valence (charge)

$$I = \text{ionic strength} = (1/2) \sum_{i}^{\text{ions}} C_i Z_i^2 \tag{5}$$

Note that the sum in the calculation of I is performed over all the ions in the solution.

The use of equation (5) gives

$$I = 1/2 \left[10^{-4.895}(1)^2 + 10^{-4.895}(1)^2\right]$$
$$= 10^{-4.895}$$

Using this in equation (4) gives

$$\log \gamma_{\pm} = -0.509 \ (1) \ \sqrt{10^{-4.895}}$$

$$= -0.001617$$

$$\therefore \quad \gamma_{\pm} = 0.9963 .$$

Using equation (3) gives

$$K_{sp} = \left(\gamma_{\pm} C_{\pm}\right)^2 = \left(0.9963 \times 10^{-4.895}\right)^2$$
$$= 1.610 \times 10^{-10}$$

Now, equation (1) can be used. That is,

$$\Delta G° = -RT \ln K_{sp} = -RT \ln 1.610 \times 10^{-10} .$$

$$= -\left(8.314 \times 10^{-3} \frac{\text{kJ}}{\text{mole °K}}\right)(298°\text{K}) \ln\left(1.610 \times 10^{-10}\right)$$
$$= 55.91 \text{ kJ/mole.}$$

b) Again using the Debye-Hückel limiting law,

$$\log \gamma_{\pm} = -0.509|Z_{+}Z_{-}|I^{1/2}$$

But here, $I = 0.010 \text{ mol dm}^{-3}$;

$$\therefore \quad \sqrt{I} = \sqrt{0.010} = 0.10$$

Consequently, $\log \gamma_{\pm} = -0.509\,(1)^2\,(0.10)$

$$= -0.0509$$

and $\qquad \gamma_{\pm} = 0.889$

Recall that K_{sp} was defined to be $K_{sp} = \left(\gamma_{\pm}\; C_{\pm}\right)^2 = \gamma_{\pm}^2\; C_{\pm}^2$.

Therefore, $C_{\pm}^2 = \dfrac{K_{sp}}{\gamma_{\pm}^2}$.

Taking the square root of both sides yields

$$\sqrt{C_{\pm}^2} = \sqrt{\frac{K_{sp}}{\gamma_{\pm}^2}}$$

or $\qquad C_{\pm} = \dfrac{\sqrt{K_{sp}}}{\gamma_{\pm}} \qquad (6)$

Substituting the respective values into equation (6) yields

$$C_{\pm} = \frac{\sqrt{1.610 \times 10^{-10}}}{0.889} = \frac{1.269 \times 10^{-5}}{0.889}$$

$$= 1.427 \times 10^{-5} \text{ mol dm}^{-3}$$

ELECTRODES

• PROBLEM 9-31

During the electrolysis of a NaCl solution using inert electrodes, the following chemical reactions are possible at the anode:

$$Cl^{-}(aq) = \frac{1}{2}\, Cl_2(g) + 1e^{-}$$

$$2H_2O(liq) = O_2(g) + 4H^{+}(aq) + 4e^{-}$$

and at the cathode:

$$Na^{+}(aq) + 1e^{-} = Na(s)$$

$$2H^{+}(aq) + 2e^{-} = H_2(g)$$

The voltage of a cell described by the first and third equations is -4.0692 V; first and fourth, -1.3583 V; second and third, -3.940 V; and second and fourth, -1.229 V. Which reaction will proceed under standard conditions?

Solution: The reactions to be compared and their respective standard electrode potentials are:

Reactions:	Standard Electrode Potentials, E°
(1) $Cl^-(aq) + Na^+(aq) = \frac{1}{2}Cl_2(g) + Na(s)$	-4.0692 V
(2) $2Cl^-(aq) + 2H^+(aq) = Cl_2(g) + H_2(g)$	-1.3583 V
(3) $2H_2O + 4Na^+(aq) = O_2(g) + 4H^+(aq) + 4Na(s)$	-3.940 V
(4) $2H_2O + 4H^+(aq) = O_2(g) + 4H^+(aq) + 2H_2(g)$	-1.229 V

The reaction that will proceed under standard conditions is the reaction that is most favored. Looking at the electrode potentials, it can be seen that reaction (4) is most favored because it has the highest (most positive) E° value.

• PROBLEM 9-32

For the reaction $2Cr(s) + 3\,Cu^{2+}(aq) \rightarrow 2Cr^{3+}(aq) + 3\,Cu(s)$ find the value of the standard cell potential. The half reactions are $Cr^3 + 3e^- \rightleftarrows Cr$ and $Cu^{2+} + 2e^- \rightleftarrows Cu$ with -0.74 volts and +0.34 volts as their respective standard reduction potentials (E°).

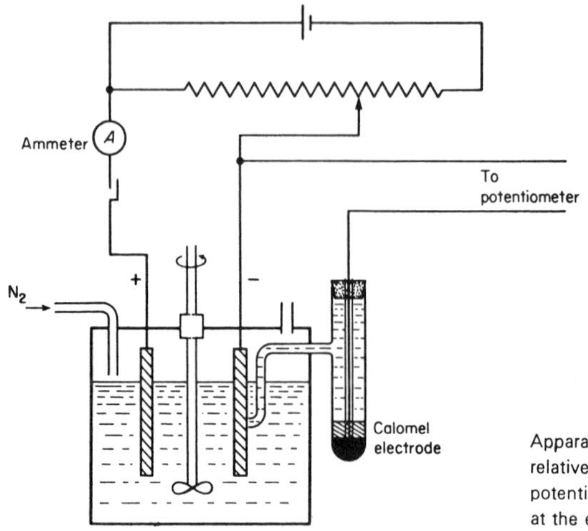

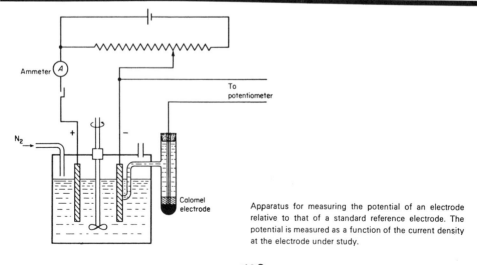

Apparatus for measuring the potential of an electrode relative to that of a standard reference electrode. The potential is measured as a function of the current density at the electrode under study.

Solution: Comparing the two half-reactions to the main reaction, we see that the Cr half-reaction is reversed. Also, we must multiply the Cr half-reaction by two and that of Cu by three so as to eliminate the electrons. Note that the reduction potentials (E°) are unaffected by these stoichiometric coefficients. This is due to the fact that all the standard potentials are already written on the same basis. This occurs because these standard potentials correspond to a free energy change on a per Faraday basis. The two half-reactions and their potentials now become:

Reactions:	E°
$2Cr \rightleftarrows 2Cr^{3+} + 6e^-$	+0.74
$3Cu^{2+} + 6e^- \rightleftarrows 3\ Cu$	+0.34
SUM: $3Cu^{2+} + 2Cr \rightleftarrows 2Cr^{3+} + 3Cu$	+1.08

E° for the first half reaction is positive because the reaction was reversed.

• PROBLEM 9-33

The chemical reaction in a "lead storage" cell of a car battery during charging involves the reduction of $PbSO_4(s)$ to $Pb(s)$ and the oxidation of $PbSO_4(s)$ to $PbO_2(s)$, both reactions occurring in the presence of $H_2SO_4(aq)$. Write the balanced reaction.

Solution: Before a balanced equation can be obtained, two balanced half reactions should be written, one for the oxidation reaction and the other for the reduction reaction. These are then added up to give the desired overall reaction equation. From the statement of the problem, the oxidation reaction is

$$PbSO_4(s) \rightarrow PbO_2(s) \qquad (1)$$

and the reduction reaction is

$$PbSO_4(s) \rightarrow Pb(s) \qquad (2)$$

Balancing the second equation involves adding a $SO_4^{2-}(aq)$ to the right hand side giving

$$PbSO_4(s) \rightarrow Pb(s) + SO_4^{2-}(aq)\ . \qquad (3)$$

The first equation also requires a $SO_4^{2-}(aq)$ on the right side, but to balance the oxygen and hydrogen atoms, $xH^+(aq)$ and $yH_2O(liq)$ are added because the reaction is occurring in neutral or acidic media.

Thus equation (1) becomes

$$PbSO_4(s) \rightarrow PbO_2(s) + SO_4^{2-}(aq) + xH^+(aq) + yH_2O(liq) \qquad (4)$$

where x and y = stoichiometric coefficients. Counting the number of hydrogen and oxygen atoms in equation (4) give

$$0 = x + 2y \quad \text{for hydrogen and}$$

$$4 = 2 + 4 + y \quad \text{for oxygen.}$$

Solving for both x and y simultaneously yield y = -2 and x = 4. Putting these values into equation (4) yields

$$PbSO_4(s) \rightarrow PbO_2(s) + SO_4^{2-}(aq) + 4H^+(aq) - 2H_2O(liq) + 2e^-$$

or $$PbSO_4(s) + 2H_2O(liq) \rightarrow PbO_2(s) + SO_4^{2-}(aq) + 4H^+(aq) + 2e^- \quad (5).$$

Note that the $2e^-$ is added to the right to balance the oxidation reaction electrically and that the $2H_2O$ is moved to the left because of the negative stoichiometry. Balancing the reduction reaction electrically, equation (3) becomes

$$PbSO_4(s) + 2e^- \rightarrow Pb(s) + SO_4^{2-}(aq) \quad . \quad (6)$$

Note the difference between the oxidation reaction and reduction reaction. In the former, the $2e^-$ is on the right while in the latter case, the $2e^-$ is on the left. Adding up equations (5) and (6) should give the desired equation as follows:

$$PbSO_4(s) + 2H_2O(liq) \rightarrow PbO_2(s) + SO_4^{2-}(aq) + 4H^+(aq) + 2e^-$$

$$PbSO_4(s) + 2e^- \rightarrow Pb(s) + SO_4^{2-}(aq)$$

OVERALL:

$$2PbSO_4(s) + 2H_2O(liq) \rightarrow PbO_2(s) + Pb(s) + 4H^+(aq) + 2SO_4^{2-}(aq) \quad .$$

Upon checking, the equation is balanced with respect to charge and mass.

IONICS

• PROBLEM 9-34

The measured voltage of the concentration cell Ag|$AgNO_3$ (0.0100m) || $AgNO_3$ (y) |Ag was 0.0650 V at 25°C. Calculate the molality y of the right-hand half-cell assuming $\gamma_\pm = 1$.

Solution: a) The cell's overall reaction is given by

$$Ag^+(y) \rightarrow Ag^+(0.0100m).$$

For this cell, the Nernst equation is

$$E = E° - \frac{RT}{nF} \ln \left(\frac{a_\pm(0.01)}{a_\pm(y)} \right) \qquad (1)$$

Here, n = 1

a = activity

E° = standard potential of the cell

F = Faraday's constant

Because of the similarity of the reactions in a concentration cell, E° = 0 and the potential is given by the non-standard conditions of the reactants and products. Therefore, equation (1) becomes

$$E = -\frac{RT}{F} \ln \left(\frac{a_\pm(0.01)}{a_\pm(y)} \right) \qquad (2)$$

By definition, the mean activity of a solute undergoing ionization in solution is given by

$$a_\pm = \gamma_\pm C_\pm$$

where $\gamma_\pm$ = mean activity coefficient

$C_\pm$ = mean ionic molal concentration

But $\gamma_\pm$ is given to be 1, therefore, $a_\pm = C_\pm$ and equation (2) becomes

$$E = -\frac{R(298)}{F} \ln \left(\frac{0.01}{y} \right) = -0.05916 \log \left(\frac{0.01}{y} \right) \text{ at } 25°\text{C}.$$

$$\text{or } \log\left(\frac{0.01}{y} \right) = -\frac{E}{0.05916} = -\frac{0.0650}{0.05916} = -1.0987;$$

From which $\frac{0.01}{y} = 7.967 \times 10^{-2}$

and $$y = \frac{0.01}{7.967 \times 10^{-2}}$$

$$= 0.1255\text{m}$$

• **PROBLEM 9-35**

For the galvanic cell $Pt|H_2(1\text{ atm})|HBr(aq, m\text{ mole liter}^{-1})|AgBr(s)|Ag$ at 25°C, the following reversible emf's were observed.

	(1)	(2)	(3)
10^4m	4.042	8.444	37.19
E (volts)	0.47381	0.43636	0.36173

(a) Write the equation for the cell process.

(b) From the data on each of the solutions (1) and (2), considered separately, calculate E° for the cell as predicted by the Debye-Hückel limiting law. Assume that molarity and molality are equal.

(c) With the aid of a graph of the results of (b), estimate the actual value of E°.

(d) Find the mean ionic activity coefficient of HBr in solution (3) from (i) the experimental data; (ii) the Debye-Hückel limiting law.

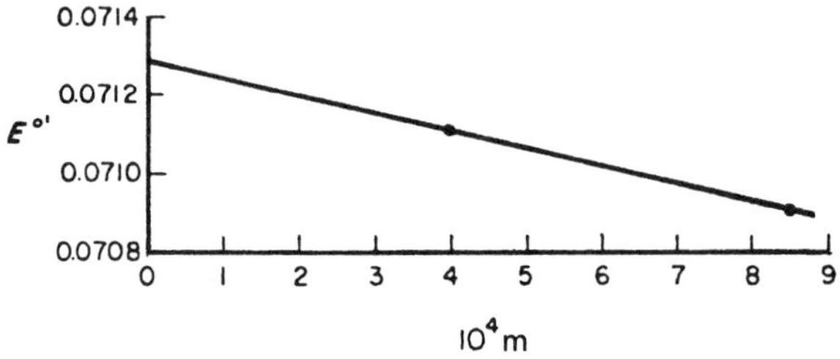

Fig. 1

Solution: a) Since this requires the overall cell reaction, it would be better to first write the two half reactions and then add them up.

The two half reactions are:

$$1/2\ H_2(g) \rightarrow H^+ + e$$

$$AgBr(s) + e \rightarrow Ag(s) + Br^-$$

The first one is the oxidation reaction and the second, reduction reaction. Adding up these half reactions give

$$1/2\ H_2(g) + AgBr(s) \rightarrow Ag(s) + H^+ + Br^- \ ,$$

which is the required equation.

b) Using the Nernst equation, the emf E, of the cell is

$$E = E° - \frac{RT}{F} \ln \left(\frac{a_{Ag}\ a_{H^+}\ _{Br^-}}{a_{AgBr}\ a_{H_2}^{1/2}} \right) \qquad (1)$$

where E° = standard emf

a = activity

F = Faradays constant

The activities of the solid phases are set equal to unity, and since the hydrogen pressure = 1 atm and consequently $a_{H_2} = 1$ equation (1) becomes

$$E = E° - \frac{RT}{F} \ln \left(a_{H^+}\ a_{Br^-}\right) \qquad (2)$$

The mean activity of ions is defined as

$$a_+ a_- = a_\pm^2$$

Introducing this mean activity into equation (2) gives

$$E = E° - \frac{RT}{F} \ln a_\pm^2$$

or

$$E = E° - \frac{2RT}{F} \ln a_\pm \qquad (3)$$

where $a_\pm$ = mean activity

But $a_\pm = \gamma_\pm$ m where $\gamma_\pm$ = mean ionic activity coefficient and m = molality, which is assumed to be equal to molarity, M. Therefore equation (3) becomes

$$E = E° - \frac{2RT}{F} \ln \left(\gamma_\pm m\right);$$

from which

$$E° = E + \frac{2RT}{F} \ln \left(\gamma_\pm m\right)$$

At 25°C,

$$E° = E + 0.1183 \left(\log \gamma_\pm + \log m\right)$$

The Debye-Hückel limiting law states that in dilute solutions,

$$\log \gamma_\pm \simeq -0.5091 \sqrt{m} \qquad (4)$$

Now let $E°' = E + 0.1183 (\log \gamma_\pm + \log m)$

Using equation (4) gives

$$E°' = E - 0.06023 \sqrt{m} + 0.1183 \log m$$

The limiting law predicts $E°' = E°$

Using the given data,

$$E°'_{(1)} = 0.47381 - 0.06023 \sqrt{\frac{4.042}{10^4}} + 0.1183 \log \frac{4.042}{10^4}$$

$$= 0.47381 - 0.0012106 - .4014$$

$$= 0.07110$$

$$E°'_{(2)} = 0.43636 - 0.06023 \sqrt{\frac{8.444}{10^4}} + 0.1183 \log \frac{8.444}{10^4}$$

$$= 0.07091$$

c) A plot of $E°'$ vs $10^4 m$ can be constructed; from which the actual $E°$ value can be obtained by extrapolating the line to $10^4\ m = 0$. The intercept at $m = 0$ gives the value of $E°$. The graph is as shown in Fig. 1.

The actual value of $E° = 0.0713$ volts.

d) (i) Recall that

$$E° = E + 0.1183 \log \gamma_{\pm} + 0.1183 \log m \quad \text{from which}$$

$$\log \gamma_{\pm} = \frac{E° - E - 0.1183 \log m}{0.1183}$$

$$= \frac{0.0713 - 0.36173 - 0.1183 \log\left(\frac{37.19}{10^4}\right)}{0.1183}$$

$$= -\ 0.0248$$

$$\therefore \quad \gamma_{\pm} = 0.944$$

(ii) From equation (4)

$$\log \gamma_{\pm} = -0.50916\sqrt{\frac{37.19}{10^4}} = -0.0311$$

$$\therefore \quad \gamma_{\pm} = 0.931$$

• PROBLEM 9-36

The mean ionic activity coefficient of an electrolyte in a dilute solution is given approximately by

$$\ln \gamma_{\pm} = -\ A\sqrt{m}$$

where m is the molality and A is a constant. Using the Gibbs-Duhem equation find the activity coefficient γ_1 of the solvent in this dilute solution in terms of A, m, and constants characteristic of the solvent and solute. Observe that

$$\ln X_1 = \ln\left(\frac{n_1}{n_1 + mv}\right) = \ln\left(\frac{1}{1 + mv/n_1}\right) \approx -\ \frac{mv}{n_1}$$

where v is the number of ions in the formula (for example v = 2 for NaCl) and n_1 is the number of moles of solvent in 1000 g of solvent. All quantities except γ_1, the unknown, can thus be expressed in terms of the variable m.

Solution: $\ln \gamma_{\pm} = -\ Am^{1/2}$ and $\ln X_1 = -\ \frac{mv}{n_1}$.

From these,

$$d \ln \gamma_{\pm} = -(1/2)\, Am^{-1/2}\, dm \quad \text{and}$$

$$d \ln X_1 = -\frac{v}{n_1}\, dm$$ by direct

differentiation with respect to m. Recall that

$$m = \text{molality}$$

$$= \frac{\text{number of moles of solute}}{1000 \text{ g of solvent}};$$

And since there are n_2 number of moles in 1000 g of water (solvent), $n_2 = m$.

For this electrolytic process,

$$a_2 = \left(a_+^p\, a_-^q\right) = \left(a_{\pm}\right)^v, \text{ where } p + q = v.$$

Therefore, $\ln a_2 = \ln \left(a_{\pm}^v\right) = v \ln a_{\pm}$.

But $a_{\pm} = \gamma_{\pm} m_{\pm}$.

Consequently,

$$\ln a_2 = v \ln (\gamma_{\pm} m_{\pm}) \tag{1}$$

Differentiating equation (1) gives

$$d \ln a_2 = v\left(d \ln \gamma_{\pm} + d \ln m_{\pm}\right) \tag{2}$$

$$= v\, d \ln \left(\gamma_{\pm} m_{\pm}\right) = v\left(d \ln \gamma_{\pm} + d \ln m\right).$$

Observe that $m_{\pm}$ is approximated by m because $\ln m_{\pm} = \ln$ (constant χ m).

The Gibbs-Duhem equation is defined to be

$$RT(X_1\, d \ln \gamma_1 + X_2\, d \ln \gamma_2) = 0;$$

from which

$$x_1\, d\ln \gamma_1 + x_2\, d\ln \gamma_2 = 0 \tag{3}$$

Multiplying equation (3) by $n_1 + n_2$ gives

$$\left(n_1 + n_2\right) X_1\, d \ln \gamma_1 + \left(n_1 + n_2\right) X_2\, d\ln \gamma_2 = 0 \tag{4}$$

observe that $\left(n_1 + n_2\right) X_1 = n_1$

and $\left(n_1 + n_2\right) X_2 = n_2$.

Therefore equation (4) becomes

$$n_1\, d\ln \gamma_1 + n_2\, d\ln \gamma_2 = 0 \tag{5}$$

Recall that $n_2 = m$.

Therefore, equation (5) becomes

$$n_1 \ \mathrm{dln}\ \gamma_1 + m \ \mathrm{dln}\ \gamma_2 = 0 \tag{6}$$

Since this is a dilute solution the quantity, γ can be approximated by the quantity a. This makes equation (6)

$$n_1 \ \mathrm{dln}\ a_1 + m \ \mathrm{dln}\ a_2 = 0$$

which turns out to be

$$n_1(\mathrm{dln}\ \gamma_1 + \mathrm{dln}\ X_1) + mv(\mathrm{dln}\ \gamma_\pm + \mathrm{dln}\ m) = 0 \tag{7}$$

by incorporating equation (2) into the last equation.

Recall that $d \ln X_1 = -\frac{v}{n_1}\, dm$ and

$$d \ln \gamma_\pm = -(1/2)\, Am^{-1/2}\, dm.$$

Therefore, equation (7) becomes

$$n_1 \ \mathrm{dln}\ \gamma_1 - vdm - (1/2)\, Avm^{1/2} dm + vdm = 0 \tag{8}$$

Solving for $\mathrm{dln}\ \gamma_1$ in equation (8) gives

$$\mathrm{dln}\ \gamma_1 = \frac{Avm^{1/2}}{2n_1}\, dm$$

Integrating both sides gives

$$\int_1^{\gamma_1} d \ln \gamma_1 = \frac{Av}{2n_1}\int_0^m m^{1/2}\, dm = \frac{Av}{2n_1}\, (2/3)\, m^{3/2} \Bigg|_0^m$$

$$\therefore \qquad \ln \gamma_1 = \frac{Av}{3n_1}\, m^{3/2}$$

Taking the exponents of both sides yields

$$e^{\ln \gamma_1} = e^{\left(\frac{Av}{3n_1} m^{3/2}\right)}$$

$$\gamma_1 = e^{\left(\frac{Av}{3n_1} m^{3/2}\right)}$$

• PROBLEM 9-37

(a) Find the mean ionic activity coefficient of $ZnCl_2$ in a 0.00500 m aqueous solution of $ZnCl_2$ at 25° by using the Debye-Hückel equation.

(b) The emf of the cell

$Zn(s)\,|\,ZnCl_2(aq,\ 0.00500\ m)\,|\,Hg_2Cl_2(s)\,|\,Hg(liq)$

is +1.2272 volt at 25°C. Find E° for this cell assuming that the Debye-Hückel equation is valid.

Solution: The Debye-Hückel equation is given by

$$\log \gamma_{\pm} = \frac{-0.509|Z_+Z_-|\sqrt{I}}{1 + \sqrt{I}} \qquad (1)$$

where γ = activity coefficient

and I = ionic strength = $1/2 \sum_i^{ions} m_i Z_i^2$

m = molality

Z = ionic valence

The summation is taken over all the different ions in the solution, multiplying the molality of each by the square of its charge. From the given data,

$$I = 1/2\ [0.00500 \times 2^2 + 0.01000 \times 1^2]$$

$$= 0.01500$$

from which $\sqrt{I} = \sqrt{0.01500} = 0.1225$

Substituting the respective values into equation (1) gives

$$\log \gamma_{\pm} = \frac{(-0.509)(2)0.1225}{1 + 0.1225} = \frac{-0.124705}{1.1225}$$

$$= -0.1111$$

and $\gamma_{\pm} = 0.774$

b) From the given cell, the two half reactions are:

$$Hg_2Cl_2(s) + 2e^- \rightarrow 2Hg(liq) + 2\ Cl^-(aq)$$

and $Zn(s) \rightarrow Zn^{2+}(aq) + 2e^-$

Thus, the overall reaction equation is obtained by adding the two half reactions. That is,

$$Hg_2Cl_2(s) + Zn(s) \rightarrow 2Hg(liq) + 2Cl^-\ (aq) + Zn^{2+}(aq)\ .$$

For this cell reaction, the Nernst equation is

$$E = E° - \frac{RT}{2F} \ln\ (a_{Zn^{2+}}\, a_{Cl^-}^2)$$

where E = emf of the cell

$E°$ = standard emf

F = Faraday's constant

a = activity

This can also be written as

$$E = E° - \frac{RT}{2F} \ln \left(a_\pm\right)^3 = E° - \frac{3RT}{2F} \ln a_\pm \qquad (2)$$

where

$$\left(a_\pm\right)^3 = a_{Zn^{2+}} \, a_{Cl^-}^2$$

But, by definition $\quad a_\pm = \gamma_\pm m_\pm$

where $\quad \gamma_\pm$ = mean ionic activity coefficient

$\quad m_\pm$ = mean ionic molality

Therefore, equation (2) becomes

$$E = E° - \frac{3RT}{2F} \ln \left(\gamma_\pm m_\pm\right)$$

$$= E° - \frac{3RT}{2F} \left[\ln \gamma_\pm + \ln m_\pm\right] \qquad (3)$$

At 25°C, equation (3) becomes

$$E = E° - (3/2) \times 0.05916 \left[\log \gamma_\pm + \log m_\pm\right] \qquad (4)$$

Before equation (4) can be used, the $m_\pm$ term must be known. This is where the Debye-Hückel theory comes in. The equation is written as

$$m_\pm = \left(m_{Zn^{2+}} \, m_{Cl^-}^2\right)^{1/3} = \left((.005) \times (2(.005))^2\right)$$

$$= \left(0.0000005\right)^{1/3}$$

$$= 0.0079$$

Using this value and $\gamma_\pm = 0.774$, equation (4) becomes

$$E = E° - (3/2) \times 0.05916 \, [\log 0.774 + \log (0.0079)]$$

$$= E° - (3/2) \times 0.05916 \, [-0.1111 - 2.102]$$

$$= E° + 0.1964.$$

The problem gives the value of E = 1.2272,

Hence $\quad E° = 1.2272 - 0.1964$

$$= 1.0308$$

● **PROBLEM** 9-38

The acidic ionization constants at 25°C of glycinium ion

$$\begin{array}{c} H_2C\text{————}C\text{—OH} \\ | \qquad\qquad \| \\ NH_3^+ \qquad\quad O \end{array}$$

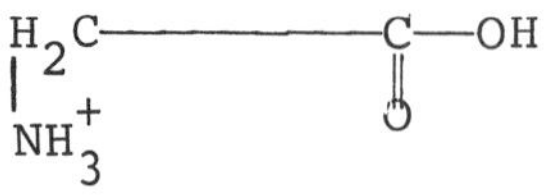

are $K_1 = 4.47 \times 10^{-3}$, $K_2 = 1.66 \times 10^{-10}$. A solution was prepared by dissolving 0.100 mole of glycine and 0.040 mole NaOH in 1000 g H_2O at 25°C.

(a) Estimate the ionic strength of this solution. Use your estimate and the Debye-Hückel equation to find the activity coefficient of each ion present in the solution.

(b) Write the equations that could be solved to give the molalities of all species present in this solution except water.

Solution: The general forms of Glycine and glycinium ion are HA and H_2A^+ respectively. The reaction equation can be represented as $0.100\ HA + 0.040\ NaOH \rightarrow Na^+ + A^- + H_2O + HA$
Balancing this equation gives

$$0.100\ HA + 0.040 NaOH \rightarrow 0.04 Na^+ + 0.04 A^- + 0.04 H_2O + 0.06 HA$$

The ionic strength (according to the Debye-Hückel theory) is defined as

$$I = 1/2 \sum_i^{\text{ions}} m_i Z_i^2 \qquad (1)$$

where Z_i = absolute value of the ionic valence (usually the charge).

m_i = molalities of the ions

$= \dfrac{\text{number of moles}}{\text{1 kg solvent}}$

Note that the sum of equation (1) is performed over all the ions present in the solution.

Substitute the given numerical data into equation (1) then the ionic strength can be estimated to be

$$I \simeq \frac{1}{2}\left[0.040(1)^2 + 0.040(1)^2\right] = 0.040$$

Note that there are 1000 g of H_2O (solvent). Therefore, there are 0.04 moles of each ion in 1000g = 1 kg; so, $m_+ = 0.04$ and $m_- = 0.04$).

For any ion with charge +Z or -Z, the Debye-Hückel law can be stated as

$$\log \gamma_\pm = \frac{(-0.509)\left(Z_i^2\right)\sqrt{I}}{1 + \sqrt{I}} \qquad (2)$$

where γ = activity coefficient.

Therefore, for a charge of +1, equation (2) becomes

$$\log \gamma_+ = \frac{(-0.509)(1)^2\sqrt{0.04}}{1 + \sqrt{0.04}} = -0.0848 .$$

Note that $\log \gamma_+ = \log \gamma_-$ because the Z_i is the absolute value of the ionic valence.

Thus, $\gamma = 0.823$ for any ion with charge ±1.

b) All the species present are

$$H_2A^+, H^+, HA, A^-, OH^- \text{ and } Na^+ .$$

Looking at the equilibrium conditions, the charge balance and the material balance, the respective equations are:

(i) Equilibrium:

$H_2A^+ \rightleftarrows H^+ + HA$ for which

$$K_1 = 4.47 \times 10^{-3} = \frac{m_{H^+}\, m_{HA}}{m_{H_2A^+}}$$

$HA \rightleftarrows H^+ + A^-$ for which

$$K_2 = 1.66 \times 10^{-10} = \gamma^2 \frac{m_{H^+}\, m_{A^-}}{m_{HA}}$$

$H_2O \rightleftarrows H^+ + OH^-$ for which

$$K = 1.00 \times 10^{-14} = \gamma^2 m_{H^+}\, m_{OH^-}$$

(ii) Charge balance:

$$m_{Na^+} + m_{H_2A^+} + m_{H^+} = m_{A^-} + m_{OH^-}$$

(iii) Material balance:

$$m_{H_2A^+} + m_{HA} + m_{A^-} = 0.100$$

$$m_{Na^+} = 0.040$$

• PROBLEM 9-39

The ionization constant of 2-thiophenecarboxylic acid (C_4H_3SCOOH or HA) is $K_a = 3.3 \times 10^{-4}$ at 25°C.

(a) Find the standard electrode potential E° for the half reaction

$$HA(aq) + e^- \rightarrow A^-(aq) + \frac{1}{2} H_2(g)$$

(b) Calculate the fraction of HA ionized in a 0.200 m aqueous solution of HA that is also 1.00 m with respect to $MgCl_2$. Make reasonable approximations in calculating activity coefficients but do not assume that they are equal to one.

Solution: a) The two electrode reactions are given as

$$HA + e^- \rightarrow 1/2\ H_2(g) + A^- \qquad (1)$$

and $$1/2\ H_2(g) \rightarrow H^+ + e^- \qquad (2)$$

OVERALL: $HA \rightleftarrows H^+ + A^-$

Note that the second equation is introduced so as to eliminate the 1/2 $H_2(g)$ in the first equation and also to provide the H^+ that is needed.

If the standard potential of reaction (1) is designated by E_1° and that of reaction (2) by E_2°,

then $$E_{cell}^\circ = E_1^\circ + E_2^\circ$$

But $E_2^\circ = 0$,

$$\therefore \quad E_{cell}^\circ = E_1^\circ$$

The Nernst equation is given by

$$E_{cell} = E_{cell}^\circ - \frac{RT}{nF} \ln K_a$$

Here, n=1

and at 25°C, $$\frac{RT}{F} \ln K_a = 0.05916 \log K_a$$

Since the reaction is in equilibrium state, $E_{cell} = 0$.

Therefore $$E_{cell}^\circ = 0.05916 \log K_a = E_1^\circ$$

or
$$E_1^\circ = 0.05916 \left(\log 3.3 \times 10^{-4}\right)$$
$$= 0.05916\ (-3.481486)$$
$$= -0.206\ V$$

b) From the Debye-Hückel theory,

$$\log \gamma_\pm \approx \frac{-0.509\ (\sqrt{I})\ Z_i^2}{1 + \sqrt{I}} \qquad (3)$$

where γ = activity coefficients

Z_i = any ion with a charge +z, or -z

I = ionic strength = $1/2 \sum_i^{ions} m_i Z_i^2$

m = molality

Z = absolute value of the ionic valence.

Note the Z_i here ≠ Z_i in equation (3). Here $Z_+ = 2$ and $Z_- = 1$.

From the given data, $I = 1/2\left[1.00 \times 2^2 + 2.0 \times 1^2\right]$

$$= 3.0$$

So $\sqrt{I} = \sqrt{3.0} = 1.732$

Consequently, $\log \gamma_{H^+} = \log \gamma_{A^-} \approx \dfrac{(-0.509)(1.732)(1)^2}{1 + 1.732}$

$$= \frac{-.8816}{2.732}$$

$$= -.3227$$

$$\therefore \quad \gamma = +.476$$

The relationship between a, γ and K_a is

$$K_a = \frac{a_{H^+}\, a_{A^-}}{a_{HA}} = \frac{\gamma^2 m_{H^+}\, m_{A^-}}{m_{HA}}$$

Therefore, $\dfrac{K_a}{\gamma^2} = \dfrac{m_{H^+}\, m_{A^-}}{m_{HA}} = \dfrac{3.3 \times 10^{-4}}{(.476)^2}$

$$= 14.6 \times 10^{-4}$$

$$= 1.46 \times 10^{-3}$$

Recall that the overall reaction is

$$HA \rightleftarrows H^+ + A^-$$

If the ionized fraction at equilibrium of H^+ and A^- is taken to be α, then the above reaction gives $0.200(\alpha)$ for H^+, $0.200(\alpha)$ for A^- and $0.200(1-\alpha)$ for HA.

From these, $1.46 \times 10^{-3} = \dfrac{0.200\alpha^2}{1-\alpha}$

or $0.200\alpha^2 = 1.46 \times 10^{-3} - 1.46 \times 10^{-3}\alpha$

This is a quadratic equation, from which

$$\alpha^2 - 7.3 \times 10^{-3} + 7.3 \times 10^{-3}\alpha = 0$$

using the quadratic formula

$$\alpha = \frac{-b \pm\sqrt{b^2 - 4ac}}{2a} ,$$

The value for α can be found.

$$\alpha = \frac{-7.3 \times 10^{-3} \pm \sqrt{(7.3 \times 10^{-3})^2 - 4(-7.3 \times 10^{-3})}}{2}$$

$$= \frac{-.0073 \pm \sqrt{0.0000533 + 0.0292}}{2}$$

$$= \frac{-\ .0073 \pm 0.17104}{2}$$

This equation will give two values for α. But the negative answer for α is impossible.

Therefore, $\alpha = +\ 0.081868 \approx 8.2 \times 10^{-2}$

Note: An easier way of doing this is to assume that $\alpha << 1$.

Therefore, $\alpha^2 = 7.3 \times 10^{-3}$

and $\alpha = \sqrt{7.3 \times 10^{-3}}$

$= 8.5 \times 10^{-2}$

The first method is more accurate; but either way is acceptable.

• PROBLEM 9-40

The acidic ionization constant of HF is 3.5×10^{-4}. The basic ionization constant of novacaine is 7×10^{-6}. A solution was prepared by dissolving 0.100 mole HF and 0.200 mole novocaine in 1000 g H_2O.

(a) Write six equations in which the unknowns are the molalities of HF, novocaine (B), F^-, novocainium ion (BH^+), H^+, and OH^-. Assume that activities are equal to molalities.

(b) By making suitable approximations (state what they are) solve these equations for the molalities of HF and H^+.

Solution: a) The ions present are

H^+, F^-, BH^+, OH^-.

Their molalities can be obtained by first looking at the equilibrium processes, the charge balance and the material balance.

These are:

(i) Equilibrium:

$HF \rightleftarrows H^+ + F^-$ for which

$$K = 3.5 \times 10^{-4} = \frac{m_{H^+}\ m_{F^-}}{m_{HF}} \qquad (1)$$

$B + H_2O \rightleftarrows BH^+ + OH^-$ for which

$$K = 7 \times 10^{-6} = \frac{m_{BH^+}\ m_{OH^-}}{m_B} \qquad (2)$$

$H_2O \rightleftarrows H^+ + OH^-$ for which

$$K = 1.00 \times 10^{-14} = m_{H^+}\ m_{OH^-} \qquad (3)$$

(ii) Charge balance:

$$m_{H^+} + m_{BH^+} = m_{OH^-} + m_{F^-} \qquad (4)$$

(iii) Material balance:

$$m_{HF} + m_{F^-} = 0.100 \qquad (5)$$

$$m_B + m_{BH^+} = 0.200 \qquad (6)$$

In all of the above, m = molality.

b) If it is assumed that

$$m_{H^+} \ll m_{BH^+} \text{ and } m_{OH^-} \ll m_{F^-} ,$$

then

$$m_{BH^+} = m_{F^-} .$$

Let the value be x. Therefore,

$$m_{HF} = 0.100 - x .$$

Also

$$m_B = 0.200 - x.$$

Multiplying equation (1) by equation (2) gives

$$\frac{m_{BH^+}m_{F^-}}{m_{HF}m_B} = 2.45 \times 10^5.$$

(Note that the $m_{H^+}m_{OH^-}$ term was replaced by $K = 1.00 \times 10^{-14}$.)

or $$\frac{x^2}{(0.100-x)(0.200-x)} = 2.45 \times 10^5 \qquad (7)$$

Since it's tedious to solve equation (7) directly, let

$$y = 0.100 - x$$

$$\therefore \quad x = 0.100 - y \text{ and } 0.200 - x = 0.100 + y$$

from which

$$2.45 \times 10^5 = \frac{(0.100 - y)^2}{y(0.100 + y)}$$

Further approximations can be made if y is assumed to be much less than 0.100. That is, assume

$$y \ll 0.100 ;$$

then

$$2.45 \times 10^5 = \frac{0.0100}{0.100y} \qquad (8)$$

Solving equation (8) for y gives

$$y = \frac{0.100}{2.45 \times 10^5 \times 0.100} = 4.1 \times 10^{-7} \text{ mol kg}^{-1}$$

But

$$m_{HF} = 0.100 - x = y = 4.1 \times 10^{-7} \text{ mol kg}^{-1}$$

Therefore

$$m_{F^-} = 0.100 - y = 0.100 \text{ mol kg}^{-1}$$

and

$$m_{H^+} = 3.5 \times 10^{-4} \times \frac{m_{HF}}{m_{F^-}}$$

$$= \frac{3.5 \times 10^{-4} \times 4.1 \times 10^{-7}}{0.100}$$

$$= 1.4 \times 10^{-9} \text{ mol kg}^{-1}$$

• PROBLEM 9-41

(a) Calculate the standard potential for the reaction $Pb(s) + 2Ag^+ = 2Ag(s) + Pb^{2+}$ given that the standard oxidation potential for the reaction $Pb = Pb^{2+} + 2e^-$ is .126 and that for $Ag = Ag^+ + e^-$ is -.7991.

(b) The half reaction $Fe = Fe^{2+} + 2e^-$ has an oxidation potential of .440 and the half reaction $Fe^{2+} = Fe^{3+} + e^-$ has an oxidation potential of - .771. Calculate the oxidation potential for the standard half cell $Fe = Fe^{3+} + 3e^-$.

Solution: (a) The half reaction which has the greater oxidation potential gets oxidized while the half reaction with the smaller oxidation potential gets reduced. Hence,

$$Pb(s) = Pb^{2+} + 2e^- \qquad \varepsilon^o = .126$$

$$Ag^+ + e^- = Ag(s) \qquad \varepsilon^o = .7991$$

Note that the sign is reversed in the second reaction since it is now written as a reduction. Also the number of electrons transferred in the second reaction is not the same as the first reaction and so the second reaction must be multiplied by 2. Therefore,

$$\begin{array}{rl} Pb(s) = Pb^{2+} + 2e^- & \varepsilon^o = .127 \\ 2Ag^+ + 2e^- = 2Ag(s) & \varepsilon^o = .7991 \\ \hline Pb(s) + 2Ag^+ = Pb^{2+} + 2Ag(s) & \varepsilon^o = .9261 \end{array}$$

This is the desired equation. Note that the standard potential of the second reaction is not multiplied by 2. This occurs because the standard potentials are equivalent to a free energy change per equivalent of electrons transferred. Hence, all standard potentials are on the same basis and can simply be added.

(b) This question is different from that in part (a). In part (a) there was an overall reaction (not a standard half reaction) which was simply the sum of the two standard half reactions. In this part, a standard half reaction is to be obtained from two other standard half reactions. Therefore, in this type of question the potentials must be weighted according to the number of electrons transferred. Hence, the net half cell will in effect be a weighted average. The following explanation should help clarify the above statements.

First, the standard potentials can be changed to standard free energy changes by the equation $\Delta G^o = -nF\varepsilon^o$ where n is the number of electrons transferred. Second, free energies are additive. Knowing this, the half reactions are written.

$$\begin{array}{ll} Fe = Fe^{2+} + 2e^- & \Delta G_1^o = -2F\ (.440) \\ Fe^{2+} = Fe^{3+} + e^- & \Delta G_2^o = -1F\ (-.771) \\ \hline Fe = Fe^{3+} + 3e^- & \Delta G_{1+2}^o = -1F\ (-.771) \quad -2F(.440) \end{array}$$

Now consider the standard half reaction $Fe = Fe^{3+} + 3e^-$ not as a sum of the two standard half reactions but by itself. Then its free energy change would be given by $\Delta G^o = -3F\varepsilon^o$. However, this is equivalent to ΔG_{1+2}^o. Therefore, the equations are equated. This yields

$$-3F\varepsilon^o = -(1)\ F(-.771) \quad -2F(.440).$$

Solving for ε^o gives

$$\varepsilon^o = \frac{-(1)(F)(-.771) \quad -2F(.440)}{-3F} = \frac{(-1)(-.771) \quad -2(.440)}{-3}$$

$$= \frac{-[(-.771)(1) + 2(.440)]}{-3} = \frac{-.771(1) + 2(.440)}{3}$$

$$= .0363$$

CHAPTER 10

CHEMICAL KINETICS

RATE OF REACTIONS

• PROBLEM 10-1

The hydrogenation of ethylene

$$C_2H_4 + H_2 \rightarrow C_2H_6$$

in the presence of mercury vapor is thought to proceed through the following steps.

$$Hg + H_2 \xrightarrow{k_1} Hg + 2H \quad (1)$$

$$H + C_2H_4 \xrightarrow{k_2} C_2H_5 \quad (2)$$

$$C_2H_5 + H_2 \xrightarrow{k_3} C_2H_6 + H \quad (3)$$

$$H + H \xrightarrow{k_4} H_2 \quad (4)$$

Assuming that H and C_2H_5 attain equilibrium determine the rate of formation of C_2H_6 in terms of the rate constants and concentrations [Hg], $[H_2]$ and $[C_2H_4]$.

Solution: For equation (3), the rate equation is

$$\frac{d[C_2H_6]}{dt} = k_3[C_2H_5][H_2] \quad (5)$$

Assume that H and C_2H_5 reach steady state concentrations. Then,

$$\frac{d[H]}{dt} = 2k_1[Hg][H_2] - k_2[H][C_2H_4] + k_3[C_2H_5][H_2]$$

$$- 2k_4[H]^2 = 0$$

$$\frac{d[C_2H_5]}{dt} = k_2[H][C_2H_4] - k_3[C_2H_5][H_2] = 0 \qquad (6)$$

and $\quad 2k_1[Hg][H_2] - 2k_4[H]^2 = 0$

Solving for [H]

$$[H] = \left(\frac{k_1[Hg][H_2]}{k_4}\right)^{\frac{1}{2}}$$

Substitute for [H] in equation (6) and solve for C_2H_5 to obtain

$$[C_2H_5] = \frac{k_2[C_2H_4]}{k_3[H_2]}\left(\frac{k_1[Hg][H_2]}{k_4}\right)^{\frac{1}{2}}$$

From equation (5)

$$\frac{d[C_2H_6]}{dt} = k_3\,\frac{k_2[C_2H_4]}{k_3[H_2]}\left(\frac{k_1[Hg][H_2]}{k_4}\right)^{\frac{1}{2}}[H_2]$$

$$= k_2[C_2H_4]\left(\frac{k_1[Hg][H_2]}{k_4}\right)^{\frac{1}{2}}$$

• PROBLEM 10-2

Determine a and b in the rate equation

$$\text{rate} = kC_A^aC_B^b$$

given the following:

Table 1:

rate, $M\ s^{-1}$	0.05	0.10	0.20	0.40
$C_{A,0}$, M	1	1	2	2
$C_{B,0}$, M	1	2	1	2

Calculate k for this reaction.

Solution: $\log \text{rate} = \log k + n \log C_i \qquad (1)$

where $\quad k$ = rate constant

n = constant, called order of reaction (a and b in this case)

C_i = concentration of substance i

Using equation (1), the order for both substances A and B can be determined. Using data from the first and third columns of table 1 and substituting the respective values into equation (1), gives

$$\log (0.05) = \log k_A + a \log 1$$

and

$$\log (0.20) = \log k_A + a \log 2,$$

keeping $(C_{B,0})$ fixed.

If the first equation is subtracted from the second, then

$$\log (0.20) - \log (0.05) = a \log 2 - a \log 1$$

$$\log (0.20/0.05) = a (\log (2/1))$$

$$0.602 = a (0.301)$$

$$\therefore \quad a = \frac{0.602}{0.301} = 2$$

Doing the same for substance B, using the first and second columns and keeping $C_{A,0}$ fixed, gives

$$\log (0.05) = \log k_B + b \log 1$$

and

$$\log (0.10) = \log k_B + b \log 2$$

If the first equation is subtracted from the second, then

$$\log (0.10) - \log (0.05) = b \log 2 - b \log 1$$

$$\therefore \quad \log \frac{0.10}{0.05} = b \log (2/1)$$

$$(0.301) = b(0.301)$$

$$\therefore \quad b = \frac{0.301}{0.301} = 1$$

Therefore, $\text{rate} = kC_A^2\, C_B$

Solving for k, yields $k = \dfrac{\text{rate}}{C_A^2 C_B}$

Using values of C_A, C_B and rate from table 1

$$k = \frac{0.05}{(1^2)(1)} = \frac{0.10}{(1^2)(2)} = \frac{0.20}{(2^2)(1)} = \frac{0.40}{(2^2)(2)}$$

from which $k = 0.05\ M^{-2}s^{-1}$ (no matter which column is chosen).

• PROBLEM 10-3

For the chemical reaction

$$H_2O + Cr_2O_7^{2-}(aq) \rightarrow 2CrO_4^{2-}(aq) + 2H^+(aq)$$

evaluate the various expressions for the rate in terms of $-dC_{Cr_2O_7^{2-}}/dt$. If the actual reaction equation for the chromate dichromate system is identical to the stoichiometric equation, write the rate equation. If C_{H_2O} is large enough to remain essentially constant, write the revised rate equation. What is the overall order of both of these rate equation?

Solution: From the chemical reaction, the rate of change of the respective ions can be represented as

$$\frac{d}{dt}\left(C_{CrO_4^{2-}}\right) = \frac{d}{dt}\left(C_{H^+}\right) = -2\frac{d}{dt}\left(C_{Cr_2O_7^{2-}}\right)$$

This is because both of the product ions are being formed twice as fast as the dichromate ion is reacting. For the water,

$$-\frac{d}{dt}\left(C_{H_2O}\right) = -\frac{d}{dt}\left(C_{Cr_2O_7^{2-}}\right)$$

because the water is reacting in a 1:1 ratio to $Cr_2O_7^{2-}$.

The complete rate equation is the second-order equation. Therefore,

$$\text{rate} = K\, C_{H_2O}\, C_{Cr_2O_7^{2-}} \quad .$$

K = rate constant

C = concentration

If the concentration of water remains constant, the revised rate equation will be the pseudo-first-order equation. Thus,

$$\text{rate} = K'\, C_{Cr_2O_7^{2-}}$$

where $K' = K\, C_{H_2O}$

A proposed mechanism for the reaction between $H_2(g)$ and $Br_2(g)$ is

$$Br_2 \underset{k_5}{\overset{k_1}{\rightleftarrows}} 2Br$$

$$Br + H_2 \xrightarrow{k_2} HBr + H$$

$$H + Br_2 \xrightarrow{k_3} HBr + Br$$

$$H + HBr \xrightarrow{k_4} H_2 + Br$$

Write expressions for dC_{HBr}/dt, dC_H/dt and dC_{Br}/dt. Assuming that $dC_H/dt = dC_{Br}/dt = 0$, solve for dC_{HBr}/dt in terms of C_{H_2}, C_{Br_2} and C_{HBr}.

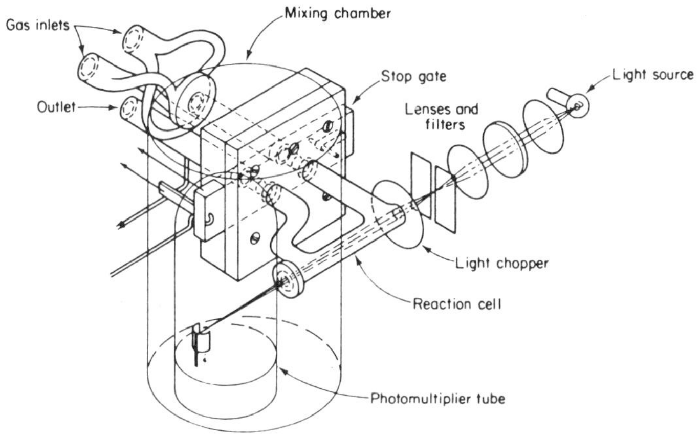

Apparatus of Johnston and Yost for study of a rapid gas reaction: isometric projection of mixing chamber, stop gate, and 2 mm diameter reaction cell, with schematic drawing of the light source, filters, and lenses.

Solution: From the second equation, $\frac{dC_{HBr}}{dt} = k_2C_{Br}C_{H_2}$.

The third equation gives $\frac{dC_{HBr}}{dt} = k_3C_HC_{Br_2}$ and the fourth gives $-\frac{dC_{HBr}}{dt} = k_4C_HC_{HBr}$.

Combining these three equations together yield

$$\frac{dC_{HBr}}{dt} = k_2C_{Br}C_{H_2} + k_3C_HC_{Br_2} - k_4C_HC_{HBr} \qquad (1)$$

Similarly,

$$\frac{dC_H}{dt} = 0 = k_2C_{Br}C_{H_2} - k_3C_HC_{Br_2} - k_4C_HC_{HBr} \qquad (2)$$

and

$$\frac{dC_{Br}}{dt} = 0 = 2k_1 C_{Br_2} - k_2 C_{Br} C_{H_2} + k_3 C_H C_{Br_2} + k_4 C_H C_{HBr}$$

$$- 2k_5 C_{Br}^2 \qquad (3)$$

Solving equations (2) and (3) simultaneously yields

$$C_{Br} = \left(\frac{k_1}{k_5}\right)^{\frac{1}{2}} (C_{Br_2})^{\frac{1}{2}}$$

and

$$C_H = k_2 \left(\frac{k_1}{k_5}\right)^{\frac{1}{2}} \frac{(C_{Br_2})^{\frac{1}{2}} \quad C_{H_2}}{k_3 C_{Br_2} + k_4 C_{HBr}}$$

Substituting C_{Br} and C_H into equation (1) gives

$$\frac{dC_{HBr}}{dt} = 2k_2 \left(\frac{k_1}{k_5}\right)^{\frac{1}{2}} \frac{C_{H_2} (C_{Br_2})^{\frac{1}{2}}}{1 + (k_4/k_3)\left(C_{HBr}/C_{Br_2}\right)}$$

• PROBLEM 10-5

For the series of competing reactions

$$H + HO_2 \xrightarrow{k_1} H_2 + O_2 \ ; \quad H + HO_2 \xrightarrow{k_2} 2OH \ ; \quad H + HO_2 \xrightarrow{k_3} H_2O + O$$

Westenberg and deHass report $k_1/k_2/k_3 = 0.62/0.27/0.11$.
Find the ratio of the products at time t.

Solution: The respective rates of all the reactions are $k_1 C_H C_{HO_2}$, $k_2 C_H C_{HO_2}$ and $k_3 C_H C_{HO_2}$

where

k_1 , k_2 and k_3 = rate constants

C = concentration.

The overall rate of the reactions is the sum of the three rates. Therefore,

$$\text{rate} = k_1 C_H C_{HO_2} + k_2 C_H C_{HO_2} + k_3 C_H C_{HO_2}$$

$$= k C_H C_{HO_2}$$

where $\quad k = k_1 + k_2 + k_3$.

The given ratio of the rate constants implies that the products of the first reaction will be formed from 62% of the reactants. For the second reaction, 27% of the reactants will form the products of the second reaction and 11% of the reactants will form the products of the third reaction.

Since the stoichiometry of the product of the second equation is 2, the ratio of the products will be

$$C_{H_2} = C_{O_2}/C_{OH}/C_{H_2O} = C_O$$

$$62\%/2 \times 27\%/11\%$$

or $$0.62/0.54/0.11$$

• PROBLEM 10-6

Assuming that $dC_C/dt = 0$ for the reactions

$$A + B \underset{k_{-1}}{\overset{k_1}{\rightleftarrows}} C$$

$$C + B \xrightarrow{k_2} D$$

find $-dC_A/dt$, $-dC_B/dt$ and dC_D/dt in terms of C_A, C_B and C_D .

Solution: $\frac{dC_C}{dt} = k_1C_AC_B - k_{-1}C_C$ from the first reaction and $-\frac{dC_C}{dt} = k_2C_CC_B$ from the second reaction. If the latter is subtracted from the former, then

$$dC_C/dt + \frac{dC_C}{dt} = k_1C_AC_B - k_{-1}C_C - k_2C_CC_B$$

Therefore, $$0 = k_1C_AC_B - k_{-1}C_C - k_2C_CC_B \qquad (1)$$

Recall that dC_C/dt is assumed to be 0

Therefore,

$$dC_C/dt = 0 = k_1C_AC_B - k_{-1}C_C - k_2C_CC_B$$

since equation (1) is also equal to zero.

Solving for C_C ,

$$k_{-1}C_C + k_2C_CC_B = k_1C_AC_B$$

$$C_C(k_{-1} + k_2C_B) = k_1C_AB_B$$

$$\therefore \quad C_C = \frac{k_1 C_A C_B}{k_{-1} + k_2 C_B} \qquad (2)$$

From the two reactions,

$$-dC_A/dt = k_1 C_A C_B - k_{-1} C_C \qquad (3)$$

$$-dC_B/dt = k_1 C_A C_B - k_{-1} C_C + k_2 C_B C_C \qquad (4)$$

$$\frac{dC_D}{dt} = k_2 C_B C_C \qquad (5)$$

Since the final answers are supposed to be in terms of C_A, C_B and C_D only, we can now substitute equation (2) into equations (3), (4) and (5) in order to eliminate C_C .

Therefore,

$$\frac{-dC_A}{dt} = k_1 C_A C_B - \frac{k_{-1} k_1 C_A C_B}{k_{-1} + k_2 C_B}$$

$$= \frac{k_1 C_A C_B (k_{-1} + k_2 C_B) - k_{-1} k_1 C_A C_B}{k_{-1} + k_2 C_B}$$

$$= \frac{k_1 C_A C_B k_{-1} + k_1 k_2 C_A C_B^2 - k_{-1} k_1 C_A C_B}{k_{-1} + k_2 C_B}$$

$$= \frac{k_1 k_2 C_A C_B^2}{k_{-1} + k_2 C_B}$$

$$\frac{-dC_B}{dt} = k_1 C_A C_B - \frac{k_{-1} k_1 C_A C_B}{k_{-1} + k_2 C_B} + \frac{k_2 C_B k_1 C_A C_B}{k_{-1} + k_2 C_B}$$

Combining them yields

$$-dC_B/dt = \frac{2k_1 k_2 C_A C_B^2}{k_{-1} + k_2 C_B}$$

Finally,

$$dC_D/dt = \frac{k_2 C_B k_1 C_A C_B}{k_{-1} + k_2 C_B} = \frac{k_1 k_2 C_A C_B^2}{k_{-1} + k_2 C_B}$$

• PROBLEM 10-7

For the reaction

$$2NO + O_2 \rightarrow 2NO_2$$

the following reaction mechanism have been suggested;

1) $NO + NO \overset{k_1}{\rightarrow} N_2O_2$

2) $N_2O_2 \overset{k_2}{\rightarrow} 2NO$

3) $N_2O_2 + O_2 \overset{k_3}{\rightarrow} 2NO_2$

a) Apply the steady state approximation to $[N_2O_2]$ and show that the rate law is given by

$$\frac{d[NO_2]}{dt} = \frac{2k_1k_3[NO]^2[O_2]}{k_2 + k_3[O_2]}$$

b) Calculate the overall activation energy for this reaction assuming that only a small fraction of the N_2O_2 formed in step 1) actually goes to form products in step 3) and most of the N_2O_2 reverts to NO in step 2). The activation energies for steps 1) through 3) are 82kJ, 205kJ and 82kJ respectively.

Solution: a) The rate law for reaction (3) is

$$\frac{d[NO_2]}{dt} = 2k_3[N_2O_2][O_2] \qquad (4)$$

For reactions (1,2,3) the rate law becomes

$$\frac{d[N_2O_2]}{dt} = k_1[NO]^2 - k_2[N_2O_2] - k_3[N_2O_2][O_2] = 0$$

Solving for $[N_2O_2]$ gives

$$[N_2O_2] = \frac{k_1[NO]^2}{k_2 + k_3[O_2]}$$

Substitute for $[N_2O_2]$ in equation (4) to obtain

$$\frac{d[NO_2]}{dt} = \frac{2k_1k_3[NO]^2[O_2]}{k_1 + k_3[O_2]}$$

b) Assume a reversible reaction.

$$2NO \underset{k_2}{\overset{k_1}{\rightleftarrows}} N_2O_2 \quad \text{or} \quad K_{1,2} = \frac{[N_2O_2]}{[NO]^2} \qquad (5)$$

and

$$N_2O_2 + O_2 \overset{k_3}{\rightarrow} 2NO_2$$

But from equation (4),

$$\frac{d[NO_2]}{dt} = 2k_3[N_2O_2][O_2] \ .$$

From equation (5), $[N_2O_2] = K_{1,2}[NO]^2$

$$\therefore \quad \frac{d[NO_2]}{dt} = 2k_3\ K_{1,2}[NO]^2[O_2]$$

$$= k[NO]^2[O_2]$$

where $k = 2k_3K_{1,2}$ = third order rate constant

or $\ln k = \ln 2 + \ln k_3 + \ln K_{1,2}$

$$\frac{d \ln k}{dT} = \frac{d \ln k_3}{dT} + \frac{d \ln K_{1,2}}{dT}$$

and $E_a = E_3 + (E_1 - E_2) = 82kJ + (82 - 205)kJ = -41kJ$

• PROBLEM 10-8

The value of the activation energy, E_a , for the thermal decomposition of gaseous acetaldehyde is 45,500 cal mole^{-1} , and the molecular diameter, σ, of a molecule of acetaldehyde is 5 x 10^{-8} cm. This decomposition is a second order reaction.

a) Determine the number of molecules colliding per milliliter per second at 800°K and 760 torr pressure

b) Calculate the second order rate constant, k, in liters mole^{-1} sec^{-1}.

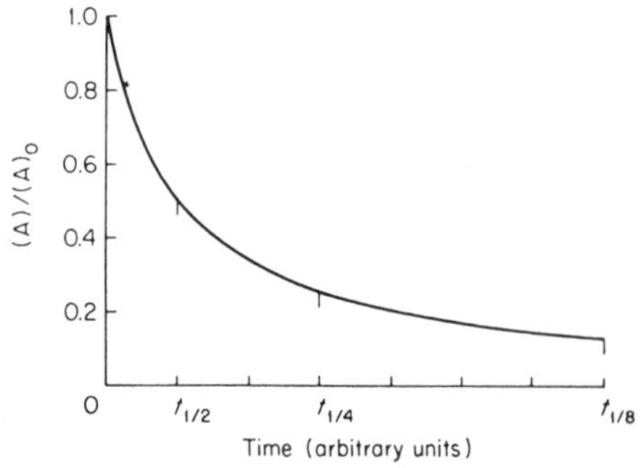

The second-order rate law. (A)/(A)$_0$ *as a function of time, showing the successive doubling of* $t_{1/2}$.

Solution: From kinetic theory of molecular collisions, the number of collisions, Z of identical molecules per unit volume per unit time is given by

$$Z = 2\left(\frac{\pi RT}{M}\right)^{\frac{1}{2}} \sigma^2 n^2 \qquad (1)$$

where σ is the collision diameter for the molecules, n is the number of molecules per unit volume

$$n = \frac{\text{number of molecules}}{\text{volume}}$$

$$= \frac{\text{number of moles x number of molecules/mole}}{\text{volume}}$$

$$= \frac{mN_0}{V}$$

where m is the number of moles, N_0 is Avogadro's number, and V is measured in cubic meters. The ideal gas law gives

$$PV = mRT \text{ or } \frac{P}{RT} = \frac{m}{V} ,$$

but $n = \frac{m}{V} N_0$ and therefore

$$n = \frac{N_0 P}{RT}$$

$$= \frac{(6.02(10^{23})\text{molec /mole}) \times (760 \text{ torr}) \times (1 \text{ atm}/760 \text{ torr})}{(0.0821 \ \ell\,\text{atm}°\text{K}^{-1}\text{mole}^{-1})}$$

$$= 9.17(10^{21}) \frac{\text{molec}}{\ell} \times 1000 \frac{\ell}{m^3} = 9.17(10^{24}) \frac{\text{molec}}{m^3}$$

and M is the molecular weight of acetaldehyde molecule.

From equation (1),

$$Z = 2 \times \left(\frac{\pi \times (8.314\text{J}/°\text{K mole}) \times (800°\text{K})}{(4.4(10^{-2}) \text{ kg/mole})}\right)^{\frac{1}{2}}$$

$$\times (5(10^{-10})\text{m})^2 \times \left((9.17(10^{24}) \frac{\text{molec}}{m^3}\right)^2$$

$$= 2 \times (4.747(10^5)\text{J/kg})^{\frac{1}{2}} \quad \times 2.5(10^{-19})\text{m}^2 \times 8.39(10^{49}) \text{ molec}^2/\text{m}^6$$

$$= 2 \times \left(4.747(10^5) \frac{\text{kg m}^2/\text{sec}^2}{\text{kg}}\right)^{\frac{1}{2}} \quad \times (2.09(10^{31}) \text{ molec}^2/\text{m}^4)$$

$$= 2 \times (688.96 \text{ m/sec}) \times 2.09(10^{31}) \text{ molec}^2/\text{m}^4$$

$$= 2.88(10^{34}) \frac{\text{molec}^2}{\text{m}^3 \text{ sec}} \times \left(\frac{1\text{m}}{100\text{cm}}\right)^3 \times \frac{1\text{cm}^3}{\text{ml}}$$

$$= 2.88(10^{28}) \frac{\text{molec}^2}{\text{sec ml}}$$

b) Also from the gas collision theory, the second-order rate constant is given by

$$k = 2 \times 10^3 N_A P \left(\frac{\pi RT}{M}\right)^{\frac{1}{2}} \sigma^2 e^{-E_a/RT} \qquad (2)$$

where N_A = the Avogadro's number, E_a is the activation energy and P is the steric factor, in this case taken as 1.

From equation (2),

$$k = \left(2 \times 10^3 \,\ell\, \text{m}^{-3}\right)\left(6.02 \times 10^{23} \text{ mole}^{-1}\right)$$

$$\left[\frac{\pi(8.31\text{J K}^{-1}\text{mole}^{-1})(800\,°\text{K})}{4.4 \times 10^{-2} \text{ kg mole}^{-1}}\right]^{\frac{1}{2}}$$

$$\times\ (5 \times 10^{-10}\text{m})^2 \left[e^{(-45500 \text{ cal mole}^{-1})/((1.987 \text{ cal } °\text{K}^{-1} \text{ mole}^{-1})}\right.$$

$$\left.\times\ (800\ °\text{K}))\right] = (2 \times 10^3)(6.02 \times 10^{23})(6.89 \times 10^2)(9.28 \times 10^{-32})$$

$$= 0.077 \text{ liter mole}^{-1} \text{ sec}^{-1}$$

• PROBLEM 10-9

The half-life for a given reaction was halved as the initial concentration of a reactant was doubled. What is n for this component?

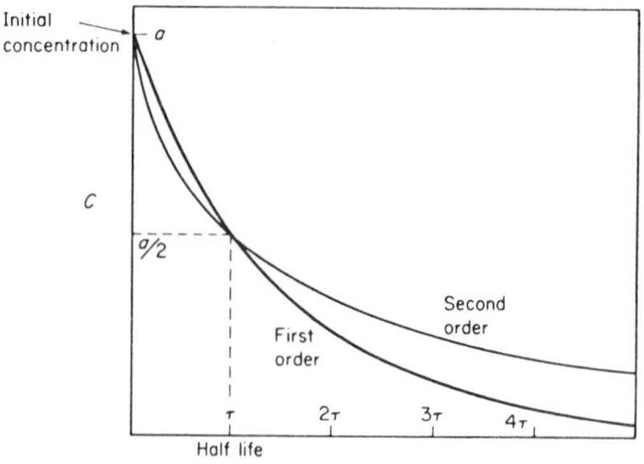

Concentration vs. time curves for first- and second-order reactions with same initial concentrations *a* and same half-lives *τ*.

Solution: The relationship between the half-life and the initial concentration of a reaction is given by

$$\log t_{1/2} = \log \left[\frac{2^{n-1} - 1}{(n-1)k}\right] - (n-1) \log C_{i,0} \qquad (1)$$

where $t_{1/2}$ = half-life period

$C_{i,0}$ = initial concentration

$n-1$ = slope of the plot $\log t_{1/2}$ against $\log C_{i,0}$

Another equation to be considered is of the form of the former, except that half-life period is halved as initial concentration is doubled. That is

$$\log\left(\frac{t_{1/2}}{2}\right) = \log \frac{2^{n-1} - 1}{(n-1)k} - (n-1) \log 2C_{i,0} \qquad (2)$$

Subtracting equation (2) from equation (1) yields

$$\log t_{1/2} - \log \frac{t_{1/2}}{2} = -(n-1) \log C_{i,0} + (n-1) \log 2C_{i,0}$$

$$\log \left(t_{1/2} \Big/ \frac{t_{1/2}}{2}\right) = (n-1) \log 2C_{i,0} - (n-1) \log C_{i,0}$$

$$\log 2 = (n-1)[\log 2C_{i,0} - \log C_{i,0}]$$

$$\log 2 = (n-1) \log \frac{2C_{i,0}}{C_{i,0}} = (n-1) \log 2$$

$$\therefore \quad n-1 = \log 2/\log 2 = 1$$

or $$n = 1 + 1 = 2$$

• PROBLEM 10-10

At 393.7°C, the second-rate constant for the decomposition of gaseous hydrogen iodide in a second order reaction is $2.6 \times 10^{-4} M^{-1} s^{-1}$. Given that the Arrhenius activation energy for the reaction is 45.6 kcal mol^{-1}, calculate the second order rate constant for this reaction from collision theory. The molecular weight of HI = 127.9 g mol^{-1}, the collision diameter = 3.5 Å and the orientation factor, P = 1.

Solution: The collision theory postulates that in order for molecules to interact, they must approach each other so closely that they can be said to be in collision. The speed of the reaction is equal to the number of collisions per second times the fraction of the collisions that are effective in producing chemical change.

Thus, according to this gas-collision theory, the second-order rate constant should be given by

$$k = 2 \times 10^3 N_A P \left(\frac{\pi RT}{M}\right)^{1/2} \sigma^2 e^{-(E_o/RT)} \qquad (1)$$

where N_A = the Avogadro's number, P is the steric or orientation factor, σ is the collision diameter and E_o is the threshold energy for the reaction, given by the expression

$$E_o = E_a - \frac{RT}{2} \qquad (2)$$

E_a is the activation energy

Substitute the respective values into equation (2) to obtain

$$E_o = 45.6 \text{ kcal mole}^{-1} - \frac{(1.987 \times 10^{-3} \text{kcal mole}^{-1} \text{°K}^{-1})(666.7 \text{ °K})}{2}$$

$$= (45.6 - 0.662) \text{kcal mole}^{-1}$$

$$= 44.94 \text{ kcal mole}^{-1}$$

From equation (1),

$$k = 2 \times (10^3 \text{liters m}^{-3})(6.02 \times 10^{23} \text{mole}^{-1})(1)$$

$$\times \left[\frac{\pi (8.31 \frac{\text{J K}^{-1}}{\text{mole}})(666.7 \text{ °K})}{127.9 \times 10^{-3} \text{kg mole}^{-1}}\right]^{1/2}$$

$$\times \left[3.5 \text{Å} \left(\frac{10^{-10} \text{m}}{1 \text{Å}}\right)\right]^2 e^{-(44.94 \text{ kcal mole}^{-1})/((1.987 \text{ cal °K}^{-1} \text{mole}^{-1})}$$

$$\times (666.7 \text{°K}))$$

$$= 1.0 \times 10^{-4} \text{ M}^{-1} \text{s}^{-1}$$

• PROBLEM 10-11

Measurement of the second order decomposition of acetaldehyde over the temperature range 700-850 °K was made and the second order rate constant was given as

T(°K)	700	730	760	790	810	840	910	1000
k_2	0.011	0.035	0.105	0.343	0.789	2.17	20.0	145

Determine by a plot the activation energy and the pre-exponential factor for the decomposition.

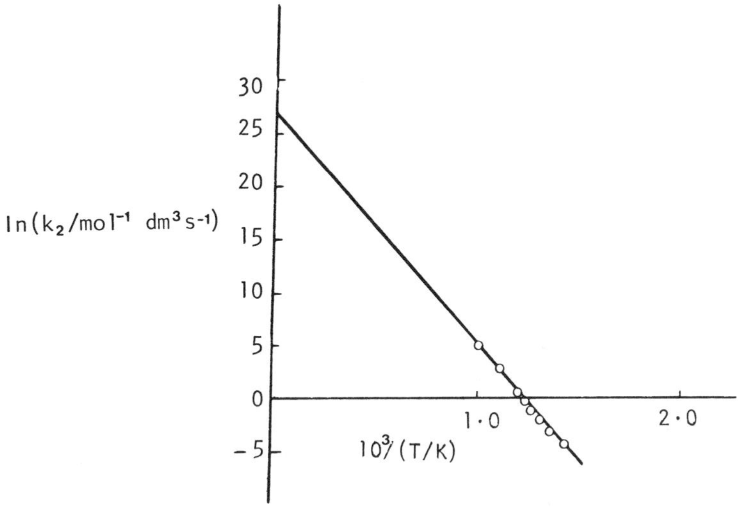

Solution: The variation of temperature with reaction rate constants is usually expressed by the Arrhenius equation,

$$k_2 = Ae^{-E_a/RT} \tag{1}$$

where A is the pre-exponential factor and E_a is the activation energy.

Equation (1) can be written in a logarithmic form as follows:

$$\ln k_2 = -\frac{E_a}{R}\frac{1}{T} + \ln A \tag{2}$$

From equation (2), it can be seen that a straight line will be obtained if the logarithm of the rate constant is plotted against the reciprocal of the absolute temperature.

From the plot, the slope is determined to be -2.207×10^4 °K

Thus $E_a = -[(8.314 J\ K^{-1} mole^{-1})(-2.207 \times 10^4\ °K)]$

$= 1.84 \times 10^5$ J mole^{-1}

$= 184$ kJ mole^{-1}

The intercept on the plot has a value of 26.95 and thus

$A = 5.06 \times 10^{11}$.

• PROBLEM 10-12

Consider the opposing second-order reactions

$$A_2 + B_2 \underset{k_{-2}}{\overset{k_2}{\rightleftarrows}} 2AB$$

Derive an expression for K in terms of k_2 and k_{-2} .

Solution: Opposing reactions proceed at equal rates when at equilibrium. Therefore, there is a net rate of change of zero for each component. The thermodynamic equilibrium constant, K can be obtained by first collecting all concentration terms on one side and all rate constants on the other side. Finally, the latter side is equated to the equilibrium constant.

From the reaction under consideration, the expression for component A at equilibrium is

$$-\frac{d}{dt}(C_{A_2}) = k_2 C_{A_2} C_{B_2} - k_{-2} C_{AB}^2 = 0 \tag{1}$$

Rearranging equation (1) yields

$$k_2 C_{A_2} C_{B_2} = k_{-2} C_{AB}^2 \tag{2}$$

Collecting all concentration terms on one side and all rate constants on the other, equation (2) becomes

$$\frac{k_2}{k_{-2}} = \frac{C_{AB}^2}{C_{A_2} C_{B_2}} \tag{3}$$

The left hand side of equation (3) is equated to the equilibrium constant. Thus, the desired expression is

$$\frac{C_{AB}^2}{C_{A_2} C_{B_2}} = \frac{k_2}{k_{-2}} = K .$$

Observe that K is the ratio of product concentrations to reactant concentrations and not vice versa.

• PROBLEM 10-13

At a temperature of 300°K it takes 12.6 min for a certain reaction to be 20% complete, and at 340°K the same reaction takes 3.20 min. Calculate the activation energy E_a for the reaction.

Solution: Write a general rate law since the order of the reaction was not specified. That is,

$$\frac{dx}{dt} = k(a-x)^n \tag{1}$$

where n = the order of the reaction, a is the initial concentration of the reactant and (a-x) is the concentration of the reactant remaining after time, t.

Rearranging equation (1) yields

$$\frac{dx}{(a-x)^n} = kdt \tag{1a}$$

Integrating equation (1a) gives

$$\frac{1}{(n-1)(a-x)^{n-1}} = kt + C \tag{2}$$

where C = the integrating constant. To evaluate C, use the condition that at t=0, x=0. Therefore, equation (2) gives

$$\frac{1}{(n-1)a^{n-1}} = C$$

Rewrite equation (2), substituting for C, to obtain

$$\frac{1}{(n-1)(a-x)^{n-1}} = kt + \frac{1}{(n-1)a^{n-1}}$$

or

$$k = \frac{1}{t(n-1)(a-x)^{n-1}} - \frac{1}{t(n-1)a^{n-1}}$$

$$= \frac{1}{t(n-1)}\left[\frac{1}{(a-x)^{n-1}} - \frac{1}{a^{n-1}}\right]$$

The reaction is (0.20) complete at the time intervals given. Therefore, when $t = t_{1/5}$, $(a-x) = 0.80a$

Write the Arrhenius equation for the rate constant as

$$k = A\exp(-E_a/RT) \tag{3}$$

where A = the constant of integration or the pre-exponential factor and E_a is the activation energy. Substitute the expression for k in equation (3) to obtain

$$Ae^{-E_a/RT} = \frac{1}{t(n-1)}\left[\frac{1}{(0.80a)^{n-1}} - \frac{1}{a^{n-1}}\right]$$

or

$$e^{-E_a/RT} = \frac{1}{t}\;\frac{1}{A(n-1)}\left[\frac{1}{(0.80a)^{n-1}} - \frac{1}{a^{n-1}}\right] \tag{4}$$

Let

$$\frac{1}{A(n-1)}\left[\frac{1}{(0.80a)^{n-1}} - \frac{1}{a^{n-1}}\right] = \text{constant} = L$$

Therefore equation (4) changes to

$$e^{-E_a/RT} = \frac{1}{t}\cdot L$$

Taking the ℓn of both sides yields

$$\ln e^{-E_a/RT} = \ln L - \ln t$$

or

$$-\frac{E_a}{RT} = \ln L - \ln t$$

At 300 °K the reaction is 20% complete in 12.6 min. Thus,

$$+\frac{E_a}{300R} = \ln 12.6 - \ln L \quad (5)$$

At 340 °K the reaction is 20% complete in 3.20 min and

$$+\frac{E_a}{340R} = \ln 3.20 - \ln L \quad (6)$$

Subtract equation (6) from equation (5) to get

$$0.04717\ E_a = \ln \frac{12.6}{3.20}$$

$$= 1.371$$

$$\therefore \quad E_a = \frac{1.371}{0.04717}$$

$$= 29.06\ kJ$$

REACTION ORDER

• PROBLEM 10-14

The partial pressure of azomethane, $CH_3N_2CH_3$ was measured as a function of time at 600°K as follows

t(sec)	0	1000	2000	3000	4000
$P_{CH_3N_2CH_3}$ (mmHg)	8.2×10^{-2}	5.72×10^{-2}	3.99×10^{-2}	2.78×10^{-2}	1.94×10^{-2}

a) Show that the decomposition, $CH_3N_2CH_3 \rightarrow CH_3CH_3 + N_2$, is a first-order reaction in azomethane.

b) Determine the rate coefficient at 600°K.

Solution: Plot $\ln(P/P_o)$ vs time, t. P_o is the vapor pressure of azomethane at 600°K. Since the plot gives a straight line, the reaction is first order, with a slope of $-k_1$. From the graph, the slope is -3.6×10^{-4}. Thus the rate constant $k_1 = 3.6 \times 10^{-4}$ s.

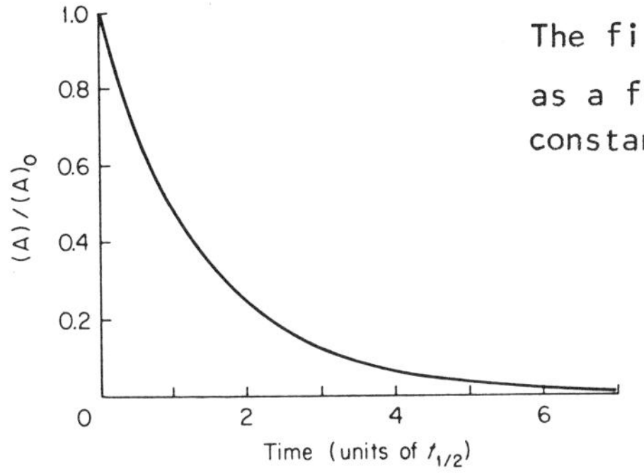

The first-order rate law. $(A)/(A)_0$ as a function of time, showing the constancy of $t_{\frac{1}{2}}$.

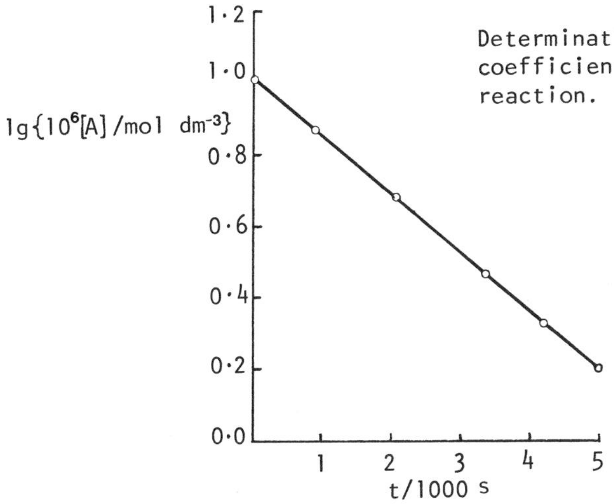

Determination of the rate coefficient for a first-order reaction.

• PROBLEM 10-15

Two equimolar solutions A and B with equal volume of solutions are mixed together and the reaction A + B = C takes place. After 1 hr, A is 75% reacted. Calculate how much of A will not react after 2 hrs if a) the reaction is first order in A and zero order in B. b) the reaction is first order in both A and B and c) the reaction is zero order in both A and B.

Solution: For a first order reaction the rate equation is written as

$$-\frac{d(A)}{dt} = k(A)$$

or $$-\frac{d(A)}{(A)} = kdt \tag{1}$$

Let $(A)_1$ = concentration of A at $t = t_1$

and $(A)_2$ = concentration of A at $t = t_2$

Integrating equation (1) using the above limits yields

$$-\int_{(A)_1}^{(A)_2} \frac{d(A)}{(A)} = k\int_{t_1}^{t_2} dt$$

$$\ln \frac{(A)_1}{(A)_2} = k(t_2 - t_1) \qquad (2)$$

Assume that $t_1 = 0$ and that the initiated concentration of $A = (A)_o$, equation (2) becomes

$$\ln \frac{(A)_o}{(A)} = kt \; .$$

Taking exponents of both sides gives

$$e^{\ln\frac{(A)_o}{(A)}} = e^{kt}$$

and

$$\frac{(A)_o}{(A)} = e^{kt}$$

Solving for (A) yields

$$(A) = (A)_o \; e^{-kt}$$

Taking ln of both sides gives

$$\ln(A) = \ln(A)_o \; e^{-kt}$$

$$= -kt + \ln(A)_o$$

or

$$\log(A) = \frac{-kt}{2.303} + \log(A)_o \qquad (3)$$

a) In this problem $(A)_o$ = 100% and (A) = 25% when t = 1 hr.

Therefore, solve equation (3) for k as follows

$$\log 0.25 = \frac{-k(3600 \text{ sec})}{2.303} + \log 1$$

$$-\; 0.602 = -1563.18k \text{ sec} + 0$$

and $k = 3.85 \times 10^{-4} \text{ sec}^{-1}$

Now, use this value of k to solve equation (3) for (A) when t = 2 hrs.

Therefore

$$\log A = \frac{(-3.85 \times 10^{-4}\ sec^{-1})(7200\ sec)}{2.303} + 0$$

$$= -1.2036$$

and $$A = 6.26 \times 10^{-2}$$

$$= 6.26\%$$

b) Here use the second order equation to find k.

The second order equation is written as

$$kt = \frac{1}{(A)} - \frac{1}{(A)_o} \qquad (4)$$

$$k(3600\ sec) = \frac{1}{0.25} - 1$$

$$k = \frac{3}{3600\ sec}$$

$$k = 8.33 \times 10^{-4}\ sec^{-1}$$

Use this value of k to solve for A in equation (4). From equation (4),

$$(8.33 \times 10^{-4}\ sec^{-1})(7200\ sec) = \frac{1}{(A)} - 1$$

$$(A) = 1.429 \times 10^{-1}$$

$$= 14.3\%$$

c) The reaction continues at constant rate. Since 75% reacts in 1 hr., the reaction will be complete before 2 hrs. Therefore the answer to this section is 0%.

• PROBLEM 10-16

Chloroform reacts according to the following equation in the presence of sodium methoxide in methanol solution.

$$CHCl_3 + OMe^- \rightleftarrows CCl_3^- + MeOH \text{ (fast)}$$

$$CCl_3^- \rightarrow CCl_2 + Cl^- \text{ (slow)}$$

and $$CCl_2 \rightarrow \text{products (fast)}$$

An experiment was done to measure the order of the slow step with respect to CCl_3^- and to determine the amount of Cl^- produced in time, t at 59.7°C by titration with 0.0100 N $AgNO_3$,

V, ml being required. The following results were obtained.

t (min)	V, ml
0	1.71
4	3.03
9	4.49
15	5.97
22	7.39
30	8.87
41	10.48
50	11.7
∞	15.98

Show that the reaction is first order and determine the rate constant.

Solution: One way to determine the order of the reaction is to plot log $(V_\infty - V)$ vs t. A straight line would be obtained if the reaction is first order. From the slope of the plot, the value of k can be calculated.

Another method is to use the equation

$$k = \frac{2.303}{t} \log \frac{V_\infty - V_o}{V_\infty - V}$$

For $t = 4$ min

$$k = \frac{2.303}{4 \text{ min}} \log \frac{15.98 - 1.71}{15.98 - 3.03}$$

$$= 0.0243 \text{ min}^{-1}$$

For $t = 4$ min to $5 = 50$ min

k = 0.0243, 0.0241, 0.0236, 0.0231, 0.0232, 0.0233 and 0.0241

Since k shows constancy then it can be said that the reaction is first order. And the value for k, taken as an average of all the values, is approximately 0.0237.

• PROBLEM 10-17

Consider the gaseous decomposition reaction of cyclopentene to H_2 and cyclopentadiene:

$$c\text{-}C_5H_8 = H_2 + c\text{-}C_5H_6$$

(a) How is dP/dt related to $-dC_{C_5H_8}/dt$? (b) If the reaction is first-order, what are the units on k? (c) Derive the first-order integrated rate equation in terms of $P_{C_5H_8,0}$ and P.

Solution: a) In a given reaction, the total pressure is the

sum of the partial pressures. That is

$$P = \Sigma P_i$$

where P = total pressure

P_i = partial pressure of component i

subscript i = the species, which are C_5H_8, H_2 and C_5H_6 in this problem.

For this problem,

$$P = P_{C_5H_8} + P_{H_2} + P_{C_5H_6}$$

The stoichiometry of the reaction is such that

$$P_{H_2} = P_{C_5H_6} = P_{C_5H_8,0} - P_{C_5H_8}$$

where $P_{C_5H_8,0}$ = partial pressure of C_5H_8 at time zero

$$\therefore \quad P = P_{C_5H_8} + 2(P_{C_5H_8,0} - P_{C_5H_8})$$

Now

$$P = P_{C_5H_8} + 2(P_{C_5H_8,0} - P_{C_5H_8}) = 2P_{C_5H_8,0} - P_{C_5H_8} \qquad (1)$$

Therefore differentiating (1) yields

$$\frac{dP}{dt} = -\frac{dP_{C_5H_8}}{dt} = k\, P_{C_5H_8} \qquad (2)$$

but

$P_{C_5H_8} = k\, C_{C_5H_8}$, so

$$\frac{dP_{C_5H_8}}{dt} = k\,\frac{dC_{C_5H_8}}{dt}\,, \text{ hence } \frac{dP}{dt} = -\frac{dP_{C_5H_8}}{dt} = -k\,\frac{dC_{C_5H_8}}{dt}$$

b) Observe that the units of k are 1/time, where time is in seconds.

c) From equation (2),

$$-\frac{dP_{C_5H_8}}{dt} = k\, P_{C_5H_8}$$

$$\therefore \quad \frac{dP}{dt} = k\,P_{C_5H_8} = k(2P_{C_5H_8,0} - P)$$

Rearranging and then integrating both sides, gives

$$\ln\left[P_{C_5H_8,0} \Big/ (2P_{C_5H_8,0} - P)\right] = kt$$

• PROBLEM 10-18

In a reaction between sodium thiosulfate and n-propyl bromide at 37°C, the amount of unreacted thiosulfate was measured by titration with I_2. Data for the I_2 titer in cm^3 of 0.02572 N iodine per 10.02 cm^3 sample of reaction mixture is given below.

t(sec)	0	1110	2010	3192	5052	7380	11232	78840
I_2(titer)	37.63	35.20	33.63	31.90	29.80	28.04	26.01	22.24

Write a balanced equation for the reaction; show that the reaction is second order and determine the rate constant.

Solution: The reaction equation can be written as

$$C_3H_7Br + S_2O_3^{2-} \rightarrow C_3H_7S_2O_3^- + Br^-$$

$$I_2 + 2S_2O_3^{2-} \rightarrow 2I^- + S_4O_6^{2-}$$

Let the initial concentrations at t=0 be "a" mole cm^{-3} of $S_2O_3^{2-}$ and "b" moles cm^{-3} of C_3H_7Br

But $\quad a = \dfrac{I_2 \text{ consumed at } t = 0}{\text{Volume } S_2O_3^{2-}}$

$$= \frac{37.63 \times 0.02572N \times \dfrac{1 \text{ mole } I_2}{\text{eq transferred}}}{10.02}$$

$$= 0.09659 \text{ M}$$

$$b = \frac{\text{total } S_2O_3^{2-} \text{ consumed}}{\text{Volume } S_2O_3^{2-}}$$

$$= \frac{(37.63 - 22.24)0.02572M}{10.02}$$

$$= 0.03950 \text{ M}$$

After a time t, x mole cm^{-3} of $S_2O_3^{2-}$ and C_3H_7Br will have reacted forming x mole cm^{-3} of $C_3H_7S_2O_3^-$ and of Br^-.

Therefore, the concentration of $S_2O_3^{2-}$ at time t

$$(a-x) = \frac{0.02572\ V_{I_2}}{10.02}$$

and the concentration of C_3H_7Br at time t

$$(b-x) = \frac{0.02572(V_{I_2} - 22.24)}{10.02}$$

and $(a-b) = 0.05709$ M

The integrated second order rate law is

$$\frac{1}{a-b} \ln \frac{b(a-x)}{a(b-x)} = k_2 t$$

and

$$k_2 = \frac{1}{t(a-b)} \ln \frac{b(a-x)}{a(b-x)}$$

$$= \frac{1}{(.05709M)t} \ln \left[\frac{(0.03950M)\left(\frac{.02572\ V_{I_2}}{10.02}\right)}{(.09659M)\left(\frac{.02572(V_{I_2} - 22.24)}{(10.02)}\right)} \right]$$

$$= \frac{1}{(.05709M)t} \ln \left[\frac{(0.03950)(V_{I_2})}{(.09659)(V_{I_2} - 22.24)} \right]$$

The values of k_2 in liters $mole^{-1}$ sec^{-1} evaluated at the different concentration levels are 0.001657, 0.001643, 0.001643, 0.001649, 0.001655, 0.001618 and 0.001618 respectively. This confirms that the reaction is second order because of the consistency of k values.

The rate constant can be assumed to be an average of the above values of k_2 . It is equal to .001640 ℓ $mole^{-1}$ sec^{-1} .

COMPLEX REACTIONS

• PROBLEM 10-19

For the set of reactions

$$A + B \underset{k_{-1}}{\overset{k_1}{\rightleftarrows}} C \qquad C + B \overset{k_2}{\rightarrow} D$$

find $-dC_A/dt$, $-dC_B/dt$, dC_C/dt and dC_D/dt.

Solution: The rate equation for a number of reactions in a complex mechanism is written as a sum of the rate equations for the simple reactions making up the complex mechanism.

So, for the substance A,

$$-\frac{dC_A}{dt} = k_1 C_A C_B - k_{-1} C_C$$

Note that the rate equation for A contains two terms (in spite of the fact that it appears only once). This is because it reacts in and is formed by this reaction, as indicated by the arrows going in opposite directions.

Using the same criterion, substance B should contain three terms because it reacts in and is formed by the first reaction. In addition to these, it reacts in the second equation. Therefore,

$$-\frac{dC_B}{dt} = k_1 C_A C_B - k_{-1} C_C + k_2 C_C C_B$$

Similarly,

$$\frac{dC_C}{dt} = k_1 C_A C_B - k_{-1} C_C - k_2 C_C C_B \ .$$

The substance D appears only once in the second equation. Since it is being formed, its rate equation is represented by

$$\frac{dC_D}{dt} = k_2 C_C C_B \ .$$

• PROBLEM 10-20

Consider the following mechanism describing enzyme catalysis:

$$E + S \underset{k_{-1}}{\overset{k_1}{\rightleftarrows}} X \underset{k_{-2}}{\overset{k_2}{\rightleftarrows}} E + P$$

where E is the enzymatic site, S is the substrate, X is the enzyme substrate complex and P is the product of the reaction. Derive the rate equation for this process assuming

$dC_X/dt = 0$ and discuss the results for the reaction during the initial stages.

Solution: The rate equation for this mechanism is written as the sum of the rate equations for the simple reactions that make up the complex mechanism. Therefore, the rate equation for the enzyme substrate complex X, will contain four terms. That is

$$\frac{dC_X}{dt} = 0 = k_1C_EC_S - k_{-1}C_X - k_2C_X + k_{-2}C_EC_P \qquad (1)$$

where C = concentration

k_1, k_{-1}, k_2, k_{-2} are rate constants

In the same manner,

$$\frac{dC_P}{dt} = k_2C_X - k_{-2}C_EC_P \qquad (2)$$

Now, let $C_E + C_X = C_{E,0}$, $V_X = k_2C_{E,0}$,

$$V_P = k_{-1}C_{E,0},\ K_S = \frac{k_{-1} + k_2}{k_1} \text{ and } K_P = \frac{k_{-1} + k_2}{k_{-2}}$$

Consequently, eliminating C_X and C_E gives

$$\frac{dC_P}{dt} = \frac{(V_S/K_S)C_S - (V_P/K_P)C_P}{1 + (C_S/K_S) + (C_P/K_P)} \qquad (3)$$

Or instead of using these substitutions, it might be easier to solve for C_X in equation (1) and substitute its expression into equation (2). That is

$$0 = k_1C_EC_S - k_{-1}C_X - k_2C_X + k_{-2}C_EC_P$$

$$\therefore \quad k_{-1}C_X + k_2C_X = k_1C_EC_S + k_{-2}C_EC_P$$

$$C_X = \frac{k_1C_EC_S + k_{-2}C_EC_P}{k_{-1} + k_2}$$

Substituting this into equation (2) gives

$$\frac{dC_P}{dt} = k_2\left[\frac{k_1C_EC_S + k_{-2}C_EC_P}{k_{-1} + k_2}\right] - k_{-2}C_EC_P \qquad (4)$$

Now what is done is to get the same denominator for both terms, so $k_{-2}C_EC_P$ is multiplied by

$$\frac{k_{-1} + k_2}{k_{-1} + k_2}$$

Hence,

$$\frac{dC_P}{dt} = k_2\left[\frac{k_1C_EC_S + k_{-2}C_EC_P}{k_{-1} + k_2}\right] - k_{-2}C_EC_P\left[\frac{k_{-1} + k_2}{k_{-1} + k_2}\right]$$

$$= \frac{k_2k_1C_EC_S}{k_{-1} + k_2} + \frac{k_2k_{-2}C_EC_P}{k_{-1} + k_2} - \frac{k_{-2}k_{-1}C_EC_P}{k_{-1} + k_2} + \frac{k_2k_{-2}C_EC_P}{k_{-1} + k_2}$$

Let $K_S = \frac{k_{-1} + k_2}{k_1}$ and $K_P = \frac{k_{-1} + k_2}{k_{-2}}$

Therefore,

$$\frac{dC_P}{dt} = \frac{k_2}{K_S} C_EC_S + \frac{k_2C_EC_P}{K_P} - \frac{k_{-1}C_EC_P}{K_P} - \frac{k_{-2}C_EC_P}{K_P}$$

Now, $C_{E,0} = C_E + C_X$, So $C_E = C_{E,0} - C_X$

Hence,

$$\frac{dC_P}{dt} = \frac{k_2C_S[C_{E,0}-C_X]}{K_S} + \frac{k_2C_P}{K_P}[C_{E,0}-C_X] - \frac{k_{-1}[C_{E,0}-C_X]}{K_P} - \frac{k_2C_P}{K_P}$$

$$\times [C_{E,0}-C_X]$$

$$= \frac{k_2C_SC_{E,0}}{K_S} - \frac{k_2C_SC_X}{K_S} + \frac{k_2C_PC_{E,0}}{K_P} - \frac{k_2C_PC_X}{K_P} - \frac{k_{-1}C_PC_{E,0}}{K_P} + \frac{k_{-1}C_PC_X}{K_P}$$

$$- \frac{k_{-2}C_PC_{E,0}}{K_P} + \frac{k_2C_PC_X}{K_P}$$

Let $k_{-1}C_{E,0} = V_P$ and $k_2C_{E,0} = V_S$. Then

$$\frac{dC_P}{dt} = \frac{V_SC_S}{K_S} - \frac{k_2C_SC_X}{K_S} + \frac{V_SC_P}{K_P} - \frac{k_2C_PC_X}{K_P} - \frac{V_PC_P}{K_P} + \frac{k_{-1}C_PC_X}{K_P} - \frac{C_PV_S}{K_P}$$

$$+ \frac{k_2C_PC_X}{K_P}$$

$$= \frac{V_S}{K_S} C_S - \frac{V_P}{K_P} C_P + \frac{k_{-1}C_PC_X}{K_P} - \frac{k_2C_SC_X}{K_S}$$

Now, substitute in the value of C_X which was determined earlier. After simplifying, the same result will be found as in equation (3).

If the measurements of the reaction rate are made during the early stages of the reaction, C_P will be nearly zero and the rate equation simplifies to give the Michaelis-Menten equation:

$$\frac{dC_P}{dt} = \frac{(V_S/K_S)C_S}{1 + (C_S/K_S)} = \frac{V_S}{1 + (K_S/C_S)}$$

If $C_S < K_S$, the reaction rate is first-order with respect to C_S and if $C_S > K_S$, the reaction rate is zero-order with respect to C_S. In both cases the reaction is dependent on V_S, which is first-order with respect to $C_{E,0} \approx C_E$. The Michaelis constant for the substrate, K_S, represents the value of C_S necessary to reduce the maximum reaction rate, V_S, by a factor of two. The rate constant for the product reaction, k_2, is known as the turnover constant. Casting the rate equation into the Lineweaver-Burk linear form gives

$$\left(\frac{dC_P}{dt}\right)^{-1} = \left(\frac{K_S}{V_S}\right)C_S^{-1} + V_S^{-1}$$

Thus a plot of $(dC_P/dt)^{-1}$ against C_S^{-1} will be linear, having an intercept of V_S^{-1} and a slope of K_S/V_S.

• PROBLEM 10-21

The Gibbs adsorption coefficient Ψ for an adsorbate on the surface of an adsorbent is related to the surface tension, γ, and the activity of the adsorbate, a_2 , by the expression

$$\Psi = -\frac{a_2}{RT}\frac{d\gamma}{da_2} = -\frac{1}{RT}\frac{d\gamma}{d(\ln a_2)}$$

If glycerol raises the surface tension of water as it is added, will the former be positively or negatively adsorbed?

Solution: Be definition, if Ψ is negative, then glycerol will be negatively adsorbed.

Assuming that this is a dilute solution, the γ term is essentially unity. Using the expression for the activity,

$a_i = \gamma_i x_i$, where

γ_i = activity coefficient for substance i. Then $\gamma_2 = 1$, and $a_2 = x_2$. Thus the a_2 term can be approximated by x_2. Therefore,

$$\Psi = -\frac{x_2}{RT}\frac{d\gamma}{dx_2} \quad (1)$$

where a_2 = activity

γ = surface tension

x_2 = mole fraction (or composition)

R = universal gas constant

T = temperature

Since $\frac{d\gamma}{dx_2}$ is positive, Ψ will have a negative value. Consequently, glycerol will be negatively adsorbed.

• PROBLEM 10-22

The luminescent reaction of luciferin catalyzed by the enzyme luciferase obtained from the crustacean Cypridina was measured at an enzyme concentration of 10^{-9}M. The initial luciferin concentration is given as cm^3 of 8.0×10^{-5}M luciferin in 20 cm^3 of reaction mixture.

Luciferin conc.	0.04	0.06	0.08	0.10	0.20	0.40	0.90
Initial rate (15°)	15	19	23	26	44	56	76
Millivolts per minute (22°C)	18	22	33	37	62	91	123

The conversion factor from millivolt reading of the photoelectric integrator to moles of luciferin reacted was 8.6×10^{-12} $mol \cdot mV^{-1}$ at 22°C and 7.7×10^{-12} at 15°C. For this reaction, estimate ΔH, ΔS and $\Delta H°$, $\Delta S°$ for the formation of the enzyme-substrate complex. What standard state is used?

Solution: A simple mechanism that describes an enzyme catalysis may be represented by

$$E + S \underset{k_{-1}}{\overset{k_1}{\rightleftarrows}} ES \overset{k_2}{\rightarrow} E + P$$

where E = enzymatic site
S = the substrate
ES = the enzyme-substrate complex
P = product of the reaction

If $k_{-1} >> k_2$, that is, if the rate of dissociation of the enzyme-substrate complex is much greater than the rate of its decomposition to form products, then the heat and entropy of formation of the complex can be obtained by using the Michaelis constant, K_M .

This is given by the expression

$$\frac{d \ln K_M}{dT} = \frac{\Delta H^\circ}{RT^2} \qquad (1)$$

from which

$$\Delta G^\circ = -RT \ln K_M \qquad (2)$$

and

$$\Delta S^\circ = - \frac{\Delta G^\circ - \Delta H^\circ}{T} \qquad (3)$$

ΔH = heat of formation

ΔG = Gibbs free energy change

R = universal gas constant

T = temperature

ΔS = entropy of formation

The superscript in these equations refer to standard condition which for this problem can be taken to be 1 atm pressure and 15°C.

Before the above relations can be used, K_M must be determined by using the relation

$$\frac{V}{[S]} = \frac{V_M}{K_M + [S]}$$

or

$$\frac{[S]}{V} = \frac{1}{V_M} [S] + \frac{K_M}{V_M}$$

where $[S]$ = concentration of substrate, in this case luciferin

V = initial rate

V_M = maximum rate

The plot of $\frac{[S]}{V}$ against [S] should give a slope of $\frac{1}{V_M}$ and and an intercept of $\frac{K_M}{V_M}$. Then K_M is found.

Note that

$$K_M(\text{mols liter}^{-1}) = K_M(\text{ml stock}) \times \frac{\text{molarity stock}}{\text{volume solution}} .$$

The K_M values are 0.24 ml stock and 0.34 ml stock at 15°C and 22°C respectively. Converting these to mols liter^{-1} gives

$$K_M = \frac{0.24 \times 8.0 \times 10^{-5}}{20} = 0.096 \times 10^{-5} \text{ at } 15°C$$

$$\text{and } K_M = \frac{0.34 \times 8.0 \times 10^{-5}}{20} = 0.136 \times 10^{-5} \text{ at } 22°C$$

All values are tabulated in table 1.

Table 1:

[S] (ml stock)	0.04	0.06	0.08	0.10	0.20	0.40	0.90
$V_{15°}$ (mV min^{-1})	15	19	23	26	44	56	76
$V_{22°}$ (mV min^{-1})	18	22	33	37	62	91	123
$\frac{[S]}{V_{15°}} \times 10^3$	2.67	3.16	3.48	3.85	4.55	7.14	11.84
$\frac{[S]}{V_{22°}} \times 10^3$	2.22	2.73	2.42	2.70	3.23	4.40	7.32

	15°	22°
V_M (mV min^{-1})	93	169
K_M (ml stock)	0.24	0.34
K_M (mols liter^{-1}) $\times 10^6$	0.96	1.36

From equation (1)

$$\Delta H° = \frac{RT_1T_2}{T_2-T_1} \ln \frac{K_M(T_2)}{K_M(T_1)}$$

$$= \frac{1.987 \times 288 \times 295}{295 - 288} \ln \frac{0.34}{0.24}$$

$$= 8400 \text{ cal/mol}$$

This is the amount of heat for the dissociation of the complex.

$$\therefore \quad \Delta H°_{formation} = - 8400 \text{ cal mol}^{-1} .$$

Using equation (2)

$$\Delta G° = - 1.987 \times 288 \ln 9.6 \times 10^{-7}$$

$$= 7930 \text{ cal/mole}$$

$$\therefore \quad \Delta G^\circ_{formation} = -\,7930 \text{ cal mol}^{-1}$$

From equation (3)

$$\Delta S^\circ = \frac{-7930 + 8400}{288} = 1.63 \text{ cal } ^\circ K^{-1} \text{ mol}^{-1}$$

$\Delta S^\circ_{formation} = -1.63$ cal $^\circ K^{-1} mol^{-1}$. The negative sign is due to the fact that upon association entropy decreases. The heat of activation for the formation of product from the enzyme substrate complex can be determined from the effect of temperature on k_2 (the turnover number)

$$k_{2\ (15^\circ C)} = \frac{V_M}{\text{enzyme concentration}}$$

$$= \frac{93 \text{ mV min}^{-1} \times 7.7 \times 10^{-12} \text{mol mV}^{-1}}{0.02 \text{ liter} \times 10^{-9} \text{mol liter}^{-1} \times 60 \text{ sec min}^{-1}}$$

$$= 0.597 \text{ sec}^{-1}$$

Similarly,

$$k_{2\ (22^\circ C)} = \frac{169 \times 8.6 \times 10^{-12}}{0.02 \times 10^{-9} \times 60}$$

$$= 1.211 \text{ sec}^{-1}$$

$$\Delta H \text{ of activation} = E_a - RT \qquad (4)$$

for liquids and solids

where E_a = energy of activation

$T = (T_1+T_2)/2$

Approximating E_a from the k_2 values gives

$$E_a = \frac{RT_2T_1}{T_2 - T_1} \ln\left(\frac{k_{(T_2)}}{k_{(T_1)}}\right)$$

$$= \frac{1.987 \times 288 \times 295}{295 - 288} \ln\left(\frac{1.211}{0.597}\right)$$

$$= 17000 \text{ cal mol}^{-1}$$

Substitute the value of E_a into equation (4) to get

$$\Delta H \text{ of activation} = 17000 - 1.987 \times 291.5$$

$$= 16400 \text{ cal mol}^{-1}$$

Using the transition state theory,

$$\Delta S_{288^\circ K} \text{ of activation} = \frac{\Delta H}{T} + R \ln\left(\frac{k_2 h}{kT}\right)$$

where $h = 6.62 \times 10^{-27}$ erg sec = Planck's constant

$k = 1.38 \times 10^{-16} \frac{erg}{°K}$ = Boltzmann's constant

$$\therefore \Delta S_{288°K} = \frac{16400}{288}$$

$$+ 1.987 \ln\left[\frac{0.597 \text{ sec}^{-1} \times 6.62 \times 10^{-27} \text{ erg sec}}{1.38 \times 10^{-16} \frac{\text{erg}}{°K} \times 288°K}\right]$$

$$= -2.54 \text{ cal deg}^{-1} \text{ mol}^{-1}$$

FAST REACTIONS

• PROBLEM 10-23

Williams and Petrucci studied the system

$$Ni(NCS)^{+} + NCS^{-} \underset{k_r}{\overset{k_f}{\rightleftarrows}} Ni(NCS)_2$$

at 25°C in methanol using a pressure-jump technique and obtained the following data:

$C_{Ni(NCS)_2}$, M	0.001	0.002	0.005	0.010	0.025	0.05	0.10
τ, ms	4.08	3.74	2.63	1.84	1.31	0.88	0.67

Determine k_f, k_r and K. τ is the relaxation time.

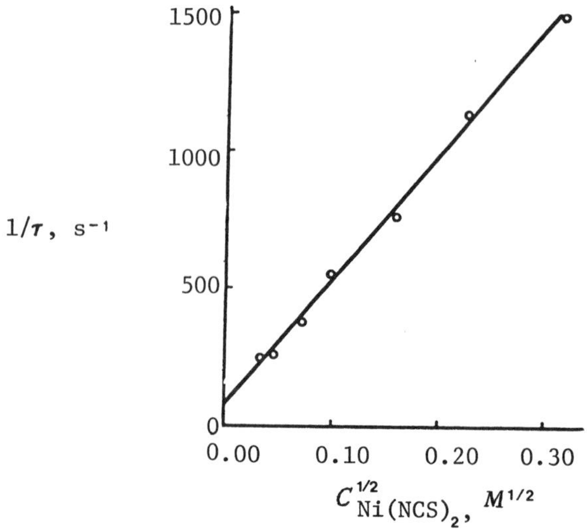

Solution: The rate equation for this system is

$$\frac{dC_{Ni(NCS)_2}}{dt} = k_f C_{Ni(NCS)^+} C_{NCS^-} - k_r C_{Ni(NCS)_2}$$

At equilibrium, $k_f C_{Ni(NCS)^+,e} C_{NCS^-,e} - k_r C_{Ni(NCS)_2,e} = 0$

For a small increase in $C_{Ni(NCS)_2}$, $\Delta C_{Ni(NCS)_2}$,

what is written is

$$C_{Ni(NCS)_2} = C_{Ni(NCS)_2,e} + \Delta C_{Ni(NCS)_2}$$

$$C_{NCS^-} = C_{NCS^-,e} - \Delta C_{Ni(NCS)_2}$$

$$C_{Ni(NCS)^+} = C_{Ni(NCS)^+,e} - \Delta C_{Ni(NCS)_2}$$

The rate equation for the decay of $\Delta C_{Ni(NCS)_2}$ is

$$\frac{d\Delta C_{Ni(NCS)_2}}{dt} = k_f\left(C_{Ni(NCS)^+,e} - \Delta C_{Ni(NCS)_2}\right)\left(C_{NCS^-,e} - \Delta C_{Ni(NCS)_2}\right)$$

$$- k_r\left(C_{Ni(NCS)_2,e} + \Delta C_{Ni(NCS)_2}\right)$$

$$= k_f\left(C_{Ni(NCS)^+,e} C_{NCS^-,e} - C_{NCS^-,e}\Delta C_{Ni(NCS)_2} - C_{Ni(NCS)^+,e}\Delta C_{Ni(NCS)_2} + \Delta C^2_{Ni(NCS)_2}\right) - k_r\left(C_{Ni(NCS)_2,e} + \Delta C_{Ni(NCS)_2}\right)$$

$$\therefore \frac{d\Delta C_{Ni(NCS)_2}}{dt} = -\left(k_f C_{Ni(NCS)^+,e} + k_f C_{NCS^-,e} + k_r\right) \times \Delta C_{Ni(NCS)_2} \qquad (1)$$

It is known that the displacement from equilibrium at time t is

$$\Delta C_i = \Delta C_{i,0}\, e^{-t/\tau} \qquad (2)$$

where $\Delta C_{i,0}$ = initial displacement from equilibrium.

If equation (2) is differentiated then

$$\frac{d(\Delta C_i)}{dt} = -\Delta C_i \frac{1}{\tau} \qquad (3)$$

Comparing equation (3) to equation (1) gives

$$\frac{1}{\tau} = k_r + k_f (C_{Ni(NCS)^+,e} + C_{NCS^-,e})$$

with $C_{Ni(NCS)^+,e} = C_{NCS^-,e}$. As for the third component,

$$C_{Ni(NCS)_{2,e}} = C_{Ni(NCS)_2} \left(1 - \frac{\alpha}{100}\right)$$

where $C_{Ni(NCS)_2}$ is the total (associated plus dissociated) concentration and α is the percent dissociation. Assuming that K will be large, and therefore that α will be small,

$$K = \frac{k_f}{k_r} = \frac{C_{Ni(NCS)_2,e}}{[C_{Ni(NCS)^+,e}]^2}$$

$$\approx \frac{C_{Ni(NCS)_2}}{[C_{Ni(NCS)^+}]^2}$$

and the formula for the relaxation time becomes

$$\frac{1}{\tau} = k_r + 2(k_f k_r)^{\frac{1}{2}} \; C^{\frac{1}{2}}_{Ni(NCS)_2}$$

A plot of $1/\tau$ against $C^{\frac{1}{2}}_{Ni(NCS)_2}$, see the Fig. is linear with a slope of 4600 $M^{-\frac{1}{2}} s^{-1}$ and an intercept of $k_r = 78\ s^{-1}$. The value of k_f is

$$k_f = \left[\frac{(\text{slope})}{2k_r^{\frac{1}{2}}}\right]^2 = \left[\frac{4600}{(2)(78)^{\frac{1}{2}}}\right]^2 = 6.8 \times 10^4\ M^{-1}\ s^{-1}$$

and the value of K is

$$K = \frac{6.8 \times 10^4}{78} = 870 .$$

• PROBLEM 10-24

Consider the water dissociation reaction

$$H_2O \rightleftarrows H^+ + OH^-$$

in which the equilibrium is disturbed. It is found that the relaxation time for the return to equilibrium at 25°C is 37μs. Calculate the rate coefficients for the forward and backward reactions.

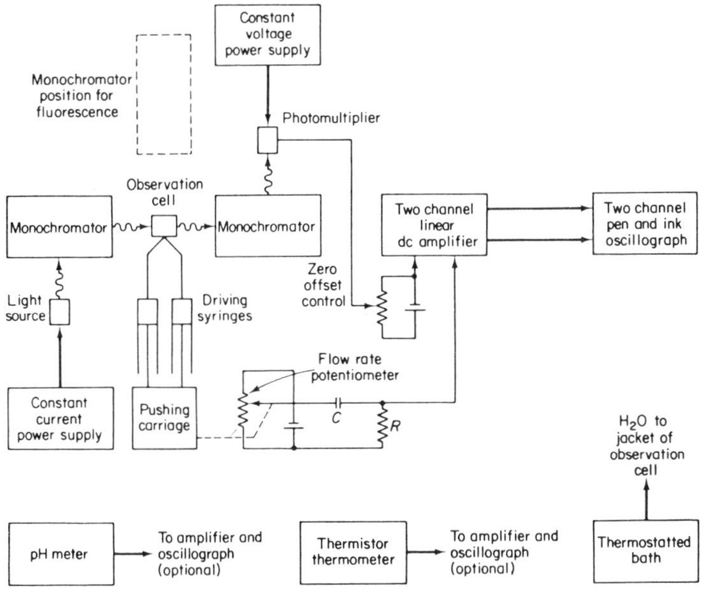

Block diagram of stopped-flow apparatus of type used to study rapid reactions in solution.

Solution: When a reaction is displaced slightly from equilibrium, the return to equilibrium is first order in the displacement from equilibrium. The rate of approach to equilibrium is proportional to the displacement from equilibrium, and the relaxation time, τ is used to characterize the rate of return to equilibrium. The forward rate is $k_1[H_2O]$. The backward rate is $k_2[H^+][OH^-]$. Therefore, the rate equation becomes

$$\frac{d(H_2O)}{dt} = k_2(H^+)(OH^-) - k_1(H_2O) \tag{1}$$

At equilibrium equation (1) changes to

$$0 = k_2(H^+)_{eq}(OH^-)_{eq} - k_1(H_2O)_{eq}$$

In terms of the displacement, $\Delta(H_2O)$ from equilibrium, equation (1) can be written by introducing

$$(H^+) = (H^+)_{eq} - \Delta(H_2O) \tag{2}$$

$$(OH^-) = (OH^-)_{eq} - \Delta(H_2O) \tag{3}$$

$$(H_2O) = (H_2O)_{eq} + \Delta(H_2O) \tag{4}$$

Substituting equations (2), (3) and (4) into equation (1) gives

$$\frac{d\Delta(H_2O)}{dt} = k_2[(H^+)_{eq} - \Delta(H_2O)][(OH^-)_{eq} - \Delta(H_2O)]$$

$$- k_1[(H_2O)_{eq} + \Delta(H_2O)]$$

Now, make the assumption that $(H^+)_{eq}(OH^-)_{eq}$ displacement from equilibrium is small

$$\therefore \quad \frac{d[\Delta(H_2O)]}{dt} = k_2[(H^+)_{eq}(OH^-)_{eq} - (H^+)_{eq}(+\Delta(H_2O))$$

$$- \Delta(H_2O)(OH^-)_{eq} + \Delta(H_2O)^2]$$

$$- k_1[(H_2O)_{eq} + \Delta(H_2O)]$$

$$= - k_2[+(H^+)_{eq}(+\Delta(H_2O)) + \Delta(H_2O)(OH^-)_{eq} - \Delta(H_2O)^2] - k_1\Delta(H_2O)$$

$$+ [k_2(H^+)_{eq}(OH^-)_{eq}] - [k_1(H_2O)_{eq}]$$

or $$\frac{d[\Delta(H_2O)]}{dt} = -\Delta(H_2O)\left\{k_2[(H^+)_{eq} + (OH^-)_{eq}] + k_1\right\} = \frac{-\Delta(H_20)}{\tau}$$

where τ = the relaxation time. Observe that the term $[\Delta(H_2O)]^2$ has been neglected. Therefore

$$\frac{1}{\tau} = k_1 + k_2[(H^+)_{eq} + (OH^-)_{eq}] \quad (5)$$

The equilibrium constant for the reaction is

$$K = \frac{(H^+)(OH^-)}{(H_2O)}$$

$$= \frac{k_1}{k_2}$$

$$= \frac{K_w}{(H_2O)}$$

where K_w = the dissociation constant for water.

Thus,

$$K = \frac{1.0 \times 10^{-14}}{55.5}$$

$$= 1.8 \times 10^{-16}$$

At equilibrium

$$k_1(H_2O)_{eq} = k_2(H^+)_{eq}(OH^-)_{eq}$$

or $$k_1 = k_2K \quad (6)$$

From equation (5)

$$\frac{1}{\tau} = k_2 + k_2[(H^+)_{eq} + (OH^-)_{eq}]$$

Therefore, since $(H^+)_{eq}(OH^-)_{eq} = K_w$ and $(H^+)_{eq} = (OH^-)_{eq}$

$$\frac{1}{\tau} = k_2[K + \sqrt{K_w} + \sqrt{K_w}]$$

$$= k_2[1.8 \times 10^{-16} + (2 \times 10^{-7})]$$

$$\cong 2 \times 10^{-7}\ k_2$$

and

$$k_2 = \frac{1}{(37 \times 10^{-6} s)(2 \times 10^{-7})}$$

$$= 1.4 \times 10^{11}\ M^{-1}\ s^{-1}$$

Substitute k_2 into equation (6) to obtain

$$k_1 = (1.4 \times 10^{11})(1.8 \times 10^{-16})$$

$$= 2.5 \times 10^{-5}\ s^{-1}$$

• PROBLEM 10-25

The following mechanism is proposed for the photodimerization of substance A:

$$A + h\nu \xrightarrow{k_1} A^*$$

$$A^* + A \xrightarrow{k_2} A_2$$

$$A^* \xrightarrow{k_3} A + h\nu'$$

Here, h = Planck's constant and

ν = Frequency of incident light

Derive the expression for the quantum yield of A_2 .

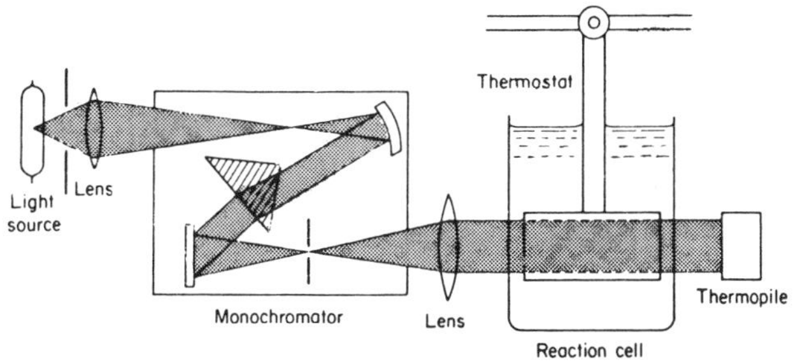

Arrangement for photochemical investigations.

Solution: The quantum yield of A_2 is the number of molecules of reactants consumed or product generated per quantum absorbed. That is

$$\frac{d(C_{A_2})/dt}{I}$$

where I = intensity of the light absorbed. So, beginning with the expression for the rate of change of the concentration of A* gives

$$\frac{dC_{A*}}{dt} = k_1 I - k_2 C_{A*} C_A - k_3 C_{A*} \tag{1}$$

where C = concentration

k_1, k_2 and k_3 = rate constants

Assuming steady-state conditions, equation (1) is set equal to zero because the steady-state approximation assumes that the concentrations of certain intermediate substances reach constant values. That is

$$\frac{dC_{A*}}{dt} = k_1 I - k_2 C_{A*} C_A - k_3 C_{A*} = 0 \tag{2}$$

Rearranging equation (2) to solve for C_{A*} yields

$$C_{A*} = \frac{k_1 I}{k_2 C_A + k_3} \tag{3}$$

The expression for the formation of A_2 is given by

$$\frac{d}{dt}(C_{A_2}) = k_2 C_{A*} C_A \tag{4}$$

The C_{A*} term in equation (4) is given by equation (3). Substituting this expression into equation (4) gives

$$\frac{d(C_{A_2})}{dt} = k_2 \frac{k_1 I}{k_2 C_A + k_3} C_A \tag{5}$$

Recall that the quantum yield is

$$\left(\frac{dC_{A_2}}{dt}\right)/I .$$

Hence, equation (5) changes to

$$\left(\frac{dC_{A_2}}{dt}\right)/I = \frac{k_2 k_1 C_A}{k_2 C_A + k_3}$$

• PROBLEM 10-26

The rate of a first order reaction increases from $r = 1.5 \times 10^{-2}\ sec^{-1}$ to $r_c = 4.6\ sec^{-1}$ at 260°C when a catalyst is added to the reaction. Calculate the decrease in the activation enthalpy H, assuming S°, the activation entropy, is not affected by the catalyst.

Solution: A catalyst provides an alternative path for many reactions. When the reactions follow this alternative path, either the value of enthalpy, H or entropy S, or both are altered in such a way that it lowers the free energy barrier for the reaction. The reaction would then proceed at a more rapid rate.

The rates of the two reactions with subscript c to denote the catalyzed reactions are

$$r = r_o\, e^{-G°/RT} \qquad (1)$$

and $$r_c = r_o\, e^{-G_c°/RT} \qquad (2)$$

where r_o is a constant

Dividing equation (2) by equation (1) gives

$$\frac{r_c}{r} = \frac{e^{-G_c°/RT}}{e^{-G°/RT}} = e^{-G_c°/RT}\ e^{G°/RT}$$

Taking the ln of both sides yields

$$\ln \frac{r_c}{r} = \frac{G° - G_c°}{RT}$$

or

$$RT \ln \frac{r_c}{r} = G° - G_c°$$

But $G° = H - TS°$

Therefore, $$RT \ln \frac{r_c}{r} = H - H_c - T(S° - S_c°) \qquad (3)$$

Assuming that S° is not affected by the catalyst, S° will be equal to $S_c°$ and $S° - S_c° = 0$. Therefore, equation (3) becomes

$$H - H_c = RT \ln \frac{r_c}{r}$$

$$= \left(1.987\ \frac{cal}{mole\ °K}\right)\left(533°K\right)\ \ln \frac{4.6}{0.015}$$

$= 6063$ cal/mole

$= 6.063$ kcal/mole

• PROBLEM 10-27

	Without Catalyst(k), sec^{-1}	With Catalyst (k_c), sec^{-1}
$T_1 = 473°K$	1.76×10^{-2}	6.10
$T_2 = 573°K$	0.804	88.1

The reaction rate of a first-order reaction at a constant pressure of 1 atm is shown in the table above. Calculate the value of H and S° with and without catalyst, assuming that they do not change with temperature.

Solution: The reaction rate theory as put forward by Arrhenius, gives the variation of the rate constant, k with temperature as represented by the expression

$$\frac{d \ln k}{dT} = \frac{H}{RT^2} \qquad (1)$$

where H = the enthalpy increase per mole needed to raise the reactants to a state of activation. Integrating equation (1) gives

$$\int_{k_1}^{k_2} d \ln k = \frac{H}{R} \int_{T_1}^{T_2} \frac{dT}{T^2}$$

Therefore,

$$\ln \frac{k_2}{k_1} = - \frac{H}{R} \left(\frac{1}{T_2} - \frac{1}{T_1} \right)$$

or

$$R \ln \frac{k_2}{k_1} = - H \left(\frac{1}{T_2} - \frac{1}{T_1} \right) \qquad (2)$$

For the uncatalyzed reaction, equation (2) becomes

$$1.987 \times 10^{-3} \frac{\text{kcal}}{\text{mole °K}} \ln \frac{0.804}{1.76 \times 10^{-2}} = - H \left(\frac{1}{573} - \frac{1}{473} \right)$$

$$1.987 \times 10^{-3} \frac{\text{kcal}}{\text{mole °K}} (3.82) = - H (- 3.689 \times 10^{-4} \text{ °K}^{-1})$$

Hence,

$$H = \frac{1.987 \times 10^{-3} \ \frac{\text{kcal}}{\text{mole°K}} \ (3.82)}{3.689 \times 10^{-4} \ °K^{-1}}$$

$$= 20.6 \ \text{kcal/mole}$$

For the catalyzed reaction, equation (2) gives

$$R \ln \frac{(k_2)_c}{(k_1)_c} = -H_c\left(\frac{1}{T_2} - \frac{1}{T_1}\right)$$

The subscript c denotes catalyst.

Thus $1.987 \times 10^{-3} \ \frac{\text{kcal}}{\text{mole °K}} \ \ln \frac{88.1}{6.10} = -H \ (-3.689 \times 10^{-4})$

$$5.30 \times 10^{-3} \ \frac{\text{kcal}}{\text{mole °K}} = 3.689 \times 10^{-4} \ H \ .$$

and

$$H = \frac{5.30 \times 10^{-3} \ \frac{\text{kcal}}{\text{mole °K}}}{3.689 \times 10^{-4} \ °K^{-1}}$$

$$= 14.4 \ \text{kcal/mole}$$

The rate constant is given by

$$k = e^{-(H-TS°)/RT}$$

Taking the ln of both sides gives

$$\ln k = \ln e^{-(H-TS°)/RT} = \frac{-H + TS}{RT}$$

or $\quad RT \ln k = -H + TS°$.

Therefore

$$S° = R \ln k + \frac{H}{T} \tag{3}$$

For the uncatalysed reaction equation (3) becomes

$$S° = 1.987 \ln 1.76 \times 10^{-2} + \frac{20600 \ \text{cal/mole}}{473 \ °K}$$

$$= -8.027 + 43.551$$

$$= 35.5 \ \text{eu}$$

For the catalysed reaction equation (3) gives

$$S° = 1.987 \ln 6.10 + \frac{14400 \ \text{cal/mole}}{473 \ °K}$$

$$= 34.0 \ \text{eu}$$

CHAPTER 11

COLLOIDS AND SURFACE CHEMISTRY

ADSORPTION

• PROBLEM 11-1

Atoms of argon gas are being adsorbed onto a uniform surface of a certain crystal and the adsorbed atoms are freely mobile. Calculate
a) the adsorption coefficient using the Langmuir adsorption isotherm by treating the adsorbed phase as a two-dimensional gas.
b) $\theta(P,T)$ for $P = 1$ atm, $\theta = 200^\circ K$ and $\Delta\varepsilon_0$(adsorption) = 0.35 eV.

Solution: The equation that relates the amount of gas adsorbed on a surface to the pressure of the gas at constant temperature is called the adsorption isotherm. One such isotherm is the Langmuir adsorption isotherm, given by

$$\theta = \frac{b(T)P}{1 + b(T)P} \qquad (1)$$

where θ = the fraction of the surface area covered by adsorbed molecules at any time and P is the pressure. $b(T)$ is the adsorption coefficient and is given in terms of statistical mechanics as

$$b(T) = Q(T)e^{-\mu^0/kT} \qquad (2)$$

where Q = the partition function.

For a mobile two-dimensional adsorbed gas, there is free translational motion in the xy plane of the crystal surface and with a vibration of magnitude of $5 \times 10^{12} sec^{-1}$ perpendicular to the surface.

The partition function of the argon gas is given by

$$Q(T) = \left(Q_{x,trans.}Q_{y,trans.}Q_{z,vib}\right)e^{-\Delta\varepsilon_0/kT} \qquad (3)$$

where $Q_{x,trans.},Q_{y,trans.}$ = the translational partition function in the x- and y-plane respectively. $Q_{z,vib.}$ is the vibrational partition function in the z-plane.

$$Q_{x,trans.} = Q_{y,trans.} = \frac{(2\pi mkT)^{\frac{1}{2}}a}{h} \qquad (4)$$

where h = Planck's constant. For two degrees of translational freedom, equation (4) is squared, and since a^2 = area, A, equation (4) changes to

$$Q_{x,trans.}Q_{y,trans.} = \frac{2\pi mkTA}{h^2}. \quad A \text{ is in } m^2.$$

$$\therefore \quad Q_{trans.} = \frac{2\pi(40\times10^{-3}kg)(1.3805\times10^{-23}J\,°K^{-1})(200°K)(A)}{(6.022\times10^{23}mole^{-1})(6.62\times10^{-34}J\text{-}sec)^2}$$

$$= 2.629 \times 10^{21}A.$$

$$Q_{z,vib.} = \frac{e^{-h\nu/2kT}}{1 - e^{-h\nu/kT}}$$

$$= \frac{e^{h\nu/2kT}}{e^{h\nu/kT} - 1}$$

$$\frac{h\nu}{2kT} = \frac{(6.62\times10^{-34}J\text{-}sec)(5\times10^{12}\ sec^{-1})}{2(1.3805\times10^{-23}J\,°K^{-1})(200°K)}$$

$$= 0.60.$$

Therefore

$$Q_{z,vib.} = \frac{e^{0.60}}{e^{1.20} - 1}$$

$$= 0.785$$

$$\frac{\Delta\epsilon_0}{kT} = \frac{(0.35eV)(1.602\times10^{-19}J/eV)}{(1.3805\times10^{-23}J\,°K^{-1})(200°K)}$$

$$= 20.31.$$

Thus $e^{-\Delta\epsilon_0/KT} = e^{-20.31}$

$$= 1.515 \times 10^{-9}.$$

From equation (3),

$$Q(T) = (2.629\times10^{21}A)(0.785)(1.515\times10^{-9})$$

$$= 3.13 \times 10^{12}A$$

$$\frac{\mu^0}{kT} = \frac{-kT\ \ln\left[\left(\frac{2\pi mkT}{h^2}\right)^{3/2}\frac{RT}{LP}\right]}{kT}$$

where L = Avogadro's number and P is the pressure. Simplification of the above equation yields

$$\frac{\mu^0}{kT} = -\ln\left[\left(\frac{2\pi mkT}{h^2}\right)^{3/2}\frac{RT}{LP}\right]$$

$$= -\ln\left\{\left[\frac{2\pi(40\times10^{-3}kg\ mole^{-1})(1.3805\times10^{-23}J\,°K^{-1})(200\,°K)}{(6.022\times10^{23}mole^{-1})(6.62\times10^{-34}J\text{-}s)^2}\right]^{3/2}\left[\frac{(0.082\times10^{-3}m^3atm\,°K^{-1}mol^{-1})(200\,°K)}{(6.022\times10^{23}mol^{-1})(1\ atm)}\right]\right\}$$

$$= -\ln[(1.35 \times 10^{32})(2.72 \times 10^{-26})]$$

$$= -\ln(3.672 \times 10^6)$$
$$= -15.12$$
$$e^{\mu^0/kT} = e^{-15.12}$$
$$= 2.72 \times 10^{-7} .$$

From equation (2) the adsorption coefficient is

$$b(T) = Q(T)e^{\mu^0/kT}$$
$$= (3.13 \times 10^{12}A)(2.72 \times 10^{-7})$$
$$= 8.51 \times 10^5 A$$

where A = the area of the surface in m^2.

b) The fraction of occupied sites on the surface of the crystal, θ, is given by equation (1). Therefore,

$$\theta = \frac{(8.51 \times 10^5 A)(1 \text{ atm})}{1 + 8.51 \times 10^5 A} .$$

• PROBLEM 11-2

The data below are for the adsorption of CO on charcoal at 273K. Confirm that they fit the Langmuir isotherm, and find the constant K and the volume corresponding to complete surface coverage.

p/mmHg	100	200	300	400	500	600	700
V/cm^3	10.2	18.6	25.5	31.4	36.9	41.6	46.1

Mass of sample of charcoal: 3.022g; in each case V has been corrected to 1 atm.

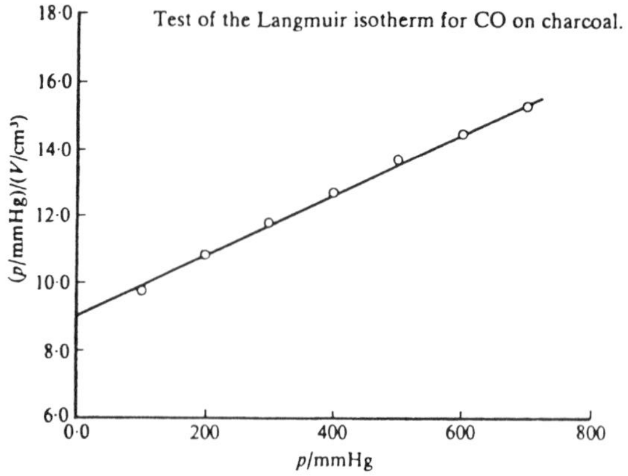

Solution: The Langmuir isotherm is given by $\theta = \frac{Kp_A}{1 + Kp_A}$ where p_A = pressure of A, K = ratio of the rate constant for adsorption to that for desorption. That is, $k_a/k_d = K$ from the above equation,

$$Kp_A = \theta + Kp_A\theta . \quad (1)$$

$$\theta = \frac{\text{number of adsorption sites filled}}{\text{number of adsorption sites available}} .$$

Let $\theta = V/V_\infty$ where V_∞ represents complete coverage. Then, equation (1) becomes

$$\frac{p_A}{V} = \frac{1}{KV_\infty} + \frac{p_A}{V_\infty} .$$

A plot of p_A/V versus p_A should give a straight line of slope $1/V_\infty$ and intercept $1/KV_\infty$.

From the given data, the following table is drawn, from which the graph will be plotted.

P	100	200	300	400	500	600	700
p_A/V	$\frac{100}{10.2}=9.8$	$\frac{200}{18.6}=10.8$	$\frac{300}{25.5}=11.8$	$\frac{400}{31.4}=12.7$	$\frac{500}{36.9}=13.6$	$\frac{600}{41.6}=14.4$	$\frac{700}{46.1}=15.2$

The values are plotted below.

$$\text{Slope of the line} = \frac{15.2 - 9.8}{700 - 100} = \frac{5.4}{600} \frac{\frac{1}{\text{mm Hg cm}^3}}{\frac{1}{\text{mm Hg}}}$$

$$= 0.0090 \text{ cm}^{-3} .$$

Since slope $= 0.009 \text{ cm}^{-3} = 1/V_\infty$,

$$V_\infty = \frac{1}{0.009\text{cm}^3} = 111 \text{ cm}^3 .$$

The intercept is approximately 9.0 as shown on the graph.

$$\text{intercept} = 9.00 = \frac{1}{KV_\infty} = \frac{1}{(K)(111)}$$

$$K = \frac{1}{(9)(111)}$$

$$= 0.001 \text{ mm Hg}^{-1}$$

• PROBLEM 11-3

The data for the adsorption of oxygen on smooth iron at -183 °C, as investigated by Armbruster and Austin[J. Am. Chem. Soc., 68, 1347 (1946)], is given below.

t,sec	V, cm^3
1380	0.167
3000	0.272
4260	0.330
7320	0.408
10020	0.432

where V = the volume adsorbed on a particular specimen of iron up to time t, and $V_e = 0.451\ cm^3$ is the volume adsorbed at equilibrium. Show that the adsorption rate follows first-order kinetics and determine the rate constant, k.

Solution:

t, sec	V, cm^3	V_e	(V_e-V)	$\ln(V_e-V)$
1380	0.167	0.451	0.284	-1.259
3000	0.272	0.451	0.179	-1.720
4260	0.330	0.451	0.121	-2.112
7320	0.408	0.451	0.043	-3.147
10020	0.432	0.451	0.019	-3.963

Plot $\ln(V_e-V)$ vs t. Obtain a straight line with a slope of -k. The value of k is estimated to be about $1.38 \times 10^{-4}\ sec^{-1}$.

• PROBLEM 11-4

Curve (a) shows the adsorption profile of N_2 on Fe at $-195°C$ and (b) shows the adsorption profile of Br_2 on SiO_2 at $79°C$. P_0 is the vapor pressure of the adsorbate in both cases. Explain why the two curves differ in shape.

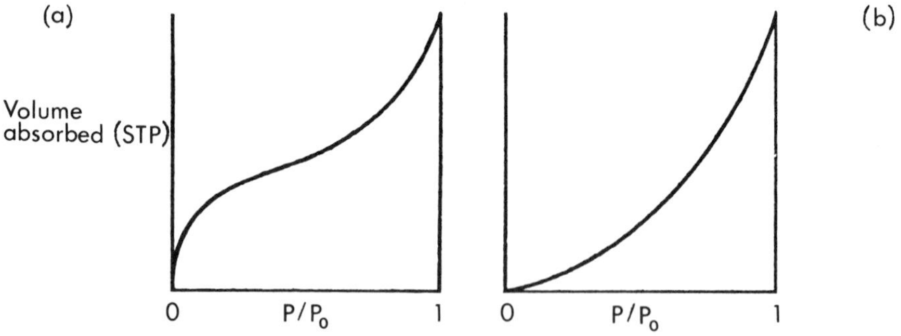

Solution: The two isotherms represent physical adsorption. Instead of the pressure, the relative pressure P/P_0 is used as a coordinate.

P_0 is the vapor pressure of the adsorbate (substance that is adsorbed) at the temperature of the isotherm. Adsorption occurs on the surface of a solid because of the attractive forces of the atoms or molecules in the surface of the solid. Physical adsorption is due to the operation of these forces between the solid surface and the adsorbate molecules that are similar to the van der Waals forces between molecules.

In curve (a) the first layer of molecules is adsorbed more strongly than the other layers; that is, the attractive forces between N_2 and Fe is much greater than the attraction between N_2 and N_2. As P/P_0 approaches unity the amount adsorbed increases rapidly and several superimposed layers of adsorbate are deposited on the surface. A temporary leveling off occurs as the first layer is completed.

In curve (b), there is more attraction between Br_2 and Br_2 than between Br_2 and SiO_2. The quantity of the adsorbate rises smoothly with pressure and the curve does not exhibit any special feature indicating the completion of the monomolecular layer.

• PROBLEM 11-5

The following data was obtained for the adsorption of aqueous acetic acid on charcoal.

c_0, molarity of acetic acid in solution before addition to charcoal	c_e, molarity of acetic acid remaining in solution at equilibrium	m, grams of charcoal
0.503	0.434	3.96
0.252	0.202	3.94
0.126	0.0899	4.00
0.0628	0.0347	4.12
0.0314	0.0113	4.04
0.0157	0.00333	4.00

Show that these data is in accordance with the Freundlich adsorption isotherm,

$$\frac{x}{m} = kc_e^{1/n}$$

where x = the number of grams of acetic acid adsorbed and k and n are constants.
Estimate the constants k and n. In all cases the volume of the solution in contact with the charcoal was 200 ml.

Solution: Adsorption from solution does not in general appear to lead to layers more than one molecule thick. For many cases the experimental data can be fairly well represented by an empirical isotherm proposed by Freundich.

$$\frac{x}{m} = kc_e^{1/n} . \quad (1)$$

Here, x and m are the masses of the substances adsorbed (adsorbate) and of the substances on which the adsorption takes place (adsorbent) respectively. c_e is the concentration of the solution at equilibrium and n is an empirical constant usually greater than unity. Freundlich equation then implies that if log x/m is plotted against log c_e, a straight line will be obtained with a slope of 1/n.

Let x = number of grams adsorbate (CH_3COOH) adsorbed

$$= \left[(c_0 - c_e)\text{mole/liter}\right][0.200 \text{ liter}][60.0 \text{ g/mole}] .$$

From equation (1)

$$\log\frac{x}{m} = \log k + \frac{1}{n}\log c_e$$

c_0	c_e	x	$\frac{x}{m}$	$\log\left(\frac{x}{m}\right)$	$\log c_e$
0.503	0.434	0.828	0.209	-0.680	-0.362
0.252	0.202	0.600	0.152	-0.818	-0.695
0.126	0.0899	0.433	0.1083	-0.965	-1.046
0.0628	0.0347	0.337	0.0818	-1.087	-1.459
0.0314	0.0113	0.241	0.060	-1.222	-1.950
0.0157	0.00333	0.148	0.037	-1.430	-2.478

Plot $\log \left(\frac{x}{m}\right)$ vs $\log c_e$ to get a straight line. The intercept

for $c_e = 1(\log c_e = 0) = \log k$. Therefore, $\log k = 9.448 - 10 =$

-0.552 and $k = 0.28$, slope $= 1/n = 0.355$ and $n = 2.82$.

● **PROBLEM** 11-6

Explain the cleansing action of soap.

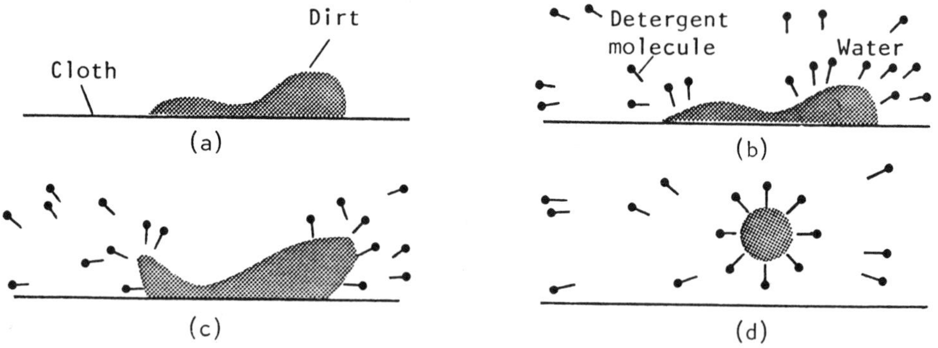

Solution: Two important classes of colloids are hydrophilic (water loving) and hydrophobic (water hating) colloids. These are colloids in which the dispersing medium is water. Soaps' cleansing ability is due to the fact that they (soaps) can stabilize hydrophobic colloids.

Hydrophobic colloids are stabilized by their adsorption to other hydrophobic colloids on their surfaces. These adsorbed groups contain a hydrophilic portion which interacts with water, thus stabilizing the colloid. Soaps contain substances such as sodium stearate which has a structure like

$$\underbrace{CH_3(CH_2)_{16}}_{\substack{\text{Hydrophilic} \\ \text{end}}}\overset{\overset{\displaystyle O}{\displaystyle \|}}{C}O^{-}Na^{+}$$

Hydrophobic end   Hydrophilic end

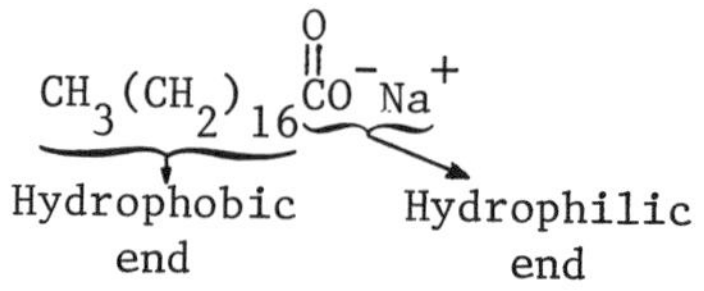

Sodium stearate has a polar end that is hydrophilic and a non-polar end that is hydrophobic. The hydrophilic end interacts with the water while the hydrophobic end interacts with the dirt on the clothes. The schematic representation of this soap action is illustrated in the diagram. In (a) there is dirt on a piece of cloth and in (b) the soap molecules in water attach their hydrophobic tails to the dirt and their hydrophilic head remains at the oil-water interphase where it interacts with water. In (c) this interaction permits the molecules to lift the dirt, breaking it into small portions and surrounding it. Finally in (d) the soap molecules hold the dirt so that it can be washed away.

● **PROBLEM** 11-7

The surface tension, γ, of an aqueous solution of butyric acid is related at $18°\,C$ to the bulk concentration, c, by the equation

$$\gamma_0 - \gamma = 29.8 \text{ dyne/cm } \log(1 + 19.64 \text{ M}^{-1}c)$$

where γ_0 is the surface tension of pure water. Calculate the excess concentration S, of solute per square centimeter of surface when c = 0.01 M. Use Gibbs adsorption equation. Determine the limiting value of S as c becomes infinite.

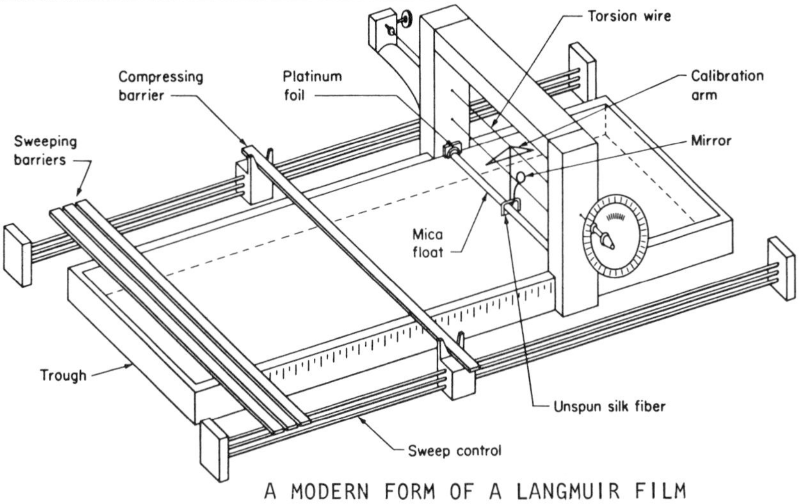

A MODERN FORM OF A LANGMUIR FILM BALANCE FOR MEASURING SURFACE TENSION CAUSED BY A SURFACE FILM.

Solution: $\gamma_0 - \gamma = 29.8$ dyne/cm $\log(1 + 19.64M^{-1}c)$. To convert logarithms in base 10 to natural logarithms the following conversion is used:

$$2.303 \log x = \ln x.$$

The reason for the nesessity of this conversion is to use the readily known formula for the derivative of ln x. Hence

$$\gamma_0 - \gamma = 29.8\left(\frac{1}{2.3026}\right)\ln\,(1 + 19.64c).$$

Therefore,

$$-\frac{d\gamma}{dc} = (29.8)\text{dyne/cm}\ (.4343)\left(\frac{1}{1+ 19.64c}\right)(19.64). \qquad (1)$$

The Gibbs adsorption equation is given by

$$S = \frac{-c}{RT}\ \frac{d\gamma}{dc} \qquad (2)$$

where S = the excess concentration of solution per square centimeter of surface and c is the concentration. From equation (1),

$$\frac{d\gamma}{dc} = \frac{-0.4343 \times 29.8 \text{ dyne/cm} \times 19.64M^{-1}}{1 + 19.64\ M^{-1}\ c}$$

$$= \frac{-254 \text{ dyne cm}^{-1} M^{-1}}{1 + 19.64\ M^{-1}c}$$

Rearranging equation (2) to solve for S yields

$$S = -\frac{c}{RT} \cdot \frac{d\gamma}{dc}$$

$$= \frac{(254c)\ \text{dyne}\ M^{-1}\text{cm}^{-1}}{RT(1 + (19.64M^{-1})c)}$$

$$= \frac{254\ \text{dyne}\ M^{-1}\text{cm}^{-1} \times 0.01\ M}{(8.314 \times 10^7 \frac{\text{erg}}{°K\ \text{mole}}\ (291°K) \times (1 + 19.64M^{-1}x0.01M)}$$

$$S = 8.79 \times 10^{-11}\ \text{moles cm}^{-2}$$

(b)

$$S = \frac{254c}{RT(1+19.64\ c)} = \frac{254c}{RT+19.64RTc}$$

To calculate the limit of S as c approaches infinity, divide the right side of the above equation by the highest power of c. Hence,

$$\lim_{c\to\infty} S = \frac{254c/c}{RT/c + 19.64RTc/c} = \frac{254}{RT/c + 19.64\ RT}$$. Now, as $c \to \infty$, $RT/c \to 0$. Therefore,

$$\lim_{c\to\infty} S = \frac{254\ \text{dyne}\ M^{-1}\ \text{cm}^{-1}}{19.64\ RT}$$

$$= \frac{254\ \text{dyne}\ M^{-1}\ \text{cm}^{-1}}{(19.64M^{-1})(8.31 \times 10^7)\frac{\text{erg}}{°K\ \text{mole}})(291°K)}$$

$$= 5.34 \times 10^{-10}\ \frac{\text{moles}}{\text{cm}^2}.$$

• PROBLEM 11-8

The amount of N_2 adsorbed on charcoal is a constant 0.894 cm^3 (STP) g^{-1} at P = 4.60 atm and 194° K and at P = 35.4 atm and 273°K. Calculate ΔH_v, the isosteric heat of adsorption, ΔS_v and ΔG_v for the adsorption at 273°K. Briefly discuss the determining factors for ΔS_v and how it relates to the adsorbent.

Solution: The Clausius-Clapeyron equation for an ideal gas will be used to calculate ΔH_v. Thus,

$$\ln\left(\frac{P_2}{P_1}\right) = \frac{-\Delta H_v}{R}\left[\frac{1}{T_2} - \frac{1}{T_1}\right] \tag{1}$$

Substituting the respective values into equation (1) gives

$$\ln \frac{35.4}{4.60} = \frac{-\Delta H_v}{(8.314J°K^{-1}mol^{-1})}\left[\frac{1}{273} - \frac{1}{194}\right]$$

$$2.04 = \frac{-\Delta H_v}{8.314J°K^{-1}mol^{-1}}\left[-1.49 \times 10^{-3}\ °K^{-1}\right]$$

Solving for ΔH_v yields

$$\Delta H_v = \frac{-2.04(8.314J\ mol^{-1})}{-1.49 \times 10^{-3}}$$

$$= 11383 \text{ J mol}^{-1} .$$

The heat adsorbed is conventionally taken to be negative. Therefore, ΔH_v is negative, given by

$$\Delta H_v = -11383 \text{ J mol}^{-1}$$

$$\Delta G_v = RT \ln P$$

$$= (8.314 \text{J}^\circ\text{K}^{-1}\text{mol}^{-1})(273^\circ\text{K}) \ln 35.4 \text{ atm}$$

$$= 8095 \text{ J mol}^{-1}$$

$$\Delta S_v = \frac{\Delta H - \Delta G}{T}$$

$$= \frac{-11383 - 8095}{273}$$

$$= -71.34 \text{ J K}^{-1}\text{mol}^{-1} .$$

ΔS_v is defined in terms of $\bar{S}_s$ and S_G. Thus $\Delta S_v = S_G - \bar{S}_s$ where $\bar{S}_s$ = a two dimensional entropy for the adsorbate and it depends on the fraction of covered sites. $\bar{S}_s$ has a tranlational portion given by

$$\bar{S}_s, \text{tr} = R \ln\left(\frac{MTb}{\theta}\right) + 63.8 \text{ cal}^\circ \text{K}^{-1}\text{mol}^{-1}$$

where b = the surface area per molecule and θ is the fraction of covered sites of the surface. Therefore ΔS_v increases and $\bar{S}_s$ decreases when θ increases.

ΔS_v would decrease if the specific area of the charcoal were greater since $\theta = v/v_m$ decreases and $\bar{S}_s$ increases.

• PROBLEM 11-9

An equation similar to $dP/P = (\Delta H/R)(dT/T^2)$ describes the temperature dependence of the amount of gas adsorbed on the surface of a solid. Find ΔH(adsorption) for N_2 at 1 atm if 155 cm^3 (measured at STP) is adsorbed by 1 g of charcoal at 88° K, and 15 cm^3 at 273° K.

Solution: By definition, the analoguous equation to the given one is

$$\frac{dV}{V} = \frac{\Delta H}{R}\frac{dT}{T^2} , \tag{1}$$

where V = volume
dV = change in volume
ΔH = enthalpy change
T = temperature
R = gas constant
dT = change in temperature.

Integrating equation (1) gives

$$\ln V\Big|_{V_1}^{V_2} = -\frac{\Delta H}{R}\frac{1}{T}\Big|_{T_1}^{T_2}$$

$$\ln V_2 - \ln V_1 = -\frac{\Delta H}{R}\left(\frac{1}{T_2} - \frac{1}{T_1}\right)$$

$$\ln \frac{V_2}{V_1} = -\frac{\Delta H}{R}\left(\frac{1}{T_2} - \frac{1}{T_1}\right) . \qquad (2)$$

Solving equation (2) for ΔH and substituting the data gives

$$\Delta H = \frac{-R \ln(V_2/V_1)}{\frac{1}{T_2} - \frac{1}{T_1}} = \frac{-(8.314 \text{ J mol}^{-1}\text{K}^{-1})\ln(155/15)}{\frac{1}{88 \text{ K}} - \frac{1}{273 \text{ K}}} = -2.52\frac{\text{kJ}}{\text{mol}}$$

GIBB'S ADSORPTION ISOTHERM

• PROBLEM 11-10

At 25 °C, the mean activity coefficient $\gamma_\pm$ of KCl in aqueous solution of 0.002 molal is 0.9648. Calculate the size droplets of 0.002M KCl solution at 25 °C that would be in equilibrium with a plane surface of pure water.

Solution: By definition, the activity of KCl(aq) is given by

$$a_{KCl}(aq) = \gamma_\pm^2 m^2 \qquad (1)$$

where m = the molality and $\gamma_\pm$ is the mean activity coefficient.

One form of the Gibbs adsorption isotherm equation is given by

$$\Gamma = -\frac{1}{kT}\frac{d\gamma}{d \ln a_{KCl}} \qquad (2)$$

where Γ = the concentration of adsorbed component of the solution at the interface, and k = Boltzmann's constant, which is the gas constant in ergs divided by Avogadro's number.
Substitute equation (1) into equation (2) to obtain

$$\Gamma = -\frac{1}{2kT}\frac{d\gamma}{d \ln \gamma_\pm m}$$

$$= -\frac{\gamma_\pm m}{2kT}\frac{d\gamma}{d(\gamma_\pm m)}$$

At low concentrations, $\frac{d\gamma}{d(\gamma_\pm m)} = \frac{d\gamma}{dm}$. Therefore,

$$\Gamma = -\frac{\gamma_\pm m}{2kT}\frac{d\gamma}{dm} \qquad (3)$$

At 20°C the surface tension of water = 72.75 dyne cm^{-1} and that for a 0.74 wt.% KCl solution (0.100m) = 72.99 dyne cm^{-1}

$$\frac{d\gamma}{dm} = \frac{0.240}{0.100}$$

$$= 2.40 \text{ dyne cm}^{-1} \text{ molal}^{-1}$$

From equation (3),

$$\Gamma = \frac{-(0.9648)(0.002)(2.40 \text{ dyne cm}^{-1}\text{molal}^{-1})}{2(1.3805 \times 10^{-16})(298)}$$

$$= -5.60 \times 10^{10} \text{ molecules cm}^{-2} .$$

The negative sign indicates that as the concentration of the salt solution increases, so does the surface tension and that a thin film of water covers the salt solution.

SURFACE FORCES

• PROBLEM 11-11

a) Derive an expression for the interaction of a molecule in the gas phase with an extended solid surface. Use this expression to calculate the interaction between krypton gas and krypton solid. In deriving the expression assume that there exist an attractive potential energy between the gas molecules and each atom of the solid surface in the form of $U = -Ar^{-6}$, where A relates to Lennard-Jones expression in the form

$$A = 4 \epsilon \sigma^6/r^6 \; . \; \sigma = 0.36 \text{ nm}$$

and

$$\epsilon/k = 171^\circ K .$$

b) Determine the temperature at which the attractive potential energy equal (3/2)kT.

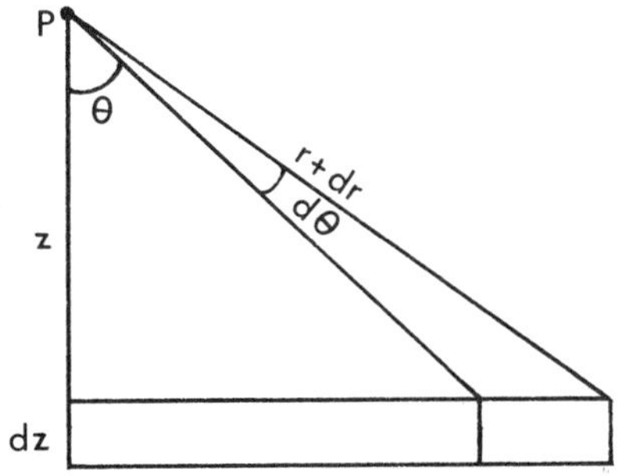

Solution: Consider the gaseous molecule at point P, a distance z from a solid surface with a thickness dz. Suppose a ring of thickness dz is cut out from the solid surface, then, the width of the ring is given by $dr/\sin\theta$, and the radius is $r \sin\theta$. Therefore, the volume of the ring is $2\pi rdrdz$. If it is also considered that there are N molecules per unit volume in the solid ring, then the energy of interaction between the gaseous molecule and those in the ring is given by $2\pi N\, U(r)\, rdrdz$.

For the whole solid surface, the energy of interaction between the gaseous molecule and the whole solid is

$$U(z) = 2\pi Ndz \int_z^\infty u(r)\, rdr$$

$$= -\; 2\pi Ndz \int_z^\infty A/r^6 \; rdr$$

$$= -\ 2\pi N\ Adz\left[\frac{1}{-\ 4r^4}\right]_z^\infty$$

$$= \frac{-\ \pi N\ Adz}{2z^4} \qquad (1)$$

There are also variations in the energy of interaction of the gaseous molecule and the solid surface with the vertical distance. This is given by the expression

$$U(z) = \frac{-\ \pi NA}{2}\int_z^\infty \frac{dz}{z^4}$$

$$= \frac{\pi NA}{6}\left[\frac{1}{z^3}\right]_z^\infty$$

$$= \frac{-\ \pi NA}{6z^3}\ .$$

For the krypton gas, the potential energy is given by

$$U(r) = -\ Ar^{-6}$$

and

$$A = -\ \frac{U(r)}{r^{-6}}$$

But

$$U(r) = \frac{-4\epsilon\sigma^6}{r^6}$$

Therefore,

$$A = \frac{4\epsilon\sigma^6}{r^6\ r^{-6}}$$

$$= 4\epsilon\sigma^6$$

$$= 4(171\ °K)(1.3805\times 10^{-23}\ \frac{J\ °K^{-1}}{molecule})(0.36nm)^6$$

$$= 2.06\ \times\ 10^{-23}\ \frac{J\ nm^6}{molecule}\ .$$

For solid krypton, crystallization occurs in a cubic-closest packed structure with $a_0 = 0.5721$ nm. Thus with four atoms per unit cell,

$$N = \frac{4}{a_0^3} = \frac{4}{(0.5721\ nm)^3}$$

$$= 21.4\ \ nm^{-3}\ .$$

From equation (1),

$$U(z) = \frac{-\pi(21.4\ nm^{-3})\left(2.06\times 10^{-23}\ \frac{J\ nm^6}{molecule}\right)}{6z^3}$$

$$= \frac{-\ 2.31\ \times\ 10^{-22}\ J\ nm^3\ molecule^{-1}}{z^3}$$

The negative sign indicates that the attractive force decreases as the distance from the surface increases.

b) $U(z) = (3/2)kT.$

$$T = \frac{(2/3)U(z)}{k}$$

The absolute value of the energy is used since the direction of the force is not being considered. What is wanted is just the temperature when the attractive force is (3/2)kT.

$$= \frac{2/3(2.31 \times 10^{-22} \text{ J nm}^3 \text{molecule}^{-1})}{z^3 (\text{nm})^3 \left(1.3805 \times 10^{-23} \frac{\text{J}°\text{K}^{-1}}{\text{molecule}}\right)}$$

$$= \frac{1.1115 (\text{nm})^3}{z^3 10^{-1} \frac{(\text{nm})^3}{°\text{K}}} = \frac{11.115 °\text{K}}{z^3}$$

• PROBLEM 11-12

In an experiment to analyze a solution for the presence of Cl^-, $AgNO_3$ was added to the solution. The solution was then heated for a short time and then cooled and filtered, by which time the Cl^- precipitated as AgCl. Give an explanation of why the solution was heated.

Solution: During the filtration it is necessary not to allow colloid particles to pass through the filter along with the AgCl precipitate. There is no way this can be accomplished during the simple filtration process. Thus the AgCl particles had to be coagulated by heating it. During the heating, there is an increased molecular motion of the particles which leads to an increase in particle collisions. The particles stick together and grow into larger particles. This process thus assures the absence of colloid-sized particles that could pass through the filter.

• PROBLEM 11-13

At some stage during the commercial making of cottage cheese, milk is heated with hydrochloric acid. Explain why milk curdles during this process.

Solution: Milk is made up of colloids such as butter fat suspended in it. By heating milk with hydrochloric acid which is an electrolyte, it makes the butter fat and the rest of the colloids, that are suspended in the milk, coagulate.

• PROBLEM 11-14

Explain why highly saline water flowing into a reservoir will hasten the sedimentation of silt, thereby shortening the lifetime of the reservoir.

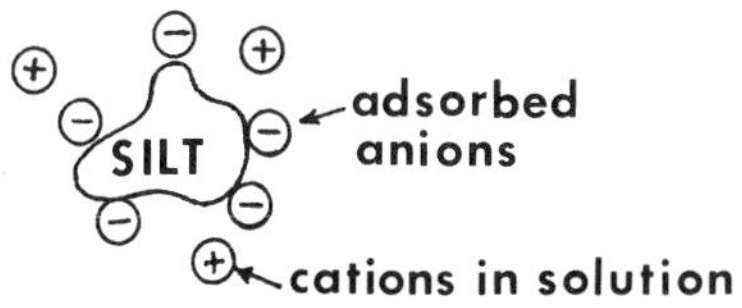

Fig. 1

Solution: Silt is suspended in water as a hydrophobic colloid. Hydrophobic means "water hating". The silt is being stabilized

in the water by the adsorption of ions on their surface as shown in figure 1.

These adsorbed ions interact with water. Therefore, the highly saline water flowing into the reservoir acts as an electrolyte. This electrolyte contains charges that are opposite to the charges adsorbed on the silt. It will have the effect of "neutralizing" the charge of ions on the silt. This causes the silt to coagulate and settle out of the reservoir. The silt will continue to settle out until the reservoir is filled with it and cannot take any more saline water.

OSMOTIC PRESSURE

• PROBLEM 11-15

The following data are available for the solutions of γ globulin in 0.15M NaCl at 37°C

c, concentration of γ globulin, g per 100 ml	π, osmotic pressure, mm H_2O
19.27	453
12.35	253
5.81	112

Calculate the molecular weight of the γ globulin.

Solution: The osmotic pressure of non-electrolyte can be represented by a power series in the concentrations. That is,

$$\pi = (RT/M)c + BC^2 + BC^3 + \ldots \qquad (1)$$

where c = the mass concentration. In dilute solutions, equation (1) can be truncated to give

$$\frac{\pi}{c} = \frac{RT}{M} + BC \qquad (2)$$

The value of B for particular solvents and temperatures may be set equal to zero. Therefore, equation (2) becomes

$$\frac{\pi}{c} = \frac{RT}{M} \qquad (3)$$

A plot of π/c vs c should give a straight line in the region of low concentration. The intercept at $c \to 0$ yields RT/M, from which the molecular weight is determined.

For the first solution

$$\frac{\pi}{c} = \frac{453 \text{ mm } H_2O}{19.27 \text{ g dl}^{-1}}$$

$$= 23.5 \text{ mm } H_2O \text{ dl g}^{-1} .$$

Similarly, for the other two solutions,

$$\frac{\pi}{c} = 20.5 \text{ and } 19.3 \text{ mm } H_2O \text{ dl g}^{-1} .$$

From the plot of π/c vs c, the intercept at $c \to 0$ gives 18.6 mm H_2O dl g^{-1}

$$\lim_{c \to 0} \left(\frac{\pi}{c}\right) = 18.6 \text{ mm } H_2O \text{ dl g}^{-1}$$

as

$$= \frac{(18.6\text{mm } H_2O \text{ dl } g^{-1})(0.100 \text{ liter dl}^{-1})}{(13.56\text{mm } H_2O \text{ torr}^{-1})(760 \text{ torr atm}^{-1})}$$

$$= 1.804 \times 10^{-4} \text{ liter atm g}^{-1}$$

and

$$M = RT/\lim(\pi/c)$$

$$= \frac{(0.08206 \text{ liter atm } ^\circ K^{-1} \text{mole}^{-1})(310\ ^\circ K)}{1.804 \times 10^{-4} \text{ liter atm g}^{-1}}$$

$$M = 1.41 \times 10^{5} \text{ g mole}^{-1} .$$

DIALYSIS

• PROBLEM 11-16

Explain why dialysis stabilizes some colloidal dispersions.

Solution: Dialysis is the separation of small solute particles from colloid particles by means of a semi-permeable membrane. The semi-permeable membrane, called the dialysis membrane, allows ions to pass through the membrane but not colloid particles. Usually the colloidal dispersion is enclosed in a sack made of the dialyzing membrane and then the sack is immersed in distilled water. The ions that promote coagulation will pass through the membrane into the water, on prolonged contact with the water. The colloidal suspensions will not pass through. In this manner the colloid particles are stabilized.

TYNDALL PROPERTIES

• PROBLEM 11-17

Explain why colloids are translucent and are able to scatter light, but solutions are transparent.

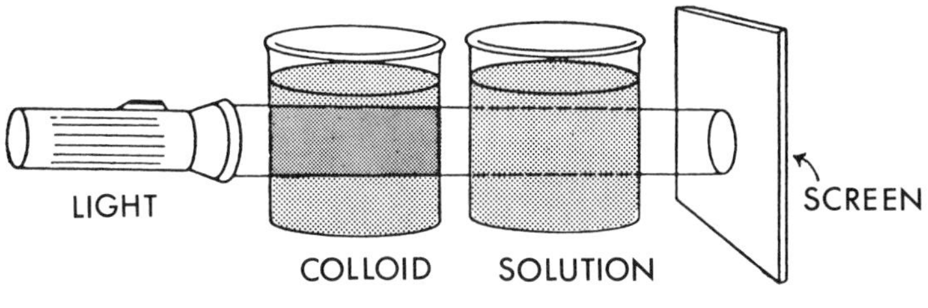

Solution: Colloid particles are small but they are large enough to scatter light effectively. When light passes through a medium in which colloid particles are present, such particles interfere with the motion of the light and cause part of its energy to be scattered in all directions. Consequently the colloids appear cloudy or opague. This effect is known as Tyndall effect as illustrated in the figure. In contrast, the dispersed particles of a solution do not scatter light.

• PROBLEM 11-18

A sintered glass filter with a uniform pore diameter of 0.20 μm is filled with water at 20° C. Estimate the pressure that would be necessary to blow the capillary water out of the pores of the filter. How would you design an apparatus to measure the distribution of pore sizes in a filter.

Solution: a) As a direct consequence of surface tension, there exist a difference in pressure across any curved liquid surface given by

$$\Delta P = \frac{2\gamma}{r} \tag{1}$$

where ΔP = the pressure difference between the concave and convex side of the liquid surface. γ is the surface tension of the liquid and r is the radius of the pore. The surface tension of water at 20° C is 72.75 dyne cm^{-1}.
Therefore from equation (1)

$$\Delta P = \frac{2(72.75 \text{ dyne/cm})(10^{-5}\text{N/dyne})(10^{2} \text{ cm/m})}{\frac{1}{2}(0.20 \times 10^{-6}\text{m})(1.013 \times 10^{5} \text{ N}\cdot\text{m}^{-2}\text{/atm})}$$

$$= 14.4 \text{ atm.}$$

b) The study of pore size distributions has been done with a mercury porosimeter. Mercury under nitrogen pressure up to 4000 atm is forced into the pores of the filter material and the volume penetrated is determined by electrical measurements.
The distribution function D is given in terms of the volume V and radius r of the pore. Thus

$$dV = D(r)dr \tag{2}$$

From equation (1),

$$r = \frac{2\gamma}{P}$$

Differentiate both sides to obtain

$$dr = \frac{-2\gamma}{P^2}\, dP$$

Substitute for dr in equation (2) to get

$$dV = \frac{-2D(r)\gamma\ dP}{P^2} \tag{3}$$

But

$$\frac{2\gamma}{P} = r$$

Thus, equation (3) becomes

$$dV = \frac{-rD(r)\ dP}{P}$$

or

$$D(r) = -\left(\frac{P}{r}\right)\frac{dV}{dP} \quad .$$

CHAPTER 12

QUANTUM CHEMISTRY

ATOMIC STRUCTURE

• PROBLEM 12-1

Which of the following ions possess a rare gas electronic configuration? (a) Ca^{2+}; (b) In^{+}; (c) Ga^{3+}; (d) Sc^{3+}; (e) Se^{2-}

Solution: The rare gases (also known as the noble or inert gases) are the elements in the "last" (far right) group of the periodic table. They are He, Ne, Ar, Kr, Xe, and Rn. All the rare gases have completely filled atomic orbitals in accordance with the octet rule. The octet of electrons (eight) in the outermost shell of an atom or ion represents an especially stable arrangement. The electronic configuration of the rare gases are,

He $1s^2$

Ne $1s^2\ 2s^2\ 2p^6$

Ar $1s^2\ 2s^2\ 2p^6\ 3s^2\ 3p^6$

Kr $1s^2\ 2s^2\ 2p^6\ 3s^2\ 3p^6\ 3d^{10}\ 4s^2\ 4p^6$

Xe $1s^2\ 2s^2\ 2p^6\ 3s^2\ 3p^6\ 3d^{10}\ 4s^2\ 4p^6\ 4d^{10} 5s^2\ 5p^6$

Rn $1s^2\ 2s^2\ 2p^6\ 3s^2\ 3p^6\ 3d^{10}\ 4s^2\ 4p^6\ 4d^{10}\ 4f^{14}\ 5s^2\ 5p^6\ 5d^{10}$
$6s^2\ 6p^6$

Now, the electronic configurations of the listed ions with those of the rare gases are compared. The electronic configuration of the ions are:

ION	ELECTRONIC CONFIGURATION
(a) Ca^{2+}	$1s^2\ 2s^2\ 2p^6\ 3s^2\ 3p^6$

(b) In^+ $1s^2\ 2s^2\ 2p^6\ 3s^2\ 3p^6\ 3d^{10}\ 4s^2\ 4p^6\ 4d^{10}\ 5s^2$

(c) Ga^{3+} $1s^2\ 2s^2\ 2p^6\ 3s^2\ 3p^6\ 3d^{10}$

(d) Sc^{3+} $1s^2\ 2s^2\ 2p^6\ 3s^2\ 3p^6$

(e) Se^{2-} $1s^2\ 2s^2\ 2p^6\ 3s^2\ 3p^6\ 3d^{10}\ 4s^2\ 4p^6$

Observe that Ca^{2+} and Sc^{3+} have the same configuration as Ar and Se^{2-} has the same configuration as Kr. Therefore,

Ca^{2+}, Sc^{3+} and Se^{2-} possess rare gases electronic configurations while In^+ and Ga^{3+} do not.

• PROBLEM 12-2

Calculate the energy of a hydrogen atom in its ground state (n = 1) using the mass of the electron rather than the reduced mass of the hydrogen atom.

Solution: The eigenvalues for the energy of the hydrogen atom or hydrogenlike atom are given by

$$E = -\frac{m_e e^4 Z^2}{2(4\pi\varepsilon_0)^2 \hbar^2 n^2} \qquad (1)$$

where E = energy

m_e = mass of electron

Z = the atomic number of hydrogen atom

$(-Ze^2/4\pi\varepsilon_0 r)$ = potential energy. r is the distance between the nucleus and electron.

$\hbar$ = constant = $\frac{h}{2\pi}$, where h is Planck's constant

n = quantum number, in this case 1.

e = electronic charge.

Since $\hbar = \frac{h}{2\pi}$, equation (1) changes to

$$E = -\frac{2\pi^2 m_e e^4}{(4\pi\varepsilon_0)^2 h^2} \qquad (2)$$

The negative sign indicates that the electron in a hydrogen or hydrogenlike atom has less energy than when it is free. Substitution of the respective values into equation (2) gives

$$E = -\frac{2\pi^2(9.1095\times 10^{-31}\text{kg})(1.6022\times 10^{-19}\text{C})^4(0.899\times 10^{10}\text{Nm}^2\text{C}^{-2})^2}{(6.6262\times 10^{-34}\ \text{J s})^2}$$

$$= -2.1802 \times 10^{-18}\ \text{J}$$

or $$E = -\frac{2.1802\times 10^{-18}\ \text{J}}{1.6021\times 10^{-19}\ \text{J eV}^{-1}}$$

$= -13.61$ eV where eV is electron volts.

• PROBLEM 12-3

Calculate the average separation of the electron and the nucleus in the ground state of the hydrogen atom.

Solution: The ground state wavefunction of a hydrogen atom is the wavefunction corresponding to the lowest energy. It is spherically symmetrical, and decays exponentially with the distance from the nucleus. This is represented by

$$\psi = \left(\frac{1}{\pi a_0^3}\right)^{1/2} e^{-r/a_0} \qquad (1)$$

where ψ = wavefunction

a_0 = a collection of fundamental constants. It has the dimensions of length and a magnitude of 53 pm. It is called the Bohr radius.

r = distance between the electron and the nucleus.

The problem requires the evaluation of the expectation of r.

$\psi^*(p)\psi(p)$ dxdydz is the probability of a particle appearing at the point, p if the three-dimensional volume is dxdydz. The requirement that the particle must be somewhere in the universe is the sum over the probabilities that it appears in every element dxdydz into which the universe can be divided. Therefore, the mean position is given by

$$\langle p\rangle = \int \psi^*(p)p\psi(p)d\tau \qquad (2)$$

where $d\tau$ is the infinitesimal region of finding the particle.

It is more convenient to work in polar coordinates and use

$d\tau = r^2 dr \sin\theta \, d\phi$, allowing r to range from 0 to ∞, θ from 0 to π, and φ from 0 to 2π. Therefore, equation (2) for the expectation value of r becomes

$$\langle r \rangle = \int_0^\infty dr \left[r^2 \left[r \left(\frac{1}{\pi a_0^3} \right) e^{-2r/a_0} \right] \right] \int_0^\pi d\theta \sin\theta \int_0^{2\pi} d\phi \qquad (3)$$

Since $\int_0^\pi \sin\theta \, d\theta \int_0^{2\pi} d\phi = 2(2\pi) = 4\pi$,

equation (3) becomes

$$4\pi \int_0^\infty r^3 \left(\frac{1}{\pi a_0^3} \right) e^{-2r/a_0} dr.$$

But $\frac{1}{\pi a_0^3}$ is a constant. Therefore,

$$\langle r \rangle = \frac{4\pi}{\pi a_0^3} \int_0^\infty r^3 \, e^{-2r/a_0} \, dr$$

$$= \frac{4}{a_0^3} \left[6 \left(\frac{a_0}{2} \right)^4 \right]$$

$$= \frac{3}{2} a_0 .$$

Recall that $a_0 = 53$ pm. Hence

$$\langle r \rangle = \frac{3}{2}(53) = 79.5 \text{ pm}.$$

• PROBLEM 12-4

List the orbitals for hydrogenlike atoms in order of increasing energy.

Solution: The wave function ψ is physically significant only if it is continous, single valued and the integral of the square of the function has a finite value. These ψs exist only for certain values of energy, E called eigenvalues. The corresponding ψs are called eigenfunctions.

For a hydrogenlike atom, the eigenvalues for the energy are given as

$$E = - \frac{m_e Z^2 e^4}{2n^2 \hbar^2 (4\pi\varepsilon_0)^2} \quad \text{for} \quad n = 1,2,3,... \qquad (1)$$

where m_e = the mass of the electron, e is the electronic charge, $\hbar = \frac{h}{2\pi}$, where h = Planck's constant and n is the principal quantum number. The negative sign indicates that the electron in a hydrogenlike atom has a lower energy than a free electron.

Equation (1) indicates that the energies are inversely proportional to the square of n and they are only a function of n. Thus all orbitals having the same value of n will have the same energy.

1s	orbital has n = 1
2s, 2p	orbitals have n = 2
3s, 3p, 3d	orbitals have n = 3
4s, 4p, 4d, 4f	orbitals have n = 4
5s, 5p, 5d, 5f	orbitals have n = 5

Thus the orbitals in order of increasing energy can be written as

$$1s < 2s = 2p < 3s = 3p = 3d < 4s = 4p = 4d = 4f < 5s = 5p$$

$$= 5d = 5f = 5g < \text{etc.}$$

• PROBLEM 12-5

What is the electronic configuration for the ground state of Cr and its oxidation state?

Solution: The "address" of any electron in an atom is given by the four quantum numbers n, ℓ, m and s and according to the Pauli principle, no two electrons in an atom may have the same four quantum numbers. Whenever the ground state of an atom is specified, it refers to electrons in the lowest possible energy level. Each orbital holds two electrons of opposite spin. The electrons can be put in each level starting with the lowest level and using exponents to indicate the number of electrons in the 1s, 2s, 2p, 3s, 3p etc., orbitals. This results in an electron configuration of the atom. s orbital can hold a maximum of two electrons; p orbitals can hold up to a maximum of six electrons, the d orbitals, 10 electrons and the f orbitals can hold 14 electrons.

Cr has 24 electrons, so its electronic configuration can be written as

$$1s^2\ 2s^2\ 2p^6\ 3s^2\ 3p^6\ 4s^2\ 3d^4.$$

There is a major exception to the rules for filling orbitals. The filled and half-filled d and f orbitals are favored over the next s and p orbitals. This results in the electronic configuration of Cr as

$$1s^2\ 2s^2\ 2p^6\ 3s^2\ 3p^6\ 4s^1\ 3d^5$$

The 3d orbitals are filled before the 4p orbitals.

The oxidation state of an atom corresponds to the number of electrons that can easily be removed and the number of electrons needed to complete a shell.

• PROBLEM 12-6

The number of orbital electrons in the atoms of Ce and O are 58 and 8 respectively. Write the quantum numbers for the fifty eighth (58th) and the eighth (8th) electrons in these two atoms.

Solution: There are four quantum numbers that must be specified to characterize an electron in an atom. These are the principal quantum number, n, the angular momentum quantum number, ℓ, the magnetic quantum number, m and the spin quantum number, s. n takes on only integer values of 1, 2, 3, 4 ..., and ℓ has values from 0 to n-1. This means that when n = 1, ℓ can have only one value, $\ell = 0$ and when n = 2, $\ell = 0, 1$. The values of m range from $-\ell$ to $+\ell$ or a total of $(2\ell + 1)$ values. When $\ell = 0$, there is only one value for m, and that is m = 0. For $\ell = 1$, there are 3 values of m, namely m = -1, 0, +1 and for $\ell = 3$, there are seven values of m, which are m = -3, -2, -1, 0, +1, +2, +3. The spin quantum number s takes on only two values, -1/2 or +1/2.

The electron configuration of Ce can be written as:

$$1s^2\ 2s^2\ 2p^6\ 3s^2\ 3p^6\ 4s^2\ 3d^{10}\ 4p^6\ 5s^2\ 4d^{10}\ 5p^6\ 6s^2\ 4f^2.$$

Notice the priority filling of the d subshells. This process of filling up orbitals by electrons is called the aufbau process. A mnemonic device for the remembering of the filling order is as follows:

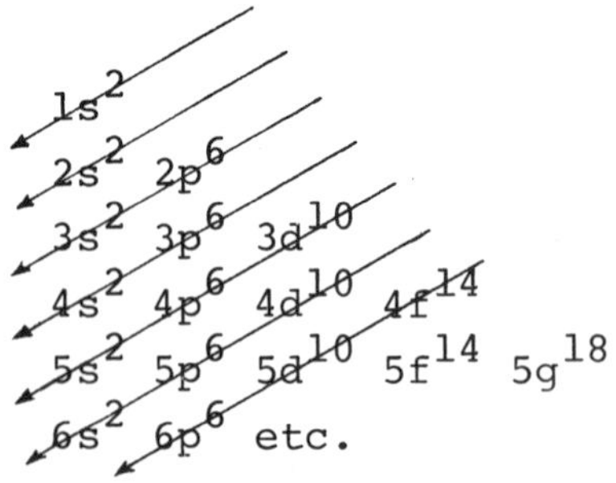

All that need be done is to move from one arrow to the next. Start at the tail of the first arrow (the one on top) and move to its head. Then move on to the tail of the second arrow and follow it to the head. Repeat this process and you will have the correct filling order.

In the above configuration the numerals represent the number of major shell, while the letters, s, p, d, and f represent ℓ = 0, 1, 2, and 3 respectively.

The last two electrons of Ce all enter the 4f subshell. The numerals indicate the number of major shell, n = 4 and $\ell = 3$ since f stands for $\ell = 3$. Since $\ell = 3$, m can have 7 values -3, -2, -1, 0, +1, +2, +3. By convention the first of the two electrons in the f subshell will be assigned an $m = +3$ and so the second and last electron will have an $m = +2$. The spin quantum number s can only take on two values $-1/2$ and $+1/2$, thus the last electron in the f subshell will have a spin of $+1/2$. The four quantum numbers of the 58th electron in Ce are:

$$n = 4, \ \ell = 3, \ m = +2 \text{ and } s = +1/2$$

O will have an electron configuration of $1s^2\ 2s^2\ 2p^4$ since it has eight orbital electrons. The eighth electron is the last of the four electrons to enter the 2p subshell. Once again the two in front of p indicate the number of major shell, i.e. $n = 2$ and the letters s and p indicate an $\ell = 0$ and 1 respectively. Thus $\ell = 1$ since 2p is the subshell the eighth electron enters. With $\ell = 1$, m has three values, namely $m = -1, 0, +1$, and by convention $m = +1$ and $s = -1/2$. Thus the four quantum numbers for the eighth electron in oxygen are $n=2$, $\ell = 1$, $m = +1$ and $s = -\frac{1}{2}$.

• PROBLEM 12-7

You are given that the ionization energy of a hydrogen atom is 13.527 eV, calculate the second ionization energy of a helium atom. The general equation for the lines in the emission spectra of one electron system such as H, He^+, Li^{2+} and Be^{3+} is given as

$$\bar{\nu} = Z^2 R_H \left(\frac{1}{n_1^2} - \frac{1}{n_2^2} \right)$$

where $\bar{\nu}$ = the wave numbers of emission lines and Z is the nuclear charge of the atom concerned.

Solution: The ionization energy of a gaseous neutral atom or a gaseous ion is defined as the energy needed to completely remove an electron from the atom or the ion in its ground state. The helium atom is composed of a nucleus of charge $+2(Z = 2)$ and two electrons. The first ionization energy of helium atom is energy required for the process:

$$He(g) \rightarrow He^+(g) + e^-$$

The second ionization energy is then the energy required to remove the lone electron from $He^+(g)$ and is given by

$$He^+(g) \rightarrow He^{2+}(g) + e^-$$

$$\bar{\nu} = Z^2 R_H \left(\frac{1}{n_1^2} - \frac{1}{n_2^2} \right) \qquad (1)$$

where R_H = the Rydberg constant, Z is the nuclear charge, and n_1, n_2 are integers corresponding to the lower and upper electronic levels respectively, and are responsible for the spectral lines. The energy for the ionization potential, E is given by

$$E = h\nu$$

$$E = h\frac{c}{\lambda}$$

But $$\bar{\nu} = \frac{1}{\lambda},$$

$$\therefore \quad E = hc\bar{\nu}$$

Equation (1) for the energies associated with the electronic transitions in any one electron system becomes

$$E = hcZ^2R_H\left(\frac{1}{n_1^2} - \frac{1}{n_2^2}\right) \tag{2}$$

The ionization energy for hydrogen atom is also given as 13.527 eV. This is the energy needed to completely remove the electron from the hydrogen atom in its ground state, and $n_1 = 1$ for the atom in the ground state. $n_2 = \infty$ for the state in which the electron is completely removed from the atom.

Equation (2), substituting $n_1 = 1$, $n_2 = \infty$ and $Z = 1$ for hydrogen atom, becomes

$$E = I_H = hcR_H \tag{3}$$

where I_H = the ionization energy of hydrogen. Similarly, the second ionization energy of He^+, using equation (2), with Z = 2, becomes

$$E = I_{He^+} = 4hcR_H \tag{4}$$

But from equation (3),

$$hcR_H = I_H$$

$\therefore$ Equation (4) becomes

$$I_{He^+} = 4I_H$$

$$= 4(13.527\ \text{eV})$$

or $$I_{He^+} = 54.108\ \text{eV}.$$

The diagram shows the wavelength range for the different colors in the visible spectrum. When alkali metal and alkaline earth-containing materials are heated in a bunsen burner flame, they emit unique colors of light. These colors are used as qualitative tests for the presence of these elements. What color flame would one expect to see if a potassium compound such as potassium chloride is heated in a bunsen burner flame, given that potassium containing materials emit light of frequency 7.41×10^{14} sec^{-1}.

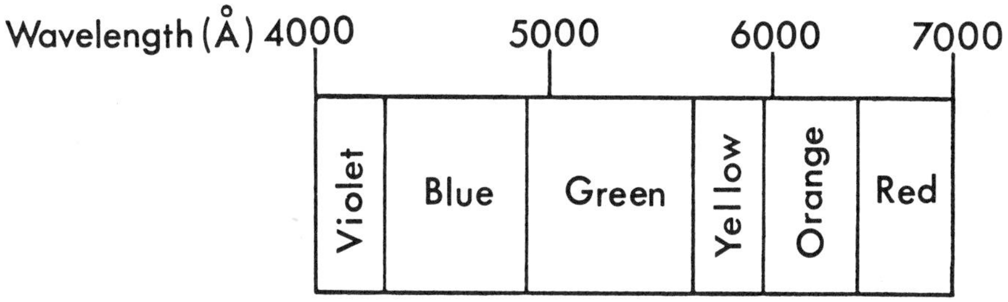

Solution: The wavelength corresponding to different colors are given in the diagram. Thus, an equation that relates frequency to wavelength is used. One such equation is

$$\nu = \frac{c}{\lambda} \tag{1}$$

where ν = the frequency of radiation or the number of cycles/sec, c is the speed of light and λ is the wavelength with units of centimeters.

Rearranging equation (1) to solve for λ yields

$$\lambda = \frac{c}{\nu}$$

$$= \left(\frac{3.00 \times 10^{10} \text{ cm sec}^{-1}}{7.41 \times 10^{14} \text{ sec}^{-1}}\right)\left(\frac{10^8 \text{Å}}{1 \text{ cm}}\right)$$

or $\lambda = 4048$ Å

In the diagram, the wavelength of 4048 Å falls within the violet spectrum and so potassium-containing materials imparts a violet color to the bunsen burner flame.

Use the figure to decide what color flame would indicate the presence of barium in a sample of unknown composition. Barium atoms can undergo an electronic transition of energy 3.62×10^{-12} erg if a barium-containing material is heated on a bunsen burner flame.

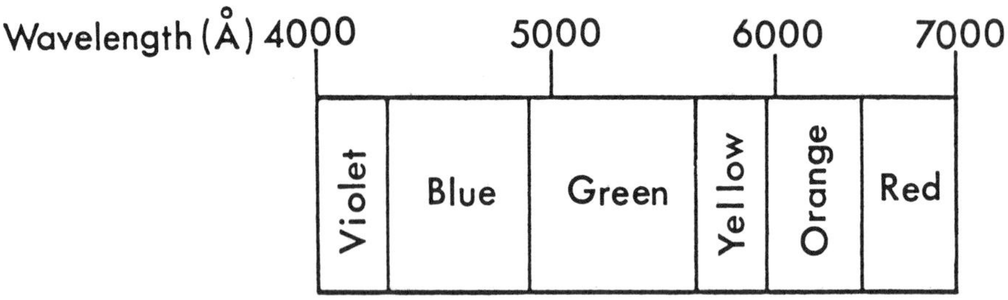

Solution: In this problem, since the energy of barium atoms is given, the wavelength can be determined. Then the figure can be used to match the corresponding color flame that will be seen. Energy relates to frequency according to the equation

$$E = h\nu. \quad (1)$$

But $\nu = \frac{c}{\lambda}$. Therefore equation (1) changes to

$$E = h\frac{c}{\lambda}.$$

Rearranging it to solve for λ yields

$$\lambda = \frac{hc}{E}$$

$$= \frac{(6.6 \times 10^{-27} \text{ erg sec})\left(3.0 \times 10^{10} \frac{\text{cm}}{\text{sec}}\right)\left(\frac{10^8 \text{ Å}}{1 \text{ cm}}\right)}{3.62 \times 10^{-12} \text{ erg}}$$

or $\lambda = 5469$ Å

Matching $\lambda = 5469$ Å with colors in the diagram, it falls in the green spectrum. This means that one would expect a green flame if a sample containing barium is heated on a bunsen burner flame.

• PROBLEM 12-10

The diagram illustrates a section of the spectrum of hydrogen atoms. Suppose that there is an electronic transition from the fifth to the tenth electronic level in hydrogen atom, in what region of the spectrum would one look for the resulting spectral line?

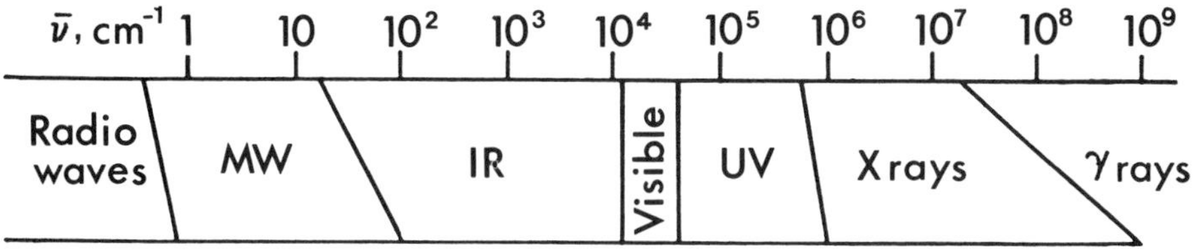

Solution: The wavelengths, λ, or wave numbers, $\bar{\nu}$ of the lines in the visible region of the hydrogen-atom spectrum can be expressed as

$$\frac{1}{\lambda} = \bar{\nu} = R_H\left(\frac{1}{n_1^2} - \frac{1}{n_2^2}\right) \tag{1}$$

where n_1 and n_2 are integers associated with the lower and upper electronic levels respectively, which are involved in the electron transitions of the spectral lines. R_H is the Rydberg constant with a value of $R_H = 1.10 \times 10^5\ cm^{-1}$. In this problem $n_1 = 5$ and $n_2 = 10$. From equation (1), the wave number is

$$\bar{\nu} = 1.10 \times 10^5\ cm^{-1}\left(\frac{1}{5^2} - \frac{1}{10^2}\right)$$

$$\bar{\nu} = 3.3 \times 10^3\ cm^{-1}$$

The electromagnetic spectrum of the diagram is searched to find the line corresponding to this wave number. This line appears in the infrared region. It is a member of the Pfund series for which $n_1 = 5$ and $n_2 = 6, 7, 8, 9, \ldots$.

The other spectral line series observed for the hydrogen atom and named after those who discovered them are:

(i) Lyman series $n_1 = 1$ $n_2 = 2,3,4,5, \ldots$

(ii) Balmer series $n_1 = 2$ $n_2 = 3,4,5,6, \ldots$

(iii) Paschen series $n_1 = 3$ $n_2 = 4,5,6,7, \ldots$

(iv) Brackett series $n_1 = 4$ $n_2 = 5,6,7,8, \ldots$

The hydrogen atom is in its ground state when the electron in the first electronic level ($n_1 = 1$) and all other higher levels are called excited states. Only the Lyman series involves transitions from the ground state.

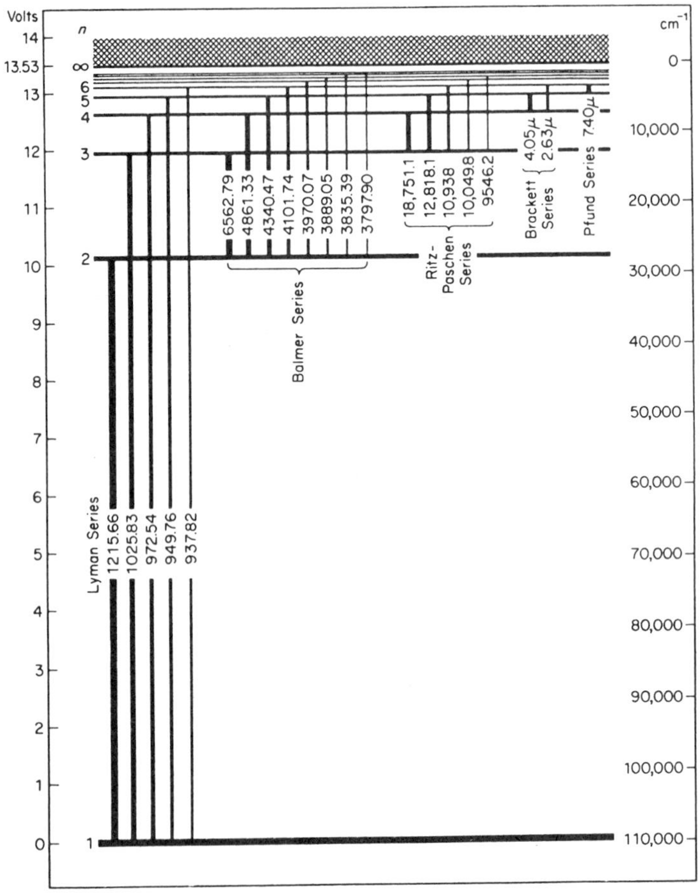

Energy levels of the hydrogen atom. The wavelengths of spectral lines corresponding to the transitions are given in Ångstrom units (1Å = 0.1 nm).

• PROBLEM 12-11

The wavelengths of lines in emission and absorption spectra are measured by a spectroscope which is calibrated from the sodium-D-lines. These are two of the lines in the yellow emission from heated sodium metal. Calculate the energy of the electronic transition associated with one of the sodium-D-lines whose wavelength is 5890 Å.

Solution: The energy, E of a light beam travels in quanta of energy, hν called photons and it relates to the frequency or wavelength according to the equation

$$E = h\nu = \frac{hc}{\lambda}, \qquad (1)$$

since $\nu = \frac{c}{\lambda}$. h is Planck's constant, ν is the frequency, λ is the wavelength and c is the speed of light. Thus, for a wavelength of 5890 Å, the energy associated with it is computed by equation (1) as follows:

$$E = \frac{(6.6 \times 10^{-27} \text{ erg sec})\left(3.0 \times 10^{10} \frac{\text{cm}}{\text{sec}}\right)}{5890 \text{ Å}\left(\frac{10^{-8} \text{ cm}}{1 \text{ Å}}\right)}$$

or $E = 3.36 \times 10^{-12}$ erg

• PROBLEM 12-12

Calculate the value of the Rydberg constant for the hydrogen atom, predict the wavelengths of the first four transitions in the Lyman series, and find the ionization potential of the atom.

Solution: The permitted energies of the hydrogen atom are

$$E_n = -\left(\frac{m e^4}{32\pi^2 \varepsilon_0^2 \hbar^2}\right)\left(\frac{1}{n^2}\right) \tag{1}$$

where n = 1,2,3, ... These are principal quantum numbers. m = mass of electron, $\hbar = h/2\pi$ and h = Planck's constant.

Equation (1) can be viewed as

$$R\left(\frac{1}{n^2}\right)$$

where R = Rydberg constant given by

$$\frac{m e^4}{32\pi^2 \varepsilon_0^2 \hbar^2} = \frac{m e^4}{8h^2 \varepsilon_0^2} \tag{2}$$

For better accuracy, the m should be interpreted as the reduced mass of the electron. It's given by

$$m = \frac{m_e m_p}{m_e + m_p} \tag{3}$$

where $m_e = 9.110 \times 10^{-31}$ kg

$$m_p = 1.673 \times 10^{-27} \text{ kg}$$

Equation (3) then becomes

$$m = \frac{(9.110 \times 10^{-31})(1.673 \times 10^{-27})}{(9.110 \times 10^{-31}) + (1.673 \times 10^{-27})}$$

$$= 9.105 \times 10^{-31} \text{ kg.}$$

The Rydberg constant can now be evaluated from equation (2) since all the constants are known.

$$\therefore \quad R = \frac{m e^4}{8h^2 \varepsilon_0^2} = \frac{(9.105 \times 10^{-31} \text{ kg})(1.602 \times 10^{-19} \text{ C})^4}{8(6.626 \times 10^{-34} \text{ J s})^2(8.854 \text{ x } 10^{-12} \text{ F m}^{-1})^2}$$

$$= \frac{(9.105 \times 10^{-31})(1.602 \times 10^{-19})^4 \text{ kg C}^4}{8(6.626 \times 10^{-34})^2(8.854 \times 10^{-12})^2(\text{J sec})^2(\text{F m}^{-1})^2}$$

$$= \frac{(9.105 \times 10^{-31})(6.5864 \times 10^{-76})\text{kg C}^4}{8(4.3904 \times 10^{-67})(7.8393 \times 10^{-23})\text{J}^2 \text{ sec}^2 \text{ F}^2\text{m}^{-2}}$$

Since 1F = 1C/V and 1V = 1J/C

$$R = \frac{(9.105 \times 10^{-31})(6.5864 \times 10^{-76})\text{kg C}^4}{8(4.3904 \times 10^{-67})(7.8393 \times 10^{-23})\text{J}^2 \text{ sec}^2 \text{ C}^4 \text{ J}^{-2}\text{m}^{-2}}$$

$$= 2.178 \times 10^{-18} \text{ J}$$

Note that R is in J. If it is required in cm^{-1}, then divide by hc, where c = speed of light.

$$\text{Therefore} \quad R = \frac{2.178 \times 10^{-18} \text{ J}}{\left(6.626 \times 10^{-34} \text{ J sec} \times 2.998 \times 10^{10} \frac{\text{cm}}{\text{sec}}\right)}$$

$$= 1.096 \times 10^5 \text{ cm}^{-1}$$

The inverse wavelength of every line in the spectrum can be written as the difference of two terms, each of the form R/n^2. That is,

$$\frac{1}{\lambda} = \frac{R}{n_1^2} - \frac{R}{n_2^2} \qquad (4)$$

where λ = wavelength

n_1 = 1 for the Lyman series

$n_2 = n_1 + 1, n_1 + 2, n_1 + 3, \ldots$

For the first four transitions, n_1 is always 1 while n_2 = 2, 3, 4, and 5. Therefore,

$$\frac{\left[R\left(\frac{1}{n_1^2} - \frac{1}{n_2^2}\right)\right]}{10^5 \text{ cm}^{-1}}$$

values for each n_2 are 0.8220, 0.9742 , 1.028 and 1.052. consecutively and their corresponding λ/nm are 121.6, 102.6, 97.29 and 95.01.

To convert from R/cm^{-1} to λ values, take the reciprocal and multiply by 100 to convert to a per nm basis. i.e.

$$\frac{1}{.822} = 1.216 \times 100 = 121.6.$$

This conversion comes about by the following

$$R = .822/10^5 \text{ cm}^{-1} \times 10^5 = .822 \text{ cm}^{-1}$$

$$\lambda = \frac{1}{R} = 1.216(10^{-5})\text{cm} \times \frac{10^{-7} \text{ nm}}{\text{cm}} \times \frac{1}{10^{-9} \text{ nm}}$$

$$= 121.6/\text{nm}.$$

Therefore, the results are 121.6, 102.6, 97.29 and 95.01.

For the ionization potential, I (or the energy required to remove an electron from the ground state atom), take $n_1 = 1$ and $n_2 = \infty$ (this corresponds to the zero binding energy) which is 1.096×10^5 cm^{-1} in this problem.

$$\therefore \quad I = 1.096 \times 10^5 \text{ cm}^{-1} = 13.60 \text{ eV}$$

• PROBLEM 12-13

Use the Russell-Saunders coupling to determine whether the transition between the 3s and 4s atomic orbitals is permitted for Na.

Solution: It was indicated before that the four quantum numbers n, ℓ, m and s determine the energy levels of a particular atom with a single orbital electron. When there is more than one orbital electron, the Russell-Saunders coupling is used to determine the energy levels. This coupling is expressed as

$$n^{(2s'+1)}L_J$$

where n = the major energy level of the atom in question and it can take on values of n = 1, 2, 3, ... corresponding to the ground state energy level, the next higher one, the second higher one, etc. respectively. S' corresponds to the spins, s_i of all the orbital electrons which are combined algebraically. Thus $S' = \Sigma s_i$. S' can have values of 0,

$\frac{1}{2}$, 1, $\frac{3}{2}$, etc. L represents a vectorial combination of all the angular momentum quantum numbers, ℓ_i, of the orbital electrons known as ℓ-ℓ coupling. Thus

$$L = \ell_1 + \ell_2, \ell_1 + \ell_{2-1}, \ldots, |\ell_1 - \ell_2|.$$

L can take on values of 0, 1, 2, 3, ... which correspond to S, P, D, F etc. respectively in letters.

L and S' can be coupled vectorially to give a quantum number J, where

$$J = L + S', L + S'-1, L + S'-2, \ldots, |L - S'|$$

or a total of (2S'+1) values of J for each value of L. An energy level of $1^2S_{\frac{1}{2}}$ can be interpreted as having n = 1, L = 0, J = $\frac{1}{2}$ and 2S' + 1 = 2 or S' = $\frac{1}{2}$. For $2\ {}^3P_o$, it can be said that n = 2, L = 1, J = 0 and S' = 1; also if an energy level is designated as $4^2F_{7/2}$, it means that n = 4, L = 3, J = 7/2 and S' = ½. (2S' + 1) is often called the multiplicity of the energy state. The energy level indicated by $1^2S'_{\frac{1}{2}}$ is read as "one doublet S a half."

There are selection rules, that govern transitions between energy levels in one atom, since only some transitions are allowed. Only the transitions that are allowed by the following selection rules

$$\Delta S' = 0 \qquad \text{(a)}$$

$$\Delta L = 0, \pm 1, \text{ but } L = 0 \not\leftrightarrow L = 0 \qquad \text{(b)}$$

$$\Delta J = 0, \pm 1, \text{ but } J = 0 \not\leftrightarrow J = 0 \qquad \text{(c)}$$

$$\Delta \ell = \pm 1 \qquad \text{(d)}$$

are possible. $\not\leftrightarrow$ means a forbidden transition.

The ground state of Na has an electron configuration of 3S'. This corresponds to ℓ = 0 and ℓ = +1/2. This, in turn, gives L = 0. The multiplicity is 2S' + 1 = 2, giving

$$S' = \frac{1}{2}$$

$$J = L + S'$$

$$= 0 + \frac{1}{2}$$

$$= |0 - \frac{1}{2}|$$

or

$$J = \frac{1}{2}$$

This gives the term symbol for the ground state of Na as $^{2}S'_{\frac{1}{2}}$. In this problem we have two ground states, the 3s and 4s, so our transition is between two ground states, that is, $^{2}S'_{\frac{1}{2}} \longleftrightarrow {}^{2}S_{\frac{1}{2}}$ selection rule (a) is satisfied because the transition is occuring between "doublets." Selection rule (b) is not satisfied because this transition involves an $L = 0 \longleftrightarrow L = 0$ transition which is forbidden. Thus, this transition is not allowed or permitted.

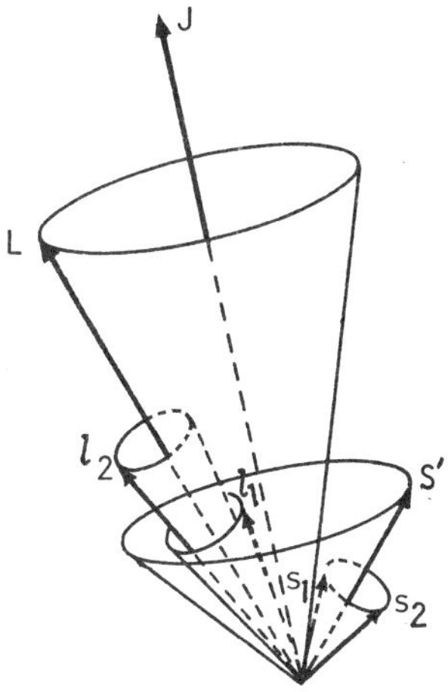

AN EXAMPLE OF RUSSELL SAUNDERS COUPLING. THE l_1 AND l_2 COMBINE TO FORM A RESULTANT L. THE s_1 AND s_2 FORM A RESULTANT S'. L AND S' PRECESS ABOUT THEIR RESULTANT J.

• PROBLEM 12-14

The Russell-Saunders coupling of the angular momenta of two atomic orbitals gives rise to a quantum number L in which all the angular quantum numbers, ℓ_i, are combined vectorially. That is,

$$L = \ell_1 + \ell_2,\ \ell_1 + \ell_2 - 1,\ \ldots,\ |\ell_1 - \ell_2|$$

What will be the values of L when a p and a d electron interact?

Solution: When writing the electron configuration of an atom, the subshells are usually represented by symbols such as

1s , 2p, 3d, 4f, etc.

The numbers, 1, 2, 3, 4, etc. represent the number of major shells K, L, M, N, etc. while the letters, s, p, d, and f stand for $\ell = 0$, 1, 2 and 3, respectively.

For a p electron then, $\ell = 1$ and for a d electron,

$\ell = 2$. The values of L for the interaction between the p and d electrons are given by

$$L = \ell_1 + \ell_2,\ \ell_1 + \ell_2 - 1,\ \ldots,\ |\ell_1 - \ell_2|$$

where $\ell_1 = 1$ and $\ell_2 = 2$. Therefore,

(a) $L = \ell_1 + \ell_2 = 1 + 2 = 3,$

(b) $L = \ell_1 + \ell_2 - 1 = 1 + 2 - 1 = 1 + 1 = 2,$

(c) $L = |\ell_1 - \ell_2| = |1 - 2| = |-1| = 1$

Thus L = 3, 2, 1 which are denoted by the letters F, D, and P respectively.

MOLECULAR STRUCTURE

• PROBLEM 12-15

Draw the Lewis dot formulas for the formation of: (a) N_2 from two N atoms; (b) Na_2 from two Na atoms; (c) HBr from H plus Br.

Solution: Lewis dot formula is based on the fact that union between atoms can be attained from sharing of electrons in pairs. There can be no more than eight electrons surrounding an atom, the electron octet rule, for purposes of stability. Nevertheless there are a few exceptions to this rule. To draw Lewis structures, knowledge of covalence (electron sharing) principle is required. For Nitrogen atom, N, there are five electrons in the outer shell and they can be represented by dots as

$$:\overset{\bullet}{\underset{\bullet}{N}}\bullet$$

To satisfy the octet rule, N must acquire three more electrons. If it joins another N atom, they both can donate three electrons each to the formation of a covalent triple bond.

Therefore,

(a) $:\overset{\bullet}{\underset{\bullet}{N}}\bullet + :\overset{\bullet}{\underset{\bullet}{N}}\bullet \rightarrow :N:::N:$

Similarly for Na_2 and HBr.

(b) Na• + Na• → Na:Na

(c) $H\bullet + \bullet\overset{\bullet\bullet}{\underset{\bullet\bullet}{Br}}: \rightarrow H:\overset{\bullet\bullet}{\underset{\bullet\bullet}{Br}}:$

• PROBLEM 12-16

Draw Lewis structures with all appropriate resonance forms, for each of the following: (a) SO_2; (b) NO_2^-;

Solution: There are molecules in which the arrangement of atoms is not adequately described by a single Lewis structure. Therefore, all the possible Lewis structures are used to represent them. This concept is called resonance. It does not imply that the two or more forms are different or that the molecule really exists in different forms. There is only one form of the molecule. The only differences are in how the arrangements of electrons are represented.

(a) SO_2,

These structures satisfy the octet rule because each atom is surrounded by eight electrons. A bond represents two electrons.

(b) NO_2^-

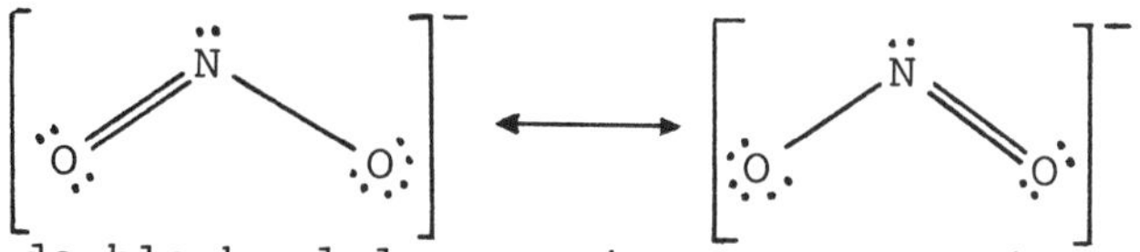

The double-headed arrow is used to indicate that both structures are resonance forms. Note that the arrangement of the nuclei is the same in both structures differing only in the placement of the electrons.

• PROBLEM 12-17

Assuming that the bond angles around the central carbon are tetrahedral in all cases, arrange the following compounds in the expected order of increasing polarity: (a) CF_3Cl; (b) CF_4; (c) CF_2Cl_2; (d) CF_2H_2; (e) CH_4.

Solution: Polarity results when one atom in a compound exerts greater attraction for a shared electron pair than the other atom, causing the shared electron pair to be displaced to the one atom. A measure of polarity is obtained from the electronegativity difference between the atoms in the compoud. The higher the difference between any two atoms, the polar the bond becomes. The halogens on the far right hand part of the periodic table have very high electronegativities so that if any of halogrns form bonds with atoms to the left or middle of the table then we can expect a large difference in electronegativities.

In compound (a) three flourine atoms which are highly electronegative and one chlorine atom which is also very electronegative form bonds with one carbon atom. One would expect then that the shared electron pairs of the compoud would be somewhat shared equally between the two electronegative atoms. In compounds (c) and (d) the central carbon atoms form bonds with equal number of Cl_2 and F_2; and H_2 and F_2, respectively. Compound (c) should be more polar because the electronegativity difference between the F_2 and H_2 bond is greater than that between the F_2 and Cl_2 bond. If the bond angles around the central carbon are tetrahedral, then the structures of the compunds are as follows:

Equal sharing of a pair of electrons occurs between atoms which are identical Therefore there is no polarity between such atoms. However, it is possible for a molecule to contain bonds which are polar and yet still be nonpolar itself. This comes about because of the geometry of the molecule. The overall polarity of the molecule is found by combining the polarity of the individual bonds of the molecule vectorially. In certain molecules, i.e. CH_4, CF_4, the geometry allows the vectors to cancel, producing a nonpolar molecule.

(a)

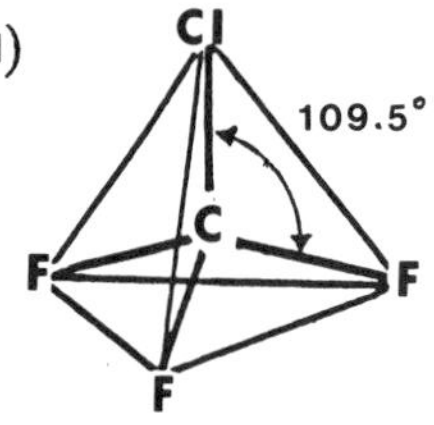

CF_3Cl

(b)

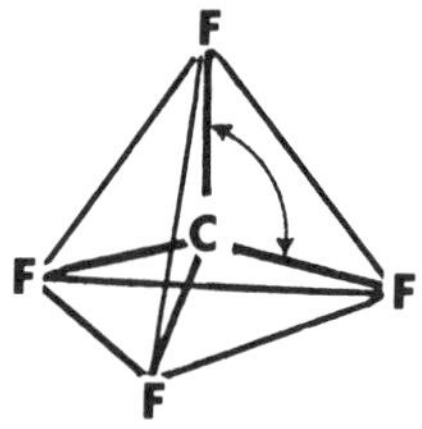

CF_4

(c)

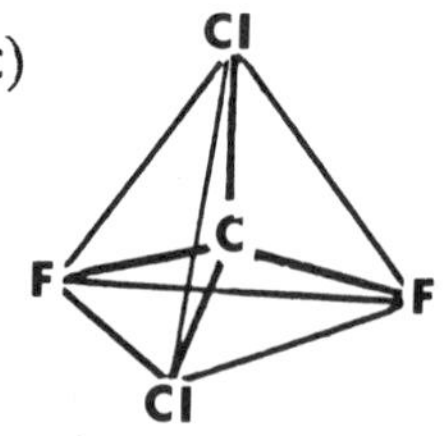

CF_2Cl_2

(d)

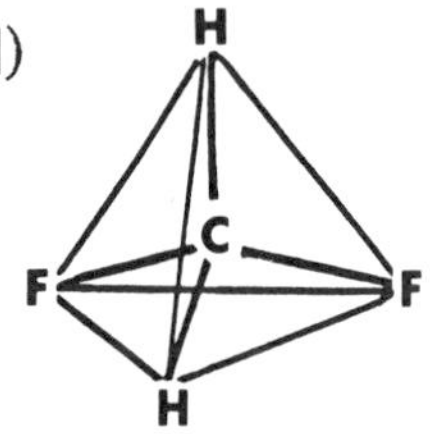

CF_2H_2

(e)

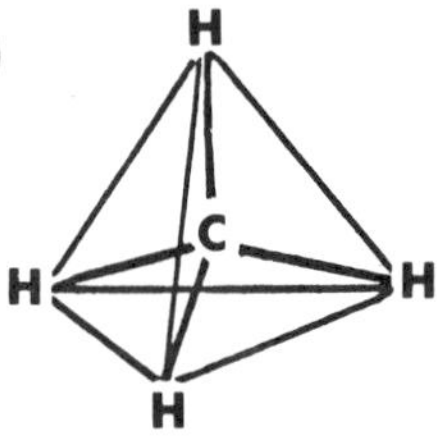

CH_4

• PROBLEM 12-18

In the following series of compounds, which metal would you expect to have the highest actual positive charge: (a) ZnS; (b) SrO; (c) $CdBr_2$? Explain.

Solution: The measure of the polarity of the bond between two atoms is by way of electronegativity difference. The electronegativity difference between Zn and S in ZnS is about 1.0, and that between Cd and Br in $CdBr_2$ is about 1.3. The difference is highest between Sr and O in SrO; about 2.5. The shared electron pairs in SrO are displaced more toward chlorine than are the shared electron pairs to the respective anions in the other compounds and thus the SrO bonds would be more polar than the other compounds meaning that Sr has a larger positive charge than the other metals.

• PROBLEM 12-19

When potassium metal (K) is burned in dry air or dry oxygen, bright yellow potassium superoxide (KO_2) is formed. What is the ground state electronic configuration of the superoxide ion (O_2^-) in potassium superoxide on the basis of molecular orbital theory?

Solution: In the same way that electrons in atoms exist in allowed energy states called atomic orbitals, electrons exist in molecules in allowed energy states called molecular orbitals. An arrangement of these electrons can be seen by considering a simple diatomic molecule of hydrogen. The electronic configuration of H_2 is $1s^2$.

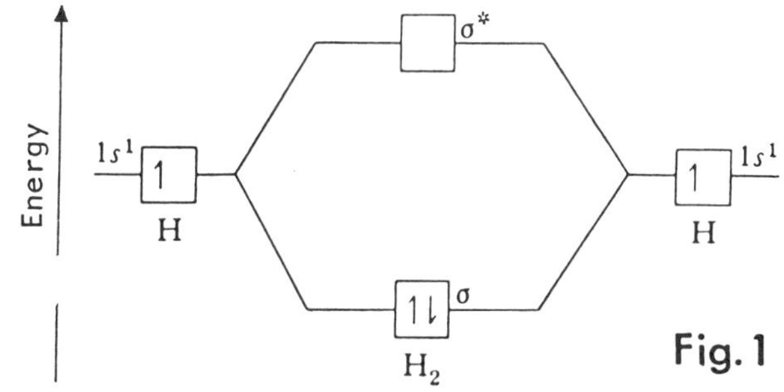

Fig. 1

From figure 1, one 1s orbital of a hydrogen atom combines with one 1s orbital of the other hydrogen atom to form two molecular orbitals. One of the combination leads to the bonding orbital called σ, which is a lowering of energy. The other orbital leads to instability (due to a raising of energy) and is called the antibonding orbital σ*.

Now consider the formation of Li_2 from two Li atoms. The electronic configuration of the Li atom is $1s^2\ 2s^1$. When two Li atoms combine, there could be a possible interaction between the 1s orbital of one Li atom and the 2s orbital of the other atom. But such an interaction is of no importance since atomic orbitals combine most effectively with other atomic orbitals of similar energy. The energy difference between the 1s and 2s orbitals is too great for any possible interaction, thus the energy-level diagram for Li_2 molecule is as shown in figure 2. Only the 2s elec-

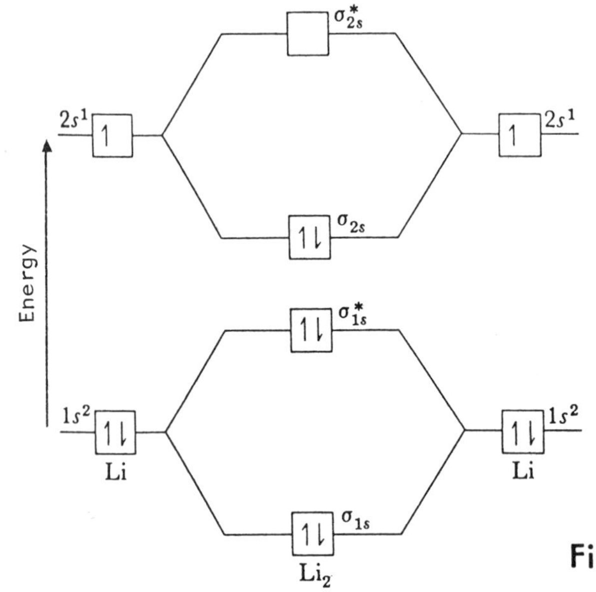

Fig. 2

trons contribute to bonding in the Li_2 molecule. The molecular orbitals are labelled with subscripts to indicate the set of atomic orbitals from which they are formed.

Whenever an atom has a completed s, p, or d level, the electrons in those orbitals do not contribute to bonding. If the electronic configuration is written to include the p atomic orbitals, combination of the s and p orbitals can lead to nonzero overlap. When the p orbitals overlap in bonding, they change sign about the bond axis. The molecular orbitals thus formed are labeled π.

The bonding in the diatomic molecule of O_2^- can now be described. O_2^- is an A_2 type molecule. There are 17 electrons in O_2^- (eight from each of the two O atoms and one from the net charge). Four of these are not valence electrons and are not involved in bonding. Therefore, there are 13 electrons to feed into our molecular orbitals. The resulting ground state electronic configuration is

$$KK(\sigma_s)^2(\sigma_s^*)^2(\pi_{x,y})^4(\sigma_z)^2(\pi_x^*)^2(\pi_y^*)^1$$

Note: $(\pi_x^*)^2(\pi_y^*)^1$ could also be written as $(\pi_{x,y}{}^*)^3$

and that the symbol KK represents the four inner electrons (two from each O atom) that are not involved in bonding.

• **PROBLEM 12-20**

Why does the electronegativity of the halogens decrease with increasing atomic number?

Solution: The halogens are the elements in group 7 of the periodic table. These are (from top to bottom) F, Cl, Br, I and At. Electronegativity refers to the tendency of an atom to attract electrons to itself in a chemical bond. One measure of electronegativity of an atom is its ionization potential, because atoms with high ionization potentials also show a strong attraction for electrons in bonds. The atomic numbers increase as we go down the group, and since ionization potentials decrease with increasing atomic number, there is an overall decrease in electronegativity as one goes down the group. It is not surprising to see elements lose their tendency to attract electrons as they become "clouded" (higher atomic number), since it is easier to remove electrons from the more "clouded" elements.

• **PROBLEM 12-21**

How many σ and π bonds are there in N_2?

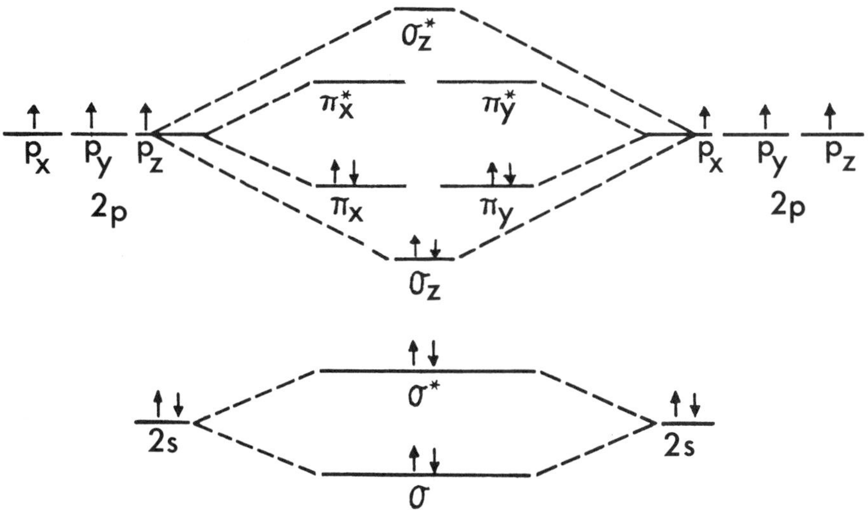

Solution: The ground state electronic configuration of N_2 is

$$KK(\sigma_s)^2(\sigma_s^*)^2(\pi_{x,y})^4(\sigma_z)^2$$

The antibonding character of the σ_s^* molecular orbital cancels the bonding character of the σ_s molecular orbital. This leaves four electrons in the $\pi_{x,y}$ orbitals and two electrons in the σ_z orbital. Thus, the N_2 molecule has three net bonds (one σ and two π). This triple bond accounts for the unusual stability of N_2. The Lewis structure of N_2 is :N≡N: , with three covalent bonds and two lone pairs. The two lone pairs fill the σ_s and σ_s^* molecular orbitals, while the triple bond results from two π bonds $(\pi_{x,y})^4$ and one σ bond $(\sigma_z)^2$.

Note: In any Lewis structure, a single bond in terms of molecular orbital theory is a σ bond, a double bond is a σ and π bond, and a triple bond is a σ and 2π bonds.

If one knows the number of bonds, (by writing the Lewis structure) that hold atoms together, then one can figure out the number of σ and π bonds by filling in the molecular orbitals (formed by the overlap of atomic orbitals) according to molecular orbital theory. There are five valence electrons for each nitrogen atom. There are two 1s orbitals which are not involved in bonding and they are represented by KK. Since N_2 has two identical atoms, the ground state electronic configuration for each atom is identical. The filling in of molecular orbitals can be represented as follows:

Note that the p_z orbitals from each atom bond in such a way that yields a σ bond.

• PROBLEM 12-22

The rotational spectrum of HF has lines 41.9 cm^{-1} apart. Calculate the moment of inertia and the bond length of this molecule.

Solution: The rotational constant of the molecule is given by

$$B = \frac{h}{8\pi^2 I} \qquad (1)$$

where h = Planck's constant.

I = moment of inertia

The spacing between the lines is given to be 41.9 cm^{-1}. This is also equal to 2B. Therefore,

$$B = \frac{41.9}{2} = 20.95\ cm^{-1}$$

$$= 20.95\ cm^{-1} \times 2.998\ cm\ sec^{-1}$$

$$= 6.281 \times 10^{11}\ sec^{-1}.$$

Rearranging equation (1) to solve for I yields,

$$I = \frac{h}{8\pi^2 B} = \frac{(6.626 \times 10^{-34}\ J\ sec)}{8\pi^2(6.281 \times 10^{11}\ sec^{-1})}$$

$$= 1.336 \times 10^{-47}\ kg\ m^2$$

The bond length is given by

$$r = \left(\frac{I}{\mu}\right)^{\frac{1}{2}} \qquad (2)$$

where $$\mu = \frac{M_H M_F}{M_{HF} L}.$$

Here M = molecular weight (atomic wt.)

L = Avogadro's number.

Hence, $$\mu = \frac{(1)\text{g mole}^{-1}(19)\text{g mole}^{-1}}{(20)\text{g mole}^{-1}(6.02 \times 10^{23}\text{ mole}^{-1})} = 0.158 \times 10^{-23}\text{g}$$

or $\mu = 0.158 \times 10^{-26}$ kg.

Using the calculated values in equation (2) yields

$$r = \left(\frac{1.336 \times 10^{-47}\text{ kg m}^2}{0.158 \times 10^{-26}\text{ kg}}\right)^{\frac{1}{2}}$$

$$= (8.456 \times 10^{-21}\text{ m}^2)^{\frac{1}{2}}$$

$$= 9.196 \times 10^{-11}\text{ m} \times 10^{9}\text{ nm/m}$$

$$= 9.196 \times 10^{-2}\text{ nm}$$

• PROBLEM 12-23

The ion Ti^{3+} has one unpaired electron. Calculate the contribution of the spin of this electron (a) to the magnetic moment of the ion and (b) to the molar magnetic susceptibility of Ti^{3+} at 298 K.

Solution: a) The quantum number, s of Ti^{3+} is equal to $\frac{1}{2}$. The contribution of the spin of this electron to the magnetic moment of the ion is given by

$$\mu = g\sqrt{s(s+1)}\ \hbar$$

$$= g\sqrt{\tfrac{1}{2}(\tfrac{1}{2}+1)}\,\hbar$$

$$= g\frac{\hbar}{2}\sqrt{3}$$

$$= \sqrt{3}\ \frac{gh}{4\pi} = \sqrt{3}\beta \qquad (1)$$

Note that $\hbar = h/2\pi$ and h = Planck's constant. $\beta = gh/4\pi$ is known as the Bohr magneton. Therefore,

$$\mu = \sqrt{3}(0.927 \times 10^{-20} \text{ erg. gauss}^{-1})$$

$$= 1.606 \times 10^{-20} \text{ erg gauss}^{-1}$$

b) The contribution of the spin of this electron to the molar magnetic susceptibility of Ti^{3+} at 298° K is given by

$$X_m = \frac{4\beta^2 \; L \; s(s+1)}{3kT} \qquad (2)$$

where L = Avogadro's number = 6.02×10^{23}

k = constant = 1.3805×10^{-16}

T = temperature = 298° K

Since all the variables in equation (2) are known, the problem becomes a matter of mere substitution. Hence,

$$X_m = \frac{4(0.927 \times 10^{-20})^2 (6.02 \times 10^{23}) \frac{1}{2}(\frac{1}{2}+1)}{3(1.3805 \times 10^{-16})(298)}$$

$$\therefore X_m = 0.01258 \times 10^{-1}$$

$$= 1.258 \times 10^{-3}$$

• PROBLEM 12-24

The density of $SiHBr_3$ is 2.690 $g \cdot cm^{-3}$ at 25°C, its refractive index is 1.578, and its dielectric constant is 3.570. Estimate its dipole moment in debyes.

Solution: The molecular weight of $SiHBr_3$ = 28 + 1 + 3(80) = 29 + 240 = 269. The molar polarization of a substance is given by

$$P_m = \frac{\varepsilon/\phi_0 - 1}{\varepsilon/\varepsilon_0 + 2} \frac{M}{d} \qquad (1)$$

where $\varepsilon/\varepsilon_0$ = dielectric constant

M = molecular weight

d = density.

From equation (1),

$$P_m = \left(\frac{3.570 - 1}{3.570 + 2}\right)\frac{269 \text{ g mole}^{-1}}{2.690 \text{ g cm}^{-3}}$$

$$\left(\frac{2.570}{5.570}\right)\frac{269 \text{ g mole}^{-1}}{2.690 \text{ g cm}^{-3}}$$

$$\therefore \qquad P_m = 46.14 \text{ cm}^3 \text{ mole}^{-1} \qquad (2)$$

The molar refractivity R_m, is defined as

$$\left(\frac{n^2 - 1}{n^2 + 2}\right)\frac{M}{d}$$

where n = refractive index. Therefore

$$R_m = \left(\frac{(1.578)^2 - 1}{(1.578)^2 + 2}\right)\frac{269 \text{ g mole}^{-1}}{2.69 \text{ g cm}^{-3}}$$

$$= \left(\frac{1.49}{4.49}\right)100 \text{ cm}^3 \text{ mole}^{-1}$$

$$\therefore \qquad R_m = 33.184 \text{ cm}^3 \text{ mole}^{-1} \qquad (3)$$

The difference between the molar polarization and molar refractivity is related to dipole moment by

$$P_m - R_m = \frac{4\pi L}{3}\left(\frac{\mu^2}{3kT}\right) \qquad (4)$$

where L = Avogadro's constant = 6.02×10^{23} mole^{-1}

μ = dipole moment

k = Boltzmann's constant = 1.38051×10^{-16} erg K^{-1}

T = Absolute temperature

Using equations (2) and (3) the difference is

$$P_m - R_m = (46.14 - 33.184)\text{cm}^3 \text{ mole}^{-1}$$

$$= 12.956 \text{ cm}^3 \text{ mole}^{-1}$$

substitute $P_m - R_m$ into equation (4)

$$12.956 = \frac{4\pi L}{3}\left(\frac{\mu^2}{3kT}\right) \qquad (5)$$

Rearranging equation (5) to solve for μ yields

$$\mu = \sqrt{\frac{(3)(3kT)(12.956)cm^3\ mole^{-1}}{4\pi L}}$$

$$= \sqrt{\frac{9(1.38051 \times 10^{-16})erg°K^{-1}(298°K)(12.956)cm^3\ mole^{-1}}{4(3.142)(6.02 \times 10^{23})mole^{-1}}}$$

$$= \sqrt{\frac{9(1.3805 \times 10^{-16})(298)(12.956)}{4(3.142)(6.02 \times 10^{23})} \frac{erg°K^{-1}\ °K\ cm^3\ mole^{-1}}{mole^{-1}}}$$

$$= 7.97 \times 10^{-19}\sqrt{cm^3\ erg}$$

$$= 7.97 \times 10^{-19}\sqrt{cm^3\ g\ cm^2\ sec^{-2}}$$

$$= 7.97 \times 10^{-19}\sqrt{g\ cm\ sec^{-2}\ cm^4}$$

$$= 7.97 \times 10^{-19}\sqrt{dyne\ cm^2\ cm^2}$$

Since $1(esu)^2 = dyne\ cm^2$,

$$= 7.97 \times 10^{-19}\ esu \cdot cm$$

$\therefore\ \mu = 0.7972$ D

• **PROBLEM 12-25**

The dielectric constant of gaseous SO_2 is 1.00993 at 273 K and 1.00569 at 373 K, at P = 1 atm. Calculate the dipole moment of SO_2. Assume ideal gas behavior.

Solution: The molar polarization of a substance is related to the dielectric constant by

$$P_m = \frac{\varepsilon/\varepsilon_0 - 1}{\varepsilon/\varepsilon_0 + 2}\frac{M}{d} \quad (1)$$

where P = molar polarization

$\varepsilon/\varepsilon_0$ = dielectric constant

Considering the polarization of the molecule to result from permanent and induced dipole moments, equation (1) changes to the form

$$P_m = \frac{4\pi L}{3}\left(\alpha + \frac{\mu^2}{3kT}\right) \quad (2)$$

where α = polarizability of the molecule

μ = permanent dipole moment

and $\qquad L$ = Avogadro's number

A plot of P against $\frac{1}{T}$ will have a slope of

$$\frac{4\pi L\mu^2}{9k}$$

$$\frac{M}{d} = \frac{RT}{P} = 82.06\ \text{cm}^3\ °\text{K}^{-1}\ \text{mole}^{-1}(\text{T}).$$

Therefore,

$$P_m\ (\text{at } 273°\text{K}) = \left(\frac{1.00993 - 1}{1.00993 + 2}\right)(82.06)\text{cm}^3\ \text{K}^{-1}\ \text{mole}^{-1}(273)°\text{K}$$

$$= 73.99\ \text{cm}^3\ \text{mole}^{-1}$$

and

$$P_m\ (\text{at } 373\ °\text{K}) = \left(\frac{1.00569 - 1}{1.00569 + 2}\right)(82.06)\text{cm}^3\ °\text{K}^{-1}\ \text{mole}^{-1}(373)°\text{K}$$

$$= 58.10\ \text{cm}^3\ \text{mole}^{-1}$$

from these,

$$\text{slope} = \frac{P_m(\text{at } 373\ °\text{K}) - P_m(\text{at } 273\ °\text{K})}{\frac{1}{373} - \frac{1}{273}}$$

$$= \frac{(58.10 - 73.99)\text{cm}^3\ \text{mole}}{(0.00268 - 0.00366)\frac{1}{°\text{K}}}$$

$$= 16.20 \times 10^3\ \text{cm}^3\ °\text{K mole}^{-1}$$

The constant $\frac{4\pi L}{9k} = 6.090 \times 10^{39}\ \text{erg}^{-1}\ °\text{K mole}^{-1}$. Therefore,

$$\mu^2 = \frac{16.20 \times 10^3\ \text{cm}^3\ °\text{K mole}^{-1}}{6.090 \times 10^{34}\ \text{erg}^{-1}\ °\text{K mole}^{-1}} = 2.66 \times 10^{-36}\ \text{esu}^2\ \text{cm}^2$$

$$\mu = [2.66 \times 10^{-36}\ \text{esu}^2\ \text{cm}^2]^{\frac{1}{2}} = 1.63 \times 10^{-18}\ \text{esu cm}$$

$$\times 1 \times 10^{18}\ \frac{\text{D}}{\text{esu cm}}$$

and therefore $\qquad \mu = 1.63$ D

The dipole moment of HBr is 0.780 D, and its dielectric constant is 1.00313 at 273 K and 1 atm. Calculate the polarizability of the HBr molecule.

Solution: The molar polarization is defined as

$$P_m = \frac{\varepsilon/\varepsilon_0 - 1}{\varepsilon/\varepsilon_0 + 2}\frac{M}{d} \qquad (1)$$

where $\varepsilon/\varepsilon_0$ = dielectric constant

M = molecular weight

d = density

Equation (1) can also be represented as

$$P_m = \frac{4\pi L}{3}\left(\alpha + \frac{\mu^2}{3kT}\right) \qquad (2)$$

where α = polarizability

L = Avogadro's number

μ = dipole moment

Therefore,

$$\frac{\varepsilon/\varepsilon_0 - 1}{\varepsilon/\varepsilon_0 + 2}\frac{M}{d} = \frac{4\pi L}{3}\left(\alpha + \frac{\mu^2}{3kT}\right) \qquad (3)$$

$$d = \frac{\text{mass}}{\text{volume}} \text{ and } \frac{M}{d} = \frac{RT}{P}$$

From the given data,

$$P_m = \left(\frac{1.00313 - 1}{1.00313 + 2}\right)\left(\frac{82.06 \text{ cc-atm - K}^{-1}\text{ mole}^{-1}}{1 \text{ atm}}\right)(273\,°\text{K})$$

$$= 23.3 \text{ cm}^3 \text{ mole}^{-1}$$

The term

$$\frac{\mu^2}{3kT} = \frac{(0.780 \times 10^{-18} \text{ esu cm})^2}{3(1.3805 \times 10^{-16} \text{ erg K}^{-1})(273\,°\text{K})}$$

$$= \frac{(.780 \times 10^{-18})^2 \quad (\text{esu cm})^2}{3(1.3805 \times 10^{-16})(273) \text{ erg K}^{-1}\text{ K}}$$

$$= 5.381 \times 10^{-24} \frac{esu^2\ cm^2}{erg}$$

$$= 5.381 \times 10^{-24} \frac{dyne\ cm^2\ cm^2}{erg}$$

$$= 5.381 \times 10^{-24} \frac{g\ cm\ cm^2\ cm^2}{sec^2 \frac{g\ cm^2}{sec^2}}$$

$$= 5.381 \times 10^{-24}\ cm^3$$

Now using all the values above in equation (3) yield

$$23.3\ cm^3\ mole^{-1} = \frac{4\pi L}{3}(\alpha + 5.381 \times 10^{-24}\ cm^3)$$

From which

$$\alpha = \frac{23.3\ cm^3\ mole^{-1}}{\frac{4\pi L}{3}} - 5.381 \times 10^{-24}\ cm^3$$

$$= (9.235 \times 10^{-24} - 5.381 \times 10^{-24})cm^3$$

$$= 3.854 \times 10^{-24}\ cm^3$$

QUANTUM THEORY

• PROBLEM 12-27

What are the wavelengths of (a) a photon, and (b) an electron, each having kinetic energy of 1 eV?

Solution: a) The energy of a photon is given by

$$E = h\nu \tag{1}$$

where h = Planck's constant = $6.6256 \quad 10^{-34}$ Js

ν = frequency

The frequency is defined to be $\frac{c}{\lambda}$, where c = speed of light λ = wavelength.

Therefore, equation (1) becomes

$$E = h\frac{c}{\lambda}$$

or

$$\lambda = \frac{hc}{E}. \tag{2}$$

Solving equation (2) with E given as

$$1 \text{ eV} = 1.6021 \times 10^{-19} \text{ J}$$

yields

$$\lambda = \frac{(6.6256 \times 10^{-34} \text{ Js})(2.9979 \times 10^{8} \text{ m s}^{-1})}{1.6021 \times 10^{-19} \text{ J}}$$

$$= 12.398 \times 10^{-7} \text{ m}$$

$\therefore$ $\lambda = 1239.8$ nm

b) The energy of an electron is defined as

$$E = \tfrac{1}{2}mv^2. \tag{3}$$

where m = mass of electron

v = velocity.

Solving equation (3) for v gives

$$v = \left(\frac{2E}{m}\right)^{\frac{1}{2}}$$

$$= \left[\frac{(2)(1.6021 \times 10^{-19} \text{ J})}{9.110 \times 10^{-31} \text{ kg}}\right]^{\frac{1}{2}}$$

$$= 5.930 \times 10^{5} \text{ m s}^{-1}$$

The wavelength of an electron is given by $\lambda = \dfrac{h}{mv}$

$$\lambda = \frac{6.6256 \times 10^{-34} \text{ J s}}{(9.110 \times 10^{-31} \text{ kg})(5.930 \times 10^{5} \text{ m s}^{-1})}$$

$$= 1.226 \times 10^{-9} \text{ m}$$

$\therefore$ $\lambda = 1.226$ nm

• PROBLEM 12-28

For the de Broglie waves representing particles, the wavelength λ depends upon the frequency ν (i.e., the waves show dispersion). Derive the relation

$$\nu = c\left(\frac{1}{\lambda_c^2} + \frac{1}{\lambda^2}\right)^{\frac{1}{2}}$$

where $\lambda_c = h/m_e c$. You should recall that the mass of the electron depends on its speed v as

$$m = m_e \left(1 - \frac{v^2}{c^2}\right)^{-\frac{1}{2}}$$

Solution: The inertial properties of matter are determined by its total content of energy. If m is the rest mass of the body (that is, its mass when at rest with respect to any frame of reference), its total energy content is given by

$$E = mc^2 \tag{1}$$

where c is the speed of light in a vacuum.

The relationship between the mass of an electron and its speed is given as

$$m = m_e \left(1 - \frac{v^2}{c^2}\right)^{-\frac{1}{2}}, \tag{2}$$

Substitute equation (2) into equation (1)

$$E = m_e \left(1 - \frac{v^2}{c^2}\right)^{-\frac{1}{2}} c^2$$

or

$$E = \frac{m_e c^2}{\sqrt{1 - \frac{v^2}{c^2}}} \tag{3}$$

where v = velocity of the electron. Squaring both sides of equation (3) gives

$$E^2 = \frac{m_e^2 c^4}{1 - \frac{v^2}{c^2}}$$

$$E^2 \left(1 - \frac{v^2}{c^2}\right) = m_e^2 c^4$$

$$E^2 - \frac{v^2 E^2}{c^2} = m_e^2 c^4 \tag{4}$$

Momentum is defined as

$$P = mv. \tag{5}$$

But m is given as $\frac{E}{c^2}$ from equation (1). Therefore,

$$P = \frac{Ev}{c^2}$$

and squaring both sides gives

$$P^2 = \frac{E^2v^2}{c^4} \quad \text{or} \quad P^2c^4 = E^2v^2 \tag{6}$$

Substituting equation (6) into equation (4) gives

$$E^2 - P^2c^2 = m_e^2c^4$$

$$E^2 = m_e^2c^4 + P^2c^2 \tag{7}$$

or
$$E = \left(m_e^2c^4 + P^2c^2\right)^{\frac{1}{2}} \tag{8}$$

By definition, the frequency of the electron particle is given by

$$\nu = \frac{E}{h} \tag{9}$$

where ν = frequency

Using the value of E from equation (8)

$$\nu = \frac{\left(m_e^2c^4 + P^2c^2\right)^{\frac{1}{2}}}{h} = \left(\frac{m_e^2c^4 + P^2c^2}{h^2}\right)^{\frac{1}{2}}$$

$$\therefore \quad \nu = c\left(\frac{m_e^2c^2}{h^2} + \frac{P^2}{h^2}\right)^{\frac{1}{2}} \tag{10}$$

The wavelength of a de Broglie wave is defined as,

$$\lambda = \frac{h}{P}$$

Also define

$$\lambda_c = \frac{h}{m_ec}$$

where λ = wavelength, h = Planck's constant and P = the momentum of the particle, and equation (10) can be written as

$$\nu = c\left(\frac{1}{\lambda_c^2} + \frac{1}{\lambda^2}\right)^{\frac{1}{2}}$$

Alpha particles emitted from radioactive radium has an energy of 4.8 MeV (million electron volts). Calculate the de Broglie wavelength of one of these alpha particles, given the following data:

(mass of alpha particle = 6.6×10^{-24} g

$h = 6.6 \times 10^{-27}$ erg sec

$1.0 \text{ MeV} = 1.6 \times 10^{-6}$ erg

$1 \text{ erg} = 1 \text{ g cm}^2 \text{ sec}^{-2}$)

Solution: Radium is a radioactive element that emits alpha particles (helium nuclei, He^{2+}), beta particles (electrons) and gamma rays. Energy depends on frequency or wavelength according to the relation:

$$E = h\nu = \frac{hc}{\lambda} \tag{1}$$

From Einstein's formula:

$$E = mc^2 \tag{2}$$

where m = the mass of the particle and c is the speed of light; the particle's momentum is p = mc.

$$\therefore \quad p = mc = \frac{E}{c} \tag{3}$$

Substituting (1) into equation (3) yields

$$p = \frac{h}{\lambda}$$

but $\frac{h}{\lambda}$ is also equal to mv hence

$$p = \frac{h}{\lambda} = mv. \tag{4}$$

Equation (4) is the de Broglie equation. Rearranging equation (4) yields

$$\lambda = \frac{h}{mv} \tag{5}$$

The kinetic energy, KE, of the alpha particles is given as 4.8 MeV. That is,

$$KE = 4.8 \text{ MeV}.$$

But, $$KE = \frac{1}{2}mv^2$$

$$\therefore \qquad \frac{1}{2}mv^2 = 4.8 \text{ MeV}$$

and $$v^2 = \frac{2(4.8 \text{ MeV})}{m}$$

$$= \frac{(9.6 \text{ MeV})\left(\frac{1.6\times10^{-6} \text{ erg}}{1 \text{ MeV}}\right)\left(\frac{1 \text{ g cm}^2 \text{ sec}^{-2}}{1 \text{ erg}}\right)}{6.6 \times 10^{-24} \text{ g}}$$

$$= 2.32 \times 10^{18} \frac{\text{cm}^2}{\text{sec}^2}$$

and $$v = \sqrt{2.32 \times 10^{18} \frac{\text{cm}^2}{\text{sec}^2}}$$

$$v = 1.52 \times 10^9 \frac{\text{cm}}{\text{sec}}$$

This is the velocity of the alpha particles. Substituting this velocity into equation (5), we have

$$\lambda = \frac{(6.6 \times 10^{-27} \text{ erg sec})\left(\frac{1 \text{ g cm}^2 \text{ sec}^{-2}}{1 \text{ erg}}\right)}{(6.6 \times 10^{-24} \text{ g})\left(1.52 \times 10^9 \frac{\text{cm}}{\text{sec}}\right)}$$

or $$\lambda = 6.6 \times 10^{-13} \text{ cm}$$

• PROBLEM 12-30

The ejection of electrons from a metal surface by light is called the photoelectric effect, and this effect is often utilized in some burglar alarms. The diagram shows the photoelectric cell and the circuit. A beam of light shines on a metal electrode, K and causes electrons to be ejected from the surface of the metal, which acts as the cathode. The ejected electrons are attracted to the positively charged screen, W connected with the cell through a battery B and a galvanometer, G thus completing the circuit. If the light beam is blocked by a burglar's arm, the electrical circuit is broken and this sets off the alarm system. Given that the metal cathode K is made of tungsten , W, the kinetic energy of the ejected electrons is 8.0×10^{-12} ergs and the wavelength of the incident light is 1.25×10^3 Å, calculate the maximum wavelength of light that could be used for a burglar alarm. Take the Planck's constant, $h = 6.6 \times 10^{-27}$ erg sec and the speed of light $c = 3.0 \times 10^{10}$ cm sec^{-1}.

Solution: The frequency of the incident light must be

greater than a certain critical value, called the threshold frequency, before any electrons are ejected from the surface of the metal. The maximum number of electrons ejected is directly proportional to the intensity of incident light, but the maximum kinetic energy, K.E. of the electrons depends only on its frequency

$$\therefore \quad KE = h[\nu - (\nu_0)_W] \tag{1}$$

where $(\nu_0)_W$ = the threshold or critical frequency of the tungsten metal, and h is Planck's constant with a value of 6.6×10^{-27} erg sec. But $\nu = \frac{c}{\lambda}$, where λ = the wavelength of the incident light and c is the speed of light. Insert these into equation (1) changes it to

$$KE = h\left[\frac{c}{\lambda} - \frac{c}{(\lambda_0)_W}\right]$$

or

$$KE = h\left[\frac{c(\lambda_0)_W - c\lambda}{\lambda(\lambda_0)_W}\right]$$

Rearranging the above equation gives

$$KE\lambda(\lambda_0)_W = hc(\lambda_0)_W - hc\lambda$$

$$hc(\lambda_0)_W = KE\lambda(\lambda_0)_W + hc\lambda$$

$$hc(\lambda_0)_W - KE\lambda(\lambda_0)_W = hc\lambda$$

$$(\lambda_0)_W(hc - KE\lambda) = hc\lambda$$

Solving for $(\lambda_0)_W$ yields

$$(\lambda_0)_W = \frac{hc\lambda}{[(hc) - (KE \times \lambda)]} \tag{2}$$

where $(\lambda_0)_W$ = the maximum or threshold wavelength of light, and λ is the wavelength of the incident light before it reaches the threshold wavelength. From equation (2) then,

$(\lambda_0)_W$ =

$$\frac{(6.6\times10^{-27}\text{ erg sec})\left(3.0\times10^{10}\ \frac{\text{cm}}{\text{sec}}\right)(1.25\times10^{3}\ \text{Å})\left(\frac{10^{-8}\ \text{cm}}{1\text{Å}}\right)}{[6.6\times10^{-27}\text{ erg sec}]\left(3.0\times10^{10}\ \frac{\text{cm}}{\text{sec}}\right) - (8.0\times10^{\ 27}\text{ erg})(1.25\times10^{3}\ \text{Å})\left(\frac{10^{-8}\ \text{cm}}{1\ \text{Å}}\right)}$$

$$(\lambda_0)_W = \frac{2.5 \times 10^{-21} \text{ erg cm}^2}{1.0 \times 10^{-16} \text{ erg cm}}$$

$$= (2.5 \times 10^{-5} \text{ cm}) \left(\frac{1 \text{ Å}}{10^{-8} \text{ cm}}\right)$$

$$(\lambda_0)_W = 2500 \text{ Å}.$$

Thus, the maximum wavelength of light that can be used for the burglar alarm using a tungsten metal in photoelectric cell is 2500 Å. This means that ultraviolet light with frequencies between (1000 - 4000 Å) is needed, since the visible light has frequencies between 4000 - 7000 Å.

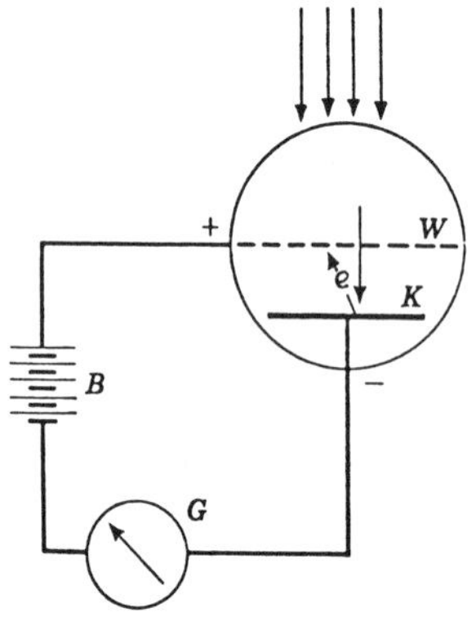

• PROBLEM 12-31

Cesium metal is used extensively as the cathode in photocells and in television cameras because it has the lowest ionization energy of all the elements and is readily ionized by light. Given that an incident light of wavelength 5000 Å is incident on a photocell containing cesium, and the threshold wavelength of the photoelectric effect is 6600 Å, calculate the kinetic energy of the ejected electrons from the surface of the cesium.

Solution: The kinetic energy, KE of a photoelectric electron is given by:

$$KE = h[\nu - (\nu_0)_{Cs}] \qquad (1)$$

where $(\nu_0)_{Cs}$ = the threshold frequency, ν is the frequency before the threshold frequency is reached and h is Planck's constant. But $\nu = \frac{c}{\lambda}$, where λ = the wavelength of the incident light and c is the speed of light.

$$\therefore \qquad \nu = \frac{\left(3.0 \times 10^{10}\ \frac{\text{cm}}{\text{sec}}\right)}{(5000\ \text{Å})\left(\frac{10^{-8}\ \text{cm}}{1\text{Å}}\right)}$$

or $$\nu = 6.0 \times 10^{14}\ \text{sec}^{-1}$$

$$(\nu_0)_{Cs} = \frac{c}{(\lambda_0)_{Cs}}$$

where $(\lambda_0)_{Cs}$ = the threshold wavelength of cesium

$$\therefore \quad (\nu_0)_{Cs} = \frac{\left(3.0 \times 10^{10}\ \frac{\text{cm}}{\text{sec}}\right)}{\left(6600\ \text{Å}\right)\left(\frac{10^{-8}\ \text{cm}}{1\ \text{Å}}\right)}$$

or $$(\nu_0)_{Cs} = 4.5 \times 10^{14}\ \text{sec}^{-1}$$

Using equation (1) gives

$$KE = (6.6 \times 10^{-27}\ \text{erg sec})[6.0 \times 10^{14}\ \text{sec}^{-1} - 4.5 \times 10^{14}\ \text{sec}^{-1}]$$

$$= 6.6 \times 10^{-27}\ \text{erg sec}(1.5 \times 10^{14}\ \text{sec}^{-1})$$

or $$KE = 9.9 \times 10^{-13}\ \text{erg}$$

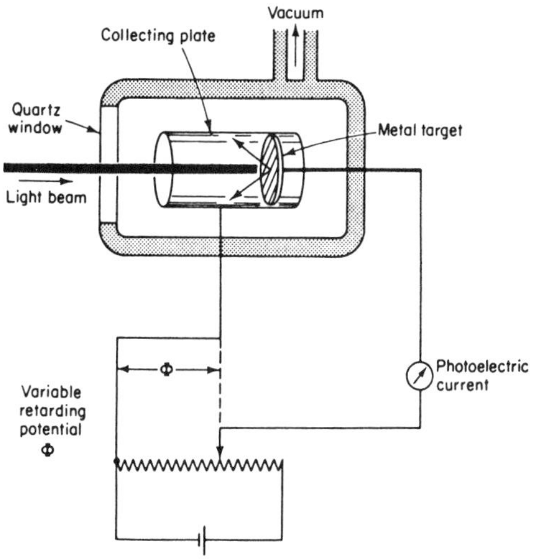

Apparatus for studying the photoelectric effect.

• PROBLEM 12-32

From Planck's Law, compute the Stefan-Boltzmann equation for the total density of black-body radiation as a function of temperature. That is,

$$E(T) = \int_0^\infty E(\nu)d\nu$$

Solution: If a collection of N oscillators having a fundamental vibration frequency ν takes up energy only in increments of $h\nu$, the allowed energies are 0, $h\nu$, $2h\nu$, $3h\nu$, ... Using the Stefan-Boltzmann equation with N_0 = the number of systems in the lowest energy state, the number N_i having an energy ε_i above this ground state is

$$N_i = N_0 \, e^{-\varepsilon_i/kT}$$

For a collection of oscillators, the average energy is given as

$$\bar{\varepsilon} = \frac{h\nu}{e^{h\nu/kT} - 1} \qquad (1)$$

Using equation (1) Planck derived an energy-distribution formula in agreement with the experimental data for black-body radiation. The energy density $E(\nu)d\nu$ is the number of oscillators per unit volume ν and $\nu + d\nu$. Planck's law then is given as

$$E(\nu)d\nu = \frac{8\pi h\nu^3}{c^3} \frac{d\nu}{e^{h\nu/kT} - 1}$$

where
- h = Planck's constant
- ν = frequency
- c = speed of light
- k = Boltzmann's constant
- T = absolute temperature

The Stefan-Boltzmann equation for the density of black-body radiation as a function of temperature is then given by

$$E(T) = \int_0^\infty \frac{8\pi h\nu^3}{c^3} \frac{d\nu}{e^{h\nu/kT} - 1} = \frac{8\pi h}{c^3} \int_0^\infty \frac{\nu^3 d\nu}{e^{h\nu/kT} - 1} \qquad (2)$$

Now, let $y = \frac{h}{kT}$, then $y^3\left(\frac{kT}{h}\right)^3 = \nu^3$, and $dy = \frac{h}{kT}d\nu$ or

$d\nu = \frac{kT}{h}dy$. Equation (2) becomes

$$E(T) = \frac{8\pi h}{c^3}\frac{k^3T^3}{h^3}\frac{kT}{h}\int_0^\infty \frac{y^3}{e^y - 1}dy$$

$$= \frac{8\pi k^4T^4}{h^3c^3}\int_0^\infty \frac{y^3}{e^y - 1}dy$$

The solution of the integral is $\frac{\pi^4}{15}$. Therefore,

$$E(T) = \left[\frac{8\pi k^4T^4}{h^3c^3}\right]\left[\frac{\pi^4}{15}\right]$$

$$= \frac{8\pi^5k^4T^4}{15h^3c^3}$$

• PROBLEM 12-33

An electron was accelerated through a potential difference of 1.00 ± 0.01 kV. What is the uncertainty of the position of the electron along its line of flight?

Solution: If the momentum of a particle is precisely specified, the position is totally uncertain. This remarkable destruction of one of the fundamentals of classical mechanics is a special case of the Heisenberg Uncertainty Principle, It states that if the momentum is known to lie within a range δp, then the position must be uncertain to an extent δz, where

$$\delta p\delta z \geq \frac{\hbar}{2} \qquad (1)$$

Here $\hbar = \frac{h}{2\pi}$ and h = Planck's constant. Note that z is the line of flight. The uncertainty of momentum can be calculated from

$$\delta p = m_e\delta v \qquad (2)$$

where δv = the uncertainty in velocity. This δv can be calculated from $\frac{1}{2}m_ev^2 = eV$.

For a potential difference of 0.99 kV,

$$v = \sqrt{\frac{2eV}{m_e}} = \sqrt{\frac{2(1.602 \times 10^{-19}C)(990V)}{9.110 \times 10^{-31}\ kg}}$$

$$= \sqrt{\frac{2(1.602 \times 10^{-19})(990)CV}{9.110 \times 10^{-31}\ kg}}$$

$$= \sqrt{3.482 \times 10^{14}\ \frac{JV^{-1}V}{kg}}$$

$$= \sqrt{3.482 \times 10^{14}\ \frac{kg\ m^2\ sec^{-2}}{kg}}$$

$$= \sqrt{3.482 \quad 10^{14}\ m^2\ s^{-2}}$$

$$\therefore \quad v = 1.866 \times 10^7\ m\ s^{-1}$$

Similarly, for a potential difference of 1.01 kV,

$$v = 1.885 \times 10^7\ m\ s^{-1}$$

Hence $\quad \delta v = (1.885 - 1.866) \times 10^7\ m\ s^{-1}$

$$= 0.019 \times 10^7\ m\ s^{-1}$$

$$= 1.9 \times 10^5\ m\ s^{-1}$$

Solving for δp in equation (2) gives

$$\delta p = (9.110 \times 10^{-31}\ kg)(1.9 \times 10^5\ m\ s^{-1})$$

$$= 17.309 \times 10^{-26}\ kg\ m\ s^{-1}$$

$$= 1.7 \times 10^{-25}\ kg\ m\ s^{-1}$$

Rearranging equation (1) to solve for δz gives

$$\delta z \geq \left(\frac{\hbar}{2}\right)\bigg/\delta p = \frac{1.054 \times 10^{-34}\ Js}{2(1.7 \times 10^{-25}\ kg\ m\ s^{-1})}$$

$$= 3.09 \times 10^{-10}\ Js/kg\ m\ s^{-1}$$

$$= 3.09 \times 10^{-10}(kg\ m^2/s^2)s/kg\ m\ s^{-1}$$

or $\quad \delta z = 3.09 \times 10^{-10}\ m = 309\ pm = 3.09\ \mathring{A}$.

Apply the Heisenberg Uncertainty Principle to estimate the kinetic energy of the electron in a hydrogen atom at a distance r from the nucleus. Then calculate the equilibrium distance r_e by minimizing the total energy E, kinetic + potential, with respect to r. Compare E calculated in this way with the experimental value of -13.59 eV.

Solution: The Heisenberg Uncertainty Principle specifies that, in simultaneous measurement of the position and momentum of a particle,

$$\Delta r \Delta p \geq \frac{h}{2\pi} \quad (1)$$

where Δr = the uncertainty in position

Δp = the uncertainty in momentum

h = Planck's constant.

Note that the right side of equation (1) can be h, $\frac{h}{2\pi}$ or $\frac{h}{4\pi}$, depending on the precise definition of Δr and Δp. For the H atom, equation (1) will be adequate.

Rearranging equation (1) to solve for Δp gives

$$\Delta p \geq \frac{h}{\Delta r 2\pi} \quad (2)$$

Recall that

$$E = \frac{1}{2}mv^2 = mv(\frac{1}{2}v), \quad (3)$$

where v = velocity

and m = mass.

But p = mv = momentum.

Substitute for p in equation (3) gives

$$E = p(\frac{1}{2}v) = \frac{p^2}{2m} \quad (4)$$

where $p^2 = m^2 v^2$

From equation (4),

$$\Delta E = \frac{(\Delta p)^2}{2m}$$

or $(\Delta p)^2 = \Delta E 2m \quad (5)$

Combining equations (2) and (5) yields

$$(\Delta p)^2 = \Delta E 2m \geq \left(\frac{h}{\Delta r 2\pi}\right)^2$$

or $$2m\Delta E(\Delta r)^2 \geq \frac{h^2}{4\pi^2} \qquad (6)$$

Rearranging equation (6) to solve for ΔE yields

$$\Delta E \geq \frac{h^2}{8m(\Delta r)^2\pi^2}$$

Therefore, the minimal energy is represented by

$$E_k = \frac{h^2}{8mr^2\pi^2}$$

Total energy is the summation of the kinetic and potential energies. That is

$$E_T = E_k + E_p$$

$$= \frac{h^2}{8mr^2\pi^2} - \frac{Ze^2}{r}$$

Recall that Z = 1 for an H. Therefore,

$$E_T = \frac{h^2}{8mr^2\pi^2} - \frac{e^2}{r} \qquad (7)$$

To find what r_e is, take the partial derivative of equation (7) with respect to r only and set it equal to zero. That is,

$$\frac{\partial E}{\partial r} = -\frac{2h^2}{8m\pi^2 r_e^3} + \frac{e^2}{r_e^2} = 0.$$

Therefore, $$r_e = \frac{h^2}{4\pi^2 me^2}$$

Using this r value in equation (7) gives

$$E = \frac{h^2}{8m\pi^2}\left(\frac{4\pi^2 me^2}{h^2}\right)^2 - e^2\left(\frac{4\pi^2 me^2}{h^2}\right)$$

$$= -\frac{2\pi^2 me^4}{h^2}$$

Here $m = 9.11 \times 10^{-28}$ g

$e = 4.80 \times 10^{-10}$ esu

and $h = 6.62 \times 10^{-27}$ erg sec. Therefore,

$$E = \frac{-2\pi^2(9.11 \times 10^{-28}\text{ g})(4.80 \times 10^{-10}\text{ esu})^4}{(6.62 \times 10^{-27}\text{ erg sec})^2}$$

$$= \frac{-2\pi^2(9.11 \times 10^{-28})(4.80 \times 10^{-10})^4\text{ g esu}^4}{(6.62 \times 10^{-27})^2(\text{erg sec})^2}$$

But 1 erg = 1 g cm^2 sec^{-2}, and 1 esu^2 = 1 dyne cm^2 = 1 g cm sec^{-2} cm^2 = g cm^3 sec^{-2}. Therefore,

$$E = -2.181 \times 10^{-11} \frac{\text{g g}^2\text{ cm}^6\text{ sec}^{-4}}{\text{g}^2\text{ cm}^4\text{ sec}^{-4}\text{ sec}^2}$$

$$= -2.181 \times 10^{-11}\text{ g cm}^2\text{ sec}^{-2}$$

$$= -2.181 \times 10^{-11}\text{ erg}$$

or $\quad E = -13.6$ eV.

Observe that this is very close to the experimental value.

• PROBLEM 12-35

A particle of mass m is confined to a one-dimensional box with the origin at the center of the box. The box extends from -L to +L. The potential energy is

$$V(x) = \begin{cases} 0, & -L \le x \le L \\ \infty, & |x| > L \end{cases}$$

(a) Write the Schrödinger equation for this problem showing separate equations for the inside and the outside of the box.
(b) Assume a solution (inside the box) of the form

$$\psi(x) = A\sin(cx) + B\cos(cx).$$

Give a rule that determines all the possible values of c, and for each possible c give the conditions on A and B that make ψ a satisfactory solution.

(c) Express the energy in terms of c.

Solution: One of the basic functions of quantum mechanics is that the motion of a particle, that is, its position as a function of space and time, is exactly described by means of a probability density function $\rho(x,y,z,t)$. By definition, the probability of finding the particle at a time t_0 in a volume element dv, surrounding the point (x_0,y_0,z_0), is given by

$$P = \rho(x_0,y_0,z_0,t_0)dv.$$

But in quantum mechanics the probability density function ρ is derived from another function ψ, which is known as the wave function. The wave function is obtained as the solution of a differential equation that is known as the Schrödinger equation. If the motion of the particle is restricted to only one dimension the Schrodinger equation takes the form

$$-\frac{\hbar^2}{2m}\frac{d^2\psi}{dx^2} + V(x)\psi = E\psi$$

where m = mass of the particle

$\hbar = \frac{h}{2\pi}$. Here h is Planck's constant.

E = time independent total energy

ψ = wave function

V = the electrostatic interaction between two particles with charges z_1 and z_2 given by $V = z_1z_2/r$. Here r is the distance between the particles.

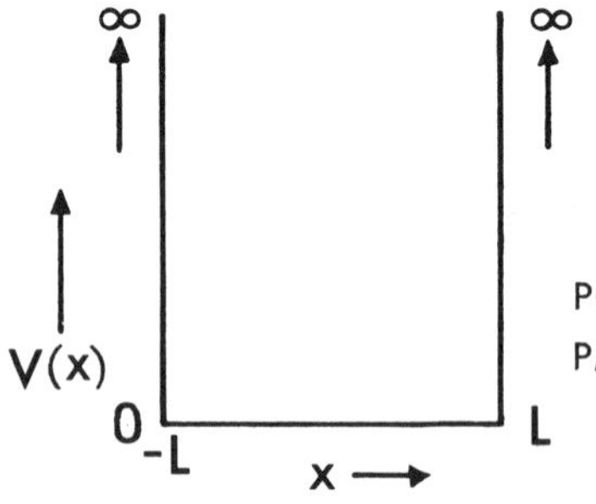

POTENTIAL FUNCTION OF THE PARTICLE IN A BOX.

Fig. 1

With reference to equation (1), a one-dimensional box is defined by a potential which is zero for $-L \leq x \leq L$ and which is infinite elsewhere (see Figure 1).

Algebraically, the potential is given by

$$V(x) = \infty \quad x < -L$$

$$V(x) = 0 \quad 0 \leq x \leq L$$

$$V(x) = \infty \quad L < x$$

The particle cannot obviously move outside the box and

$$\psi(x) = 0 \quad x < -L \quad \text{and} \quad x > L$$

Then the Schrödinger equation becomes

$$= -\frac{\hbar^2}{2m}\frac{d^2\psi}{dx^2} + V\psi = E\psi.$$

a) The Schrödinger equation for the region $x = -L$ and $x = L$ (inside the box) reduces to

$$\left(\frac{-\hbar^2}{2m}\right)\frac{d^2\psi}{dx^2} = E\psi \qquad (1)$$

since the potential is defined to be zero in this region.

After substituting in the value of $\hbar$, the Schrödinger equation for the inside of the box is

$$\left(-\frac{h^2}{8\pi^2 m}\right)\frac{d^2\psi}{dx^2} = E\psi \qquad (2)$$

For the outside, it is

$$\left(\frac{-h^2}{8\pi^2 m}\right)\frac{d^2\psi}{dx^2} + V\psi = E\psi$$

or

$$\left(\frac{-h^2}{8\pi^2 m}\right)\frac{d^2\psi}{dx^2} + \infty\psi = E\psi$$

where $V = \infty$ for the region $|x| > L$

Then $\psi = 0$ outside the box.

b) For the equation dealing with the inside of the box a possible solution is of the form

$$\psi(x) = A \sin cx + B \cos cx$$

For continuity of inside and outside functions,

$$\psi(-L) = -A \sin cL + B \cos cL = 0 \qquad (3)$$

$$\psi(+L) = A \sin cL + B \cos cL = 0 \qquad (4)$$

subtract equation (3) from equation (4)

$$2A \sin cL = 0 \qquad (5)$$

Therefore, either A = 0 or sin cL = 0, which makes

$$cL = n\pi \quad \text{for} \quad n = \pm 1, \pm 2, \ldots$$

from which

$$c = \frac{\pi n}{L}$$

Therefore, the wavefunction is given by

$$\psi = A \sin \frac{n\pi x}{L} .$$

Addition of equation (3) to equation (4) gives

$$2B \cos cL = 0$$

either B = 0 or cos cL = 0 for n = 0, ±1, ±2, ...

which makes

$$cL = \left(n - \frac{1}{2}\right)\pi$$

and

$$c = \frac{\left(n - \frac{1}{2}\right)\pi}{L} = \frac{(2n-1)\pi}{2L}$$

Therefore,

$$\psi = B \cos \left[\frac{(2n-1)\pi x}{2L}\right]$$

c)

$$E\psi = \left(\frac{-h^2}{8\pi^2 m}\right) \frac{d^2\psi}{dx^2} .$$

Also

$$\frac{d^2\psi}{dx^2} = - c^2\psi$$

$$\therefore \qquad E\psi = \left(\frac{-h^2}{8\pi^2 m}\right)(-c^2\psi)$$

and

$$E = \frac{h^2 c^2}{8\pi^2 m} .$$

Determine the energy levels and wave functions of a particle in the potential well shown by solving the Schrödinger equation.

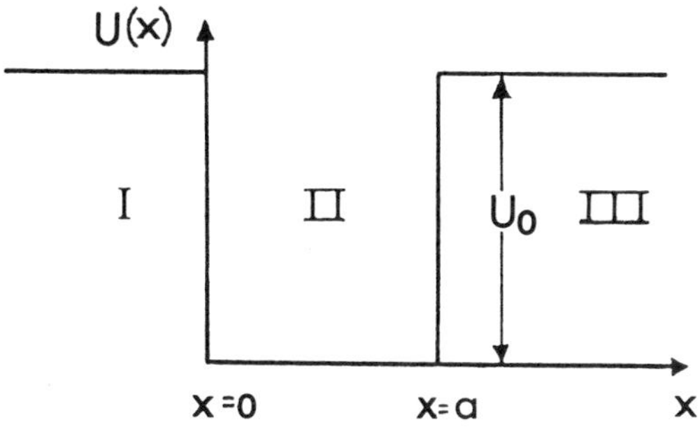

Fig. 1

Solution: In region I where $x \leq 0$, $U = U_0$. In region II, $0 \leq x \leq a$ and $U = 0$ and in region III $x \geq a$ and $U = U_0$. The Schrödinger equation is written as

$$\frac{d^2\psi}{dx^2} + \frac{8\pi^2 m}{h^2}(E - U)\psi = 0 \tag{1}$$

where ψ = the amplitude function called the wave function. Equation 1 would be solved for ψ in each of the three regions of figure 1 and the constants evaluated by the requirements that ψ and $d\psi/dx$ and therefore $(\frac{1}{\psi})(d\psi/dx)$ must be continuous at the boundaries.

Writing equation (1) for regions I and III where $U = U_0$ gives

$$\frac{d^2\psi}{dx^2} + \frac{8\pi^2 m}{h^2}(E - U_0)\psi = 0 \tag{2}$$

In region III where U = 0, equation (1) becomes

$$\frac{d^2\psi}{dx^2} + \frac{8\pi^2 m}{h^2}E\psi = 0 \tag{3}$$

Solve for ψ_I in region I, by making the following substitution. Let

$$K_1^2 = \frac{8\pi^2 m}{h^2}(U_0 - E) \tag{4}$$

Substitute equation (4) into equation (2)

$$\frac{d^2\psi}{dx_2} - K_1^2\psi = 0$$

from which

$$\psi = Ae^{K_1x} + Be^{-K_1x} \qquad (5)$$

where A and B are constants. When $x \to -\infty$ the term Be^{-K_1x} increases to infinity and B = 0 for region I. Therefore

$$\psi_I = Ae^{K_1x}$$

For region III, again

$$\psi = Ae^{K_1x} + Be^{-K_1x},$$

and as $x \to \infty$, Ae^{K_1x} increases to infinity and A = 0. Therefore $\psi_{III} = Be^{-K_1x}$. Define $B' = Be^{-K_1a}$, thus

$$\psi_{III} = B'e^{-K_1(x-a)} \qquad (6)$$

To solve for ψ in region II, the following substitution is made. Let

$$K_2^2 = +\frac{8\pi^2 mE}{h^2} \qquad (7)$$

Substitute equation (7) into equation (3) to give

$$\frac{d^2\psi}{dx_2} + K_2^2\psi = 0$$

where $\psi_{II} = C\sin(K_2x + \delta)$, C and δ = constants.

To determine the energy levels of the particles some boundary conditions would be applied to the different regions of the potential well. For regions I and II the boundary conditions are

$$\psi_I = \psi_{II} \quad \text{at} \quad x = 0$$

$$\therefore \quad \frac{d\psi_I}{dx} = \frac{d\psi_{II}}{dx} \text{ at } x = 0 \qquad (8)$$

from which

$$\psi_I\Big]_{x=0} = \psi_{II}\Big]_{x=0} = C\sin\delta \text{ and } A = C\sin\delta \qquad (9)$$

Thus $$\left.\frac{d\psi_I}{dx}\right)_{x=0} = K_1 A e^{K_1 x}$$

$$= K_1 A \quad \text{since} \quad x = 0$$

Also $$\left.\frac{d\psi_{II}}{dx}\right)_{x=0} = 0 = K_2 \cos(K_2 x + \delta)$$

$$= K_2\ C \cos\delta \quad \text{since} \quad x = 0$$

From equation (8)

$$K_1 A = K_2\ C \cos\delta \tag{10}$$

Applying boundary conditions on regions II and III gives

$$\psi_{II} = \psi_{III} \quad \text{at} \quad x = a$$

or $$\frac{d\psi_{II}}{dx} = \frac{d\psi_{III}}{dx} \quad \text{at} \quad x = a$$

$$\left.\psi_{II}\right)_{x=a} = K_2\ C \cos(K_2 a + \delta)$$

$$\left.\psi_{III}\right)_{x=a} = C \sin(K_2 a + \delta)$$

Define $B' = C \sin(K_2 a + \delta)$ (11)

$$\therefore \quad \left.\psi_{III}\right)_{x = a} = B'$$

The derivative of the wave function in regions II and III will now be evaluated at point x = a. Thus

$$\left.\frac{d\psi_{II}}{dx}\right)_{x=a} = K_2\ C \cos(K_2 a + \delta)$$

and $$\left.\frac{d\psi_{III}}{dx}\right)_{x=a} = -K_1\ B' e^{-K_1(x - a)}\Big]\ x = a$$

$$= -K_1 B'$$

$$\therefore \quad -K_1 B' = K_2\ C \cos(K_2 a + \delta) \tag{12}$$

From regions I and II boundary conditions define

$$\tan\delta = \frac{\sin\delta}{\cos\delta}$$

Using equation (9), $\sin\delta = \frac{A}{C}$ and from equation (10) $\cos\delta = \frac{K_1}{K_2}\frac{A}{C}$. Therefore,

$$\tan\,\delta = \frac{\frac{A}{C}}{\frac{K_1}{K_2}\,\frac{A}{C}}$$

$$= \frac{A}{C}\cdot\frac{K_2}{K_1}\,\frac{C}{A}$$

$$= \frac{K_2}{K_1}$$

Substitute for K_1 and K_2 from equations (4) and (7) gives

$$\tan\,\delta = \frac{\sqrt{\frac{8\pi^2 mE}{h^2}}}{\sqrt{\frac{8\pi m^2 (U_0 - E)}{h^2}}}$$

$$= \sqrt{\frac{E}{(U_0 - E)}} \qquad (13)$$

From regions II and III boundary conditions

$$\tan(K_2 a + \delta) = \frac{\sin(K_2 a + \delta)}{\cos(K_2 a + \delta)} \qquad (14)$$

From equation (II) $\sin(K_2 a + \delta) = \frac{B'}{C}$ and from equation (12) $\cos(K_2 a + \delta) = \frac{-K_1 B'}{K_2 C} = -\frac{K_1}{K_2}\frac{B'}{C}$. Substitute these values into equation (14) to give

$$\tan(K_2 a + \delta) = \frac{\frac{B'}{C}}{\frac{-K_1}{K_2}\,\frac{B'}{C}}$$

$$= -\frac{B'}{C}\,\frac{K_2}{K_1}\,\frac{C}{B'}$$

$$= -\frac{K_2}{K_1}$$

Using a trigonometry identity, define

$$\tan(K_2 a + \delta) = \frac{\tan K_2 a + \tan\,\delta}{1 - \tan K_2 a\,\tan\,\delta}$$

and $$\tan K_2 a = \frac{2 \tan \delta}{\tan^2 \delta - 1} \tag{15}$$

But from equation (7)

$$K_2 = \sqrt{\frac{8\pi^2 mE}{h^2}}$$

and from equation (13) $\tan \delta = \sqrt{\frac{E}{U_0 - E}}$ therefore equation (15) becomes

$$\tan\sqrt{\frac{8\pi^2 mEa^2}{h^2}} = \frac{2\sqrt{E/(U_0-E)}}{\frac{E}{(U_0-E)} - 1}$$

$$= \frac{2\sqrt{\frac{E}{U_0-E}}}{\frac{2E - U_0}{U_0 - E}}$$

$$= \frac{2\sqrt{\frac{E}{U_0-E}}(U_0-E)}{2E - U_0}$$

$$= \frac{2\sqrt{E(U_0-E)}}{2E - U_0} \tag{16}$$

Equation (16) is the energy equation with the number of bound states dependent on U_0. For example, when $U_0 \gg E$, the right side of the equation approaches zero. Therefore the equation becomes

$$\tan\sqrt{\frac{8\pi^2 ma^2 E}{h^2}} = 0$$

but $\tan n\pi = 0$

$$\therefore \qquad \sqrt{\frac{8\pi^2 ma^2 E}{h^2}} = n\pi$$

Squaring both sides gives

$$\frac{8\pi^2 ma^2 E}{h^2} = n^2\pi^2$$

Solving for E

$$E = \frac{n^2 h^2}{8ma^2}$$

An electron is confined to a molecule of length 1.0 nm (10 Å, about 5 atoms long). What is its minimum energy? What is the minimum excitation energy from this state? What is the probability of finding it in the region of the molecule lying between x = 0.49 nm and x = 0.51 nm? What is the probability of finding it between x = 0 and x = 0.2 nm?

Solution: Energies of a system are said to be quantized, that is, only some energies are possible because other energies correspond to untenable properties of the distribution of the particle. The Schrödinger equation accounts for those quantized energy levels. For a particle free to move in one dimension the Schrödinger equation reads

$$\left(\frac{-h^2}{2m}\right)\left(\frac{d^2}{dx^2}\right)\psi(x) + V(x)\psi(x) = E\psi(x)$$

where ψ is the wavefunction and V(x) is the potential energy of the particle, E is the total energy and $\hbar = h/2\pi$, a modification of Planck's constant. Consider an example of a particle of mass m which is free to move in a straight line between two walls separated by distance x. The potential energy V(x) of the particle is constant and taken to be zero at all points and in the path of the particle except where it hits the wall. The Schrödinger equation for the region between x = 0 and x = L, where the potential energy is zero, is

$$\left(\frac{-\hbar^2}{2m}\right)\frac{d^2\psi}{dx^2} = E\psi(x) \qquad (1)$$

and its solution is in the form

$$\psi(x) = M \cos Kx + N \sin Kx \qquad (2)$$

where $$K = \frac{\sqrt{2mE}}{\hbar} \qquad (3)$$

and M and N are constants. Since one end of the wall is at x = 0 the amplitude of the wave function using equation (2) is

$$\psi(x) = M \cos 0 + N \sin 0$$

$$= M$$

since sin 0 = 0 and cos 0 = 1.

But $\psi(0)$ must be zero for the solution to be acceptable, thus M must be zero. This means that

$$\psi(x) = N \sin Kx.$$

At the other end of the wall, the amplitude is

$$\psi(L) = N \sin KL$$

which must be zero too. But $\psi(0) = 0$ for all x if N = 0 is not acceptable, thus KL must be chosen such that sin KL = 0. This implies that KL be some integral multiple of π since $\sin\theta = 0$ when $\theta = 0, \pi, 2\pi, \ldots$ Therefore the only values of K permitted are those for which

$$KL = n\pi \quad n = 1,2,\ldots \tag{4}$$

The relation between K and E is given in equation (3). Solving for E gives

$$K^2 = \frac{2mE}{\hbar^2}$$

and

$$E = \frac{K^2\hbar^2}{2m} \tag{5}$$

Also from equation (4)

$$K = \frac{n\pi}{L}$$

Substituting for K in equation (5) shows that the energy of the system is confined to the values

$$E = \frac{n^2\pi^2\hbar^2}{2mL^2}$$

$$= \frac{n^2\pi^2h^2}{(2mL^2)(4\pi^2)}$$

$$= \frac{n^2h^2}{8mL^2} \qquad n = 1,2,\ldots \tag{6}$$

Thus the energy of the particle is quantized. The minimum energy is given as $E_2 - E_1$ where E_1 is the ground state (zero point) energy. Equation (6) would be used for calculating E_1 and E_2.

Therefore with n = 1,

$$E_1 = \frac{h^2}{8m_eL^2} = \frac{(6.626 \times 10^{-34}\ \text{J s})^2}{8(9.110 \times 10^{-31}\ \text{kg})(1 \times 10^{-9}\ \text{m})^2}$$

where m_e = mass of electron particle

$$= 6.024 \times 10^{-20}\ \text{J} = 6.024 \times 10^{-23}\ \text{kJ}$$

$$= 6.024 \times 10^{-23}\ \text{kJ} \times 6.023(10^{23})\text{mol}^{-1}$$

$$= 36.28\ \text{kJ mol}^{-1}$$

Using n = 2,

$$E_2 = \frac{2^2 h^2}{8m_e L^2} = 4 \times 6.024 \times 10^{-20} \text{ J} = 24.096 \times 10^{-20} \text{ J}$$

$$= 4 \times 36.28 \text{ kJ mol}^{-1}$$

$$= 145.12 \text{ kJ mol}^{-1}$$

Thus $E_2 - E_1 = 145.12 - 36.28$

$$= 108.84 \text{ kJ mol}^{-1}$$

The distribution of the electron particle under consideration is given by

$$\psi_n(x) = \left(\frac{2}{L}\right)^{\frac{1}{2}} \sin\left(\frac{n\pi x}{L}\right) \tag{2}$$

where n = 1.

For the first part, the region $0.49 \leq x \leq 0.51$ nm is almost infinitesimal and so the probability can be approximated by $[\psi_1^2(x = 0.50)]\delta x$ with $\delta x = 0.51 - 0.49 = 0.02$ nm. From equation (2),

$$\psi_1^2(x = 0.50) = \left(\frac{2}{L}\right)\sin^2 \frac{\pi x}{L}$$

$$= \left(\frac{2}{1.0 \times 10^{-9} \text{ m}}\right)\sin^2\left(\frac{0.5\pi}{1.0}\right)$$

$$= 2 \times 10^9 \text{ m}^{-1}$$

Therefore, the probability of being in the range 0.49 nm to 0.51 nm is

$$(2 \times 10^9 \text{ m}^{-1})(0.02 \text{ nm}) = 0.04.$$

For the second part, the region $0 \leq x \leq 0.2$ nm is not infinitesimal (on the scale of the molecule). Therefore, $\psi_1^2(x)dx$ has to be integrated numerically to get the total probability of being in that region.

The probability of being in the range x = 0 and x = 0.2 nm is therefore

$$\int_{0.0\text{nm}}^{0.2\text{nm}} \psi_1^2(x)dx = (2 \times 10^9 \text{ m}^{-1}) \int_{0.0\text{nm}}^{0.2\text{nm}} \sin^2\left(\frac{\pi x}{1.0\text{nm}}\right)dx$$

$$= (2 \times 10^9 \text{ m}^{-1})\left[\frac{1}{2}x - \left(\frac{1.0\text{nm}}{4\pi}\right)\sin\left(\frac{2\pi x}{1.0\text{nm}}\right)\right]_{0.0\text{nm}}^{0.2\text{nm}}$$

$$= (2 \times 10^9\ m^{-1})\left[(0.1nm) - \left(\frac{1.0nm}{4\pi}\right)\sin(0.4\pi)\right]$$

$$= 0.0486$$

• PROBLEM 12-38

The angular wave function for $\ell = 2$, $m = 0$ is given as

$$Y(\theta,\phi) = \left(\frac{5}{16\pi}\right)^{\frac{1}{2}}(3\cos^2(\theta) - 1)$$

and that for $\ell = 1$, $m = 1$ is

$$Y(\theta,\phi) = \left(\frac{3}{4\pi}\right)^{\frac{1}{2}}\sin\theta\cos\phi.$$

Show that these two functions are orthogonal.

Solution: Consider any dynamic system containing, say n particles. At any time the condition or state of such a system is given by the Schrödinger equation $\psi(q_1,q_2,\ldots,q_{3n},t)$ where q_i represent the coordinates of the system, t is the time and ψ is the wave function. The physical significance of ψ is not clear but $\psi^*\psi$ can be interpreted as the probability of finding a particle within a certain coordinate in space. ψ^* is the complex conjugate of ψ. For a one dimensional problem the coordinate domain is the interval between q_i and $q_i + dq_i$, for a two-dimensional problem the domain is an element of area, while the domain is an element of volume for a three dimensional problem.

If ψ is continuous and integrable, then

$$\int_{\text{all space}} \psi^*\psi\ dV = 1$$

where dV is the volume element and ψ is said to be normalized. On the other hand if

$$\int_{\text{all space}} \psi_i^*\psi_j\ dV = 0 \qquad (1)$$

for two wave functions ψ_i and ψ_j, then the two functions are said to be orthogonal.

In this problem there are two wave functions, so the integration can be carried out to see if their angular parts are zero. Then it can be concluded that the two functions are orthogonal

$$\psi^*\psi\ dV = (3\cos^2(\theta) - 1)(\sin\theta\cos\phi)\sin\theta d\theta d\phi$$

θ has values from 0 to 180° or π. ϕ takes values from 0 to 360° or 2π. Equation (1), using the limits for θ and ϕ, becomes

$$= \int_{\theta=0}^{\theta=\pi} \int_{\phi=0}^{\phi=2\pi} \left(\frac{5}{16\pi}\right)^{\frac{1}{2}} \left(\frac{3}{4\pi}\right)^{\frac{1}{2}} (3\cos^2(\theta)-1)(\sin\theta\cos\phi)\sin\theta d\theta d\phi$$

$$= \int_{\theta}^{\pi} \int_{0}^{2\pi} \left(\frac{15}{64\pi^2}\right)^{\frac{1}{2}} (3\cos^2(\theta)-1)(\sin\theta\cos\phi)\sin\theta d\theta d\phi$$

$$= \frac{\sqrt{15}}{8\pi} \int_0^{\pi} (3\cos^2(2\theta)-1)\sin^2\theta d\theta \int_0^{2\pi} \cos\phi d\phi.$$

The integral over ϕ vanishes as follows.

$$\int_0^{2\pi} \cos\phi d\phi = \sin\phi \Big|_0^{2\pi}$$

$$= \sin 2\pi - \sin 0$$

$$= 0 - 0$$

$$= 0$$

$$\therefore \quad \int \psi^*\psi = 0$$

Therefore, the two functions are orthogonal.

• PROBLEM 12-39

The wave function, ψ, in spherical coordinates is written as

$$\psi(r,\theta,\phi) = R(r)\Theta(\theta)\Phi(\phi)$$

The radial contribution R is a function of r only and R^2 represents the probability of finding the electron at points r and r + dr in space for a hydrogenlike atom. Given the values of r between 0 and $10a_0$, prepare plots of R(r) for the 1s, 2s, 3s, 3p and 3d subshells for hydrogen.

Solution: A hydrogen atom has a positive nucleus and one electron surrounding it. The Bohr radius a_0 is given as

$$a_0 = \frac{4\pi\varepsilon_0\hbar^2}{\mu e^2} \qquad (1)$$

where μ = the reduced mass for hydrogen. e is the electronic charge, ε_0 is the permittivity of vacuum and $\hbar = h/2\pi$. h is Planck's constant. The reduced mass for hydrogen is given by

$$\mu = \frac{m_n m_e}{m_n + m_e}$$

where m_e = mass of the electron and m_n is the mass of the nucleus. Therefore,

$$\frac{1}{\mu} = \frac{m_n + m_e}{m_n m_e} = \frac{m_n}{m_n m_e} + \frac{m_e}{m_n m_e}$$

$$\frac{1}{\mu} = \frac{1}{m_e} + \frac{1}{m_n}$$

But $\frac{1}{m_n}$ is negligibly small compared to $\frac{1}{m_e}$. Therefore $\frac{1}{\mu} = \frac{1}{m_e}$ and $\mu = m_e$. Equation (1) becomes

$$a_0 = \frac{4\pi\left(8.85 \times 10^{-12} \frac{C^2 s^2}{kg\ m^3}\right)\left(1.055 \times 10^{-34} \frac{kg\ m^2}{s}\right)^2}{(9.11 \times 10^{-3}\ kg)(1.602 \times 10^{-19}\ C)^2}$$

$$a_0 = (0.529 \times 10^{-10}\ m)\left(\frac{1\ \mathring{A}}{10^{-10}\ m}\right)$$

or $\quad a_0 = 0.529\ \mathring{A}$.

Values of R(r) for different orbitals can be looked up in any physical chemistry text. For 1s orbital

$$R(r) = 2\left(\frac{Z}{a_0}\right)^{3/2} e^{-Zr/a_0}$$

For hydrogen atom Z = 1 thus for

1s orbital; $\quad R(r) = 2\left(\frac{1}{a_0}\right)^{3/2} = e^{-r/a_0}$

2s orbital; $\quad R(r) = \frac{1}{2\sqrt{6}}\left(\frac{1}{a_0}\right)^{3/2}\left(2 - \frac{r}{a_0}\right)e^{-r/2a_0}$

2p orbital; $\quad R(r) = \frac{1}{2\sqrt{6}}\left(\frac{1}{a_0}\right)^{3/2}\left(\frac{r}{a_0}\right)e^{-r/2a_0}$

3s orbital; $R(r) = \frac{1}{81\sqrt{3}}\left(\frac{1}{a_0}\right)^{3/2}\left[27 - 18\frac{r}{a_0} + 2\left(\frac{r}{a_0}\right)^2\right] e^{-r/3a_0}$

3p orbital; $R(r) = \frac{4}{81\sqrt{6}}\left(\frac{1}{a_0}\right)^{3/2}\left(6 - \frac{r}{a_0}\right)\frac{r}{a_0}\, e^{-r/3a_0}$

3d orbital; $R(r) = \frac{4}{81\sqrt{30}}\left(\frac{1}{a_0}\right)^{3/2}\left(\frac{r}{a_0}\right)^2 e^{-r/3a_0}$

Values of R(r) and $\frac{r}{a_0}$ for the different orbitals are plotted in the figure.

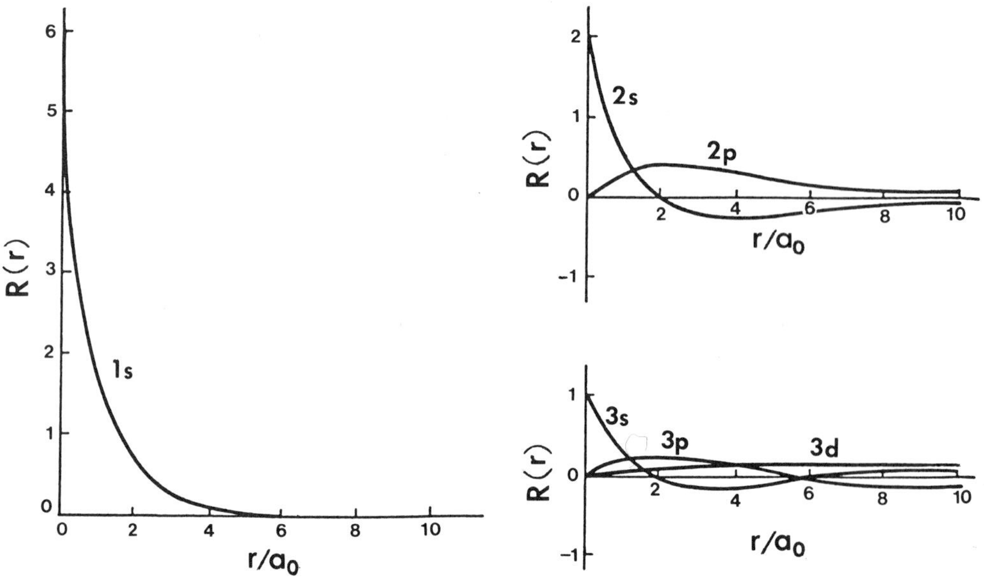

• PROBLEM 12-40

For a hydrogenlike atom the total wave function, ψ is the product of the radial contribution R, and the two angular portions Θ and Φ. The expression for ΘΦ for ℓ = 1 and m = 0 is

$$Y(\theta,\phi) = \left(\frac{3}{4\pi}\right)^{1/2} \cos\theta.$$

With the aid of an arbitrary plane through the z-axis, construct two-dimensional sketches for $Y(\theta,\phi)$ and $Y(\theta,\phi)^*Y(\theta,\phi)$. Describe the three dimensional sketches often encountered.

Solution: A hydrogenlike atom is one in which an electron having a charge of -e and mass m_e, is moving around a nucleus with mass $m_{nucleus}$ and a charge of +Ze; where Z = the atomic number. The postulated basis of all quantum mechanical behavior of matter, is given by the well known Schrödinger wave equation. This equation provides the basis for handling all problems by wave mechanics, and cannot be derived from first principles. The time-independent Schrödinger equation for a particle moving in three-dimensions can be written as

$$\frac{\partial^2\psi}{\partial x^2} + \frac{\partial^2\psi}{\partial y^2} + \frac{\partial^2\psi}{\partial z^2} + \frac{2m}{\hbar^2}(E - V)\psi = 0 \tag{1}$$

where ψ = the wave function, m is the mass of the particle, E is the total energy of the particle, V, its potential energy and $\hbar = h/2\pi$. h is Planck's constant.

For the hydrogenlike atom the nucleus has a charge Ze. Thus its potential energy is

$$\frac{-Ze}{4\pi\varepsilon_0 r},$$

where e = the electronic charge, ε_0 is the permittivity of vacuum. Equation (1) can therefore be rewritten as

$$\frac{\partial^2\psi}{\partial x^2} + \frac{\partial^2\psi}{\partial y^2} + \frac{\partial^2\psi}{\partial z^2} + \frac{2m_e}{\hbar^2}\left(E + \frac{Ze^2}{4\pi\varepsilon_0 r}\right)\psi = 0 \tag{2}$$

where m_e = the mass of the electron. Equation (2) may be solved by converting to spherical coordinates (r,θ,ϕ), whose relation to the cartesian coordinate is shown in figure 1.

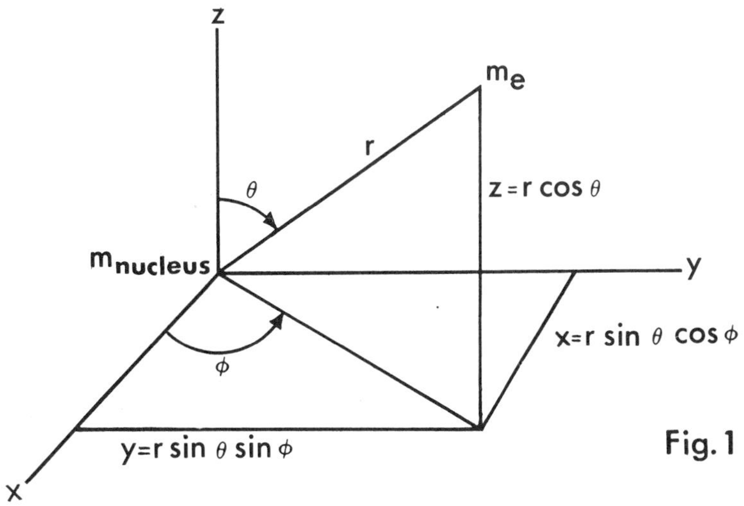

Fig. 1

Thus in terms of r,θ,ϕ, equation (2) becomes

$$\frac{1}{r^2}\frac{\partial}{\partial r}\left(r^2\frac{\partial\psi}{\partial r}\right) + \frac{1}{r^2\sin\theta}\frac{\partial}{\partial\theta}\left(\sin\theta\frac{\partial\psi}{\partial\theta}\right) + \frac{1}{r^2\sin^2\theta}\frac{\partial^2\psi}{\partial\phi^2}$$

$$+\frac{8\pi^2 m_e}{h^2}\left(E + \frac{Ze^2}{4\pi\varepsilon_0 r}\right)\psi = 0 \qquad (3)$$

which can be written as the product of

$$(r,\theta,\phi) = R(r)\Theta(\theta)\Phi(\phi) \qquad (4)$$

three functions R, Θ and Φ each dependent only on r, θ and ϕ respectively.

Equation (4) can be substituted into equation (3) to give three ordinary differential equations, each of which can be solved to give a quantum number. For the hydrogen-like atom, the quantum numbers are: a) the principle quantum number, n with acceptable solutions to equation (3) corresponding to n = 1,2,3,... b) the angular momentum quantum number, ℓ, with values 0,1,2,3,..., (n-1) and c) the magnetic quantum number, m, with acceptable values of $-\ell$, 0, $+\ell$. The total wave function ψ is a product of R, Θ and Φ. The Φ portion depends only on the magnetic quantum number m, and Θ depends on the angular momentum quantum number, ℓ, and also m.

When $\ell = 1$ and $m = 0$, then $Y(\theta,\phi) = (3/4\pi)^{\frac{1}{2}} \cos\theta$. For $\theta = 0$,

$$Y(\theta,\phi) = \left(\frac{3}{4\pi}\right)^{1/2} \cos 0$$

Since cos 0 = 1,

$$Y(\theta,\phi) = \left(\frac{3}{4\pi}\right)^{1/2}$$

Therefore, $Y(\theta,\phi) = 0.489$

and $Y(\theta,\phi)^*Y(\theta,\phi) = [Y(\theta,\phi)]^2$

$$= (0.489)^2$$

$$= 0.239$$

For $\theta = 10°$

$$Y(\theta,\phi) = \left(\frac{3}{4\pi}\right)^{1/2} \cos 10°$$

$$= 0.482$$

and $Y(\theta,\phi)^*Y(\theta,\phi) = (0.482)^2 = 0.232$.

For $\theta = 45°$

$$Y(\theta,\phi) = 0.346$$

$$Y(\theta,\phi)^*Y(\theta,\phi) = (0.346)^2 = 0.119$$

For $\theta = 90°$

$$Y(\theta,\phi) = \left(\frac{3}{4\pi}\right)^{1/2} \cos 90°. \quad \text{But } \cos 90° = 0.$$

Therefore, $Y(\theta,\phi) = 0$ and $Y(\theta,\phi)*Y(\theta,\phi) = 0$.

For $\theta = 180°$

$$Y(\theta,\phi) = -0.489 \quad \text{and} \quad Y(\theta,\phi)*Y(\theta,\phi) = +0.239$$

For $\theta = 270°$

$$Y(\theta,\phi) = 0 \;,\; Y(\theta,\phi)*Y(\theta,\phi) = 0$$

For $\theta = 360°$

$$Y(\theta,\phi) = 0.489 \;,\; Y(\theta,\phi)*Y(\theta,\phi) = 0.239$$

With these values plot the curves shown in figures 2(a) and 2(b) for $Y(\theta,\phi)$ and $[Y(\theta,\phi)*Y(\theta,\phi)]$ respectively.

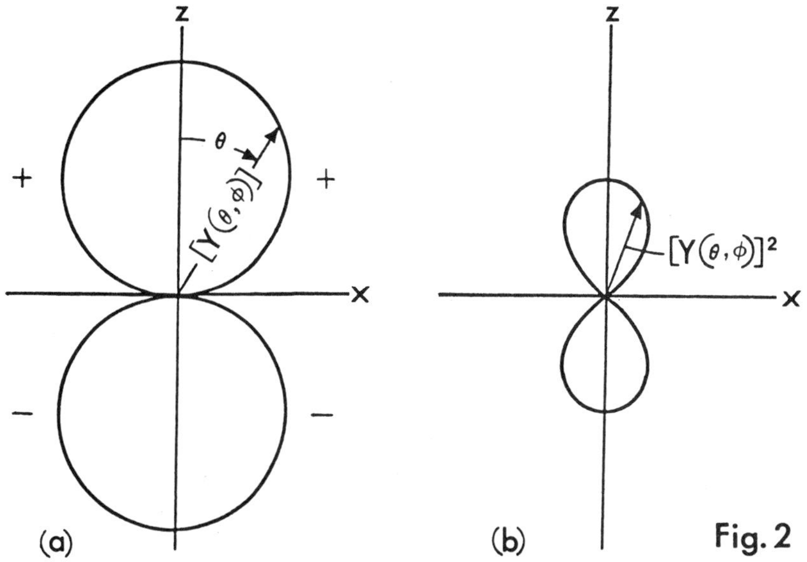

Fig. 2

If the curves in figure 2 are rotated about the z axis, three dimensional curves can be generated as shown in figure 3. They are often encountered in many textbooks.

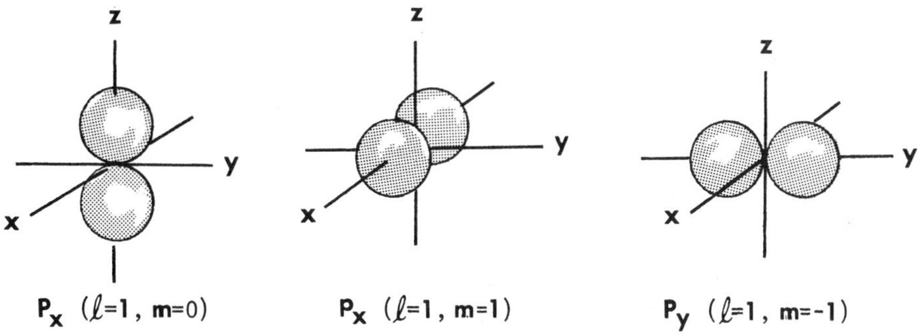

Fig. 3

The orbitals of figure 3 are called P_z, P_x and P_y orbitals because their surfaces are extended along the z-axis, x-axis, and y-axis respectively and also ℓ = 1.

• PROBLEM 12-41

Which of the following statements concerning the function of two of the four quantum numbers n and ℓ, with respect to their orbital, is/are correct.

(a) n determines the shape of an orbital
(b) ℓ determines the size of an orbital
(c) n determines the size of an orbital
(d) ℓ determines the shape of an orbital
(e) n determines the number of lobes of electron density in an orbital.

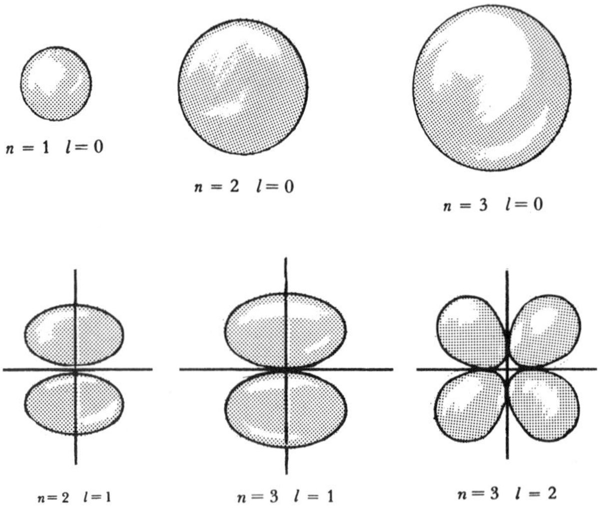

Solution: The solutions of the Schrödinger wave equation can be illustrated by means of electron probability diagrams called orbitals; six of which are shown in the figure. Looking at the first two columns of the figure, n increases but ℓ remains constant, and in the process, the size of an orbital type increases. But the shape and the number of lobes of the electron density remains unchanged. It can be said therefore, that n determines the size of orbitals whether they are spherical, dumbell or lobed, and not the shape. Statement c) is thus correct while statements a) and e) are incorrect.

Now as ℓ increases while n is kept constant, the shape of the orbitals change. Thus statement d) is correct while statement b) is incorrect. Statements c) and a) are correct.

• **PROBLEM 12-42**

Which of the following combinations of quantum numbers represent permissible solutions of the Schrödinger wave equation for the hydrogen atom:

	n	ℓ	m	s
a)	3	0	1	$-\frac{1}{2}$
b)	2	2	0	$+\frac{1}{2}$
c)	4	3	-4	$-\frac{1}{2}$
d)	5	2	2	$+\frac{1}{2}$
e)	3	2	-2	$-\frac{3}{4}$

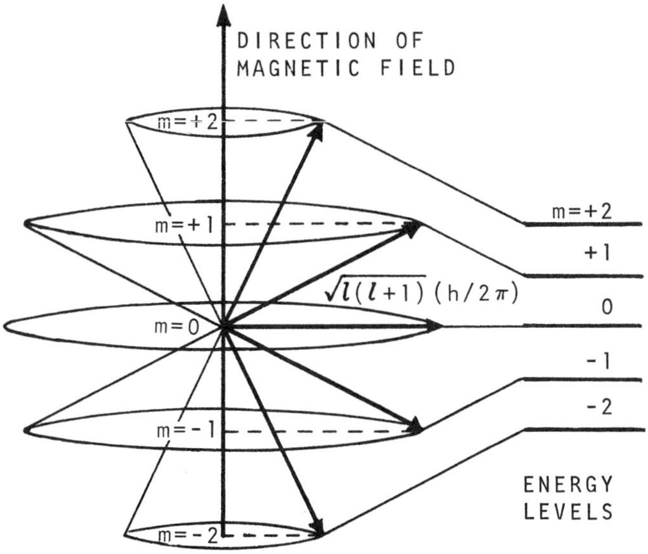

QUANTIZATION OF THE COMPONENTS OF ANGULAR MOMENTUM IN A MAGNETIC FIELD **B** FOR THE CASE $\ell=2$.

Solution: The hydrogen atom is described by four quantum numbers: n, the principal quantum number, ℓ, the angular momentum quantum number, m, the magnetic quantum number and s, the spin quantum number. Pauli exclusion principle states that, no two electrons in an atom can have the same four quantum numbers. Permissible values of the quantum numbers are:

$n = 1, 2, 3, \ldots$

$\ell = 0, 1, 2, \ldots, (n-1)$

$m = -\ell, \ldots, 0, \ldots, +\ell$

$s = -\frac{1}{2}$ or $+\frac{1}{2}$

In combination a), $\ell = 0$ and $m = 1$. This is incorrect bebause accroding to permissible values for m, it cannot be greater than zero when $\ell = 0$. In combination b), $n = 2$ and $\ell = 2$. This too is incorrect because when $n = 2$, $\ell = (n-1) = 1$, and as such ℓ cannot be greater than 1. $\ell = 3$ and $m = -4$ in combination c); but m cannot be less than -3 when $\ell = 3$ since this will be contrary to the permissible values of m. Thus, statement c) is incorrect. Combination d) is correct since it is in accordance with the permissible values of the four quantum numbers. In combination e) s is given as $-3/2$ but s cannot take any values other than $+1/2$ or $-1/2$ so combination e) is incorrect.

Only combination d) is correct and valid.

• PROBLEM 12-43

The wave function for the state of lowest energy of a one-dimensional harmonic oscillator is $\psi = Ae^{-Bx^2}$, where A is a normalization constant and $B = (\mu K)^{\frac{1}{2}}/2\hbar$. The potential energy is $U = \frac{1}{2}Kx^2$. Derive the total energy E by substituting ψ into the Schrödinger equation.

Solution: Since the wave function for the state of lowest energy of a one-dimensional harmonic oscillator is

$\psi = Ae^{-Bx^2}$,

$$\frac{d\psi}{dx} = -2ABxe^{-Bx^2} \qquad (1)$$

and

$$\frac{d^2\psi}{dx^2} = -2ABe^{-Bx^2} + 4AB^2x^2e^{-Bx^2}$$

$$= 2BAe^{-Bx^2}(-1 + 2Bx^2) \qquad (2)$$

But $\psi = Ae^{-Bx^2}$,

Therefore, equation (2) becomes

$$\frac{d^2\psi}{dx^2} = 2B\psi(-1 + 2Bx^2)$$

$$= -2B\psi + 4B^2\psi x^2 \qquad (3)$$

For one-dimensional problems, the Schrödinger equation is

$$\frac{d^2\psi}{dx^2} + \left(\frac{2\mu}{\hbar^2}\right)\left(E - U(x)\right)\psi = 0 \tag{4}$$

Note that throughout this problem,

ψ = wave function

E = total energy

U(x) = potential energy

$\hbar = \frac{h}{2\pi}$ and h = Planck's constant

μ = reduced mass

Since $\frac{d^2\psi}{dx^2}$ has been derived and U(x) and B are given, equation (4) becomes

$$-2B\psi + 4B^2x^2\psi + \frac{2\mu}{\hbar^2}(E - \tfrac{1}{2}Kx^2)\psi = 0 \tag{5}$$

or $$-2\frac{(\mu K)^{\frac{1}{2}}}{2\hbar} + \frac{4\mu Kx^2}{4\hbar^2} + \frac{2\mu E}{\hbar^2} - \frac{\mu Kx^2}{\hbar^2} = 0.$$

From this, $$\frac{2\mu E}{\hbar^2} = \frac{\mu Kx^2}{\hbar^2} + \frac{(\mu K)^{\frac{1}{2}}}{\hbar} - \frac{\mu Kx^2}{\hbar^2}$$

$$= \frac{\mu Kx^2 - \mu Kx^2 + \hbar(\mu K)^{\frac{1}{2}}}{\hbar^2}$$

$$\frac{2\mu}{\hbar^2}E = \frac{\hbar(\mu K)^{\frac{1}{2}}}{\hbar^2}$$

or $$E = \frac{\hbar(\mu K)^{\frac{1}{2}}}{2\mu} = \frac{\hbar}{2}\sqrt{\frac{K}{\mu}} \tag{6}$$

Recall that $\hbar = \frac{h}{2\pi}$

Hence equation (6) becomes

$$E = \frac{h}{2}\,\frac{1}{2\pi}\sqrt{\frac{K}{\mu}} = \frac{1}{2}h\left(\frac{1}{2\pi}\sqrt{\frac{K}{\mu}}\right)$$

$$= \frac{h}{2}\nu$$

where $\nu = \frac{1}{2\pi}\sqrt{\frac{K}{\mu}}$ = fundamental frequency.

• **PROBLEM 12-44**

Which of the following operators is Hermitian; d/dx, i d/dx, d^2/dx^2?

Solution: An operator A is said to be Hermitian (or self-adjoint) if it has the following property:

$$\int \alpha^* A\beta dx = \int \beta (A\alpha)^* dx$$

with respect to all the functions.

a) for the operator $\frac{d}{dx}$,

$$\langle \frac{d}{dx} \rangle = \int_{-\infty}^{\infty} \alpha^* \frac{d\alpha}{dx} dx$$

$$= \alpha^* \alpha \Big|_{-\infty}^{\infty} - \int_{-\infty}^{\infty} \alpha \frac{d\alpha^*}{dx} dx$$

$$= - \int_{-\infty}^{\infty} \alpha \frac{d\alpha^*}{dx} dx$$

Thus the operator $\langle d/dx \rangle$ is non-Hermitian.

b) for i $\frac{d}{dx}$,

$$\langle i \frac{d}{dx} \rangle = \int_{-\infty}^{\infty} i\alpha^* \frac{d\alpha}{dx} dx$$

$$= i\alpha^* \alpha \Big|_{-\infty}^{\infty} - \int_{-\infty}^{\infty} i\alpha \frac{d\alpha^*}{dx} dx$$

$$= - \int_{-\infty}^{\infty} i\alpha \frac{d\alpha^*}{dx} dx$$

c) for $\frac{d^2}{dx^2}$,

$$\langle \frac{d^2}{dx^2} \rangle = \int_{-\infty}^{\infty} \alpha^* \frac{d^2\alpha}{dx^2} dx = \alpha^* \frac{d\alpha}{dx} \Big|_{-\infty}^{\infty} - \int_{-\infty}^{\infty} \frac{d\alpha}{dx} \frac{d\alpha^*}{dx} dx$$

$$= - \int_{-\infty}^{\infty} \frac{d\alpha}{dx} \frac{d\alpha^*}{dx} dx$$

$$= - \frac{d\alpha^*}{dx}\Bigg|_{-\infty}^{\infty} + \int_{-\infty}^{\infty} \alpha \frac{d^2\alpha^*}{dx^2} dx$$

$$= \int_{-\infty}^{\infty} \alpha \frac{d^2\alpha^*}{dx^2} = \langle \frac{d^2}{dx^2} \rangle$$

The above results show that only b and c are Hermitian.

CHAPTER 13

THE SOLID STATE

CRYSTAL STRUCTURES

• PROBLEM 13-1

What is the plane of closest packing in the fcc and bcc structures? What is the relation between the length of cube a_0 and the closest internuclear distance in these structures?

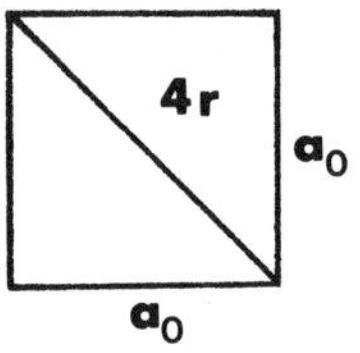

Solution: For a face-centered cubic unit cell, the plane of closest packing is 111 plane while that of a body-centered cubic unit cell is 110 plane.

There are two atoms on the face diagonal of an fcc. If r is taken to be the radius of an atom (spherical in shape) at a lattice point, then the length of a face diagonal is 4r. Note that there are 2r in each face diagonal.

From the diagram and using the Pythagorean theorem,

$$a_0^2 + a_0^2 = (4r)^2$$

or

$$2a_0^2 = (4r)^2$$

$$\therefore \quad a_0 = \frac{4r}{\sqrt{2}} = \frac{2(\sqrt{2})(\sqrt{2})r}{\sqrt{2}}$$

$$= 2\sqrt{2}\ r$$

Similarly, for a body-centered cube, the length of the body diagonal is 4r; But this time, $(4r)^2 = a_0^2 + a_0^2 + a_0^2 = 3a_0^2$ from which

$$a_0^2 = \frac{(4r)^2}{3}$$

or

$$a_0 = \frac{4r}{\sqrt{3}}$$

• PROBLEM 13-2

Tetraborane is monoclinic with a = 0.868, b = 1.014, c = 0.578 nm, $\beta = 105.9°$. Draw a diagram showing the a and c axes and the orientation of the 101 planes. Calculate the interplanar spacing for 101 based on your diagram.

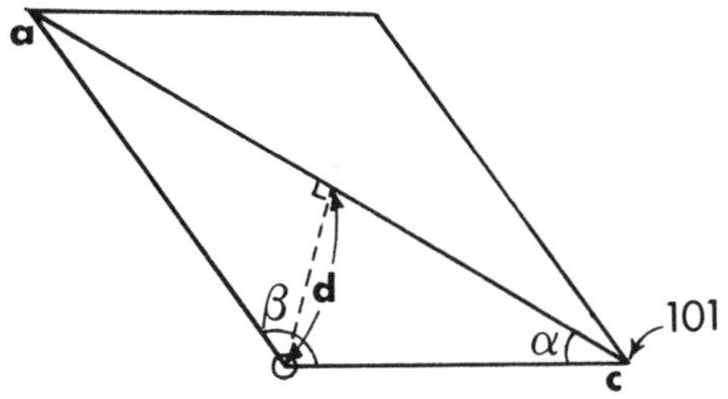

Solution: The diagram that shows a and c axes and the orientation of the 101 plane is shown below as follows:
Let the distance between the axes a and c be h. By the cosine rule,

$$h^2 = a^2 + c^2 - 2ac \cos \beta$$

or

$$h = \sqrt{a^2 + c^2 - 2ac \cos \beta} \tag{1}$$

Substituting the given values into equation (1) gives

$$h = \sqrt{(0.868)^2 + (0.578)^2 - 2(0.868)(0.578)\cos 105.9°}$$

$$= \sqrt{0.753 + 0.334 - 1.003(-0.274)}$$

$$= \sqrt{1.087 + 0.2748} = \sqrt{1.3618}$$

$$= 1.167 \text{ nm}.$$

Similarly, $a^2 = h^2 + c^2 - 2hc \cos \alpha$. (2)

From equation (2),

$$\cos \alpha = -\left(\frac{a^2 - h^2 - c^2}{2hc}\right)$$

$$= \frac{h^2 + c^2 - a^2}{2hc} \tag{3}$$

Substituting for h, c and a in equation (3) yields

$$\cos \alpha = \frac{(1.167)^2 + (0.578)^2 - (0.868)^2}{2(1.167)(0.578)}$$

$$= \frac{1.362 + 0.334 - 0.753}{1.349}$$

$$= \frac{0.943}{1.349} = 0.699$$

or

$$\alpha = \cos^{-1} 0.699 = 45.65°$$

Note that the desired distance is d. Using the relation

$$\sin \alpha = \frac{d}{c}$$

then

$$d = c \sin \alpha = (0.578)\sin 45.65°$$

$$= 0.413 \text{ nm}.$$

• PROBLEM 13-3

Sodium crystallizes in the body-centered cubic structure with $a = 4.24$ Å. Calculate the theoretical density of Na.

Solution: The content of a body-centered unit cell is $8(1/8) + 1 = 2$. In a body-centered cell, there are eight corners and their contribution is $8(1/8) = 1$. In other words, every corner of the unit cell contributes 1/8 of an atom. Also there is an atom on the body, which is not shared, making it 2 altogether.

$$d = \text{density} = \frac{ZM}{AV} \qquad (1)$$

where Z = content = 2
M = Molecular weight
A = Avogadro's number
$V = abc(1 - \cos^2\alpha - \cos^2\beta - \cos^2\gamma + 2\cos\alpha\cos\beta\cos\gamma)^{\frac{1}{2}}$

But for a cell having 90° (as in this case), $V = abc$. a,b and c are lengths of the edges. V = Volume. Therefore

$$V = (4.24\text{Å})^3 = (4.24 \times 10^{-10}\text{m})^3$$

Using (1),

$$d = \frac{(2)(23\text{ gm mol}^{-1})(10^{-3}\text{kg gm}^{-1})}{(6.022 \times 10^{23}\text{ mol}^{-1})(4.24 \times 10^{-10}\text{m})^3}$$

$$= 1.00 \times 10^3 \text{ kg m}^{-3} \ .$$

• PROBLEM 13-4

Using the following ionic radii, find the fractional void volume in (a) CsCl, (b) NaCl, (c) LiCl. Assume that the ions are hard spheres in contact.

Ion	Radius, Å
Li^+	0.60
Na^+	0.95
Cs^+	1.69
Cl^-	1.81

In CsCl the positive ions and the negative ions each comprise a simple cubic lattice. Each ion has eight oppositely charged ions as nearest neighbors. In NaCl and LiCl the ions of each sign comprise a face-centered cubic lattice. Each ion has six oppositely charged ions as nearest neighbors.

Solution: a) CsCl:

Since the CsCl is to be taken as a simple cubic lattice, the unit cell has two atoms. If the Cl^- ions are considered to be at the corners of the unit cell and the Cs^+ ion at the body, then the unit cell contains

$$1\ Cs^+ + 8(1/8)\ Cl^- = 2\ .$$

There are two possible ways to compute the length of the edge. First if the Cl^- ions are in contact along the edge, the length will be $1.81 + 1.81 = 3.62$ Å . Second, if the Cs^+ and Cl^- ions are in contact along the body diagonal, then the length of the diagonal is

$$1.81 + 2(1.69) + 1.81 = 7.00 \text{ Å} .$$

Consequently, the length of the edge is

$$\frac{7.00}{\sqrt{3}} = 4.04 \text{ Å} .$$

Since the latter value is larger, the length of the edge must be 4.04 Å .

By definition, the volume of the unit cell is given by $V = a^3$. Therefore,

$$V = (4.04 \text{ Å})^3 = 65.9 \text{ Å}^3 .$$

The ions are assumed to be spherical in shape and the volume of a sphere is given by $4/3\ \pi r^3$. For both Cs^+ and Cl^- , the volume is

$$4/3\ \pi(1.69)^3 + 4/3\ \pi(1.81)^3 = 4/3\ \pi(1.69^3 + 1.81^3)$$

$$= 4.2(4.82 + 5.9) = 45.1 \text{ Å} .$$

The fraction void is

$$\frac{65.9 - 45.1}{65.9} = \frac{65.9}{65.9} - \frac{45.1}{65.9}$$

$$= 1 - 0.684 = 0.316 .$$

b) NaCl:

Since this is a face-centered cubic lattice, it has 4 "atoms". Therefore, it contains $4\ Na^+ + 4\ Cl^-$. If the Cl^- ions are considered to be in contact along a face diagonal, then the diagonal is

$$4r = (4)(1.81) = 7.24 \text{ Å} \text{ long.}$$

As a result, the length of the edge is

$$7.24/\sqrt{2} = 5.12 \text{ Å} .$$

Secondly, if Na^+ and Cl^- are in contact along an edge, then the edge is

$$2(0.95 + 1.81) = 5.52 \text{ Å} .$$

If on the other hand the Na^+ and Cl^- are considered to be in contact along the body diagonal, this diagonal is

$$2(0.95 + 1.81) = 5.52 \text{ Å} ,$$

and the edge is

$$5.52/\sqrt{3} = 3.19 \text{ Å} \text{ long.}$$

The largest of these values must be the correct one. Consequently, the length of the edge is 5.52 Å .

The volume of the unit cell is therefore

$$(5.52 \text{ Å})^3 = 168 \text{ Å}^3 .$$

The volume of

$$4Na^+ = 4(\frac{4}{3}\ \pi\ (0.95)^3) = 14.37 \text{ Å}^3$$

while that of

$$4Cl^- = 4(\frac{4}{3}\ \pi\ (1.81)^3) = 99.37 \text{ Å}^3 .$$

The total volume of the ions is

$$14.37 + 99.37 = 113.74 \text{ Å}^3 .$$

The fraction void volume

$$= \frac{168 - 113.74}{168}$$

$$= 1 - \frac{113.74}{168} = 0.32 .$$

c) LiCl:

For this, edge contact is $2(0.60 + 1.81) = 4.82$ Å. Face diagonal contact is

$$4(1.81/\sqrt{2}) = 5.12 \text{ Å} .$$

Body diagonal contact is $4.82/\sqrt{3} = 2.78$ Å. The largest of these must be the length of the edge. Therefore, the correct one is 5.12 Å, from which

$$V = a^3 = (5.12)^3 = 134 \text{ Å}^3 .$$

Volume of the ions is given by $4(\frac{4}{3}\pi(0.60^3 + 1.81^3)) = 103$ Å^3. Therefore, the fraction void volume $= \frac{134 - 103}{134} = 1 - \frac{103}{134} = 0.23.$

• PROBLEM 13-5

Determine the coordinate number for an atom in the body-centered cubic unit cell.

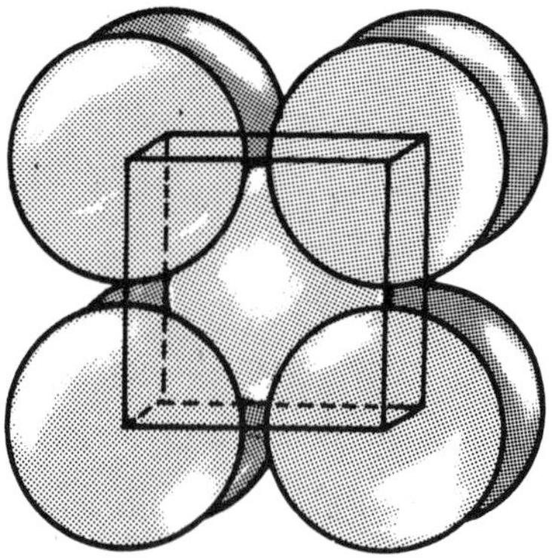

Fig. 1

Solution: Fig. 1 is an example of a body centered cubic cell. Now consider the atom in the center, it is surrounded by eight atoms. These are called the nearest neighbor atoms. In other words, the atom in the center of a body centered cubic unit cell is surrounded by eight nearest neighbor atoms.

By definition, the coordinate number of an atom in a crystal is the number of nearest-neighbor atoms. Therefore, a body centered cubic unit cell has a coordinate number of 8.

• PROBLEM 13-6

Potassium crystallizes with a body-centered cubic lattice and has a density of 0.856 g cm^{-3}. Calculate the length of the side of the unit cell a and the distance between (200), (110), and (222) planes.

Solution: a) The relationship between the theoretical density of a unit cell and its dimensions is given by

$$d = \frac{CM}{AV} \tag{1}$$

where d = density
c = the contents of the unit cell (that is the number of points contained within it).
M = the molecular weight of the substance that makes up the cell.
A = Avogadro's number.
V = volume, which is a^3 in this problem.

For a body-centered cubic unit cell, the contribution of the eight corners is 8(1/8) = 1, and that of the body-centered atom is 1. Therefore, the contents of the unit cell, c = 1 + 1 = 2. Since the molecular weight of potassium is 39.098 g mol^{-1} and Avogadro's number,

$$A = 6.02 \times 10^{23}\ mol^{-1},$$

then equation (1) becomes

$$d = \frac{(2)(39.098\ g\ mol^{-1})}{(6.02 \times 10^{23}\ mol^{-1})a^3} \tag{2}$$

But $d = 0.856\ g\ cm^{-3}$. Hence equation (2) can be written in the form

$$0.856\ g\ cm^{-3} = \frac{(2)(39.098\ g\ mol^{-1})}{(6.02 \times 10^{23}\ mol^{-1})a^3}\ .$$

Solving for a^3 yields

$$a^3 = \frac{(2)(39.098\ g\ mol^{-1})}{(6.02 \times 10^{23}\ mol^{-1})(0.856\ g\ cm^{-3})}$$

$$= \left[\frac{(78.196)}{5.15 \times 10^{23}}\right] cm^3$$

$$= 1.517 \times 10^{-22}\ cm^3$$

Therefore, $a = 5.33 \times 10^{-8}\ cm = 5.33\ \mathring{A}$.

b) The interplanar distance within a unit cell is related to its (unit cell) dimensions by

$$\frac{1}{d^2_{hkl}} = \frac{h^2}{a^2} + \frac{k^2}{b^2} + \frac{l^2}{c^2}\ .$$

But, in this problem a = b = c. Therefore

$$\frac{1}{d^2_{hkl}} = \frac{h^2}{a^2} + \frac{k^2}{a^2} + \frac{l^2}{a^2} = \frac{h^2 + k^2 + l^2}{a^2} \tag{3}$$

where d = interplanar distance between the Miller indices.
hkl = Miller indices .
Taking the reciprocal of equation (3) gives

$$d^2_{hkl} = \frac{a^2}{h^2+k^2+l^2} \tag{4}$$

and taking the square root of equation (4) yields

$$\sqrt{d^2_{hkl}} = \frac{\sqrt{a^2}}{\sqrt{h^2+k^2+l^2}}$$

$$\therefore \quad d_{hkl} = \frac{a}{\sqrt{h^2+k^2+l^2}} \qquad (5)$$

For planes of (200) Miller indices, equation (5) gives

$$d_{200} = \frac{5.33\ \mathring{A}}{\sqrt{2^2+0^2+0^2}}$$

$$= \frac{5.33\ \mathring{A}}{\sqrt{4}} = \frac{5.33\ \mathring{A}}{2} = 2.665\ \mathring{A}\ .$$

For (110) planes,

$$d_{110} = \frac{5.33\ \mathring{A}}{\sqrt{1^2+1^2+0^2}}$$

$$\therefore \quad d_{110} = \frac{5.33\ \mathring{A}}{\sqrt{2}} = 3.77\ \mathring{A}\ .$$

For (222) planes,

$$d_{222} = \frac{5.33\ \mathring{A}}{\sqrt{2^2+2^2+2^2}}$$

$$d_{222} = \frac{5.33\ \mathring{A}}{\sqrt{12}} = 1.540\ \mathring{A}\ .$$

• PROBLEM 13-7

List and explain the possible solid state defects that can occur in crystals.

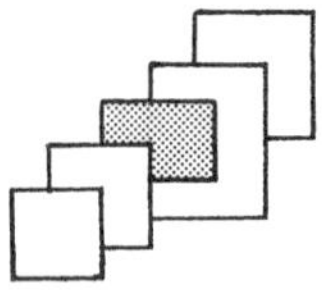

Fig. 1

Solution: The main type of solid state defects that can occur in crystals are lattice defects. There are three major types of lattice defects: lattice vacancies, lattice interstitials, and dislocations. Lattice vacancies are by far the most common of the three. They arise when some of the lattice points are unoccupied (some atoms are missing). This type of defect occurs to a small extent in all crystals, and properties such as diffusion and ionic conductivity can be explained by it.

Lattice interstitials arise if some atoms are pushed in and therefore occupy positions between lattice points. This occurs when small cations migrate into locations between normal planes of large anions.

The third type of lattice defect is dislocation. It consists of two types, edge dislocation and screw dislocation.

Edge dislocation comes about when an extra half-plane of atoms is inserted only partially in the upper half of a crystal as shown in Figure 1. The dislocation line is the shaded plane of the crystal.

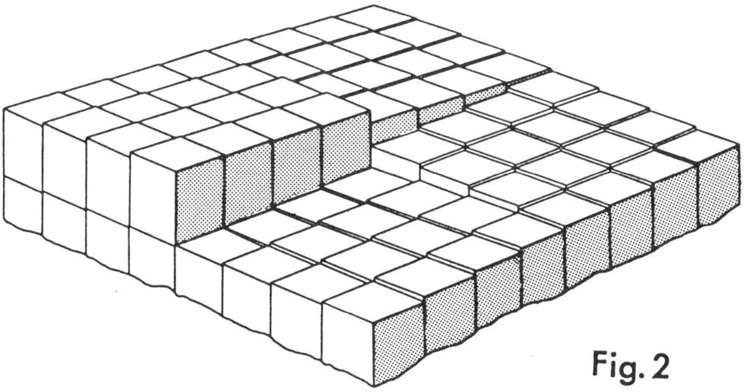

Fig. 2

As a result of this, the interatomic distances in the upper half crystal are compressed and those in the lower half-crystal are extended setting up tension. This effect is similar to moving a rug by pushing a crease down it.
Screw dislocation can be depicted when there is a fault line in a crystal and a resulting shift of the planes of the crystal relative to one another, as shown in Figure 2.
Here the atoms to the left of the fault line are being pushed up through the distance of a unit cell. The unit cells of the crystal now form a continuous spiral around the end of the fault line, which is the screw axis, and breaks through to the surface where it takes the form of a spiral ramp. The dislocation line is along the axis of the unit cell.

MILLER INDICES

• PROBLEM 13-8

Consider the plane shown in the Fig. below which intersects the x-,y- and z-axes at a,b and c, the unit cell dimensions, respectively. What are the Miller indices for this plane?

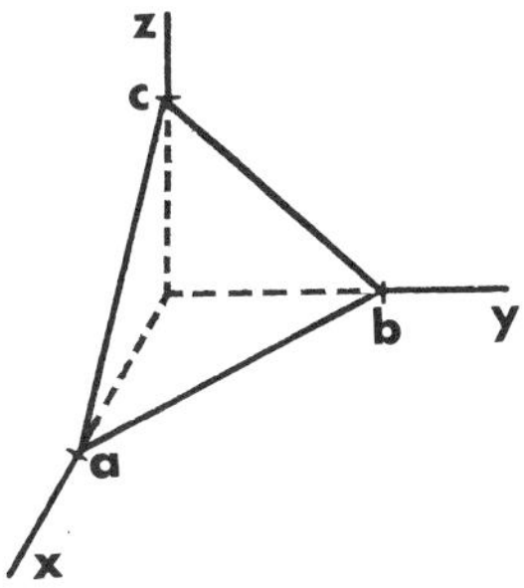

Solution: Miller indices for a plane is prepared in the following manner: (a) Make a three-column table with the three axes of the unit cell at the top of the columns.
(b) Enter in each column the intercept of the plane with that axis (this makes the first row).
(c) For the second row, invert all numbers.
(d) Then clear all fractions in the last (third) row.
Now if these steps are followed very carefully, a table as seen below would be obtained.

	1st column a	2nd column b	3rd column c	
First row:	1	1	1	the intercepts.
Second row:	$\frac{1}{1} = 1$	$\frac{1}{1} = 1$	$\frac{1}{1} = 1$	inversion of the numbers, otherwise known as reciprocals.
Third row:	1	1	1	clear fractions

Essentially, the last (third) row is the answer to our problem. (Make sure all fractions are cleared). The Miller indices (hkl) of this plane is thus (111).

• PROBLEM 13-9

Find the spacing between the planes with indices 101 in NaCl if a = 5.6402 Å .

Solution: By definition, $\frac{1}{d^2_{hkl}} = \frac{h^2 + k^2 + l^2}{a^2}$ (1)

where d = spacing

hkl = Miller indices (101 respectively in this case). Substituting the respective values into (1), yields

$$\frac{1}{d^2_{101}} = \frac{1^2 + 0^2 + 1^2}{(5.6402\ \text{Å})^2} = \frac{2}{31.81\ \text{Å}^2}$$

$$d^2_{101} = \frac{31.81\ \text{Å}^2}{2}$$

$$\therefore \quad d_{101} = \sqrt{\frac{31.81\ \text{Å}^2}{2}} = \frac{5.6402\ \text{Å}}{1.4142} = 3.9883\ \text{Å}\ .$$

Note that the general formula is

$$\frac{1}{d^2_{hkl}} = \frac{h^2}{a^2} + \frac{k^2}{b^2} + \frac{l^2}{c^2}\ ;$$

but in this problem, a = b = c .

UNIT CELLS

• PROBLEM 13-10

Determine the content for the body-centered cubic unit cell shown in the Fig. below.

Solution: There are eight corners in a body-centered cubic cell. The contribution of one corner is 1/8 of an atom. Therefore, the eight corners contribute

$$\frac{1}{8} + \frac{1}{8} + \frac{1}{8} + \frac{1}{8} + \frac{1}{8} + \frac{1}{8} + \frac{1}{8} + \frac{1}{8} = 8(\frac{1}{8}) = 1\ .$$

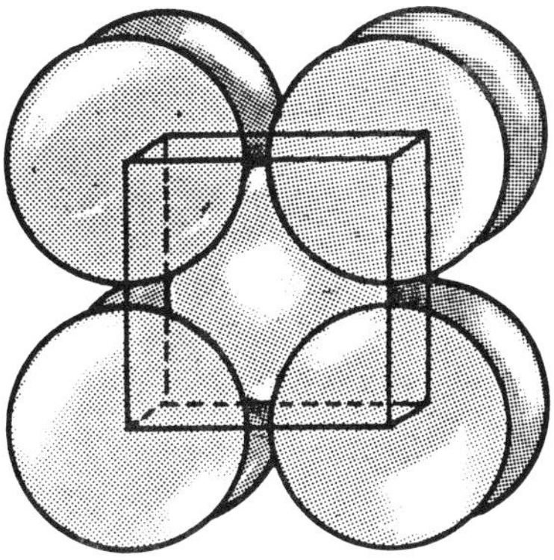

We can also see that there is one atom in the center unshared by any corner. Consequently, there are

$$[8(\frac{1}{8}) + 1] \text{ atoms} = 2 \text{ atoms}$$

in a body-centered cubic unit cell.

• PROBLEM 13-11

Polonium is the only element known to crystallize in a primitive cubic unit cell under room conditions. If $a = 3.36$ Å, find the theoretical density.

Solution: Density, $d = \frac{ZM}{AV}$.

Z = content = 1 .
M = Molecular weight
A = Avogadro's number
V = Volume = a^3 in this case .

But $V = (3.36 \text{ Å})^3 = (3.36 \times 10^{-10} \text{m})^3$

$$\therefore \quad d = \frac{(1)(209 \text{ gm/mole})(10^{-3} \text{kg/gm})}{(6.022 \times 10^{23} \text{mole}^{-1})(3.36 \times 10^{-10} \text{m})^3}$$

$$= 9.15 \times 10^3 \text{ kg/m}^3 .$$

Note that a primitive unit cell has points only at the corners of a parallelepiped. So the total contribution from all corners = 1. This is why Z = content = 1, unlike others like edge-centered, body-centered or face centered cells that have points on the edge, body and face respectively (as suggested by their names.)

• PROBLEM 13-12

Find the distance between two Po atoms that lie along a body diagonal if

$$a = 3.36 \text{ Å} .$$

Solution: Po atoms form a cubic unit cell. The distance, L, between two atoms in a cubic unit cell is

$$L = \sqrt{a^2(x_2-x_1)^2 + a^2(y_2-y_1)^2 + a^2(z_2-z_1)^2} \qquad (1)$$

where $(x_1y_1z_1)$ and $(x_2y_2z_2)$ are their respective coordinates. In this case $(x_1y_1z_1) = (000)$ and $(x_2y_2z_2) = (111)$. Substituting these values into equation (1) gives

$$L = \sqrt{(3.36)^2[(1-0)^2 + (1-0)^2 + (1-0)^2]} = 3.36\ \text{Å}\sqrt{3}$$

$$= (3.36\ \text{Å})(1.732) = 5.8197\ \text{Å} = 5.820\ \text{Å}.$$

• PROBLEM 13-13

Determine the coordination number for an atom in the primitive cubic unit cell.

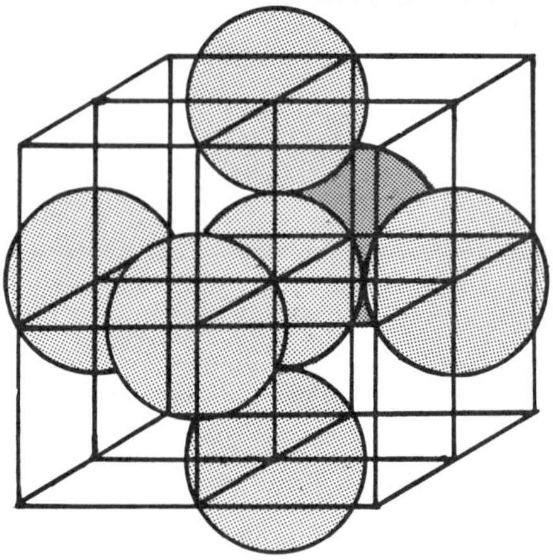

Solution: If the primitive cubic unit cell were translated to generate several unit cells as shown in the fig. below around any given atom there would be six equally-spaced nearest-neighbor atoms at a distance a. Thus coordination number = 6. Any other atoms in the crystal lattice will be at a distance greater than a from the atom under consideration.

• PROBLEM 13-14

Find the relationship between a and R for a primitive cubic unit cell and calculate R for Po if

$$a = 3.36\ \text{Å}.$$

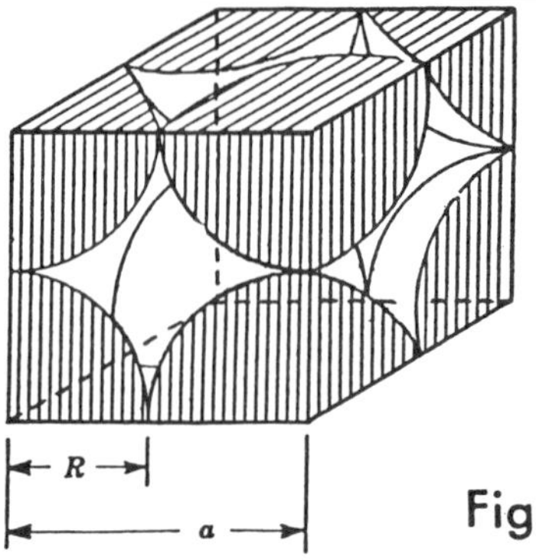

Fig. 1

Solution: By definition, R is the radius of an atom and a is the distance between the centers of two atoms which touch as shown in Fig. 1.

The relationship between a and R can be written as $R = \frac{1}{2} a$. Therefore $a = 2R$. Since

$$a = 3.36 \text{ Å}, \quad R = \tfrac{1}{2}(3.36) = 1.68 \text{ Å} .$$

• PROBLEM 13-15

Show that the void volume for structures of closest packed spheres is 25.9% in both ccp and hcp. For spheres of radius 0.100nm, calculate a_0 for ccp, and a_0, c_0 for hcp.

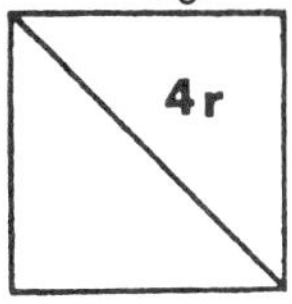

Solution: a) A cubic closest packed (ccp) unit cell has the same dimensions as the face centered cubic cell. For a face centered cubic, the length of the diagonal = 4r. Using the Pythagorean theorem,

$$(4r)^2 = a_0^2 + a_0^2$$

$$16r^2 = 2a_0^2$$

or

$$a_0 = \sqrt{\frac{16r^2}{2}} = \frac{4r}{\sqrt{2}} = \frac{2\sqrt{2}\sqrt{2}}{\sqrt{2}} r$$

$$= 2\sqrt{2}\, r .$$

The volume of this cell is therefore $(2\sqrt{2}\, r)^3 = a_0^3 = 8(\sqrt{2})^3 r^3$

$$= (8)(2)\sqrt{2}\, r^3$$
$$= 16\sqrt{2}\, r^3 .$$

Recall that the contents of a face centered unit cell add up to 4. That is, there are four spheres in the unit cell. Volume of a sphere = $4/3\ \pi r^3$. Therefore, the volume of 4 spheres is

$$4\left((4/3)\pi r^3\right) = (16/3)\pi r^3 .$$

The void volume percent is therefore

$$\frac{16\sqrt{2}\, r^3 - (16/3)\pi r^3}{16\sqrt{2}\, r^3} \times 100$$

$$= \left[\frac{16\sqrt{2}\, r^3}{16\sqrt{2}\, r^3} - \frac{16/3\ \pi r^3}{16\sqrt{2}\, r^3}\right] \times 100$$

$$= \left[1 - \frac{1\ \pi}{3\sqrt{2}}\right] \times 100$$

$$= 100 - \frac{100\pi}{3\sqrt{2}} = 25.9\%$$

$$a_0 = 2\sqrt{2}\ r = 2\sqrt{2}(0.100\ \text{nm})$$

$$= 0.282\ \text{nm} .$$

b) The hexagonal closest packed (hcp) unit cell has dimensions

$$a_0 = b_0 = 2r \quad \text{and} \quad c_0 = \frac{4\sqrt{2}}{\sqrt{3}}\ r \ .$$

Volume of the cell = area of parallelogram x height

$$= (2r)^2 \sin 60^\circ \times \frac{4\sqrt{2}}{\sqrt{3}}\ r$$

$$= 8\sqrt{2}\ r^3 \ .$$

This unit cell is occupied by two spheres. Therefore, volume of both spheres = $2((4/3)\pi r^3) = (8/3)\pi r^3$.
The void volume percent is therefore

$$\left[\frac{8\sqrt{2}\ r^3 - (8/3)\pi r^3}{8\sqrt{2} r^3}\right] \times 100$$

$$= \left[\frac{8\sqrt{2}\ r^3}{8\sqrt{2}\ r^3} - \frac{(8/3)\pi r^3}{8\sqrt{2}\ r^3}\right] \times 100$$

$$= \left[1 - \frac{\pi}{3\sqrt{2}}\right] \times 100$$

$$= 100 - \frac{100\ \pi}{3\sqrt{2}} = 25.9\% \ .$$

$$a_0 = 2r = 2(0.100) = 0.200\ \text{nm}$$

$$b_0 = 2r = 0.200\ \text{nm}$$

$$c_0 = \frac{4\sqrt{2}}{\sqrt{3}}\ r = \frac{4\sqrt{2}}{\sqrt{3}}(0.100) = \frac{0.5656}{\sqrt{3}} = 0.327\ \text{nm}$$

X-RAY CRYSTALLOGRAPHY

• PROBLEM 13-16

Magnesium oxide (M = 40.30) is cubic and has a density of 3.620 $g \cdot cm^{-3}$. An X-ray diffraction diagram of MgO powder has lines at values of $\sin\theta$ = 0.399, 0.461, 0.652, 0.764, 0.798, and 0.922. Index the pattern and determine the type of cubic structure. Calculate the wavelength of X-rays used. Assume that the number of MgO units per unit cell is the smallest consistent with the structure type.

Solution: This is a problem in which a test is conducted to determine the structure of magnesium oxide.
The test will be conducted by using the ITO method for indexing the X-ray powder pattern of the substance and inferring the dimensions of the cell.
Bragg developed a treatment of X-ray scattering by a crystal. He

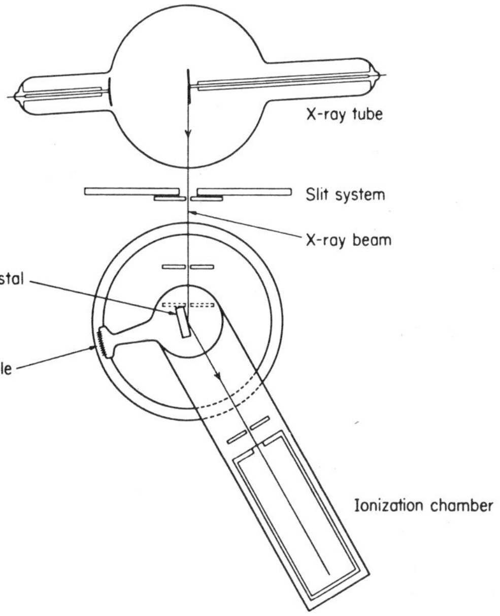

Bragg X-ray spectrometer.

showed that the scatterings of X-rays could be represented as a "reflection" by successive planes of atoms in the crystal. All the waves "reflected" by a single crystal plane will be in phase and only under certain conditions will the waves "reflected" by different underlying planes be in phase with one another. The condition is that the difference in length of path between the waves scattered from successive planes must be an integral number of wavelengths, $n\lambda$. Thus the Bragg equation or "reflection" is

$$n\lambda = 2d \sin \theta$$

where λ = the wavelength
θ = angle of incident beam of X-rays, and n is an integer; i.e., $n = 1,2,\ldots$. The value of n determines its order. Hence, the "reflection" is first order if $n = 1$, second order if $n = 2$, etc. Suppose however, that θ is fixed. Hence $\sin \theta$ is fixed. If the order is 1, then $\lambda = 2d \sin \theta$. In order to obtain the same value for λ when the order is 2, the spacing, d, must be $\frac{1}{2}$ of what it was for first order.
To circumvent this problem the equation $n\lambda = 2d \sin \theta$ is rewritten as

$$\lambda = 2d_{hkl} \sin \theta \, . \qquad (1)$$

Magnesium oxide could be based on one of the cubic lattices, simple, body-centered, or face-centered and by comparing the spacings calculated from the X-ray data with those expected for these lattices, the proper assignment of right cubic lattice can be made.
The distance between the planes (hkl) in a cubic lattice is given as

$$d_{hkl} = \frac{a_0}{(h^2 + k^2 + l^2)^{\frac{1}{2}}} \qquad (2)$$

Combining equation (2) with equation (1) gives

$$\sin^2\theta = (\lambda^2/4a_0^2)(h^2 + k^2 + l^2) \qquad (3)$$

$\lambda^2/4a_0^2$ is a constant for the crystal; therefore

$$\sin^2\theta/(h^2 + k^2 + l^2)$$

is also a constant. The observed value of $\sin\theta$ can be indexed by assigning to it the value of (hkl) for the set of planes responsible for the "reflection".

Using the first 6 lines of each cubic structure, $\frac{\sin^2\theta}{h^2+k^2+l^2}$ is computed for each and if its value is a constant for each of the (hkl), then it is that cell described by those Miller indices.

The first 6 lines of each cubic structure are:

a) Simple cubic,	(hkl):100	110	111	200	210	211
b) Body centered,	(hkl):110	200	211	220	310	222
c) Face centered,	(hkl):111	200	220	311	222	400

These values can be obtained from literatures.

Computing the

$$\frac{\sin^2\theta}{h^2+k^2+l^2}$$

value for the first two (hkl) values of each cubic structure gives

simple cubic: i) $\frac{\sin^2\theta}{h^2+k^2+l^2} = \frac{(0.399)^2}{1^2+0^2+0^2} = 0.159$

ii) $\frac{\sin^2\theta}{h^2+k^2+l^2} = \frac{(0.461)^2}{1^2+1^2+0^2} = 0.106$

Body centered: i) $\frac{\sin^2\theta}{h^2+k^2+l^2} = \frac{(0.399)^2}{1^2+1^2+0^2} = 0.0795$

ii) $\frac{\sin^2\theta}{h^2+k^2+l^2} = \frac{(0.461)^2}{2^2+0^2+0^2} = 0.0531$

Face centered: i) $\frac{\sin^2\theta}{h^2+k^2+l^2} = \frac{(0.399)^2}{1^2+1^2+1^2} = 0.0530$

ii) $\frac{\sin^2\theta}{h^2+k^2+l^2} = \frac{(0.461)^2}{2^2+0^2+0^2} = 0.0530$

The above values show that the $\frac{\sin^2\theta}{h^2+k^2+l^2}$ is a constant only for the face centered cubic structure. All the values are tabulated below.

		$\frac{\sin^2\theta}{h^2+k^2+l^2}$		
$\sin\theta$	$\sin^2\theta$	simple*	BCC*	FCC*
0.399	0.159	0.159	0.0795	0.0530
0.461	0.212	.0.106	0.0531	0.0530
0.652	0.425	0.142	0.0708	0.0530
0.764	0.584	0.145	0.0732	0.0530
0.798	0.637	0.127	0.0637	0.0530
0.922	0.850	0.141	0.0707	0.0530

The constant value indicates that MgO is face centered cubic.

Rearranging equation (3), the wavelength can be calculated. That is

$$\lambda = \sqrt{4a_0^2\left(\frac{\sin^2\theta}{h^2+k^2+l^2}\right)} \qquad (4)$$

Before equation (4) can be used, a_0 needs to be known.

$$a_0 = V^{\frac{1}{3}} \quad \text{where} \quad V = \text{volume}.$$

The volume, V can be obtained from the relation

$$V = \frac{CM}{Ad} \tag{4}$$

where C = the contents of the unit cell.
M = Molecular weight.
A = Avogadro's number.
d = density.

For an fcc unit cell, C = 4. Since all the parameters are known, equation (4) gives

$$V = \frac{(4)(40.30\ \text{g mol}^{-1})}{(6.02 \times 10^{23})\text{mol}^{-1}\ 3.620\ \text{g cm}^{-3}}$$

$$= 73.94 \times 10^{-24}\ \text{cm}^3$$

$$= 0.07394\ \text{nm}^3$$

$$\therefore \quad a_0 = V^{\frac{1}{3}} = (0.07394\ \text{nm}^3)^{\frac{1}{3}} = 0.4197\ \text{nm}.$$

Substituting for a in equation (4) gives

$$\lambda = \sqrt{(4)(0.4197)^2(0.0530)}$$

$$= \sqrt{4(0.1761)\text{nm}^2\ 0.0530}$$

$$= \sqrt{0.0373\ \text{nm}^2}$$

or $\lambda = 0.1932$ nm

• PROBLEM 13-17

Prepare a crystallographic projection for the body-centered cubic unit cell.

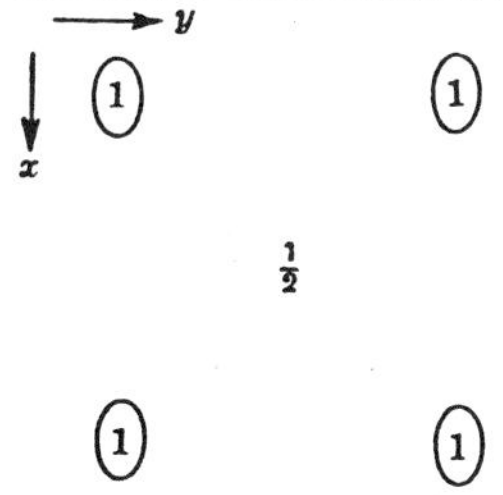

Solution: The eight corner atoms will be represented by four (1) symbols at the corners of a square and the body-centered atom will be represented by a ½ in the center of the square, see Fig. below. The above is constructed by viewing a unit cell along one of the crystallographic axes. It shows the shape of a unit cell in two dimensions, with the three-dimensional information.

• PROBLEM 13-18

If $\lambda = 1.5418\ \text{Å}$ for filtered Cu radiation, at what angle would the maximum reflection by the (200) plane of AgCl occur, assuming that

$$a = 5.5491\ \text{Å}\ ?$$

Solution: A beam of X-rays will be reflected if

$$\sin\theta = \frac{n\lambda}{2d} = \frac{\lambda}{2d_{hkl}} \qquad (1)$$

where θ = angle of reflection from the hkl plane.
n = order of reflection (an integer).
λ = wavelength of the radiation.
d_{hkl} = distance.

Looking at equation (1), $n = 1$ and $\lambda = 1.5418\ \mathring{A}$; but d_{hkl} is not given. This can be calculated using

$$\frac{1}{d^2_{hkl}} = \frac{h^2 + k^2 + l^2}{a^2}$$

where hkl = (200).
Therefore

$$\frac{1}{d^2_{200}} = \frac{2^2 + 0^2 + 0^2}{(5.5491\ \mathring{A})^2} = 0.1299\ \mathring{A}^{-2}$$

and

$$\frac{1}{d_{200}} = 0.3604\ \mathring{A}^{-1}\ .$$

Thus

$$d_{200} = \frac{1}{0.3604\ \mathring{A}^{-1}} = 2.7746\ \mathring{A}\ .$$

Now that d_{hkl} is known, substitute its value into equation (1) and solve for θ. Hence

$$\sin\theta = \frac{1.5418\ \mathring{A}}{(2)(2.7746\ \mathring{A})} = \frac{1.5418}{5.5492} = 0.279$$

and

$$\theta = \sin^{-1} 0.279.$$

$$\theta = 16.1^\circ\ .$$

• PROBLEM 13-19

A face-centered cubic structure gave the following powder pattern with X-rays of wavelength 0.1542 nm:

h	k	l	$\sin^2\theta$
1	1	1	0.0526
2	0	0	0.0701
2	2	0	0.1402
3	1	1	0.1928
2	2	2	0.2104

(a) Derive a general formula for $\sin^2\theta$ of a cubic substance in terms of wavelength, the unit cell dimension, and the Miller indices.
(b) Calculate the interplanar spacing for each of the preceding lines.
(c) From each of these lines, determine a value for the length of the unit cell edge.

Solution: (a) The interplanar distance (or spacing) is related to the dimensions of a unit cell by the formula

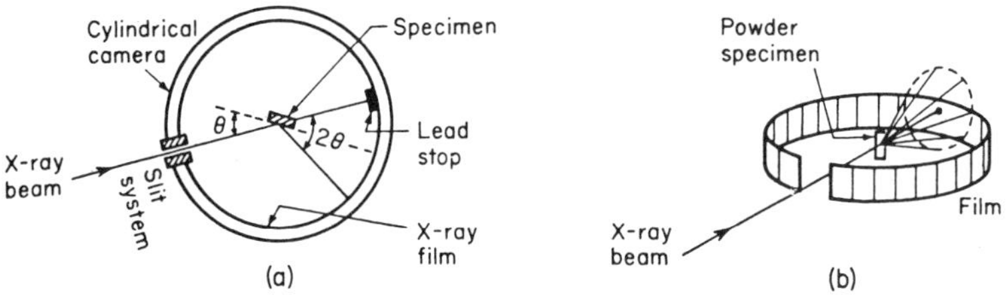

X-ray diffraction by the powder method.

$$\frac{1}{d^2_{hkl}} = \frac{h^2}{a^2} + \frac{k^2}{b^2} + \frac{l^2}{c^2} \tag{1}$$

where d_{hkl} = interplanar distance.

a,b and c = dimensions of the unit cell.

h,k and l = Miller indices.

In this particular cell under consideration, a = b = c. Therefore, equation (1) changes to

$$\frac{1}{d^2_{hkl}} = \frac{h^2}{a^2} + \frac{k^2}{a^2} + \frac{l^2}{a^2} = \frac{h^2 + k^2 + l^2}{a^2} \tag{2}$$

Taking the square root and reciprocal of equation (2) gives

$$\sqrt{d^2_{hkl}} = \sqrt{\frac{a^2}{h^2+k^2+l^2}}$$

$$\therefore \quad d_{hkl} = \frac{a}{\sqrt{h^2+k^2+l^2}} \tag{3}$$

The Bragg equation is given by

$$\lambda = 2(d/n) \sin\theta \tag{4}$$

where n = an integer known as the order of reflection.

λ = wavelength of the radiation .

In equation (4), the $d/n = d_{hkl}$; which means that higher order reflections can be treated as first order reflections from planes with spacing d/n.

Thus,

$$\lambda = 2d_{hkl} \sin\theta \ . \tag{5}$$

But

$$d_{hkl} = \frac{a}{\sqrt{h^2+k^2+l^2}}$$

Therefore, equation (5) becomes

$$\lambda = 2\frac{a}{\sqrt{h^2+k^2+l^2}} \sin\theta \tag{6}$$

Squaring both sides of equation (6) gives

$$\lambda^2 = \left[2\frac{a}{\sqrt{h^2+k^2+l^2}} \sin\theta\right]^2$$

or

$$\lambda^2 = 4\frac{a^2}{h^2+k^2+l^2} \sin^2\theta \ . \tag{7}$$

Rearranging equation (7) to solve for $\sin^2\theta$ gives

$$\sin^2\theta = \frac{\lambda^2}{4a^2}(h^2+k^2+l^2) \quad . \tag{8}$$

(b) Recall that the $\frac{h^2+k^2+l^2}{a^2}$ term in equation (8) is $\frac{1}{d^2_{hkl}}$.

Therefore, rewriting it in terms of $\frac{1}{d^2_{hkl}}$ gives

$$\sin^2\theta = \frac{\lambda^2}{4d^2_{hkl}} \tag{9}$$

Solving equation (9) for d^2_{hkl} gives

$$d^2_{hkl} = \frac{\lambda^2}{4\ \sin^2\theta} \tag{10}$$

Taking the square root of both sides, equation (10) becomes

$$d_{hkl} = \frac{\lambda}{2\ \sin\theta} = \frac{0.1542\ \text{nm}}{2\ \sin\ \theta} \tag{11}$$

Putting the $\sin\theta$ value of the first row of the table in equation (11) gives

$$d_{hkl} = \frac{0.1542\ \text{nm}}{2\sqrt{\sin^2\theta}} = \frac{0.1542\ \text{nm}}{(2)\sqrt{0.0525}}$$

$$= \frac{0.1542\ \text{nm}}{(2)(0.2293)} = 0.3362\ \text{nm} \ .$$

The others are tabulated below.

hkl	111	200	220	311	222
$\sin\ \theta$	0.2293	0.2647	0.3744	0.4391	0.4587
d_{hkl}, nm	0.3362	0.2913	0.2059	0.1756	0.1681

(c) Rearranging equation (3) to solve for a gives

$$a = d_{hkl}(\sqrt{h^2+k^2+l^2}) \tag{12}$$

Using the different d_{hkl} values and their corresponding hkl values in equation (12), a can be determined. That is

$$a = 0.3362(\sqrt{1^2+1^2+1^2}) = 0.582\ \text{nm}$$

$$a = 0.2913(\sqrt{2^2+0^2+0^2}) = 0.582\ \text{nm}$$

$$a = 0.2059(\sqrt{2^2+2^2+0^2}) = 0.582\ \text{nm}$$

$$a = 0.1756(\sqrt{3^2+1^2+1^2}) = 0.582\ \text{nm}$$

$$a = 0.1681(\sqrt{2^2+2^2+2^2}) = 0.582\ \text{nm}$$

Therefore, the required value is 0.582 nm.

SYMMETRY PROPERTIES

• PROBLEM 13-20

Tridymite, the high temperature form of SiO_2, is hexagonal with $a = 0.503$ nm and $c = 0.822$ nm. The space group is P6/mmc, and there are 4 SiO_2 units per unit cell. The Si atoms occupy positions with

C_{3v} symmetry:

$$\tfrac{1}{3},\ \tfrac{2}{3},\ z;\quad \tfrac{2}{3},\ \tfrac{1}{3},\ \bar{z};\quad \tfrac{2}{3},\ \tfrac{1}{3},\ \tfrac{1}{2}+z;\quad \tfrac{1}{3},\ \tfrac{2}{3},\ \tfrac{1}{2}-z$$

with $z = 0.44$.
The oxygen atoms occupy positions with D_{3h} - $\bar{6}m2$ symmetry:

$$\tfrac{1}{3},\ \tfrac{2}{3},\ \tfrac{1}{4};\quad \tfrac{2}{3},\ \tfrac{1}{3},\ \tfrac{3}{4}$$

The other six oxygens are in positions of C_{2h} - 2/m symmetry:

$$\tfrac{1}{2},\ 0,\ 0;\quad 0,\ \tfrac{1}{2},\ 0;\quad \tfrac{1}{2},\ \tfrac{1}{2},\ 0;\quad \tfrac{1}{2},\ 0,\ \tfrac{1}{2};\quad 0,\ \tfrac{1}{2},\ \tfrac{1}{2};\quad \tfrac{1}{2},\ \tfrac{1}{2},\ \tfrac{1}{2}$$

(a) Calculate the density of tridymite.
(b) Draw the projection of this structure on the ab plane, showing all of the atoms in at least one unit cell.
(c) Calculate the distance from a silicon atom to each of the two types of oxygen bonded to it.

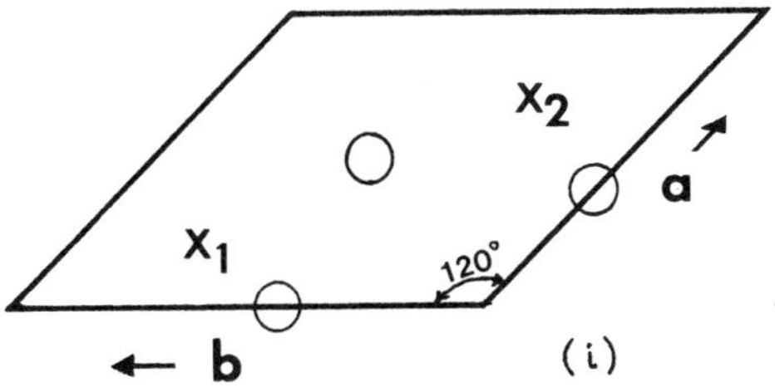

(i)

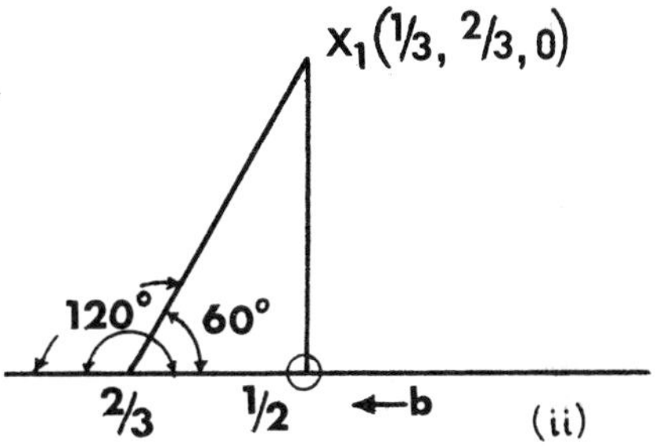

(ii)

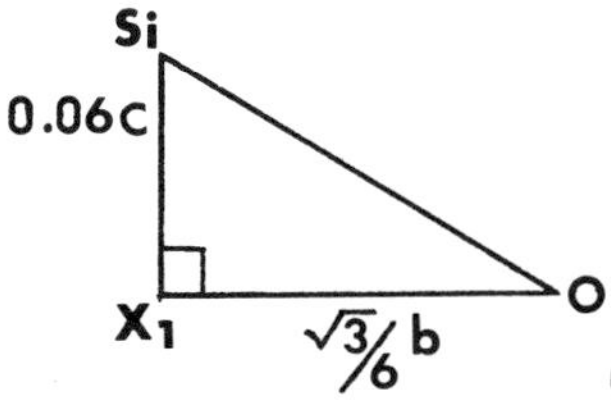

(iii)

Solution: The volume of a unit cell is given by

$$V = abc(1 - \cos^2\alpha - \cos^2\beta - \cos^2\gamma + 2\cos\alpha\cos\beta\cos\gamma)^{\frac{1}{2}}. \quad (1)$$

where V = volume
a, b and c = dimensions
α, β and γ = angles between the edges.

For the particular cell described above, equation (1) reduces to

$$V = abc(1 - \cos^2\alpha)^{\frac{1}{2}} \quad (2)$$

with $\alpha = 120°$.
Using the appropriate trigonometric identity, equation (2) takes the form

$$V = abc(\sin^2\alpha)^{\frac{1}{2}}$$

$$= abc\ \sin\alpha \quad (3)$$

Because of the hexagonal form, a = 0.503, b = 0.503 and c = 0.822.
Therefore, $V = (0.503)^2(0.822)\sin 120° = 0.180\ nm^3$

or $V = 180 \times 10^{-24}\ cm^3$.

The density of a unit cell is related to its dimensions and angles by the expression

$$d = \frac{CM}{AV} \qquad (4)$$

where

d = density
C = the contents of the unit cell (or the number of points contained within it).
M = Molecular weight.
A = Avogadro's number.
V = Volume.

C is given to be 4 and the molecular weight of SiO_2 is 28.08 + 32 = 60.08. Substituting the respective values into equation (4) gives

$$d = \frac{(4)(60.08)}{(6.02 \times 10^{23})(180 \times 10^{-24})}$$

$$= 2.218 \text{ g cm}^{-3} .$$

b) Above each C_{2h} - 2/m, oxygen in the ab plane (represented by 0) is an oxygen at $\frac{1}{2}C$. At $x_1(\frac{1}{3}a, \frac{2}{3}b)$, D_{3h} - $\bar{6}m2$ oxygen is at $\frac{1}{4}C$ and Si is at 0.44C and 0.06C.

At $x_2(\frac{2}{3}a, \frac{1}{3}b)$, D_{3h} - $\bar{6}m2$ oxygen is at $\frac{3}{4}C$ and Si is at 0.56C and 0.94C.

c) The shortest distance between them lies on the vertical to ab plane. Therefore, for x_1 vertical, distance

$$d = (0.44 - 0.25)C = 0.156 \text{ Si} - C_{2h} - 2/m \text{ oxygen.}$$

For example, distance from $(0,\frac{1}{2},0)$ oxygen to $(\frac{1}{3},\frac{2}{3},0.06)$Si is given by the distance from oxygen to x_1 on ab plane: that is,

$$\cos 60^\circ = \frac{(\frac{1}{3}a)^2 + (1/6\ b)^2 - (x_1 - 0)^2}{2(\frac{1}{3}\ a)(1/6\ b)}$$

Note that a = b. Solving for $(x_1 - 0)$ yields

$$(x_1 - 0) = \frac{\sqrt{3}}{6}\ b$$

Now $(\text{Si} - 0)^2 = (0.06\ c)^2 + \frac{3a^2}{36}$ from the figure.

$$= (0.0493)^2 + (0.1454)^2$$

$$(\text{Si} - 0) = 0.1535 \text{ nm} .$$

• PROBLEM 13-21

List and explain all the symmetry operations on molecules.

Solution: Symmetry (or lack of symmetry) is a property of all objects. Objects can be classified according to their symmetry by looking for all the operations that leave them looking the same. These are called symmetry operations. For instance, a sphere is said to be highly symmetrical because no matter how the sphere is rotated it is indistinguishable from its original state. A pencil is said to have

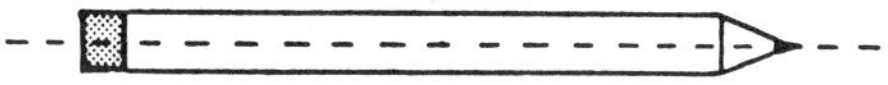

Fig. 1

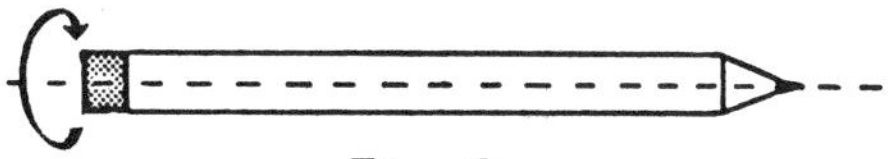

Fig. 2

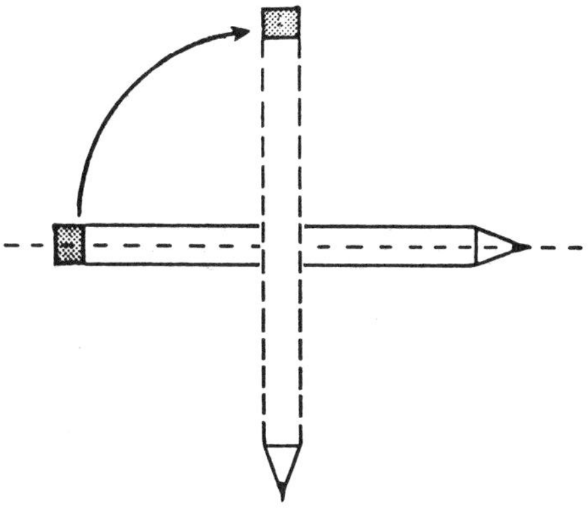

Fig. 3

Fig. 1 Original.
Fig. 2 Rotation about its length
Fig. 3 Rotation of 90° perpendicular to its length

less symmetry because although any rotation about its length will leave it identical to its original state, a rotation of 90° perpendicular to its length will not. This symmetry is shown in Figures 1 through 3.

The same principle applies to molecules. For molecules, there are five symmetry operations that can be performed on them. They are identity, rotation about an axis of symmetry, reflection through a plane of symmetry (i.e., a mirror plane), inversion through a center of symmetry, and improper rotation. Crystals contain two more unique symmetry operations, translation and screw rotation. The use of these symmetry make it possible to classify all the different types of molecules.

1) The identity operation performs no operation on the molecule. All molecules are identical to their original position if the identity operation is done. This may seem superfluous. However, it allows a molecule such as CHClBrF to be classified. This operation shall be denoted by E.

2) Rotation about an axis of symmetry is that operation which allows a molecule to be rotated through an angle of 360°/n and remain unchanged from its original condition. The molecule is then said to have an n-fold axis of symmetry. This is denoted by the symbol C_n. For instance, if a water molecule is rotated by 180° it is indistinguishable from its original state. This is shown in Figure 4.

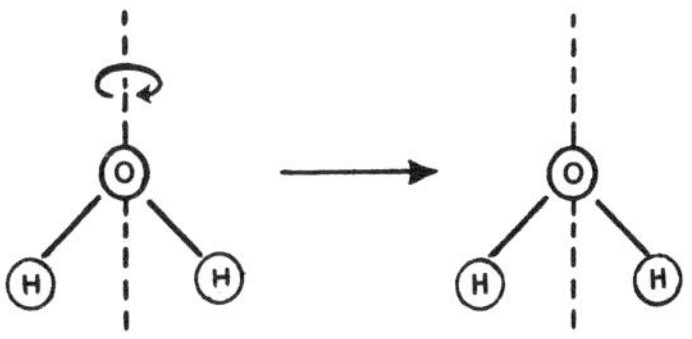

Fig. 4

Hence, the water molecule has a C_2 or two-fold axis of symmetry (360/2 = 180). If there are several axes of symmetry, the one with the highest value of n is used. This is called the principal axis of symmetry.

3) Reflection through a plane of symmetry (a mirror plane) is when reflection in a plane passing through the molecule leaves the molecule indistinguishable from its original state.

When the principal axis is contained in the mirror plane this symmetry element (operation) is denoted σ_v (the v denoting vertical).

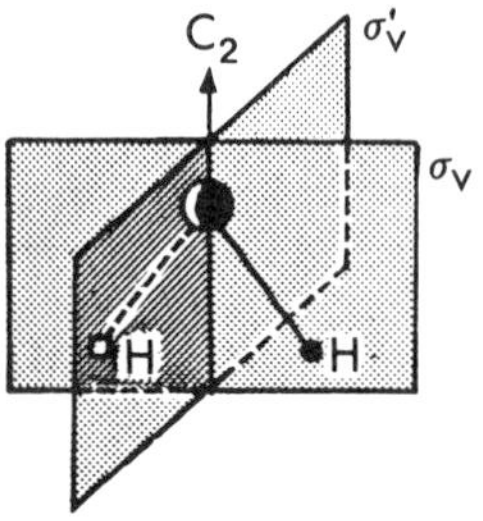

Fig. 5

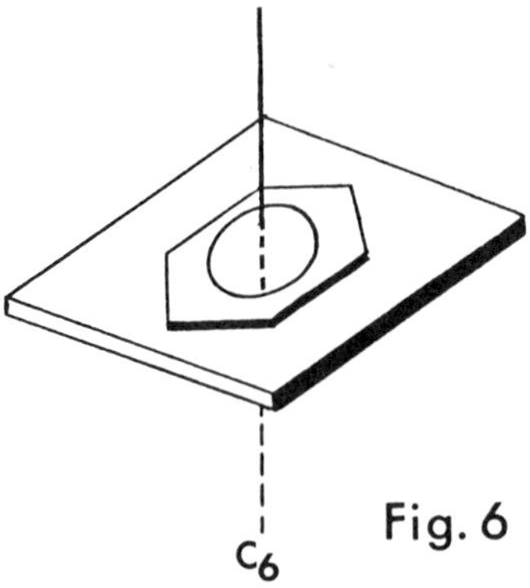

Fig. 6

For instance, the water molecule shown in Figure (5) has a twofold axis of symmetry passing through the oxygen atom. In addition to the C_2 axis, there are two σ_v planes. Both contain the C_2 axis, and one is just the H-O-H plane, while the other is perpendicular to it.
When the mirror plane is perpendicular to the principal axis (which if C_n is a vertical axis makes σ a horizontal plane), it is denoted by σ_h. An example of this is benzene, which is shown in Figure 6.
Thus benzene has a six-fold axis of symmetry. (The person observing this is looking down the axis of symmetry and seeing the benzene molecule lying flat).
There is one other σ plane, σ_d, which is much trickier and harder to see. Consider the hypothetical molecule shown in Figure 7, where all the x's lie in a plane. One can find a C_4 axis of symmetry since rotation by 90° leaves the molecule unchanged. Now the σ_v planes can also be found. (The person looking at this figure is looking down the C_4 axis, which goes from above the plane of the page and extends below it, and sees the molecule flat and in the plane of the page). They are the ones that run along the diagonals, as seen in Figure 8.

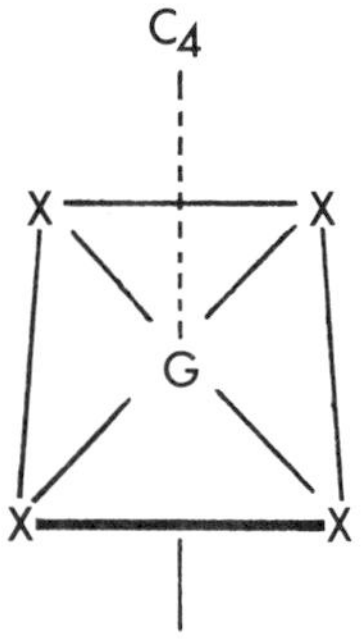

Fig. 7

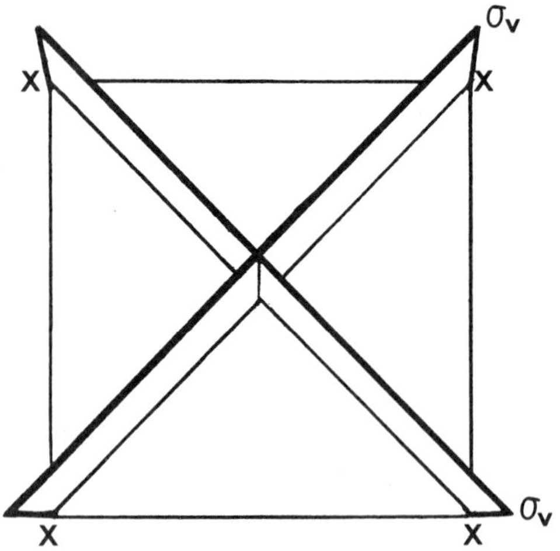

Fig. 8

There is also the horizontal σ_h plane shown in Figure 9.

Now, this molecule has other axes of symmetry besides the principal C_4 axis. The particular ones that are important for determining σ_d are the two C_2 axes.

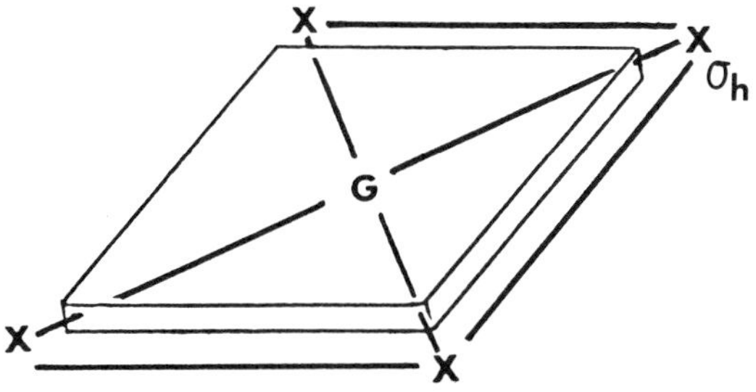

Fig. 9

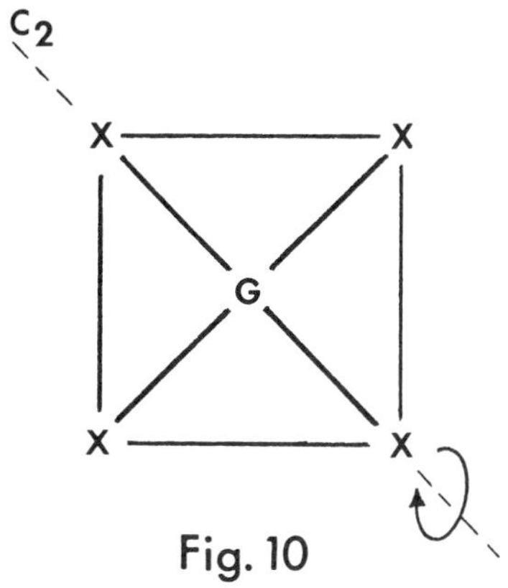

Fig. 10

Consider the molecule in Figure 10. There is a C_2 axis running along the diagonal of the molecule in the plane of the paper. If the molecule is rotated 180° around this axis, it is indistinguishable from its starting position. Likewise, for the other C_2 axis. See Figure 11.

The two σ_d planes are those planes which are vertical and contain the principal axis and also bisect the angle between the two C_2 axes (which are themselves perpendicular to the principal axis).

The overall result of all the σ planes mentioned is Figure 12.

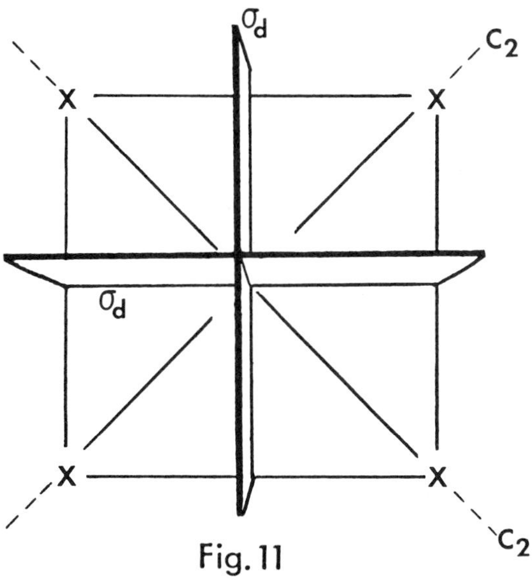

Fig. 11

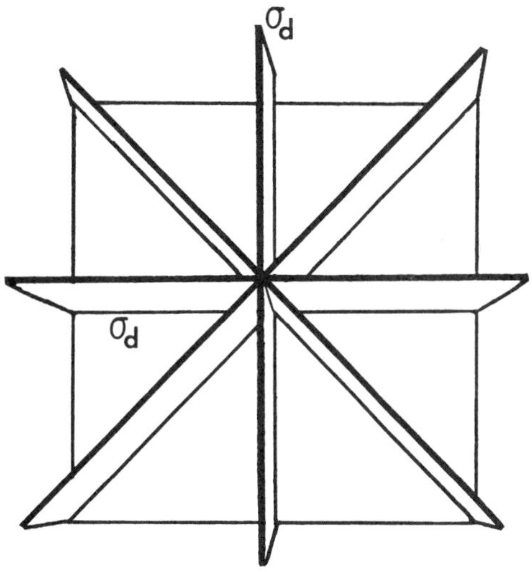

Fig. 12

4) Inversion is when the molecule is left unchanged after all its points in space are inverted. In other words, a center for the molecule can be found where, if the distance out in one direction is reversed to the opposite direction, the molecule is unchanged. For instance, in Figure 13 (where a heavy line denotes coming out of the plane of the paper and a dashed line denotes going into the plane

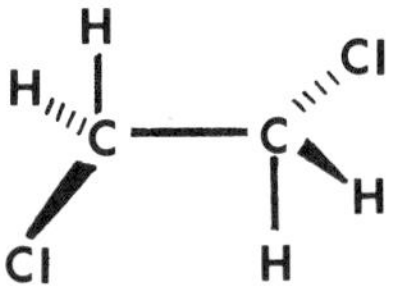

Fig. 13

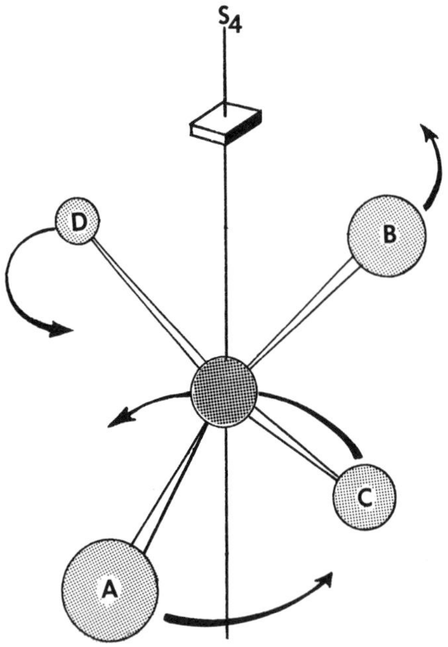

Fig. 14

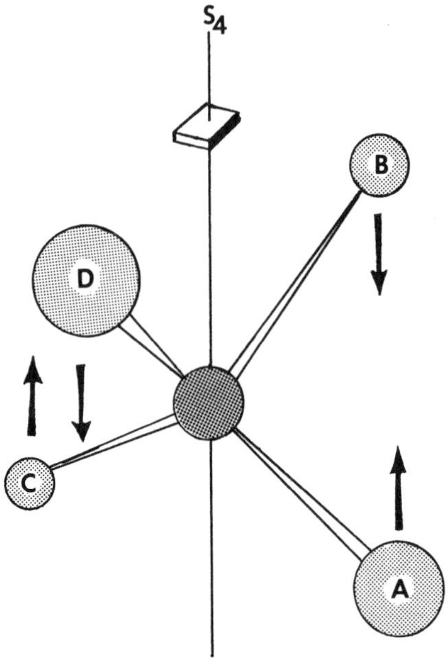

Fig. 15

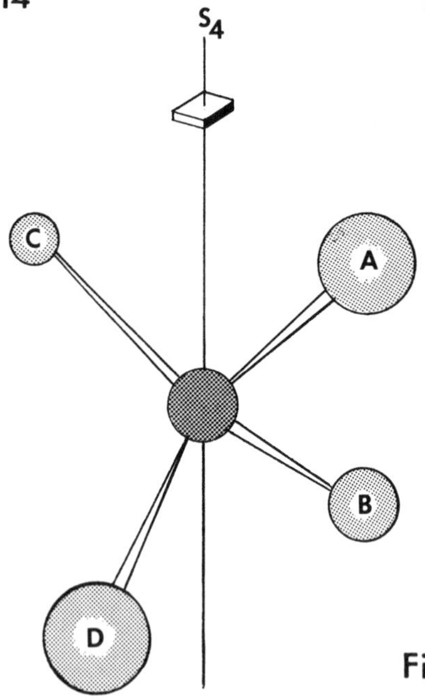

Fig. 16

of the paper) there exists a center of symmetry so the chlorine coming out of the plane on the first carbon if inverted would coincide with the chlorine on the second carbon going into the plane. Likewise, for all the other atoms. The operation is denoted by i.

5) Improper rotation (or rotary-reflection) is actually two operations. A molecule possesses it if it is unchanged after first undergoing an n-fold rotation followed by a horizontal reflection. This operation is denoted by S_n. An example of this is shown in Figures 14 through 16. The letters are really to aid the reader. For a real molecule such as CH_4 all the hydrogens are equivalent so one could not tell which one was A, B, C, or D. Hence, Figure 14 is equivalent to Figure 16.

• PROBLEM 13-22

Explain how point groups for molecules are designated from the symmetry operations.

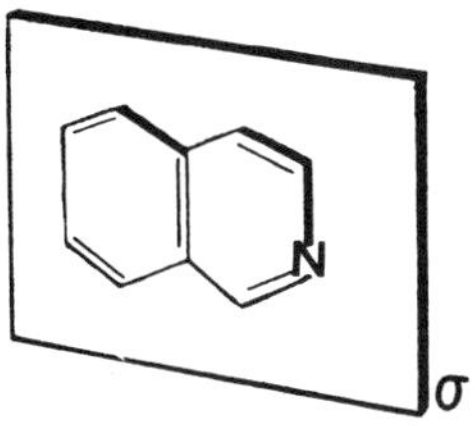

Fig. 1

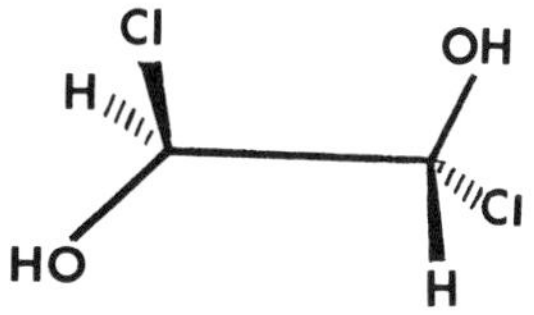

Fig. 2

Fig. 3

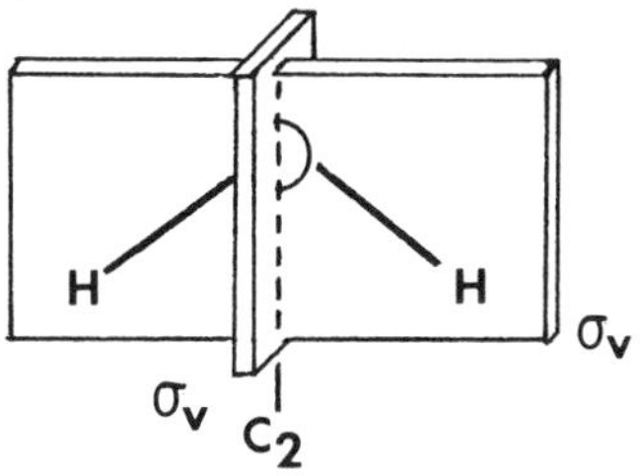

Fig. 4

Solution: Point groups are defined according to the type of symmetry elements they contain.

1) The C_s group is that group where the molecule contains only the identity element and a plane of symmetry. An example of this would be isoquinoline, shown in Figure 1.

2) The C_i group is that group where the molecule contains only the identity element and a center of inversion. An example of this is shown in Figure 2. Since all the other groups contain the identity operation it will not be explicitly mentioned for them.

3) The C_n group is that group which contains only an n-fold axis of symmetry. An example would be the compound CHClBrF, shown in Figure 3, which contains a one-fold axis of symmetry (since rotation by 360° leaves the molecule unchanged and $n = 360/360 = 1$). Hence, CHClBrF is C_1.

4) The C_{nv} group is that group which contains a C_n axis and n vertical reflection palnes σ_v. An example would be H_2O, shown in Figure 4. Hence, water is a member of the group C_{2v}.

5) The C_{nh} group is that group where the molecule contains a C_n axis and a horizontal plane of reflection. An example of this would be trans CHCl = CHCl, shown in Figure 5.

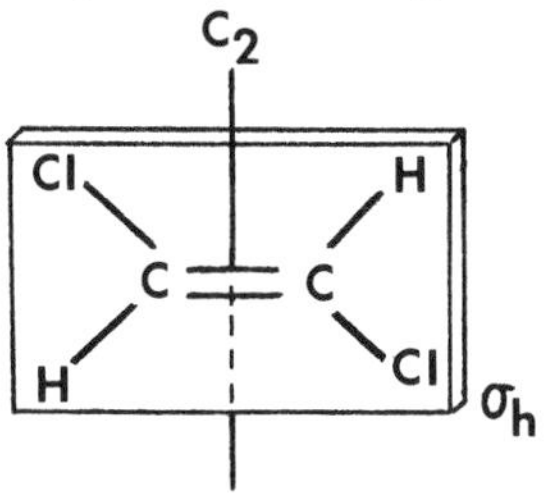

Fig. 5

This compound has a C_2 axis of symmetry and a σ_h plane of symmetry and hence it is a member of C_{2h}.

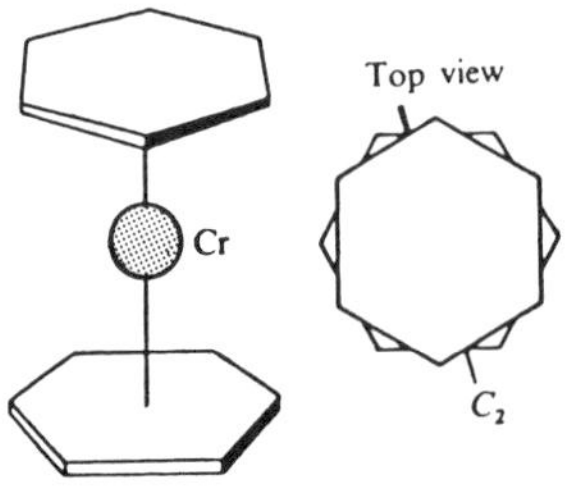

Fig. 6

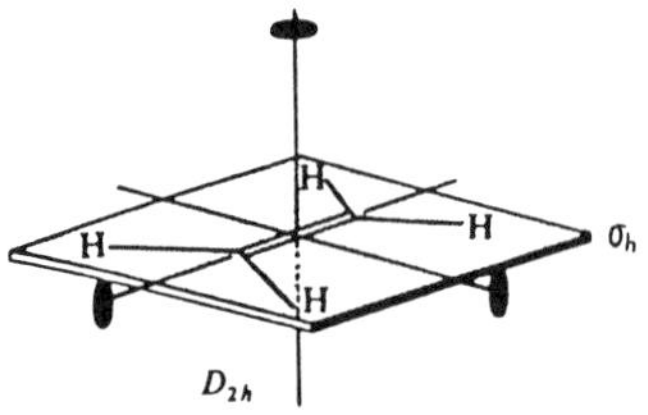

Fig. 7

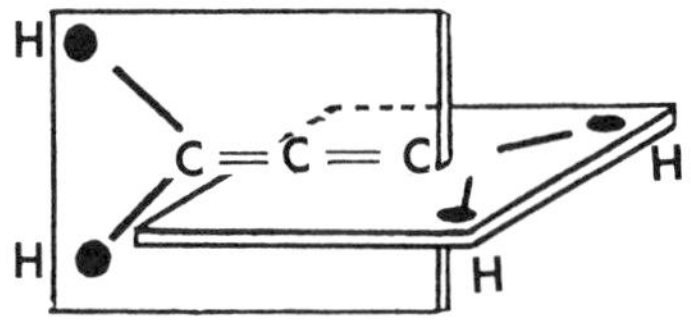

Fig. 8

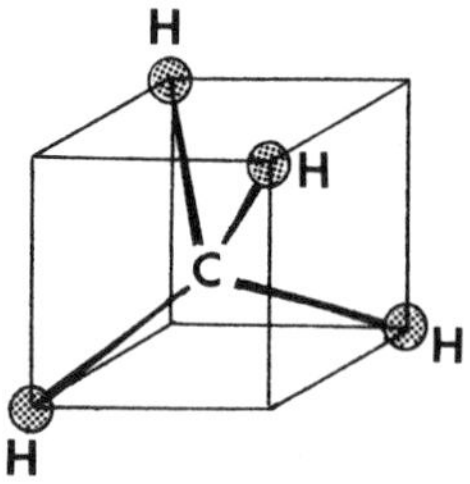

Fig. 9

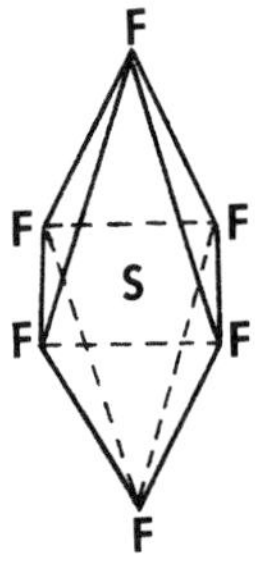

Fig. 10

6) The D_n group is that group where the molecule possesses a C_n axis and an n-two fold axes perpendicular to C_n. An example is shown in Figure 6.
Thus, this molecule is a member of D_2.
7) The D_{nh} group is that group where the molecules belong to D_n and possesses a horizontal plane of symmetry, σ_h . An example of this is ethylene, C_2H_4 shown in Figure 7.
8) The D_{nd} group is that group where the molecules belong to D_n and possesses an additional vertical plane which bisects the angles between all the adjacent C_2 axes. An example of this is allene, shown in Figure 8 which is D_{2d}. The next groups to be considered have more than one axis of symmetry where the order of rotation is greater than two. They are the octahedral and tetrahedral groups.
9) The T_d group is that group where the molecule has a regular tetrahedron shape. An example of this is methane, CH_4, shown in Figure 9. If the T_d group possesses in addition rotational symmetry, it becomes the group T. If the group T contains a center of inversion it becomes the group T_h.
10) The O_h group is that group where the molecule has a regular octahedron. An example of this is SF_6, shown in Figure 10.
If the O_h group possesses rotational symmetry it becomes the O group.

• PROBLEM 13-23

For each molecule below, determine its point group:
a) N_2 , b) PCl_5, c) NH_3 , d) C_2H_4, e) pyridine, f) pyrazine, g) hydrogen peroxide, h) cyclopropane (ignore the hydrogens), i) C_2H_5Cl(in eclipsed form), j) SF_5Cl (octahedral), k) CO .

Fig. 1

Fig. 2

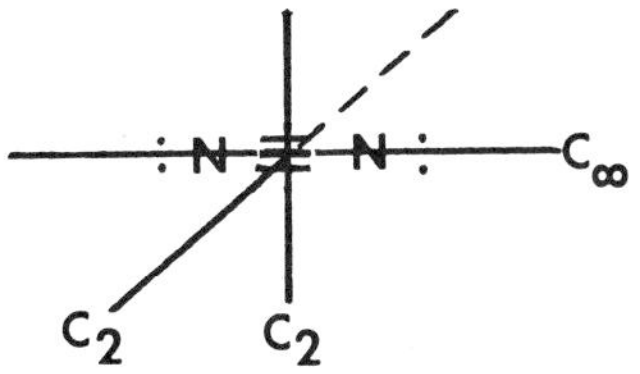

Fig. 3

Fig. 4

Solution: a) N_2 is a linear homonuclear molecule. It has the following structure shown in Figure 1 . One can draw an axis of symmetry right through the molecule as shown in figure 2. No matter how small an angle θ this molecule is rotated about this axis, the molecule is unchanged. Hence, N_2 has a C_∞ axis of symmetry. As n approaches zero, 360/n approaches infinity. The molecule also possesses n 2-fold axes. An example of two of them is shown in figure 3 where the vertical C_2 is in the plane of the paper and the other starts above the plane of the paper and extends below it. Hence, the molecule is a member of D_n. N_2 also possesses a horizontal reflection plane, σ_h, perpendicular to the principal axis as seen in Figure 4. Therefore, N_2 belongs to the group $D_{\infty h}$.

b) PCl_5 has 3 Cl atoms in a plane at 120° and two Cl atoms above and below the phosphorous atom 180° apart. The molecule is shown in Figure 5. The molecule contains a C_3 axis passing through the phosphorous atom and the two Cl atoms above and below it. It also possesses 3 C_2 axes along each P-Cl bond in the plane. Since the molecule contains a horizontal mirror plane, σ_h, the molecule belongs to the group D_{3h}. These features can be seen in Figure 6.

c) NH_3 has a structure that can be seen in Figure 7. It has a C_3 axis of symmetry that starts above the nitrogen atom and extends to the middle of the triangular base. There are also 3 vertical mirror planes, σ_v which contain the principal axis. Each of these cut through the nitrogen atom and one of the hydrogens. This is shown in Figure 8. Hence, NH_3 is a member of the group C_{3v} .

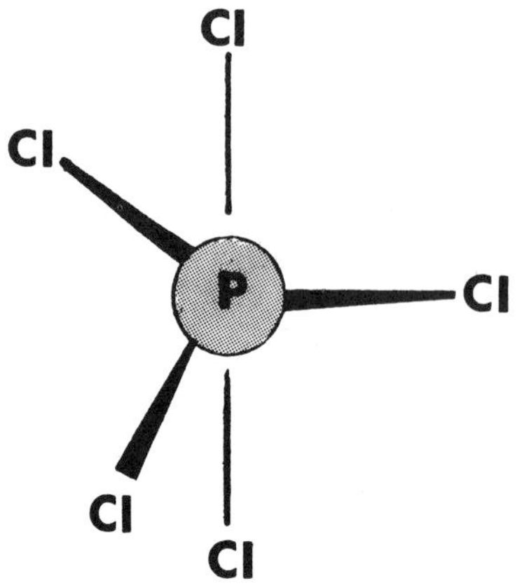

Fig. 5

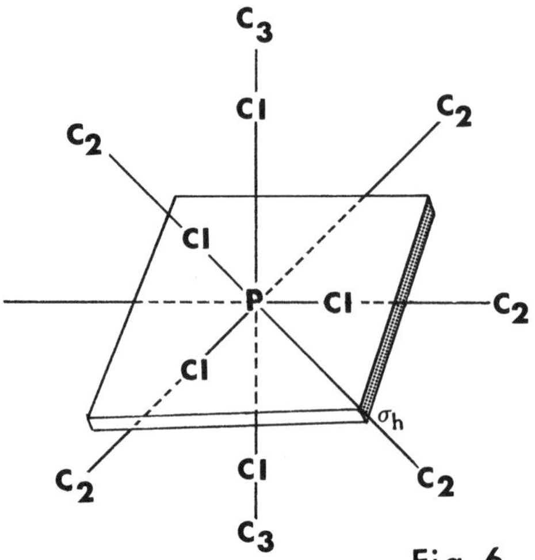

Fig. 6

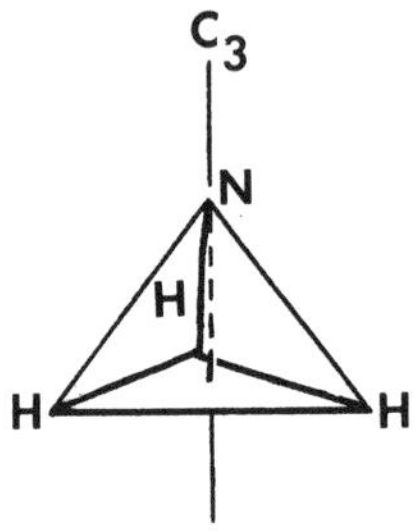

Fig. 7

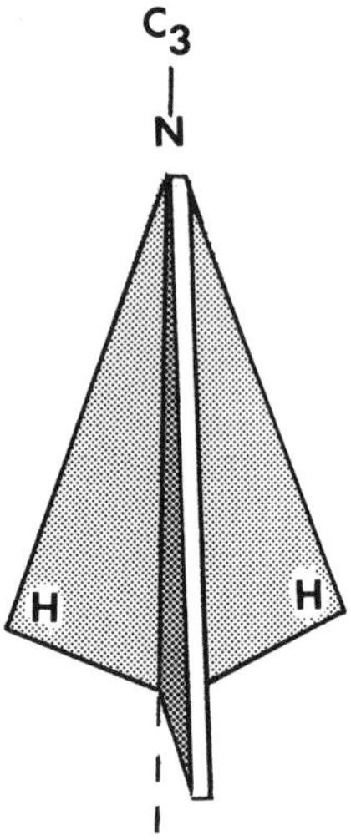

Fig. 8

d) C_2H_4 is a planar hydrocarbon molecule. Its structure is shown in Figure 9. This molecule has a principal axis starting above the plane of the molecule and extending below it. Since rotation by 180° will leave the molecule unchanged, the principal axis is a C_2 axis. There are 2 C_2 axis perpendicular to the principal axis. They lie in the plane of the molecule. Hence, the molecule is a member of D_2. In addition, the molecule contains a horizontal mirror plane, σ_h, perpendicular to the principal axis. Therefore, the molecule belongs to the group D_{2h}.

e) Pyridine is a heterocyclic aromatic compound. It has the following structure, as shown in Figure 10. A C_2 axis of symmetry can be found running through the plane of the molecule from the nitrogen atom to the opposite carbon atom. In addition, there are two vertical mirror planes σ_v, which contain the principal axis, hence pyridine is in the C_{2v} group. These features are shown in Figure 11.

f) Pyrazine is also a heterocyclic aromatic compound. Notice that there is one more nitrogen and one less carbon in its ring structure than in pyridine. The position of this new nitrogen greatly increases

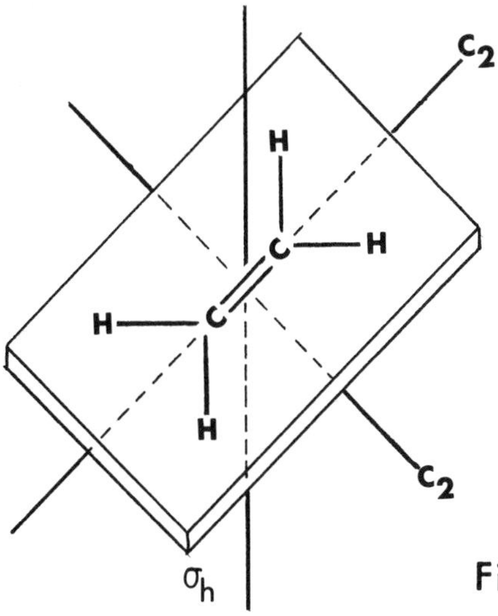

Fig. 9

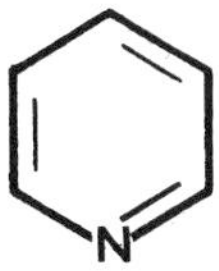

Fig. 10

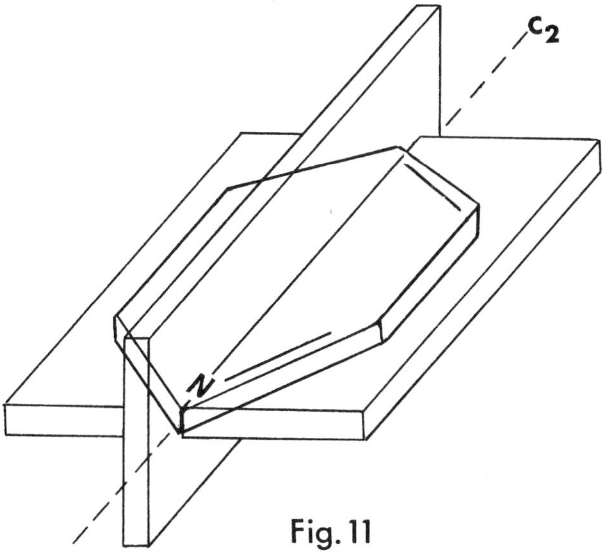

Fig. 11

the symmetry of the molecule. Its structure is seen in Figure 12. In this case, there is a C_2 axis starting above the plane of the molecule and extending below it. There are two C_2 axes perpendicular to the principal C_2 axis, which run through the plane of the molecule.

Fig. 12

In addition, there is a horizontal mirror plane running perpendicular to the principal C_2 axis. Hence, the pyrazine molecule belongs to the point group D_{2h}. These features are shown in Figure 13.

g) Hydrogen peroxide, H_2O_2, has the following structure, shown in Figure 14. The only symmetry element this molecule has is C_2. Rotating this molecule about this principal axis 180°, brings the

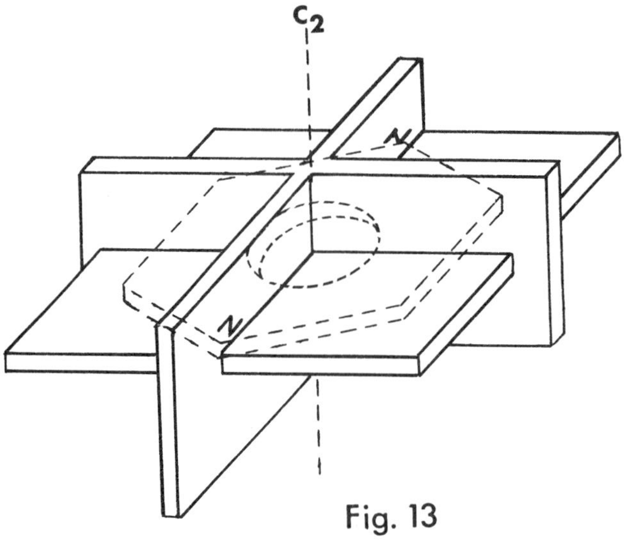

Fig. 13

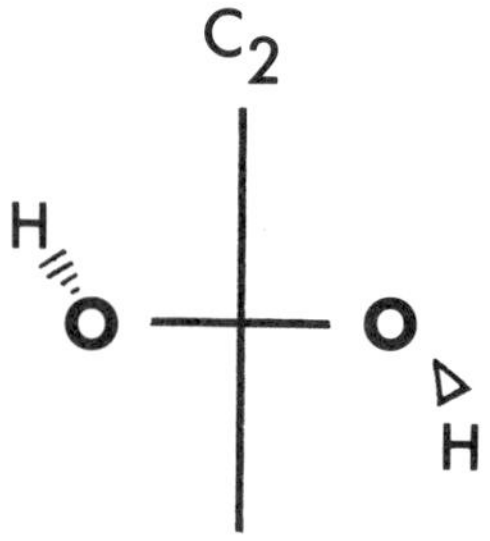

Fig. 14

hydrogen out front (on the right) to the back (on the left) and the hydrogen in the back (on the left) to the front (on the right). Hence, H_2O_2 is a member of the C_2 point group.

h) Cyclopropane without considering the hydrogens will be a planar, triangular shaped molecule. It will have a C_3 principal axis extending through the molecule from above it to below it. There will also be 3 C_2 axis perpendicular to the principal axis. They are in the plane of the molecule and run from one vertex to the opposite side. There is also a horizontal mirror plane perpendicular to the C_3 axis. These features indicate cyclopropane is of the point group D_{3h}, and they are shown in Figure 16.

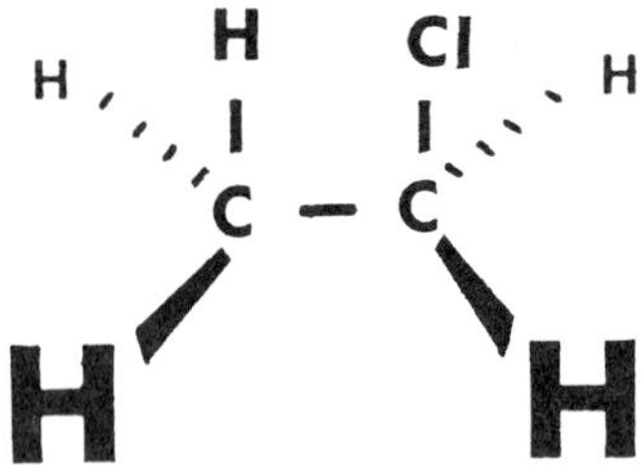

Fig. 15

i) There is only one plane of symmetry in this molecule. This plane contains the 2 carbons and the H and the Cl pointing up. If this plane is inserted what is behind the plane is the same as what is in front of it. Since this is the only symmetry element present, this molecule belongs to the point group C_s. The diagram seen in Figure 17 shows this symmetry.

j) SF_5Cl (octahedral) has the structure shown in Figure 18. There is a C_4 axis running through the Cl-S-F atoms from above the plane to below it. There are also 4 vertical reflection planes which contain this C_4 axis. Two run between a pair of flourine atoms and the other two contain two flourine atoms along a diagonal. Figure 19 illustrates this (the F, Cl, and S have been left out for clarity). The point group for SF_5Cl is thus C_{4v}.

Notice that if the chlorine atom were replaced by a flourine atom

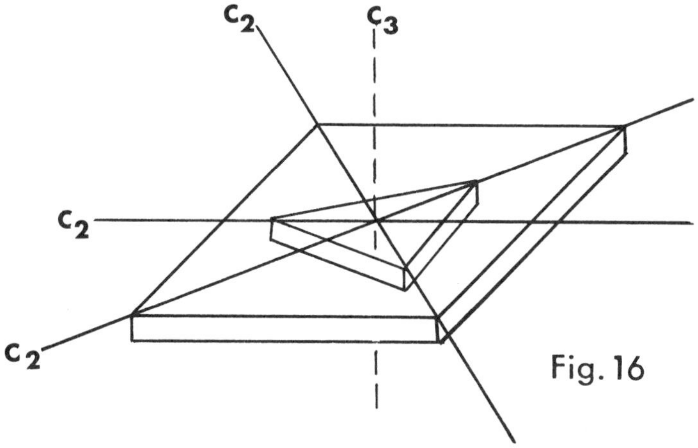

Fig. 16

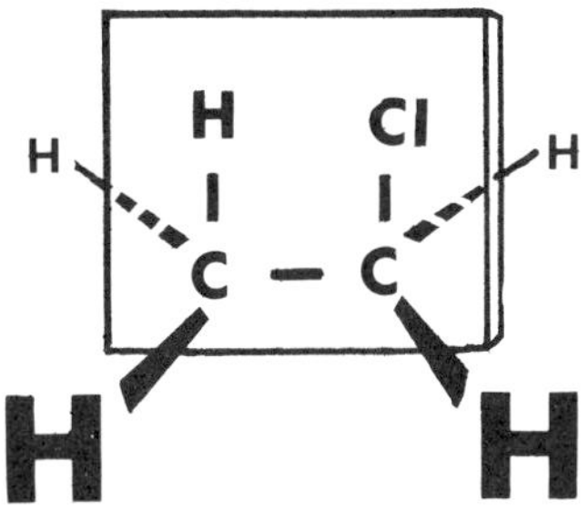

Fig. 17

the symmetry would be greatly increased and the point group would be O_h.

k) CO is a linear heteronuclear diatomic molecule. It has the structure shown in Figure 20.

One can draw an axis of symmetry right through the molecule as seen in Figure 21.

No matter how small an angle θ this molecule is rotated about this axis, the molecule is unchanged. Hence, CO has a C_∞ axis of

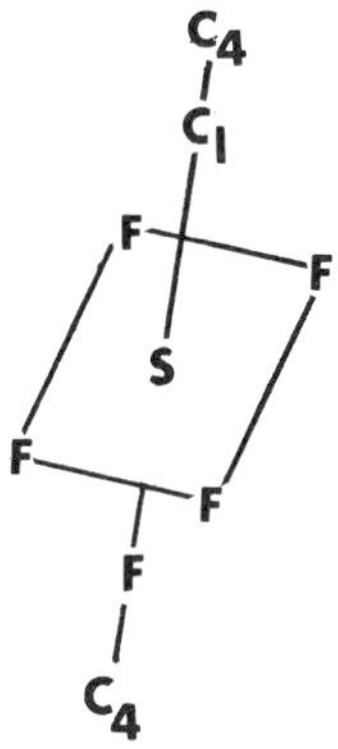

Fig. 18

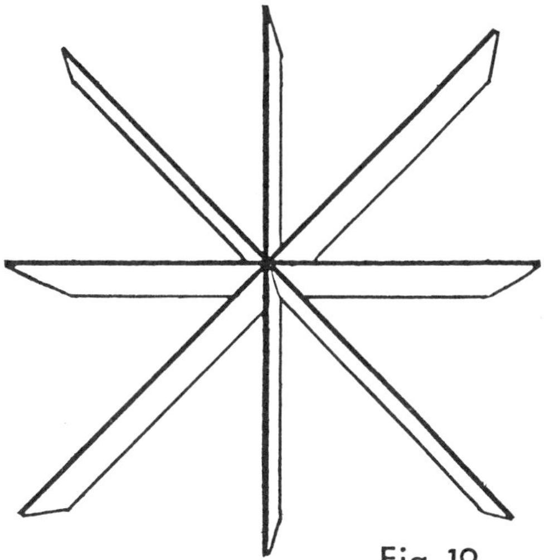

Fig. 19

Fig. 20

Fig. 21

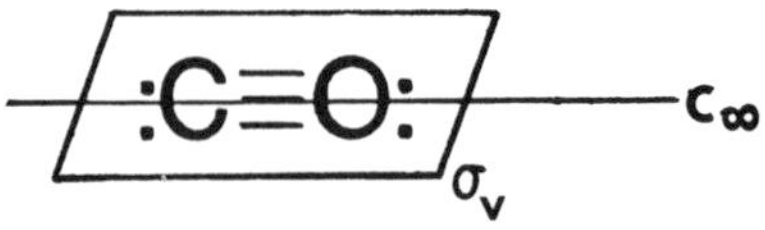

Fig. 22

symmetry. As n approaches zero, 360/n approaches infinity. In addition, any vertical plane drawn through this molecule will contain the axis of symmetry (there will be an infinite number of these planes). This is shown in Figure 22. Hence, CO belongs to the point group $C_{\infty v}$.

CHAPTER 14

NUCLEAR CHEMISTRY

ATOMIC NUCLEI

• PROBLEM 14-1

The mass of an electron is 9.109×10^{-28} g . What is the atomic weight of electrons?

Solution: Atomic weight is defined as the weight of one mole of particles. According to Avogadro, there are 6.02×10^{23} particles in one mole. The atomic weight of electrons is equal to 6.02×10^{23} times the mass of one electron. But the problem indicates that the weight of a particle is given as 9.109×10^{-28} g/particle. Therefore, atomic weight of electrons = 9.109×10^{-28} g/particle x 6.02×10^{23} particle/mole

$$= 5.48 \times 10^{-4} \text{ g/mole.}$$

Note that the unit of the final answer is g/mole (units for atomic and molecular weights). The particles cancel out. In this problem the electron is the particle.

• PROBLEM 14-2

A chemist is given an unknown element X. He finds that the element X has an atomic weight of 210.197 amu and consists of only two isotopes, ^{210}X and ^{212}X. If the masses of these isotopes are, respectively, 209.64 and 211.66 amu, what is the relative abundance of the two isotopes?

Solution: The relative abundance of the two isotopes is equal to their fraction in the element. The sum of the fractions of the isotopes times their respective masses is equal to the total atomic weight of X. The element X is composed of only two isotopes. The sum of their fractions must be equal to one.

Solving: Let y = the fraction of the 210 isotope. Since the sum of the fractions is one, 1 - y = the fraction of the 212 isotope. The sum of the fractions times their masses, equals the atomic weight of X.

$$209.64\ y + 211.66(1 - y) = 210.197;$$

$$209.64\ y + 211.66 - 211.66\ y = 210.197$$

$$-2.02\ y = -1.463$$

$$y = 1.463/2.02$$

$$y = 0.7242 = \text{fraction of } {}^{210}X.$$

$$\therefore \quad 1 - y = 0.2758 = \text{fraction of } {}^{212}X.$$

By percentage the relative abundance of ${}^{210}X$ is 72.42% and ${}^{212}X$ is 27.58%.

• PROBLEM 14-3

Chromium exists in four isotopic forms. The atomic masses and percent occurrences of these isotopes are listed in the following table:

Isotopic mass (amu)	Percent occurrence
50	4.31%
52	83.76%
53	9.55%
54	2.38%

Calculate the average atomic mass of chromium.

Solution: By definition,

$$A = \sum_{i=1}^{N} p_i M_i \,, \tag{1}$$

where A = average value, p_i = probability of occurrence of isotope i M_i = atomic mass of isotope i . Making use of the above definition and the given data, the average atomic mass of chromium can be computed.

For the four isotopes of chromium,

$M_1 = 50$ amu $\quad p_1 = 4.31\% = 0.0431$

$M_2 = 52$ amu $\quad p_2 = 83.76\% = 0.8376$

$M_3 = 53$ amu $\quad p_3 = 9.55\% = 0.0955$

$M_4 = 54$ amu $\quad p_4 = 2.38\% = 0.0238$

Hence, the average atomic mass of chromium is $A = p_1M_1 + p_2M_2 + p_3M_3 + p_4M_4 = 0.0431 \times 50$ amu $+ 0.8376 \times 52$ amu $+ 0.0955 \times 53$ amu $+ 0.0238 \times 54$ amu $= 2.155$ amu $+ 43.555$ amu $+ 5.062$ amu $+ 1.285$ amu $= 52.057$ amu.

• PROBLEM 14-4

Natural chlorine is a mixture of isotopes. Determine its atomic weight if 75.53% of the naturally occurring element is chlorine 35, which has a mass of 34.968, and 24.47% is chlorine 37, which has a mass of 36.956.

Solution: If naturally occurring chlorine contains 75.53% chlorine 35 and 24.47% chlorine 37, one mole of chlorine contains .7553 mole chlorine 35 and .2447 mole chlorine 37. The weight of one mole of chlorine is, then, equal to the sum of the weight of .7553 mole ^{35}Cl and .2447 mole ^{37}Cl.

Making use of the definition of average value gives

$$A = p_1M_1 + p_2M_2 \qquad (1)$$

where

A = atomic weight

p_i = probability of occurrence of isotope i

M_i = mass of isotope i .

In this problem, $p_1 = 0.7553$, $M_1 = 34.968$

$p_2 = 0.2447$ and $M_2 = 36.956$.

Inserting these values into equation (1) yields:

$$\text{atomic weight of Cl} = (.7553)(34.968) + (.2447)(36.956)$$
$$= 26.41 + 9.04$$
$$= 35.45 .$$

• PROBLEM 14-5

Chlorine is found in nature in two isotopic forms, one of atomie mass 35 amu and one of atomic mass 37 amu. The average atomic mass of chlorine is 35.453 amu. What is the percent with which each of these isotopes occurs in nature?

Solution: This is a mathematical problem, the solution to which centers on defining the average value properly. Consider a set of N observations or measurements, $M_1, M_2, \ldots, M_N$. Let the probability that the observation M_1 is made be p_1, the probability that the observation M_2 is made be p_2, and so on. Then, the average, A is defined as:

$$A = \sum_{i=1}^{N} p_iM_i .$$

Since, by definition, the sum of the probabilities must be one, then:

$$1 = \sum_{i=1}^{N} p_i .$$

For this problem there are two observations, hence N = 2. Let the first observation be M_1 = 35 amu and the second observation be $M_2 = 37$ amu. The average $A = 35.453$ amu. Hence,

$$A = p_1M_1 + p_2M_2 \qquad (1)$$

$35.453 \text{ amu} = p_1 \times 35 \text{ amu} + p_2 \times 37 \text{ amu}$ and

$$1 = p_1 + p_2 \,. \qquad (2)$$

In order to find the percent occurrences of these isotopes, the above equations are solved simultaneously to obtain the values of p_1 and p_2. Rearranging equation (2) gives:

$$p_2 = 1 - p_1 \,.$$

Substituting this into equation (1) yields:

$$A = p_1M_1 + p_2M_2 = p_1M_1 + (1 - p_1)M_2$$
$$= p_1M_1 + M_2 - p_1M_2$$
$$= M_2 + (M_1 - M_2)p_1$$

or,

$$p_1 = \frac{A - M_2}{M_1 - M_2} = \frac{35.453 \text{ amu} - 37 \text{ amu}}{35 \text{ amu} - 37 \text{ amu}} = 0.7735 \,.$$

Then,

$$p_2 = 1 - p_1 = 1 - 0.7735 = 0.2265 \,.$$

Thus, the isotope of mass 35 amu occurs with probability of 0.7735 or $0.7735 \times 100\% = 77.35\%$ and the isotope of mass 37 amu occurs with a probability of 0.2265 or $0.2265 \times 100\% = 22.65\%$.

In reality, the two isotopes do not have integral atomic masses, and the percent occurrences calculated above are not exactly correct.

• PROBLEM 14-6

Compute the missing mass of $^{19}_{9}F$ (atomic weight = 18.9984) when the masses of proton, neutron and electron are 1.00728, 1.00867 and 0.000549 respectively.

Solution: The total number of particles in $^{19}_{9}F$ and their total weight can be calculated. The amount of missing mass in $^{19}_{9}F$ will be the difference of this calculated weight and the given atomic weight of $^{19}_{9}F$. The subscript number 9, in $^{19}_{9}F$, indicates the atomic number of fluorine (F). Because the atomic number equals the number of protons, there are 9 protons in F. The superscript, 19, indicates the total number of particles in the nucleus. Since the nucleus is composed of protons and neutrons, and there are 9 protons, there are 10 neutrons present. In a neutral atom, the number of electrons equals the number of protons. Thus, there are 9 electrons. The total number of particles is, thus, 28. The mass and quantity of each particle is now known. Calculating the total weight contribution of each type of particle:

$$\begin{aligned} \text{Protons:} \quad & 9 \times 1.00728 = 9.06552 \\ \text{Neutrons:} \quad & 10 \times 1.00867 = 10.0867 \\ \text{Electrons:} \quad & 9 \times 0.000549 = \underline{0.004941} \\ & \text{Total mass} = 19.1572 \,. \end{aligned}$$

It is given that the mass of the fluorine atom is 18.9984. Therefore, the missing mass is 19.1572 - 18.9984 = 0.1588 amu.

• PROBLEM 14-7

The natural abundance of neon is 90.92% $^{20}_{10}Ne$ (19.99244 u), 0.257% $^{21}_{10}Ne$ (20.99395 u) and 8.82% $^{22}_{10}Ne$ (21.99138 u). Calculate the average atomic weight for natural neon gas.

Solution: The average atomic weight for natural neon gas can be calculated by dividing the sum of the products of the percentages times the atomic weights by the sum of the percentages.

The mathematical representation of this is

$$\frac{\Sigma\, p_i a_i}{\Sigma\, p_i} \qquad (1)$$

where p_i = percentage of the ith component and

a_i = atomic weight of the ith component.

Inserting the numerical data into equation (1) gives:

$$\frac{(0.9092)(19.99244) + (0.00257)(20.99395) + (0.0882)(21.99138)}{0.9092 + 0.00257 + 0.0882}$$

$$= \frac{18.177126 + 0.0539544 + 1.9396397}{0.9092 + 0.00257 + 0.0882}$$

$$= \frac{20.17072}{0.99997}$$

$$= 20.171325 \text{ u} \,.$$

• PROBLEM 14-8

The mass of an atom of hydrogen having one proton and one electron is 1.0072766 + 0.0005486 = 1.0078252 u. What fraction of the total mass of a hydrogen atom is contained within the nucleus? Contrast this answer to that for the fraction of the atomic volume (r = 0.529 Å) occupied by the nucleus if

$$r = (1.5 \times 10^{-15} \text{m})A^{\frac{1}{3}}$$

is valid, where r = radius of a nucleus

A = mass number .

Solution: The total mass of the atom is 1.0072766 + 0.0005486 =

1.0078252 u. Observe that 1.0072766 is the mass of proton and 0.0005486 is the mass of electron.

As a result, the fraction of atomic mass is given by

$$\frac{1.0072766}{1.0078252} = 0.9994557 .$$

The fraction of volume is defined as the ratio of the volume of nucleus to that of the atom. That is,

$$\frac{[(1.5 \times 10^{-5})1^{\frac{1}{3}}]^3}{(0.529 \times 10^{-10})^3}$$

$$= \frac{22.7985 \times 10^{-45}}{1 \times 10^{-30}}$$

$$= 22.7985 \times 10^{-15}$$

$$= 2.3 \times 10^{-14} .$$

• PROBLEM 14-9

List (a) isotopes, (b) isobars and (c) isotones among the following nuclides:

$$^{15}_{8}O,\ ^{14}_{7}N,\ ^{13}_{6}C,\ ^{12}_{5}B,\ ^{14}_{8}O,\ ^{13}_{7}N,\ ^{15}_{7}N,\ ^{16}_{8}O,\ ^{18}_{9}F,\ ^{17}_{9}F$$

Solution: Before these nuclides can be classified as either isotopes, isobars or isotones, it is important to state clearly what they mean.

Isotopes are nuclides having the same number of protons in the nucleus. That is, the atomic numbers are the same.

Isobars are nuclides having the same number of neutrons and protons in the nucleus. In other words, they have equal mass numbers and these represent the number of nucleons in the nucleus.

Isotones are nuclides having the same neutron number in the nucleus. That is, they have equal amount of neutrons in the nucleus. (Note that a typical nuclide is represented by the symbol $^{m}_{p}X$ or $_{p}X^{m}$. m is the mass number, p is the atomic number and X is the elemental chemical symbol corresponding to the value of p.)

Now that these terminologies have been well defined, the nuclides can be categorized very easily.

a) The isotopes are $^{13}_{7}N$, $^{14}_{7}N$ and $^{15}_{7}N$;

$^{14}_{8}O$, $^{15}_{8}O$ and $^{16}_{8}O$;

$^{17}_{9}F$ and $^{18}_{9}F$.

b) The isobars are $^{13}_{6}C$ and $^{13}_{7}N$;

$^{14}_{7}N$ and $^{14}_{8}O$;

$^{15}_{7}N$ and $^{15}_{8}O$.

c) The isotones are $^{13}_{7}N$ and $^{14}_{8}O$;

$^{12}_{5}B$, $^{13}_{6}C$, $^{14}_{7}N$ and $^{15}_{8}O$;

$^{15}_{7}N$, $^{16}_{8}O$ and $^{17}_{9}F$.

INTERACTION OF RADIATION WITH MATTER

• PROBLEM 14-10

Given that lead has a density of 11.3×10^{3} kg m^{-3} and a mass absorption coefficient for 3.0 MeV, γ's corresponding to a half thickness of 16 g cm^{-2}, calculate the percent decrease in activity at a depth of 1 cm.

Solution: All the processes by which γ-rays interact with matter lead to exponential attenuation, which is characterized by a half thickness and an absorption coefficient μ .

If I_0 is the incident intensity of a beam of γ-rays, then the intensity I transmitted through a thickness x cm of absorber is given by

$$I = I_0 e^{-\mu x} \tag{1}$$

The linear absorption coefficient μ is a function of the energy of the γ-rays and of the absorbing medium. The half thickness $x_{\frac{1}{2}}$ is defined as the thickness of absorber required to absorb one half of the incident photons, that is, the thickness required to make $I = \frac{1}{2} I_0$. It is related to μ by the equation

$$x_{\frac{1}{2}} = \frac{0.693}{\mu}.$$

The absorber thickness are frequently given in terms of surface density ρx , expressed in grams per square centimeter, where ρ = the density. Thus equation (1) can be written as

$$I = I_0 e^{-(\mu/\rho)\rho x} .$$

The ratio $\frac{\mu}{\rho}$ is called the mass absorption coefficient.

The mass absorption coefficient for this problem has a value given by

$$\frac{0.693}{16 g\ cm^{-2}}$$

$$= (4.33 \times 10^{-2} cm^2 g^{-1})\left(\frac{1m}{100\ cm}\right)^2\left(\frac{1000g}{1kg}\right)$$

$$= 4.33 \times 10^{-3} m^2 kg^{-1}$$

$$\therefore \quad \mu(\text{linear}) = \mu(\text{mass absorption})\rho$$

$$= (4.33 \times 10^{-3} m^2 kg^{-1})(11.3 \times 10^3 kg\ m^{-3})$$
$$= 48.9 m^{-1} .$$

Using equation (1) yields

$$I = I_0 \exp(-48.9 m^{-1})(1 \times 10^{-2} m)$$
$$= 0.613\ I_0 .$$

The decrease in activity at a depth of $1 \times 10^{-2} m$ is therefore

$$1 - 0.613 = 0.387$$

or

$$= 38.7\%$$

• PROBLEM 14-11

Determine the approximate energy-loss rate of 3 Mev alpha particles in air, given that the mean energy-loss rate of 3 Mev protons in air is 12.5×10^{-2} Mev/cm .

Solution: Particles such as protons or alpha particles, interact by virtue of their electric charge with the atomic electrons of the medium through which they are passing. As a result, part of the kinetic energy of the moving particle is transferred to the electron, thus slightly decreasing the velocity of the moving particle. The rate at which a particle loses energy along its path, -dE/dx, is given by

$$-\frac{dE}{dx} = \frac{4\pi e^4 z^2}{m_0 \bar{V}^2} NZ\left[\ln \frac{2m_0 \bar{V}^2}{I(1-\beta^2)} - \beta^2\right] \qquad (1)$$

where z = the charge of the moving particle whose average velocity is $\bar{V}$, m_0 and e are the rest mass and charge of an electron respectively. N is the number of stopping atoms per cm^3, and Z is their atomic number. β is the ratio $\bar{V}/c$, where c = the velocity of light. I is the average energy required to excite or ionize the atoms of the stopping material.

For particles whose velocities are much smaller than c, the terms containing β may be ignored. Also the logarithmic term will vary rather slowly with $\bar{V}$. Thus equation (1) may be written in an approximate form as

$$-\frac{dE}{dx} \propto \frac{MZ^2}{E} \qquad (2)$$

where M and E = the mass and energy of the moving particle respectively. The $\propto$ is a proportionality sign. Equation (2) can also be written as

$$-\frac{dE}{dx} = \frac{4\pi Z^2 e^4 N}{m_0 \bar{V}^2} . \qquad (3)$$

Since the range in a particular stopping medium is known, the range of another particle of different mass and charge can be calculated by using the subscript 1 for protons and 2 for alphas. According to equation (3),

$$\frac{-dE_1/dx_1}{dE_2/dx_2} = \frac{4\pi Z_{11}^2 e^4 N_1}{M_0 \bar{V}_1^2} \frac{m_0 \bar{V}_2^2}{4\pi Z_{12}^2 e^4 N_2}$$

$$= \frac{Z_{11}^2 N_1 \bar{V}_2^2}{Z_{12}^2 N_2 \bar{V}_1^2} \qquad (4)$$

where $Z_{11} = 1$ and $Z_{12} = 2$. Since $E = m\bar{V}^2$, $E_1 = 3\text{Mev}$, $E_2 = 3\text{Mev}$, $m_1 = 1$ and $m_2 = 4$, $E_1 = 3 = 1\bar{V}_1^2$. Therefore, $\bar{V}_1^2 = 3$. Also $E_2 = 3 = 4\bar{V}_2^2$. Therefore $\bar{V}_2^2 = 0.75$. Using equation (4) gives

$$-\frac{dE_2}{dx_2} = (12.5 \times 10^{-2}) \frac{(4)(3)}{(1)(0.75)}$$

$$= 2 \text{ Mev/cm}$$

• PROBLEM 14-12

Calculate the ratio of energy loss when a 4 Mev alpha particle travelling through carbon collides with nuclei (scattering) to the energy loss when it collides with bound electrons.

Solution: If a particle of energy E and momentum $p = m\bar{V}$ is deflected through an angle θ, the nonrelativistic energy loss in the forward direction is equal to

$$E = \frac{m(\bar{V} \sin\theta)^2}{2} = \frac{p^2 \sin^2\theta}{2m} \qquad (1)$$

The probability $P(\theta)d(\theta)$ of an incident particle's being scattered through an angle between θ and $d\theta$ is given by

$$P(\theta)d(\theta) = \frac{\pi Z_1^2 Z_2^2 e^4 \sin\theta}{8E^2 \sin^4 \theta/2} \qquad (2)$$

The energy loss, $\Delta\bar{E}$, averaged over all deflections is the probability of the energy loss, Eq. (2), times the energy loss, Eq. (1)

$$\Delta\bar{E} = \int \Delta E(\theta)P(\theta)d\theta$$

$$= \frac{p^2}{2m} \frac{\pi Z_1^2 Z_2^2 e^4}{8E^2} \int \frac{\sin^3\theta}{\sin^4 \frac{\theta}{2}} d\theta \qquad (3)$$

Equation (3) is integrated with the upper limit of $\theta = \pi$, which is the maximum angle when the incident particle is deflected 180°. The lower limit will be designated by θ_{min} for purposes of integration.

Integrating Eq. (3) between these limits gives

$$-\Delta E = \frac{p^2}{2m} \frac{\pi Z_1^2 Z_2^2 e^4}{E^2} 2\left[\ln\left(\frac{2}{\theta_{min}}\right) + \frac{\theta_{min}^2}{4} - 1\right] \quad (4)$$

The minimum angle, θ_{min}, is related to the closest distance to which a particle of velocity $\bar{V}$ can approach a nucleus of charge Z_2. Experimental and theoretical evidence indicates that this distance is a function of the size and charge of the nucleus as well as of the velocity and charge of the incident particle. In general, the distance approximates the size of the nucleus (2×10^{-12} cm), and the angle θ_{min} for light elements is about 10^{-6} radians. The term $\theta_{min}^2/4$ and the -1 in the brackets of Eq. (4) may be neglected in comparison to the $\ln(2/\theta_{min})$ term.

$$-\Delta E = \frac{p^2}{2m} \frac{\pi Z_1^2 Z_2^2 e^4}{E^2} 2\left[\ln\left(\frac{2}{\theta_{min}}\right)\right] \quad (5)$$

The energy loss due to scattering over an interval dx is obtained by multiplying the right-hand side of equation (5) by $N_1\,dx$, where N_1 = the number of particles per cubic centimeter and E is substituted for $p^2/2m$ to give

$$-\frac{dE}{dx} = \frac{2\pi Z_1^2 Z_2^2 e^4 N_1}{E} \ln(2/\theta_{min}) \quad (6)$$

The ratio of scattering losses to collision losses, dE_s/dE_c, is

$$\frac{-dE_s/dx}{-dE_c/dx} = \frac{\dfrac{2\pi Z_1^2 Z_2^2 e^4 N_1}{E} \ln\left(\dfrac{2}{\theta_{min}}\right)}{\dfrac{4\pi Z_1^2 e^4 N}{m_0 \bar{V}^2} \ln\left(\dfrac{2m_0\bar{V}^2}{I}\right)}$$

Substituting the following values: $\theta_{min} = 8 \times 10^{-5}$, $Z_1 = 2$, $I \cong 80$, $\bar{V} = 1.40 \times 10^9$ cm/sec, $m_0 = 9.11 \times 10^{-28}$g, $Z_2 = 6$, $N = 3.01 \times 10^{23}$ electrons/g, $N_1 = 0.5 \times 10^{-23}$ nuclei/g, $E = 4$, and $2m_0\bar{V}^2 = (2)(9.11 \times 10^{-28})(1.40 \times 10^9)^2(6.24 \times 10^5) = 22.3 \times 10^{-4}$ Mev, and cancelling the Z_1, π, and e^4 terms, gives

$$\frac{dE_s}{dE_c} = \frac{(2)(6)^2(0.5)(10^{-23})/4 \ln\left(2/(8 \times 10^{-5})\right)}{(4)(3.01)(10^{-23})/(11.15 \times 10^{-4})\ln(2230/80)}$$

$$= 2.5 \times 10^{-3}$$

• PROBLEM 14-13

Calculate the total and average binding energies and the packing fraction for $^{12}_{6}C$.

BINDING ENERGY PER NUCLEON AS A FUNCTION OF MASS NUMBER

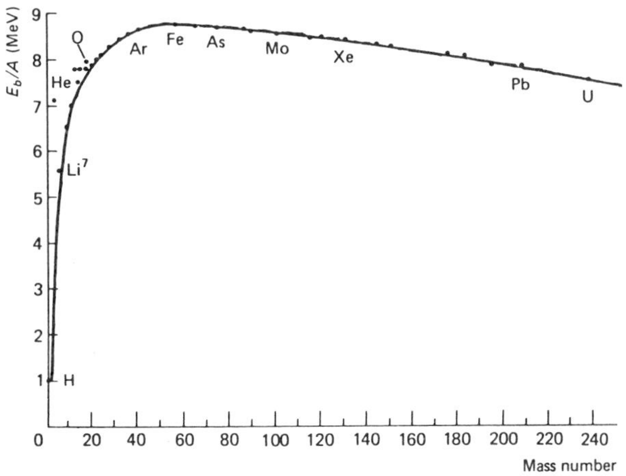

Solution: The general form of representing a particular nuclear reaction is given by

$$^{A}_{Z}X = Z\,^{1}_{1}H + (A - Z)\,^{1}_{0}n \qquad (1)$$

where X = elemental chemical symbol corresponding to the value of Z.

Z = atomic number

A = protons + neutrons = mass number.

Consequently, for $^{12}_{6}C$, the reaction is

$$^{12}_{6}C = 6\,^{1}_{1}H + 6\,^{1}_{0}n\ . \qquad (2)$$

For a nucleus, the average binding energy is defined as the total binding energy divided by the value of A. The total binding energy is the energy for reaction (1) as calculated from the difference in the rest masses of products and reactants. Therefore, the average binding energy for reaction (2) is given by

$$\frac{\Delta(\text{mass})}{12} = \frac{6(1.007825) + 6(1.008665) - 12.000000}{12}$$

$$= \frac{0.098940\ u}{12}$$

1u = 1 amu, $\Delta E = (\Delta m)c^2$ where c is the speed of light. Therefore,

$$\frac{0.09894\ \text{amu} \times 1.6605(10^{-24})\text{g amu}^{-1} \times (2.997925(10^{10})\text{cm sec}^{-1})^2 \times 10^{-7}\text{J sec}^{-1}}{1.6022(10^{-19})\text{J ev}^{-1} \times 10^{6}\ \text{ev Mev}^{-1}}$$

$= 92.163$ Mev

Thus, $\frac{\Delta(\text{mass})}{12} = \frac{92.163 \text{ Mev}}{12}$

$= 7.680$ Mev

The packing fraction is given by

$$pf = \frac{(M - A)10^4}{A} \tag{3}$$

where pf = packing fraction. M - A = mass excess = mass of the nuclide in u less the mass number. In this problem, observe that M = A. As a result, equation (3) yields

$$pf = \frac{(12 - 12)10^4}{12}$$

$$= \frac{(0)10^4}{12}$$

or $\quad pf = 0$

• PROBLEM 14-14

Calculate the recoil energy of an atom of mass 10, following emission of a 2 Mev gamma ray.

Solution: The energy equivalent to one mass unit is $E = mc^2 = 931 \times 10^6$ ev.

$$E_r = \frac{(2 \times 10^6)^2}{1862 \times 10^6 \times 10} = 214 \text{ ev},$$

where E_r = recoil energy

or, alternatively,

$$E_r = \frac{E_\gamma^2}{2\ Mc^2}$$

$$= \frac{4 \times 10^{12} (\text{ev})^2}{2 \times 10 \frac{\text{g}}{\text{mole}} \times \frac{\text{mole}}{6.02 \times 10^{23} \text{ molec}} \times 9 \times 10^{20} \frac{\text{cm}^2}{\text{sec}^2}}$$

$$= \frac{4 \times 10^{12} (\text{ev})^2}{\frac{180 \times 10^{20} \text{ ergs}}{6 \times 10^{23} \text{ molecules}} \times \frac{\text{ev}}{1.6 \times 10^{-12} \text{ ergs}}}$$

$$= \frac{4 \times 10^{12} \text{ ev}}{186.2 \times 10^8 \text{ recoil}}$$

$$E_r = 214 \text{ ev/recoil}$$

• PROBLEM 14-15

Given a 25 Mev proton, compute its velocity and the energy associated with this velocity.

Solution: When the energy equivalent of the rest mass of the particle is considerably greater than the energy of the particle, nonrelativistic mechanics applies. The rest mass energy, in electron volts, for any particle is

$$E = m_0c^2 = \frac{\text{atom-wt}}{\text{Avogadro's number}} \times c^2 \times \frac{1}{1.602 \times 10^{-12} \frac{\text{erg}}{\text{ev}}}$$

where c = the speed of light.
For the proton,

$$E = \frac{1.008 \text{ g}}{\text{g-atom}} \times \frac{1}{6.023 \times 10^{23} \frac{\text{atoms}}{\text{g-atom}}} \times \left(2.9979 \times 10^{10} \frac{\text{cm}}{\text{sec}}\right)^2 \times \frac{1}{1.602 \times 10^{-12} \frac{\text{erg}}{\text{ev}}}$$

$$E = 1.008 \text{ g} \times \frac{\text{cm}^2}{\text{sec}^2} \times 931 \times 10^6 \frac{\text{ev}}{\text{erg}}$$

$$E \cong 931 \times 10^6 \text{ ev}$$

Since this is far in excess of the given energy of the particle, non-relativistic mechanics applies, and

$$E = \tfrac{1}{2} m\bar{V}^2$$

$$25 \times 10^6 \text{ ev} = \tfrac{1}{2} m_p\bar{V}^2$$

where m_p = the mass of the proton

$$\bar{V}^2 = 50 \times 10^6 \text{ ev} \times 1.6 \times 10^{-12} \frac{\text{ergs}}{\text{ev}} \times \frac{1}{1.67 \times 10^{-24} \text{ g}}$$

The dimensions of the erg in the CGS system are $m\ell^2t^{-2}$, and the velocity of a 25 Mev proton is, in centimeters per second,

$$\bar{V} = \sqrt{50 \times 10^{18} \frac{\text{cm}^2}{\text{sec}^2}} \cong 7 \times 10^9 \frac{\text{cm}}{\text{sec}}$$

The energy of an electron with the same velocity is

$$E = \tfrac{1}{2} m_e \bar{V}^2 = \tfrac{1}{2} \times 9.11 \times 10^{-28} \text{ g} \times \left(7 \times 10^9 \frac{\text{cm}}{\text{sec}}\right)^2$$

where m_e = the mass of the electron.

$$E = 225 \times 10^{-10} \text{ erg} \times \frac{\text{ev}}{1.6 \times 10^{-12} \text{ erg}}$$

or $E \cong 14{,}000$ ev .

NUCLEAR REACTIONS

• PROBLEM 14-16

Complete the following nuclear equations.

(a) ${}_7N^{14} + {}_2He^4 \rightarrow {}_8O^{17} + \ldots$

(b) ${}_4Be^9 + {}_2He^4 \rightarrow {}_6C^{12} + \ldots$

(c) ${}_{15}P^{30} \rightarrow {}_{14}Si^{30} + \ldots$

(d) $_1H^3 \rightarrow {}_2He^3 + \ldots$

Solution: The rules for balancing nuclear equations are: (1) the superscript assigned to each particle is equal to its mass number and the subscript is equal to its atomic number or nuclear charge; (2) a free proton is the nucleus of a hydrogen atom, and is therefore written as $_1H^1$; (3) a free neutron has no charge and is therefore assigned zero atomic number. Its mass number is one and its notation is $_0n^1$; (4) an electron, β^-, has zero mass and its atomic number is -1, hence the notation $_{-1}e^0$; (5) a positron has zero mass and its atomic number is +1, hence the notation $_{+1}e^0$; (6) an alpha particle (α-particle) is a helium nucleus, and is represented by $_2He^4$ or α; (7) Gamma radiation (γ) is a form of light, and has no mass and no charge; (8) in a balanced equation, the sum of the subscripts must be the same on both sides of the equation; the sum of the superscripts must also be the same on both sides of the equation.

In equation (a), $_7N^{14} + {}_2He^4 \rightarrow {}_8O^{17} + \ldots$, the sum of the subscripts on the left is $(7 + 2) = 9$. The subscript of one of the products is 8, thus, the other product must have a subscript or net charge of 1. The sum of the superscripts on the left is $(14 + 4) = 18$. The superscript of one of the products is 17, thus the other product on the right must have a superscript or mass number of 1. The particle with a +1 nuclear charge and a mass number of 1 is the proton, $_1H^1$.

In equation (b), $_4Be^9 + {}_2He^4 \rightarrow {}_6C^{12} + \ldots$, the nuclear charge of the second product particle (that is, its subscript) is $(4 + 2) - 6 = 0$. The mass number of the particle (its superscript) is $(9 + 4) - 12 = 1$. Thus, the particle must be the neutron, $_0n^1$.

In equation (c), $_{15}P^{30} \rightarrow {}_{14}Si^{30} + \ldots$, the nuclear charge of the second particle is $15 - 14 = +1$. Its mass number is $30 - 30 = 0$. Thus, the particle must be the positron, $_{+1}e^0$.

In equation (d), $_1H^3 \rightarrow {}_2He^3 + \ldots$, the nuclear charge of the second product is $1 - 2 = -1$. Its mass number is $3 - 3 = 0$. Thus, the particle must be a β^- or an electron $_{-1}e^0$.

Therefore, the correct balanced equations are

a) $_7N^{14} + {}_2He^4 \rightarrow {}_8O^{17} + {}_1H^1$

b) $_4Be^9 + {}_2He^4 \rightarrow {}_6C^{12} + {}_0n^1$

c) $_{15}P^{30} \rightarrow {}_{14}Si^{30} + {}_{+1}e^0$

d) $_1H^3 \rightarrow {}_2He^3 + {}_{-1}e^0$

• PROBLEM 14-17

A 1-cm cube (1.46 g) of carbon tetrachloride is irradiated to produce ^{35}S by the reaction

$$^{35}_{17}Cl + ^{1}_{0}n \rightarrow ^{35}_{16}S + ^{1}_{1}H$$

The thermal neutron flux, normal to one face of the sample, is $10^9\ cm^{-2}sec^{-1}$. Given that the total absorption cross section for chlorine is 33.8 barns and the isotopic cross section for the reaction is 0.19 barn, calculate the number of ^{35}S atoms formed in 24 hrs.

Solution: The number of radioactive reactions per unit time is given by

$$I_0 - I = I_0(1 - e^{-n\sigma_t x}) \qquad (1)$$

where I = the intensity of incident particles per unit time after travelling a target thickness x, n is the number of target nuclei per cubic centimeter of target and σ_t is the total cross section.

Since total cross sections must be used in equation (1), then only the total number of reactions may be obtained directly. This can be multiplied by the ratio of the isotopic cross section to the total cross section, to obtain the number of reactions of a particular kind.

To be able to use equation (1), the number of chlorine atoms per cubic centimeter of sample, n, must be calculated. Therefore,

$$n = \left(\frac{1.46g\ CCl_4}{153.8g\ mol^{-1}CCl_4}\right)(4)(6.02 \times 10^{23}mol^{-1})$$

$$= 2.28 \times 10^{22}$$

From equation (1), the total number of neutrons absorbed in the CCl_4 sample in 24 hrs is

$$I - I_0 = 10^9 cm^{-2}sec^{-1} \times (24hrs)\left(\frac{3600sec}{1hr}\right)\left[1-\exp(-2.28x10^{22}x33.8x10^{-24}cm^2)\right]$$

$$= 8.64 \times 10^{13}cm^{-2}[0.537\ cm^2]$$

$$= 4.64 \times 10^{13}$$

The percent isotopic abundance for the naturally occurring ^{35}Cl nuclide is given in tables of constants as 75.53. Therefore, the fraction of neutrons absorbed that lead to the neutron, proton reactions in ^{35}Cl is

$$\frac{(0.19\ barn)(0.7553)}{33.8}$$

$$= 4.24 \times 10^{-3}$$

The total number of reactions to produce the number of ^{35}S atoms is found by multiplying the 4.24×10^{-3} by the ratio of the partial cross section to the total cross section. Therefore, the number of ^{35}S atoms formed is

$$4.24 \times 10^{-3}(4.64 \times 10^{13})$$

$$= 1.96 \times 10^{11}.$$

• PROBLEM 14-18

A sheet of gold 0.3mm thick and $5cm^2$ in area with a density of $19.3g\ cm^{-3}$ is exposed to a thermal neutron flux of 10^7 neutrons per cm^2 per second. Given that the capture cross section of ^{197}Au for thermal neutrons is 99 barns, calculate the number of radioactive ^{198}Au nuclei produced per second in the gold. Neglect any other neutron reaction with gold and take the atomic weight of gold to be 197.2.

Solution: The probability of a nuclear process is generally expressed in terms of a cross section, σ which has the dimensions of area. For a beam of particles striking a thin target, that is, a target in which the beam is slowed down only infinitesimally, the cross section for a particular process is given by

$$R_i = I\, n\, \sigma_i x \tag{1}$$

where R_i = the number of processes of the type under consideration occurring in the target per unit time, I is the number of incident particles per unit time, n is the number of target nuclei per cubic centimeter of target, σ_i is the cross section for the processes and x is the target thickness in cm. If instead of a thin target, there is a thick target where the incident particle beam is slowed down or attenuated, the attenuation $-dI$ in the infinitesimal thickness dx is given by

$$-dI = In\sigma_t\, dx \tag{2}$$

Here σ_t is the total cross section. Integrating equation (2) gives

$$I = I_0 e^{-n\sigma_i x}$$

and

$$I_0 - I = I_0(1 - e^{-n\sigma_i x}) \tag{3}$$

where I = the intensity of the beam after traversing a target thickness x, I_0 is the incident intensity, and $I_0 - I$ is the number of reactions per unit time which is what this problem requires. Since the density of gold is $19.3g\ cm^{-3}$ and its atomic weight is 197.2, therefore

$$n = \frac{19.3g\ cm^{-3}}{197.2g\ mole^{-1}} \times 6.02 \times 10^{23} mol^{-1}$$

$$= 5.89 \times 10^{22}\ nuclei/cm^3$$

$$x = 0.03\ cm$$

$$I_0 = \left(10^7\ \frac{neutrons}{cm^2 sec}\right)(5\ cm^2)$$

$$= 5 \times 10^7\ \text{neutrons per sec}\ .$$

Using these values in equation (3) yields

$$I_0 - I = 5 \times 10^7 (1 - e^{-5.89\times10^{22}\times99\times10^{-24}\times0.03})$$

$$= 5 \times 10^7 (0.1604)$$

$= 8.02 \times 10^6$ ^{198}Au nuclei formed per second.

• PROBLEM 14-19

Calculate ΔE for the proposed basis of an absolutely clean source of nuclear energy

$$^{11}_{5}B + ^{1}_{1}H \rightarrow ^{12}_{6}C \rightarrow 3\ ^{4}_{2}He$$

Atomic masses: $^{11}B = 11.00931$, $^{4}He = 4.00260$, $^{1}H = 1.00783$.

Solution: The energy of nuclear reactions, ΔE, is calculated from the difference between the masses of products and reactants in accordance with the Einstein Law. Einstein's Law can be stated as $\Delta E = \Delta mc^2$, where Δm = the difference in the masses of the products and the reactants, and c is the speed of light (3×10^{10} cm/sec). The total reaction here can be written as

$$^{11}_{5}B + ^{1}_{1}H \rightarrow 3\ ^{4}_{2}He .$$

Δm is equal to the mass of $^{11}_{5}B$ and $^{1}_{1}H$ subtracted from the mass of $3\ ^{4}_{2}He$. The mass of $3\ ^{4}_{2}He$ is equal to 3 times the mass of $^{4}_{2}He$. Thus,

$$\Delta m = (3 \times m \text{ of } ^{4}_{2}He) - (m \text{ of } ^{11}_{5}B + m \text{ of } ^{1}_{1}H)$$

$$= (3 \times 4.00260) - (11.00931 + 1.00783)$$

$$= 12.0078 - 12.01714 = - 9.34 \times 10^{-3} \text{ g/mole.}$$

Now, using Δm to solve for ΔE yields

$$\Delta E = \Delta mc^2 = - 9.34 \times 10^{-3} \text{ g/mole} \times (3.0 \times 10^{10} \text{ cm/sec})^2$$

$$= - 9.34 \times 10^{-3} \text{ g/mole} \times 9.0 \times 10^{20} \text{ cm}^2/\text{sec}^2$$

$$= - 8.406 \times 10^{18} \text{ g cm}^2/\text{mole sec}^2$$

$$= - 8.406 \times 10^{18} \text{ ergs/mole.}$$

There are 4.18×10^{10} ergs in 1 kcal, thus ergs can be converted to kcal by dividing the number of ergs by the conversion factor, 4.18×10^{10} ergs/kcal.

$$\text{no. of kcal} = \frac{- 8.406 \times 10^{18} \text{ ergs/mole}}{4.18 \times 10^{10} \text{ ergs/kcal}}$$

$$= - 2.01 \times 10^{8} \text{ kcal/mole.}$$

ΔE for this reaction is $- 2.01 \times 10^{8}$ kcal per mole.

Calculate the Q value of the following reaction

$$^{106}_{46}Pd + ^{1}_{0}n \rightarrow ^{106}_{45}Rh + ^{1}_{1}H + Q$$

$$^{106}_{45}Rh \rightarrow ^{106}_{46}Pd + \beta^- + \bar{\nu} + 3.54 \text{ MeV}$$

The product $^{106}_{45}Rh$ decays with a half-life of 30 seconds and 3.54 MeV β particles are emitted to the ground state of ^{106}Pd.

Solution: Just like chemical reactions, nuclear reactions are accompanied by energy changes. Some reactions are exothermic, and some are endothermic. When energy is evolved, it appears as kinetic of the escaping particles and of the product nucleus. The change in kinetic energy in a nuclear reaction is called the Q value. Q values may be calculated from atomic masses, if they are known; but if they are not known it is often possible to calculate the Q value provided that the product nucleus is radioactive and decays back to the initial nucleus with known decay energy.

$$^{106}_{46}Pd + ^{1}_{0}n \rightarrow ^{106}_{45}Rh + ^{1}_{1}H + Q \qquad (1)$$

$$^{106}_{45}Rh \rightarrow ^{106}_{46}Pd + \beta^- + \bar{\nu} + 3.54 \text{ MeV} \qquad (2)$$

Here β^- is an electron and $\bar{\nu}$ is an antineutrino.

Adding equations (1) and (2) gives

$$^{1}_{0}n \rightarrow ^{1}_{1}H + \beta^- + \bar{\nu} + Q + 3.54 \text{ MeV}.$$

This is equivalent to the transformation of a neutron into a proton, an electron, together with an antineutrino and an energy change. Writing an energy balance on the net change gives

$$M_n \rightarrow M_{^1H} + Q + 3.54 \text{ MeV} \qquad (3)$$

where M_n = mass of neutron and $M_{^1H}$ is mass of proton

$M_n = 1.008665$ mass units

$M_{^1H} = 1.007825$ mass units

Therefore, using equation (3) yields

$$Q \text{ value} = (M_n - M_{^1H}) - 3.54 \text{ MeV}$$

$$= \left[(1.008665 - 1.007825)\text{amu} \times \left(\frac{931.5 \text{ MeV}}{1 \text{ amu}}\right)\right] - 3.54 \text{ MeV}$$

$$= (0.7824 - 3.54) \text{ MeV}$$

$$= -2.76 \text{ MeV}.$$

• PROBLEM 14-21

Calculate the yield, the threshold energy and the projectile energy for the reaction

$$^{58}_{26}\text{Fe}\left(^{3}_{2}\text{He},\ ^{2}_{1}\text{H}\right)^{59}_{27}\text{Co}$$

if the masses are 57.9333, 3.01603, 2.0140 and 58.9332 u, respectively.

Solution: The yield of the reaction is defined as the negative of the energy for a nuclear transformation reaction. This energy is calculated by subtracting the sum of the rest masses of the reactants from the sum of the rest masses of the products. That is,

$$Q = -\Delta(\text{mass}) \qquad (1)$$

where Q = the yield

$$\Delta(\text{mass}) = (\text{rest masses of products}) - (\text{rest masses of reactants}).$$

Substitute the given data into equation (1) to obtain

$$Q = -\Delta(\text{mass}) = -\left[(58.9332 + 2.0140) - (57.9333 + 3.01603)\right]$$

$$= -\left[60.9472 - 60.94933\right]$$

$$= -\left[-0.00213\right]$$

$$\therefore \quad Q = 0.0021 \text{ u} = 1.96 \text{ MeV}$$

Observe that $\Delta(\text{mass})$ is negative. Because of this, the threshold energy, which is given by

$$E_{thr} = \frac{(M_{proj} + M_{target})\,\Delta(\text{mass})}{M_{target}}$$

has no meaning.

The projectile energy is given by

$$E_{proj} = \frac{(M_{proj} + M_{targ})U_{proj}}{M_{targ}} \qquad (2)$$

where U_{proj} for $^{3}_{2}\text{He}$ is given as

$$U_{Proj} = \frac{(1.92 \text{ MeV})(P_{targ})}{A_{targ}^{\frac{1}{3}} + 1.44} \qquad (3)$$

P is the number of protons in the nucleus, otherwise known as the atomic number.

A = mass number or the number of protons and neutrons in the nucleus.

From equation (3),

$$U_{proj} = \frac{(1.92)(26)}{58^{\frac{1}{3}} + 1.44} = 9.40 \text{ MeV}$$

Using this value of U_{proj} in equation (2) gives

$$E_{proj} = \frac{(3 + 58)(9.40)}{58}$$

or $$E_{proj} = 9.89 \text{ MeV} .$$

RADIOACTIVITY

• PROBLEM 14-22

2.000 picogram (pg) of ^{33}P decays by $^{0}_{-1}\beta$ emission to 0.250 pg in 75.9 days. Find the half-life of ^{33}P.

Solution: The half-life is defined as the time it takes for ½ of the amount of a certain compound present to decompose. For example, if a substance has a half-life of 1 day, after one day there will only be ½ of the original amount left. When given the original and final amount of a substance, after a given time has elapsed, the number of half-lives that have passed can be found. This is done by dividing the original amount by the final amount and determining how many factors of 2 are present in the quotient. The half-life is then found by dividing the time elapsed by the number of twos. Mathematically, this is done as follows:

Solving for the half-life of ^{33}P :

$$\frac{\text{original amount}}{\text{final amount}} = \frac{2.000 \text{ pg}}{0.250 \text{ pg}} = 8$$

Obtaining the number of 2's in the quotient yields

$8 = 2 \times 2 \times 2$; Therefore 3 half-lives have passed.

One is given that these half-lives elapse in 75.9 days. Consequently, the half-life of ^{33}P is

$$\text{half-life} = \frac{75.9 \text{ days}}{3} = 25.3 \text{ days}.$$

• PROBLEM 14-23

One curie is defined as the amount of material, which is equivalent to one gram of radium, that gives 3.7×10^{10} nuclear disintegrations per second. The half-life of ^{210}At is 8.3 hr. How many grams of astatine (At) would equal one curie?

Solution: The half life is defined as the time it takes for one half of the amount of a radioactive substance to disintegrate. To find the number of grams of ^{210}At that would be equal to 1 curie, first find the number of disintegrations of ^{210}At per second. Then solve for the number of moles necessary and from that solve for the number of grams.

Solving:

(1) determine the half-life in seconds. This unit is used because curies are measured in disintegrations per second.

$t_{\frac{1}{2}}$ = 8.3 hr x 60 min/hr x 60 sec/min = 29880 sec

(2) Solving for the number of disintegrations of ^{210}At in 1 curie.

Let x = the total number of nuclei of ^{210}At in 1 curie, x/2 the number of nuclei left after 1 half-life, 29880 sec. The following ratio can be set up:

$$\frac{(^{210}At) \text{ number of nuclei after 1 half-life}}{\text{half-life}} = 3.7 \times 10^{10} \text{ dis/sec.}$$

One can solve this ratio for x, the original number of nuclei present.

$$\frac{x/2}{29880 \text{ sec}} = 3.7 \times 10^{10} \text{ dis/sec}$$

$$\frac{x}{2} = 29880 \text{ sec} \times 3.7 \times 10^{10} \text{ dis/sec}$$

$$x = 2 \times 29880 \text{ sec} \times 3.7 \times 10^{10} \text{ dis/sec} = 2.21 \times 10^{15} \text{ dis.}$$

Thus, 2.21×10^{15} dis of ^{210}At are equal to 1 curie.

(3) Solving for the number of moles. There are 6.02×10^{23} nuclei per mole. Therefore, the number of moles present is equal to the number of disintegrations divided by 6.02×10^{23}.

$$\text{no. of moles} = \frac{2.21 \times 10^{15} \text{ nuclei}}{6.02 \times 10^{23} \text{ nuclei/mole}} = 3.67 \times 10^{-9} \text{ moles}$$

(4) One solves for the number of grams necessary by multiplying the number of moles by the molecular weight of ^{210}At(MW = 210).

$$\text{no. of grams} = 210 \text{ g/mole} \times 3.67 \times 10^{-9} \text{ moles}$$

$$= 7.71 \times 10^{-7} \text{ g.}$$

This would be the number of grams necessary at $t = t_{\frac{1}{2}}$.

• PROBLEM 14-24

The half-life, $t_{\frac{1}{2}}$ of $^{220}_{86}Rn$ is given as 54.5 sec. Calculate the mass of $^{220}_{86}Rn$ which is equivalent to 1 millicurie.

Solution: The rate of emission from a sample of a particular radioactive substance is proportional to the number of nuclei remaining, consequently the rate is continuously decreasing. Expressing this mathematically gives

$$\frac{-dN}{dt} = \lambda N \qquad (1)$$

which reads:

number decaying per sec = a proportionality constant λ, characteristic of the isotope times the number of nuclei remaining, N .

If at some particular time there are N_0 nuclei in the sample, then an expression can be found for N, the number remaining at any later time t, by integrating equation (1). That is,

$$\int -\frac{dN}{N} = \int \lambda\, dt$$

$-\ln N = \lambda t +$ constant of integration. To evaluate the constant, let N_0 be the number of nuclei present at some arbitrary zero time. When $t = 0$

$$-\ln N_0 = \text{constant of integration}$$

Therefore $$-\ln N = \lambda t - \ln N_0$$

or $$\ln N_0 - \ln N = \lambda t$$

$$\ln\left(N_0/N\right) = \lambda t$$

Therefore $$\frac{N_0}{N} = e^{\lambda t}$$

or $$\frac{N}{N_0} = e^{-\lambda t} \qquad (2)$$

and $$\ln(N/N_0) = \ln e^{-\lambda t}$$

$$= -\lambda t \qquad (3)$$

A relationship between the decay constant λ and the half-life $t_{\frac{1}{2}}$ can be found from equation (3). At time $t_{\frac{1}{2}}$, the number of nuclei remaining is exactly one half of the initial number, so that the ratio N/N_0 is numerically equal to one half

$$t_{\frac{1}{2}} = \left[-\ln \tfrac{1}{2}\right]/\lambda$$

$$= \left[\ln(1/\tfrac{1}{2})\right]/\lambda$$

$$= \left[\ln 2\right]/\lambda$$

$$= 0.693/\lambda$$

Therefore $$t_{\frac{1}{2}} = \frac{0.693}{\lambda} \qquad (4)$$

from which $$\lambda = \frac{0.693}{t_{\frac{1}{2}}}$$

$$= \frac{0.693}{54.5 \text{ sec}}$$

$$= 1.27 \times 10^{-2} s^{-1} .$$

Using equation (1) and the definition of a curie given as

$$\frac{-dN}{dt} = 3.7 \times 10^7 \text{ sec}^{-1},$$

N can be calculated as follows:

$$N = \frac{-(dN/dt)}{\lambda}$$

$$= \frac{3.7 \times 10^7 \text{ sec}^{-1}}{1.27 \times 10^{-2} \text{ sec}^{-1}}$$

$$= 2.91 \times 10^9$$

Converting this number to moles and mass gives:

$$\left(\frac{2.91 \times 10^9}{6.02 \times 10^{23} \text{mol}^{-1}}\right)(220 \text{ g mol}^{-1})$$

$$= 106 \times 10^{-14} \text{ g} = 106 \times 10^{-17} \text{ kg}$$

or $$= 1.06 \times 10^{-15} \text{ kg} .$$

• PROBLEM 14-25

A slow neutron flux of 10^{12} neutrons per cm^2 bombards a sample of cobalt for a period of six months. Given that the cross section of ^{59}Co is 21.7 barns and ^{60}Co has a half-life of 5.26 years, calculate the net activity of the cobalt sample.

Solution: The average rate of radioactive decay is proportional to the number of radioactive atoms, N, present and is given by

$$-\frac{dN}{dt} = \lambda N \tag{1}$$

where λ = the decay constant analogous to the first-order rate constant. The rate of formation of the nuclides is given by the product of the cross section σ, the neutron flux density φ and the concentration N_0. That is, rate of formation = $\sigma\varphi N_0$. Therefore the net rate of formation is

$$\frac{dN}{dt} = \sigma\varphi N_0 - \lambda N \tag{2}$$

$$= R - \lambda N$$

where $R = \sigma\varphi N_0$ (3)

or $$\frac{dN}{R - \lambda N} = dt \tag{4}$$

Integrating equation (4) between $t = 0, N = 0$ and $t = t, N = N$ gives

$$\int_{N=0}^{N=N} \frac{dN}{R - \lambda N} = \int_{t=0}^{t=t} dt$$

$$-\frac{1}{\lambda} \ln \frac{R - \lambda N}{R} = t$$

Solving for N gives

$$-\lambda t = \ln\left(\frac{R - \lambda N}{R}\right)$$

$$= \ln\left(1 - \frac{\lambda N}{R}\right)$$

$$e^{-\lambda t} = e^{\ln(1 - \lambda N/R)}$$

$$= 1 - \frac{\lambda N}{R}$$

$$\frac{\lambda N}{R} = 1 - e^{-\lambda t}$$

or

$$N = \frac{R(1 - e^{-\lambda t})}{\lambda} \qquad (5)$$

Recall that $R = \sigma\varphi N_0$. Therefore, substituting for R in equation (5) gives

$$N = \frac{\sigma\varphi N_0(1 - e^{-\lambda t})}{\lambda}$$

$$= \frac{\sigma\varphi N_0}{\lambda}(1 - e^{-\lambda t}) \qquad (6)$$

$$N_0 = \left(\frac{8.9\text{g } ^{60}\text{Co}}{\text{cm}^3}\right)\left(\frac{1 \text{ mol}}{59 \text{ g}}\right)\left(\frac{6.02 \times 10^{23} \text{ molecules}}{1 \text{ mole}}\right)$$

$$= 9.08 \times 10^{22} \text{ molecules cm}^{-3} .$$

But $$t_{\frac{1}{2}} = \frac{0.693}{\lambda}$$

where $t_{\frac{1}{2}}$ = half-life

$$\therefore \lambda = \frac{0.693}{t_{\frac{1}{2}}}$$

$$= \frac{0.693}{(5.26 \text{ years})\left(\frac{365 \text{ days}}{1 \text{ year}}\right)\left(\frac{24 \text{ hrs}}{1 \text{ day}}\right)\left(\frac{3600 \text{ sec}}{1 \text{ hr}}\right)}$$

$$= 4.2 \times 10^{-9} \text{ sec}^{-1}$$

Using equation (6) yields

$$N = (2.17 \text{ barns})\left(\frac{10^{-24}\text{cm}^2}{1 \text{ barn}}\right)\left(\frac{10^{12}}{\text{cm}^2\text{-sec}}\right)\left(9.08\times10^{22}\text{cm}^{-3}\right)\left(1 - e^{-0.693t/5.6}\right)$$

$$= 8.82 \times 10^{19} \frac{\text{atoms}}{\text{cm}^3} .$$

From equation (1),

$$-\frac{dN}{dt} = (4.2 \times 10^{-9} \text{ sec}^{-1})\left(8.82 \times 10^{19} \frac{\text{atoms}}{\text{cm}^3}\right)\left(\frac{1 \text{ cm}^3}{9 \text{ g}}\right)$$

$$= 4.11 \times 10^{10} \frac{\text{atoms}}{\text{sec}} .$$

Therefore, the number of radioactive material or the curies in the ^{60}Co sample is obtained by using the definition of the curie, which is 3.7×10^{10} disintegrations per second.

That is, $$\frac{4.11 \times 10^{10}}{3.7 \times 10^{10}}$$

$$= 1.10 \frac{\text{curies}}{\text{g}} \times \text{number of grams.}$$

Note that the value 1.10 curies/g is the specific activity.

N^{13} decays by β^+ emission. The maximum kinetic energy of the β^+ is 1.19 MeV. What is the nuclidic mass of N^{13}?

Solution: In the emission of a β^+ particle, the daughter nuclide has a Z value one unit less than the parent with no change in A (mass). Thus,

$$_ZP^A \rightarrow {}_{Z-1}D^A + \beta^+ ,$$

where P and D are the parent and daughter nuclides, respectively. The emitted positron (β^+) is unstable and is usually consumed after being slowed down by collisions. This is shown in the following reaction

$$\beta^+ + \beta^- \rightarrow 2\gamma .$$

The gamma (γ) radiation is a form of light. It has no mass and no charge.

In this reaction, 2 photons of light are produced.

The reaction in this problem is

$$_7N^{13} \rightarrow {}_6C^{13} + \beta^+$$

In this type of process, a simple difference of whole atom masses is not desired. Whole atom masses can be used for mass difference calculations in all nuclear reactions, except in β^+ processes where there is a resulting annihilation of two electron masses (one β^+ and one β^-). Thus,

$$\text{mass difference} = (M_n \text{ for } _7N^{13}) - (M_n \text{ for } _6C^{13}) - M_e$$

$$= [(M \text{ for } _7N^{13}) - 7M_e] - [(M \text{ for } _6C^{13}) - 6M_e] - M_e$$

$$= (M \text{ for } _7N^{13}) - (M \text{ for } _6C^{13}) - 2M_e$$

$$= (M \text{ for } _7N^{13}) - 13.00335 - 2(0.00055)$$

$$= (M \text{ for } _7N^{13}) - 13.00445$$

Here, M_n is the nuclear mass (mass of neutrons and protons), M is the atomic mass, and M_e is the mass of an electron. This expression is equal to the mass equivalent of the maximum kinetic energy of the β^+.

$$\frac{1.19 \text{ MeV}}{931.5 \text{ MeV/amu}} = 0.00128 \text{ amu}$$

Then, 0.00128 amu = (M for $_7N^{13}$) - 13.00445 or,

$$M \text{ for } _7N^{13} = 13.00445 + 0.00128 = 13.00573 \text{ amu}.$$

• PROBLEM 14-27

Calculate Δm, the difference in mass between the final and initial nuclei in grams per mole for the emission of a γ ray, $^{19}_{8}O^*$ (excited state) $\rightarrow$ $^{19}_{8}O$ (ground state) $+ \gamma$ ($\Delta E = 1.06 \times 10^8$ kcal/mole).

Solution: Δm can be solved for by using Einstein's Law, which relates Δm and ΔE.
This law is given by

$$\Delta E = \Delta mc^2 ,$$

where ΔE = the energy, Δm is the change in mass, and c is the speed of light, 3×10^{10} cm/sec. When using Einstein's Law, the ΔE, in kcal/mole, must be first converted to ergs/mole. There are 4.18×10^{10} ergs in one kcal, therefore one converts kcal to ergs by multiplying the number of kcal by 4.18×10^{10} ergs/kcal.

$$\text{no. of ergs} = 4.18 \times 10^{10} \text{ ergs/kcal} \times 1.06 \times 10^8 \text{ kcal/mole}$$

$$= 4.43 \times 10^{18} \text{ ergs/mole.}$$

Solving for Δm,

$$\Delta m = \frac{\Delta E}{c^2}, \text{ where } \Delta E = 4.43 \times 10^{18} \text{ ergs/mole}$$

$$c = 3 \times 10^{10} \text{ cm/sec}$$

$$\text{ergs} = \frac{\text{g cm}^2}{\text{sec}^2}$$

$$\therefore \quad \Delta m = \frac{4.43 \times 10^{18}}{(3 \times 10^{10})^2} \frac{\text{g}}{\text{mole}}$$

$$\Delta m = 4.92 \times 10^{-3} \text{ g/mole} .$$

When a γ particle is emitted, one knows that the final state weighs less than the initial state, therefore,

$$\Delta m = - 4.92 \times 10^{-3} \text{ g/mole.}$$

• PROBLEM 14-28

Calculate the weight, W, in grams of 1.00 millicurie of ^{14}C from its half life of 5720 years.

Solution: The decay of a radioactive substance follows the exponential law

$$N = N_0 e^{-\lambda t} , \qquad (1)$$

where N = the number of unchanged atoms at time t, N_0 is the number present at t = 0, and λ is the characteristic decay constant for the substance. The characteristic rate of radioactive decay may be given in terms of the half-life $t_{\frac{1}{2}}$, which is the time required for an initial number of atoms N, to be reduced in half. Thus, at the time $t = t_{\frac{1}{2}}$, $N = N_0/2$. Equation (1) thus becomes

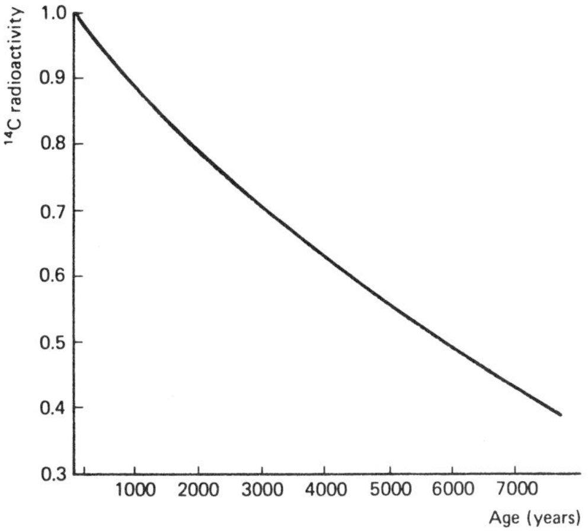

$$\frac{N_0}{2} = N_0 e^{-\lambda t_{\frac{1}{2}}}$$

or

$$\tfrac{1}{2} = e^{-\lambda t_{\frac{1}{2}}}$$

and

$$\ln \tfrac{1}{2} = -\lambda t_{\frac{1}{2}} \ .$$

from which

$$t_{\frac{1}{2}} = \frac{\ln 2}{\lambda}$$

$$= \frac{0.693}{\lambda} \qquad (2)$$

If the decay rate, $-\frac{dN}{dt}$, is set proportional to the number of atoms present: then

$$\frac{-dN}{dt} = \lambda N$$

$$= \frac{\lambda \text{ W in g}}{14 \text{ g mole}^{-1}} \times 6.02 \times 10^{23} \text{ mole}^{-1} \qquad (3)$$

Solving for λ in equation (2) yields

$$\lambda = \frac{0.693}{t_{\frac{1}{2}}}$$

$$= \frac{0.693}{(5720 \text{ years})\left(\frac{365 \text{ days}}{1 \text{ year}}\right)\left(\frac{24 \text{ hrs}}{1 \text{ day}}\right)\left(\frac{3600 \text{ sec}}{1 \text{ hr}}\right)}$$

$$= 3.83 \times 10^{-12} \text{ sec}^{-1} \ .$$

But $\frac{-dN}{dt}$ = 1.00 millicurie

= 3.700×10^7 disintegrations per second.

Therefore, from equation (3),

$$W = \frac{-dN/dt \ (14)}{(3.83 \times 10^7 \text{ sec}^{-1})(6.02 \times 10^{23})}$$

$$= 2.24 \times 10^{-4} \text{ g} \ .$$

• PROBLEM 14-29

How many alpha particles per second would be emitted from 4×10^{-12} g of ^{210}Po ($t_{\frac{1}{2}}$ = 138 days)?

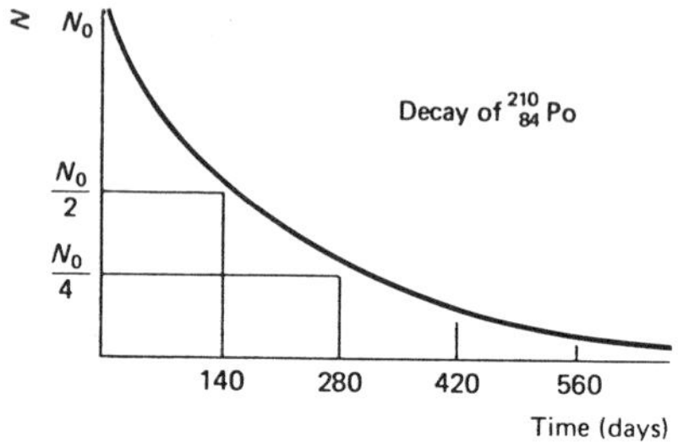

Solution: When given the mass and the half-life of a substance, one can find the number of disintegrations per second (dN/dt) by using the following equation:

$$\frac{dN}{dt} = -\frac{\ln 2}{t_{\frac{1}{2}}} \times N ,$$

where $t_{\frac{1}{2}}$ is the half-life in second, N is the original number of nuclei.

(1) Solving for the half-life in seconds:

$$t_{\frac{1}{2}} = 138 \text{ days} \times 24 \text{ hr/day} \times 60 \text{ min/hr} \times 60 \text{ sec/min}$$

$$= 1.192 \times 10^7 \text{ sec} .$$

(2) Determining the number of nuclei present. One is given that there was originally 4×10^{-12}g of ^{210}Po present. The number of nuclei present is found by multiplying the number of moles by Avogrado's number (6.02×10^{23}), the number of nuclei in one mole. The number of moles is found by dividing 4×10^{-12} g by the molecular weight of ^{210}Po. (MW = 210).

$$\text{no. of moles} = \frac{4 \times 10^{-12} \text{ g}}{210 \text{ g/mole}} = 1.905 \times 10^{-14} \text{ moles}$$

$$\text{no. of nuclei} = 1.905 \times 10^{-14} \text{ moles} \times 6.022 \times 10^{23} \text{ nuclei/mole}$$

$$= 1.147 \times 10^{10} \text{ nuclei}$$

(3) Solving for dN/dt ,

$$\frac{dN}{dt} = -\frac{\ln 2}{t_{\frac{1}{2}}} \times N$$

$N = 1.147 \times 10^{10}$ nuclei

$t_{\frac{1}{2}} = 1.192 \times 10^7$ sec

$\ln 2 = 0.693$

$$\frac{dN}{dt} = -\frac{0.693}{1.192 \times 10^7 \text{ sec}} \times 1.147 \times 10^{10} \text{ nuclei}$$

$$= -666.94 \text{ nuclei/sec}$$

Because dN/dt is negative, it means that the change in the number of nuclei per unit time is caused by disintegrations of the nuclei. This is the disintegration rate at $t = 0$.

• PROBLEM 14-30

A lead foil 1 cm^2 in area and 1 mm thick is bombarded by a flux of thermal neutrons equal to $10^8 \text{ sec}^{-1} \text{ cm}^{-2}$. Given that the cross section, σ of lead is 0.18 barn and its density $= 11.3 \times 10^3 \text{ kg m}^{-3}$, calculate the number of radioactive nuclei formed per second.

Solution: For a beam of particles striking a given target, the number of nuclei formed is given by the equation

$$I_0 - I = I_0(1 - e^{-n\sigma_t x}) \qquad (1)$$

where I = the intensity of the beam after passing through a target thickness x, I_0 is the incident intensity and $I_0 - I$ is the number of reactions per unit time. n is the number of nuclei present per m^3, and since the atomic weight of lead is given, n is equal to (weight of lead) $\times$ (Avogadro's number) $\div$ the atomic weight. Therefore

$$n = \frac{(11.3 \times 10^3 \text{ kg m}^{-3})(6.02 \times 10^{23} \text{ nuclei mol}^{-1})}{(207 \text{ g mol}^{-1})\left(\frac{10^{-3} \text{ kg}}{1 \text{ g}}\right)}$$

$$= 3.29 \times 10^{28} \text{ nuclei/m}^3$$

$$x = 1 \text{ mm}\left(\frac{10^{-3} \text{ m}}{1 \text{ mm}}\right)$$

$$= 1 \times 10^{-3} \text{ m} .$$

The intensity of the incident beam is

$$I_0 = (\text{flux}) \times (\text{area})$$

$$= (10^8 \text{sec}^{-1} \text{cm}^{-2}) \times (1 \text{ cm}^2)$$

$$= 10^8 \text{ sec}^{-1} .$$

Therefore, from equation (1)

$$I_0 - I = 10^8[1 - \exp(-3.29 \times 10^{28} \text{m}^{-3})(0.18 \times 10^{-24} \text{cm}^2)\left(\frac{1 \text{ m}}{100 \text{ cm}}\right)^2 (1 \times 10^{-3} \text{m})]$$

$$= 10^8[1 - \exp(-5.9 \times 10^{-4})]$$

$$= 5.9 \times 10^4 \text{ lead nuclei formed per second.}$$

• PROBLEM 14-31

A sample of bristle cone pine wood of age 7,000 ± 100 years, known by counting growth rings, possesses an activity of 6.6 d (disintegrations)/minute-g of carbon. Calculate the exact age of the wood sample from radiochemical evidence.

Solution: Radioactive decay is related to the rate of disintegration and the half-life by the following equation:

$$q_t = q_0\ (0.5)^{t/t_{1/2}}$$

where q_t is the rate of disintegration of the substance containing carbon, q_0 is the rate of disintegration of carbon (14 d/min-g), t is the time elapsed during the reaction, and $t_{1/2}$ is the half-life of the element concerned. For carbon, $t_{1/2}$ = 5730 yrs. Here one needs to solve for t.

$$q_t = q_0\ (0.5)^{t/t_{1/2}}$$

q_t = 6.6 d/min-g

q_0 = 14 d/min-g

t = ?

$t_{1/2}$ = 5730 yrs

$$6.6 \text{ d/min-g} = 14 \text{ d/min-g} \times (0.5)^{t/5730}$$

$$\frac{6.6 \text{ d/min-g}}{14 \text{ d/min-g}} = 0.5^{t/5730}$$

$$.471 = 0.5^{t/5730}$$

$$\log .471 = t/5730 \text{ yrs} \times \log 0.5$$

$$-.327 = t/5730 \times (-.301)$$

$$\frac{-.327}{-.301} = \frac{t}{5730 \text{ yrs}}$$

$$t = \frac{.327 \times 5730 \text{ yrs}}{.301} = 6225.0 \text{ yrs.}$$

Therefore, the tree is 6,225 years old.

• PROBLEM 14-32

The radioactive decay constant for radium is 1.36×10^{-11}. How many disintegrations per second occur in 100 g of radium? The molecular weight of radium is 226 g/mole.

Solution: The number of disintegrations per second of a given amount of a particular element can be determined by using the following equation.

$$D = \lambda N$$

where D = the number of disintegrations per second, λ is the decay constant and N is the number of atoms present.

In this problem λ is given and N must be determined before solving for D. Given that 100 g of radium is present, the number of moles present is determined by dividing 100 g by the molecular weight of radium. Therefore,

$$\text{no. of moles} = \frac{100 \text{ g}}{226 \text{ g/mole}} = 0.442 \text{ moles} .$$

There are 6.02×10^{23} particles per mole; Thus, calculate the number of atoms (N) in 0.442 moles as follows:

$$N = (0.442 \text{ moles})(6.02 \times 10^{23} \text{ atoms/mole})$$
$$= 2.66 \times 10^{23} \text{ atoms}$$

Consequently, solving for D yields

$$D = \lambda N = (1.36 \times 10^{-11})(2.66 \times 10^{23}) = 3.62 \times 10^{12} \text{ dis/sec.}$$

• PROBLEM 14-33

Calculate the maximum kinetic energy of the β^- emitted in the radioactive decay of He^6 .

Solution: To solve this problem, one must first know that β^- is an electron of negative unit charge and zero mass. Thus, the equation for this particular decay process is

$$^6_2He \rightarrow {}^6_3Li + \beta^- . \quad \text{Or} \quad {}_2He^6 \rightarrow {}_3Li^6 + {}_{-1}e^0 .$$

The kinetic energy of the β^- particle comes from the difference in mass (or energy, $E = mc^2$), between products and reactants. To compute the mass change during this process, only the whole atomic mass of He^6 and Li^6 need be considered. Once the difference in mass is known, a conversion factor is used (931. MeV = 1 amu). Thus

Mass of He^6	=	6.01890	amu
Mass of Li^6	=	6.01513	amu
loss in mass	=	0.00377	amu

Energy equivalent = (931 MeV/1 amu)(0.00377 amu) = 3.51 MeV.

Therefore, the maximum kinetic energy of the β^- particle is 3.51 MeV.

• PROBLEM 14-34

The first step in the radioactive decay of $^{238}_{92}U$ is $^{238}_{92}U = {}^{234}_{90}Th + {}^4_2He$. Calculate the energy released in this reaction. The exact masses of $^{238}_{92}U$, $^{234}_{90}Th$, and ^4_2He are 238.0508, 234.0437 and 4.0026 amu, respectively.

(1.0073 amu = 1.673×10^{-24} g.)

Solution: The energy released in this process can be determined from the change in mass that occurs. Energy and mass are related by the following equation,

$$\Delta E = \Delta mc^2$$

where, ΔE is the change in energy, Δm is the change in mass and c is the speed of light (3.0×10^{10} cm/sec). Δm is found by subtracting the mass of $^{238}_{92}U$ from the sum of the masses of $^{234}_{90}Th$ and $^{4}_{2}He$.

$$\Delta m = (234.0437 \text{ amu} + 4.0026 \text{ amu}) - 238.0508 \text{ amu}$$
$$= -.0045 \text{ amu}.$$

(Note that amu is called atomic mass unit, and is defined such that the mass of the particular carbon atom having six neutrons and six protons is exactly 12.00000u .)

Energy is expressed in ergs (g-cm^2/sec^2), therefore, Δm must be converted to grams before solving for ΔE.

That is,

$$\Delta m = (-.0045 \text{ amu}) \frac{(1.673 \times 10^{-24} \text{ g})}{(1.0073 \text{ amu})} = -0.00747394 \times 10^{-24} \text{ g}$$
$$= -7.47 \times 10^{-27} \text{ g}.$$

Solving for ΔE :

$$\Delta E = (-7.47 \times 10^{-27} \text{ g})(3.0 \times 10^{10} \text{ cm/sec})^2$$
$$= -6.72 \times 10^{-6} \text{ g cm}^2/\text{sec}^2 = -6.72 \times 10^{-6} \text{ erg}$$

The negative sign indicates that 6.72×10^{-6} ergs are released in the decay process.

• PROBLEM 14-35

You add radioactive material whose activity per unit mass was 45.5 $s^{-1}g^{-1}$ to a liquid and then dilute it so the activity per unit mass was 6.5 $s^{-1}g^{-1}$. What is the dilution factor and the original amount of radioactive material? Assume 100 mg of radioactive material was added.

Solution: The dilution factor is simply the ratio of the activities since the activity is proportional to the concentration. Hence,

$$\text{dilution factor} = \frac{45.5 \text{ s}^{-1}\text{g}^{-1}}{6.5 \text{ s}^{-1}\text{g}^{-1}} = 7.0$$

Let X be the original amount of material

X* be the amount of radioactive material added

Since the activity per unit mass decreased seven times (dilution factor = 7), the mass must have increased seven times. Therefore,

$$X + X^* = 7.0X^*$$

$$X = 7.0X^* - X^* = 6.0X^* = 6.0\ (100\text{mg}) = 600\ \text{mg}$$

• PROBLEM 14-36

> You are a chemist employed by a geological company to date the age of rocks by radioactive testing. You are told by an assistant that the sample he just handed to you contains a substantial quantity of ^{40}Ar. Through analysis you discover the sample contains 3 percent K (by weight), that there is $95.0 \times 10^{-7}\ \dfrac{m^3 \text{ of } ^{40}Ar}{\text{kg sample}}$ at STP, and the $^{40}Ar/^{36}Ar$ ratio is an incredible 75,200. Determine the age of the sample. How do you do it? The percent abundance of ^{40}K is 0.0118.

Solution: This problem is not a simple decay process where an element decays by one type of decay. It is actually a complex process which uses two different modes of decay, electron capture and beta decay. Therefore, the equation used to find the time of decay is not the simple decay equation but rather a complex one of the following form.

$$t = \frac{1}{\lambda_{EC} + \lambda_{\beta-}} \ln \left[1 + \frac{\left(\lambda_{EC} + \lambda_{\beta-}\right) N_{40,Ar}}{\left(\lambda_{EC}\right) N_{40,K}} \right] \qquad (1)$$

where

t = time of decay

λ_{EC} = decay constant for electron capture

$\lambda_{\beta-}$ = decay constant for beta decay

$N_{40,Ar}$ = number of atoms of ^{40}Ar

$N_{40,K}$ = number of atoms of ^{40}K

For $^{40}_{19}K$, $\lambda_{EC} = 5.85 \times 10^{-11}\ y^{-1}$ and $\lambda_{\beta-} = 4.72 \times 10^{-10}\ y^{-1}$

It is obvious from equation (1) that it is necessary to find $N_{40,Ar}$ and $N_{40,K}$. Remember, in solving this problem there will be ^{40}Ar which was formed by decay of ^{40}K, but there will also be ^{40}Ar which was not formed from decay of ^{40}K.

To calculate the number of moles of ^{40}Ar/kg sample, use the ideal gas law. Hence,

$$n = \frac{PV}{RT} = \frac{(1 \text{ atm})(95.0 \times 10^{-7} \text{ m}^3/\text{kg sample})}{\left(82.1 \frac{\text{cm}^3 \text{ atm}}{{}^{o}\text{K mol}}\right)\left(\frac{1\text{m}}{100 \text{ cm}}\right)^3 \left(273^{o}\text{K}\right)}$$

$$= 4.24 \times 10^{-4} \text{ mol/kg sample}$$

The number of atoms of ^{40}Ar/kg sample can now be found by multiplying by Avogadro's number. Hence,

$$N_{40,Ar} = 4.24 \times 10^{-4} \text{ mol/kg sample} \times 6.02252 \times 10^{23} \text{ atoms/mol}$$

$$= 2.5535 \times 10^{20} \text{ atoms/kg sample}$$

As stated earlier, not all of the ^{40}Ar was derived from the ^{40}K. This must now be corrected for. In a normal sample of Ar, the ratio of $^{40}Ar/^{36}Ar$ is 296. For the sample this ratio was 75,200. This ratio for the sample represents the total amount, that is, the normal ratio plus the ratio from the decay of ^{40}K. Therefore, by subtracting the normal amount from the total, and then dividing this difference by the total, the fraction of ^{40}Ar derived from ^{40}K can be found. Hence,

$$\frac{(75{,}200 - 296)}{75{,}200} = .996$$

This is now the correction factor to be multiplied in front of $N_{40,Ar}$ to find $N_{40,Ar}$ from the decay of ^{40}K. Hence,

$$N_{40,Ar} = 2.5535 \times 10^{20} \text{ atoms/kg sample} \times .996$$

$$= 2.5433 \times 10^{20} \text{ atoms/kg sample}$$

Next, the number of atoms/kg sample must be found. It is known that the percent of potassium (by weight) in 1 kg sample is 3%. Therefore, the fraction of potassium in 1000 g is $\frac{(3 \times 10^{-2})}{\text{kg sample}}$ (1000 g). Hence, the number of moles/kg sample of potassium is

$$\frac{\frac{(3 \times 10^{-2})(1000 \text{ g})}{\text{kg sample}}}{39.1 \frac{\text{g}}{\text{mol}}} = .767 \frac{\text{mol}}{\text{kg sample}} \text{ K}$$

However, not all of the potassium in the sample is ^{40}K. The percent abundance of ^{40}K is 1.18×10^{-2}. Hence, the fraction of ^{40}K in the sample is 1.18×10^{-4}. Therefore, the number of

$\frac{\text{moles of } ^{40}K}{\text{kg sample}}$ is given by,

$$.767 \text{ mol/kg sample} \times 1.18 \times 10^{-4} = 9.05 \times 10^{-5} \text{ mol/kg sample}$$

The number of atoms of ^{40}K/kg sample can now be found by multiplying by Avogadro's number. Hence,

$$N_{40,K} = 9.05 \times 10^{-5} \text{ mol/kg sample} \times 6.02252 \times 10^{23} \text{ atoms/mol}$$

$$= 5.4504 \times 10^{19} \text{ atoms/kg sample}$$

All the information required in equation (1) has been found. Therefore,

$$t = \frac{1}{\lambda_{EC} + \lambda_{\beta-}} \ln \left[1 + \frac{\left(\lambda_{EC} + \lambda_{\beta-}\right) N_{40,Ar}}{\left(\lambda_{EC}\right) N_{40,K}} \right]$$

$$= \frac{1}{5.85 \times 10^{-11} y^{-1} + 4.72 \times 10^{-10} y^{-1}} \times$$

$$\ln \left[1 + \frac{\left(5.85 \text{x} 10^{-11} y^{-1} + 4.72 \text{x} 10^{-10} y^{-1}\right)\left(2.5433 \text{x} 10^{20} \text{atoms/kg sample}\right)}{\left(5.85 \times 10^{-11} y^{-1}\right)\left(5.4504 \times 10^{19} \text{ atoms/kg sample}\right)} \right]$$

$$= \frac{1}{5.305 \times 10^{-10} y^{-1}} \times$$

$$\ln \left[1 + \frac{\left(5.305 \text{x} 10^{-10} y^{-1}\right)\left(2.5433 \text{x} 10^{20} \text{atoms/kg sample}\right)}{\left(5.85 \text{x} 10^{-11} y^{-1}\right)\left(5.4504 \text{x} 10^{19} \text{ atoms/kg sample}\right)} \right]$$

$$= \frac{1}{5.305 \times 10^{-10} y^{-1}} \ln \left[1 + \frac{1.3492 \times 10^{11}}{3.1885 \times 10^{9}} \right]$$

$$= \frac{1}{5.305 \times 10^{-10} y^{-1}} \ln [43.32]$$

$$= 7.10 \times 10^{9} y$$

• PROBLEM 14-37

^{146}Ce decays by beta emission to ^{146}Pr, with $t_{1/2} = 14$ min; the ^{146}Pr decays in turn to stable ^{146}Nd with $t_{1/2} = 25$ min. A sample consists initially of 0.5mCi of pure ^{146}Ce. Calculate the activity of ^{146}Ce and of ^{146}Pr present 30 minutes later. Is this a case of secular equilibrium?

Solution: This problem illustrates consecutive radioactive decay. An initial species decays to a second species which undergoes radioactive decay. The sequence of decays for this problem can be represented as

$$^{146}Ce \xrightarrow{\lambda_1} {}^{146}Pr \xrightarrow{\lambda_2} {}^{146}Nd$$

where λ_1, λ_2 represent the first and second decay constants respectively.

The equation dealing with such sequential decay is given by

$$D_2 = \frac{\lambda_1 D_1^0}{\lambda_2 - \lambda_1}\left(e^{-\lambda_1 t} - e^{-\lambda_2 t}\right) \qquad (1)$$

where

λ_1 = first decay constant

λ_2 = second decay constant

D_1^0 = initial amount of the first species

D_2 = amount of the second species at some time t

t = any arbitrary time

It is obvious that in order to calculate the activity of ^{146}Pr (the second species), it is necessary to calculate both decay constants, λ_1, λ_2. This can be done because the half-life of each decay is given. For the first decay the following equation can be written,

$$D_1 = D_1^0 e^{-\lambda_1 t} \qquad (2)$$

Now the half-life is defined as the time necessary to reduce the initial concentration in half. That is, when $t = t_{1/2}$ $D_1 = \frac{1}{2} D_1^0$. Then equation (2) becomes

$$\frac{1}{2} D_1^0 = D_1^0 e^{-\lambda_1 t_{1/2}}$$

which rearranges to

$$\frac{\frac{1}{2} D_1^0}{D_1^0} = e^{-\lambda_1 t_{1/2}} \qquad (3)$$

Taking natural logarithms of both sides and solving for λ_1, equation (3) becomes

$$\lambda_1 = \frac{.693}{t_{1/2}} .$$

Since $t_{1/2} = 14$ min, $\lambda_1 = 0.0495\ \text{min}^{-1}$.

The second decay constant, λ_2, must now be found. It does not matter that the initial concentration of the second species is unknown. At the half-life, $t_{1/2}$, only half the concentration remains. Hence, as was done with the first species,

$$\lambda_2 = \frac{.693}{t_{1/2}}$$

Since $t_{1/2} = 25$ min, $\lambda_2 = 0.027\ \text{min}^{-1}$.

The activity of ^{146}Ce is to be found after 30 minutes. Since the initial concentration is given, equation (2) can be used. Therefore,

$$D_1 = D_1^0 e^{-\lambda_1 t} = 0.5\ \text{mCi}\ e^{-(0.0495\ \text{min}^{-1})(30\ \text{min})}$$

$$= 0.113\ \text{mCi}$$

The activity of ^{146}Pr is to be found after 30 minutes. In this case it is necessary to use equation (1) which relates the activity of the second species to the initial activity of the first species. Therefore

$$D_2 = \frac{\lambda_1 D_1^0}{\lambda_2 - \lambda_1}\left(e^{-\lambda_1 t} - e^{-\lambda_2 t}\right)$$

$$= \frac{(0.0495\ \text{min}^{-1})(0.5\ \text{mCi})}{(0.027\text{min}^{-1} - .0495\text{min}^{-1})}\left(e^{-(0.0495\ \text{min}^{-1})(30\ \text{min})} - e^{-(.027\ \text{min}^{-1})(30\ \text{min})}\right)$$

$$= \frac{0.02475\ \text{min}^{-1}\ \text{mCi}}{-0.0225\ \text{min}^{-1}}\ (.227 - .445)$$

$$= .240\ \text{mCi}$$

Secular equilibrium is when the activity of the first species does not change over several half-lives of the second species. That is, $D_2 = D_1^0$. This occurs when $\lambda_2 \gg \lambda_1$.

Considering the process

$$^{146}Ce \xrightarrow{\lambda_1} {}^{146}Pr \xrightarrow{\lambda_2} {}^{146}Nd$$

if $\lambda_2 \gg \lambda_1$ then ^{146}Ce has not appreciably decayed. Therefore, the activity of the first species is regarded as being constant. In this problem $\lambda_1 = 0.0495\ min^{-1}$ and $\lambda_2 = .027\ min^{-1}$. Therefore, $\lambda_1 > \lambda_2$, and hence, there is no secular equilibrium.

• PROBLEM 14-38

Calculate the Coulombic barrier in the bombardment of ^{209}Bi with alpha particles.

Solution: In bombarding a nucleus with a charged particle an energy barrier is encountered. This is due to the Coulombic repulsion which develops between the charged particle and the nucleus. An empirical formula to calculate this Coulombic barrier is given by

$$E_{barrier} = \frac{0.96\ zZ}{A_{particle}^{1/3} + A_{target}^{1/3}}$$

where

z = charge number of the particle

Z = atomic number of the target

$A_{particle}$ = mass of the particle

A_{target} = mass of the target

$E_{barrier}$ = Coulombic barrier measured in MeV

For the bombardment of ^{209}Bi with alpha particles, $z = 2$, $Z = 83$, $A_{particle} = 4$ and $A_{target} = 209$. Therefore,

$$E_{barrier} = \frac{(0.96)(2)(83)}{(4)^{1/3}+(209)^{1/3}} = 21.2\ MeV$$

• PROBLEM 14-39

Calculate the barrier potential and threshold energy for an alpha particle colliding with a ^{14}N nucleus.

Solution: In a collision of a particle with a nucleus a certain minimum energy must be imparted from the kinetic energy of the particle in order for a reaction to take place. This energy is called the threshold energy.

The following reaction is relevant to this problem.

$$^{14}_{7}N + ^{4}_{2}He \longrightarrow ^{1}_{1}H + ^{17}_{8}O$$

In order to calculate the threshold energy it is necessary to calculate the change in mass due to the collision. This is done by summing the mass of the products and summing the mass of the reactants, and then subtracting the mass of the reactants from the mass of the products. The mass of hydrogen is 1.0078252 amu and the mass of oxygen is 16.999133 amu. (Note these are the atomic masses of the specific isotopes and not the common atomic masses which are averages of all the isotopes.) Therefore, the sum of the products is 18.006958 amu.

The mass of nitrogen is 14.0030744 amu and the mass of helium is 4.0026036 amu. (Note, again these are the atomic masses of the specific isotopes.) Therefore, the sum of the reactants is 18.005678 amu.

The change in the mass as a result of the collision is 18.006958 amu - 18.005678 amu = 0.00128 amu. To calculate the energy equivalent of this mass change, Einstein's equation is used. It states

$$\Delta E = (\Delta m)c^2$$

where

ΔE = energy change

Δm = change in the mass

c = speed of light

Note the mass in the above equation is not in dimensions of amu but rather kg (g in the cgs system). Hence,

$$\Delta E = 0.00128 \text{ amu} \times 1.66057 \times 10^{-27} \frac{\text{kg}}{\text{amu}} \times (2.997925 \times 10^8 \frac{\text{m}}{\text{s}})^2$$

$$\times \frac{1\text{eV}}{1.602189 \times 10^{-19} \text{ J}} \times \frac{1\text{MeV}}{10^6 \text{eV}}$$

$$= 1.19\text{MeV (Remember 1J} = 1 \text{ kg m}^2/\text{s}^2)$$

To calculate the barrier potential an empirical formula is used. It is given by

$$E_{barrier} = \frac{0.96 \ zZ}{A^{1/3}_{particle} + A^{1/3}_{target}}$$

where

$E_{barrier}$ = barrier potential (in MeV)

z = charge number of the particle

Z = atomic number of the target

$A_{particle}$ = mass of the particle

A_{target} = mass of the target

For the bombardment of ^{14}N with alpha particles, z = 2, Z = 7, $A_{particle}$ = 4, and A_{target} = 14. Therefore,

$$E_{barrier} = \frac{(0.96)(2)(7)}{(4)^{1/3} + (14)^{1/3}}$$

$$= 3.36 \text{ MeV}$$

• PROBLEM 14-40

The maximum weekly dose for the hands and forearms, assuming a mass of 4kg and a surface area of 800 cm^2, is 1.5 rem. How long would it take for a person to receive this dose from a 10 millicurie source emitting a 2.5 MeV gamma ray? The distance between the source and the receiving surface is 10 cm. Assume no radiation is absorbed by the air.

Solution: The curie is equal to 3.700×10^{10} disintegrations/sec. Therefore, the number of gamma rays emitted is equal to

$$10 \text{ millicurie} \times 10^{-3} \frac{\text{curie}}{\text{millicurie}} \times 3.7 \times 10^{10} \text{ s}^{-1} \text{ curie}^{-1}$$

$$= 3.7 \times 10^{8} \text{ s}^{-1}$$

The next step is to calculate the flux which reaches the receiving surface. If the source is considered to be a point, then the rays move out in all directions forming a sphere. The total area covered by these rays is given by the equation for the surface area of a sphere. This is $4\pi r^2$ where r is the distance between the source and the receiving surface. Hence, the flux is

$$\frac{3.7 \times 10^{8} \text{ s}^{-1}}{4\pi(10 \text{ cm} \times 1\text{m}/100 \text{ cm})^2} = \frac{3.7 \times 10^{8} \text{ s}^{-1}}{.1257\text{m}^2}$$

$$= 2.94 \times 10^9 \ s^{-1} \ m^{-2}$$

This is the radiation flux. What is wanted is the energy flux. Therefore, this flux is multiplied by the energy of the source. Hence,

$$2.5 \text{ MeV} \times \frac{10^6 \text{eV}}{\text{MeV}} \times 1.602189 \times 10^{-19} \frac{\text{J}}{\text{eV}} \times 2.94 \times 10^9 \ s^{-1} \ m^{-2}$$

$$= 1.18 \times 10^{-3} \ \text{Js}^{-1} \ m^{-2}$$

The dosage rate is found by multiplying the energy flux by the surface area of the receiving surface. Therefore,

$$\text{dosage rate} = 1.18 \times 10^{-3} \ \text{J s}^{-1} \ m^{-2} \times 800 \ \text{cm}^2 \times (1\text{m}/100 \ \text{cm})^2$$

$$= 9.44 \times 10^{-5} \ \text{J s}^{-1}$$

The next step often confuses the student unfamiliar with the units of radiation. The following discussion will help. The unit called the roentgen is defined for ionizing radiation which is incident in air. It is not based on the actual amount of energy absorbed by the receiving source. It is therefore defined as the amount of ion pairs formed in air. Hence,

$$1\text{r} = 1.61 \times 10^{15} \text{ ion pairs/kg of air},$$

or upon conversion,

$$1\text{r} = 2.57976 \times 10^{-4} \ \text{C/kg}.$$

The unit of radiation which is based upon the actual energy absorbed is the rad. 1 rad = 1.00×10^{-2}J absorbed/kg of receiving source. The rad unit is used for all types of radiation (not just ionizing radiation). In considering damage done to living tissue, other factors besides energy release, are important. Hence each type of radiation has its relative biological effectiveness (rbe). For α particles rbe = 20, and for γ radiation, rbe = 1. The product of the dose in rads and the rbe factor is equal to the roentgen-equivalent in man, rem.

Hence, the 1.5 rem given in the problem can now be converted into energy terms.

$$\frac{1.5 \text{ rem}}{1 \text{ rbe}} = 1.5 \text{ rad} \quad \text{and } 1.5 \text{ rad} \times 1.00 \times 10^{-2} \frac{\text{J}}{\text{kg rad}}$$

$$= 1.5 \times 10^{-2}\ \text{J/kg}$$

Now the receiving source has a mass of 4 kg. Therefore, the permitted dose is

$$1.5 \times 10^{-2}\ \text{J/kg} \times 4\ \text{kg} = 6 \times 10^{-2}\ \text{J}\ .$$

The time needed to achieve this does is found by dividing the dose by the dosage rate,

$$\frac{6 \times 10^{-2}\ \text{J}}{9.44 \times 10^{-5}\ \text{J s}^{-1}} = 6.36 \times 10^{2}\ \text{sec} \times \frac{1\ \text{min}}{60\ \text{sec}} = 10.6\ \text{min}$$

CHAPTER 15

MACROMOLECULES

LIGHT SCATTERING

• PROBLEM 15-1

For a solution of cellulose trinitrate (M = 140,000) in acetone, $dn/dc = 0.105\ cm^3 \cdot g^{-1}$ and $n_0 = 1.3589$. Calculate the ratio of intensities of transmitted to incident light at wavelengths of 400 and 700 nm through 1.00 cm thickness of a solution of the polymer containing 2.00 g per 100 cm^3.

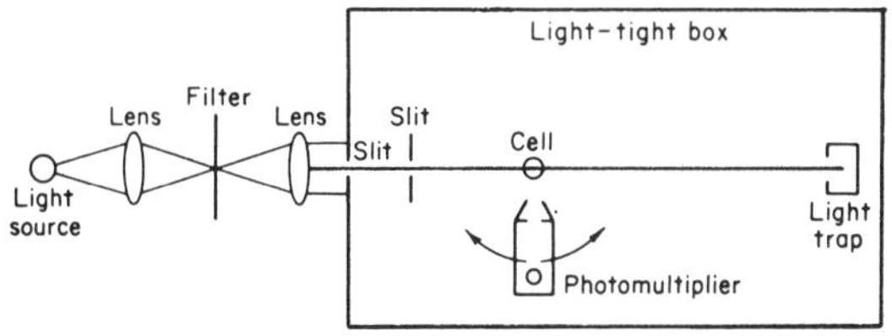

Diagram of the basic construction of a light-scattering apparatus.

Solution: The relationship between the refractive index increment, the number of molecules per cm^3 and the intensity scattered from solution in excess of that scattered by solvent is given by

$$\frac{i}{I_0} = \frac{2\pi^2 n_0^2 (1 + \cos^2\theta)(dn/dc)^2 Mc}{N \lambda^4 r^2}$$

where

i = intensity

I_0 = intensity of incident unpolarized light

n_0 = refractive index of solvent

$\frac{cN}{M}$ = number of molecules per cm^3

$\frac{dn}{dc}$ = refractive index increment

r = distance from the scattering molecule

θ = angle measured from the emergent beam

λ = wavelength .

If the above expression is integrated over all angles to obtain the total scattered intensity, it is found that the transmitted intensity is given by

$$I = I_0 e^{-\tau x} \qquad (1)$$

where I = transmitted intensity
τ = turbidity
x = thickness of the cell in the direction of the incident beam.

Observe that
$$\tau = \frac{32\pi^3 n_0^2 (dn/dc)^2 Mc}{3N \lambda^4}$$
and x = 1 cm thick.

Equation (1) can be rearranged to give

$$I/I_0 = e^{-\tau x} \qquad (2)$$

where I/I_0 = ratio of intensities of transmitted to incident light.

Solving for τx gives

for λ = 400 cm,
$$\tau x = \frac{(3130 \times 10^{-23})(1 \text{ cm})}{256 \times 10^{-20} \text{ cm}^4}$$
$$= 0.0122$$

Therefore, $I/I_0 = e^{-\tau x} = e^{-0.0122}$
$= 0.988$.

For λ = 700,
$$\tau x = \frac{(3130 \times 10^{-23})(1 \text{ cm})}{2401 \times 10^{-20} \text{ cm}^4}$$
$$= 0.0013$$

Therefore, $I/I_0 = e^{-\tau x} = e^{-0.0013} = 0.999$

MELTING POINTS

• PROBLEM 15-2

List the following materials in the probable order of their increasing crystalline melting points and justify your answer. Do not consider molecular length as a factor

(a) $\text{-(NH-(CH}_2)_6\text{-NH-}\overset{O}{\overset{\|}{C}}\text{-(CH}_2)_8\text{-}\overset{O}{\overset{\|}{C}}\text{)}_n$

(b) $\text{-(NH-(CH}_2)_6\text{-NH-}\overset{O}{\overset{\|}{C}}\text{-NH-(CH}_2)_8\text{-NH-}\overset{O}{\overset{\|}{C}}\text{)}_n$

(c) $\text{-(NH-(CH}_2)_6\text{-NH-}\overset{O}{\overset{\|}{C}}\text{-NH-CH}_2\text{-}$  $\text{-CH}_2\text{-NH-}\overset{O}{\overset{\|}{C}}\text{)}_n$

(d) $\text{-(NH-(CH}_2)_6\text{-NH-}\overset{O}{\overset{\|}{C}}\text{-(CH}_2)_4\text{-}\overset{O}{\overset{\|}{C}}\text{-)}_n$

(e) $\text{-(O-(CH}_2)_6\text{-}\overset{O}{\overset{\|}{C}}\text{-)}_n$

What factors must be considered before making such a relative comparison?

Solution: The factors to be considered before making such comparisons are

1) Chain flexibility due to the composition of the backbone. The flexibility of a straight carbon chain polymer can be considerably increased if some of the carbon atoms are replaced by those of oxygen and considerably reduced if some of the carbon atoms are replaced by phenyl group. Such a variation is caused primarily by the variation of freedom of rotation about the -O-, -C- and —⟨O⟩— groups.

2) The number of -CH$_2$- units between functional groups and

3) molecular patterns.

Using these factors, arrange the functional groups in order of their increasing melting points, from lowest to highest.

$$\text{esters}(-O-), \quad \text{amide } (-\overset{\overset{\text{H}}{|}}{\underset{\underset{\text{O}}{||}}{N}}-C-), \quad \text{urea}(-NH-\overset{\overset{\text{O}}{||}}{C}-NH-)$$

Therefore, lowest to highest melting points are:

e)   because of ester linkage
a)   because of amide linkage
d)   amide linkage closer together
b)   this has urea linkages
c)   this has urea linkages and phenyl group.

● PROBLEM 15-3

a)   List (and explain very briefly) the factors that should be considered in deciding which of any two macromolecules (or polymers) will have a higher melting point.
b)   Order the following polymers in order of increasing melting point (lowest to highest):

(1)   -CH$_2$ - CH -   (2)   -CH$_2$ - CH -   (3) -CH$_2$ - CH   (4) -CH$_2$ - $\overset{\overset{CH_3}{|}}{\underset{\underset{⟨O⟩}{|}}{C}}$ -
        | | |
       ⟨O⟩   ⟨O⟩-CH$_3$ ⟨O⟩
                                                                |
                                                          CH$_2$ - CH$_3$

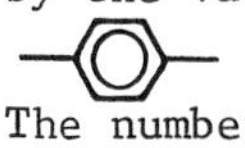

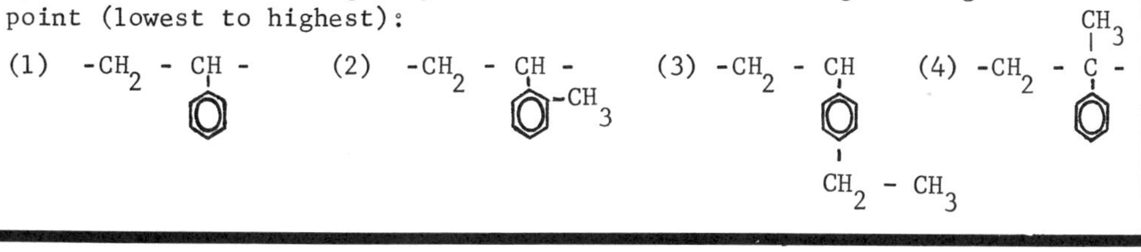

Solution: a)   There are lots of factors to be considered in deciding whether a polymer has a high or low melting point. These factors include molecular weight, repeat units or the groups that make up the macromolecule, molecular packing, chain flexibility, spatial orientation of functional groups (or the presence of pendants) and crosslinking effect.

(i)   Molecular weight:
      The higher the molecular weight of a substance the higher the melting point.
(ii)   Repeat units or groups that make up the polymers:
      The melting point of a polymer is high or low, depending on the groups present in the molecule. For example, a polymer that has a

group will have a higher melting point than one that has an -O-group because of the freedom of rotation about the latter group.
(iii) Molecular Packing: Polymers that have well-packed, parallel molecules have higher intermolecular attractions and therefore higher melting points than those that have molecules that are not well arranged.
(iv) Chain flexibility:

The more flexible the polymer chains are, the more easily segments of the chain will acquire translational motion and hence the lower the melting point. In other words, the stiffer a polymer chain is, the higher the melting point.
(v) Spatial orientation of functional groups: (Pendants)

Pendant groups are those that are attached as appendages to the backbone. They increase the melting point of the polymer when introduced. For example the melting point of

$$-CH_2 - CH_2 - CH_3 \quad \text{is} \quad 75^\circ C,$$

that of
$$-CH_2 - \underset{}{\overset{CH_3}{\overset{|}{CH}}} - CH_2 - CH_3 \quad \text{is} \quad 196^\circ C \quad \text{and}$$

that of
$$-CH_2 - \underset{\underset{CH_3}{|}}{\overset{CH_3}{\overset{|}{C}}} - CH_2 - CH_3 \quad \text{is} \quad 350^\circ C\ .$$

Note that polymers that have appendages which do not have "substituents" have lower melting points as shown above. This is because of the steric influence and higher intermolecular forces.
(vi) Crosslinking effect:

Crosslinked polymers have higher melting points than either branched or linear polymers.

b) Considering the factors listed above, the order of increasing melting point of the following polymers is (lowest to highest) (3), (1), (2) and (4).

MOLECULAR WEIGHT DETERMINATION

• PROBLEM 15-4

a) Briefly discuss the limitation of end-group analysis for molecular weight determination.

b) Fifty grams of a polyester was separated into homogeneous molecular weight fractions by sedimentation. The carboxylic end-groups in each fraction were titrated by base with the following results:

Weight of fraction (grams):	1	10	25	9	5
Moles of base titrant:	10^{-3}	10^{-4}	10^{-5}	10^{-6}	10^{-7}

Determine the weight average and the number average molecular weights of the 50 gram sample.

Solution: a) The determination of molecular weight of a macromolecule (or polymer) is done by numerous methods of which one of them is End-group analysis. Amongst others are light scattering, colligative properties, etc.
The End-group analysis is the limitation of long chains to end groups

of macromolecules (or polymers). The functional group analysis requires that a known amount of determinable groups per molecule be present, for example, the determination of amino groups in polyesters and polyamides. The limitation of end-group analysis is that chemical methods for molecular weight determination become insensitive at molecular weights higher than about 25000, as the fraction of end groups become too small to be detected with precision. Therefore, the viscosity is increased as well as the effect of crosslinking.

b) The weight average molecular weight is given by

$$\bar{M}_w = \frac{\Sigma W_i M_i}{\Sigma W_i} = \frac{\Sigma N_i M_i^2}{\Sigma N_i M_i} = \Sigma w_i M_i \qquad (1)$$

where $\bar{M}_w$ = weight average molecular weight

M_i = molecular weight of the ith species;

W_i = weight of material with molecular weight M_i ;

N_i = number of moles with molecular weight M_i ;

w_i = weight fraction of molecules of the ith species.

From the given data, total weight = 50 grams. Therefore,

$$w_1 = \frac{1}{50},\ w_2 = \frac{10}{50},\ w_3 = \frac{25}{50},\ w_4 = \frac{9}{50} \text{ and } w_5 = \frac{5}{50}.$$

The corresponding molecular weights using the relation that molecular weight = weight/moles are

$$M_1 = \frac{1}{10^{-3}} = 10^3,\ M_2 = \frac{10}{10^{-4}} = 10^5,\ M_3 = \frac{25}{10^{-5}} = 25 \times 10^5,$$

$$M_4 = \frac{9}{10^{-6}} = 9 \times 10^6 \text{ and } M_5 = \frac{5}{10^{-7}} = 5 \times 10^7$$

Inserting these values into equation (1) gives

$$\bar{M}_w = \Sigma w_i M_i = \frac{1}{50} \times 10^3 + \frac{10}{50}\times 10^5 + \frac{25}{50}\times 25\times 10^5 + \frac{9}{50}\times 9\times 10^6 + \frac{5}{50}\times 5\times 10^7$$

$$= 20 + 20000 + 1250000 + 1620000 + 5000000$$

Therefore

$$\bar{M}_w = 7890020.$$

The number average molecular weight is defined as

$$\bar{M}_n = \frac{1}{\Sigma(w_i/M_i)}$$

$$= \frac{1}{\frac{0.02}{10^3} + \frac{0.2}{10^5} + \frac{0.5}{2.5\times 10^6} + \frac{0.18}{9\times 10^6} + \frac{0.1}{5\times 10^7}}$$

$$= \frac{1}{0.00002+0.000002+0.0000002+0.00000002+\frac{.1}{5\times 10^7}}$$

Therefore

$$\bar{M}_n = \frac{1}{0.000022222}$$

or

$$\bar{M}_n = 45045$$

Physical Constants of Proteins at 20° in Water

Protein	$S \times 10^{13}$, s	$D \times 10^{11}$ $m^2 s^{-1}$	$\bar{v}$, $cm^3 g^{-1}$
Beef insulin	1.7	15	0.72
Lactalbumin	1.9	10.6	0.75
Ovalbumin	3.6	7.8	0.75
Serum albumin	4.3	6.15	0.735
Serum globulin	7.1	4.0	0.75
Urease	18.6	3.4	0.73
Tobacco mosaic virus	185	0.53	0.72

The physical constants of proteins at 20° in water are given in the table above. The table tabulates values of the sedimentation coefficient S, the diffusion coefficient D, and the partial specific volume $\bar{v}$, for various proteins. Using these data estimate the maximum molecular weight of ovalbumin. State any assumption(s) made.

Solution: Assuming that ovalbumin is spherical, the molecular weight may be estimated from diffusion coefficient. This diffusion coefficient is related to frictional coefficient f, by the expression

$$D = \frac{RT}{Nf} \tag{1}$$

where D = diffusion coefficient
R = universal gas constant
T = temperature
N = Avogadro's number
f = frictional coefficient

Equation (1) was first obtained by Einstein.
For spheres and nonturbulent flow, the frictional coefficient is given by

$$f = 6\pi\eta r \tag{2}$$

where η = coefficient of viscosity = .001005 Js/m^3
r = radius of the sphere .

Combining equations (1) and (2) yields

$$D = \frac{RT}{N6\pi\eta r} . \tag{3}$$

Since the estimation of molecular weight of the particle is needed, the expression

$$\frac{M\bar{v}}{N} = \frac{4}{3}\pi r^3 \tag{4}$$

is used, where M = molecular weight
$\bar{v}$ = partial specific volume .

Solving for r in equation (4) gives

$$r^3 = \frac{3M\bar{v}}{4\pi N}$$

$$r = \left(\frac{3M\bar{v}}{4\pi N}\right)^{\frac{1}{3}} \qquad (5)$$

Substituting this expression for r in equation (3) gives

$$D = \frac{RT}{N6\pi\eta\left(\frac{3M\bar{v}}{4\pi N}\right)^{\frac{1}{3}}}$$

$$= \frac{RT}{N6\pi\eta}\left(\frac{4\pi N}{3M\bar{v}}\right)^{\frac{1}{3}} \qquad (6)$$

Solving equation (6) for M with the given data yields

$$7.8 \times 10^{-11} m^2 s^{-1} = \left[\frac{(8.31\ J\ K^{-1} mol^{-1})(293K)}{(6.02 \times 10^{23} mol^{-1})6\pi(0.001005 J\ m^{-3} s)}\right]$$

$$\times \left[\frac{4\pi(6.02 \times 10^{23} mol^{-1})}{3M(0.75 \times 10^{-3} m^3 kg^{-1})}\right]^{\frac{1}{3}}$$

and

$$M = 69.0\ kg\ mol^{-1}$$

$$= 69000\ g\ mol^{-1}$$

• **PROBLEM 15-6**

The density of water at 20° is 0.9982 g cm^{-3}. Using the data in the table given below, calculate the molecular weight of serum albumin.

Physical Constants of Proteins at 20° in Water

Protein	$S \times 10^{13}$, s	$D \times 10^{11}$, $m^2 s^{-1}$	$\bar{v}$, $cm^3 g^{-1}$
Beef insulin	1.7	15	0.72
Lactalbumin	1.9	10.6	0.75
Ovalbumin	3.6	7.8	0.75
Serum albumin	4.3	6.15	0.735
Serum globulin	7.1	4.0	0.75
Urease	18.6	3.4	0.73
Tobacco mosaic virus	185	0.53	0.72

Solution: The equation on which this calculation is based may be derived by setting the force of the centrifugal field on the particle equal to the frictional force, f(dr/dt), where f is the frictional coefficient of the molecule and dr/dt is the speed of sedimentation. The force of the field on a particle of mass m and partial specific volume $\bar{v}$ suspended in a medium of density ρ is

$$m(1 - \bar{v}\rho)\omega^2 r = \frac{M}{N}(1 - \bar{v}\rho)\omega^2 r \qquad (1)$$

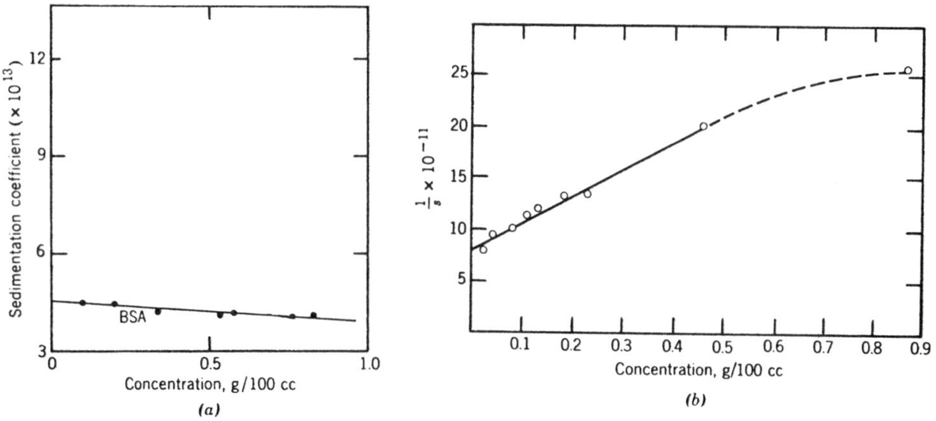

(*a*) The effect of concentration on the sedimentation coefficient of bovine serum albumin (BSA; Kegeles and Gutter[60]) ; Kahler[62])
(*b*) Kahler's data plotted as $1/s$ versus c.

where $(1 - \bar{v}\rho)$ = buoyancy factor
M = molecular weight
$\omega^2 r$ = centrifugal acceleration
N = Avogadro's number .

The sedimenting molecule or particle will be accelerated by the field until its velocity is such that the frictional force is equal to the force of the field. That is

$$f \frac{dr}{dt} = \frac{M}{N} (1 - \bar{v}\rho)\omega^2 r$$

or

$$\frac{dr/dt}{\omega^2 r} = \frac{M}{N} \frac{(1 - \bar{v}\rho)}{f} \quad . \tag{2}$$

By definition, $\frac{dr/dt}{\omega^2 r} = S$, where S = sedimentation coefficient.

Using the relation obtained by Einstein,

$$D = \frac{RT}{Nf} ,$$

or

$$f = \frac{RT}{DN} \tag{3}$$

where
f = frictional coefficient
D = diffusion coefficient
R = universal gas constant
T = absolute temperature,

the combination of equations (2) and (3) will yield

$$S = \frac{M}{N} \frac{(1 - \bar{v}\rho)}{(RT/DN)}$$

$$= \frac{M}{N} (1 - \bar{v}\rho) \frac{DN}{RT}$$

$$= \frac{M(1 - \bar{v}\rho)D}{RT}$$

Solving for M gives

$$M = \frac{SRT}{D(1 - \bar{v}\rho)} \quad .$$

Using the table given above,

$$M = \frac{(4.3 \times 10^{-13} s)(8.31\ J\ K^{-1} mol^{-1})(293\ K)}{(6.15 \times 10^{-11} m^2 s^{-1})[1 - (0.735 \times 10^{-3} m^3 kg^{-1})(0.9982 \times 10^3 kg\ m^{-3})}$$

$= 64.0\ kg\ mol^{-1}$

$= 64000\ g\ mol^{-1}$

• PROBLEM 15-7

For horse hemoglobin in water solution at 20° C, $D = 6.3 \times 10^{-7} cm^2 \cdot s^{-1}$, $s = 4.41 \times 10^{-13} s$, $\bar{v} = 0.749\ cm^3 g^{-1}$, $\rho = 0.9982\ g \cdot cm^{-3}$. Calculate the molecular weight.

Solution: The hemoglobin sedimenting particle will be accelerated by the field until its velocity is such that the frictional force is equal to the force of the field. That is

$$f \frac{dr}{dt} = \frac{M}{N}(1 - \bar{v}\rho)\omega^2 r$$

or

$$\frac{dr/dt}{\omega^2 r} = \frac{M(1 - \bar{v}\rho)}{Nf} \tag{1}$$

where
M = molecular weight
N = Avogadro's number
f = frictional coefficient
$(1 - \bar{v}\rho)$ = buoyancy factor
dr/dt = speed of sedimentation
$\omega^2 r$ = centrifugal acceleration.

The speed of sedimentation divided by the centrifugal acceleration is called the sedimentation coefficient S. Therefore, equation (1) becomes

$$S = \frac{M(1 - \bar{v}\rho)}{Nf} \tag{2}$$

The diffusion coefficient D, is defined as

$$D = \frac{RT}{Nf}$$

Solving for f gives,

$$f = \frac{RT}{DN} \tag{3}$$

Substitute this expression for f into equation (2) to obtain

$$S = \frac{M(1 - v\rho)}{N(RT/DN)}$$

Solving for M gives

$$M = \frac{RTS}{D(1 - \bar{v}\rho)} \tag{4}$$

Since all the variables in equation (4) are known, the molecular weight of the horse hemoglobin in water solution is

$$M = \frac{(8.31 \times 10^7 erg\ K^{-1} mol^{-1})(293K)(4.41 \times 10^{-13} sec)}{(6.3 \times 10^{-7} cm^2 sec^{-1})[1 - (0.749 cm^3 g^{-1})(0.9982 cm^{-3} g)]}$$

$$= \frac{17043.81}{1 - 0.7477} \text{ g mol}^{-1} = \frac{17043.81}{0.2523} \text{ g mol}^{-1}$$

$$= 67553.745 \text{ g mol}^{-1} \cong 67554 \text{ g mol}^{-1}$$

• PROBLEM 15-8

The relative viscosity of a polymer solution containing 1.00g of polymer in 100 cm^3 is 2.800. A solution half as concentrated has a relative viscosity of 1.800.

(a) Calculate the intrinsic viscosity. (Assume that a graphical treatment would give a straight line, and calculate the intercept analytically).

(b) If the appropriate values of K and a in the Mark-Houwink equation are 5.00×10^{-4} and 0.600, calculate the molecular weight of the polymer.

Solution: a) Viscosity measurements provide an additional method of molecular weight estimation. It was determined by Einstein that for a dilute suspension of spheres in a viscous medium

$$\lim_{\varphi \to 0} \frac{(\eta/\eta_0) - 1}{\varphi} = 2.5 \qquad (1)$$

where η and η_0 are the viscosities of the solution or suspension and pure solvent, respectively, and φ is the volume fraction of the solution occupied by the spheres. The fraction η/η_0 is the relative viscosity η_r, and $[(\eta/\eta_0)-1]$ is called the specific viscosity η_{sp}. For polymer solutions the concentration c is usually given as grams per cubic centimeter and $\eta_{sp}/100c$ is called the reduced visocity. The limiting value of the reduced viscosity as c approaches zero is the intrinsic visocity $[\eta]$.

By definition,

$$\frac{1}{c}(\eta_r - 1) = kc + [\eta] \qquad (2)$$

where

$$c = \text{concentration}$$

$$k = \frac{1/c_1(\eta_{r_1} - 1) - 1/c_2(\eta_{r_2} - 1)}{c_1 - c_2}$$

Since c_1 is given to be 1.00 g dl^{-1} and $c_2 = 0.5g\ dl^{-1}$,

$$\frac{1}{c_1}(\eta_{r_1} - 1) = \frac{1}{1}(2.800 - 1) = 1.800$$

and

$$\frac{1}{c_2}(\eta_{r_2} - 1) = \frac{1}{0.5}(1.800 - 1) = 1.600$$

Now, solving for k gives

$$k = \frac{1.800 - 1.600}{1.0 - 0.5}$$

$$k = 0.400\ g^{-2}\ dl^2$$

Since equation (2) is linear,

$$[\eta] = \frac{1}{c_1}(\eta_{r_1} - 1) - kc_1 \quad (3)$$

and

$$[\eta] = \frac{1}{c_2}(\eta_{r_2} - 1) - kc_2\ . \quad (4)$$

From equation (3)

$$[\eta] = 1.800 - 0.400(1.0)$$
$$= 1.400\ g^{-1}\ dl,$$

and equation (4) gives

$$[\eta] = 1.600 - 0.400(0.5)$$
$$= 1.400\ g^{-1}\ dl.$$

b) The dependence of the intrinsic viscosity on the molecular weight of a series of samples of the same polymer in a given solvent and at a constant temperature is given by equation (2) written in the form

$$[\eta] = KM^a \quad (5)$$

The exponent a can vary depending on the stiffness of the polymer and together with K they are treated as constants that may be determined by measuring the intrinsic viscosities of a series of polymer samples for which the molecular weights have been measured by another method; i.e., light scattering.

Taking the log of both sides of equation (5) gives

$$\log[\eta] = \log(KM^a)$$
$$= \log K + \log M^a$$

$$\log[\eta] = \log K + a \log M \quad (6)$$

Rearranging equation (6) to solve for $\log M$ gives

$$\log[\eta] - \log K = a \log M$$

or

$$a \log M = \log\ [\eta]/K$$

$$\log M = \frac{(\log[\eta]/K)}{a}$$

$$= \left(\log \frac{1.400}{5.00 \times 10^{-4}}\right) \Big/ 0.600$$

$$= \frac{3.447}{0.600} = 5.745$$

$$\therefore \quad M = 5.56 \times 10^5 g\ mol^{-1}\ .$$

• PROBLEM 15-9

It is desired to produce poly(methylmethacrylate) in bulk at 60° C with $\bar{M}_n = 10^5$. The initiator is 1% (wt) AIBN based on monomer and n-butyl mercaptan is to be used as a chain transfer agent. What (wt) percent of mercaptan is required (based on monomer wt)?

Data: k_d (AIBN) = 9×10^{-6} sec^{-1}

$\epsilon = 0.5$

$C_{SH} = 0.66$

$k_p/k_t^{\frac{1}{2}} = 1.61$

Solution: By definition,

$$\frac{1}{\bar{X}_n} = C_M + \frac{C_{SH}[SH]}{[M]} + \frac{k_t}{k_p^2}\frac{V_p}{[M]^2} + C_I\frac{k_t}{k_p^2 \epsilon k_d}\frac{V_p^2}{[M]^3} \qquad (1)$$

where C_M = transfer constant due to monomer

C_{SH} = transfer constant due to solvent

[SH] = concentration of solvent molecules

[M] = concentration of monomer molecules

k_t = termination rate constant

k_p = propagation rate constant

V_p = rate of generation of polymer (usually during propagation)

C_I = transfer constant due to initiator

k_d = decomposition rate constant

ϵ = initiator efficiency

$\bar{X}_n$ = number average degree of polymerization

The V_p term in equation (1) is defined as

$$V_p = k_p\left(\frac{\epsilon k_d[I]}{k_t}\right)^{\frac{1}{2}}[M] = \frac{k_p}{k_t^{\frac{1}{2}}}(\epsilon k_d[I])^{\frac{1}{2}}[M] \qquad (2)$$

Basis for calculation: 100% monomer. That is [M] = 1.

[I] is given to be 0.01 or 1% . Substitute [I] and the numerical data into equation (2) to get

$$\begin{aligned} V_p &= (1.61)[(0.5)(9 \times 10^{-6})(0.01)]^{\frac{1}{2}}(1) \\ &= 1.61(0.0000045 \times 0.01)^{\frac{1}{2}} \\ &\cong 0.000342 . \end{aligned}$$

Observe that $\left(\frac{k_p}{k_t^{\frac{1}{2}}}\right)^2 = (1.61)^2 = 2.592$ or $\frac{k_p^2}{k_t} = 2.592$.

$$\frac{k_t}{k_p^2} = \frac{1}{2.592} = 0.3858 .$$

Rewriting equation (1) using the numerical data yields

$$\frac{1}{\bar{X}_n} = C_M + \frac{(0.66)[SH]}{1} + \frac{(0.3858)(0.000342)}{1^2}$$

$$+ C_I \frac{0.3858}{0.5(9 \times 10^{-6})} \frac{(.00000012)}{1^3} \qquad (3)$$

In this problem, C_M and C_I are to be neglected because transfer is by solvent (mercaptan) only. Therefore equation (3) becomes

$$\frac{1}{\bar{X}_n} = \frac{(0.66)[SH]}{1} + \frac{(0.3858)(0.000342)}{1^2} \qquad (4)$$

Observe that the [SH] term in equation (4) is the required percentage. Using the given $\bar{M}_n$ value, $\bar{X}_n$ can be computed.

By definition,

$$\bar{M}_n = m\,\bar{X}_n \qquad (5)$$

where $\bar{M}_n$ = number average molecular weight

m = molecular weight of the monomer

The monomer of poly(methylmethacrylate) is methylmethacrylate, whose molecular formula is $CH_2 = C(CH_3)COOCH_3$ or

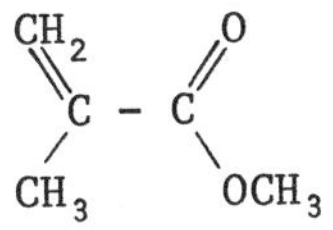

From this formula, m = 12 + 2 + 24 + 15 + 32 + 15 = 100 .

Rearranging equation (5) to solve for $\bar{X}_n$ gives

$$\bar{X}_n = \frac{\bar{M}_n}{m} = \frac{10^5}{10^2} = 10^3 .$$

Inserting this into equation (4) gives

$$\frac{1}{10^3} = \frac{0.66[SH]}{1} + \frac{(0.3858)(0.000342)}{1^2}$$

or

$$0.001 = 0.66[SH] + 0.000132 \qquad (6)$$

Rearranging equation (6) yields

$$0.66[SH] = 0.001 - 0.000132 = 0.000868$$

$$\therefore \quad [SH] = \frac{0.000868}{0.66} = 0.0013151$$

or

$$[SH] = 0.13151\% .$$

• PROBLEM 15-10

Given that $\bar{X}_n = 100$ for each of the following macromolecules: polystyrene, polycaprolactam and nylon (66), otherwise known as poly(hexamethylene adipamide), compute $\bar{M}_n$ for each of them.

Solution: The number average molecular weight of a polymer is the product of the molecular weight of the monomer that make up the polymer and the number average degree of polymerization. This is mathematically defined as

$$\bar{M}_n = m\bar{X}_n \, , \qquad (1)$$

where $\bar{M}_n$ = number average molecular weight

m = molecular weight of the monomer

$\bar{X}_n$ = number average degree of polymerization.

If more than one monomer make up the polymer, then m = mean of the molecular weights.

For polystyrene, the monomer is represented as

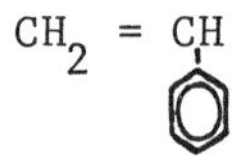

Therefore, $m = 12 + 2 + 12 + 6(12) + 5(1) + 1 = 104$.

Consequently,

$$\begin{aligned} \bar{M}_n &= m\bar{X}_n \\ &= (104)(100) \\ &= 10400 \end{aligned}$$

For polycaprolactam, the monomer is represented as

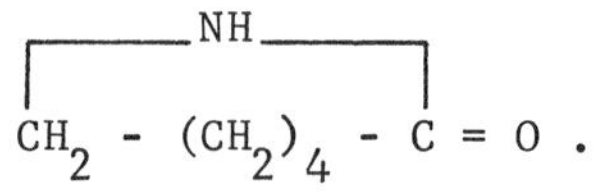

Therefore, $m = 12 + 2 + 4(12) + 4(2) + 12 + 14 + 1 + 16 = 113$

Consequently,

$$\begin{aligned} \bar{M}_n &= m\bar{X}_n \\ &= (113)(100) \\ &= 11300 \, . \end{aligned}$$

Finally, the monomers for nylon (66) are represented as $NH_2 - (CH_2)_6 - NH_2$ and $HOOC - (CH_2)_4 - COOH$. Their molecular weights are

$$14 + 2 + 6(12) + 6(2) + 14 + 2 = 116$$

and

$$1 + 16 + 16 + 12 + 4(12) + 4(2) + 12 + 16 + 16 + 1 = 146 \text{ respectively.}$$

Therefore, m = mean molecular weight =

$$\frac{116 + 146}{2} = 131$$

Observe that to make a reccurence unit, one H_2O per monomer is eliminated. As a result, effective $m = 131 - 18 = 113$.

Consequently,

$$\begin{aligned} \bar{M}_n &= m\bar{X}_n \\ &= (113)(100) \\ &= 11300 \, . \end{aligned}$$

The number average and weight average molecular-weights are defined as

$$\bar{M}_n = \frac{\Sigma N_i M_i}{\Sigma N_i} = \frac{1}{\Sigma(w_i/M_i)}$$

and

$$\bar{M}_w = \frac{\Sigma W_i M_i}{\Sigma W_i} = \frac{\Sigma N_i M_i^2}{\Sigma N_i M_i} = \Sigma w_i M_i$$

respectively, where

M_i = molecular weight of the ith species
N_i = moles of molecules with molecular weight M_i
W_i = weight of material with molecular weight M_i
w_i = weight fraction of molecules of the ith species.

Derive equations analogous to the ones above for the number average, $\bar{X}_n$, and weight average, $\bar{X}_w$, degree of polymerization.

Solution: In any given macromolecule (or polymer), the molecular weight of the ith species is defined as the product of the molecular weight of the monomer that make up the large molecule and its degree of polymerization. Mathematically, this can be represented as

$$M_i = mX_i \tag{1}$$

where m = molecular weight of a monomer.
X_i = degree of polymerization of the ith species.

Note that if there are more than one monomer that make up the macromolecule, m will be the mean molecular weight of the monomers. Also, note that $X_i \neq \bar{X}_n$. X_i is not an average.

By definition, $\bar{M}_n = m\bar{X}_n$. (2)

But $\bar{M}_n = \frac{\Sigma N_i M_i}{\Sigma N_i}$. Therefore, equation (2) becomes

$$m\bar{X}_n = \frac{\Sigma N_i M_i}{\Sigma N_i} \tag{3}$$

Combining equations (1) and (3) gives

$$m\bar{X}_n = \frac{\Sigma N_i m X_i}{\Sigma N_i} .$$

Observe that m is a constant. Therefore, it can be taken out of the summation sign to obtain

$$m\bar{X}_n = m\frac{\Sigma N_i X_i}{\Sigma N_i}$$

or

$$\bar{X}_n = \frac{\Sigma N_i X_i}{\Sigma N_i} .$$

Using a similar procedure as the one above,

$$\bar{M}_w = m\bar{X}_w \tag{4}$$

But

$$\bar{M}_w = \frac{\Sigma N_i M_i^2}{\Sigma N_i M_i} .$$

Therefore, equation (4) changes to

$$m\bar{X}_w = \frac{\Sigma N_i M_i^2}{\Sigma N_i M_i} \qquad (5)$$

Combining equations (1) and (5) gives

$$m\bar{X}_w = \frac{\Sigma N_i m^2 X_i^2}{\Sigma N_i m X_i}$$

$$= \frac{m^2 \Sigma N_i X_i^2}{m \Sigma N_i X_i}$$

$$= \frac{m \Sigma N_i X_i^2}{\Sigma N_i X_i}$$

Therefore

$$\bar{X}_w = \frac{\Sigma N_i X_i^2}{\Sigma N_i X_i}$$

• PROBLEM 15-12

A suspension contains equal numbers of particles with molecular weights 10,000 and 20,000. Calculate $\bar{M}_N$ and $\bar{M}_m$. A suspension contains equal masses of particles with molecular weights 10,000 and 20,000. Calculate $\bar{M}_N$ and $\bar{M}_m$.

Solution: a) When there is a range of molecular weights, different experimental methods for estimating it yield different types of average molecular weights. The number average molecular weight $\bar{M}_N$ is equal to the weight of the whole sample divided by the number of molecules in it.

That is,
$$\bar{M}_N = (\sum_i N_i M_i)/\sum_i N_i \qquad (1)$$

where N_i = number of i particles or molecules

M_i = molecular weight of the ith particle.

Since there are only two particles, equation (1) becomes

$$\bar{M}_N = \frac{N_1 M_1 + N_2 M_2}{N_1 + N_2} \qquad (2)$$

But the suspension contains equal number of particles. Therefore, $N_1 = N_2$. Equation (2) can be written as

$$\bar{M}_N = \frac{N_1 M_1 + N_1 M_2}{N_1 + N_1}$$

$$= \frac{N_1(M_1 + M_2)}{2N_1}$$

with $M_1 = 10,000$ and $M_2 = 20,000$,

$$\bar{M}_N = \frac{N_1(10000 + 20000)}{2N_1}$$

$$= \frac{30000}{2}$$

$$= 15000$$

The mass (or weight) average molecular weight is given by

$$\bar{M}_m = \frac{\Sigma m_i M_i}{\Sigma m_i} = \frac{\Sigma N_i M_i^2}{\Sigma N_i M_i} \tag{2}$$

$$\bar{M}_m = \frac{N_1(10000)^2 + N_2(20000)^2}{N_1(10000) + N_2(20000)} .$$

But $N_1 = N_2$,

$$\bar{M}_m = \frac{N_1((10000)^2 + (20000)^2)}{N_1(10000 + 20000)}$$

$$= \frac{100000000 + 400000000}{30000}$$

$$= \frac{500000000}{30000}$$

$$\bar{M}_m = \frac{50000}{3} = 16666.7 .$$

b) Since there are twice as many particles of MW = 10000 as there are particles of MW = 20000, $N_1 = 2N_2$. Equation (1) then becomes

$$\bar{M}_N = \frac{2N_2(10000) + N_2(20000)}{2N_2 + N_2}$$

$$\bar{M}_N = \frac{N_2(40000)}{3N_2} = \frac{40000}{3}$$

$$= 13333.3$$

With similar conditions,

$$\bar{M}_m = \frac{2N_2(10000)^2 + N_2(20000)^2}{2N_2(10000) + N_2(20000)}$$

$$= \frac{2N_2 100000000 + N_2 400000000}{2N_2 10000 + N_2 20000}$$

$$= \frac{N_2(600000000)}{N_2(40000)}$$

$$= 15000$$

A non-homogeneous polymer system is composed according to the following fractional distribution

Wt. fraction	0.05	0.20	0.35	0.20	0.15	0.05
Mol. Wt.$\times 10^{-5}$	1	2	3	4	6	7

Compute $\bar{M}_n$, $\bar{M}_w$, and $\bar{M}_w/\bar{M}_n$ for this system.

Solution: The mathematical definitions of $\bar{M}_n$ and $\bar{M}_w$ are

$$\bar{M}_n = \frac{\Sigma N_i M_i}{\Sigma N_i} = \frac{1}{\Sigma(w_i/M_i)}$$

and

$$\bar{M}_w = \frac{\Sigma W_i M_i}{\Sigma W_i} = \frac{\Sigma N_i M_i^2}{\Sigma N_i M_i} = \Sigma w_i M_i$$

respectively, where

M_i = molecular weight of the ith species
N_i = moles of molecules with molecular weight M_i
W_i = weight of material with molecular weight M_i
w_i = weight fraction of molecules of the ith species
$\bar{M}_n$ = number average molecular weight
$\bar{M}_w$ = weight average molecular weight.

Substitute the given data into the expression for $\bar{M}_n$ to get

$$\bar{M}_n = \frac{1}{\Sigma(w_i/M_i)} = \frac{1}{\frac{0.05}{10^5} + \frac{0.20}{2\times10^5} + \frac{0.35}{3\times10^5} + \frac{0.20}{4\times10^5} + \frac{0.15}{6\times10^5} + \frac{0.05}{7\times10^5}}$$

$$= \frac{1}{0.0000005 + 0.000001 + 0.000001167 + 0.0000005 + 0.00000025 + 0.00000007143}$$

Therefore $\bar{M}_n \cong 285700$

In a similar manner,

$$\bar{M}_w = \Sigma w_i M_i = (0.05)(10^5) + (0.20)(2\times10^5) + (0.35)(3\times10^5) + (0.20)(4\times10^5) + (0.15)(6\times10^5) + (0.05)(7\times10^5)$$

$$= 5000 + 40000 + 105000 + 80000 + 90000 + 35000$$

$$= 355000$$

For this system, the ratio

$$\frac{\bar{M}_w}{\bar{M}_n} = \frac{355000}{285700}$$

$$\cong 1.242$$

• PROBLEM 15-14

From $\bar{M}_n = \Sigma N_i M_i / \Sigma N_i$, show that $\bar{M}_n = 1/\Sigma\left(\frac{w_i}{M_i}\right)$ and from $\bar{M}_w = \Sigma W_i M_i / \Sigma W_i$ that $\bar{M}_w = \Sigma w_i M_i$.

Solution: a) One of the definitions of $\bar{M}_n$ is

$$\bar{M}_n = \frac{\Sigma N_i M_i}{\Sigma N_i} \tag{1}$$

where $\bar{M}_n$ = number average molecular weight

M_i = molecular weight of the ith species

N_i = moles of molecules with molecular weight M_i

By definition, $N_i = W_i/M_i$. Therefore, equation (1) changes to

$$\bar{M}_n = \frac{\sum \frac{W_i}{M_i} M_i}{\sum \frac{W_i}{M_i}} = \frac{\Sigma W_i}{\sum \frac{W_i}{M_i}} \tag{2}$$

But $W_i = w_i W_t = w_i \Sigma W_i$ where w_i = weight fraction of molecules of the ith species. W_t = total weight.

Inserting these into equation (2) changes it to

$$\bar{M}_n = \frac{\Sigma W_i}{\sum \frac{w_i \Sigma W_i}{M_i}}$$

Observe that the ΣW_i is a constant. Therefore,

$$\bar{M}_n = \frac{1}{\Sigma(w_i/M_i)} .$$

The weight average molecular weight is given by

$$\bar{M}_w = \frac{\Sigma W_i M_i}{\Sigma W_i} \tag{3}$$

But $W_i = w_i W_t = w_i \Sigma W_i$. Therefore equation (3) becomes

$$\bar{M}_w = \frac{\Sigma(w_i \Sigma W_i) M_i}{\Sigma W_i} \tag{4}$$

Observe that the ΣW_i = constant. Therefore, equation (4) becomes

$$\bar{M}_w = \Sigma w_i M_i$$

a) It is desired to make nylon (66) with $\bar{M}_n = 20000$. Assuming that the reaction goes to completion, find $F_A(0)/F_B(0)$.

b) What weight fraction of the product will have a degree of polymerization of 200.

Solution: The active monomers of nylon (66) are $NH_2 - (CH_2)_6 - NH_2$ and $HOOC - (CH_2)_4 - COOH$

The number average molecular weight is given by

$$\bar{M}_n = m\bar{X}_n \qquad (1)$$

where $\bar{M}_n$ = number average molecular weight

m = molecular weight of the monomer.

Note that m = mean molecular weight in this case since there is more than one monomer.

$\bar{X}_n$ = number average degree of polymerization

$$= (1 + 1/r)/(1 + 1/r - 2P_A) \qquad (2)$$

where

$$r = \frac{F_A(0)}{F_B(0)} .$$

So computing $\bar{X}_n$ from equation (1) helps in computing r from equation (2). Note that $P_A = 1$ since the reaction is assumed to go to completion.

The molecular weight of the first monomer is

$$14 + 2 + 72 + 12 + 14 + 2 = 116$$

and that of the second is $1 + 44 + 48 + 8 + 44 + 1 = 146$.

Therefore $m = \dfrac{116 + 146}{2} = 131$. To make a recurrence unit, one H_2O per monomer is eliminated. Therefore effective $m = 131 - 18 = 113$.

Rearranging equation (1) to solve for $\bar{X}_n$ gives

$$\bar{X}_n = \frac{\bar{M}_n}{m} = \frac{20000}{113} = 176.99 = 177$$

Since $P_A = 1$, equation (2) changes to the form

$$\bar{X}_n = \frac{1 + 1/r}{1 + 1/r - 2} = \frac{1 + 1/r}{1/r - 1}$$

or

$$177 = \frac{1 + 1/r}{1/r - 1} = \frac{(r + 1)/r}{(1 - r)/r} = (1 + r)/(1 - r)$$

Therefore,

$$1 + r = 177 - 177r$$

or

$$178r = 176$$

From which $$r = \frac{F_A(0)}{F_B(0)} = \frac{176}{178}$$
$$= 0.9887$$

b) The degree of polymerization is defined as X = (number of repeat units)(number of monomers/repeat unit).

Therefore $$200 = X\ (2)$$
or
$$X = 100$$

By definition
$$w_X = \frac{Xr^{(X-1)/2}(1 - r)^2}{1 + r} \tag{3}$$

Inserting the values for r and X into equation (3) gives

$$w_X = \frac{100(0.9887)^{(100-1)/2}(1 - 0.9887)^2}{1 + 0.9887}$$
$$= \frac{100(0.9887)^{49.5}(0.0113)^2}{1.9887}$$
$$= \frac{100(0.5698)(0.0001276)}{1.9887}$$
$$= 0.00366\ .$$

• PROBLEM 15-16

a) Given the system

$$2RA_4 + 3R'A_3 + 50R''A_2 + 60R''''B_2\ ,$$

determine the extent of reaction, P_A, of substance A and the number average degree of polymerization, $\bar{X}_n$ at incipient gelation.

b) Determine the most probable maximum weight fraction of an ARB condensation process when a tenth of the A functions remain unreacted.

Solution: a) In any given system, if $\alpha(i)$ is the probability that a section containing i(BR''B-AR'A) units has formed, then

$$\alpha(i) = P_A P_B \rho [P_A P_B (1-\rho)]^i \tag{1}$$

where P_B = extent of reaction of substance B

ρ = (number of A functions in branch units)/$F_A(0)$

$F_A(0)$ = total number of functional groups of substance A

However, α, the total probability, is what we are interested in. Accordingly,
$$\alpha = \sum_{i=0}^{\infty} \alpha(i) \tag{2}$$

Substituting the expression for $\alpha(i)$ from equation (1) into equation (2) yields

$$\alpha = \sum_{i=0}^{\infty} P_A P_B \rho [P_A P_B (1 - \rho)]^i \tag{3}$$

Recall that, in mathematics, any expression of the form $\sum_{i=0}^{\infty} x^i$ is equal to $1/(1-x)$ (for $x < 1$). As a result, equation (3) becomes

$$\alpha = P_A P_B \rho \left[\frac{1}{1 - P_A P_B (1 - \rho)}\right]$$

$$= \frac{r P_A^2 \rho}{1 - r P_A^2 (1 - \rho)} \qquad (4)$$

where $r = \frac{P_B}{P_A} = \frac{F_A(0)}{F_B(0)}$

By definition, α at the critical point is given by

$$\alpha_c = \frac{1}{b - 1}$$

where b = the functionality of the branch unit. When there are more than one species of branch units, α_c is computed using an average b. Therefore, $b \cong 3.44$ and $\alpha_c \cong 0.41$.

$$\rho = \frac{\text{number of A functions in branch unit}}{F_A(0)} = \frac{9 + 8}{117} = 0.145 .$$

$$r = \frac{F_A(0)}{F_B(0)} = \frac{117}{120} = 0.975.$$

Using all the values in equation (4) gives

$$0.41 = \frac{(0.975)P_A^2(0.145)}{1 - (0.975)P_A^2(1 - 0.145)}$$

$$= \frac{0.1414 P_A^2}{1 - 0.975 P_A^2 + 0.1414 P_A^2}$$

$$= \frac{0.1414 P_A^2}{1 - 0.8336 P_A^2}$$

Therefore, $0.41 - 0.3418\ P_A^2 = 0.1414\ P_A^2$

or

$$0.4832\ P_A^2 = 0.41$$

From which $P_A \cong 0.921$. The number average degree of polymerization at incipient gelation is given by

$$\bar{X}_n = \frac{b(1+r-\rho r) + 2r\rho}{b(1+r-r\rho-2rP_A) + 2r\rho}$$

Therefore

$$\bar{X}_n = \frac{3.44(1+0.975 - 0.1414) + 0.2828}{3.44(1+0.975-0.1414-1.794) + 0.2828}$$

$$\cong 16.0 .$$

b) The weight fraction distribution function of any X-mer is given by

$$w_X = X(1 - P_A)^2\ P_A^{X-1} \qquad (5)$$

where P_A = extent of reaction of A functions. Since 1/10 = 0.1

of A functions remain unreacted, $P_A = 1 - 0.1 = 0.9$. Consequently, equation (5) changes to

$$w_X = X(1 - 0.9)^2(0.9)^{X-1}$$

or

$$w_X = X(0.01)(0.9)^{X-1} \qquad (6)$$

Observe that there are two unknowns in equation (6), w_X and X. Therefore another equation with the two unknowns must be found. Then, there will be two equations and two unknowns and both X and w_X can be found.

Take the ln of both sides of equation (6) to obtain

$$\ln w_X = \ln(0.01X) + (X-1)\ln(0.9)$$
$$= \ln(0.01) + \ln X + X\ln(0.9) - \ln(0.9) .$$

Taking the derivative of both sides yields

$$\frac{1}{w_X}\, dw_X = \left[\frac{1}{X} + \ln(0.9)\right] dX \qquad (7)$$

The mathematical implication of the maximum probable weight fraction is that $dw_X/dX = 0$. Consequently, equation (7) takes the form

$$\frac{dw_X}{dX} = 0 = \frac{w_X}{X} + w_X \ln(0.9)$$

thus giving the second equation with two unknowns, or

$$\frac{w_X}{X} = -w_X \ln(0.9) \qquad (8)$$

Dividing both sides of equation (8) by w_X gives

$$\frac{1}{X} = -\ln(0.9)$$
$$= -(-0.10536)$$

therefore

$$X = \frac{1}{0.10536}$$

or

$$X = 9.49$$

Now that X is found, use equation (6) to compute w_X. That is

$$w_X = 9.49(0.1)^2(0.9)^{9.49-1}$$
$$= (9.49)(0.01)(0.9)^{8.49}$$

or

$$w_X = 0.0388 .$$

• PROBLEM 15-17

Figure 1 shows Schlieren patterns for an ultracentrifuge experiment with fumarase at 50,400 rpm. The distance from the axis of the ultracentrifuge to the boundary was 5.949 cm in the top photograph and 6.731 cm in the bottom photograph taken 70 minutes later. Calculate the sedimentation coefficient.

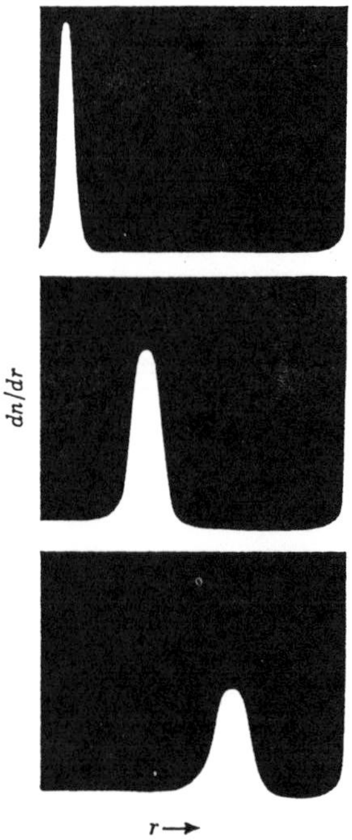

Fig. 1

Solution: By definition, the sedimentation coefficient S, is given as

$$S = \frac{dr/dt}{\omega^2 r} \tag{1}$$

where $\omega^2 r$ = centrifugal acceleration

dr/dt = velocity of sedimentation .

Rearranging equation (1) gives

$$S\,dt = 1/\omega^2\ dr/r \tag{2}$$

If a boundary is r_1 cm from the axis of the centrifuge at time t_1 and r_2 cm from the axis at time t_2, equation (2) may be integrated as

$$S\int_{t_1}^{t_2} dt = 1/\omega^2 \int_{r_1}^{r_2} dr/r$$

$$St\,\Big|_{t_1}^{t_2} = 1/\omega^2\ \ln r\,\Big|_{r_1}^{r_2}$$

or

$$S(t_2 - t_1) = 1/\omega^2 [\ln r_2 - \ln r_1]$$

$$S(t_2 - t_1) = 1/\omega^2\ \ln r_2/r_1$$

Therefore

$$S = \frac{1}{\omega^2 (t_2 - t_1)}\ \ln r_2/r_1\ .$$

Observe that $(t_2 - t_1)$ = 70 minutes

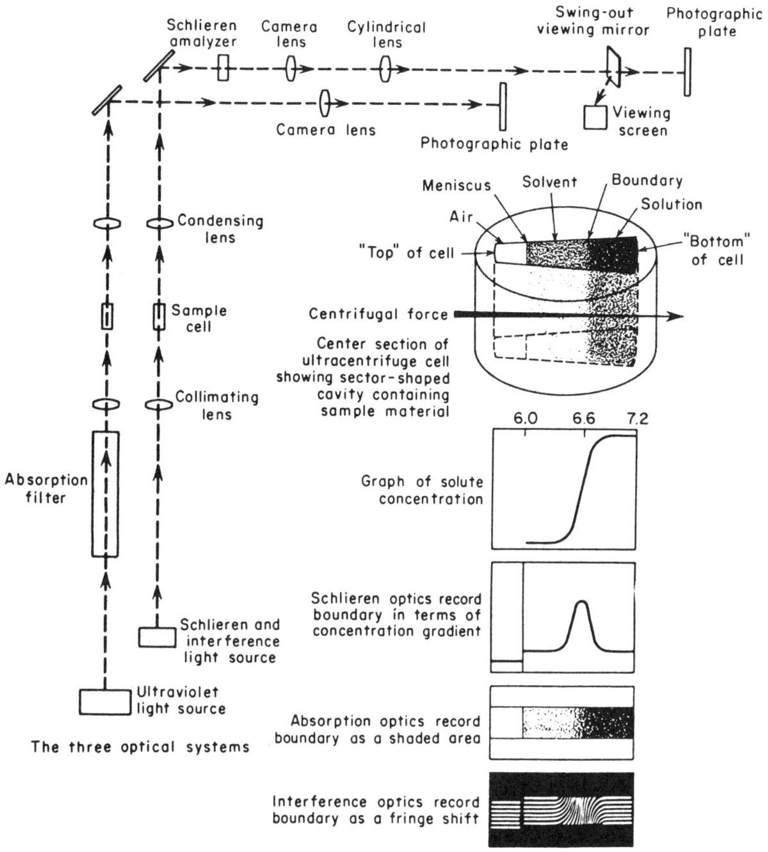

Summary of methods used for study of high polymer molecules in the analytical ultracentrifuge.

$$r_2 = 6.731 \text{ cm}$$

$$r_1 = 5.949 \text{ cm} .$$

Since the speed of the rotor was 50,400 rpm, $\omega^2 = 2.79 \times 10^7$. Using these values,

$$S = \frac{1}{(2.79\times10^7)(70 \text{ min})(60 \text{ sec/min})} \ln \frac{6.731}{5.949}$$

Therefore $S = 10.5 \times 10^{-13}S = 10.5$ svedbergs. Note that $10^{-13}S = 1$ svedberg.

• PROBLEM 15-18

Discuss the ways in which molecular weights can be controlled in addition polymerization.

Solution: The following equations will be used as the basis for discussing control of molecular weights.

$$\nu = \frac{V_p/k_p}{V_t/k_p + C_M[M][A] + C_{SH}[SH][A] + C_I[I][A]} \qquad (1)$$

and

$$\frac{1}{\bar{X}_n} = C_M + \frac{C_{SH}[SH]}{[M]} + \frac{k_t V_p}{k_p^2 [M]^2} + C_I \frac{k_t}{k_p^2 \varepsilon k_d} \frac{V_p^2}{[M]^3} \qquad (2)$$

where C_M = transfer constant due to monomer

ν = kinetic chain length

C_{SH} = transfer constant due to solvent

$[SH]$ = concentration of solvent molecules

$[M]$ = concentration of monomer molecules

k_t = termination rate constant

k_p = propagation rate constant

V_p = rate of generation of polymer (usually during propagation)

C_I = transfer constant due to initiator

k_d = decomposition rate constant

ε = initiator efficiency.

$\bar{X}_n$ = number average degree of polymerization.

V_t = rate of loss of active species.

$[A]$ = total concentration of active species.

The ways to be considered are: i) control by transfer to monomer and initiator: If the terms corresponding to polymerization, transfer to monomer and transfer to initiator are kept in equation (2), the resulting equation for $\bar{X}_n$ is quadratic in V_p. For example, this behavior has been observed in benzoyl peroxide initiated polymerization of styrene. Transfer to initiator increases rapidly with increasing rate while that to monomer is constant. The transfer to monomer is negligibly small.

ii) Transfer to Solvent:
In this case, equation (2) reduces to

$$\frac{1}{\bar{X}_n} = \frac{1}{(\bar{X}_n)_0} + C_{SH} \frac{[SH]}{[M]}$$

if proper conditions are chosen to minimize other types of chain transfer. This is easier to solve than a quadratic.

iii) Transfer to Polymer:
This produces no new molecules but leads to the formation of branches on existing polymer molecules. This has no bearing on the kinetic chain length.

RUBBER ELASTICITY

• PROBLEM 15-19

Suppose you have a weight on a rubber band so as to keep it under constant tension. If you then heat the rubber band, will the weight rise or fall? Give a thermodynamic answer.

Solution: For a closed system of constant composition that does only pressure-volume work, the first and second laws of thermodynamics for a reversible process may be combined with the definition of entropy into the differential form of the first law to obtain:

$$dU = TdS - PdV \tag{1}$$

where
U = internal energy
T = temperature
S = entropy
P = pressure
V = volume

For the problem at hand, a similar differential equation can be written in the form

$$dU = TdS + Kd\ell \tag{2}$$

where $-Kd\ell$ = the work done to stretch the rubber a distance $d\ell$ under a tension K. Using the same interpretation above, the enthalpy analog is therefore $H = U - K\ell$ and the Gibbs Free energy analog is

$$G = H - TS = (U - K\ell) - TS = U - K\ell - TS .$$

Differentiating the last equation gives

$$dG = dU - Kd\ell - \ell dK - TdS - SdT . \tag{3}$$

From equation (2), $+ Kd\ell = dU - TdS$. Therefore, rewriting equation (3) gives

$$dG = + Kd\ell - Kd\ell - \ell dK - SdT = -\ell dK - SdT \tag{4}$$

Applying the Euler reciprocity relation to dG, then

$$\left(\frac{\partial \ell}{\partial T}\right)_K = \left(\frac{\partial S}{\partial K}\right)_T .$$

When the rubber is stretched, S decreases while K increases. Consequently, the $(\partial \ell/\partial T)_K$ term is negative. Hence length decreases when temperature increases under constant tension.

TENSILE STRENGTH

• PROBLEM 15-20

Explain why nylon (66) has higher tensile strength than polyethylene.

Solution: Of all the properties that explain the tensile strength of a given substance, by far the most important is the intermolecular bonding forces.
Nylon (66) has a higher tensile strength than polyethylene because of the effect of hydrogen bonding. The

$$\overset{\displaystyle O}{\overset{\|}{-NHC-}}$$

group in nylon (66) provide sites for hydrogen bonding. The energy ranges from about 5 kcal/mole to 10 kcal/mole. In polyethylene, there are only $-CH_2-$ units. These $-CH_2-$ units have only weak van der Waals forces associated with them. The bonding energies range from only (about) 0.5 kcal/mole to 5 kcal/mole.

The probability that one end of a polymer chain lies at a distance r from the origin (regardless of direction) is given by the Gaussian distribution,

$$W(r)dr = \left(\frac{\beta}{\pi^{\frac{1}{2}}}\right)^3 e^{-\beta^2 r^2} \; 4\pi r^2 dr \; .$$

Calculate the most probable value of r.

Solution: Essentially, the problem gives a distribution function and what is needed is to maximize the function. In other words, maximizing this function is equivalent to finding the most probable value of r.

In order to maximize this function, the derivative with respect to r is taken and then it is set equal to zero. The function is

$W(r) = \left(\frac{\beta}{\pi^{\frac{1}{2}}}\right)^3 e^{-\beta^2 r^2} \; 4\pi r^2$. The $\left(\frac{\beta}{\pi^{\frac{1}{2}}}\right)^3$ term is constant.

Therefore,

$$W'(r)dr = \left(\frac{\beta}{\pi^{\frac{1}{2}}}\right)^3 \left[e^{-\beta^2 r^2} \; (4\pi r^2)' + (4\pi r^2)(e^{-\beta^2 r^2})'\right]$$

$$= \left(\frac{\beta}{\pi^{\frac{1}{2}}}\right)^3 \left[e^{-\beta^2 r^2} \; (4\pi 2r) + (4\pi r^2)(e^{-\beta^2 r^2})(-\beta^2 2r)\right]$$

$$= \left(\frac{\beta}{\pi^{\frac{1}{2}}}\right)^3 \left[(e^{-\beta^2 r^2})(8\pi r) + (e^{-\beta^2 r^2})(-8\pi\beta^2 r^3)\right]$$

Factoring out $e^{-\beta^2 r^2}$ and setting the expression equal to zero yields,

$$\left(\frac{\beta}{\pi^{\frac{1}{2}}}\right)^3 (e^{-\beta^2 r^2})[8\pi r + - \; 8\pi\beta^2 r^3] = 0$$

Factoring out $8\pi r$ yields,

$$\left(\frac{\beta}{\pi^{\frac{1}{2}}}\right)^3 (e^{-\beta^2 r^2})(8\pi r)[1 + - \; \beta^2 r^2] = 0$$

Dividing both sides of the equation by

$$\left(\frac{\beta}{\pi^{\frac{1}{2}}}\right)^3 (e^{-\beta^2 r^2})(8\pi r)$$

gives

$$1 + -\beta^2 r^2 = 0 \ .$$

This now yields,

$$1 = \beta^2 r^2$$

or

$$r^2 = \frac{1}{\beta^2} \ .$$

Therefore, the most probable value of r is,

$$r = \sqrt{\frac{1}{\beta^2}} = \frac{1}{\beta} = \beta^{-1} \ .$$

• PROBLEM 15-22

> Prove that the mean square end-to-end length of a linear polymer chain with free rotation about the bonds of the chain is
>
> $$\overline{r^2} = Na^2$$
>
> where N is the number of bonds of length a. Hence calculate the root mean square end-to-end length of a linear polystyrene molecule with a molecular weight of 10^5. The bond length is 0.25 nm.

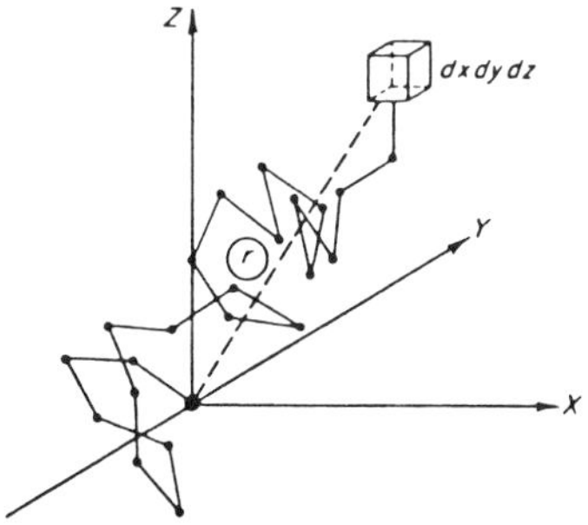

Conformation of a freely rotating polymer chain of 23 links with one end at origin. Analog of a random walk in three dimensions.

Fig. 1

Solution: Figure 1 shows a specific example of a polymer with free rotation about its bonds. In this case, the number of bonds, N, is 23. As can be seen, this is the same case as that of a single molecule starting from the origin and moving at random with a fixed distance before changing direction. If r is the distance between the origin and the other end of the polymer, then the probability that the end falls within volume element dxdydz is given by the Gaussian distribution,

$$W(x,y,z)dx\,dy\,dz = \left(\frac{\beta}{\pi^{\frac{1}{2}}}\right)^3 e^{-\beta^2 r^2}\,dxdydz \qquad (1)$$

The volume element dxdydz expressed in terms of r (where

$$r^2 = x^2 + y^2 + z^2)$$

is given by $4\pi r^2 dr$. Therefore, equation (1) becomes

$$W(r)dr = \left(\frac{\beta}{\pi^{\frac{1}{2}}}\right)^3 e^{-\beta^2 r^2}\,4\pi r^2 dr \qquad (2)$$

Analogously to mean square velocity of a gas in three dimensions, the mean square end-to-end length of the polymer is given by

$$\overline{r^2} = \int_0^\infty r^2\,W(r)dr = \int_0^\infty r^2 \left(\frac{\beta}{\pi^{\frac{1}{2}}}\right)^3 e^{-\beta^2 r^2}\,4\pi r^2 dr\,. \qquad (3)$$

Taking the constants out of the integral and combining all terms in r yields

$$\overline{r^2} = 4\pi\left(\frac{\beta}{\pi^{\frac{1}{2}}}\right)^3 \int_0^\infty e^{-\beta^2 r^2}\,r^4 dr \qquad (4)$$

To solve this equation the following substitution is used.

Let $x = \beta^2 r^2$, then $dx = \beta^2 2rdr$, $x^2 = \beta^4 r^4$,

$$r = \sqrt{\frac{x}{\beta^2}}$$

Since

$$r = \sqrt{\frac{x}{\beta^2}}$$

and

$$dx = \beta^2 2rdr,\quad dx = 2\beta^2\sqrt{\frac{x}{\beta^2}}\,dr$$

Equation (4) now becomes

$$\overline{r^2} = 4\pi\left(\frac{\beta}{\pi^{\frac{1}{2}}}\right)^3 \int_0^\infty e^{-x}\left(\frac{x^2}{\beta^4}\right)\left(\frac{dx}{(2\beta^2)\left(\sqrt{\frac{x}{\beta^2}}\right)}\right) \tag{5}$$

Simplifying the above expression yields

$$\overline{r^2} = 4\pi\left(\frac{\beta}{\pi^{\frac{1}{2}}}\right)^3 \int_0^\infty \left(\frac{e^{-x}}{\beta^4}\right) x^2\left(\frac{dx}{2\beta\sqrt{x}}\right)$$

Taking all the constants outside of the integral sign yields,

$$\overline{r^2} = 4\pi\left(\frac{\beta}{\pi^{\frac{1}{2}}}\right)^3\left(\frac{1}{\beta^4}\right)\left(\frac{1}{2\beta}\right)\int_0^\infty e^{-x}\,\frac{x^2}{\sqrt{x}}\,dx \tag{6}$$

Simplifying equation (6) gives

$$\overline{r^2} = \frac{2}{\sqrt{\pi}\,\beta^2}\int_0^\infty x^{3/2}\,e^{-x}\,dx \tag{7}$$

Equation (7) has an integral which is of a type called the gamma function, $\Gamma(n)$. That is, the gamma function has the general type of integral

$$\int_0^\infty x^{n-1}\,e^{-x}\,dx\ .$$

It can be evaluated given that,

$$\Gamma\left(\frac{1}{2}\right) = \sqrt{\pi},\quad \Gamma(1) = 1,\quad \text{and}\quad \Gamma(n+1) = n\Gamma(n).$$

Equating equation (7) and the general integral it can be seen that the $\frac{3}{2}$ in equation (7) is equal to n-1 in the general integral. Hence, $n = \frac{5}{2}$.

The gamma function is now evaluated at n = 5/2. Since the only values given are for $\Gamma(1)$ and $\Gamma\left(\frac{1}{2}\right)$, $\Gamma\left(\frac{5}{2}\right)$ must be broken up into these terms. Therefore,

$$\Gamma\left(\frac{5}{2}\right) = \Gamma\left(1 + \frac{3}{2}\right)\ .$$

Using the fact that

$$\Gamma(n+1) = n\Gamma(n), \ \Gamma\left(1+\frac{3}{2}\right) \text{ becomes } \frac{3}{2}\Gamma\left(\frac{3}{2}\right).$$

Likewise

$$\frac{3}{2}\Gamma\left(\frac{3}{2}\right) = \frac{3}{2}\Gamma\left(1+\frac{1}{2}\right) = \left(\frac{3}{2}\right)\left(\frac{1}{2}\right)\Gamma\left(\frac{1}{2}\right)$$

However

$$\Gamma\left(\frac{1}{2}\right) = \sqrt{\pi}$$

and therefore

$$\Gamma\left(\frac{5}{2}\right) = \left(\frac{3}{2}\right)\left(\frac{1}{2}\right)(\sqrt{\pi}) = \frac{3}{4}\sqrt{\pi}$$

Equation (7) can now be solved.

$$\overline{r^2} = \left(\frac{2}{\sqrt{\pi}\,\beta^2}\right)\left(\frac{3}{4}\sqrt{\pi}\right) = \frac{3}{2\beta^2} \ .$$

Now

$$\beta^{-1} = a\left(\frac{2N}{3}\right)^{\frac{1}{2}}$$

since a is the bond length in the chain and N is the number of bonds. Therefore,

$$\overline{r^2} = \frac{3}{2}\beta^{-2} = \frac{3}{2}\left(\beta^{-1}\right)^2 = \frac{3}{2}\left[a\left(\frac{2N}{3}\right)^{\frac{1}{2}}\right]^2 = \frac{3}{2}a^2\frac{2N}{3} = a^2N \ .$$

What is to be calculated now is root mean square end-to-end length and not the mean square length. The monomer unit which makes up the polystyrene molecule is styrene. Its formula is $C_6H_5-C_2H_3$ and its molecular weight is 104. Hence, to find the number of these units, divide the molecular weight of polystyrene by the molecular weight of styrene. Therefore, the number of units is

$$10^5/104 = 962 \text{ units.}$$

The root mean square length is therefore,

$$(\overline{r^2})^{\frac{1}{2}} = (962)^{\frac{1}{2}}(0.25 \text{ nm}) = 7.75 \text{ nm.}$$

• PROBLEM 15-23

Calculate the most probable value of the chain length of normal $C_{20}H_{42}$ given the C-C bond length of 0.15 nm and the bond angle of 109°28'.

Solution: If a molecule has the typical zig-zag shape of a carbon backbone, then the length of a unit link of the backbone can be found using the following equation.

$$a = \ell\left(\frac{1 + \cos\alpha}{1 - \cos\alpha}\right)^{\frac{1}{2}}$$

where

a = length of a unit link of the backbone

ℓ = C-C bond length

α = bond angle .

To put 28' into decimal notation, divide 28' by 60'/degree. Hence, 109°28' is now equal to 109.467°.

Therefore,

$$a = 0.15 \text{ nm}\left(\frac{1 + \cos 109.467°}{1 - \cos 109.467°}\right)^{\frac{1}{2}}$$

$$= 0.15 \text{ nm}\left(\frac{1 + -0.333}{1 - -0.333}\right)^{\frac{1}{2}}$$

$$= 0.106 \text{ nm}$$

For $C_{20}H_{42}$ there are twenty carbon atoms in the chain but there are nineteen bonds. The most probable value of the chain length is given by

$$r = \beta^{-1} = a\left(\frac{2N}{3}\right)^{\frac{1}{2}}$$

where N = number of links in the backbone.

Therefore,

$$r = 0.106 \text{ nm}\left(\frac{2(19)}{3}\right)^{\frac{1}{2}} = 0.377 \text{ nm}.$$

Consider a segment of length a in a freely orienting polymer chain. Under the influence of a force F the segment acquires an orientation in the x direction. Show that the average value of the x component of a is

$$\langle a_x \rangle = a\left(\coth \frac{aF}{kT} - \frac{kT}{aF}\right)$$

$$= a\mathcal{L}\left(\frac{aF}{kT}\right)$$

where $\mathcal{L}$ is the Langevin function.

How large a force would be required at 300°K to elongate a linear polystyrene chain, whose molecular weight is 10^5, by 20%? The bond length is 0.25 nm.

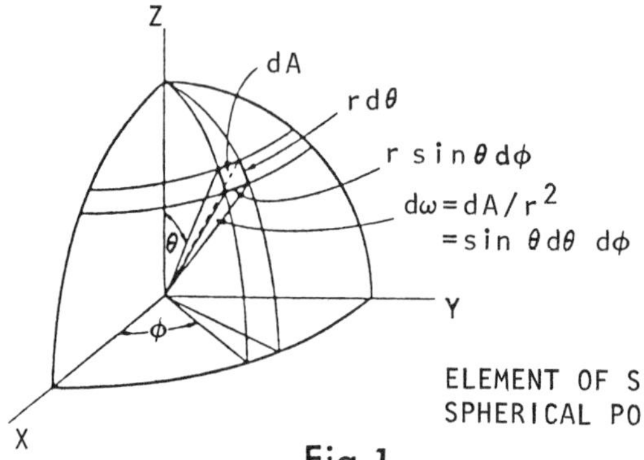

Fig. 1

Solution: In order to solve this problem it will be necessary to define a solid angle, ω. Assume that a sphere is drawn whose distance from the origin is radius r. Then the solid angle, ω, is defined as the ratio of the area of a spherical surface to the square of the radius. That is,

$$\omega = A/r^2 .$$

Since the total surface area of the sphere is $4\pi r^2$,

$$\omega = \frac{4\pi r^2}{r^2} = 4\pi .$$

This can be shown as follows. The differential in the solid angle, dω, is equal to the differential in the spherical surface area, dA, divided by the radius squared, r^2. That is,

$$d\omega = dA/r^2$$

From figure 1 it can be seen that

$$dA = (r \sin\theta \, d\phi)(r d\theta) = r^2 \sin\theta \, d\theta \, d\phi \quad .$$

Hence,

$$d\omega = dA/r^2 = r^2 \sin\theta \, d\theta \, d\phi / r^2 = \sin\theta \, d\theta \, d\phi \qquad (1)$$

From figure 1 it is seen that $d\phi$ can vary from 0 to 2π. Therefore, integrating equation (1) with respect to $d\phi$ between 0 and 2π yields,

$$d\omega = \int_0^{2\pi} \sin\theta \, d\theta \, d\phi = \sin\theta \, d\theta \int_0^{2\pi} d\phi = \sin\theta \, d\theta \, [\phi]_0^{2\pi}$$

$$= 2\pi \sin\theta \, d\theta$$

Now, θ can vary between 0 and π. However, the integral which is $\cos\theta$ will have a maximum value at $\theta = 0$, a minimum value at $\theta = \pi$, and have a value of 0 at $\theta = \pi/2$. Therefore, the integral must be evaluated as follows:

$$d\omega = 2\pi \sin\theta \, d\theta$$

$$\omega = \int_0^{\pi} 2\pi \sin\theta \, d\theta = 2\pi \int_0^{\pi} \sin\theta \, d\theta = 2\pi \, [-\cos\theta]_0^{\pi} \qquad (2)$$

$$= 2\pi\left[-\cos\theta \Big|_0^{\pi/2} + - \cos\theta \Big|_{\pi/2}^{\pi}\right]$$

$$= 2\pi[(-\cos \pi/2) - (-\cos 0) + (-\cos \pi) - (-\cos \pi/2)]$$

$$= 2\pi[0 - (-1) + (- -1) - 0]$$

$$= 2\pi[1 + 1]$$

$$= 4\pi$$

Having an understanding of what a solid angle is, the solution to the problem can now be shown. For a freely oriented polymer chain of length a, oriented at an angle θ to a force F, the potential energy is given by $U = -Fa \cos\theta$. This is because the potential is minus the displacement times the component of the force in the direction of the displacement.

According to the Boltzmann distribution law, the probability of a molecule having energy, ε, is given by

$$p(\varepsilon) = (\text{constant})e^{-\varepsilon/kT} .$$

Hence, the probability (at the given potential) of the x component of a being in solid angle $d\omega$ is given by the Boltzmann distribution as

$$p(U) = Ae^{-U/kT} .$$

Therefore, the average value of the x-component of a is given by,

$$\langle a_x \rangle = \frac{\int_0^{4\pi} A \exp\left(\frac{Fa\cos\theta}{kT}\right) a\cos\theta \, d\omega}{\int_0^{4\pi} A \exp\left(\frac{Fa\cos\theta}{kT}\right) d\omega} \qquad (3)$$

The limits were chosen because, as was shown, $d\omega$ varies from 0 to 4π. To solve this equation, let $x = Fa/kT$ and $y = \cos\theta$. Then upon making the appropriate substitutions, and removing all the constants outside of the integral sign, equation (3) becomes

$$\langle a_x \rangle = \frac{aA \int_0^{4\pi} \exp(xy) y \, d\omega}{A \int_0^{4\pi} \exp(xy) \, d\omega}$$

which simplifies to

$$\langle a_x \rangle = \frac{a \int_0^{4\pi} \exp(xy) y \, d\omega}{\int_0^{4\pi} \exp(xy) d\omega} \qquad (4)$$

Now as was already stated $d\omega = 2\pi \sin\theta \, d\theta$ where θ varies from 0 to π. In addition, since $y = \cos\theta$, $dy = -\sin\theta \, d\theta$. Therefore,

$$d\omega = 2\pi \sin\theta \, d\theta = -2\pi \, dy.$$

Equation (4) now becomes

$$\langle a_x \rangle = \frac{a \int \exp(xy)\, y(-2\pi)\, dy}{\int \exp(xy)(-2\pi)\, dy} \tag{5}$$

Notice the limits were purposely left out in equation (5). This is because the integration is not being carried out with respect to $d\omega$, but rather dy. However, since $y = \cos\theta$, when $\theta = 0$, $y = 1$ and when $\theta = \pi$, $y = -1$. Equation (5) now becomes

$$\langle a_x \rangle = \frac{2\pi a \int_{1}^{-1} -ye^{xy}\, dy}{2\pi \int_{1}^{-1} -e^{xy}\, dy} \, . \tag{6}$$

Remembering that

$$\int_a^b -f(x)\,dx = \int_b^a f(x)\,dx \, ,$$

equation (6) now becomes

$$\langle a_x \rangle = \frac{a \int_{-1}^{1} ye^{xy}\, dy}{\int_{-1}^{1} e^{xy}\, dy} \tag{7}$$

The denominator is calculated as follows. Since the integration is carried out with respect to dy, x is treated as a constant. An integral of the form

$$\int_a^b e^{ay}\, dy$$

has the solution

$$\frac{1}{a} e^{ay} \Big|_a^b \quad .$$

Therefore,

$$\int_{-1}^{1} e^{xy}\, dy = \frac{1}{x} e^{xy} \Big|_{-1}^{1} = \frac{1}{x}\left[e^{1(x)} - e^{-1(x)}\right] = \frac{e^x - e^{-x}}{x} \quad . \tag{8}$$

The numerator must be integrated by parts. Remember that

$$\int udv = uv - \int vdu \; .$$

Therefore, for the integral

$$\int_{-1}^{1} e^{xy}\, y\, dy \; ,$$

let $u = y$ and $dv = e^{xy}$ dy. Then $du = dy$ and

$$v = \int e^{xy}\, dy = \frac{e^{xy}}{x}$$

(as shown above). Therefore,

$$\int_{-1}^{1} e^{xy}\, ydy = y\,\frac{e^{xy}}{x}\Big|_{-1}^{1} - \int_{-1}^{1} \frac{e^{xy}}{x}\, dy \; . \tag{9}$$

The first term in equation (9) is evaluated as follows

$$y\,\frac{e^{xy}}{x}\Big|_{-1}^{1} = \frac{(1)\; e^{1(x)}}{x} - \frac{(-1)\; e^{-1(x)}}{x} = \frac{e^x + e^{-x}}{x} \; .$$

The second term in equation (9) has a constant $\frac{1}{x}$ term in the integral. Removing this outside the integral sign yields the same integral as equation (8). The second term in equation (9) is thus

$$\frac{1}{x}\left(\frac{e^x - e^{-x}}{x}\right) \; .$$

Equation (9) is thus,

$$\int_{-1}^{1} e^{xy}\, ydy = \frac{e^x + e^{-x}}{x} - \frac{e^x - e^{-x}}{x^2} \quad . \tag{10}$$

Substituting equation (10) for the numerator in equation (7) and equation (8) for the denominator in equation (7) yields

$$<a_x> = \frac{a\left(\frac{e^x + e^{-x}}{x} - \frac{e^x - e^{-x}}{x^2}\right)}{\frac{e^x - e^{-x}}{x}}$$

$$= a\left(\frac{\frac{e^x + e^{-x}}{x}}{\frac{e^x - e^{-x}}{x}} - \frac{\frac{e^x - e^{-x}}{x^2}}{\frac{e^x - e^{-x}}{x}}\right)$$

$$= a\left[\frac{e^x + e^{-x}}{e^x - e^{-x}} - \frac{1}{x}\right]$$

$$= a\left(\coth x - \frac{1}{x}\right) \qquad (11)$$

Remembering that $x = Fa/kT$ and substituting yields

$$<a_x> = a\left(\coth \frac{Fa}{kT} - \frac{kT}{Fa}\right)$$

$$= a\mathcal{L}\left(\frac{aF}{kT}\right) \qquad (12)$$

The Langevin function, $\mathcal{L}(x)$, can be expanded in a power series. Since

$$e^v = 1 + v + \frac{v^2}{2!} + \frac{v^3}{3!} + \ldots$$

the function

$$\frac{e^x + e^{-x}}{e^x - e^{-x}} - \frac{1}{x}$$

can be expanded as follows.

$$\frac{e^x + e^{-x}}{e^x - e^{-x}} - \frac{1}{x} =$$

$$\frac{1 + x + \frac{x^2}{2!} + \frac{x^3}{3!} + \ldots + 1 + -x + \frac{x^2}{2!} - \frac{x^3}{3!} + \ldots}{1 + x + \frac{x^2}{2!} + \frac{x^3}{3!} + \ldots - (1 - x + \frac{x^2}{2!} - \frac{x^3}{3!} + \ldots)} - \frac{1}{x}$$

$$= \frac{2 + \frac{2x^2}{2!} + \ldots}{2x + \frac{2x^3}{3!} + \ldots} - \frac{1}{x} = \frac{2 + x^2 + \ldots}{2x + \frac{x^3}{3} + \ldots} - \frac{1}{x}$$

$$= \frac{2 + x^2 + \ldots}{x(2 + \frac{x^2}{3} + \ldots)} - \frac{1}{x} = \frac{1}{x}\left(\frac{2 + x^2 + \ldots}{2 + \frac{x^2}{3} + \ldots}\right) - \frac{1}{x}$$

What is now desired is to simplify the term in parentheses. The fraction appears to be the ratio of two simple power expansions. Therefore it is equated to a general form of a power expansion. That is,

$$1 + kx + \ell x^2 + \ldots = \frac{2 + x^2 + \ldots}{2 + \frac{x^2}{3} + \ldots}$$

Cross multiplying yields

$$(1 + kx + \ell x^2 + \ldots)(2 + \frac{x^2}{3} + \ldots) = 2 + x^2 + \ldots$$

$$2 + 2kx + 2\ell x^2 + \frac{x^2}{3} + \ldots = 2 + x^2 + \ldots$$

$$2 + 2kx + (2\ell + \frac{1}{3})\, x^2 + \ldots = 2 + x^2 + \ldots$$

Equating the coefficients on both sides of the equation, it can be seen that the right side has no terms in x, and hence on the left side $k = 0$. On the right side the coefficient before the x^2 is 1 and on the left side it is $2\ell + \frac{1}{3}$. Hence,

$$1 = 2\ell + \frac{1}{3}\,,\ 2\ell = \frac{2}{3}\,,\ \text{and therefore } \ell = \frac{1}{3}\,.$$

Therefore, the general power series which replaces the term

$$\frac{2 + x^2 + \ldots}{2 + \frac{x^2}{3} + \ldots}$$

is given by

$$1 + \frac{1}{3} x^2 + \ldots$$

Therefore, the Langevin function, $\mathcal{L}(x)$, can be expressed as

$$\frac{e^x + e^{-x}}{e^x - e^{-x}} - \frac{1}{x} = \frac{1}{x}\left(1 + \frac{1}{3} x^2 + \ldots\right) - \frac{1}{x}$$

$$= \frac{1}{x} + \frac{x}{3} + \ldots - \frac{1}{x}$$

$$= \frac{x}{3} + \ldots$$

The approximate value of x/3 will be used here.

For a linear polystyrene chain, the functional unit is $C_6H_5 - C_2H_3$ and its molecular weight, 104. The total molecular weight of the chain is 10^5. Therefore, the number of units is equal to $10^5/104 = 962$. There is one less bond than units, therefore the number of bonds is 961.

The fraction of elongation upon stretching is given by

$\frac{\langle a_x \rangle}{a}$. In this case, $\frac{\langle a_x \rangle}{a} = 0.20$.

Since $\mathcal{L}(x) = \frac{x}{3}$ and $x = \frac{aF}{kT}$, $\mathcal{L}\left(\frac{aF}{kT}\right) = \frac{aF}{3kT}$

Therefore,

$$\frac{\langle a_x \rangle}{a} = 0.20 = \frac{aF}{3kT}$$

and

$$F = 0.20 \left(\frac{3kT}{a}\right)$$

$$= 0.20 \left(\frac{3 \times 1.381 \times 10^{-23}\ \text{J/°K} \times 300\text{°K}}{0.25 \times 10^{-9}\ \text{m}}\right)$$

$$= 9.94 \times 10^{-12} \text{ newtons}$$

This is the force needed to stretch one bond. Since there are 961 bonds, the total force is

$$9.94 \times 10^{-12}\ \text{N/bond} \times 961 \text{ bonds} = 9.55 \times 10^{-9}\ \text{N}$$

INDEX

Numbers on this page refer to PROBLEM NUMBERS, not page numbers

Numbers on this page refer to <u>PROBLEM NUMBERS</u>, not page numbers

Numbers on this page refer to PROBLEM NUMBERS, not page numbers

Numbers on this page refer to **PROBLEM NUMBERS**, not page numbers

Numbers on this page refer to PROBLEM NUMBERS, not page numbers

Numbers on this page refer to PROBLEM NUMBERS, not page numbers

Numbers on this page refer to <u>PROBLEM NUMBERS,</u> not page numbers

Numbers on this page refer to PROBLEM NUMBERS, not page numbers

Numbers on this page refer to PROBLEM NUMBERS, not page numbers

Numbers on this page refer to PROBLEM NUMBERS, not page numbers

Numbers on this page refer to PROBLEM NUMBERS, not page numbers

Numbers on this page refer to **PROBLEM NUMBERS**, not page numbers

Numbers on this page refer to PROBLEM NUMBERS, not page numbers